AMERICAN ORIENTAL SERIES

VOLUME 40

Index to Journal of the American Oriental Society,

Volumes 21 to 60

AMERICAN ORIENTAL SERIES

VOLUME 40

AMERICAN ORIENTAL SOCIETY
NEW HAVEN, CONNECTICUT
1955

Index to Journal of the American Oriental Society,

Volumes 21 to 60

Compiled by

EDWARD H. SCHAFER

ISIDORE DYEN

HELEN E. FERNALD

HAROLD W. GLIDDEN

AMERICAN ORIENTAL SOCIETY
NEW HAVEN, CONNECTICUT
1955

LITHOPRINTED IN THE UNITED STATES OF AMERICA BY
CUSHING - MALLOY, INC., ANN ARBOR, MICHIGAN, 1955

CONTENTS

I. Index of Authors 1

III. Index of Subjects 25

III. Index of Books Reviewed 127

IV, Index of Words 139

V. Index of Passages 159

VI. Index of Abstracts and Titles of Papers read at Society Meetings 165

PREFACE

In 1940 a Committee on the Centennial Celebration of the Society reported to the Executive Committee that it was desirable, as part of the celebration, to prepare an index to volumes 21 to 60 of the Journal.

The American Council of Learned Societies, to whose officers and committees we express our gratitude, provided encouragement and funds for the initial stages of the work on the Index. The three geographical sections were compiled by Doctors Helen E. Fernald (Far East), Isidore Dyen (South Asia), and Harold W. Glidden (Near East). These sections were arranged in unified alphabets for the various subdivisions of the Index by Professor Edward H. Schafer of the University of California, Berkeley; he put much other labor into preparing the copy for printing. Thanks are owed to several scholars for aid during the manufacture; we should name especially Mrs. Hans H. Frankel (Chang Ch'ung-ho) who inserted the Chinese characters by kind permission of the East Asiatic Library of the University of California, Berkeley.

The Secretary-Treasurer and various Editors of the Society have put much thought into the production of the Index. The labors of all concerned will have their reward if, as we hope, Oriental scholarship is furthered by the volume.

I. INDEX OF AUTHORS

ABBOTT, Justin E. The Bhikshugīta or Mendicant's Song. The Parable of the Repentant Miser, 46 289-296
------. Indian Inscriptions on the Fire Temple at Bāku, 29 299-304
------. Mālobā, the Marāthā Saint, 40 300-306
------. The Maratha Poet-saint Dāsopant Digambar, 42 251-279
------. The 300th Anniversary of the Birth of the Maratha King Shivaji, 50 159-163
ABBOTT, Nabia. An Arabic Papyrus Dated A.H. 205, 57 312-315
------. Persian Documents from Mughal India, 59 371-374
ADLER, Cyrus. A New Hebrew Press, 41 225-229
------. East and West, (Presidential address delivered before the Society at New York, April 1924), 44 177-185
------. Paul Haupt, 47 1-2
------, J. A. Bewer, H. Hyvernat and S. Zeitlin. In Memoriam: Jacob Hoschander, 54 87-88
------, and M. Burrows. Felix M. Warburg, In Memoriam, 58 505
AITKEN, W. E. M. Notes on a Collation of some Unpublished Inscriptions of Ashurnazirpal, 32 130-134
AIYAR, L. V. Ramaswami. The History of Tamil ṟ, 58 664-668
ALBRIGHT, William Foxwell. A Babylonian Geographical Treatise on Sargon of Akkad's Empire, 45 193-245
------. Gilgames and Engidu, Mesopotamian Genii of Fecundity, 40 307-335
------. How Well can we Know the Ancient Near East? 56 121-144
------. Islam and the Religions of the Ancient Orient, 60 283-301
------. New Light on Magan and Meluḫa, 42 317-322
------. Ninib-Ninurta, 38 197-201
------. Notes on Egypto-Semitic Etymology. III, 47 198-237
------. Notes on the Topography of Ancient Mesopotamia, 46 220-230
------. Some Cruces in the Langdon Epic, 39 65-90
------. Some Unexplained Cuneiform Words, 35 394-398
------. The Babylonian Antediluvian Kings, 43 323-329
------. The Babylonian Sage Ut-Napištim Rûqu, 38 60-65
------. The Conclusion of Esarhaddon's Broken Prism, 35 391-393
------. The Eighth Campaign of Sargon, 36 226-232
------. The Home of Balaam, 35 386-390
------. The Name and Nature of the Sumerian God Uttu, 42 197-200
------. Uttu, the Sumerian God of Commerce, 40 73-74
------, and P. E. Dumont. A Parallel between Indic and Babylonian Sacrificial Ritual, 54 107-128
------, review of W. F. Badè, Some Tombs of Tell en-Nasbeh, 52 52-53
------, review of Carl Bezold, Babylonisches-assyrisches Glossar, 48 177-182
------, review of Arvid Bruno, Gibeon, 45 181-182
------, review of E. Douglas van Buren, Clay Figurines of Babylonia and Assyria, 51 175-177
------, review of G. Contenau, La civilisation phénicienne, 48 76-80
------, review of E. Ebeling, B. Meissner and E. Weidner, Die Inschriften der altassyrischen Könige, 48 90-93
------, review of Z. S. Harris, Development of the Canaanite Dialects, 60 414-422
------, review of Amelia Hertz, Die Kultur um den persischen Golf und ihre Ausbreitung, 51 67-70
------, review of Anton Jirku, Die Wanderungen der Hebräer im 3. und 2. Jahrtausend v. Chr., 48 183-185
------, review of D. D. Luckenbill, Ancient Records of Assyria and Babylonia, I and II, 48 93-95
------, review of H. H. von der Osten and E. Schmidt, The Alishar Hüyük, Season of 1927, Part I, 51 173-175
------, review of T. Eric Peet, A Comparative Study of the Literatures of Egypt, Palestine, and Mesopotamia, 52 51-52
------, review of F. Petrie, Ancient Gaza I. Tell el-Ajjûl, 53 285-287
------, review of M. Rostovtzeff, A. Bellinger and C. Welles (eds.), The Excavations of Dura-Europos. Preliminary Report of Sixth Season... Oct. 1932 - Mar. 1933, 57 318-321
------, review of Ernst Sellin, Wie wurde Sichem eine israelitische Stadt?, 45 182-184
------, review of E. A. Speiser, Mesopotamian Origins, 51 60-66
------, review of L. C. Watelin and S. Langdon, Excavations at Kish, III, 52 54
ALLEN, Albert Henry. The Vaṭa-sāvitrī-vrata, according to Hemādri and the Vratārka, 21 53-66
ARCHER, John Clark, review of J. A. Subhan, Sufism, its Saints and Shrines, 59 274-275
ARNOLD, Edward V. The Rig Veda and Atharva Veda, 22 309-320
ARNOLD, William R. Additional Palmyrene Inscriptions in the Metropolitan Museum of Art, New York, 26 105-112
------. Solomon's Horse-Trade, 26 104
ASAKAWA, K. Notes on Village Government in Japan After 1600, I, 30 259-300
------. Notes on Village Government in Japan After 1600, II, 31 151-216
ATKINS, Samuel D. A Vedic Hymn to the Sun-god Sūrya. (Translation and exegesis of Rig-Veda 1.115), 58 419-434
BABB, M. J., review of Walter Eugene Clark, The Āryabhaṭīya of Āryabhaṭa, An Ancient Indian Work on Mathematics and Astronomy, 51 51-52
BACHHOFER, Ludwig. Herrscher und Münzen der späten Kushānas, 56 429-439
------, review of Joseph Hackin, Recherches archéologiques au Col de Khair khaneh près de Kābul, 57 326-329
------, review of Joseph Hackin, Recherches archéologiques en Asie Centrale (1931), 57 329-331
------, review of Kern Institute's Annual Bibliography of Indian Archaeology for the Year 1932. Vol. VII, 57 331-335
BAILEY, H. W. The Rāma Story in Khotanese, 59 460-468
BARBOUR, Philip Lemont. Buruçaskī, a Language of Northern Kashmir, 41 60-72
BARRET, LeRoy Carr. The Contents of the Kashmirian Atharva-Veda, books 1-12, 46 8-14
------. The Kashmirian Atharva Veda, book one. Edited with critical notes, 26 197-295
------. The Kashmirian Atharva Veda, book two. Edited, with critical notes, 30 187-258
------. The Kashmirian Atharva Veda, book three. Edited, with critical notes, 32 343-390
------. The Kashmirian Atharva Veda, book four. Edited, with critical notes, 35 42-101
------. The Kashmirian Atharva-Veda, book five. Edited with critical notes, 37 257-308
------. The Kashmirian Atharva Veda, book seven. Edited with critical notes, 40 145-169
------. The Kashmirian Atharva-Veda, book eight. Edited with critical notes, 41 264-289
------. The Kashmirian Atharva Veda, book nine. Edited with critical notes, 42 105-146
------. The Kashmirian Atharva Veda, book ten. Edited with critical notes, 43 96-115

------. The Kashmirian Atharva Veda, book eleven. Edited with critical notes, 44 258-269
------. The Kashmirian Atharva Veda, book twelve. Edited with critical notes, 46 34-48
------. The Kashmirian Atharva Veda, book thirteen. Edited with critical notes, 48 34-65
------. The Kashmirian Atharva Veda, book fourteen. Edited with critical notes, 47 238-249
------. The Kashmirian Atharva Veda, book fifteen. Edited with critical notes, 50 43-73
------. The Kashmirian Atharva Veda, book eighteen. Edited with critical notes, 58 571-614
------. Note on Pāippalāda 6.18, 41 318-319
------. Three Pāippalāda Fragments, 54 70-74
------. Two Pāippalāda Manuscripts, 50 104-111
------, review of M. Bloomfield and F. Edgerton, Vedic Variants, Volume I, The Verb, 51 73-76
------, review of Maurice Bloomfield, Franklin Edgerton, and Murray B. Emeneau, Vedic Variants. Volume III: Noun and Pronoun Inflection, 55 110-112
------, review of W. Caland, The Śatapatha Brāhmaṇa, Kāṇvīya Recension, 48 89-90
------, review of W. Caland, Das Śrāuta-sūtra des Āpastamba, aus dem Sanskrit übersetzt, 44 139-140
------, review of W. Caland, Das Śrāutasutra des Āpastamba, achtes bis fünfzehntes Buch, aus dem Sanskrit übersetzt, 46 272-273
------, review of Alfred Hillebrandt, Vedische Mythologie, 50 74-75
------, review of A. A. Macdonell, Hymns from the Rigveda, 43 429-430
------, review of Hannes Sköld, The Nirukta, 47 335-336
------, review of Edward J. Thomas, Vedic Hymns, 43 428-429
BARTON, George Aaron. An Androgynous Babylonian Deity, 21 185-187
------. Ancient Babylonian Expressions of the Religious Spirit, 37 23-42
------. The Archaic Inscription in Découvertes en Chaldée, Plate 1bis, 42 338-342
------. The Babylonian Calendar in the Reigns of Lugal-anda and Urkagina, 31 251-271
------. The Contributions of Morris Jastrow Jr. to the History of Religion, 41 327-333
------. A Correction, 45 323
------. The Expression of the Comparative Degree in Sumerian, 43 243-244
------. The Form and Nature of E-PA at Lagash, 43 92-95
------. The Genesis of the God Eshmun, 21 188-190
------. Hilprecht's Fragment of the Babylonian Deluge Story, 31 30-48
------. Identification of Sign No. 572 of Barton's Babylonian Writing, 46 311-312
------. Interpretation of the Archaic Tablet of the E. A. Hoffman Collection, 23 21-28
------. Kugler's Criterion for Determining the Order of the Months in the Earliest Babylonian Calendar, 33 297-305
------. Lexicographical Notes, 44 271-272
------. The names of two Kings of Adab, 33 295-296; 34 facing p. 228
------. A New Babylonian Parallel to a part of Genesis 3, 39 287
------. A New Collation of the Blau Monuments, 24 388-389
------. A New Inscription of Entemena, 51 262-265
------. A New Inscription of Libit-Ishtar, 45 154-155
------. A North Syrian Poem on the Conquest of Death, 52 221-231
------. Note on Dr. Peters' Notes and Suggestions, 41 150-151
------. Notes on an Archaic Inscription Published by Father Scheil, 22 126-128
------. An Obscure Passage in the Hittite Laws, 53 358-359
------. On the Anticipatory Pronominal Suffix before the Genitive in Aramaic and Akkadian, 47 260-262
------. On the Babylonian Origin of Plato's Nuptial Number, 29 210-219
------. On Binding-Reeds, Bitumen, and Other Commodities in Ancient Babylonia, 46 297-302
------. On the Etymology on Ishtar, 31 355-358
------. On an Old Babylonian Letter Addressed "to Lushtamar," 29 220-223
------. On the Pantheon of Tyre, 22 115-117
------. On the Significance of Compound Postpositives in Early Sumerian, 43 317-322
------. On the Vocalization of the Ideogram ŠES-AB^{ki}-MA, 46 310-311
------. The Origin of the Thought-Pattern which Survives in Baptism, 56 155-165
------. The Place of the Amorites in the Civilization of Western Asia, 45 1-38
------. The Problem of the Origin and Early History of the Deity NIN-IB (NIN-URTA, NIN-URASH), 46 231-236
------. Recent Researches in the Sumerian Calendar, 33 1-9
------. Religious Conceptions Underlying Sumerian Proper Names, 34 315-320
------. The Second Liturgical Poem from Ras Shamra, 55 31-58
------. Some Notes on the Blau Monuments, 22 118-125
------. Some Observations on the Origin of the Babylonian Syllabary, 54 75-79
------. Takku, 37 163-164
------. Tammuz and Osiris, 35 213-223
------. Three Objects in the Collection of Mr. Herbert Clark, of Jerusalem, 27 400-401
------. Two New Hebrew Weights, 24 384-387
------. When the Goddess Nin-shakh became a God, 47 268-269
------. Whence Came the Sumerians? 49 263-268
------. A Word with Reference to 'Emperor'-Worship in Babylonia, 37 162-163
------, review of W. F. Albright, The Archaeology of Palestine and the Bible, 52 197-199
------, review of C. J. Ball, The Book of Job, a Revised Text and Version, 45 177-179
------, review of C. Bezold, Ninive und Babylon, 46 317
------, review of E. A. Wallis Budge, Babylonian Life and History, 46 318
------, review of C. J. Gadd, The Fall of Nineveh, the Newly Discovered Babylonian Chronicle, 46 316-317
------, review of C. J. Gadd, A Sumerian Reading Book, 46 316
------, review of R. Koldewey, Das wieder erstehende Babylon, 4th ed., 48 95-96
------, review of S. Langdon, The Babylonian Epic of Creation, 45 179-181
------, review of S. Langdon, Oxford Edition of Cuneiform Inscriptions, vols. I and II, 46 315-316
------, review of S. A. B. Mercer, Études sur les origines de la religion de l'Égypte, 53 169-170
------, review of I. M. Price, The Great Cylinder Inscriptions A & B of Gudea, 48 84-87
------, review of Anna Schneider, Die Anfänge der Kulturwirtschaft: Die Sumerische Tempelstadt, 43 249-250
------, review of J. K. Shryock, Desire and the Universe, a Study of Religions, 55 479-482
------, review of E. Hershey Sneath (ed.), Religion and the Future Life, the Development of the Belief in the Life after Death, 43 250-251
------, review of L. W. Waddell, Historical Origin and Economic Purpose of the Tower of Babel and the Name "Shinar," 43 251-253
------, review of W. L. Wardle, Israel and Babylon, 46 314
BATES, M. S. Problems of Rivers and Canals under Han Wu Ti (140-87 B.C.), 55 303-306

BELVALKAR, Shrimad Krishna. Stage-emendations in the Uttara-Rāma-charita, 34 428-433

BENDER, Harold H. The Etymology and Meaning of Sanskrit garūtmant, 42 203-204

------. Lithanian klónas, kluonas 'a place where something is spread out', 40 353-355

------. On the Naturalistic Background of the 'Frog-hymn', Rig-Veda 7.103, 37 186-191

------. Two Lithuanian Etymologies, 42 186-188

------, review of, Streitberg-Festgabe, 45 324-328

------, review of Ernst Arbman, Rudra. Untersuchungen zum altindischen Glauben und Kultus, 43 56-60

------, review of K. Būga, Lietuvių kalbos žodynas. 1 sąsiuvinis, 44 140-141

------, review J. W. Hauer, Die Anfänge der Yogapraxis im alten Indien, 43 60-65

------, review of Norbert Jokl, Linguistisch-kulturhistorische Untersuchungen aus dem Bereiche des Albanischen, 43 427-428

BEN YEHUDA, E. Three Notes on Hebrew Lexicography, 37 324-327

BERGMAN, Abraham. The Israelite Occupation of Eastern Palestine in the Light of Territorial History, 54 169-177

BERNHEIMER, Richard. A Literary Description of the Most Primitive Type of Vault, 59 109-110

------. Vitae prophetarum, 55 200-203

BEWER, Julius A., see ADLER, Cyrus

BINGHAM, Woodbridge. Wên Ta-ya: the First Recorder of T'ang History, 57 368-374

BISHOP, C. W. The Chronology of Ancient China, 52 232-247

------. The Elephant and its Ivory in Ancient China, 41 291-306

BLAKE, Frank R. Aaron Ember, 1878-1926, 46 182-184

------. A Bibliography of the Philippine Languages. Part I, 40 25-70

------. The Bisayan Dialects, 26 120-136

------. Comparative Syntax of the Combinations formed by the Noun and its Modifiers in Semitic, 32 135-267

------. Contributions to Comparative Philippine Grammar, 27 317-396

------. Contributions to Comparative Philippine Grammar, II. The Numerals, 28 199-253

------. The Development of Symbols for the Vowels in the Alphabets Derived from the Phoenician, 60 391-413

------. Differences between Tagalog and Bisayan, 25 162-169

------. Expression of Case by the Verb in Tagalog, 27 183-189

------. The Expression of Indefinite Pronominal Ideas in Hebrew, 34 115-228

------. Expression of the Ideas "to be" and "to have" in the Philippine Languages, 30 375-391

------. Hebrew חֲמִשָּׁה , חֲמִשִּׁים , 26 117-119

------. The Hebrew Metheg, 32 78-102

------. The Internal Passive in Semitic, 22 45-54

------. A New Method of Syntactical Arrangement, 41 467-471

------. The Part played by the Publications of the United States Government in the Development of Philippine Linguistic Studies, 42 147-170

------. The So-Called Intransitive Verbal Forms in Hebrew, 24 145-204

------. Studies in Semitic Grammar, 35 375-385

------. The Tagalog Ligature and Analogies in other Languages, 29 227-231

------. The Tagalog Verb, 36 396-414

------. The Word זדה in the Siloam Inscription, 22 55-60

------. Vocalic r, l, m, n in Semitic, 31 217-222

------, review of Najeeb Mitry Saleeby, The Language of Education of the Philippine Islands, 46 61-71

BLOCH, Joshua. Richard James Horatio Gottheil 1862-1936, 56 472-489

BLOOMFIELD, Leonard. On some Rules of Pāṇini, 47 61-70

BLOOMFIELD, Maurice. The Dohada or Craving of Pregnant Women: a Motif of Hindu Fiction, 40 1-24

------. The Hittite Language, 41 195-209

------. The Home of the Vedic Sacrifice, 48 200-224

------. The Mind as Wish-car in the Veda, 39 280-282

------. Notes on the Divyāvadāna, 40 336-352

------. On a possible pre-Vedic Form in Pāli and Prākrit, 41 465-466

------. On certain Work in Continuance of the Vedic Concordance, 29 286-298

------. On False Ascetics and Nuns in Hindu Fiction, 44 202-242

------. On ṛcīṣama, an Epithet of Indra, 21 50-52

------. On Recurring Psychic Motifs in Hindu Fiction, and the Laugh and Cry Motif, 36 54-89

------. On the Etymology and Meaning of the Sanskrit Root varj, 35 273-288

------. On the Relative Chronology of the Vedic Hymns, 21 42-49

------. On Vedic dhénā "prayer", "song", 46 303-308

------. The Śālibhadra Carita. A Story of Conversion to Jaina Monkhood, 43 257-316

------. Some Rig-Veda Repetitions, 31 49-69

------, review of Walter Neisser, Zum Wörterbuch des Ṛgveda, 45 157-172

BOAK, A. E. R. and WORRELL, W. H., review of H. E. Winlock and W. E. Crum, The Monastery of Epiphanius at Thebes, 47 85-87

BOBRINSKOY, G. V. A Line of Brāhmī (?) Script in a Babylonian Contract Tablet, 56 86-88

------. The Rite of dantadhāvana in Smṛti Literature, 52 163-167

BODDE, Derk. A Perplexing Passage in the Confucian Analects, 53 347-351

------. Types of Chinese Categorical Thinking, 59 200-219

------, review of Rudolph Löwenthal (with the assistance of Ch'en Hung-shun, Ku T'ing-ch'ang, and William W. Y. Liang), The Religious Periodical Press in China, 60 584-585

BOLLING, G. M. The Çāntikalpa of the Atharvaveda, 33 265-278

------. The Relation of the Vedic Forms of the Dual, 23 318-324

BONNER, Campbell. Palladas and Jewish Reflection upon the Beginnings of Man, 55 196-199

BORTON, Hugh, review of Robert Karl Reischauer and Jean Reischauer, Early Japanese History (c. 40 B.C. - A.D. 1167), 59 143-146

BRADEN, Charles S., A. H. Lybyer and H. G. May. Frederick Carl Eiselin, In Memoriam, 58 550-551

------ and Wm. R. Mc Govern. [Leslie Elmer Fuller, In Memoriam], 57 214

BRADLEY, Cornelius Beach. Graphic Analysis of the Tone-accents of the Siamese Language, 31 282-289

------. Some Features of the Siamese Speech and Writing, 44 11-28

------. The Tone-Accents of Two Chinese Dialects, 35 199-206

BREASTED, James Henry. The First Expedition of the Oriental Institute of the University of Chicago, 40 282-285

------. The Place of the Near Orient in the Career of Man and the Task of the American Orientalist, 39 159-184

BRIGGS, G. W. Episode in the Wanderings of Śiva, 53 357-358

------. The Indian Rhinoceros as a Sacred Animal, 51 276-282

------, review of J. Abbot, The Keys of Power, 53 186

------, review of William Crooke, Religion and Folklore of Northern India, 47 189-192

------, review of N. K. Dutt, Origin and Growth of Caste in India, 53 181-186

------, review of G. S. Ghurye, Caste and Race in India, 53 181-186

------, review of L. S. S. O'Malley, Indian Caste Customs, 53 181-186

------, review of Vasant G. Rele, The Mysterious Kundalini, 48 185
BROWN, George William. Note on Angarôs, in Montgomery's 'Aramaic Incantation Texts from Nippur,' 41 159-160
------. The Possibility of a Connection between Mitanni and the Dravidian Languages, 50 273-305
------. Prāṇa and apāna, 39 104-112
------, review of T. G. Aravamuthan, An Account of the Tamil Academies, 51 338-339
------, review of V. R. Ramachandra Dikshitar, Studies in Tamil Literature and History, 52 80-81
------, review of Nripendra Kumar Dutt, The Aryanization of India, 51 336-338
------, review of Brahmachari Gitanand, The Gita Idea of God, 52 82
------, review of H. D. Griswold, The Religion of the Rigveda, 47 187-189
------, review of Robert Ernest Hume, The Thirteen Principal Upanishads, 52 81-82
------, review of S. G. Mohiuddin Qadri, Hindustani Phonetics, 52 79-80
------, review of L. A. Waddell, The Indo-Sumerian Seals Deciphered, 47 284-285
BROWN, W. Norman. The Beginnings of Civilization in India, 59 Sup. 32-44
------. Change of Sex as a Hindu Story Motif, 47 3-24
------. A Comparative Translation of the Arabic Kalīla wa-Dimna, Chapter VI, 42 215-250
------. An Old Gujarātī Text of the Kālaka Story, 58 5-29
------. The Pañcatantra in Modern Indian Folklore, 39 1-54
------. Proselyting the Asuras. (A Note on Rig Veda 10.124), 39 100-103
------. The Sources and Nature of pūruṣa in the Puruṣasūkta (Rigveda 10.91), 51 108-118
------. and Muhammed A. Simsar. Late Mughul Illustrations to the Iqbāl-nāmah'i Jahāngīrī, 58 354-365
------, J. K. Shryock and J. A. Montgomery. Max Leopold Margolis, 52 105
------, review of, Indian Studies in Honor of Charles Rockwell Lanman (by numerous contributors), 50 171-174
------, review of Justin E. Abbott, Bhānudās, 47 280
------, review of Justin E. Abbott, The Poet-Saints of Maharashtra. No. 6, Stotramala: A Garland of Hindu Prayers, 50 271
------, review of Justin E. Abbott, Tukaram. Translation from Mahipati's Bhaktalilamrita, 51 289-290
------, review of Lord Chalmers, Buddha's Teachings, being the Sutta-Nipāta or Discourse Collection, 54 218-219
------, review of Ananda K. Coomaraswamy, Elements of Buddhist Iconography, 57 115-117
------, review of Ananda K. Coomaraswamy, La Sculpture de Bodhgayā, 57 115-117
------, review of Ananda K. Coomaraswamy, The Transformation of Nature in Art, 54 216-218
------, review of Ananda K. Coomaraswamy, Yakṣas, Parts I and II, 51 286-288
------, review of Franklin Edgerton, The Elephant-Lore of the Hindus, 52 89-90
------, review of R. E. Enthoven, The Folklore of Bombay, 46 265-267
------, review of Johannes Hertel, Bharaṭakadvātriṃśikā, 46 72-75
------, review of Johannes Hertel, ed., Indische Erzähler. Vols. 1-12, 46 71-75
------, review of Johannes Hertel, The Panchākhyānavārttika. Part I, 46 72-75
------, review of C. A. Högman, L'Inde et son âme, 49 95
------, review of Helen M. Johnson, Triṣaṣṭiśalākāpuruṣacaritra. Vol. I. Ādīśvaracaritra, 52 86-88
------, review of Margaret Macnicol, Poems by Indian Women, 46 267
------, review of T. N. Ramachandran, Buddhist Sculptures from a Stupa near Goli Vilage, Guntur District, 52 90
------, review of T. N. Ramachandran, Tiruparuttikunram and its Temples, 54 438-440
------, review of Benjamin Rowland, Jr., The Wall-Paintings of India, Central Asia, and Ceylon, 58 484-485
------, review of Hiranand Sastri, Indian Pictorial Art as developed in Book-Illustrations, 57 118-119
------, review of Ralph Lilley Turner, A Comparative and Etymological Dictionary of the Nepali Language, 51 288-289
BUCKLER, Francis W. Firdausī's Shāhnāmah and the Genealogia Regni Dei, 55 Supp. 1, 1-21
------, review of F. W. Hasluck, Christianity and Islam under the Sultans, 53 73-75
------, review of Muhammad Nāzim, The Life and Times of Sultan Maḥmūd of Ghazna, 53 75-76
BULL, Ludlow, E. A. Speiser and A. T. Olmstead. James Henry Breasted, 1865-1935, 56 113-120
------. see also Gottheil, Richard J. H.
BURLINGAME, E. W. Sources of Pāli Commentaries, 38 267-268
BURROWS, Millar. The Complaint of Laban's Daughters, 57 259-276
------. I Have Written on the Door (Lachish Letter IV), 56 491-493
------. see also Adler, C.
BUTTENWIESER, Moses. Blood Revenge and Burial Rites in Ancient Israel, 39 303-321
BYRNE, Eugene H. Easterners in Genoa, 38 176-187
CARNOY, A. J. The Iranian Gods of Healing, 38 294-307
------. Iranian Views of Origins in Connection with Similar Babylonian Beliefs, 36 300-320
------. Pre-Aryan Origins of the Persian Perfect, 39 117-121
CARR, Denzel. The New Official Romanization of Japanese, 59 99-102
CASANOWICZ, I. M. The Collection of Oriental Antiquities at the United States National Museum, 23 44-47
------. Jewish Amulets in the United States National Museum, 36 154-167
------. Notes on Some Usages of רְבֵן , 30 343-346
------. Two Jewish Amulets in the United States National Museum, 37 43-56
CHAN, Wing-Tsit, review of Robert J. Kerner, Northeastern Asia, A Selected Bibliography, 2 vols., 60 429-432
CHANDLER, J. S. The Forthcoming Tamil Lexicon, 44 134-137
------. Names of God in the Tamil Language which Denote his Oneness, 45 115-118
CHAPIN, Helen B. The Ch'an Master Pu-tai, 53 47-52
------. The Gion Shrine and the Gion Festival, 54 282-289
CH'EN, Kenneth. Matteo Ricci's Contribution to, and Influence on, Geographical Knowledge in China. 59 325-359
CHIERA, Edward. A New Creation Story, 41 459-460
------ and Speiser, E. A. Selected "Kirkuk" Documents, 47 36-60
CHOMSKY, William. The Plural of Nouns in the (ק)טֹרֶת Formations, 54 425-428
CHUNG, Kei Won, and G. F. Hourani. Arab Geographers on Korea, 58 658-661
CLACK, Robert Wood, review of Yoshitomo Okamoto, Jūrokuseiki sekaichizu jō no Nihon, 60 275-278
CLARK, Walter Eugene. Māgadhī and Ardhamāgadhī, 44 81-121
------. A Note on Pargiter's Ancient Indian Historical Tradition, 43 130-131
------. Śākadvīpa and Śvetadvīpa, 39 209-242
------. Some Misunderstandings about India, 46 193-201
------, L. C. Goodrich, A. T. Olmstead and J. K. Shryock. Berthold Laufer; In Memoriam, 54 349-351

------, review of Franklin Edgerton, The Mīmānsā Nyāya Prakāśa or Āpadevī: A Treatise on the Mīmānsā System by Āpadeva, 51 53-54
------, review of A. Berriedale Keith, Classical Sanskrit Literature, 46 76-77
------, review of G. K. Nariman, Priyadarśikā, A Sanskrit Drama by Harsha, 46 77-78
------, review of F. E. Pargiter, Ancient Indian Historical Tradition, 43 132-141
------, review of Edward J. Thompson and Arthur Marshman Spencer, Bengali Religious Lyrics, Śakta, 46 270-272
CLAY, Albert T. The Antiquity of Babylonian Civilization, 41 241-263
------, Gobryas, Governor of Babylonia, 41 466-467
------, Name of the Socalled Deity Za-mal-mal, 37 328-329
------, A New King of Babylonia, 41 313
------, The Origin and Real Name of NIN-IB, 28 135-144
------, Professor Jastrow as an Assyriologist, 41 333-336
------, A Rejoinder to Professor Barton, 45 119-151
------, The So-Called Fertile Crescent and Desert Bay, 44 186-210
------, and Montgomery, James A.: Bibliography of Morris Jastrow Jr., 41 337-344
COHEN, Boaz, review of E. Goodenough, By Light Light, 56 500-505
------, review of S. L. Skoss (ed.), The Hebrew-Arabic Dictionary of the Bible known as Kitab Jami Al-Alfaz, 60 108-110
COHON, Samuel S., review of H. Thackeray, Josephus the Man and the Historian, 53 176-178
COMFORT, Howard. Supplementary Sigillata Signatures in the Near East, 58 30-60
------, review of C. Bonner (ed.), A Papyrus Codex of the Shepherd of Hermas, 56 103-104
CONANT, Carlos Everett. Grammatical Notes on the Isinai Language (Philippines), 35 289-292
------, Indonesian l in Philippine Languages, 36 181-196
------, Monosyllabic Roots in Pampanga, 31 389-394
------. Notes on the Phonology of the Palau Language, 35 1-15
------. Notes on the Phonology of the Tirurai Language, 33 150-157
------. The RGH Law in Philippine Languages, 31 70-85
COOMARASWAMY, Ananda K. Ābhāsa, 52 208-212
------. Angel and Titan: an Essay in Vedic Ontology, 55 373-419
------. Chāyā, 55 278-283
------. Daṇḍarāsa, vaṃśanartin, and caturaśratva, 48 281-283
------. The "Four Causes" in the Bhagavad Gītā, 57 415-416
------. Indian Architectural Terms. A review of P. K. Acharya, Indian Architecture According to the Mānasāraśilpaśāstra, and A Dictionary of Hindu Architecture, 48 250-275
------. The Indian Origin of the Buddha Image, 46 165-170
------. Mudrā, muddā, 48 279-281
------. The Old Indian Vīṇā, 51 47-50
------. Pali kaṇṇikā = Circular Roof-plate, 50 238-243
------. The Parts of a vīṇā, 50 244-253
------. The Parts of a vīṇā, 57 101-103
------. A Passage in the Uttara-Rāma-Carita of Bhavabhūti, 49 61
------. The Persian Wheel, 51 283-284
------. Ratha-chidra, 51 172
------. Reactions to Art in India, 52 213-220
------. The Sun-kiss, 60 46-67
------. Upavīṇa, 51 284-285
------. Viṣṇudharmottara, chapter XLI, 52 13-21
------, review of The Cultural Heritage of India. A Symposium of some 100 Authors, 57 426-428
------, review of Journal of the Indian Society of Oriental Art. Vol. I, Pts. 1 and 2, 54 222
------, review of P. K. Acharya, A Dictionary of Hindu Architecture, 48 250-275
------, review of P. K. Acharya, Indian Architecture According to the Mānasāraśilpaśāstra, 48 250-275
------, review of S. Krisnaswami Aiyangar, Manimekhalai in its historical setting, 49 71-72
------, review of Ludwig Bachhofer, Early Indian Sculpture, 51 58-59
------, review of R. D. Banerji, Basreliefs of Bādāmī, 49 191-193
------, review of Benimadhab Barua, Gayā and Buddha-Gayā, 57 191-193
------, review of B. Bhattacharyya, The Indian Buddhist Iconography, 46 187-189
------, review of N. K. Bhaṭṭaśāli, Iconography of Buddhist and Brahmanical sculptures in the Dacca Museum, 50 82
------, review of Laurence Binyon, The Poems of Nizami, 49 339
------, review of Laurence Binyon, The Spirit of Man in Asian Art, 55 325-329
------, review of Phanindra Nath Bose, Pratimā-Māna-Lakṣaṇam, 50 266-267
------, review of P. N. Bose, Principles of Indian Śilpaśāstra; with the text of Mayaśāstra, 49 69-70
------, review of W. Norman Brown, The Kālaka Story: Texts, history, legends, and miniature paintings of the Jain Hagiographical work the Kālakācāryakathā, 53 305-307
------, review of G. Coedès, Études cambodgiennes, XIX. La date du Bàyon, 50 264-265
------, review of H. Cousens, Chalukyan architecture, 49 331
------, review of Henry Cousens, Somanātha and Other Mediaeval temples in Kāṭhiāwāḍ, 53 187
------, review of Mrs. Rhys Davids, What was the Original Gospel in Buddhism? 58 679-686
------, review of Lefebure des Noëttes, L'Attelage et le cheval de selle à travers les âges: contribution à l'histoire de l'esclavage, 52 84-86
------, review of A. Foucher, On the Iconography of the Buddha's Nativity, 55 323-325
------, review of O. C. Gangoly, Masterpieces of Rajput painting, 49 72-73
------, review of G. T. Garratt, The Legacy of India, 57 426-428
------, review of Alice Getty, Gaṇeśa, 57 428-429
------, review of Hermann Goetz, Geschichte der indischen Miniaturmalerei, 54 440-442
------, review of V. Goloubew, Ajanta. Les peintures de la première grotte, 47 278-279
------, review of F. H. Gravely and T. N. Ramachandran, Catalogue of the South Indian Metal Images in the Madras Government Museum, 53 187-188
------, review of Georges Groslier, Les collections khmères du Musée Sarrault à Phnom Penh, 52 83-84
------, review of Martin Hürliman, India: the landscape, the monuments, and the people, 49 190-191
------, review of Albert Ippel, Indische Kunst und Triumphalbild, 52 83
------, review of Stella Kramrisch, Indian Sculpture, 54 219-221
------, review of Robert Lachmann, ed., Zeitschrift für Vergleichende Musikwissenschaft, 54 223
------, review of A. H. Longhurst, Pallava Architecture, Parts I and II, 49 70-71
------, review of A. H. Longhurst, Pallava Architecture, Part III, 50 266
------, review of Sappho Marchal, Costumes et parures khmers d'après les Devatā d'Angkor Vat, 49 73
------, review of Sappho Marchal, Dances cambodgiennes, 49 73
------, review of N. C. Mehta, Studies in Indian Painting, 47 275-278

------, review of Paul Mus, Barabuḍur, 57 336-343
------, review of Paul Mus, Le Buddha paré: son origine indienne. Çakyamuni dans le Mahāyānisme moyen, 50 263-264
------, review of C. K. Ogden and I. A. Richards, The Meaning of Meaning, 53 298-303
------, review of Vasudeva Poduval, Kathakali (pp. 13), and Diagrams of Hand Poses in Kathakali (pp. 2 and 24 plates), 51 180
------, review of I. A. Richards, Mencius on the Mind, 53 298-303
------, review of William Rothenstein, Ancient India, 46 253-256
------, review of A. Sakisian, La miniature persane, 50 81
------, review of H. K. Sastri, Two Statues of Pallava Kings and Five Pallava Inscriptions in a Rock Temple at Mamallapuram, 49 70-71
------, review of T. Gaṇapati Śāstrī, Samarāṅganasūtradhāra by King Bhojadeva, Volume II, 49 69
------, review of Philippe Stern, Le Bayon d'Angkor et l'evolution de l'art khmer, 49 330-331
------, review of J. Ph. Vogel, Indian Serpent Lore, or the Nāgas in Hindu Legend and Art, 49 186-190
------, review of J. Ph. Vogel, La sculpture de Mathurā, 51 54-58
------, review of E. H. Warmington, The Commerce between the Roman Empire and India, 51 180-182
------, review of Richard Wilhelm, (tr.), The Secret of the Golden Flower: a Chinese Book of Life, 53 303-305
------, review of J. V. S. Wilkinson, The Lights of Canopus: Anvār i Suhailī, 50 170-171
------, review of J. V. S. Wilkinson, The Shāh Nāmah of Firdausī, 52 254-255
CREEL, Herrlee Glessner. Bronze Inscriptions of the Western Chou Dynasty as Historical Documents, 56 335-349
------, Confucius and Hsün-tzu, 51 23-32
------. I 彝, as Equivalent to Tao 道, 52 22-34
------, review of Roswell S. Britton (ed.), The Couling-Chalfant Collection of Inscribed Oracle Bones, Drawn by Frank H. Chalfant, 56 528-529
CUMMINGS, Thomas F. The Irreducible Minimum in Learning a Foreign Language, 43 81-84
DANTON, G. H., review of Leang K'i-Tch'ao (Liang Ch'i-ch'iao), La Conception de la Loi et les Theories des Legistes a la veille de Ts'in, Trs. Intro. et Notes par Jean Escarra et Robert Germain, 49 76-78
DAIVD, A. Wie Šú.Gé.-tum zu lesen ist? 43 426
DAVIDOWITZ, H. S., review of Adolf Weiss, Mose ben Maimon. Führer der Unschlüssigen, 48 190-191
DAVIDSON, D. S. Is the Boomerang Oriental? 55 163-181
------. Northwestern Australia and the Question of Influences from the East Indies, 58 61-80
DAVIDSON, Israel, review of B. Halper, Descriptive Catalogue of the Genizah Fragments in Philadelphia, 45 332-334
DEAN, James E. The Old Syriac Calendar, 54 129-142
DEB, Harit Krishna. India and Elam, 42 194-197
------. Rājaśekhara on Śiśunāka, 45 72-75
DELLA VIDA, Giorgio Levi. A Neopunic Inscription in England, 60 578-579
------. A Phoenician Fragment from Rhodes, 60 260-264
------, review of P. K. Kitti, History of the Arabs, 59 121-126
DIMAND, Maurice Sven. Samanid Stucco Decoration from Nishapur, 58 258-261
DINSHAW, Viccaji. Deccan Parallels to the Burj-Namah, 35 293-296
DOMINIAN, Leon. The Geographical Foundation of Turkey's World Relation, 36 168-180
------. The Site of Constantinople a Factor of Historical Value, 37 57-71
DONALDSON, Dwight M. Ibn Jubayr's Visit to al-Medina, 50 26-42
DOUGHERTY, Raymond P. Ancient Teimâ and Babylonia, 41 458-459
------. Nabonidus and Belshazzar, 45 354
------. Nabonidus in Arabia, 42 305-316
------. The Sealand of Arabia, 50 1-25
------. Writing upon Parchment and Papyrus among the Babylonians and the Assyrians, 48 109-135
------, review of E. Unger, Babylon - Die Heilige Stadt, 52 54-55
DUBS, Homer H. The Attitude of Han Kao-tsu to Confucianism, 57 172-180
------. The Conjunction of May 205 B.C., 55 310-313
------. "Nature" in the Teaching of Confucius, 50 233-237
------. The Victory of Han Confucianism, 58 435-449
DUMONT, P. E. The Avyakta Upaniṣad, 60 338-355
------. The Indic God Aja Ekapād, the One-legged Goat, 53 326-334
------. Vedic anyedyúḥ and ubhayedyúḥ (ubhayadyúḥ), 59 425-430
------, and W. F. Albright. A Parallel between Indic and Babylonian Sacrificial Ritual, 54 107-128
------, review of W. Caland, Pañcaviṃśa-Brāhmaṇa, The Brāhmaṇa of the Twenty-five Chapters, 52 387-390
------, review of C. V. Vaidya, History of Sanskrit Literature. Vol. I. Śruti (Vedic) Period, 52 391-392
------, review of J. M. van der Hoogt, The Vedic Chant studied in its Textual and Melodic Form, 52 390-391
DUYVENDAK, J. J. L., review of A. J. H. Charignon, A propos des voyages aventureux de Fernand Mendez Pinto, recueillies et complétées par Mlle. M. Médard, 57 343-348
------, review of John K. Shryock, The Origin and Development of the State Cult of Confucius, 55 330-338
------, review of J. K. Shryock, The Study of Human Abilities, the Jen Wu Chih of Liu Shao, 59 280-282
DYEN, Isidore. A Dubious Old Persian Tablet in Philadelphia, 56 91-93
EDGERTON, Franklin. The Aorist in Buddhist Hybrid Sanskrit, 57 16-34
------. Buddhist Sanskrit saṃdhā, saṃdhi(-nirmocana), 57 185-188
------. Counter-rejoinder to Professor Fay, 40 100-102
------. Edward Washburn Hopkins, 1857-1932, 52 311-315
------. Endingless Noun Case-forms in Prakrit, 59 369-371
------. The Epic triṣṭubh and its Hypermetric Varieties, 59 159-174
------. Evil-Wit, No-Wit, and Honest-Wit, 40 271-275
------. The Goat and the Knife: an Automatic Solution of an Old Crux, 59 366-368
------. A Hindiism in Sanskrit, 38 206-207
------. Hindiisms in Sanskrit again: a reply to Professor Fay, 40 84-89
------. The k-suffixes of Indo-Iranian. Part I, The k-suffixes in the Veda and Avesta, 31 93-150, 296-342
------. The Kashmirian Atharva Veda, book six. Edited, with critical notes, 34 374-411
------. The latest work on the Kauṭilīya Arthaśāstra, 48 289-322
------. Maurice Bloomfield, 1855-1928, 48 193-199
------. Notes, mainly Textual, on Tantrākhyāyika, book II, 38 273-293
------. On the Doubling of Consonants in the Seam of Certain Pāli Compounds, 41 462-465
------. Pañcadivyādhivāsa or Choosing a King by Divine Will, 33 158-166
------. Rome and (?) Antioch in the Mahābhārata, 58 262-265
------. Samādhi "hostage," and Related Matters from Kauṭilya, 60 208-216
------. The Sanskrit Ghost-word *paḍviṅśa, 51 170-171
------. Sources of the Filosofy of the Upaniṣads, 36 197-204
------. Studies in the Veda, 35 240-246
------. Studies in the Veda, 40 89-92

------. The Upaniṣads: What do they Seek, and Why? 49 97-121
------, review of Justin E. Abbott, The Poet-Saints of Maharashtra, 50 76-77
------, review of Leonard Bloomfield, Language, 53 295-297
------, review of S. N. Dasgupta, Hindu Mysticism, 48 87-88
------, review of Surendranath Dasgupta, A History of Indian Philosophy, Vols. I and II, 52 248-252
------, review of P. S. Deshmukh, The Origin and Development of Religion in Vedic Literature, 55 319-323
------, review of P. E. Dumont, L'Īśvaragītā. Le chant de Śiva, 54 306-310
------, review of E. H. Johnston, The Buddhacarita: or, Acts of the Buddha, 57 422-425
------, review of A. Berriedale Keith, A History of Sanskrit Literature, 50 77-79
------, review of Embar Krishnamacharya, Tattvasaṁgraha of Śāntarakṣita, with the Commentary of Kamalaśīla, 49 66-67
------, review of St. Fr. Michalski-Iwienski, Bhagavadgītā, 43 65-67
------, review of Motilal Lādhāji Oswāl, Hemacandrācārya-viracitā Anyayogavyavachedikā, tadvyākhā ca śrī-Malliṣeṇa-sūripraṇītā Syādvādamañjarī, 49 67-68
------, review of Louis Renou, Études de grammaire sanskrite. Première série, 56 362-364
------, review of Louis Renou, La valeur du parfait dans les hymnes védiques, 49 64-66
------, review of Lakshman Sarup, Fragments of the Commentaries of Skandasvāmin and Maheśvara on the Nirukta, 50 175-176
------, review of Lakshman Sarup, Indices and Appendices to the Nirukta, with an Introduction, 50 175-176
------, review of F. Otto Schrader, The Kashmir Recension of the Bhagavad Gītā, 52 68-75
------, review of Vishnu S. Sukthankar, The Mahābhārata, for the first time critically edited, 48 186-190
------, review of Vishnu S. Sukthankar, The Mahābhārata, 49 282-284
------, review of Vishnu S. Sukthankar, The Mahābhārata, Ādiparvan: Fascicule 5, 52 252-254
------, review of Vishnu S. Sukthankar, The Mahābhārata. Ādiparvan: Fascicule 7, 56 360-362
------, review of Bal Gangadhar Tilak, Śrīmad Bhagavadgītā Rahasya or Karma-Yoga-Śāstra. Translated from the original Marathi by Bhalchandra Sitaram Sukthankar, 56 525-528
------, review of A. von Le Coq and E. Waldschmidt, Die buddhistische Spätantike in Mittelasien, Sechster Teil: Neue Bildwerke II. Mit einem Beitrag über die Darstellung und den Stil der Wandgemälde aus Qyzil bei Kutscha. 49 62-64
------, review of A. von Le Coq and Ernst Waldschmidt, Die buddhistische Spätantike in Mittelasien, Siebenter Teil: Neue Bildwerke III, including essays by Friederich Sarre, Otto Kümmel and Heinrich Lüders, 53 360-361
------, review of Walter Wust, Stilgeschichte und Chronologie des Ṛgveda, 49 276-282
------, review of Walter Wust and others, Studia Indo-Iranica. Ehrengabe für Wilhelm Geiger zur Vollendung des 75. Lebensjahres 1856-21. Juli-1931, 52 76-79
------, review of Walther Wust, Vergleichendes und etymologisches Wörterbuch des Alt-Indoarischen (Altindischen). Lieferung 1-3, 56 364-370
EDGERTON, William F. On the Origin of Certain Coptic Verbal Forms, 55 257-267
------, review of August Köster, Das antike Seewesen, 44 77-79
------. Egyptian Phonetic Writing, 59 403
EDWARDS, Clara Cary. Relations of Shah Abbas the Great, of Persia, with the Mogul Emperors, Akbar and Jahangir, 35 247-268
------. Two Popular Religious Poems in the Azerbaijani Dialect, 39 113-116
EFROS, Israel. An Emendation to Jer. 4.29, 41 75
------. Textual Notes on the Hebrew Bible, 45 152-154
EITAN, Israel. Three 'im Particles in Hebrew, 54 295-297
------. Two Onomatological Studies, 49 30-33
EMENEAU, M. B. Another Example of the Echo-word Motif in Dravidian Folk-tales, 59 503-505
------. Confusion in Prakrit between the Sanskrit Prepositions prati and pari, 51 33-39
------. An Echo-word Motif in Dravidian Folk-tales, 58 553-570
------. Kṣemendra as kavi, 53 124-143
------. A Story of Vikrama's Birth and Accession, 55 59-88
------. Toda Garments and Embroidery, 57 277-289
------. Was there Cross-cousin Marriage among the Śākyas? 59 220-226
------, review of A. Aiyappan, Social and Physical Anthropology of the Nayadis of Malabar, 59 129-133
------, review of W. V. Grigson, The Maria Gonds of Bastar, 59 129-133
------, review of H. I. Poleman, A Census of Indic Manuscripts in the United States and Canada, 59 133-135
------, review of Anthony Xavier Soares, Portuguese Vocables in Asiatic Languages, 60 112-114
ENSLIN, Morton S. "Luke" and Paul, 58 81-91
EPSTEIN, J. N. Zum magischen Texte (Journal of the American Oriental Society 1912, p. 434 seq.), 33 279-280
EWING, Arthur H. The Çāradā-tilaka Tantra, 23 65-76
------. The Hindu Conception of the Functions of Breath; a Study in Early Hindu Psycho-physics, 22 249-308
FAIRBANK, J. K. The Manchu Appeasement Policy of 1843, 59 469-484
------, review of Earl H. Pritchard, The Crucial Years of Early Anglo-Chinese Relations, 1750-1800. Research Studies of the State College of Washington, Vol. IV, Nos. 3-4, 57 353-357
FARIS, Nabih Amin, review of M. Féghali, Contes, légendes, coutumes populaires du Liban et de Syrie, 56 509-510
------, review of P. H. Mamour, Polemics on the Fatimi Caliphs, 56 509
------, see also Glidden, Harold Walter.
FAUST, Richard A., review of John F. Embree, Suye Mura - A Japanese Village, 60 432-435
FAY, Edwin W. Indo-Iranian Word-studies, 31 403-413
------. Indo-Iranian Word-studies (ii), 34 329-343
------. Indo-Iranica, 40 121-125
------. Notes on Indo-Iranian Words, 39 206-207
------. Phonetic and Lexical Notes, 40 81-84
------. Rejoinder to Professor Edgerton, 40 93-100
------. Studies of Sanskrit Words, 27 402-417
------. The Vedic Hapax suśiśvi-s, 32 391-392
------. The Vedic Posterius - pitvam, cover (night), 39 261-264
FEIGIN, Samuel I. The Oldest Occurrence of Niqum, 59 107-108
------. A Purchase Contract from the Time of Samsu-Iluna, 55 284-293
------. Upî near Ishchali 59 106-107
FENG, H. Y., and J. K. Shryock. The Black Magic in China known as Ku 蠱, 55 1-30
------ and Shryock, J. K. Chinese Mythology and Dr. Ferguson, 53 53-65
FENOLLOSA, Ernest F. Notes on the Japanese Lyric Drama, 22 129-137
FERGUSON, John C. The Abolition of the Competitive Examinations in China, 27 79-87
------. Chinese Mythology; A Reply, 54 85-87
FERNALD, Helen E. The Horses of T'ang T'ai Tsung and the Stele of Yu, 55 420-428
------. A New Chinese Bronze in the University Museum, Philadelphia, 51 16-22
FINKEL, Joshua. A Risāla of al Jāḥiẓ, 47 311-334
FISH, T. A Nippur Tablet of Ur III, 56 494
FOOTE, T. C. The Cherubim and the Ark, 25 279-286

------. The Metrical Form of the Songs of Degrees, 27 108-122
------. The Old Testament Expression zanâh ahrê, 22 64-69
------. The Two Unidentified Names in the Moabite Stone, 22 61-63
------. Visiting Sins upon the Innocent, 28 309-316
FRAUWALLNER, E. Untersuchungen zum Mokṣadharma, 45 51-67
FRIEDLAENDER, Israel. The Heterodoxies of the Shiites in the Presentation of Ibn Ḥazm, 28 1-80, 29 1-183
FRY, Allan Harrison, review of Barend Faddegon, Studies in Pāṇini's Grammar, 59 135-138
FURLANI, Giuseppe. Contributions to the History of Greek Philosophy in the Orient, Syriac Texts IV: A Syriac Version of the λόγος κεφαλαιώδης περὶ ψυχῆς πρὸς Τατιανόν of Gregory Thaumaturgus, 35 297-317
------. A Short Physiognomic Treatise in the Syriac Language, 39 289-294
GALE, Esson M. The Citatory Element in the Composition of the Yen T'ieh Lun, 51 266-275
------, review of Berthold Laufer, The Domestication of the Cormorant in China and Japan, Field Museum of Natural History publication no. 300: Anthropological series, Vol. XVIII, No. 3, 52 267-269
------, review of John K. Shryock, The Temples of Anking and their Cults, 52 98-100
GARDINER, Alan H. The Egyptian Origin of Some English Personal Names, 56 189-197
GARDNER, Fletcher. Bamboo Writings from Mindoro and Palawan, 60 271-272
------. Three Contemporary Incised Bamboo Manuscripts from Hampangan Mangyan, Mindoro, P. I., 59 496-502
GASKILL, Gussie Esther. On Certain Foreigners who assisted in the suppression of the T'aip'ing Rebellion in Chehkiang, 57 246
GATES, Jean. Model Emperors of the Golden Age in Chinese Lore, 56 51-76
GAVIN, Frank. The Sleep of the Soul in the Early Syriac Church, 40 103-120
------. Some Notes on Early Christian Baptism, 46 15-22
GEHMAN, Henry S. Adhi √brū and adhi √vāc in the Veda, 36 213-225
------. Ādisati, anvādisati, anudisati, and uddisati in the Peta-Vatthu, 43 410-421
------. The Armenian Version of I. and II. Kings and its Affinities, 54 53-59
------. The Garrett Sahidic Manuscript of St. Luke, 55 451-457
------. A Pālism in Buddhist Sanskrit, 44 73-75
------. The Relations Between the Hebrew Text of Ezekiel and that of the John H. Scheide Papyri, 58 92-102
------, review of E. A. W. Budge, The Bandlet of Righteousness, 53 293-295
------, review of S. A. B. Mercer, The Ethiopic Text of the Book of Ecclesiastes, 52 260-263
......, review of C. Schmidt, Kephalaia, I, 56 520-522
------, review of H. Thompson, The Gospel of St. John According to the Earliest Coptic Manuscript, 46 286-287
------, review of Mizraim, ed. N. Reich, 53 292-293
GINSBERG, H. L. A Further Note on the Aramaic Contract Published by Bauer and Meissner, 59 105
------. The So-Called Šĕṿâ Medium in the Light of the Christian Palestinian Idiom, 53 352-356
GLIDDEN, Harold Walter. The Lemon in Asia and Europe, 57 381-396
------. A Note on Early Arabian Military Organization, 56 88-91
------. Some Supplementary Arabic Literature on the Lemon, 60 97-99
GLUECK, Nelson. The Theophany of the God of Sinai, 56 462-471
GÖTZE, Albrecht. Accent and Vocalism in Hebrew, 59 431-459
------. Cuneiform Inscriptions from Tarsus, 59 1-16
------. The n- Form of the Ḫurrian Noun, 60 217-223
------. Some Notes on the Corpus Inscriptionum Chaldaicarum, 55 294-302
------. The t- form of the Old Babylonian Verb, 56 297-334
------. The Tenses of Ugaritic, 58 266-309
------, review of Giuseppe Furlani, La Religione degli Hittiti, 58 475-476
------, review of B. Lansberger, Die Serie ana ittišu, 59 265-271
------, review of Edgar H. Sturtevant, A Hittite Glossary. Second Edition, 57 109-111
------, review of A. Ungnad, Subartu, 57 104-109
------, review of H. H. von der Osten, The Alishar Hüyük. Seasons of 1930-32, 59 510-515
GOLDMAN, Hetty. The Sandon Monument of Tarsus, 60 544-553
GOLOMSHTOK, Eugene A., review of Emile Licent, S.J., Comptes Rendus de Onze Années (1923-1933) de Séjour et D'Exploration dans le Bassin du Fleuve Jaune, du Pai Ho, et des Autres Tributaires du Golfe du Pei Tcheu ly, 57 449-451
------, review of G. N. Roerich, The Animal Style among the Nomads of Northern Tibet, Seminarium Kondakovianum, 53 89-91
GOODRICH, L. Carrington. Early Prohibitions of Tobacco in China and Manchuria, 58 648-657
------. Some Bibliographical Notes on Eastern Asiatic Botany, 60 258-260
------, review of Berthold Laufer, The American Plant Migration Part I, The Potato, prepared for publication by C. Martin Wilbur, 59 142-143
------, review of Elmer D. Merrill and Egbert H. Walker, A Bibliography of Eastern Asiatic Botany, 59 138-142
------, review of Arthur de Carle Sowerby, Nature in Chinese Art 60 580-584
------, see also Clark, Walter
GOTTHEIL, Richard J. H. Achmed Taimur Pasha, The [o] dor Nöldeke, and Eduard Sachau: an Appreciation, 51 104-107
------. Al-Ḥasan ibn Ibrāhīm ibn Zūlāḳ, 28 254-270
------. An Answer to the Dhimmis, 41 383-457
------. A distinguished Family of Fatimide Cadis (al-Nu'-mān) in the Tenth Century, 27 217-296
------. A Door from the Madrasah of Barḳūḳ, 30 58-60
------. A Fragment on Astrology from the Genizah, 47 302-310
------. Fragments Treating of Medicine from the Cairo Genizah, 50 112-124
------. A Further Fragment on Astrology from the Genizah, 49 291-302
------. Ignaz Goldziher, 42 189-193
------. Ignazio Guidi - Selected Bibliography, 55 458-463
------. Mohammed 'Abdu, late Mufti of Egypt, 28 189-197
------. Morocco as it is Today, 54 231-239
------. The Origin and History of the Minaret, 30 132-154
------. The Peshiṭta Text of Gen. 32, 25, 33 263-264
------. Seven Unpublished Palmyrene Inscriptions, 21 109-111
------. A Supposed Work of al-Ghazālī, 43 85-91
------. Two Forged Antiques, 33 306-312
------, A. V. W. Jackson and L. S. Bull. The Life and Work of Max Leopold Margolis, 52 106-109
------, review of C. C. Torrey, The History of the Conquest of Egypt, North Africa and Spain by Ibn 'Abd Al-Ḥakam, 43 144-148
GRAY, Louis H. The Bhartṛharinirveda of Harihara, now first Translated from the Sanskrit and Prākrit, 25 197-230
------. Contributions to Avestan Syntax, the Preterite Tenses of the Indicative, 21 112-145
------. Contributions to Avestan Syntax, the Subordinate Clause, 22 145-176

------. The Dūtāṅgada of Subhaṭa, now first Translated from the Sanskrit and Prākrit, 32 58-77
------. Fifteen Prākrit-Indo-European Etymologies, 60 361-369
------. The Indian God Dhanvantari, 42 323-337
------. Iranian Miscellanies, 33 281-294
------. A List of the Divine and Demonic Epithets in the Avesta, 46 97-153
------. Notes on the Old Persian Inscriptions of Behistun, 23 56-64
------. On Certain Persian and Armenian Month-Names as Influenced by the Avesta Calendar, 28 331-344
------. The Parsī-Persian Burǰ-Nāmah, or Book of Omens from the Moon, 30 336-342
------. Śivarāma's Commentary on the Vāsavadattā, 24 57-63
------. The Viddhaśālabhañjikā of Rājaśekhara, now first Translated from the Sanskrit and Prākrit, 27 1-71
------. Yasna LVII: an Essay in Text-reconstruction, 58 310-323
------, review of L. O. Fossum, A Practical Kurdish Grammar, 44 80
------, review of M. Winternitz, Geschichte der indischen Litteratur. Dritter Band, 43 332-336
GRAYZEL, Solomon, review of S. Baron, A Social and Religious History of the Jews, 58 482-483
GRICE, Ettalene M. Selected Bibliography of Albert T. Clay, 45 295-300
GRIERSON, George A. A few Notes on the First Half of the Twenty-fifth Volume of JAOS. (Letter to the Corresponding Secretary), 25 339-340
------. Letter: Representation of Tones in Oriental Languages, 41 235
------. Note on Professor Prince's Article on the English-Rommany Jargon in vol. xxviii, 2, of the Journal of the American Oriental Society, 29 232-235
------. Shāhbāzgaṛhī uthānaṃ; Śaurasēnī locative in ē, 42 211-212
GRIEVE, Lucia C. G. The Collecting of Coins in India, 47 185-186
------. The Dasara Festival at Satara, India, 30 72-76
------. Some Folk-stories of Rāmdās the Last of the Sages, 25 185-188
GRIFFIS, William Elliot, review of Helen C. Gunsaulus, Japanese Sword-Mounts, 45 88-91
------, review of Karl Haushofer, Japan und die Japaner, 46 81-82
GRIMM, Karl J. The Meaning and Etymology of the Word תּוּשִׁיָּה in the Old Testament, 22 35-44
------. The Polychrome Lion Recently Found in Babylon, 22 27-34
VON GRÜNEBAUM [or Grunebaum], Gustave. The Early Development of Islamic Religious Poetry, 60 23-29
------, review of E. Tyan, Histoire de l'organisation judiciaire en pays d'Islam, 59 519-522
GUEST, Rhuvon. An Arabic Papyrus of the 8th Century, 43 247-248
GUPTA, Charu Chandra Dasa. The Variant Reading of Rāmāyaṇa 7.46.21, 54 297-299
HAAS, George C. O. Addenda to the Bibliography of A. V. Williams Jackson, 58 473
------. Bibliography of A. V. Williams Jackson, 58 241-257
------. Recurrent and Parallel Passages in the Principal Upanishads and the Bhagavad-Gītā, 42 1-43
------, review of S. M. Edwardes, Kharsheji Rustamji Cama, 1831-1909. A Memoir, 43 256
------, review of Irach Jehangir Sorabji Taraporewala, Seclections from Avesta and Old Persian (First Series). Part I, 43 255-256
HADDAD, Elias, see Spoer, H. Henry
HAGERTY, M. J. Two Unlisted Chüan of the Yung-lo-ta-tien, 52 179-181
HALKIN, A. S. The Ḥashwiyya, 54 1-28
------, review of C. C. Torrey, The Jewish Foundation of Islam, 54 209-212
HALL, Ardelia Ripley. The Early Significance of Chinese Mirrors, 55 182-189
HALL, H. U., review of W. E. Armstrong, Rossel Island: An Ethnological Study, 49 182-185
HALLOCK, Frank H., review of A. Z. Aešcoly, Les noms magiques dans les apocryphes chrétiens des éthiopiens, 55 109-110
HALLOWELL, A. Irving, review of Ivor H. N. Evans, Studies in Religion, Folk-Lore, and Custom in British North Borneo and the Malay Peninsula, 45 92-93
HALPER, B., review of E. Bräunlich, Bisṭām Ibn Qais, ein vorislamischer Beduinenfürst und Held, 43 436-437
------, review of H. A. R. Gibb, The Arab Conquests in Central Asia, 43 434-435
------, review of Joseph Hobeika, Explication de la liturgie syriaque par saint Jean Maron, 43 435-436
HAMILTON, Clarence H. Hsüan Chuang and the Wei Shih Philosophy, 51 291-308
------. K'uei Chi's Commentary on Wei-shih-er-shih-lun, 53 144-151
------, review of D. T. Suzuki (tr.), The Laṅkāvatāra Sūtra: A Mahayana Text, 53 87-89
------, review of D. T. Suzuki, Studies in the Laṅkāvatāra Sūtra, 52 91-93
HARRIS, R. Laird: A Mention of Pottery Glazing in Proverbs, 60 268-269
HARRIS, Zellig S. A Conditioned Sound Change in Ras Shamra, 57 151-157
------. A Hurrian Affricate or Sibilant in Ras Shamra, 55 95-100
------. Expression of the Causative in Ugaritic, 58 103-111
------. The Structure of Ras Shamra C, 54 80-83
------, review of R. P. Dougherty, The Sealand of Ancient Arabia, 54 93-95
HARTMANN, Gerda. Symbols of the nidānas in Tibetan Drawings of the "Wheel of Life," 60 356-360
HAUPT, Paul. Arabic Doublets, 43 422-423
------. Arabic u = r, 43 423-424
------. Arab. ṭâhamah = çánaxah, Heb. çaḥnâ, 43 424-425
------. Armageddon, 34 412-427
------. Askari, 'soldier', and Lascar, 'sailor', 36 417-418
------. Assyrian lânu, 'aspect' — Arabic láun, 'color,' 37 253-255
------. The Beginning of the Babylonian Nimrod Epic, 22 7-12
------. Christopher Johnston, 36 339-341
------. The Ending of the Semitic Genitive, 45 311-315
------. The Etymology of Cabinet, 28 108-111
------. The Etymology of Egypt. ṯsm, greyhound, 45 318-320
------. The Five Assyrian Stems la'u, 32 17-20
------. Heb. ărz, cedar, Ass. irêšu, balsamic juice, 45 322-323
------. Heb. kĕ, like, and kî, as, 45 316-318
------. Heb kōhén and qahál, 42 372-375
------. Heb. qîṭôr a doublet of 'ašán, 42 375-377
------. The Hebrew Terms for Gold and Silver, 43 116-127
------. The Introductory Lines of the Cuneiform Account of the Deluge, 25 68-75
------. The Name Istar, 28 112-119
------. The Names of the Hebrew Vowels, 22 13-17
------. The Origin of the Name Veadar, 45 320-322
------. Some Difficult Passages in the Cuneiform Account of the Deluge, 32 1-16
------. The Sumerian Affixes TAM and KAM, 42 301-304
------. Sumerian gul-gik, 'obstinate refusal,' 38 66-68
------. Tones in Sumerian, 37 309-323
------. Well and Field = Wife, 36 418-420
------. Xenophon's Account of the Fall of Nineveh, 28 99-107
HAYDON, A. Eustace, review of Kenneth Saunders, The Heritage of Asia, 54 103-104

HEIDEL, Alexander. The Problem of Mummu in the Babylonian Epic of Creation Reconsidered, 58 545
HIRSCHFELD, Hartwig. A Hebraeo-Sufi Poem, 49 168-173
------. The Marriages of Hosea, 48 276-277
HIRTH, Friedrich. Early Chinese Notices of East African Territories, 30 46-57
------. Mr. Kingsmill and the Hiung-nu, 30 32-45
------. The Mystery of Fu-lin, Pt. I, 30 1-31
------. The Mystery of Fu-lin, Pt. II, 33 193-208
------. The Story of Chang K'ien, China's Pioneer in Western Asia. Text and Translation of Chap. 123 of the Shih-chi, with Introduction and notes, 37 89-132; Chronological Synopsis, 133-136; Index, 137-152
HITTI, P. K. Correction to JAOS 59. 522, 60 272
------. Recent Publications in Arabic or Dealing with the Arabic World, 54 435-438
------, review of al-Ruwwād, 49 327
------, review of N. M. al-'Aẓm, Riḥlah fi Bilād al-'Arab al-Sa'īdah, 59 526
------, review of J. K. Birge, The Bektashi Order of Dervishes, 59 522-523
------, review of O. Farrukh, Das Bild des Frühislam in der arabischen Dichtung, 59 525-526
------, review of Michel Féghali, Syntaxe des parlers arabes actuels du Liban, 49 328-329
------, review of A. A. A. Fyzee, al-'Hiyādatu'-l-Āmirīya, 59 527
------, review of H. A. R. Gibb, The Damascus Chronicle of the Crusades, 52 265-267
------, review of S. Goitein (ed.), Ansāb al-Ašrāfof al-Balāḏuri, 57 322, 324-325
------, review of R. Grousset, Histoire des croisades et du royaume franc de Jérusalem, 56 510, 512
------, review of R. Grousset, Histoire des croisades, II, 57 322, 325
------, review of A. S. Halkin, Moslem Schisms and Sects, 56 510, 512-513
------, review of M. Ḥamīd-Allāh, Documents sur la diplomatie musulmane à l'époque du Prophète et des khalifes orthodoxes, 57 326
------, review of S. Ḥimādah, Monetary and Banking System of Syria, 56 511, 514
------, review of S. Ḥimādah, al-'Niẓām al-Iqtiṣādi fi 'l-'Irāq, 59 526
------, review of Anīs Ḫūri al-Maqdisi (tr.), al-Ḏikra, 49 85, 86-87
------, review of A. Ḫūri al-Maqdisi, Dīwān ibn-al-Sā'āti, vol. I, 59 529
------, review of A. Ḫūri al-Maqdisi, Taṭawwur al-Asālīb al-Naṯrīyah fi 'l-Adab al-'Arabi, 56 511, 514-515
------, review of Anīs Ḫūri al-Maqdisi, Umarā' al-Ši'r al-'Arabi fi 'l-'Aṣr al-'Abbāsi, 53 79-81
------, review of W. Ivanow (ed.), Diwan of Khaki Khorasani, 56 510, 513
------, review of W. Ivanow (tr.), True Meaning of Religion, 56 510, 513
------, review of W. Ivanow (ed.), Two Early Ismaili Treatises, 56 510, 513
------, review of J. Jabbūr, 'Aṣr ibn-abi-Rabī'ah, vol. I, 56 511, 515
------, review of P. Kahle, M. Muṣṭafa and M. Sobernheim (eds.), Badā'i' al-Zuhūr fi Waqā'i' al-Duhūr, by ibn-Iyās, 54 213
------, review of D. S. Kasir, The Algebra of Omar Khayyam, 52 267
------, review of M. Krause (ed. and tr.), Die Sphärik von Menelaos aus Alexandrien in der Verbesserung von Abū Naṣr Manṣūr B. 'Ali B. 'Irāq, 59 524-525
------, review of Muḥammad Kurd-'Ali, Kitāb Ḫiṭaṭ al-Šām, 46 321-322
------, review of Muḥammad Kurd-'Ali, Kitāb Ḫiṭaṭ al-Šām, 51 178-179
------, review of R. Levy (ed. and tr.), the Ma'ālim al-Qurba fi Aḥkām al-Ḥisba of ibn-al-Uḫuwwah, 59 523-524
------, review of Šayḫ 'Abd-al-Qādir al-Maġribi, al-Bayyināt fi al-Dīn wa-'l-Ijtimā' wa-'l-Adab wa-'l-Ta'rīḫ, 47 78-79
------, review of S. Mahmassani, Les idées économiques d'Ibn Khaldoun, 53 81
------, review of 'Abbās Maḥmūd, al-Islām wa-'l-Tajdīd fi Miṣr, 56 511, 513-514
------, review of Louis Massignon, Recueil de textes inédits concernant l'histoire de la mystique en pays d'Islam, 51 179
------, review of E. Montet, Choix de proverbes, dictons, maximes et pensées de l'Islam, 57 326
------, review of J. A. Montgomery, Arabia and the Bible, 54 302-303
------, review of D. Munro, The Kingdom of the Crusades, 56 510, 512
------, review of F. C. Murgotten, The Origins of the Islamic State, 46 274-284
------, review of A. R. Nykl (ed.), al-Niṣf al-Awwal min Kitāb al-Zahrah of Muḥammad ibn-abi-Sulaymān al-Iṣfahāni, 54 215-216
------, review of A. Nykl, The Dove's Neck-Ring about Love and Lovers, 52 58-59
------, review of Naoum Elias Palak, Majmū' al-Alfāẓ al-Suryānīyah min al-'Arabīyah al-'Āmmīyah fi mā bayn al-Nahrayn wa-Ḫuṣūṣan al-'Arabīyah al-Āmidīyah, 47 77-78
------, R. Paret, Zur Frauenfrag in der arabischen-islamischen Welt, 57 326
------, review of Dāwūd Qurbān (tr.), al-'Uṣūr al-Qadīmah, 49 85, 87-88
------, review of H. Ritter (ed.), Kitāb Firaq al-Šī'ah of al-Nawbaḫti, 54 214
------, review of H. Ritter (ed.), Kitāb al-Wāfi bi-'l-Wafāyāt of ibn-Aybak al-Ṣafadi, 54 214-215
------, review of J. Ruska, Das Buch der Alaune und Salze, 57 325
------, review of A. J. Rustum, The Royal Archives of Egypt and the Disturbances in Palestine, 1834, 59 528
------, review of A. Rustum, The Royal Archives of Egypt and the Origins of the Egyptian Expedition to Syria 1831-1841, 57 322, 324
------, review of A. J. Rustum, The Royal Archives of Egypt and the Origins of the Egyptian Expedition to Syria, 1831-41, 59 528
------, review of Ḫalīl Sa'd, As'ad Ḫayrallāh and Paul Erdman, al-Mu'jam al-'Aṣri fi 'l-Inkilīzi wa-'l-'Arabi (Centennial English-Arabic Dictionary), 49 85-86
------, review of 'A. Sarfarāz, A Descriptive Catalogue of the Arabic, Persian and Urdu Manuscripts in the Library of the University of Bombay, 57 322-323
------, review of J. F. Scheltema, The Lebanon in Turmoil, 43 338-347
------, review of M. Schloessinger (ed.), Ansāb al-Ašrāf of al-Bālaḏuri, vol. IV B, 59 528
------, review of Ḥ. al-Šihabi, Lubnān fi 'Ahd al-Umarā' al-Šihābīyīn, ed. A. Rustum and F. al-Bustāni, 56 511, 515-516
------, review of: al-Ṣūli, Kitāb al-Awrāq, ed. H. J. Dunne, 57 322, 323-324
------, review of Khalil A. Totah, Contribution of the Arabs to Education, 47 282-284
------, review of E. Tyan, Historie de l'organisation judiciaire en pays d'Islam, 59 527
------, review of Ṭūbīyah al-'Unaysi, Tafsīr al-Alfāẓ al-Daḫīlah fi 'l-Luġah al-'Arabīyah, 2nd ed. by T. al-Bustāni, 53 79
------, review of H. B. van Hoesen and F. K. Walker, Bibliography: Enumerative and Historical, 49 327
------, review of A. J. Wensinck, Concordance et indices de la tradition musulmane, 56 510-512

------, review of Q. Zurayq (ed.): ibn-al-Furāt, Ta'rīh, vol. IX, 57 322, 323-324
------, review of Q. Zurayq and N. 'Izz al-Dīn (eds.), Ta'rīḫ ibn-al-Furāt, IX, 59 527-528
------, review of Q. Zurayq, (ed.), The Yazīdis, Past and Present, 56 511, 514
HODOUS, Lewis. The Reception of Spring, observed in Foochow, China, 42 53-58
HOMMEL, Fritz. The Oldest Dome-Structure in the World, 41 230-234
HOPKINS, Clark. The Palmyrene Gods at Dura-Europos, 51 119-137
HOPKINS, E. Washburn. Allusions to the Rāma-story in the Mahābhārata, 50 85-103
------. Aspects of the Vedic Dative, 28 360-406
------. The Background of Totemism, 38 145-159
------. A Buddhistic Passage in Manu, 43 244-246
------. The Buddhistic Rule against Eating Meat, 27 455-464
------. The Divinity of Kings, 51 309-316
------. Epic Chronology, 24 7-56
------. The Fountain of Youth, 26 1-67
------. The Fountain of Youth. Second Paper, 26 411-415
------. Further Notes on Automatic Conflagrations, the Hindu Method of Counting, and the Period of Pregnancy, 24 390-391
------. A Handful of Books from India, 49 52-55
------. In Memoriam (Edward Elbridge Salisbury), 22 1-6
------. Indic and Indian Religious Parallels, 37 72-84
------. Indra and other Gods of War and Fertility Combined, 37 85-86
------. Indra as God of Fertility, 36 242-268
------. Mythological Aspects of Trees and Mountains in the Great Epic, 30 347-374
------. Note on Professor Toy's Article on Message-Sacrifices, 26 416
------. Notes on the Çvetāçvatara, the Buddhacarita, etc., 22 380-389
------. The Oath in Hindu Epic Literature, 52 316-337
------. On the Hindu Custom of Dying to Redress a Grievance, 21 146-159
------. The Origin of the Ablative Case, 38 47-59
------. The Original Rāmāyaṇa, 46 202-219
------, Phrases of Time and Age in the Sanskrit Epic, 23 350-357
------. Priestly Penance and Legal Penalty, 44 243-257
------. Remarks on the Form of Numbers, the Method of Using them, and the Numerical Categories found in the Mahābhārata, 23 109-155
------. Sanskrit Kabāiras or Kubāiras and Greek Kabeiros, 33 55-70
------. Sanskrit te for tvām, 51 285
------. The Sniff-kiss in Ancient India, 28 120-134
------. Two Notes on the Rig Veda, 25 336-338
------. The Universality of Religion, 25 332-335
------. Words of Defamation in Sanskrit Legal Language, 45 39-50
------. Yoga-technique in the Great Epic, 22 333-379
------, review of N. C. Bandhyopadhyaya, Development of Hindu Polity, Part I, 49 52
------, review of N. C. Bandhyopadhyaya, Kātyāyana-Mata-Saṅgraha, 49 53
------, review of N. C. Bandhyopadhaya, Kautilya, 49 52
------, review of S. K. Belvalkar and R. D. Ranade, History of Indian Philosophy, 49 54-55
------, review of K. N. Das, History of Bengali Literature, 49 54
------, review of Johannes Hertel, Die Arische Feuerlehre, I Teil, 49 177-178
------, review of Johannes Hertel, Die Methode der Arischen Forschung, 49 177-178
------, review of Pandurang Vaman Kane, History of Dharmaśāstra (Ancient and Mediaeval, Religious and Civil Law), 51 80-84
------, review of S. V. Karandikar, Hindu Exogamy, 49 53
------, review of Ryukan Kimura, A History of the Terms Hīnayāna and Mahāyāna and the Origin of Mahāyāna Buddhism, 49 53
------, review of Bimal Churn Law, Ancient Indian Tribes, 49 177-178
------, review of Bimala C. Law, Women in Buddhist Literature, 49 52
------, review of Sylvain Lévi, L'Inde et le monde, 49 177-178
------, review of R. C. Majumdar, The Outline of Ancient Indian History and Civilisation, 49 55
------, review of G. N. Mallik, The Philosophy of Vaishnava Religion, vol. I, 49 54
------, review of Kâlidâs Nâg, Les théories diplomatiques de l'Inde ancienne et l'Arthaçâstra, 44 76-77
------, review of H. Oldenberg, Das Mahābhārata. Seine Entstehung, sein Inhalt, seine Form, 43 54-56
------, review of Beni Prasad, The State in Ancient India, 49 52-53
------, review of Beni Prasad, Theory of government in Ancient India, 49 52-53
------, review of R. D. Ranade, A Constructive Survey of Upanishadic Philosophy, 47 274-275
------, review of S. N. Mojumdar Śāstrī, Ancient India as described by Ptolemy, 49 55
------, review of V. S. Sukthankar, The Mahābhārata, 51 179-180
HOURANI, George F., see Chung, Kei Won
HOWARD, Harry N. Preliminary Materials for a Survey of the Libraries and Archives of Istanbul, 59 227-246
HOWLAND, Felix, review of A. Christensen, Contributions à la dialectologie iranienne. (Dialecte Guilāke de Recht, dialectes de Fārizānd, de Yaran et de Natanz), 52 65-67
------, review of G. Morgenstierne, An Etymological Vocabulary of Pashto, 52 65, 67-68
HOYT, Sarah F. The Etymology of Religion, 32 126-129.
------. The Holy One in Psalm 16, 10, 32 120-125
------. The Name of the Red Sea, 32 115-119
HSÜ TI-SHAN. The History of the Canon of the Chinese Classics, 44 273-284
HUANG K'uei-yuen and J. K. Shryock. A Collection of Chinese Prayers, translated with Notes, 49 128-155
HUME, Edward H. Note on the Adaptation of a Chinese Character to Political Change 46 58-60
HUMMEL, Arthur W. Ts'ung Shu, 51 40-46
HUSIK, Isaac. Maimonides and Spinoza on the Interpretation of the Bible, 55 Supp. 1, 22-40
------, review of P. M. Bouyges, Notes sur les philosophes arabes connus des latins au moyen âge, 45 329-331
------, review of H. A. Wolfson, Crescas' Critique of Aristotle, 50 166-168
HUSSEY, Mary Inda. A Conveyance of Land Dates in the Reign of Ellilbâni, 36 34-36
------. A Galet of Eannatum, 38 264-266
------. A Supplement to Brünnow's Classified List of Cuneiform Ideographs, 22 201-220
------. Tablets from Drêhem in the Public Library of Cleveland, Ohio, 33 167-179
HUXLEY, Henry Minor. Syrian Songs, Proverbs, and Stories; Collected, translated, and annotated, 23 175-288
HYATT, J. Philip. The Deity Bethel and the Old Testament, 59 81-98
HYDE, W. W., review of W. H. Buckler and D. M. Robinson, Sardis, VII, I: Greek and Latin Inscriptions, 53 178-180
HYVERNAT, Henry, see Adler, Cyrus
JACKSON, Abraham Valentine Williams. The Allegory of the Moths and the Flame, translated from the Manṭiq aṭ-Ṭair of Farīd ad-Dīn 'Attār, 36 345-347
------. Contributions to the Knowledge of Manichaeism, 44 61-72
------. The Doctrine of the Bolos in Manichaean Eschatology, 58 225-234

------. The Doctrine of Metempsychosis in Manichaeism, 45 246-268
------. The Etymology of some Words in the Old Persian Inscriptions, 38 121-124
------. The Great Behistun Rock and some Results of a Re-examination of the Old Persian Inscriptions on it, 24 77-95
------. The Location of the Farnbāg Fire, the most Ancient of the Zoroastrian Fires, 41 81-106
------. The Magi in Marco Polo and the Cities in Persia from which they came to Worship the Infant Christ, 26 79-83
------. Notes from India: Letters to the Corresponding Secretary, 22 321-332
------. Notes from India, Second Series. — A Visit to Ujjain — Bhartṛhari's Cave — Legends of King Vikrama. (Letters to the Corresponding Secretary), 23 307-317
------. Notes of a Journey to Persia, 25 176-184
------. On the Manichaean Word Nōxvīr in Turfan Pahlavi, 47 193-197
------. On a Pahlavi Bowl-Inscription Deciphered by the Late E. W. West, 28 345-348
------. On a Passage in Bāṇa's Harṣacarita, 50 129-131
------. On Sanskrit l = Avestan d, 25 175
------. On Turfan Pahlavi miyazdagtāčīh, as Designating a Manichaean Ceremonial Offering, 49 34-39
------. The Personality of Mānī, the Founder of Manichaeism, 58 235-240
------. The Religion of the Achaemenian kings. First Series. The Religion according to the Inscriptions, 21 160-184
------. A Sketch of the Manichaean Doctrine Concerning the Future Life, 50 177-198
------. Studies in Manichaeism, 43 15-25
------. Textual Notes on the Old Persian Inscriptions, 27 190-194
------. Time Analysis of Sanskrit Plays. Second Series, 21 88-108
------. Traces of Biblical Influences in the Turfan Pahlavi Fragment M. 173, 56 198-207
------, review of Reuben Levy, Persian Literature. An Introduction, 44 138-139
------, see also Gottheil, Richard J. H.; Torrey, Charles Cutler; Yohannan, Abraham
JACOBI, Hermann. The Dates of the Philosophical Sūtras of the Brahmans, 31 1-29
JACOBSEN, Thorkild. The Assumed Conflict Between Sumerians and Semites in Early Mesopotamia, 59 485-495
JASTROW, Morris Jr. Another Fragment of the Etana Myth, 30 101-131
------. An Assyrian Law Code, 41 1-59
------. Did the Babylonian Temples have Libraries? 27 147-182
------. The God Ašur, 24 282-311
------. Ḫuruppâti, 'betrothal gifts,' 41 314-316
------. In Memoriam: William Hayes Ward, 36 233-241
------. Old and Later Elements in the Code of Hammurapi, 36 1-33
------. The Revolt in Arabia, 36 420
------. Sumerian and Akkadian Views of Beginnings, 36 274-299
------. The Sumerian View of Beginnings, 36 122-135
------. The Teating of Garments as a Symbol of Mourning, with especial reference to the Customs of the Ancient Hebrews, 21 23-39
------. Wine in the Pentateuchal Codes, 33 180-192
JEFFREY, Arthur, review of Dissertationes in honorem Dr. Eduardi Mahler, 59 517-519
------, review of B. Lewis, The Origins of Ismā'īlism, 60 426-429
JOHNSON, Helen M. Conversion of Vikrama Saṃvat Dates, 58 668-669
------. The Date of Divālī, 59 506-508
------. Historical References in Hemacandra's Mahāvīracaritra, 45 301-310
------. The Lemon in India, 56 47-50
------. The Lemon in India. Correction, 56 384
------. The Story of the Thief Rāuhiṇeya in the Mahāvīracaritra of Hemacandra, 44 1-10
------, review of Charaṇavijaya, Trishashṭiśalākā-purushacharitram-mahākāvyam, by Śrī-Hemachandra-āchārya. Parvan First, 59 275-276
------, review of Jarl Charpentier, The Indian Travels of Apollonius of Tyana, 55 316-318
------, review of C. D. Dalal, Lekhapaddhati, 46 270
------, review of Barend Faddegon, The Pravacana-sāra of Kunda-kunda Ācārya, together with the commentary Tattva-dīpikā, by Amṛtacandra, 56 523-525
------, review of Helmuth v. Glasenapp, Der Jainismus, 46 268-269
------, review of Johannes Hertel, On the Literature of the Shvetāmbaras of Gujarat, 46 75-76
------, review of Chimanlal J. Shah, Jainism in North India. 800 B. C. — A. D. 526, 52 392-395
------, review of A. J. Sunavala, Vijaya Dharma Sūri, 45 328
------, review of Çrī Vijaya Indra Sūri, Reminiscences of Vijaya Dharma Sūri, 45 328
------, review of A. N. Upadhye, Pravacanasāra, Śrī Kundakundācarya's, 56 523-525
------, review of Maurice Winternitz, A History of Indian Literature. Vol. II. Buddhist Literature and Jain Literature. Translated from the original German by Mrs. S. Ketkar and Miss H. Kohn, 56 371-373
JOHNSON, Jotham. Observation of the Equinox at Petra, 55 464-465
------, review of R. H. Mc Dowell, Coins from Seleucia on the Tigris, 56 517, 518
------, review of R. Mc Dowell, Stamped and Inscribed Objects from Seleucia on the Tigris, 56 517-518
------, review of M. I. Rostovtzeff (ed.), The Excavations at Dura-Europos. Preliminary Report of Fifth Season of Work, October 1931-March 1932, 55 210-214
JOHNSTON, Christopher. Assyrian qanânu 'to coil'; and xarâpu 'to abound', 29 224-226
------. The Fall of Nineveh, 22 20-22
------. The Marburg Collection of Cypriote Antiquities, 22 18-19
------. Note on two Assyrian Words Hitherto Unexplained, 22 23-26
------. Šamaš-šum-ukîn the Eldest Son of Esarhaddon, 25 79-83
JURJI, Edward Jabra. The Illuministic Sufis, 57 99-101
------. The Išrāqi Revival of al-Suhrawardi, 60 90-94
------, review of O. Spies and S. K. Khatak, Three Treatises on Mysticism by Shihābuddin Suhrawerdī Maqtūl, 56 516-517
KALMYKOW, A. Iranians and Slavs in South Russia. 45 68-71
KATRE, S. M. Epic iyāt and Blends of Aorist and Optative Forms, 57 316-317
KENNEDY, George A. A Study of the Particle Yen, 60 1-22; 193-207
KENT, Roland G. Addendum on a Difficult Old Persian Passage, 41 74-75
------. Addendum on the Record of Darius's Palace at Susa, 53 166
------. Cattle-tending and Agriculture in the Avesta, 39 329-333
------. The Chronology of Certain Indo-Iranian Sound-changes, 33 259-262
------. Classical Parallels to a Sanskrit Proverb, 33 214-216
------. Linguistic Science and the Orientalist, Presidential Address delivered at meetings of the Society in Ann Arbor, Apr. 24, 1935, 55 115-137
------. More Old Persian Inscriptions, 54 34-52
------. Note on Atharva-Veda XX, 127, 10, 34 310-312

------. Note on Yasna 34.11, 47 267-268
------. Old Persian Jottings, 58 324-330
------. The Present Status of Old Persian Studies, 56 208-225
------. The Recently Published Old Persian Inscriptions, 51 189-240
------. The Record of Darius's Palace at Susa, 53 1-23
------. The Restoration of Order by Darius, 58 112-121
------. Studies in the Old Persian Inscriptions, 35 321-352
------. A Syntactical Shift in an Avestan Passage, 48 277-279
------. The Textual Criticism of Inscriptions, 40 289-299
------, review of C. Autran, Introduction a l'étude critique du nom propre grec, 46 249-252
------, review of Jacques Duchesne-Guillemin, Études de Morphologie iranienne I. Les Composés de l'Avesta, 57 429-431
------, review of Ernst Herzfeld, Altpersische Inschriften, 59 126-129
------, review of T. Hudson-Williams, A Short Grammar of Old Persian, with a Reader, 57 193-194
------, review of A. V. Williams Jackson, Zoroastrian Studies: the Iranian Religion and Various Monographs, 49 286-289
------, review of Friedrich Wilhelm König, Relief und Inschrift des Koenigs Dareios I am Felsen von Bagistan, 58 675-679
------, review of Enno Littmann, Morgenländische Wörter im Deutschen, 46 248-249
------, review of Karl Lokotsch, Etymologisches Wörterbuch der europäischen (germanischen, romanischen und slavischen) Wörter orientalischen Ursprungs, 49 93-94
------, review of A. Meillet, Trois Conférences sur les Gāthā de l'Avesta, 46 273-274
------, review of Jal Dastur Cursetji Pavry, The Zoroastrian Doctrine of a Future Life from Death to the Individual Judgment, 48 285-286
------, review of L. A. Waddell, The Phoenician Origin of Britons, Scots and Anglo-Saxons, 45 172-174
------, see also Ogden, Charles J.
KERNS, J. Alexander and Benjamin Schwartz. The Laryngeal Hypothesis and Indo-Hittite, Indo-European Vocalism, 60 181-192
KNOWLES, Lillian E., review of André Beaujard, Sei Shonagon, son Temps et son Oeuvre (une femme de lettres de l'ancien Japon). Avec une préface de M. Michel Revon, 57 133-134
KOHLER, K. The Sabbath and Festivals in Pre-Exilic and Exilic Times, 37 209-223
KOHUT, George Alexander. Blood Test as Proof of Kinship in Jewish Folklore, 24 129-144
------. Some Oriental Analogues to the Ballad of King John and the Abbot of Canterbury, 22 221-226
KOO, Telly H. The Constitutional Development of the Western Han Dynasty, 40 170-193
KRAELING, Carl H. A Mandaic Bibliography, 46 49-55
------. The Mandaic God Ptahil, 53 152-165
------. The Origin and Antiquity of the Mandaeans, 49 195-218
------, review of J. Kroll, Gott und Hölle, 53 290-292
------, review of E. L. Sukenik, Ancient Synagogues in Palestine and Greece, 55 107-109
KRAELING, Emil G. The Death of Sennacherib, 53 335-346
------. The Tower of Babel, 40 276-281
KRAMER, Samuel N. Dr. Chiera's List of Duplicates to de Genouillac's Textes religieux sumériens, 54 407-420
------. Langdon's Historical and Religious Texts from the Temple Library of Nippur — Additions and Corrections, 60 234-257
------. New Tablets from Fara, 52 110-132
KRAUSS, S., review of G. Beer, Mishna Manuscript Codex Kaufmann A. 50, 51 78-80
KREY, A. C., review of R. B. Yewdale, Bohemond I, Prince of Antioch, 45 174-175
KROGMAN, W. M., review of H. Field, Arabs of Central Iraq, 57 189-191
KÜMMEL, Otto, see Book Reviews, Le Coq
LACH, Donald F. The Chinese Studies of Andreas Müller, 60 564-575
LACHEMAN, Ernest R. New Nuzi Texts and a New Method of Copying Cuneiform Tablets, 55 429-431
------. SU = Šiqlu, 57 181-184
LADD, George Trumbull. A Death Ceremonial of the "Kapola Bania" Caste, 22 227-236
LANGDON, Stephen H. An Assyrian Grammatical Treatise on an Omen Tablet; C.T. 20, pp. 39-42, 27 88-103
------. Critical Notes Upon the Epic of Paradise, 36 140-145
------. An Early Babylonian Tablet of Warnings for the King, 28 145-154
------. Evidence for an Advance on Egypt by Sennacherib in the Campaign of 701-700 B.C., 24 265-274
------. The Name of the Ferryman in the Deluge Tablets, 23 48-50
------. Notes on the Annals of Ašurbanipal (V. Rawlinson, pp. 1-10), 24 96-102
------. The Supposed Variant of AH. 82, 7-14, 1042. Where is it? Its Probable Contents, 26 98-103
LANMAN, Charles R. Bharata's Treatise on Dramaturgy (Nāṭya-śāstra), 40 359-360
------. The Buddhist Sacred Texts: a Plea for the Prompt Undertaking of the Work of Making the Most Ancient Ones Accessible to the Occident, with a Word as to Methods and Helps, 38 333
------. India and the West with a Plea for Team-work among Scholars, 40 225-247
------. Phrase-words and Phrase-derivatives, 40 194-198
------. The Sanskrit Passive-stem, 40 199
LATOURETTE, K. S. American Scholarship and Chinese History, 38 97-106
LAU, R. J. Ābēl (אָבֵל) in the Bible, 27 301-302
------. Supplement to the Old Babylonian Vocabularies, 27 297-300
LAUFER, Berthold. Burkhan, 36 390-395
------. Burkhan (Brief Notes), 37 167-168
------. Columbus and Cathay, and the Meaning of America to the Orientalist, 51 87-103
------. In Memoriam, Édouard Chavannes, 38 202-205
------. The Lemon in China and Elsewhere, 54 143-160
------. Lun Yü, IX, 1, brief note, 54 83
------. On the Possible Oriental Origin of our Word Booze, 49 56-58
------. Origin of Tibetan Writing, 38 34-46
------. An Unpublished MS. Dictionary of the Manchu Language, prepared by Stanislas Julien, 40 140; see also Thayer, Gordon W.
------. The Vigesimal and Decimal Systems in the Ainu Numerals, with some remarks on Ainu Phonology, 37 192-208
------, review of Thomas F. Carter, The Invention of Printing in China and Its Spread Westward, 47 71-76
------, review of Henri Cordier, Mélanges d'histoire et de géographie orientales, 45 185
------, review of Hsiang Yüan-pien, Noted Porcelains of Successive Dynasties, revised, translated and annotated by Kuo Pao-ch'ang and John C. Ferguson, 52 93-95
------, review of Harry Ignatius Marshall, The Karen People of Burma: a Study in Anthropology and Ethnology, 45 185-187
------, review of Mrs. Leslie Milne, The Home of an Eastern Clan. A Study of the Palaungs of the Shan States, 45 187-189
------, review of George N. Roerich, Trails to Inmost Asia. Five Years of Exploration with the Roerich Central Asian Expedition, 52 95-97
------, review of T. B. Roorda, (Editor), Choix d'objets d'art d'Extrême-Orient conservés dans les Pays Bas, 43 337
------, review of Lucian and Christine Scherman, Im Stromgebiet des Irrawaddy, Birma und seine Frauenwelt, 45 189-191

LENT, Frederick. The Life of St. Simeon Stylites: A Translation of the Syriac Text in Bedjan's Acta Martyrum et Sanctorum, Vol. IV, 35 103-198
LEON, Harry J. The Synagogue of the Herodians, 49 318-321
LEVITAN, Isidore S. Dr. Efros' Emendation of Jer. 4.29, 41 316
LEVY, Reuben. A Note on the Marsh Arabs of Lower Iraq, 44 130-133
LEWY, Hildegard, review of E.-M. Cassin, L'adoption à Nuzi, 59 118-120
------, review of F. Thureau-Dangin, Textes mathématiques babyloniens, 60 105-107
LEWY, Julius. Notes on Pre-Ḫurrian Texts from Nuzi, 58 450-461
------, review of I. J. Gelb, Inscriptions from Alishar and Vicinity, 57 434-438
LICHTI, Otto. Das Sendschreiben des Patriarchen Barschuschan an den Catholicus der Armenier, 32 268-342
LINFIELD, H. S. The Dependence of the Talmudic Principle of Asmakhta on Babylonian Law, 40 126-133
LITTMANN, Enno. Arde'et: The Magic Book of the Disciples, 25 1-48
------. Specimens of the Popular Literature of Modern Abyssinia, 23 51-55
LUCE, Stephen Bleecker. A Note on 'The Year's Work in Oriental Archaeology,' 37 86-87
------. The Year's Work in Oriental Archaeology, 36 348-354
LUCKENBILL, Daniel D. The Name Hammurabi, 37 250-253
LÜDERS, Heinrich, see Book Reviews, Le Coq
LUTZ, Henry F. A Cassite Liver-Omen Text, 38 77-96
------. The DD-emblem of Osiris, 39 196-205
------. The Ḫagoroth of Genesis 37, 42 208-209
------. The Hebrew Word for 'to sew,' 40 71-72
------. The Helmet of Eannatum, 38 68-69
------. Ḳû, "thread, cord" in Egyptian, 42 209-210
------. The Meaning of Babylonian bittu, 42 206-207
------. A Nilometer in the Egyptian Collection of the Museum of Anthropology and Ethnology of the University of California, 43 49
------. Nin-Uraš and Nippur, 42 210-211
------. A Note on the Closing Lines of the Story of the Shipwrecked Sailor, 45 156
------. A Note Regarding the Garment Called بَدَنٌ and its Etymology, 42 207
------. The Oldest Monumental Evidence of a Dome-structure, 39 122
------. On the Reading of the Date-formula of the Fourth Year of Gimil-Sin, 37 330-331
------. The Root ידל, edelu in Egyptian, 42 202-203
------. Sanduarri, King of Kundi and Sizû, 42 201-202
------. A Stone Group of Amset and Hapi, 46 312-313
LYBYER, A. H. The Four Quadrants of Asia (Presidential Address), 41 190-191
------. The Travels of Evliya Effendi, 37 224-239
------. See also Braden, Charles S.
LYON, David G. Notes on the Hammurabi Monument, 25 266-278
------. The Seal Impressions on an Early Babylonian Contract (Harvard Semitic Museum, No. 109), 27 135-141
------. The Structure of the Hammurabi Code, 25 248-265
------. When and Where was the Code of Hammurabi Promulgated? 27 123-134
MC COWN, C. C. A New Deity in a Jerash Inscription, 54 178-185
------, review of E. Sukenik and L. Mayer, The Third Wall of Jerusalem, 52 56-58
MC GOVERN, Wm. R., see Braden, Charles S.
MACKAY, Ernest. Bead Making in Ancient Sind, 57 1-15
MAC KINLAY, William E. W. Some Minor Languages of Luzon, 25 170-174
MC PHERSON, William B. Gideon's Water-lappers, 22 70-75
MACHT, David I. A Pharmacological Note on Psalm 58_9, 42 280-285
MAJUMDAR, D. N. Totemism and Origin of Clans, 50 221-232
MALONE, Carroll B. Current Regulations for Building and Furnishing Chinese Imperial Palaces, 1727-1750, 49 234-243
------, review of Maurice Adam, Yuen Ming Yuen, L'Oeuvre Architecturale des Anciens Jésuites au XVIII Siècle, (C. B. Malone), 57 126-127
------, review of Luther Carrington Goodrich, The Literary Inquisition of Ch'ien-lung, 55 477-479
MANNING, Clarence Augustus. The Legend of Kostryuk, 46 23-33
------. Prester John and Japan, 42 286-294
------. Yermak Timofeyevich in Russian Folk Poetry, 43 206-215
MARCUS, Ralph. An Armenian-Greek index to Philo's Quaestiones and De Vita Contemplativa, 53 251-282
------, review of J.-B. Frey (ed.), Corpus inscriptionum judaicarum, 56 505-506
MARGOLIS, Max L. Additions to Field from the Lyons Codex of the Old Latin, 33 254-258
------. Complete Induction for the Identification of the Vocabulary in the Greek Versions of the Old Testament with its Semitic Equivalents, 30 301-312
------. The Washington MS. of Joshua, 31 365-367
------, review of D. S. Blondheim, Les Parlers judéo-romans et la Vetus Latina, 49 82-84
------, review of J. A. Montgomery, A Critical and Exegetical Commentary on the Book of Daniel, 49 78-82
MARTINOVITCH, Nicholas N. Arabic, Persian and Turkish Manuscripts in the Columbia University Library, 49 219-233
------. Crusius or Orosius, 51 171-172
------. The Life of Mohammad Paolo Zaman, the Persian Painter of the XVIIth Century, 45 106-109
------. A New Manuscript of Ali Riza Abbasi, 44 270-271
------. The Turkish chalabī, 54 194-199
------, review of Iran, vol. I (1926), 49 91-93
------, review of T. W. Arnold and A. Grohmann, The Islamic Book, 50 82-84
------, review of F. Babinger, Die Geschichtsschreiber der Osmanen und ihre Werke, 48 286-287
------, review of E. Blochet, Musulman Painting, 51 71-73
------, review of F. W. Buckler, Harunu'l-Rashid and Charles the Great, 52 61-63
------, review of A. Coomaraswamy, Mughal Painting, 51 71
------, review of M. Dimand, A Guide to an Exhibition of Islamic Miniature Painting, 55 105
------, review of M. S. Dimand, A Handbook of Mohammedan Decorative Arts, 51 84-85
------, review of L. Fekete, Türkische Schriften aus dem Archive des Palatins Nikolaus Esterhazy 1606-1645, ed. by Prince Paul Esterhazy, 53 82-83
------, review of G. Jarring, Studien zu einer osttürkischen Lautlehre, 55 105-106
------, review of P. Kahle, Die verschollene Columbus-Karte von 1498 in einer türkischen Weltkarte von 1513, 55 106-107
------, review of I. Manninen, Die Finnisch-Ugrischen Völker, 53 84-85
------, review of the Mīr 'Ali Šīr 500th Anniversary Memorial Volume, issued by the USSR Academy of Sciences, 49 185-186
------, review of Helmut Ritter, Karagös. Türkische Schattenspiel, 46 284-285
------, review of A. Vahid Bey, A Condensed Dictionary, English-Turkish, 46 185-186
------, review of G. Weil, Tatarische Texte, 52 63

------, review of C. E. Wilson, The Haft Paikar (The Seven Beauties) by Nizami of Ganja, 46 285-286
------, review of Yusuf Ziya, Arier und Turanier, 53 83-84
MATTHEWS, Charles D. The Kitāb Aimān al-'Arab wa-Ṭalāqiha fi'l-Jāhilīya of an-Najīramī, 58 615-637
------. Manuscripts and a Mamlūk Inscription in the Lansing Collection in the Denver Public Library, 60 370-382
------. A Muslim Iconoclast (ibn Taymīyyeh) on the "Merits" of Jerusalem and Palestine, 56 1-21
MATTHEWS, I. G., review of C. C. Torrey, Pseudo-Ezekiel and the Original Prophecy, 52 368-373
MAY, Herbert Gordon. The Sacred Tree on Palestine Painted Pottery, 59 251-259
------, see also Braden, Charles S.
MAYNARD, J. A., review of G. A. Barton, Archaeology and the Bible, 49 182
MEDARD, M. Note on the Review of A Propos des Voyages aventureaux de Fernard Mendez Pinto, 58 473-474
MEEK, Theophile James. Babyloniaca, 43 353-357
------. The Co-ordinate Adverbial Clause in Hebrew, 49 156-159
------. The Hebrew Accusative of Time and Place, 60 224-233
------. Lapses of Old Testament Translators, 58 122-129
------. A Votive Inscription of Ashurbanipal, 38 167-175
------, review of G. A. Barton, Semitic and Hamitic Origins, 54 300-302
------, review of J. Billiet, Cachets et cylindres-sceaux de style sumérien archaïque et de styles dérivés du Musée de Cannes, 53 70
------, review of R. P. Dougherty, Goucher College Cuneiform Inscriptions, I: Archives from Erech. Time of Nebuchadrezzar and Nabonidus, 45 91-92
------, review of T. Fish, Catalogue of Sumerian Tablets in the John Rylands Library, 53 71
------, review of S. Langdon, Oxford Editions of Cuneiform Inscriptions, Vol. I, Sumerian and Semitic Religious and Historical Texts; Vol. II, Historical Inscriptions, containing principally the Chronological Prism, W-B. 444, 44 287-290
------, review of I. Mendelsohn, Legal Aspects of Slavery in Babylonia, Assyria and Palestine, 53 72-73
------, review of L. Waterman, Royal Correspondence of the Assyrian Empire, I-III, 53 68-70
MENDELSOHN, I. The Conditional Sale into Slavery of Freeborn Daughters in Nuzi and the Law of Ex. 21:7-11, 55 190-195
------. Gilds in Babylonia and Assyria, 60 68-72
MERCER, Samuel A. B. Divine Service in Early Lagash, 42 91-104
------. 'Emperor' - Worship in Babylonia, 36 360-380
------. 'Emperor' - Worship in Babylonia — a Reply, 37 331
------. The Malediction in Cuneiform Inscriptions, 34 282-309
------. The Oath in Cuneiform Inscriptions, 33 33-50
METHENY, J. Renwick. Road Notes from Cilicia and North Syria, 28 155-163
MICHELSON, Truman. Additions to Bloomfield's Vedic Concordance, 29 284-285
------. Asokan Notes, 36 205-212
------. The Interrelation of the Dialects of the Fourteen-Edicts of Asoka. 1: General Introduction and the Dialect of the Shāhbāzgarhi and Mansehra Redactions, 30 77-93
------. The Interrelation of the Dialects of the Fourteen-Edicts of Asoka. 2: The Dialect of the Girnār Redaction, 31 223-250
------. Linguistic Archaisms of the Rāmāyaṇa, 25 89-145
------. The Locative Singular of Masculine and Neuter i and u Stems in Śaurasenī Prākrit, 41 461-462
------. Note on Māgadhī ahake, 41 459
------. Once more Shāhbāzgarhi uthanaṃ, 41 460-461
------. Vedic, Sanskrit, and Middle Indic, 33 145-149
------, review of D. R. Bhandarkar, Asoka, 46 256-264
------, review of Alfred C. Woolner, Asoka Text and Glossary, 46 264-265
MILES, George C. Turkish pala "Sword" and its Derivatives, 50 254-260
MILLS, Lawrence H. The Pahlavi Text of Yasna ix. 49-103, Edited with the Collation of all the NSS., also Deciphered, 23 1-18
------. The Pahlavi Text of Yasna ix. 49-103 for the First Time Critically Translated, 24 64-76
------. The Pahlavi Text of Yasna XVII, Edited with all the MSS. Collated, 26 68-78
------. Vohumanah in the Gáthas, 21 67-87
MOGADHAM, M. E. A Note on the Etymology of the Word checkmate, 58 662-664
MONTGOMERY, James A. Additional Notes on the Ras Shamra Texts, 53 283-284
------. Adverbial kúlla in Biblical Aramaic and Hebrew, 43 391-395
------. Alleged Intensive Noun-Formations in Semitic, 46 56-58
------. Arabia Today, 47 97-132
------. An Aramaic Ostrakon from Nippur and the Greek Obolos, 29 204-209
------. Babylonian niš 'oath' in West-Semitic, 37 329-330
------. Hebraica, 58 130-139
------. In Memoriam: Albert T. Clay, 45 289-294
------. A Jewish Mortuary Amulet, 38 140-141
------. A Magical Bowl-Text and the Original Script of the Manichaeans, 32 434-438
------. The Nominal Prefix n in some Hebrew Names, 43 50-51
------. Notes on Early Aramaic Inscriptions, 54 421-425
------. Notes on the Mythological Epic Texts from Ras Shamra, 53 97-123
------. Origin of the Ethiopic Gerund, 48 283-284
------. Postage Stamps of the Hijâz, 37 87-88
------. Ras Shamra Notes. II, 54 60-66
------. Ras Shamra Notes III, 55 89-94
------. Ras Shamra Notes IV: The Conflict of Baal and the Waters, 55 268-277
------. Ras Shamra Notes V, 56 226-231
------. Ras Shamra Notes VI: The Danel Text, 56 440-445
------. Report on an Aramaic Boundary Inscription in Cilicia, 28 164-167
------. Some Early Amulets from Palestine, 31 272-281
------. The 'two youths' in the LXX to Dan. 6, 41 316-317
------. The Words 'law' and 'witness' in South Arabic, 37 164-165
------, review of The Encyclopaedia of Islām, No. 28, 45 336
------, review of al-Muqtaṭaf and its press, 46 92-93
------, review of Studien zur Geschichte und Kultur des Nahen und Fernen Ostens Paul Kahle zum 60 Geburtstag überreicht von Freuden und Schülern aus dem Kreise des Orientalischen Seminars der Universität Bonn. Edited by W. Heffening and W. Kirfel; 23 monographs, 55 472-473
------, review of I. Abrahams, The Glory of God, 47 88-89
------, review of P. J. André, L'Islam et les races, vols. I and II, 46 89-90
------, review of Mohammad Barakatullah, The Khilafet, 45 336
------, review of H. Bauer, Das Alphabet von Ras Schamra, 53 167-168
------, review of H. Bauer and P. Leander, Grammatik des Biblisch-Aramäischen, 51 317-320
------, review of H. Bauer and P. Leander, Kurzgefasste Grammatik des Biblisch-Aramäischen, 51 317, 320
------, review of R. H. Charles, A Critical and Exegetical Commentary on the Book of Daniel, 51 317, 323-327
------, review of Michel Féghali and Albert Cuny, Du genre grammatical en sémitique, 45 335

------, review of Gaudefroy-Demombynes, Le pèlerinage à la Mekke, 46 88, 91
------, review of C. A. Hawley, A Critical Examination of the Peshitta Version of the Book of Ezra, 43 432-433
------, review of J. Hempel, Die althebräische Literatur und ihr hellenistisches Nachleben, 55 208-210
------, review of P. Hitti, An Arab-Syrian Gentleman, 50 261-262
------, review of P. Hitti, Kitāb al-I'tibār li-Usāmah ibn-Munqid, 51 327-328, 329-332
------, review of P. Hitti, The Origins of the Druze People and Religion, 50 261, 262-263
------, review of J. J. Jibrān, al-Badā'i' wa-'l-Ṭarā'if, 46 92-93
------, review of A. C. Johnson, H. S. Gehman and E. H. Kase (eds.), The John H. Scheide Biblical Papyri: Ezekiel, 59 262-265
------, review of H. Lammens, La Syrie. Précis historique, 46 88, 90-91
------, review of P. Leander, Laut- und Formenlehre des Ägyptisch-Aramäischen, 51 317, 320-321
------, review of R. Levy, Deutero-Isaiah, 47 89-90
------, review of T. Meek, Hebrew Origins, 57 431-434
------, review of A. Mingana, Christian Documents in Syriac, Arabic and Garshūni, 49 284-286
------, review of A. Mingana, Christian Documents in Syriac, Arabic, and Garshūni, 56 499-500
------, review of Mordtmann and Mittwoch, Sabäische Inschriften, 52 194-196
------, review of Ditlef Nielsen, Handbuch der altarabischen Altertumskunde, 48 80-83
------, review of R. Paret (ed.), Orientalistische Studien Enno Littmann... überreicht, 56 104-106
------, review of W. Popper, Abū 'l-Maḥāsin ibn Taghrī Birdī's Annals, 51 327, 328-329
------, review of W. Popper, Extracts from Abū 'l-Maḥāsin ibn Taghrī Birdī's Chronicle entitled ḥawādith ad-duhūr fī madā 'l-ayyām wash-shuhūr, 51 327, 328-329
------, review of Rathjens and von Wissmann, Vorislamische Altertümer, 53 289-290
------, review of Amin Rihani, Ta'rīḫ Najd al-Ḥadīṯ wa-Mulqaḥātihi, 51 328, 332-334
------, review of M. Rostovtzeff, Caravan Cities, 53 287-288
------, review of H. H. Rowley, The Aramaic of the Old Testament, 51 317, 321-323
------, review of G. Ryckmans, Les noms propres sud-sémitiques, 55 314-316
------, review of N. Schmidt, Ibn Khaldun, Historian, Sociologist and Philosopher, 51 327, 328
------, review of Martin Thilo, Die Chronologie des Danielbuches, 47 280-281
------, review of H. Wiener, Early Hebrew History and Other Studies, 47 90-91
------, see also Brown, W. Norman; Clay, Albert T.
MOORE, George Foote. Conjectanea Talmudica, 26 315-333
MOORE, Justin Hartley. Metrical Analysis of the Pāli Itivuttaka, a Collection of Discourses of Buddha, 28 317-330
MORGENSTERN, Julian. American Culture and Oriental Studies, 48 97-108
------. The Bones of the Paschal Lamb, 36 146-153
------. The Date, Historical Background and Cultural Implications of Psalm 48, 58 527-528
------. The Etymological History of the Three Hebrew Synonyms for 'to Dance,' ḤGG, ḤLL and KRR, and their Cultural Significance, 36 321-332
------. Morris Jastrow Jr. as a Biblical Critic, 41 322-327
------. The Tent of Meeting, 38 125-139
------, review of Max Löhr, Untersuchungen zum Hexateuchproblem, I Der Priesterkodex in der Genesis, 46 82-84
------, see also Torrey, Charles Cutler
MORRIS, Margaretta. The Economic Study of Religion, 24 394-426
------. Harvest Gods of the Land Dyaks of Borneo, 26 165-175
------. The Influence of War and of Agriculture upon the Religion of Kayans and Sea Dyaks of Borneo, 25 231-247
------. Race and Custom in the Malay Archipelago, 27 195-216
MÜLLER, Valentine [or Valentin]: The Origin of the Early Dynastic Style, 58 140-147
------. The Origin of Mosaic, 59 247-250
------. Studies in Oriental Archaeology I. Plano-convex Bricks, 57 84-87
------. Types of Mesopotamian Houses, 60 151-180
------, review of W. Andrae, Die ionische Säule, 54 429-431
------, review of E. A. Speiser, Excavations at Tepe Gawra, Vol. I, 55 466-469
------, review of C. L. Wooley, Ur Excavations, II: The Royal Cemetery, 55 204-208
MÜLLER, W. Max. Remarks on the Carthaginian Deity, 32 429-433
MUMFORD, Ethel Watts. The Japanese Book of the Ancient Sword, 26 334-410
MUNRO, Dana C., review of Max Silberschmidt, Das orientalische Problem zur Zeit der Entstehung des Türkischen Reiches, 45 175-176
NEGELEIN, Julius von. Atharvaprāyaścittāni. Text mit Anmerkungen, 33 71-120
------. Atharvaprāyaścittāni. Text mit Anmerkungen, 33 121-144
------. Atharvaprāyaścittāni. Text mit Anmerkungen, 33 217-253
------. Atharvaprāyaścittāni. Vorwort und Einleitung, 34 229-277
NEISSER, Walter, review of Hermann Güntert, Der arische Weltkönig und Heiland, 45 280-288
NEWBOLD, William Romaine. A Syriac Valentinian Hymn, 38 1-33
NIES, James B. A Net Cylinder of Entemena, 36 137-139
------. Origin of MAŠ or BAR and the Development of its Meanings, 39 91-99
------. A pre-Sargonid Inscription on Limestone from Warka, 38 188-196
------. The Reading of GIŠ-ÚḪ^{ki}, 37 255-256
NORTON, Ruth. Note on Tantrākhyāyika IV, A 286, 41 76-77
NYKL, A. R. Notes on E. H. Palmer's "The Qur'ân," 56 77-84
OBERMANN, Julian J. The Archaic Inscriptions from Lachish, 58 Supp. II, 1-48
------. [Christian Snouck Hurgronje, In Memoriam], 57 215-216
------. Political Theology in Early Islam, 55 138-162
------, review of J. Montgomery and Z. Harris, The Ras Shamra Mythological Texts, 56 495-498
VON OEFELE, Felix. Ascalabotes fascicularis, in Old Babylonian Medicine, 39 284-285
------. Assyrian 'kalmat,' Arabic 'kaemlet,' 36 416
------. The Assyrian Veterinary Physician, 37 331-332
------. A Babylonian Belt Buckle, 38 308-309
------. A Babylonian Representation of a Jumping Mouse, 38 140
------. Babylonian Titles of Medical Textbooks, 37 250
------. Old Babylonian Linen Weaving, 36 415
OERTEL, Hanns. Additions to the Fifth Series of Contributions from the Jāiminīya Brāhmaṇa (JAOS. xxvi. 176 ff.), 26 306-314
------. Contributions from the Jāiminīya Brāhmaṇa to the History of the Brāhmaṇa Literature. — Fourth Series: Specimens of Verbal Correspondences of the Jāiminīya Brāhmaṇa with other Brāhmaṇas, 23 323-349
------. Contributions from the Jāiminīya Brāhmaṇa to the History of the Brāhmaṇa Literature. Fifth Series, 26 176-196
------. Contributions from the Jāiminīya Brāhmaṇa to the History of the Brāhmaṇa Literature. Sixth Series, 28 81-98

OGDEN, Charles J. Lexicographical and Grammatical Notes on the Svapnavāsavadatta of Bhāsa, 35 269-272
------. Three Turfan Pahlavi Etymologies: ḤPŠYRD, ʿŠKRWST, MNWḤMYD, 58 331-333
------ and R. G. Kent. A. V. W. Jackson, In Memoriam, 58 504-505
OGDEN, Ellen Seton. A Conjectural Interpretation of Cuneiform Texts vol. V, 81-7-27, 49 and 50, 32 103-114
------. Some Notes on the So-called Hieroglyphic-Tablet, 33 16-23
------. The Text of an Archaic Tablet in the E. A. Hoffman Collection, 23 19-20
OLIPHANT, Samuel Grant. Sanskrit dhénā = Avestan daenā = Lithuanian dainà, 32 393-413
------. The Vedic Dual: Part I., The Dual of Bodily Parts, 30 155-185
------. The Vedic Dual: Part II, The Dual in Similes, 35 16-30
------. The Vedic Dual: Part VI, The Elliptic Dual; Part VII, The Dual Dvandva, 32 33-57
OLMSTEAD, Albert Ten Eyck. The Assyrian Chronicle, 34 344-368
------. The British General Staff Maps, 39 58-59
------. The Calculated Frightfulness of Ashur Nasir Apal, 38 209-263
------. Intertestamental Studies, 56 242-257
------. New Testament Times — and Now, 53 311-325
------. Shalmaneser III and the Establishment of the Assyrian Power, 41 345-382
------. Tiglath-Pileser I and his Wars, 37 169-185
------, review of Paul Schnabel, Berossus und die babylonisch-hellenistische Literatur, 46 85-87
------, see also Bull, Ludlow; Clark, Walter
ORLINSKY, Harry M. Ḥāṣēr in the Old Testament, 59 22-37
------. Problems of Kethib-Qere, 60 30-45
OUSSANI, Gabriel. The Arabic Dialect of Baghdâd, 22 97-114
------. The Modern Chaldaeans and Nestorians, and the Study of Syriac among them, 22 79-96
OWEN, Charles A. Arabian Wit and Wisdom from abu Saʿid al-Abī's Kitab Nathr al-Durar, 54 240-275
PARISOT, J. A Collection of Oriental Jewish Songs, 24 227-264
PEAKE, Cyrus H., review of Kenneth Scott Latourette, The Chinese: Their History and Culture, 56 533-535
PERRY, Edward Delavan. Abraham Valentine Williams Jackson, 58 221-224
PETERS, John P. The Cock, 33 363-396
------. The Home of the Semites, 39 243-260
------. The Nippur Library, 26 145-164
------. Notes and Suggestions on the Early Sumerian Religion and its Expression, 41 131-149
------. Notes on Recent Theories of the Origin of the Alphabet, 22 177-198
------. The Tower of Babel at Borsippa, 41 157-159
PETERSEN, Walter. Hittite ḫ and Saussure's Doctrine of the Long Vowels, 59 175-199
------. Vedic, Sanskrit, and Prakrit, 32 414-428
PFEIFFER, Robert H. Assyrian Epistolary Formulae, 43 26-40
------, review of E. Chiera, Joint Expedition with the Iraq Museum at Nuzi, II, 51 76-78
------, review of E. Chiera, Nuzi, 49 178-180
PHILLIPS, William. The Need of an American School of Living Oriental Languages, 39 185-188
POEBEL, Arno. Another Case of the Predicative use of the Genitive in Sumerian, 58 148-150
------. The City of Aktab, 57 359-367
------. Etymology of qâtum, "Hand," 60 95-97
------. The Root Forms sī(m) and su$_{11}$(m), "to give," in Sumerian, 57 35-72
POLEMAN, Horace I. The Ritualistic Continuity of Ṛgveda X. 14-18, 54 276-281
------ and Philip Q. Roche. Aspects of Caesarean Section in India, 59 17-21
------, review of M. B. Emeneau, A Union List of Printed Indic Texts and Translations in American Libraries, 55 482-483
------, review of Fletcher Gardner and Ildefonso Maliwanag, Indic Writings of the Mindoro-Palawan Axis, 60 275
------, review of Arthur Berriedale Keith, Catalogue of the Sanskrit and Prākrit Manuscripts in the Library of the India Office. Volume II. Brahmanical and Jaina Manuscripts. With a Supplement: Buddhist Manuscripts. By F. W. Thomas, 55 214-215
------, review of Bharatan Kumarappa, The Hindu Conception of the Deity As Culminating in Rāmānuja, 55 329-330
------, review of Joseph Nadin Rawson, The Kaṭha Upaniṣad, 55 215-216
POPE, John, review of Charles S. Gardner, A Union List of Selected Western Books on China in American Libraries, 2nd Ed., 59 283-286
POPENOE, Paul. The Pollination of the Date Palm, 42 343-354
------. The Propagation of the Date Palm: Materials for a Lexicographical Study in Arabic, 35 207-212
------. Scale-Insects of the Date-Palm, 42 205-206
POPLICHA, Joseph. The Biblical Nimrod and the Kingdom of Eanna, 49 303-317
------. A Sun Myth in the Babylonian Deluge Story, 47 289-301
PORTER, Lucius C., review of Lewis Hodous, Chinese Buddhism, 46 78-81
------, review of Fritz Holm, My Nestorian Adventure, 44 290
PRICE, Ira Maurice. The Animal DUN in the Sumerian Inscriptions, 33 402-404
------. H. de Genouillac on "Lagash" and "Gírsu," 57 309-312
------. An Inscribed Eye of a Babylonian Idol, 43 51-53
------. The Laws of Deposit in Early Babylonia and the Old Testament, 47 250-255
------. Light out of Ur — the Devotion of Elamite Kings to Sumerian Deities, 51 164-169
------. The Nabopolassar Chronicle, 44 122-129
------. The Oath in Court Procedure in Early Babylonia and the Old Testament, 49 22-29
------. The Particle nam in Sumerian, 47 256-259
------. Penalties for Defaulters in Early Babylonia and the Old Testament, 48 354
------. The Relation of Certain Gods to Equity and Justice in Early Babylonia, 52 174-178
------. Some Light from Ur Touching Lagash, 50 150-158
------. The Topography of the Gudea Inscriptions, 43 41-48
PRINCE, J. Dyneley. A Brazilian Gypsey Dialect, 50 139-143
------. A Divine Lament (CT. XV. Plates 24-25), 31 395-402
------. The English-Rommany Jargon of the American Roads, 28 271-308
------. Further Notes on the So-Called Epic of Paradise, 36 269-273
------. The Gypsy Language of Denmark, 45 97-105
------. The Hymn to Bêlit, K. 257 (HT. 126-131), 24 103-128
------. A Hymn to the Goddess Kir-gí-lu (Cuneiform Texts from the British Museum, XV., Plate 23), 30 325-335
------. A Hymn to Nergal, 28 168-182
------. A Hymn to Tammuz, 30 94-100
------. The Modern Pronunciation of Coptic in the Mass, 23 289-306
------ Phonetic Relations in Sumerian, 39 265-279
------. The Pierpont Morgan Babylonian Axe-head, 26 93-97
------. A Political Hymn to Shamash, 33 10-15

------. Possible Non-Indo-European Elements in 'Hittite', 41 210-224
------. A Possible Sumerian Original of the Name Nimrod, 40 201-203
------. The So-Called Epic of Paradise, 36 90-114
------. Striking Phenomena of Sumerian, 34 321-328
------. Surviving Turkish Elements in Serbo-Croatian, 51 241-261
------. A Tammuz Fragment, 33 345-348
------. Turkic Material in Hungarian, 56 446-452
------. The Unilingual Inscriptions K. 138 and K. 3232 translated, 21 1-22
------. The Vocabulary of Sumerian, 25 49-67
PURVES, Pierre M. Nuzi Names, 58 462-471
RANKE, Hermann, review of W. C. Hayes, The Texts in the Maṣṭabeh of Se'n-wosret-'ankh at Lisht, 59 515-517
REICH, Nathaniel Julius. Coptic Ostracon Merton 1, 58 151-152
------, review of Jean Capart, L'art Égyptien, 43 430-431
------, review of von Rotter, Gough, von Buttel-Reepen and Armbruster, Die Biene in Aegypten jetzt und vor 5000 Jahren, 43 431
REICHLING, Gerard Alston. A Demotic Folk-tale the Basis of Goethe's 'Der Zauberlehrling,' 39 295-298
REIDER, Joseph. The Name Ashur in the Initials of a Difficult Phrase in the Bible, 58 153-155
------, review of William Popper, Parallelism in Isaiah, 45 82-88
REISCHAUER, Edwin O. Rōmaji or Rōmazi, 60 82-89
REISCHAUER, Robert K. The Japanese Shōen (莊園), or Manor; Some Useful Terminology, 57 78-83
REMY, Arthur F. J. The Influence of Persian Literature on the German Poet Platen, 21 40-41
RIGG, Horace Abram Jr. A Note on the Names Armânum and Urartu, 57 416-418
ROBERTSON, Edward. Rain, Dew, Snow and Cloud in Arab Proverb, 52 145-158
ROCHE, Philip Q., and Horace I. Poleman. Aspects of Caesarean Section in India, 59 17-21
ROERICH, Georges de, review of A Comparative Analytical Catalogue of the Kanjur Division of the Tibetan Tripiṭaka edited in Peking during the K'anghsi Era, and at present kept in the Library of the Otani Daigaku, Kyoto. Compiled by various scholars, Three parts, 52 395-399
------, review of Jacques Bacot, Les Çlokas Grammaticaux de Thonmi Sambhoṭa avec leurs commentaires, 51 182-185
------, review of Marcelle Lalou, Catalogue du Fonds Tibétain de la Bibliothèque Nationale, Quatrième Partie, I. Les mDo-maṅ. Buddhica, IV, 52 395-399
ROSENAU, W. Some Notes on Akathriel, 36 437
ROSMARIN, Trude Weiss. The Origin of the Alphabet of Ras Shamra and its Bearing on the Origin of the Phoenician Alphabet, 55 101-102
ROSS, Marvin Chauncey. A Pair of Lost Byzantine Doors, 60 576-578
------, review of P. Cott, Siculo-Arabic Ivories, 60 424-426
RUDOLPH, Richard C. Emu Tanggô orin sakda-i gisun sarkiyan, an unedited Manchu Manuscript, 60 554-563
RYDER, Arthur W. Kṛṣṇanātha's Commentary on the Bengal Recension of the Çakuntalā, 23 79-83
------. Note on bṛhácchandas, AV. iii.12.3, 23 77-78
------. Notes on the Mṛcchakaṭika, 27 418-454
SACHS, A. Another Occurrence of the Alleged Ancient Name of Sāmarrā, 57 419-420
SAKANISHI, Shio. The Magic Holly in Japanese Literature, 55 444-450
------. Prohibition of Import of Certain Chinese Books and the Policy of the Edo Government, 57 290-303
------, review of Masaharu Anesaki, Katam Karaniyam. Lectures, Essays and Studies, 57 448-449
------, review of André Beaujard (tr.), Les Notes de Chevet de Sei Shonagon, dame d'Honneur au Palais de Kyôto, 57 132
------, review of Kosaku Hamada and Sueji Umehara, Shiragi ko-ga no kenkyû, Report upon archaeological research in the Dept. of Literature, Kyoto Imperial University, Vol. XIII, 1934, 55 218-219
------, review of Yoshito Harada and Kingo Tazawa, Lo-Lang: a report on the excavation of Wang Hsü's tomb in the ancient Chinese colony in Korea, 54 97-99
------, review of Kazuma Kawase, Ko katsuji han no kenkyu, 59 147-148
------, review of Akio Koizumi and Shunichi Sawa, Rakuro Saikyu-bo, The Tomb of the Painted Basket and other two tombs of Lo-Lang, a report on the excavations of 1931, 56 101-103
------, review of Churyo Noda, Chou pi suan ching no kenkyu, 54 96-97
------, review of Michel Ribaud, Le Vieux Japon: "La Route de la Mer orientale," Voyage du Jeune Stanislas au Japon, ou Essais sur la Civilisation japonaise — Histoire, Religion, Philosophie, Littérature & Beaux-arts. Vol. II, 57 131
------, review of Osvald Sirén, The Chinese on the Art of Painting: Translations and Comments, 56 531-533
------, review of Daisetz Teitaro Suzuki, An Introduction to Zen Buddhism, 57 445-446
------, review of Daisetz Teitaro Suzuki, Manual of Zen Buddhism, 57 447
------, review of Daisetz Teitaro Suzuki, The Training of the Zen Buddhist Monk, 57 446-447
------, review of Ku Teng, Chinesische Malkunsttheorie in der T'ang-und Sungzeit: Versuch einer geschichtlichen Betrachtung, 56 530-531
SANDERS, Charles S. Jupiter Dolichenus, 23 84-92
SANDERS, Henry A., review of E. J. Goodspeed, D. W. Riddle and H. R. Willoughby, The Rockfeller Mc Cormick New Testament, 52 376-377
SAPIR, Edward. Hebrew 'argáz, a Philistine Word, 56 272-281
------. Hebrew "helmet," a Loanword, and its Bearing on Indo-European Phonology, 57 73-77
------. κύβδα, a Karian Gloss, 56 85
SARKISSIAN, A. O. On the Authenticity of Moses of Khoren's History, 60 73-81
SARRE, Friederich, see Book Reviews, Le Cog
SAUNDERS, A. J., review of Stephen H. Roberts, Population Problems of the Pacific, 48 74-76
SAUNDERS, Virginia. Magic in the Sanskrit Drama, 45 110-114
------. Portrait Painting as a Dramatic Device in Sanskrit Plays, 39 299-302
------. Some Allusions to Magic in Kauṭilya's Arthaśāstra, 42 75-79
------. Some Literary Aspects of the Absence of Tragedy in the Classical Sanskrit Drama, 41 152-156
------, review of Kshetreśachandra Chaṭṭopādhyāya, The Date of Kālidāsa, 49 75-76
------, review of Lakshman Sarup, The Vision of Vāsavadattā, 49 73-74
SCHANZLIN, G. L. On the Structure of Munda Words, 52 46-50
SCHAPIRO, Israel. The Hebrew Collections of the Library of Congress, 36 355-359
SCHELTEMA, J. F. Arabs and Turks, 37 153-161
SCHERMAN, L., review of Von O. Franke, Li Tschi. Ein Beitrag zur Geschichte der chinesischen Geisteskämpfe im 16. Jahrhundert, 59 276-280
SCHERMERHORN, R. A. When did Indian Materialism get its Distinctive Titles? 50 132-138
SCHILLER, A. Arthur. Coptic Ostraca of the New York Historical Society, 48 147-158
SCHMIDT, Nathaniel. Daniel and Androcles, 46 1-7
------. Early Oriental Studies in Europe and the Work of the American Oriental Society, 1842 - 1922, Presidential Address delivered in Chicago, April 1922, 43 1-14
------. Is Canticles an Adonis Litany? 46 154-164

------. The Manuscripts of ibn Khaldun, 46 171-176
------. Problems Concerning the Origin of Some of the Great Oriental Religions, 53 191-214
------. The Two Recensions of Slavonic Enoch, 41 307-312
------. Traces of Early Acquaintance in Europe with the Book of Enoch, 42 44-52
------, review of Margolis, Montgomery, Hyde, F. Edgerton, Meek and Schoff, The Song of Songs. A Symposium, 46 189-192
------, review of H. T. Obbink, De godsdienst in zijn verschijningsvormen, 54 303-306
SCHOFF, Wilfred H. Aloes, 42 171-185
------. Camphor, 42 355-370
------. Cinnamon, Cassia and Somaliland, 40 260-270
------. The Eastern Iron Trade of the Roman Empire, 35 224-239
------. The Name of the Red Sea, 33 349-362
------. Nard, 43 216-228
------. Navigation to the Far East under the Roman Empire, 37 240-249
------. Regencies in Babylon, 42 371-372
------. Some Aspects of the Overland Oriental Trade at the Christian Era, 35 31-41
------. Tamil Political Divisions in the First Two Centuries of the Christian Era, 33 209-213
------, review of Émile Chassinat, Un papyrus médical copte, 45 76-82
SCHRÖDER, E. E. W. Gs. A Phoenician Alphabet on Sumatra, 47 25-35
SCHROEDER, Eric, review of I. Stchoukine, La Peinture iranienne, 57 120-121
SCHUYLER, Montgomery, Jr., Bibliography of Kālidāsa's Mālavikāgnimitra and Vikramorvaçī, 23 93-101
------. A Bibliography of the plays of Bhavabhūti and of Kṛṣṇamiśra, 25 189-196
------. The Editions and Translations of Çakuntalā, 22 237-248
------. Notes on the Making of Palm-Leaf Manuscripts in Siam, 29 281-283
SCHWARTZ, Benjamin. The Hittite and Luwian Ritual of Zarpiya of Kezzuwatna, 58 334-353
------ and J. Alexander Kerns. The Laryngeal Hypothesis and Indo-Hittite, Indo-European Vocalism, 60 181-192
SCOTT, Mrs. Samuel Bryan. Harvest Festivals of the Land Dyaks, 29 236-280
------. Mohammedanism in Borneo, 33 313-344
SEIDEL, M. Û as an Old Plural Ending of the Hebrew Noun, 37 165-167
SEIPLE, William G. Polysyllabic Roots with Initial p in Tagalog, 25 287-301
SELLERS, Ovid R., review of W. F. Albright, The Excavation of Tell Beit Mirsim, I, 53 66-68
SHAFER, Robert. The Vocalism of Sino-Tibetan, 60 302-337
SHRYOCK, J. K. Brief Communication, on a complete bibliography of Laufer's works, and a Biographical Memoir of Laufer by Latourette, and remarks on the work of Sadajiro Sugiura at the Univ. of Penna., 57 421
------. Two Far Eastern Bibliographical Notes, 57 421
------. The Use of the Word An 安, 58 156-166
------ and Feng, H. Answer to Ferguson's Chinese Mythology: A Reply, (54 85-87), 54 87
------, review of L'Adoption Universelle des Caractères Latins, Dossiers de la Coopération Intellectuelle. Société des Nations, Institut International de Coopération Intellectuelle, Paris, 55 338-339
------, review of Jubiläumsband herausgegeben von der Deutschen Gesellschaft für Natur-und Völkerkunde Ostasiens, Teil I, (43 authors) 53 336-364
------, review of Nanking Journal, Vol. I, No. 1, University of Nanking, 1931, 52 190-191
------, review of The New Orient: Vol. II, The Far East, 1933, 54 316
------, review of Progress of Chinese Studies in the United States of America, Bull. No. 1 of the Committee on the Promotion of Chinese Studies, 1931, Edited by Kenneth S. Latourette, 51 340-341
------, review of A Volume on Tangut (Hsi Hsia) Studies. Bull. of the National Library of Peiping, Vol. 4, No. 3, 1932, 52 189-190
------, review of L. C. Arlington and Harold Acton, Famous Chinese Plays, 57 442-443
------, review of Leigh Ashton (ed.), Chinese Art, 56 373
------, review of Florence Ayscough, Chinese Women Yesterday and Today, 58 691-692
------, review of M. S. Bates, An Introduction to Oriental Journals in Western Languages, 53 361-362
------, review of F. X. Biallas (ed.), Monumenta Serica; Journal of Oriental Studies of the Catholic University of Peking, Vol. I, No. 1, 56 379-380
------, review of Laurence Binyon, Painting in the Far East, 4th ed., 55 341-342
------, review of George Bounakoff, The Oracle Bones of Honan, 56 376-377
------, review of J. J. Brandt, Introduction to Literary Chinese, 57 351-352
------, review of J. J. Brandt, Modern Newspaper Chinese, 57 195
------, review of Roswell S. Britton, The Chinese Periodical Press: 1800-1912, 54 316-317
------, review of Clara M. Candlin, The Herald Wind, 54 316
------, review of Cyril Drummond Le Gros Clark, The Prose-Poetry of Su Tung-p'o, 56 95-96
------, review of Walter E. Clark, Two Lamaistic Pantheons, 2 vols., 58 695-696
------, review of Sir J. C. Coyajee, Cults and Legends of Ancient Iran and China, 57 198-200
------, review of H. G. Creel, The Birth of China, 57 348-349
------, review of H. G. Creel, Chang Tsung-ch'ien, and Richard C. Rudolph, Editors, Literary Chinese: Vol. I, the Hsiao Ching, 59 153-155
------, review of H. G. Creel, Literary Chinese by the Inductive Method, Vol. II, 60 116-117
------, review of H. G. Creel, Studies in Early Chinese Culture, 58 688-690
------, review of George H. Danton, The Culture Contacts of the United States and China, 52 193-194
------, review of H. H. Dubs, Hsuntze; the Moulder of Ancient Confucianism, 49 88-91
------, review of Pierre DuPont, Catalogue des Collections Indochinoises, in Musée Guimet, 56 380
------, review of G. Ecke and P. Demiéville, The Twin Pagodas of Zayton, 56 373-374
------, review of E. D. Edwards, Chinese Prose Literature of the T'ang Period, 58 687-688
------, review of E. D. Edwards, Chinese Prose Literature, Vol. II, 60 586-587
------, review of S. Elisséeff, C. S. Gardner and J. R. Ware (eds.), Harvard Journal of Asiatic Studies, Vol. I, No. 1, 56 381-382
------, review of Jean Escarra, Le Droit Chinois, 57 203
------, review of Lieutenant-Colonel B. Favre, Les Sociétés Secrétes en Chine, 53 362
------, review of Filippo de Filippi, An Account of Tibet; The Travels of Ippolito Desideri, S. J., 1712-1727, with an Introduction by C. Wessels, S. J., The Broadway Travellers series, 52 400-401
------, review of Walter Fuchs, Beiträge zur mandjurischen Bibliographie und Literatur, 58 693
------, review of Esson M. Gale, Basics of the Chinese Civilization, 54 227
------, review of Charles S. Gardner, Chinese Traditional Historiography, 59 152-153

------, review of Charles S. Gardner, A Union List of Selected Western Books on China in American Libraries, 52 192-193
------, review of Charles S. Gardner, A Union List of Selected Chinese Books in American Libraries, 53 92-93
------, review of David C. Graham, "A Preliminary Report of the Hanchow Excavation," Reprinted from the Journal of the West China Border Research Society, 1934, 56 98-99
------, review of Marcel Granet, Chinese Civilization, Translated from the French by Kathleen E. Innes and Mabel R. Brailsford, 51 186-188
------, review of E. Haenisch, Lehrgang der chinesischen Schriftsprache, 53 361
------, review of Erich Haenisch, Monggo Han Sai Da Sekiyen; Die Mandschufassung von Secen Sagang's Mongolischer Geschichte, 54 315
------, review of Clarence H. Hamilton, Wei-shih-er-shih-lun, 60 115-116
------, review of Yoshito Harada and Kazuchika Komai, Mu-yang-ch'ang; Han and Pre-Han Sites at the Foot of Mount Lao-t'ieh in South Manchuria, Archaeologia Orientalis, Vol. II, 52 191-192
------, review of Henry H. Hart, The Hundred Names, 54 225-226
------, review of Henry H. Hart, Seven Hundred Chinese Proverbs, 58 690
------, review of Henry H. Hart, The West Chamber, 57 205-206
------, review of A. Eustace Haydon (Editor), Modern Trends in World Religions, Chapters by Sprengling, Pratt, Allen, Joshi, Kaplan, Natarajan, Hodous, and Hu Shih, 55 224
------, review of Albert Herrmann, Historical and Commercial Atlas of China, 57 200-201
------, review of Lewis Hodous, (ed.), Careers for Students of Chinese Language and Civilization, 53 364-365
------, review of Lewis Hodous, Folkways in China, 50 169-170
------, review of D. C. Holtom, The National Faith of Japan, 60 587-588
------, review of Rudolph P. Hommel, China at Work, 58 690-691
------, review of Paul Houo-ming-tse, Preuves des Antiquités de Chine, 52 191
------, review of J.-J. Hospitalier, Grammaire Laotienne, 58 692-693
------, review of Hu Shih, The Chinese Renaissance, 55 223-224
------, review of Witold Jablonski, Les "Siao-ha(i-eu)l-yu" de Pekin; un essai sur la poésie populaire en Chine, 56 375-376
------, review of R. D. Jameson, Three Lectures on Chinese Folklore, 52 399-400
------, review of Katashi Kakinuma, Catalogue of the Library of the South-Manchurian Railway, 56 381
------, review of Ku Chieh-kang, The Autobiography of a Chinese Historian, Being the Preface to a Symposium on Ancient Chinese History (Ku Shih Pien), translated and annotated by Arthur W. Hummel, 52 100
------, review of Étienne Lamotte, La Somme du Grand Vehicule, 60 115-116
------, review of K. S. Latourette, A History of the Expansion of Christianity, 57 438-440
------, review of Kenneth S. Latourette (Ed.), Progress of Chinese Studies in the United States of America, Bull. No. 1 of the Committee on the Promotion of Chinese Studies, 1931, (J. K. Shryock), 51 340-341
------, review of John Hazedel Levis, Foundations of Chinese Musical Art, 57 201-202
------, review of Walter Liebenthal, The Sutra of the Lord of Healing, 57 207
------, review of Chungshee H. Liu, A Study of the Tattooing Custom among the Li of Hainan Island, 57 198
------, review of C. B. Malone, "History of the Peking Summer Palaces under the Ch'ing Dynasty," University of Illinois Bull., Vol. XXXI, No. 41, June 12, 1934, 54 443
------, review of Benjamin March, Some Technical Terms of Chinese Painting, 56 382-383
------, review of Georges Margoulies, Petit Précis de Grammaire Chinoise écrite, 56 97
------, review of M. Médard, Le Choei-king Tchou et l'ancienne géographie Indo-chinoise, 56 96-97
------, review of Bernard Miall and Franz Kuhn, Chin P'ing Mei (translated), 2 vols., 60 278-280
------, review of J. A. Muller, Apostle of China: Samuel Isaac Joseph Schereschewsky, 58 696-697
------, review of Cyrus H. Peake, Nationalism and Education in Modern China, 53 93-94
------, review of P. D. and Ione Perkins, Lafcadio Hearn: A Bibliography of His Writings, 54 444
------, review of D. L. Phelps, Omei Illustrated Guide Book, 57 349-350
------, review of Shio Sakanishi, Kyogen, 59 150
------, review of Kitamura Sawakichi, Grundriss der Ju-Lehre, 57 196-198
------, review of Kurakichi Shiratori (ed.), Memoirs of the Research Department of the Toyo Bunko, No. 4, 56 377--378
------, review of J. Siguret (Tr.) Territoires et Populations des Confins du Yunnan, 57 350-351
------, review of Jadunath Sinha, Indian Realism, 59 151-152
------, review of W. E. Soothill, The Lotus of the Wonderful Law, 51 185
------, review of W. E. Soothill and L. Hodous, A Dictionary of Chinese Buddhist Terms, 58 694-695
------, review of D. T. Suzuki, Essays in Zen Buddhism: Second Series, 54 223-225
------, review of Ssu-yü Teng and Knight Biggerstaff, An Annotated Bibliography of Selected Chinese Reference Works, 57 350
------, review of Nancy Lee Swann, Pan Chao: Foremost Woman Scholar of China, 53 91-92
------, review of To-Yuen Hoh, Guide to Chinese Reference Books (in Chinese), 59 156
------, review of Tun Li-ch'en, Annual Customs and Festivals in Peking, tr. and annotated by Derk Bodde, 57 204
------, review of L. Austine Waddell, The Buddhism of Tibet, 55 225
------, review of H. G. Quaritch Wales, Ancient Siamese Government and Administration, 55 340
------, review of Wang Tch'ang-tche, S. J., La Philosophie Morale de Wang Yang-ming, 57 352-353
------, review of James R. Ware, Vocabularies to the Elementary Chinese Texts used at Harvard University, 57 195-196
------, review of James R. Ware, Vocabularies to the Intermediate Chinese Texts used at Harvard University, 58 692
------, review of Langdon Warner, Buddhist Wall-Paintings, 59 155-156
------, review of Alan W. Watts, The Spirit of Zen, 57 204-205
------, review of Harry Emerson Wildes, Aliens in the East, 59 149-150
------, review of Richard Wilhelm, A History of Chinese Civilization, tr. by Joan Joshua, 50 168-169
------, review of H. R. Williamson, Wang An Shih, A Chinese Statesman and Educationalist of the Sung Dynasty, Vol. I, 56 99-101
------, review of H. R. Williamson, Wang An Shih, Vol. II, 57 440-442
------, review of Genevieve Wimstatt, Selling Wilted Peonies, 57 206
------, review of K. A. Wittfogel, Wirtschaft und Gesellschaft Chinas; Erster Teil; Produktivkräfte, Producktions und Zirkulationsprozess, 53 363

------, review of Stuart N. Wolfenden, Outlines of Tibeto-Burman Linguistic Morphology, 51 339-340
------, review of K. Wulff, Chinesische und Tai, 55 340-341
------, review of Erwin von Zach, Übersetzungen aus dem Wên Hsüan, 56 94
------, see also Brown, W. Norman; Clark, Walter E.; Feng Han-yi
SHUI, T. T., review of Georg Jacob and Hans Jensen, Das chinesische Schattentheater, 55 220-223
SIMCOX, Carroll E. The Rôle of Cyrus in Deutero-Isaiah, 57 158-171
SIMSAR, Mehmet A. Three Rare Manuscripts from the John Frederick Lewis Collection, 57 88-94
------ and W. Norman Brown. Late Mughul Illustrations to the Iqbāl-nāmah'i Jahāngīrī, 58 354-365
SKOSS, Solomon. A Study of the Uses of Letter "Yōd" by David ben Abraham al-Fāsī, 58 167-172
------, review of J. Obermann, The Arabic Original of Ibn Shāhīn's Book of Comfort, 56 506-508
SLOANE, Ely Bannister. [letter on the 'Ali-Illāhis and Yazīdis], 33 ii-iii
SMITH, J. M. Powis, review of Mayer Sulzberger, The Status of Labor in Ancient Israel, 45 184-185
SMITH, Maria Wilkins, review of Emile Benveniste, The Persian Religion according to the Chief Greek Texts, 52 186-189
------, review of Herman Lommel, Die Religion Zarathustras, 53 85-86
------, review of Cursetji Erachji Pavry, Iranian Studies, 49 174-176
SMITH, Myron Bement. Correction to JAOS 59 397, 60 100
SOMMER, F. E. Documents from Mughal India, 60 99-100
SPEISER, E. A. Addendum on the Phrase מן חם ועד חוט, 54 299
------. The Beginnings of Civilization in Mesopotamia, 59 Supp. IV, 17-31
------. A Figurative Equivalent for Totality in Akkadian and West-Semitic, 54 200-203
------. A Letter of Saushshatar and the Date of the Kirkuk Tablets, 49 269-275
------. A New Hurrian Pronominal Form, 60 264-267
------. In Memoriam: Edward Chiera, Raymond P. Dougherty, 53 308-309
------. New Kirkuk Documents Relating to Security Transactions, 52 350-367
------. New Kirkuk Documents Relating to Security Transactions (concluded), 53 24-46
------. Notes on Hurrian Phonology, 58 173-201
------. Notes to Recently Published Nuzi Texts, 55 432-443
------. Recent Assyriological Publications of the Oriental Institute of the University of Chicago, 54 431-434
------. Studies in Hurrian Grammar, 59 289-324
------. Studies in Semitic Formatives, 56 22-46
------, review of T. Bauer, Die Ostkanaanäer, 49 325-326
------, review of G. Bergsträsser, Einführung in die semitischen Sprachen, 50 269-271
------, review of V. Gordon Childe, The Most Ancient East, 50 79-81
------, review of G. Contenau, Manuel d'archéologie orientale, I, 49 323-325
------, review of Martin David, Die Adoption im altbabylonischen Recht, 49 182
------, review of Adolf Dirr, Einführung in das Studium der kaukasischen Sprachen, 50 268-269
------, review of Driver and Miles, The Assyrian Laws, 56 107-108
------, review of H. Frankfort, Archeology and the Sumerian Problem, 53 359-360
------, review of Giuseppe Furlani, Religione dei Yezidi, 51 334-335
------, review of C. J. Gadd and Leon Legrain, Ur Excavations, Texts. I: Royal Inscriptions, 49 322-323
------, review of E. Grant (ed.), The Haverford Symposium on Archaeology and the Bible, 58 670
------, review of P. W. Ireland, 'Iraq: A Study in Political Development, 59 117-118
------, review of P. Koschaker, Über einige griechische Rechtsurkunden aus den östlichen Randgebieten des Hellenismus, 52 255-257
------, review of Mallowan and Rose, Excavations at Tall Arpachiyah, 1933, 56 109-110
------, review of J. Obermeyer, Die Landschaft Babyloniens im Zeitalter des Talmuds und des Gaonats, 50 267-268
------, review of R. H. Pfeiffer, The Archives of Shilwateshup, son of the King, 52 257-260
------, review of E. Schmidt, Excavations at Tepe Hissar, Damghan, 59 115-117
------, review of Edgar H. Sturtevant, A Comparative Grammar of the Hittite Language, 54 206-208
------, review of William H. Worrell, A Study of Races in the Ancient Near East, 49 181
------, review of G. E. Wright, The Pottery of Palestine from the Earliest Times to the End of the Early Bronze Age, 58 671-673
------, see also Bull, Ludlow; Chiera, Edward
SPOER, H. Henry. Arabic Magic and Medicinal Bowls, 55 237-256
------. Arabic Magic Bowls II: an Astrological Bowl, 58 366-383
------. Description of the Case of the Roll of a Samaritan Pentateuch, 27 105-107
------. Five Poems by Nimr ibn 'Adwān, 43 177-205
------. Iḥdaidun wal-Rūle: Folk-lore Story from Bethlehem, 52 168-173
------. Notes on Bloody Sacrifices in Palestine, 25 312-313
------. Notes on some Palmyrene Tesserae, 27 397-399
------. On Bloody Sacrifices in Palestine, 27 104
------. Palmyrene Inscriptions found at Palmyra in April, 1904, 25 314-319
------. Palmyrene Tesserae, 26 113-116
------. Some Hebrew and Phoenician Inscriptions, 28 355-359
------. Two Unpublished Palmyrene Inscriptions, 29 203
------ and Elias Haddad: Folklore and Songs from Qubebe, 48 225-249
------ and Elias N. Haddad, Folklore and Songs from el-Qubēbe, 50 199-213
------, review of H. Granquist, Marriage Conditions in a Palestinian Village, 53 76-78
------, review of Sir W. Haig, Comparative Tables of Muhammadan and Christian Dates, 53 175
------, review of P. Kahle, Der Leuchtturm von Alexandria, 52 59-61
------, review of M. Smith, Studies in Early Mysticism in the Near and Middle East, 53 173-175
SPRENGLING, Martin, review of R. Paret, Die legendäre Maghāzī-Literatur, 52 263-265
VON STAEL-HOLSTEIN, Baron A. Notes on Two Lama Paintings, 52 338-349
------. Notes on Two Lama Paintings (see 52 338-349), Explanation of simultaneous publication of, in Bull.of the National Library of Peiping, 1932, 53 189
STAPLES, W. E. The Second Column of Origen's Hexapla, 59 71-80
STEHLE, Dorothy. Sibilants and Emphatics in South Arabic, 60 507-543
------, review of W. Leslau, Lexique Soqoṭri, 60 110-112
STEPHENS, Ferris J. Did the Early Semites of Asia Minor use the Alphabet? 49 122-127
------. A Newly Discovered Inscription of Libit-Ishtar, 52 182-185
------. Notes on Cappadocian Tablets, 46 179-181
------, review of J. G. Lautner, Altbabylonische Personenmiete und Erntearbeiterverträge, 58 476-481

STINESPRING, William F. Hadrian in Palestine, 129/130 A.D., 59 360-365
STRATTON, Alfred William. A Dated Gandhāra Figure, 24 1-6
STURTEVANT, Edgar H. Analogical Creation and Contamination as Illustrated by Lapses, 57 135-150
------. The Development of the Stops in Hittite, 52 1-12
------. A Hittite Text on the Duties of Priests and Temple Servants, 54 363-406
------. Indo-European bh Corresponds to Hittite p, 50 125-128
------. The Misuse of Case Forms in the Achaemenian Inscriptions, 48 66-73
------. Notes on Hittite and Indo-European Pronouns and Morphology, 47 174-184
------. Phonetic Law and Imitation, 44 38-53
------. Two Hittite Words, 56 282-287
STUTTERHEIM, Willem. The Meaning of the Hindu-Javanese caṇḍi, 51 1-15
SUKTHANKAR, V. S. An Assyrian Tablet Found in Bombay, 40 142-144
------. Studies in Bhāsa, 40 248-259
------. Studies in Bhāsa, 41 107-130
------. Studies in Bhāsa, III, 42 59-79
SUTER, Rufus. The Words san i fen shen in the Inscription on the Nestorian Monument at Hsi-an-fu, 58 384-393
SVERDRUP, George Jr. A Letter from the Mahdi Muhammad Aḥmad to General C. G. Gordon, 31 368-388
SWANN, Dr. Nancy Lee. Biography of the Empress Têng, a Translation from the Annals of the Later Han Dynasty, (Hou Han Shu, Chüan 10a, 後漢書.卷十上), 51 138-159
------. A Woman Among the Rich Merchants: The Widow of Pa, 巴寡婦清, (3rd century B.C.), 54 186-193
------, review of Lucy Driscoll and Kenji Toda, Chinese Calligraphy, 55 473-476
SWEET, Alfred H., review of Gilberte Hla-Dorge, Une Poetesse Japonaise au XVIII siècle, Kaga No Tchiyo-Jo, 57 130-131
------, review of N. Matsudaira, Les Fêtes Saisonnières au Japon, (Province de Mikawa), Étude descriptive et sociologique, 57 127-129
TEDESCO, Paul. 'Geben' und 'Nehmen' im Indischen, 43 358-390
------. Neu-Persisch yāzdāh, 42 295-300
THAYER, Gordon W. The John G. White Collection, Cleveland Public Library, 36 421-422
------. A rare work by Sir Henry Miers Elliot, 41 73-74
------, review of Stanislas Julien, Dictionary of the Manchu Language, unpublished MS. in the John G. White Collection, Cleveland Public Library. (Account quoted from letter of Dr. Berthold Laufer), 40 140
TITIEV, Mischa. The Sun-kiss among the Hopi Indians, 60 270
TOLMAN, H. C. An Erroneous Etymology of New Persian pādšāh, in Relation to the pr. n. Πατιζεῖθης (Hdt. 3.61), 40 200-201
------. Persian words in the Glosses of Hesychius, 41 236-237
------. A Possible Restoration from a Middle Persian Source of the Answer of Jesus to Pilate's Inquiry 'What is Truth?' 39 55-57
TOMITA, Kojiro, review of Langdon Warner, The Craft of the Japanese Sculptor, 56 536
TORREY, Charles Cutler. The Aḥīrām Inscription of Byblos, 45 269-279
------. An Arabic Papyrus Dated 205 A.H., 56 288-292
------. An Aramaic Inscription from Cilicia, in the Museum of Yale University, 35 370-374
------. An Aramaic Inscription from the Jawf, 54 29-33
------. Epigraphic Notes, 28 349-354
------. Four Palmyrene Epitaphs, 25 320-323
------. Hebrew and Aramaic from Beth Shemesh, 55 307-310
------. An Inscription of Eliba'al, King of Byblos, 46 237-240
------. The Letters Prefixed to Second Maccabees, 60 119-150
------. The Loss of the Urumia Concordance of the Peshitta, 43 128-129
------. The Mosaic Inscription at 'Ain Dūk, 40 141-142
------. A New Phoenician Grammar, 57 397-410
------. Note on the Line of Brāhmī (?) Script on a Babylonian Tablet, 56 490-491
------. Notes on a Few Inscriptions, 29 192-202
------. Notes on the Aramaic Contract Published by Bauer and Meissner, 58 394-398
------. The Outlook for American Oriental Studies, 38 107-120
------. Pehlevi Inscriptions from Yale Collections, 52 201-207
------. A Phoenician Royal Inscription, 23 156-173
------. Semitic Epigraphical Notes, 24 205-226
------. The So-called Original Hebrew of Sirach, 40 219-220
------. A Specimen of Old Aramaic Verse, 46 241-247
------. The Story of a Friend in Need. The Arabic Text Edited from the Vienna Manuscript of el-Ghuzūlī and Translated for the First Time, 26 296-305
------. Stray Notes on the Aramaic of Daniel and Ezra, 43 229-238
------. Two Letters from Professor Porter in Regard to the Bod-'Aštart Stones in Beirut, 25 324-331
------. "Yāwān" and "Hellas" as Designations of the Seleucid Empire, 25 302-311
------. The Zahar and Kalamu Inscriptions, 35 353-369
------, A. V. W. Jackson and J. Morgenstern: Richard J. H. Gottheil, In Memoriam, 57 251-252
------, review of The Macdonald Presentation Volume, 54 89, 90-91
------, review of J. C. Chabot, Choix d'inscriptions de Palmyre, 43 141-144
------, review of D. Diringer, Le iscrizioni antico-ebraiche palestinesi, 55 469-470
------, review of M. Kamil, Des Josef ben Gorion (Josippon) Geschichte der Juden, 59 260-262
------, review of E. Littman, Syriac Inscriptions, 55 470-471
------, review of T. Menzel (ed.), Festschrift Georg Jacob, 54 89-90
TOY, Crawford H. Creator Gods, 23 29-37
------. An Early Form of Animal Sacrifice, 26 137-144
------. Recent Discussions of Totemism, 25 146-161
------. Remarks on the Hebrew Text of Ben-Sira, 23 38-43
TUTTLE, Edwin H. Armenian hariur, 46 60
------. Dravidian and Nubian, 52 133-144
------. Dravidian "bone," 58 472
------. Dravidian Notes, 46 177-178
------. Dravidian Notes, 46 309-310
------. Dravidian Notes, 57 304-308
------. Dravidian Notes, 59 103-104
------. Dravidian *geli and Aryan *gili, 49 60-61
------. Dravidian wrīghia "rice," 47 263-266
------. The History of Tamil R, 57 411-415
------. Sanskrit ṣṭhīv-, 46 60
------, review of Denys Bray, The Brāhūī Language. Part II, The Brāhūī Problem. Part III: Etymological Vocabulary, 56 350-360
------, review of K. Ramakrishnaiah, Studies in Dravidian Philology, 57 112-115
TYNG, D. The Confucian Utopia, 54 67-69
UNGNAD, A. Review of Staatliche Museen zu Berlin, Vorderasiatische Abteilung. Keilschrifturkunden aus Boghazköi. Bde. I-V, 43 67-72
VANDERBURGH, Frederick A. Babylonian Legends, BM Tablets 87535, 93828 and 87521, CT XV, Plates 1-6, 32 21-32
------. A Business Letter of Anu-šar-uṣur, 36 333-336

------. A Hymn to Bêl (Tablet 29644, CT. XV, Plates 11 and 12), 29 184-191
------. A Hymn to Bêl (Tablet 29623, CT. XV, Plates 12 and 13), 30 61-71
------. A Hymn to Mullil. Tablet 29615, CT. XV, Plates 7, 8 and 9, 30 313-324
------. Three Babylonian Tablets, Prince Collection, Columbia University, 33 24-32
VANOVERBERGH, Morice. Animal Names in Iloko, 48 1-33
------. Iloko anatomy, 49 1-21
------. Iloko pathology, 49 244-262
------. Plant Names in Iloko, 47 133-173
VASCHALDE, Arthur A., review of A. Mingana, Commentary of Theodore of Mopsuestia on the Lord's Prayer, and on the Sacraments of Baptism and the Eucharist, 54 91-93
------, review of A. Mingana, Woodbrooke Studies, vols. III and V, 53 170-173
------, review of M. Sprengling and W. C. Graham, Barhebraeus' Scholia on the Old Testament, 52 374-375
VERDANSKY, George. Notes on the History of the Uigurs in the Late Middle Ages, 56 453-461
------. On the Origins of the Antae, 59 56-66
VRIES, J. D. L. de. On Compounds of the Type goghná and gáviṣṭi, 48 166-176
WALDSCHMIDT, Ernst, see Book Reviews, Le Coq
WARE, James R. Notes on the History of the Wei Shu, 52 35-45
------. Old Persian niyaθrārayam, Bh. 1.64, 44 285-287
------. Studies in the Divyāvadāna, 48 159-165
------. Studies in the Divyāvadāna, 49 40-51
------. Transliteration of the Names of Chinese Buddhist Monks, 52 159-162
------. Transliteration of the Names of Chinese Buddhist Monks, three corrections to article in Vol. 52, pp. 160, 162, 52 269
------. The Wei Shu and the Sui Shu on Taoism, 53 215-250
------. The Wei Shu and the Sui Shu on Taoism, Corrigenda and Addenda to JAOS 53, 217-249, 54 290-294
------, review of Vasudev Gokhale, Pratītyasamutpādaśāstra des Ullangha, kritisch behandelt und aus dem Chinesischen ins Deutsche übertragen, 54 314-315
------, review of Marcel Granet, Festivals and Songs of Ancient China, 54 100-103
------, review of Étienne Lamotte (ed. & tr.), Saṃdhinirmocanasūtra, l'explication des mystères, Texte tibétain édité et traduit (James R. Ware), 57 122-124
------, review of F. W. Thomas (tr.), Tibetan Literary Texts and Documents concerning Chinese Turkestan. Part I: Literary Texts, 57 125-126
------, review of Gustave-Charles Toussaint, Le Dict de Padma, Padma thang yig, Ms. de Lithang, traduit du Thibétain, 54 311-313
WARREN, William F. Babylonian and Pre-Babylonian Cosmology, 22 138-144; 23 opp. p. 388
------. Problems still Unsolved in Indo-Aryan Cosmology, 26 84-92
------. Where was Śākadvīpa in the Mythical World-view of India? 40 356-358
WATERMAN, Leroy. The Curse in the 'Paradise Epic,' 39 322-328
------. Oriental Studies in the Present World Picture, 58 403-412
------. Some Determining Factors in the Northward Progress of Levi, 57 375-380
------. Some Historical and Literary Consequences of Probable Displacement in I Kings 1-2, 60 383-390
------, review of G. Cameron, History of Early Iran, 56 519-520
WELKER, Marian, review of M. E. L. Mallowan, The Excavations at Tall Chagar Bazar, 58 673-674
WENLEY, A. G., review of R. W. Swallow, Ancient Chinese Mirrors, 57 443-445
WEST, Edward W. A Transliteration and Translation of the Pahlavi Treatise 'Wonders of Sagastān' (Sīstān), 36 115-121
WESTON, Sidney Adams. The Kitâb Masâlik an-Naẓar of Sa'īd ibn Ḥasan of Alexandria, 24 312-383
WIESCHHOFF, Heinz A. Concepts of Right and Left in African Cultures, 58 202-217
WOLFE, R. E. Questions Relating to the Origin of the Israelite Sabbath, 59 402
WOLFENSEN, Louis B. The Infixes la, li, lo in Tagalog, 27 142-146
------. The Pi'ēl in Hebrew, 27 303-316
WOOD, Howland, review of Nalini Kanta Bhattasali, Coins and Chronology of the Early Independent Sultans of Bengal, 43 253-254
------, review of Fr. Schjöth, Currency of the Far East. The Schjöth Collection at the Numismatic Cabinet of the University of Oslo, Norway, 51 341-342
WOODS, James Haughton. The Yoga-sūtras of Patañjali as Illustrated by the Comment entitled the Jewel's Lustre or Maṇiprabhā. Translated, 34 1-114
WORRELL, William H. An Account of Schools for Living Oriental Languages Established in Europe, 39 189-195
------. The Case of Muhammad, 48 136-146
------. The Consonants Z and Ẓ in Egyptian Colloquial Arabic, 34 278-281
------. A Coptic Ostracon, 34 313-314
------. The Demon of Noonday and some Related Ideas, 38 160-166
------. Ink, Oil and Mirror Gazing Ceremonies in Modern Egypt, 36 37-53
------. The Pronunciation of Coptic, 50 144-149
------, review of M. Cohen, Études d'éthiopien méridional, 52 380-382
------, review of W. H. T. Gairdner, Egyptian Colloquial Arabic, 47 336-337
------, review of W. H. T. Gairdner, The Phonetics of Arabic, 46 318-320
------, review of H. F. R. Günther, Rassenkunde des jüdischen Volkes, 50 164-165
------ and H. C. Youtie; review of A. A. Schiller, Ten Coptic Legal Texts, 52 377-380
------, see also Boak, A. E. R.
YANAGA, Chitoshi. Source Materials in Japanese History: The Kamakura Period, 1192-1333, 59 38-55
YERKES, Royden Keith, Index to Volumes 21-40 of the Journal, 44 313-384
------, review of G. B. Gray, Sacrifice in the Old Testament, 47 79-83
------, review of W. O. E. Oesterly, The Jewish Background of the Christian Liturgy, 47 79, 83-84
YLVISAKER, S. C. Dialectic Differences between Assyrian and Babylonian and some Problems they Present, 33 397-401
YOHANNAN, Abraham. Another Old Syriac Reference to Zoroaster, 43 239-242
------. A Manuscript of Gul ū Naurūz, a Seventeenth Century Persian Romance, in the Library of Columbia University, 23 102-108
------. A Manuscript of the Manāfi' al-Ḥaiawān in the Library of Mr. J. P. Morgan, 36 381-389
------. Some Remarks Regarding the Pronunciation of Modern Syriac, 25 76-78
------ and Jackson, A. V. W. Some Persian References to Zoraster and his Religion, 28 183-188
YOUTIE, Herbert C. A Gnostic Amulet with an Aramaic Inscription, 50 214-220
------, see also Worrell, William H.
ZIRKLE, Conway, review of H. Danthine, Le palmier-dattier et les arbres sacrés, 60 422-424
ZWEMER, Samuel M. A New Census of the Moslem World, 44 29-37
------, review of C. Snouck Hurgronje, Mekka in the Latter Part of the Nineteenth Century, tr. J. H. Monahan, 52 383-387

II. INDEX OF SUBJECTS

Â, father of Gilgameš, a figure of the Attis type? 40 308
Abasa and Sacaea, identified with Kuria Muria Islands, 35 40, 238
Abaṭur, Mandaean deity identified with Iranian Rašnu, 53 163, 165
'Abbāsid Caliphs, regarded Pippin and Charlemagne as their vassals, 47 364
'Abd-Allāh, Wahhābi chief, beheaded in Constantinople after his defeat by Muḥammad 'Ali, 37 157
'Abd-al-Raḥmān, Šarīf, his career in Borneo as founder of the Malay Kingdom of Pontianak, 33 318-319
'Abdu, Muḥammad (1850-1905), mufti of Egypt, life of, 28 189-197
Ābhāsa, the meaning of, 52 208-210; implications of term regarding psychological conception of relation of painting to sculpture and relief, 52 210-212
Abhayākara, an Indian magician represented on a Tibetan painting of a Panchen Lama, 52 347
Abhayakumāra, feud of Pradyota and, 45 307; refuses crown, 45 308
Abhidharmakośaśāstra, see Vasubandhu
Abībaʻal, king of Byblos, 45 278
Ablative case, origin of, 38 47-59; paucity of special forms, 47, meaning of, 47 f., pronominal forms, 48, 53-56, Greek-tos, Sanskrit-tas, Latin-tus, 48-52, 56, representation of ablative-idea by other means, 56-59
Ablution, see Baptism
Abyssinia, establishment of kingdom of, 35 34; noonday demon, belief in, 38 163-164; see also Ethiopia
Academies, supporting Asiatic studies in 17th cent., see Asiatic Studies in Europe
Academy of Sciences of the USSR: Mīr 'Ali Šīr 500th Anniversary Memorial Volume [N. Martinovitch], 49 185-186
Accent, definition of; use of this term as contrasted with "tone," 37 309-314
Achaemenids, Achaemenid, history Jewish knowledge of, 43 234-235; inscriptions, misuse of case forms in, 48 66-73; prices in Babylonia in later period were double what they had been under Neo-Babylonian rule, 52 305
Religion: apotheosis of kings occurs from time of Cyrus, 52 305; in Old Persian and non-Iranian inscriptions, 21 160-184; the Persian religion described by Herodotus, 52 186 f.
Achamoth derived from Aeons, teaching of Secundus, 38 26-29
Act of Truth, in the oath of the epic, 52 317-328; utilized to change sex, 47 19 f.
Acts, Book of: author used Pauline Epistles, 58 83-91; Luke-Acts not earlier than end of 1st cent., 84
Ethiopic: Bibliothèque Nationale eth. 26 (15th cent.) MS of Acts has a text of Antiochene type with close affinities to the Syriac and the Sahidic, 49 353; London Polyglot text revised after Vulgate in Rome, 49 353; Platt's version revised after Arabic, 49 353
'Ād, Arab tribe, not from genuine Arab tradition, 60 288; tribe of Luqmān and of Midianite Yahweh-worshippers of Sinai, 35 386-387
Adab, first settled as a fishing-place by an Asiatic-Elamite people, 54 78; inscriptions of Lugaldaudu and Mêsitug from, 33 295-296; 34 facing p. 228
Adad-apal-iddina, marriage alliance with Assyria, 38 209
Adad-bêl-ukîn, Assyrian governor, 34 349
Adad-nirâri III, reorganization of Assyrian empire under, 34 351-352; subjects Babylonia under Šamaš-mudammiq and Nabû-šum-iškun, 38 211-212
Adam, as primeval man, belief in his divinity among the Ḫaṭṭābīyah, 29 104; created from 4 elements plus soul, according to Syrians, 32 271, 311
Adami, Biship of Aleppo, exposer of fictitious Kitāb Dīwān Miṣr, 33 310
Adams, Will, see Japan, Geography
ādān (Muslim call to prayer), copied from Christians and Jews, 30 133-135
Addād (contrasts), doctrine of common to al-Šalmaġāni and Nuṣayris, 29 116, 127
Ādīśvaracarītra, contents of, 52 87
Ādityas, nature of the, 45 281 f.; serpents consubstantial with, 55 405 f.
Ādivarāha-Peumāl shrine, identification of two reliefs, 49 71
"Αδωδος = Adonis, 22 115-117
Adonis, = Sem. Tammuz, 35 222; identified with Ugaritic deity 'Alēyân, 53 104-105, 107; legends concerning him applied to Isaiah, 55 201-202; see also Pakeidas, Tammuz, Ešmun
Adonis myth, paralleled in Ugaritic poem describing the death and resurrection of Al'eyn, 52 229; Vellay on, 26 413 f.
Adonis-Ešmun-Tammuz, worshipped at Tyre, 22 115-117
Adoption, in Japan in Tokugawa period, for purpose of inheritance, 31 177, 178
Adulis, trade of, 35 229
'Adwān, Transjordan tribe dispossessed by the banu-Saḫr, 43 178
Aelia Capitolina, planned by Hadrian in A. D. 130, 59 363
Aemilius Sura (Roman historian), his idea of five world-empires has a common origin with that in Daniel, 59 422
Aeons, Valentinus's doctrine of reconstructed, 38 22-24
Aesop, and the Pañcatantra, 45 351; Fables, tr. by P. Trigault into Chinese, import into Japan prohibited, 57 292-294
Aesthetics of Indian art, 54 217 f.
'Afar Language, see Hamitic
Afdīyā va-Sāyakīh-ī Damīg-ī Sagastān (Wonders of Sagastān), Pahlavi treatise, transliteration and translation of, 36 115-121
Afghanistan, Afghans, Afghan, treaties with Turkey and Iran since 1921, 49 368-369; language, change of d to l in, 25 339; see also Calendar, Persian
Afrasiyab, King of Chin (ancient Chinese state of Ch'in?), use of war elephants by an ally of, as told in the Shâhnâma, 41 294
Africa, earliest Chinese accounts refer to Alexandria, Berbera, Socotra and Zanzibar, 30 46-57; early Chinese notices of, 30 46-57, earliest, in Wei-lio, refers to Wu-ch'ih-san = Alexandria, Egypt, 46-47, accounts of Po-pa-li in the T'ang-shu, Yu-yang-tsa-tsu, and Chau Ju-kua's Chu-fan-chih identify it as Barbarik or Berbera, 47-51, products of Berbera, 48, 49-50, Chau Ju-kua's description of Chung-li, identifies it as Somaliland, in particular the island of Socotra, 51-54, products of, 52, accounts by Chau Ju-kua of Ts'êng-pa, = Zanzibar?, and the trade in ivory, ambergris, and Chinese porcelain, 55-57, coins and broken celadon wares testify to Chinese medieval trade with Somali coast, 55-57; early trade with, in iron fr. India, 35 229-230, 232, 237-238; giraffe sent to China from, see abstract, J.J.L. Duyvendak; Ptolemy's conception of a southern continent connecting the land beyond the Gulf of Tong-King with Africa, below Zanzibar, 37 246-249
Africa, West, animals sacrificed there as messengers to deity, 26 416
African cultures, concepts of right and left in, 58 202-217
African languages, modern, European schools for study of, 39 193-195
Afzul Khan, Shivaji's killing of, 50 159-162, a Muhammedan saint, 162 f.
Agade, may have been founded and ruled in 1st dynasty by Amorites, 45 13
Age of persons, Chinese, how reckoned, 51 140 n.14
Agni, as peculiarly vidathyá, 48 219; as savior, 45 287; as the 'Spider', 55 398; Agni characteristics found in Puruṣa, 51 108-114; endlessness of, 55 411-417; in Vṛtra's power, 55 385; production of, by twirling, 55 376; relation to Indra as god of fertility, 36 250 f., 260, 263; traits in common with Viśvarūpa, 55 389

Agnikṣetra, prāṇas in relation to, 22 284-286, 294, 304; prāṇas in the, 22 281 f.; shape, 22 249

Agriculture, influence on religion of Kayans and Sea Dyaks of Borneo, 25 231-247

Chinese: Date of planting told to the husbandman by the position of the image of T'ai Sui in the Ceremony of Reception to Spring 42 57-58; in early Han period; in Ta-yüan 37 95; in An'hsi, 97; in T'iaó-chih, 97; in military colony at Lun-t'ou, 116

Ahab of Israel, his part in the Aramaean confederation against Shalmaneser III, 41 366-367

Ahalyā, interpretation of, 36 264

Ahap-Porul of Iraiyanār, dates of the work and its commentary, 51 339

Āhavanīya Fire, location in mouth, 22 290; prāṇa correlated with, 22 273; prāṇas as bricks of, 22 294 f.

Ahaziah, co-regent with Ahab, 47 357

Ahi, see Loloish

Ahi, identified with Vṛtra, 55 390 f.

Ahi Budhnya and Aja Ekapād, 53 326 f., 329, 331

Ahiṃsa in Buddhism and Brahmanism, 27 455-464

Aḥiqar Story, goes back to Assyrian original in the reign of Esarhadon; Syriac versions assumed present form under the Parthians, 56 242-243; relation to Babylonian wisdom literature, 38 64-65; Assyrian proverbs in, 64-65

Aḥîrâm Inscription, dated in early 11th cent. B.C., 48 80

Ahl al-Ḥadīt, see Aṣḥāb al-Ḥadīt

Ahmet Paşa, wazir of Bayazid II, MS of his will in Lewis collection, 56 413

Ainu, numerals, analysis of, 37 192-198; decimal principle followed from 11 to 19, a vigesimal system from 20 on, 194-196; influence of Japanese, 194, 199, 201, 203-204, 207; list of numerals, 195; relations with the Manchu, 196-198; phonetics of Ainu, 198-208; words in Yezo and Saghalin dialects compared with each other and with the Kuril dialect, 200-208; Ainu an isolated language at present, 206, 208; Yezo purer than Saghalin, 203, 208; subject to the Manchus for two centuries, 37 196-198; of Saghalin, tradition of the loss of their ancient books at sea, 45 191

Airyaman, as healer, 38 294 f.

Airyana Vaējah, in Azarbaijan, 25 181

Aiyer, Velandai Gopala, his views on the beginning of the Kali Yuga and the date of the Mahābhārata war, 24 6 f., 21, 52-55

Aja Ekapād, the Indic god, 53 326-334

Ajanta, art of Cave I, 47 278 f.; fragments of a painting of a "Wheel of Life" found at, 60 356; human face with extra pair of eyes represented the six senses, one of the nidānas, in painting at, 360

A-Kamba, concepts of right and left among the, 58 204, 208 f., 211 f.

Akbar, relations with Shāh 'Abbās the Great, 35 247-268

Akkadian, history of use of term as name of a language, 39 143; see also Calendar

History: as Turanians, struggle with early Iranians, 35 295; boundaries of at time of Isin dynasty, 45 222; East-Semitic origin of, 45 15; Naram-Sin defeated Menes of Egypt, dynasty of dated 3000-2800 B.C., 39 150

Language: â in palḫâku, "I fear," coresponds to ô in Heb. ānôkî, 40 221-222; accent fell on same syllables which are shown by lengthening to have been stressed in early Hebrew, 59 445; anticipatory pronominal suffix, non-Semitic origin of, 47 260-262; archaisms in texts of Nebuchadrezzar II, 33 401; anumma, "and now," shows that following action is influenced by the preceding; inanna, closely related in meaning to anumma (q.v.), but emphasizes the temporal element, 56 308-310; Assyrian dialect arose from early separation of Assyrian from Akkadians of N Babylonia, 58 451; causative stem in Cappadocian Tablets, 46 180; changes caused by Hurrian substratum, 50 270; co-ordinate adverbial, clause in, 53 69; dialectic differences between Assyrian and Babylonian, 33 397-401; dš > zz occurs down to al-'Amārnah age, 35 395; insertion of nasals as compensation for gemination, 41 177; internal passive in, 22 45ff.; -iš, adverbial ending, from išu, "existence," 45 314, 355; -ni not general mark of subjunctive in Cappadocian texts, 56 414; Nuzi dialect shows influence of Ḫurrian passival concept of the verb, 56 403; Old Akkadian related to Semitic dialect of Cappadocia, which dates from ca. 2500 B.C., 48 357; Old Babylonian distinguished between sibilants derived from Sem. ṭ and from Sem. ṣ, 56 409-410; originated in Amurrū, 41 257-258; orthography of Old Akkadian essentially the same as Sumerian; does not express length of vowels or doubled consonants, 57 48-49; permansive is identical with the infinitive in all conjugations except the Qal, where it is derived from the intransitive participle, 44 167-168; pi, bi, mi etc. used to render West-Sem. w, 37 252; t- form of the Old Babylonian verb: In dependent clauses: a future perfect, 56 319-321, reflexive-reciprocal meaning, 323-324, 332, separative meaning, 324-332, Sumerian influence on, 332-333, aspective character of, 333-334, in independent clauses: has function of a tense in coördinated (šumma) clauses, 56 302, denotes perfect action still affecting the situation, 312, 333, restricted use with neg., 316, not used with bašû, 316-317, not used with dative suffixes, 317-319, 331, emphatic use of in imperative, 319; tendency to double consonant after stressed short vowel is inherited from Sumerian, 57 49, V̄C replaced by V̆CC under Sumerian influence, 49, final -n in roots changes to -m, but rarely vice-versa, 59, change of a, u to o in late times, 71 n. 95; texts before Šamši-Adad I show no distiction between voiced and voiceless stops, due to Hurrian influence, 48 90-91; vocalic n, 45 359; wide divergence between N and S dialects in 2nd millennium B.C., 41 12; written before time of Sargon of Agade, 41 257-258; see also Semitic Languages

Literature: epistolary formulae, 43 26-40; royal texts copy Babylonian style from ca. 1800 B.C. on; prevalence of Babylonian dialect due to importation of Babylonian scribes, 48 92

Religion: creation, conceptions of, how differing from Sumerian, 36 274-290, 295-299; see also Babylonia

Texts: AH 82, 7-14, 1042, probable contents of supposed variant cylinder of, 26 98-103; Akkadian version of the restoration of order by Darius, 58 119-121; Alişar Hüyük texts, notes to Gelb's publication of, 57 434-438; ana ittišu series composed between Hammurabi and Akkad period, 59 266, notes to Landsberger's ed. of, 265-271; Annals of Ashurbanipal, notes on, 24 96-102; Annals of Ashurbanipal, three text types in, 52 304; Anu-šar-uṣur, business letter of, with translation, 36 333-336; Assyrian and Babylonian Letters (HARPER), trans. of No. 870, 25 81-83; axe-head, inscribed, of Nazimaruttaš, 26 94, of Ḫattiš in Morgan collection, 93-97; broken Prism of Esarhaddon, translation of, 35 391-393; CT XV, pl. 1-6, with translation, 32 21-32; creation account, translation and analysis of, 36 279-290; Deluge Story, notes to difficult passages in, 32 1-16; Deluge Story, translation and notes on Hilprecht's fragment of, 31 30-48; Deluge Story, translation of the beginning of, 25 68-75; Ditennûtu texts from Nuzi, 53 24-46; Early Babylonian warning to king against injustice, translit, and translat., 28 145-154; Etana Myth, Pittsfield fragment, with translation, 30 101-131; from Tarsus, 59 5-16; geographical text describing empire of Sargon of Agade cannot be ascribed to his time, 51 359; Gilgameš Epic, beginning of, 22 7-12; Hammurabi Code, errors in, 32 132-133; Hammurabi Code, notes to, 25 266-278; Hammurabi Code, notes to, 27 123-134; Hymn to Šamaš, with translation, 33 10-15; Kassite liver-omen text with translation, 38 77-96; letter of Sauššatar, King of Mitanni, to Itḫia, 49 270-275; Malazgird inscription of Tiglath-Pileser I, occasion of its setting up, 37 176; Nabû-kudurri-uṣur, inscribed paving-stone of from Babylon, 22 28-29; Neo-Babylonian contract from Bombay, 40 142-144; Nuzi documents, with translation, 47 36-60; Nuzi tablets

date ca. 1500 B.C, 49 273, 360; Nuzi texts, notes to, 55 432-443; Nuzi, three legal and commercial documents from, 55 431; Old Akkadian letter KT 135 (Istanbul), continuation of in Yale University, 59 399-400; Old Akkadian texts from pre-Ḫurrian Nuzi (Gasúr), notes to, 58 450-461; omen tablet in CT 20, pp. 39-42, grammatical treatise in, translit. and translat., 27 88-103; Sargon III, 8th campaign of, notes to, 36 226-232; Standard Inscription of Ashurbanipal, errors in, 32 130-132, 134; Syllabary, Elamite-Babylonian (?), 32 103-114; tablets in University of Illinois collection, 46 345; Tell al-'Amārnah texts found in 1933-1934, notice of, 56 414; temple receipt from reign of Mardukbêl-zêr, 41 313; text of Darius Susa no. 15 Scheil, 54 47-50; text of Artaxerxes Susa no. 28 Scheil, 54 52; VR 47, errors in, 32 133; votive inscription of Nebuchadrezzar on eye of idol, 43 51-53; votive text of Ashurbanipal from temple of Ningal at Ḥarrān, 38 167-175; Watelin and Langdon, Excavations at Kish, III, pp. 17-19, lines 2,3,6, corrections to, 52 54; see also Sign-lists

Akšak, a part of Upî, 59 107 n. 6

Aksou, panorama of city of, see Yüan Ming Yüan

Aksum, Kingdom of, allied with Romans against Himyarites, 35 35

Àktab, Babylonian city near Nippur and belonging to Isin, 57 363-365

'Alā' al-Dīn Fīrūz Šāh of Bengal, his existence proved from coins, 43 254

al-Ābi, abu-Sa'īd, see Kitāb Naṯr al-Durar

Alani and the Antae, 59 60-66

Alans, people of An-ts'ai or Suk-tak, formerly called the Aorsi, 30 35, 41, 42-45; see also Hsiung-nu

Alauddin Firoz Shah, existence discovered from coins, 43 254;

Albania, Albanians, see Calendar, Persian

Alchemy, Chinese, Taoist medicine and diet recipes, 53 216-217; 223-227; 233, 239, 240, 246, 247, 248, 249

Aleni, Jules, books (in Chinese) by, prohibited in Japan, 1630-1720, 57 290-294

Aleppo, did not come into Semitic hands until after the reign of Sargon of Agade's son Rimuš, 45 24; site and names of, 41 364 n. 39

Alexander Polyhistor, may have got his Babylonian material from some unknown Hellenistic source, 43 326; quotations from him in Eusebius of value for criticism of LXX, 56 251-252

Alexander the Great, quest of the water of life, 26 19 f.; started custom in western regions of using elephants in war, 41 293, found no wild elephants in countries west of India, 293

Alexandria, Egypt, called Wu-ch'ih-san by early Chinese, 30 46-47; trade with Genoa in the 12th cent., 38 179-182, 184

Alexandropolis (Arachosia, or Kandahar), end of route travelled by Isidore of Charax, 35 36

'Alēyân, Ugaritic deity, identified with Adonis, 53 104-105, 107

'Ali, miracles of, 29 42-43, 69-71; as demiurge, 127; traditions concerning him have a strong Shī'ite tinge, 59 123

'Ali ibn-'Īsa, see Taḏkirat al-Kaḥḥālīn

'Alids, see Shī'ites

'Ali-Illāhis, common origin with Yazīdis, 33 ii-iii

Alişar Hüyük, Chronology: Period I, Early Bronze (3rd millennium); II, Late and Middle Bronze; III, transition from Bronze to Iron (end of 2nd millennium); to Achaemenid period, 51 174-175; dating and coördination of stratification, 59 510-515

Allah, among Dyaks of Kotei, see Mahatara

al-Madā'in, Persia, site of the Nestorian colony, built by Khosru I after the fall of Antioch, for his Christian captives, 30 5-15; described in the Sui-shu, 30 5; the see of Nestorian patriarchs, 30 5, 9-15, 30; confused at first by the Chinese with Fu-lin (Syria) the original country of the Nestorians, 30 13-14; formed of Ctesiphon and Seleucia (Su-lin), 33 197-198; the see of Nestorian Patriarchs in Ctesiphon, 198, 201-202; confused at first by Chinese with Fu-lin, the original home of the Nestorians, 198-199, 201

al-Maqrīzi, account of Korea, see Korea, Arab geographers on

al-Mas'ūdi, account of Korea, see Korea, Arab geographers on

Al Modain, see al-Madā'in

Aloes, a product of Chung-li (Socotra), 30 52-53; description of the aromatic resinous products known as, and used for incense, 42 172-179; favored by the Chinese, 172-173; the su-ho-yu of Chinese Annals, obtained fr. Arabia, 176; aloe wood from Indo-China, 177-178, 181, 182; Chinese "sinking incense", 173, 178, 179, 181; Ceylon received it fr. Burma-Yünnan in 6th cent., 180; 'aloes of Kita' best Chinese, and those fr. Champa and Khmer, 180; Sumatra the center of trade in, 180; grow in the mountains of Kamrun, bet. India and China, 181; used among Chinese for embalming the dead, 182; see also Chau Ju-kua

Alphabet, Comparison of theories on origin of prior to 1901, 22 177-198; Letter-names compared, 22 191-198; may have developed from astrological symbols, 43 169-170; some new evidence on the history of, 56 406;

Arabic: Vowel-point system based on Nestorian, 60 408-409

Armenian: Independent vowel writing borrowed from Greek, 60 400

Avestan: Vowel signs developed under both Greek and Semitic influence, 60 399-400; Greek influence later than in Indian alphabets, perhaps via Armenia, 400-401, 411

Batak: Written from bottom to top on bamboo strips, 47 29-30; reached Sumatra 700-650 B.C. from Phoenician prototype, 47 31-35

Canaanite: Uniformity of alphabet not complete by time of Israelite invasion of Palestine, 58 Supp. II, 4-5; in use during most of 2nd millennium B.C., 58 Supp. II, 7

Chinese: ideographs for signs of the zodiac correspond to some western alphabetic forms, 43 169-170

Ethiopic: Indian influence on system of representing vowels, 60 409-410, 412; left-to-right direction of script may be due to Coptic or Greek influence, 410

Georgian: independent vowel writing borrowed from Greek, 60 400

Greek: borrowed from a cursive Phoenician script of ca. 800 B.C., 60 420-421; vowel signs arose from consonants not distinguished from following vowels; vowel values of vowel signs developed on acrophonic principle, 60 398-399

Hebrew: Nestorian is basis of Tiberian vowel system, 60 404-408

Kharoṣṭhi: vowel system borrowed from Greek, 60 399, 400-401, 411

Lachish: two groups, oldest belonging to Hyksos period, 58 Supp. II, 4-5; script orientated toward north, 7, 8; inscriptions, reading of, 8-41; older script related to, but not identical with, the Phoenician, 43-48

Manchu: vowel signs derived from Syriac matres lectiones, 60 411

Mandaean: complete development of vowel writing due to Nestorian stimulus, 60 404

Mongol: vowel signs derived from Syriac matres lectiones, 60 411

Palmyrene: related to that on Syro-Mandaean incantation bowls, 32 437

Phoenician: adapted to Phoenician language in 14th or 13th cent. B.C., 48 80; derived from the Ugaritic alphabet, 55 102; in 9th cent. B.C. had the same form from Moab to Cilica; writing usually on papyrus or skin, 46 239-240; in Sumatra, 47 25-35; origin, possibly Babylonian, 22 177-198; unknown in Phoenicia and Syria ca. 1400 B.C., 22 179

Semitic: progress in decipherment of, 56 128-130;

(North) possible influence on cuneiform script of Cappadocian texts, 49 122-127; matres lectiones begin with early Canaanite inscriptions in 10th cent. B.C., 60 396; independent development of in Old Aramaic, 397; consistent use of may have started in a single alphabet and spread to others, 397; vowellessness due to creation of signs on acrophonic principle, 53 387
Siamese: derivation from Semitic and Indian, 44 15-28
South Arabic: not earliest known representative of the alphabet, 48 82
Syriac: Estrangelo-like form on incantation bowls from Nippur, related to Palmyrene and Manichaean scripts, 32 437; vowel signs: originated in Syriac script beginning in 8th cent. A.D., 60 401: Nestorian system of dots is modification of Jacobite system borrowed from Greek, 401; probably arose through glossing of Syriac words with Greek transcriptions, 401-402, 412; development of Nestorian from older Semitic dot system, 402; Jacobite adoption of Greek vowel letters due to necessity for pronouncing Greek proper names, 412
Syro-Mandaean: similar to Manichaean Turkish, 32 437-438
Tibetan: derived fr. central India about 630 A.D., 38 34-38, 43-46
Ugaritic: cuneiform alphabet and linear script of Byblos are two different systematizations of the same alphabet, 58 Supp. II, 2; developed from Babylonian syllabary in middle of 2nd millennium B.C., 55 101-102; is the original of the Phoenician alphabet, 55 102
Uigur: vowel signs derived from Syriac matres lectiones, 60 411
al-Qazwīnī, account of Korea, see Korea, Arab geographers on
Altar, early Sumerian types of, 42 100-101
Amalric, Latin king of Jerusalem, correspondance with ibn-Duḫḫān and invasion of Egypt, 41 438
Amanus Mts., mentioned in texts of Gudea period, 43 44
Amarāvatī sculptures representing Nāgas, 49 189 f.
Ambergris (Chinese, o-mo), usual name in China lung-hsien, "Dragon's Spittle", an ancient product of Po-pa-li (Berbera), 30 48, 49; a product of Chung-li (Socotra), 52, 53; found on the African east coast, 54-55; a product of Zanzibar, 49, 52
America, Latin dissertation on pre-Columbian discovery of, printed in 1757, 52 310
American Oriental Society, work of in period 1842-1922, 43 11-14
American School of Living Oriental Languages, the need for one voiced in 1919, 39 144-145, 185-188
American School of Oriental Research, Jerusalem, closed in 1915, 36 351
'Am hā-'āreṣ, Jewish peasant class, growth of their conflict with the clergy, 52 307
Amharic Language, see Semitic Languages
Amitābha Buddha, as founder of the line of Panchen Lamas, 52 346-347
'Amm, Arabian god perpetuated in Hebrew and Amorite theophorous names, 45 5
Ammon, see Transjordan
Amorites, see Amurru
Amos, Book of, strophic structure in, 59 421
Amri culture, characteristics, 59 Sup. 35 f.; affiliations with Obeid culture, 59 Sup. 40; survivals at Ghazi Shah, 59 Sup. 41 f.
Amṛtodaya, Māgadhī in the 44 101
Amset and Hapi, sons of Horus or Osiris, stone statues of in University of California, 46 312-313
Amshaspands, in the Gāthās, 49 287
Amulets
Forged: gold, reputed to have come from Irbid, 33 307-308
Gnostic: with Aramaic inscription in Greek letters, of 3rd cent. A.D., 50 214-220
Jewish: in the U.S. National Museum, 36 154-167; mortuary, on silver foil, 38 140-141; Palestinian, early, 31 272-281; two from Tunis in the U.S. National Museum, 37 43-56
Amurru, Amorites, Amorite
History: Barton's criticism of Clay's theories on, 45 1-38; best-known foreign country to Sumerians of Gudea's time; accounts of it in his texts, 43 44; civilization did not exist before time of Sargon; was East-Semitic, 45 15, 25, 27, 37; constituted 1st dynasty of Agade; found in Palestine 2500 B.C., 45 13; culture was indigenous and synchronous with that of earliest Egypt, 41 263; empire of in 4th millennium B.C., 41 256; extended from Babylonia to the Mediterraean; capital at Mâri in 4th millennium B.C.; ruled Babylonia, 44 186-188; home of, Clay's rejoinder to Barton's criticism of his views on, 45 122 ff.; home of Semitic Babylonians, 41 255; Indo-Europeans among, 45 38 n. 85; name applied by Babylonians to Semites from Arabia; were somatically and culturally non-Semitic, 47 363; name taken from Amurru, a city on the Syrian coast, 38 248-249; Pan-Amurrism not supported by comparative mythology, 43 173; personal names related to Arabic and Hebrew, 45 5; were pre-Hellenic invaders from the Aegean and Crete, 38 336
Language: akin to Sabaean, 47 363; nothing known about it, but was probably East-Semitic, 45 17, 19, 37; two early dialects of, 45 124 n. 2, 126
Religion: Amurru, deity, his worship spread through Near East from Mâri, 44 196; myth of marriage of god Martu to Namrat, from Sumerian tablet in Nippur collection, 43 164; their deities in Babylonia since dynasty of Isin, 28 138-144
Anāhita, identified with Ištar, 36 302-304; in Old Persian inscriptions, 21 169
Analects of Confucius, now dated as earlier than the first few chapters of the Shu-ching, 56 54, 58: describes the titanic work of Yü, 54, 59: Yao and Shun mentioned, 54: references to model emperors scarce, 70; place in the Canon, 44 282
Analogical creation as illustrated by lapses, 57 135-150
Analogy, operation of in Hebrew numerals, 26 117-119
Analyses, of Chinese Bronzes, metal analysis of an early tsun, 51 20-21; metallographic examination, 21-22
'Anat-'Aštart, Canaanite goddess of fate and chthonic deity closely corresponding to Ereškigal (Mamītu), 50 339
Anatolia, see Alişar Hüyük, Art and Architecture
Anatta doctrine of Buddhism, 49 351 f.
Ancestor Worship, in China, genealogies kept in connection with, 52 233-234, 236, 238, 239-240
An Ch'ing Miao, 安 青 苗 , see God of the Green Sprouts of Rice
Andhra kings, importance of Bay of Bengal trade under, 37 245
Andhras, personality materials for the ages preceding 1000 B.C. of the, 48 348
Androcles and the Lion, of Aulus Gellius's Noctes Atticae, appears to be of Jewish origin, 41 183; possible factual basis of story, 46 4-5
Androgyny, Ištar androgynous, 21 185-187
Anesaki, Dr. Masaharu, elected honorary member of AOS, 1934, 54 333
Angel and Titan: essay in Vedic ontology, 55 373-419
Anglo-Saxon works in Cleveland Public Library, 36 421
An-hsi, 安 息 , (Parthia), west of Yüeh-chih, 37 96; described by Chang Ch'ien, 97-98; its people shrewd traders, 97; coins of; records of, on leather, 97; its relation to T'iao-chih (Chaldea), 97; Chinese legendary traditions maintained by old people in, 97; assistant ambassador sent to, by Chang Ch'ien, 102; regular missions to, 103-104; welcome given Chinese embassy by, 107; royal capital of, 107; Parthians visit China with gifts, 107; visited by traveller Hui-ch'ao, 33 203-204; see also Names, Geographical
Animal sacrifice, at harvest feast of the Land Dyaks, 29 250-256; in Devi festival in the Maratha country, 30 74 f.
Animal Style in Tibet, see Book Reviews, Roerich
Animism, survival of among Indonesian Muslims, 33 327-328, 331, 334

Ankh, on Hebrew seals, 29 193-194
Añkorian periods of art, 49 330 f.
Anna, sister of Dido, relation to Tanit, 32 432
Annam, Chinese tombs at Vinh-yen, note on, 57 332
Anšar and Kišar, character of; Anšar not connected with Aššur, 24 304-311
An-si, see An-hsi
Antae, the origins of the, 59 56-66, 58 527
Anthropology, American, early man fr. Asia, 51 97-98; physical, importance of in study of ancient Near East, 39 174-175; see also Japan, Japanese; Religion, Primitive
Antila, traditional island, confused with "Zipangu"(?), 60 276
Antioch, capital of Ta-ts'in, or Syria, 30 1; patriarchs of, 6-15, 30; ruined by earthquake, 525 A.D., sacked by Persians, 540 and 611 A.D., 6, 8; chalice of, discovery of, 36 351-352; dated A.D. 120-140 by Barton, 49 182; (?) in the Mahābhārata, 58 262-265; in the story of Oponia, 42 293-294
Antioch-on-the-Chrysorhoas, see Gerasa
Antioch-on-the-Orontes, Simeon Stylites buried there in church of Constantine, 35 196; Antioch-on-the-Orontes, see also Mosaics
Antiochus Epiphanes, cuneiform and biblical sources referring to him, 56 247-250
Antiochus VII Sidetes in II Maccabees, 60 125-126
Antiquities, see under Archeology, Art and Architecture, and under names of various countries, museums and collections
Antiquities and ancient ceremonies and customs, a study of in Kamakura times, source materials for, 59 43, 44, 52
An-ts'ai, 奄 蔡, country of the Aorsi, or Alans, a nomad nation on the banks of a 'great Marsh' (the Palus Maeotis), described by Chang Ch'ien, 37 96; north of Parthia, 97; regular missions to, 103-104; oldest notice of, 30 38; more knowledge of acquired later, 38-39; conquered by the Hsiung-nu, 43-45; see also Names, Geographical; Hsiung-nu
An-tun, see Marcus Aurelius: Ta-ts'in
Anu-šar-uṣur, overseer of temple of E-ana in Uruk in 7th year of Cyrus, 36 336
Anuṣṭubh, metre in Vedas, 21 46 f.; popular and hieratic, 22 309-320
Anvāhāryapacana Fire, vyāna correlated with, 22 273
Anyang, climate at, in late Shang, similar to that today, see abstract, K.A. Wittfogel; discoveries of earliest known specimens of carved ivory at, 41 297; finds at, dated by oracle bone inscriptions; many Shang bronzes from, 56 346 n. 33; see also Oracle Bones
An Yu Kung, ancestral hall in the Yüan Ming Yüan, see Yüan Ming Yüan
Ao, 鰲, the fabulous sea monster on which K'uei Hsing rides, 49 138 n. 5
Aorsi, people of An-ts'ai, also called Alans, 30 35, 40, 43-45; as middlemen in the trade across Asia, 33, n. 1
Apabhraṃśa, endingless noun case-forms in, 59 370 f.
Āpadeva's Mīmāṅsā Nyāya Prakāśa, 48 340
Apāna, as a form of breath in Hindu literature, 22 249-308; etymology and location, 39 104-112
Āpastamba, approximate date of, 51 81 fn.
Aphraates, homilies of, considerable Jewish influence in, 38 330-331; soul, his teaching on, 40 103-104, 106, 109 ff.
Aphrodite, Cypriote, possible connection with Ugaritic Ašerat, "Lady of the Sea," 53 107-109
Apocalypse of Paul, shows Iranian conception of redemption of the soul, 51 364-365
Apocalyptic Works, Jewish, background in Alexandra of Lykophon and in Demotic Chronicle, 56 245
Apocrypha and Pseudepigrapha, Old Testament, I Macc. (Heb.) written between 105 and 63 B.C., 56 248-249; Prayer of Azariah dated in 2nd-1st cent. B.C., 56 249; Words of Mattathiah dated in 1st cent. B.C., 56 249; II Macc., date of; a contemporary historical document, 56 250-251; Enoch literature, began shortly before rule of Antiochus Epiphanes, 56 251; Herodian, 256; III, Macc., written in reign of Ptolemy VII Physkon, 56 252; Judith, written in 134 B.C.; interpretation of figures in, 56 252-253; Jubilees, relationship to Enoch, 56 253; 23:11-32 written after time of Pompey, 255; Testament of the 12 Patriarchs, numerous interpolations in, 56 253-254; Psalms of Solomon, historical background of, 56 255; Enoch Similitudes, mentions Pacorus's invasion of Palestine in 40 B.C., 56 255-256; IV Macc. dates from beginning of Christian era, 56 256-257; IVth Sibylline Oracle dates in A.D. 80-81; written by Palestinian Christian Jew at Antioch or Cyrrhus; second oldest noncanonical Christian document, 56 257; see also under names of individual books
Apocryphal Christianity in the Ethiopic magic Book of the Disciples, 25 1-48
Apollo, cock sacred to, 33 381
Apologos, see al-Ubullah
al-'Aqabah (Transjordan) and Ma'ān obtained from the Hijaz in 1925, 47 110-111
Arabia, Arabs, Arabian, Arabic, Arabic numerals, source of, 50 174; dessication of Arabia, 45 4-5; see also Alphabet, Art and Architecture (Islamic), Blood-revenge, Bowls (magic), Burial Customs, Festivals, Folklore, Inscriptions, Judaeo-Arabic, Manuscripts, Marriage (Palestinian), Marsh Arabs, Medicine, Oath, Papyri, Proverbs, Science, Sealand of Arabia, Semites, Semitic, Songs, South Arabia, Umayyads
Agriculture: agents for the transmission of the lemon from India to the rest of the Near East and Europe, 54 158-160; citrus fruit, not native to Arabian Peninsula, 57 381-382; date culture, lexicography of, 35 207-212; spices of, critique of classical accounts of, 40 260-270
Historiography: origins of in old accounts of Arab feudal wars; world-history is of Jewish and Christian inspiration, 59 125
History: background of the revolt against Turkey in 1916, 37 153-161; conquest of Central Asia, note on, 43 434; first mentioned in stele of Shalmaneser III as following Aramaeans into the Fertile Crescent, 41 366; geographers in the 9th-15th cents., on Korea, 58 658-661; home of Semites, 45 3-7; Jews not settled there at an early date and were not at a high cultural level, 54 211-212; military organization, the ḫamīs as an ancient unit of, 56 88-91; most of Arabia paid tribute to Assyria and Neo-Babylonia, 42 371; names, personal, related to Hebrew and Amorite, 45 5; northern part ruled by Nabonidus from Taymā', 42 313-316; not home of Semites, 45 123 ff.; part of Arabia included in Neo-Babylonian Empire, 41 459; Persia under the Arabs; tr. of account by Hui-ch'ao, 33 204-205, Little Fulin, the new country of the Arabs, tr. of account by Hui-ch'ao, 205-206, note of attacks on Byzantium, 206, capital removed fr. their native country to Little Fu-lin (Syria), 205, 207-208; revolt against Turkey during World War I, 36 420; sent Mo-i (Muawia) to besiege the capital of Fu-lin, 30 16, merchants assemble in Ta-ts'in, 14, defeat of Persia and Fu-lin by, 16, composition of an Arab embassy, 30; works on modern Arabia, 47 98-100; participation in World War I, 47 103-106; divisions of, modern, 47 112-116; modern politics of, 47 116-131
Language: accent does not best preserve that of primitive Semitic, 59 456; Baghdad, modern dialect of (phonetics, morphology, lexicon), 22 97-114, loan-words in, 109-111; Egyptian dialect: a-vowel colored by contiguous consonants, 34 279, ẓ and z in, 278-281, "heavy" vowels tend to give rise to emphatic consonants, 280-281; "Emphatics" are ordinary sounds changed by pressure articulation, 46 319-320; g for j in Cairene pronunciation is primitive, and is not under Boheiric influence, 46 319; grammar, not influenced by Greek logic, 59 124; passive construction in, 22 47ff.; root doublets in, 43 422-423; verbs of stative form are never of direct affective type, 53 401; vocalic similarities of modern Palestinian dialect to Hebrew, 48

361; w and r, alternation of in roots, 43 423-424; w = Heb. n; n = Heb. r, 424; VIIth stem perf. form derived from imperf. by dropping prefix, 31 218
Literature: collection of in Cleveland Public Library, 36 421-422; lemon mentioned in Arabian Nights and other early literature, 54 157, 158; poetry, pre-Islamic, absence of religious elements in due to stylistic tradition, 59 123; religious motive never an accepted one in early period, 60 22; religious tendency increased after Hārūn al-Rašīd's accession in A.D. 786, 24, 28-29; had source in popular poetry, 27-28, and was introduced into love-poetry, 27-28; received first recognition in poetry of abu-'l-'Atāhiyah, 29
Palaeography: MS of late 13th or early 14th cent., peculiarities of script in, 41 385
Religion: astrological beliefs of Persian Muslims in Indian not held by Arabs there, 35 294-295; Christian Arabs, their heretical teaching on the soul; Jewish character of their beliefs, 40 113ff.; converted to Christianity by Simeon Stylites, 35 136, 168; mourning customs and ceremonial nudity, 21 23-39; religion not lacking among pre-Islamic Arabs, 59 123
Texts: al-Qubaybah, Palestine, modern folklore and songs from, 48 238-249; 50 199-213; Baybars, reservoir inscription of, dated A.H. 707, 60 376-377; Beirut dialect, songs, proverbs and stories in, 23 175-288; Bethlehem dialect, story of Iḥdayd and the She-Ghoul in, 52 168-173; ibn-Ḥajar's account of the al-Nu'mān family of Fāṭimid qāḍis, text and trans., 27 238-296; Kitāb Aymān al-'Arab of al-Najīrami, 58 615-637; Kitāb Masālik al-Naẓar of Sa'īd ibn-Ḥasan of Alexandria, text and tr., 24 312-383; Kitāb Radd 'ala Ahl al-Ḏimmah wa-man Tabi'ahum of Ġāzi ibn-al-Wāsiṭi, with translation, 41 383-457; Mahdi, letter from to Gen. Gordon, with translation, 31 368-388; papyrus from Alexandria dated A.H. 205, 56 288-292; papyrus published by Torrey in JAOS 56 288-292, corrected translation of, 57 312-315; poems by Nimr ibn-'Adwān, with translation and commentary, 43 177-205; Qā'idah fi Ziyārat Bayt al-Maqdis of ibn-Taymīyah, text of 18th-cent. Landberg MS of, with notes and summary, 56 1-21; Wit and wisdom, translation of al-Ābi's Kitāb Naṯr al-Durar, pt. II, 54 240-275
Trade: Arab monopoly of the iron and cinnamon trade bet. India and the Roman Empire, 35 230-231, 236-239, Indian steel used in Damascus blades, 232; earliest ref. to lemon of India made by Arabic geographers of 10th cent. A.D., 54 157, 158; introduced camphor to western world, 42 358; knowledge of trade winds in the Indian Ocean, 37 241; middlemen in the camphor trade, 42 358, 361, 364-365, in the trade in frankincense, 365-366; trade in storax, etc., with China and Malasia, 42 176; trade in white cotton cloth with Zanzibar, according to Chinese records, 30 56; trade with Eastern Asia; influence in Borneo, 33 313-344; traded between China and the Roman Empire, 35 32, 35-36
Aramaeans, Aramaean, Aramaic, see also Art and Architecture, Bowls, Inscriptions, Ostraka, Seals, Semites
History: appear as nomad Ḫabīru in 2nd millennium B.C., 48 184; contests with Assyria under Shalmaneser III, 41 347, 350, 351, 356, 358, 365-367, 381-382; Suḫu and Ḫindanu overcome by Nabopolassar in 616 and 613 B.C., 44 123-124, 125; take cities of Pitru and Mutkinu on Euphrates from Aššur-rabi, 38 211; their rise in North Mesopotamia and their wars with Ashurnasirpal II, 38 218, 222-225, 228, 229-230, 238, 239, 240, 244, 245, 256; threaten Assyria and are defeated by Tiglath-Pileser I, 37 176-177, 180-181, cause downfall of Assyrian Empire, 182
Language: anticipatory pronominal suffix, non-Semitic origin of, 47 260-262; Christian-Palestinian interstitial vowel of plural still pronounced down to Byzantine times, 53 355; earliest evidence of its use in Judaea is an inscribed jar handle of 5th-4th cent. B.C. from Beth Shemesh, 55 309-310; Egyptian Jews did not abandon it, 60 131-134; emphatic ending written in O.T. both -ā' and -āh due to scribal inconsistency, 51 322-323; internal passive of Hebrew origin, 22 46ff.; -īt, adverbial ending, cf. Akk. -iš, from išu, "existence," 45 314, 355; the language of Fu-lin, spoken by the Nestorians in Persia, India, Tartary and China, as well as Syria, Mesopotamia, & Chaldaea, 30 24; mixed constructions in, 35 382-385; multiplicative numerals in, 35 381-382; no Eastern and Western dialect in Biblical Aramaic, 51 323; no spirantization of stops before Achaemenid period, 60 421; pᵊ'īl functions as stative participle, 58 287-288; scribes and language among Neo-Babylonians and Assyrians, 48 127-131, 133-135; syllabic meter, early, 46 241-247
Literature: Aḥîqar Romance, parallels with Syriac version, 38 65
Religion: see Ninmarada
Texts: Behistun inscription version has passage not found in other versions, 33 283-284; incantation texts from Nippur, Indian names in, 41 159-160; notes to Aramaic incantation text from Nippur, 33 279-280; notes to Egyptian Aramaic contract on papyrus published by Bauer and Meissner, 58 394-398; 'Nwšt in Murašû indorsement to be read Enmaštu, 28 135-138; Ostrakon, commercial, from Nippur, 5th cent. B.C., 29 204-209; papyrus contract published by Bauer and Meissner, note to, 59 105; "Passover papyrus" from Elephantine, restoration and translation of, 60 120-122; reconstructed text of letters prefixed to II Maccabees, with translation, 60 141-150; Syro-Mandaean incantation bowls from Nippur, 32 434-438
Arame, Ḫaldian ruler and traditional king of Armenia, 41 349, 360, King of Gûsi, 41 353, 369
Arbuda, foe of Indra, 36 253 f.
Archeology, see also under names of various countries and regions
Africa, East Coast: Chinese coins and celadon shards found on Somali coast, 30 54-57
Chinese: brush-inscribed characters on oracle bones and Shang pottery, 56 335 n.2; finds at Anyang dated by oracle bones, many Shang bronzes, 346 n.33; coins and shards of celadons found on Somali coast testify to medieval trade with China, 30 54-57; see also Mu-yang-ch'eng, Paper money; (Chou Period), see also Hanchow Ssu-ch'uan; (Han Period, in Korea), see also Lo-Lang; (Neolithic), see also Pig; Sheep; Water-buffalo; Fowl; Rice; Wine; Plough
Indian and oriental: books on in Cleveland Public Library, 36 421
Korean: review of Hamada and Umehara's study of the ancient tiles of the Silla dynasty, 55 218-219; review of Harada's report on excavations of Lo-Lang, 54 97-99; see also Lo-Lang
Manchurian: notes on excavations of Mu-yang-ch'eng, see also Book Reviews, Harada
Archers, see Military
'Archipiélago Filipino, El,' on Bisayan dialects, 26 121
Architecture, see Art and Architecture and under names of various architectural subjects
Archiv für Keilschriftforschung, announcement its founding by E. Weidner, 43 79-80
Archives, Chinese, of early Chou, 52 235, custom of keeping genealogical records in ancient China, 233-234, 236, 238, 239-240, destruction of ancient records in 771 B.C.?, 235-236, records of Shang, 241
Arde'et, Ethiopic magic book, text and translation of, 25 1-48
Ardeshir III (Artaxerxes), difficulties in ascending the throne; his refuge in "Fu-lin", 33 200-202
Ardhamāgadhī, and Māgadhī, 44 81-121; what it is, 105-110; characters in drama speaking, 110-114
Ardhanārī, the figure of, 54 222
Ares, cock sacred to, 33 381
Aretas III, discovery of his probable palace and sanctuary at Petra, 52 286
Arhats, eighteen on the pagodas of Zayton, 56 374
Arianism, opposed by Bar-Šûšan, 32 270, 307

Aristeas, pseudonymous work; chiefly valuable for sources copied, 56 252
Aristotelian Psychology, basis of Nestorian teaching on the sleep of the soul, 40 109, 116
Aristotle, Syriac work on his Categories by Sergius of Rīš'aynā, 35 298
Ark of the Covenant, had no cherubim, 25 286; had no original connection with the Tent of Meeting, 38 134
Armageddon, origin and meaning of the name, 34 412-415
Armânum, country situated around Pir Hüseyn, NE of Diyarbekir, 57 417
Armenia, Armenians, Armenian-Greek index to Philo's Quaestiones and De Vita Contemplativa, 53 251-282; originally a Semitic country, 39 254-255, 260; see also Calendar (Persian)
Religion: accused of retaining Jewish customs, 32 273, 276-277, 335-336; begin day in morning, 32 271; celebrate Christmas and Epiphany on Jan. 6, 32 272, 276, 320-323; converted by Simeon Stylites, 35 136; converted to Christianity by St. Gregory in 863 of the Alexandrian Era, 32 331; customs criticized by Bar-Šūšan, 32 268-342; fast on Friday instead of Saturday, 32 271; follow Arabs in sacrifice and circumcision, 32 340; follow Chalcedonians Nestorians in manner of making sign of the cross, 32 340; follow Jews and pagans in making offerings to the dead, 32 339-340; practices condemned by Syrian Fathers, 32 335-336; Simony among clergy, 32 326-328
Arms, Armor, weapons of the people of Po-pa-li (Berbera), 30 48; migration of laminated plate armor through Near East, Far East, into America, 51 100; see also Crossbows, Halberds, Swords
Japanese: Tr. of the "Complete Manual of the Old Sword", by an unknown author, pub. in Yeddo in 1793, 26 334-410
Sumerian: Eannatum, helmet of furnished with visor, 38 68-69
Arnold's views on Vedic dual endings, 23 319-321
Arrapḫa, see Itḫia
Arsaniah, one of women at tomb of Christ, according to Turfan Pahlavi account of Crucifixion, 39 55
Arshtāt (?) in the Old Persian inscriptions, 21 169
Art and Architecture, mosaic, technique of originated in the highlands of Anatolia, 59 247-250; vault, primitive method of building described by Theophilus Presbyter (10th cent.), 59 109-110; see also Seals
Anatolian, southern: objects listed in tribute and plunder lists of Assyria, 38 236, 239
Aramaean: of Ša-Dikanni, a sub-Assyrian style, 38 222-223, of Bît-Zamâni, 238-239, of Bît-Adini, 246-247
Asian: analysis of psychological attitude towards art, east and west compared, 55 325-329; origin of certain Burmese tapestries and Acheik patterns may be traced to China, then to Persia? 45 190
Assyrian: Kalḫu reliefs depicting Ashurnasirpal's campaigns in southern Anatolia, 38 236, 241-243; wall-paintings, 22 31-32
Babylonian: belt buckle, bronze, in Metropolitan Museum of Art, 38 308-309; enameling of bricks, 22 29-34; jumping mouse, green slate figure of, 38 140; polychrome lion from Babylon, 22 27-34
Buddhist: 25 collotype reproductions of old masters illustrating Suzuki, Essays in Zen Buddhism: Second Series, mentioned in Book Reviews, Suzuki
Byzantine: doors, bronze inlaid with gold, taken from Brusa in 1326 by Timur, 60 576-578
Chinese: bronze drums of South China and nearby regions, 45 186; building materials for Chinese imperial palaces, 1727-1750, a description of a MS. book giving regulations, prices and man-hours for work at Yüan Ming Yüan, Jehol, Wan Shou Shan, Hsiang Shan, the Yung Ho Kung (Lama Temple) at Peking, etc., also furnishings of, 49 234-243; regulations for timbers and boards, 236-237, price lists for diff. kinds of woods, 238, 240, wood carvers and furniture makers, records of materials allowed for finishing woods and stone, 237, 239, regulations for stone work, sizes, materials, work days, time allowed for carving by diff. classes of artizans, 237, for transportation of stone and cost, 239, finishing with wax, varnish, carving, painting, materials, and amounts, 237, 239, metal work, 239, straw mats and awnings, 239-240, price lists of bamboo and paper, brick and tile, 240, foundry rules for bronze work and casting of sacrificial vessels, religious objects and ornaments for temples, 240, 242, cost of glazed roof tiles, with and without transportation fr. factory, 240-241, price lists for all sorts of builders' and furnishers' materials, 241-242, regulations for painting of palaces and temple interiors, with cost per sq. ft., 237, 242, "Western Ocean" articles, 242, protection from birds, 241; Feng Yang, 汾陽, name of a palace built at Ch'in Lo Hsien in 608 A.D. 49 142 n.7; Han mirrors, form and decoration, 55 185, 186-187, mirror in its toilet-box, with other fittings, excavated at Lo-Lang, 188; ivory objects of Shang and Chou, 41 295-297, the elephant in ancient art and pictograph, 298; legends represented on the Shantung sculptures; giant swallowing a child (soul), 56 65, Shan-hai-ching made to accompany a book of art, 66, designs on the nine tripods of Yü, 74; painted basket from tomb at Lo-Lang, Korea, description, 56 102-103; pre-Han, carved rafters and painted red pillars mentioned (in the Han-shu), 54 188, pavilion called Nü Huai Ch'ing T'ai, 女懷清臺, erected to the widow of Pa, 192, n.22; T'ang designs in flat relief on border and end of stone sculpture of horse "Autumn Dew", 55 427, evidence of the painting of sculpture in T'ang period, 428; Taoist cult pictures on doors, 54 293; tower of great height proposed, in Wei period, for holding intercourse with divinities of heaven, 53 237-238; see also Flying Gallop, Hanchow, Ssu-ch'uan, Liu-i, Lo-Lang, Mu-yang-ch'eng, pagodas, sculpture, shadow-theater; Han, see also Lacquer Ware; Glass; Silk; Gold & Silver, Ornaments; Toilet Articles; Divination; Mirrors; Tortoise-shell; Pottery; Coins
Christian: Campanile an adaptation of the minaret, 30 151-154; Chalice of Antioch dated A.D. 120-140 by Barton, 49 182; Chalice of Antioch, discovery of, 36 351-352
Cilician: Sandon monument from Tarsus, represents a rock-sculpture of ca. 150 B.C., 60 544-553
Egyptian: statues of Amset and Hapi in University of California, 46 312-313; Tall al-'Amārnah, sculptor's studio at, 36 350
Etruscan: jewelry in Marburg collection, 22 18-19
Greek: order in artistic compositions first appears in protohistoric period (ca. 700 B.C.), due to internal social and political developments; parallels in Mesopotamia and Egypt, 58 140-147
Hittite: at Carchemish, 38 246-247; relief at Çoban Tepe, 28 159, 161-162
Indian: Rajput painting not realistic, 55 328
Islamic: À cheval perspective in painting is Asiatic, not specifically Chinese, 52 254-255; Dome of the Rock had no dome before the time of 'Abd-al-Malik, 56 5, 12; earliest known use of exterior architectural faience at Sīn, near Iṣfahān, 60 100; earliest mosques had no minaret, which was not always used in later times, 30 133-138; Harāt, center of Timurid painting in 15th and early 16th cent., 50 81; Madrasah of Barqūq in Cairo, modern copy of inscribed door from, 30 58-60; minaret, origin and history of, 30 132-154; Mongol miniatures in the Morgan Manāfi' al-Ḥayawān, 36 388-389; Nīšāpūr pottery begins at end of 8th and beginning of 9th cent., 58 258, stucco panel from Sabz Pūšān, arabesque-like character of its ornament; Sasanian elements in; dates in second half of 10th cent. A.D., 258-261, Imām Zādah Karrar at Būzan, its stuccos are early 'Abbāsid in date, 260-261, stuccos from Friday mosque at Nāyin date from early 10th cent., 260-261; Painting: fine line developed out of Islamic calligraphic style, 57 120, asymmetric composition of Mongol period derives from older Iranian formulae, 120-121, linear, calligraphic characteristics of Mongol and Timurid style derived from pre-Mongol pottery painting,

121; Stalactite cupola, earliest dated (A.D. 1132) example of at Sīn, near Isfahān, 59 397-398; textiles, printed and painted, from al-Fusṭāṭ, 53 394; Zamān, Muḥammad Paolo, Persian painter, life of, 45 106-109; see also Mosque, Mosques

Japanese: Hotei (Chinese Pu-tai) as subject for paintings, prints, netsuke, etc., 53 48; the magic holly used as a motive in surimono, 55 447, holly in paintings by Otsu artists, 448, holly on netsuke and textiles, 448, sword-guards by the Hiiragiya, 449; shown at the festival of Gion matsuri, 54 286-287, floats carved by famous artists and decorated with tapestries, embroideries, etc., 287, carvings by Jingoro, 289; the tsuba, 45 90; see also Jingoro

Jewish: pictorial art in synagogues tolerated outside Palestine, 55 108-109; Dura synagogue represents a distinct type, 55 109

Korean: roof-tiles of Silla, 55 218-219

Manichaean: passage in Turfan Pahl. Frag. M. 47 shows interest in painting and calligraphy, 49 354

Mesopotamian: dome goes back to early prehistoric times, 56 110

Near Eastern: order in artistic compostions first appears in Early Dynastic in Egypt and Mesopotamia, due to internal social and political developments; parallels in Greece, 58 140-147; Scorpion-man in, 52 288; (Hellenistic) Rabbinical references to early basilicas and stoas, 50 338

Parthian: gold jewelry from Seleucia-on-the-Tigris, 52 301; mixture of Hellenistic, Assyrian and Sumerian elements, 49 369; rock sculptures at al-'Imādīyah (Āšib), 38 219 n. 28

Persian: Chinese influence on, 36 177-178; Īwān originated from long-room house in warm climates, 60 168

Phoenician: objects in Assyrian tribute and plunder lists, 38 250

Sasanian: notice of relief and inscription at Biricik, 28 158

Syrian: Antioch-on-the-Orontes, mosaics from show shift from painting style to abstraction, 59 399; objects described in Assyrian tribute and plunder lists, 38 215, 219, 225, 234, 250; 41 373; Syro-Hittite, of Lubarna, 38 247

Turkish: Chinese influence on, 36 177-178

Arthaśāstra, advice to conquerors, 53 388; allusions to magic in the, 42 75-79; the appellation Lokāyata in the, 50 135; heading of Topic 123, 60 208-216; notes to Meyer's translation of the, 48 289-322, editions and translations, 290-294, relative age of the, 294; samādhi-mokṣa and śamaḥ saṃdhiḥ samādhiḥ, 60 208-216

Aruru, Sumerian female divine element, called Ištar by Akkadians, 36 284-285

Arvad, city of Syrian coast, later representative of Amurru, 38 249

Āryabhaṭīya, date of the, 47 364; place system and algebra of, 51 51 f.

Aryans, invasion of India, date of, 47 187 f.; the original home of the, 48 358; see also Indo-Europeans

Aryaramna inscription and the date of Zarathuštra, 53 202

Ārṣa, the terms Ardhamāgadhī and, 44 81 f., 105, 108

Asa, basis of his reforms in Ex. 33: 12-34:28 and Num. 10: 29-32, 38 128

Aṣa in the Gāthās, 21 75 f., 81-87

'Asad, Palmyrene god, of Arab origin, 57 319

Asakawa, Prof., contribution of to Chinese studies in America, 38 105

Asaṅga, Indian Buddhist philosopher, 4th cent. A.D., 51 292, author of the Mahāyānasaṁparigrahaśāstra, 295-296, 299, 302-303, and of the Yogācāryabhūmiśāstra, 297, 301, Chinese trs. of his works, 295-296, 297-299; note on tr. of his work, by Prof. Lamotte, 60 115-116

Asar, Sumerian solar-fertility god later identified with Marduk and related to Osiris, 39 196-205, originally a West-Sem. deity? 204

al-Aš 'ari, see Risālah fi Istiḥsān al-Ḫawḍ fi 'l-Kalām

Ascalon ('Asqalān), not to be visited by Muslims as a sacred spot, 56 5, 15

Asceticism in the Mahābhārata, 22 333-379

Ascetics, Hindu stories of false, 44 202-242

Aṣḥāb al-Ḥadīt, forerunners of the Ḥanbalites, 54 15, 18, 23, points of difference from Ḥanbalites, 20-21, passive or negative attitude on theological problems, 22-23, called Ḥašwīyah, 24, various divisions of, 24-25

Ashurbanipal, Annals of, notes on, 24 96-102; three text types in, 52 304

Ashurnasirpal II, annals and campaigns of, 38 216-263, army, reorganization of, 217, political situation in Assyria at his accession, 217-218, policy of frightfulness, 224 ff., estimate of his rule, 253 ff., confused with Ashurbanipal, 257-258; possible foreign origin of, 38 210-211; see also Menagerie

Asia, Asiatic, influence of Asia on America, 51 87-103, interest in India and China led to Columbus' discovery of America, 88, natives called "Indians", 89, Columbus' expeditions and movements determined by his notions of Asiatic geography, 89-90, stories in Columbus' diary said told him by Indians he imagined fr. his own knowledge of Euro-Asiatic tales, 90-96, tale of the dog-headed people, 91-94, story of the woman's kingdom, 91-93, 94, 95, the one-eyed people, 93, 94, tale of cannibals, 93, 94, people with tails, 95; tradition of the fountain of perpetual youth, 95-96, fable of the long-eared people, 96, excitement over discovery of America and theories as to origin of its peoples, 96-97, Chinese influence in America not direct, by sea, but gradual by infiltration over land route, 97, early man in America via Bering Strait or the Aleutions, 25,000-20,000 B.C., 98, culture in America evolved independently before Columbian times, 98, contacts and undercurrents of Asiatic thought swept to N. America in historic times, i.e. scapulimancy, bear ceremonialism, shamanism, 99-100, backgammon, football, the composite bow, the moccasin, laminated armor, ivory carvings, decorative motives, 100; migration of folklore and myth, i.e. the story of the magic flight or obstacle pursuit, 101; trials of bridegroom to win bride, war bet. pigmies and cranes, creation of Earth through an animal diving into water for mud, concept of hare in moon, of frog in moon, of magical devices for seeing long distances, 102-103; Asian art, the essence, 55 325-327; relation of geographical divisions to history, 41 190-191

Asia Minor, geography and trade of, 36 168-180; history of the cock in, 33 380-383; archeology, see Alisar Hüyük, Tarsus

Asiatic Studies in Europe, knowledge spread by Marco Polo, 43 3; a Spanish-Japanese Vocabulario, 1595, 4, 17th cent. studies mostly grammatical and lexicographical; works of missionaries in China (Matteo Ricci, etc.) not then known in Europe, nor Gaubil's tr. of the Shu-ching, 1669; Kircher, Duret, Martini, on Chinese characters and geography; studies in Japanese language by Rodriguez, and by Collado, 6, 18th cent. Chinese studies on the language, hist. of the Huns, grammatical studies of Manchurian, Mongolian, Tibetan and Indo-Chinese, and a grammar of Japanese, 8, the founding of Royal Academies which supported oriental studies, 1603-1819, and Journals, 8-9, 19th cent. works of Rémusat on Chinese, 1811-1829; de Rosny, Humboldt and Siebold on Japanese, 9; school for study of Japanese opened in St. Petersburg about 1701 by Denby, first Jap. to go to Russia, 42 290; schools for teaching living Oriental languages, 39 189-195; see also Chinese Studies in Europe; Müller, Andreas

Asiatic Studies in the U.S.A., internat'l relations bet. East and West, 44 177-185; modern Asiatic Societies founded, especially American Oriental Society in 1843; conditions of the time and influence upon other learned societies 43 11-13, leading sinologists and students of Japan, Tibet and Siam in AOS, 12, relations bet. AOS, the Royal Asiatic Society, and the Société Asiatique, 13; oriental archeology, 36 348-354; schools needed, 39 144-145, 185-188; see also Chinese Studies in the U.S.A.

Aširta (= Aštar, Ištar), worship of carried to South Arabia, where she became the god 'Attar, 45 135

Asklepios, cock sacrificed to, 33 381

Asmaktā, Talmudic principle of legal obligation, Babylonian element in, 40 126-133

al-Asmar, Ni'mat Allāh, his edition of ibn-al-Habbārīyah's text of Kalīlah and Dimnah is made from a good MS, 42 394
Asoka, Fourteen-Edicts of, dialect of Girnār redaction, 31 223-250; interrelation of dialects of, 30 77-93, dialect of Shāhbāzgarhi and Mansehra redactions, 81-93; on the killing of animals, 27 460
Asokan dialects, interrelation with Sanskrit, 46 257 f.; their evidence on relationship of Middle Indic to Vedic and Sanskrit, 33 145-148
Asokan inscriptions, notes on the Minor Pillar Edicts, 46 264; notes on the Pillar Edicts, 46 261-263; notes on the Rock Edicts, 46 258-261; notes on the "Separate Edicts," 46 263-264
Asokan notes, 36 205-212, etymology of Shb. niraṭhriyaṃ, Mans. nirathrīya, 210, Shāhbāzgarhi and Mansehra phonetics, 210 f., Girnar likhāpayisaṃ, 211, Māgadhan kachati, 211 f., Shb. śruneyu, 212, nāsaṃtaṃ, 205, asvatha-saṃtaṃ, 205 f., Girnār athā, 207, on the gender of pālanā, sukhīyanā, and dasaṇā, 207-209, Delhi-Sivalik lāja, siya, Girnar karu, gerunds in tu, ti, 209, locative singular of a-stems, 209 f.
Ass-worship in Anatolia, Egypt, Rome and Iran, 40 331-333
Assemani, Joseph Simonius, Maronite author, works of, 22 94
Assemani, Stephanus Evodius, Maronite author, works of, 22 94
Assimilation and analogy, 57 136-140
Aššur (deity), form, character and etymology of, 24 282-311
Aššur (Qal'at Šarqāt), occupied before 3000 B.C.; Aeneolithic pottery at, 48 91-92; abandoned as capital of Assyria under Ashurnasirpal II in favor of Kalḫu, 38 256-257; possibly never a Sumerian city, 58 451
Aššur-bânia-uṣur, rab BI.LUL under Shalmaneser III, 34 346, 348
Aššur-bêl-kalâ, ruled over Amurru, 38 209
Aššur-bêl-uṣur, Assyrian governor of Kirurri and Kalḫu, 34 349-350
Aššur-eṭel-ilâni, reigned until 622 B.C., 22 20
Aššur-iṣka-dannin, turtânu under Sargon II, 34 349
Assyria, Assyrians, Assyrian, army, seige methods of, 38 243; cock unknown there before the middle of the 7th cent. B.C., 33 392-393, 395; elephants in, about 1100 B.C., 41 291 (see also Obelisk, Black, of Shalmaneser II); greatest cultural gift of Assyria to the ancient world was provincial organization, 38 254-255; see also Akkadian, Art and architecture, Babylonia, Calendar, Guilds, Medicine, Mesopotamia
History: Arabia, tribute collected from, 42 371; Assyrian Canon dates must be reduced to agree with the accession of Hosea in 729 and the death of Tiglath-Pileser in Jan., 726 B.C., 44 159; Assyrian Chronicle, text, translation and commentary, 34 344-368; campaigns of rulers from death of Tiglath-Pileser II to end of reign of Ashurnasirpal, 38 209-263; elements among the Ḫabîru, 48 184; eponym list begins with accession of Adad-nirâri III in 911 B.C., 38 211-212; fall of empire predicted by Isaiah, 42 371-372; fall of the empire according to the Nabopolassar Chronicle, 44 124-129; Nabopolassar Chronicle account of campaign against Ḫarrān in 610 B.C. confirmed by letter of Nebuchadrezzar, 46 362; Nineveh, account of fall of in Xenophon (Anab. 3 4, 7), 28 99-107; Nineveh, fall of, 22 20-22; Provincial governors, careers of, 34 345ff.; Sennacherib's advance on Egypt, 701-700, 24 265-274; Shalmaneser III and the foundation of Assyrian power, 41 345-382; State already existed at beginning of 3rd millennium B.C., 45 208; Tiglath-Pileser I, campaigns of, 37 169-185; see also under names of rulers, governors, etc.
Language, see Akkadian
Literature: wisdom literature, influence of on Aḥîqar Romance, 38 64-65
Religion: Aššur, originally patron deity of A-usar; not connected with Anšar, 24 282-311; see also Babylonia
Society: sexual immorality common, 41 10; veiling of women practised before 1000 B.C., 41 11, 34-38
Topography: 38 209-263 (with maps); topographical lists begin with Tiglath-Pileser I, 38 258
Aštart, possibly androgynous, 21 187; represented in Palestine as nude goddess holding serpent to her vulva, 51 176; worship of in Israel, 46 157, 163; worshipped by Semites as Queen of Heaven, 37 212-213; see also 'Anat
Astrologer (Grand), T'ai-shih, see Ssu-ma T'an, Ssu-ma Ch'ien
Astrology, see also Bowls, magic
Chinese: see Alphabet
Greek: Babylonian influence on, 33 293;
Islamic: lunar omens of Babylonian origin, 35 294-295
Judaeo-Arabic: Genizah texts, with translation, 47 302-310, 49 291-302
Parsi-Persian: Burj-Nāmah, book of moon-omens, text and translation, 30 336-342; moon and serpent calendars, text and translation, 33 286-293
Zoroastrian: lunar omens of Babylonian origin, 35 294-295
Astronomy
Babylonian: see Kidinas and Naburianus
Chinese: Conjuction of the 5 planets in May 205 B.C., 55 310-313, reasons for Pan Ku's mistake in placing it in 207 B.C., 310, 311-313, date of the "triumph of the Han dynasty", 312-313, constellations tung-ching and kuei, 310-311; some records of eclipses in the ancient texts may be interpolations, 52 233; see also Chou pi suan ching.
Japanese, see Yoshimune
Aṣṭādhyāyī of Pāṇini, date of, 59 404 f.
'Ašūrā' festival in Persian, two popular Azarbayjani poems recited in connection with, 39 113-116
Asuras, proselyting the, a note on Rig-Veda 10.124, 39 100-103, the Asura pitṛ of vs. 3, 100 f., conflict between Asuras and Devas, 101 f., translation of hymn, 102 f.
Asûšu-namir, a reflex of Tammuz, connected with the crescent moon, 39 86-88
Aśvaghoṣa's dramas, affinities of Bhāsa's Prākrit with that of, 40 259
Aśvins, as saviors, 45 287; Aśvins and Cyavana, the story of, 26 45-67
Atash-Behram, the founding of an, 49 174-176
Atharvaprāyaścittāni, indices and corrections, 33 217-253; preface, 34 229-233, introduction, 233-266, textual criticism and date, 267-270, parallel passages in other texts, 270-277; text with notes, 33 71-120; text with notes, 33 121-144
Ātharvaśiras Upaniṣad, literary stratum, 23 67
Atharva-Veda, history of the 12-syllable verse, 22 316-318; philosophic materials of, 39 148; prāṇa-series in the, 22 257 f., 278-280; Atharva-Veda Paippalāda, a manuscript of the, at Poona, 48 340 f.; description of two manuscripts of the Paippalāda, 50 104-111; principle of magic power of knowledge in the Upaniṣads, 49 97-121; and Rig-Veda, relative dates of, 22 309-320; Śāntikalpa of the, 33 265-278, text, 267-278; Whitney's material on, 44 157
Kashmirian: book one, edited with critical notes, 26 197-295; book two, edited with critical notes, 30 187-258; book three, edited with critical notes, 32 343-390; book four, edited, with critical notes, 35 42-101; book five, edited with critical notes, 37 257-308; book six, edited with critical notes, 34 374-411; book seven, edited with critical notes, 40 145-169; book eight, edited with critical notes, 41 264-289; book nine, edited with critical notes, 42 105-146; book ten, edited with critical notes, 43 96-115; book eleven, edited with critical notes, 44 258-269; book twelve, edited with critical notes, 46 34-48; book thirteen, edited with critical notes, 48 34-65; book fourteen, edited with critical notes, 47 238-249; book fifteen, edited with critical notes, 50 43-73; book eighteen, edited with critical notes, 58 571-614; books 1-12, contents of, 46 8-14
Atirat, Arabian goddess posited by Barton, did not exist, 45 135-136
Atlantis, identified with southwestern Spain; called ^{mât}Anâku,

"Tin Land" by Sargon of Agade and Tarsîsu (Heb. Taršîš) by Esarhaddon; Taršîš later confused with Gades, 43 163
Ātman, and Brahman, and animism, 52 82; Ātmán-Bráhman equation, 36 197-202; and the Buddhist position, 57 339; its dwelling-place, 22 265; in the Mokṣadharma story of world creation and dissolution, 45 54-63; prāna and the sun as paths of, 22 264; in the Upaniṣads, 49 112-116; of Upaniṣads, 22 386; and the vital breaths, 22 249 f.; 22 267, 270, 272
Atonement, Day of, changed from first to 10th day of 7th month, 37 220-223, originally a New Year's festival, 223; Pharisee-Sadducee dispute over manner of high priest's entering Holy of Holies; background existed already in days of Zechariah, 47 358-359
'Attar, South Arabian god, masculinization of Aširta-Ištar, 45 135
'Aṭṭār, Farīd al-Dīn, translation of his allegory of the moths and the flame, 36 345-347
Aulus Gellius, see Androcles and the Lion
Auramazda, in Old Persian and non-Iranian inscriptions, 21 163-180
Australia, cultural traits peculiar to northwest, 58 66-69; influences from the East Indies, 58 61-80; Malays in, 58 71-78; missile-sticks, 55 164-166; polished chisels, 58 70; totemism, 38 147-150
Austronesian, some changes of original t and s in, 38 71
"Autumn Dew", see Horses of T'ang T'ai Tsung
Avalokiteśvara, as spiritual founder of line of Dalai Lamas of Tibet, 52 339, 341, 346-347
Avāna as a form of breath in Hindu literature, 22 249-308
Avesta, Avestan, in Achaemenian inscriptions (?), 21 172-175; cattle-tending and agriculture in, 39 329-333, Geiger's views, 329; terminology, 330 f.; conclusions, 333; observations in Azerbaijan, 25 181-183; see also Calendar, Persian; Gathas
Language: compounds, 57 430 f.; Avestan d = Sanskrit l, 25 175; use of instrumental as accusative or nominative, 23 57-60; instrumental as subject, 48 285 f.; k-suffixes, 31 304-310; meaning of past tenses of the indicative, 21 112-145; passage (Yasna 49.4), a syntactical shift in, 48 277-279; syntax, subordinate clauses, 22 145-176; compared with other Indo-European languages, 22 145-175; transcription, Justi's and new standard, 21 191; treatment of IE. k̑s, 40 82; Yazd pronunciations employs aspirates rather than spirants, 25 184
Religion: location of Farnbāg fire, 41 81-106; location of three oldest fire-temples, 41 82; divine and demonic epithets in, 46 97-153
Texts: history, 39 331 f.; Pahlavi text of Yasna ix. 49-103, edited with collation, 23 1-18; critically translated, 24 64-76; Yasna xvii, Pahlavi text of, edited, 26 68-78; Yasna lvii: an essay in text-reconstruction, 58 310-323
Avyakta Upaniṣad, text and translation, 60 338-355
Awnings, see Mats
ibn-'Adwān, Nimr, five poems by, 43 177-205
Awsān (Arabian tribe), called Seres by the Romans, 35 237, connected with Zayla', 237-238
'Ayn Dūq, near Jericho, 5th-cent. inscribed Hebrew mosaic from, 40 141-142
abu-'l-'Aynayn, saint near Rāmallāh (Palestine), descended from Adonis, 60 300
Ayco, king mentioned by von Suchem (1350), was Haitum I, king of Lesser Armenia (1226-1270), 55 103
Azarbaijan, was the Avestan Airyana Vaējah, 25 181; severity of winters in, 25 182; dogs of, 25 182-183
Azarbayjani dialect, see Turkish texts
Azaria of Julfah, see Calendar, Persian
Azazel, chief of demons dwelling in wilderness around Jerusalem, 37 222
al-'Aẓm, Nazīh al-Mu'ayyad: Riḥlah fi Bilād al-'Arab al-Sa'īdah [P. Hitti], 59 526
Aztecs, used bronze and copper implements, 39 163
Azuma Kagami, 吾 妻 鏡 , value of, as source for study of Kamakura period, 59 38-39, 45
Babai, his teaching on the soul, 40 107
Babel, Tower of, is the ziggurat E-ur-imin-an-ki at Borsippa (Birs Nimrūd) 40 276-281; identified with the ziggurat at Borsippa, 41 157-159; was an eight-staged ziggurat, 43 252
Babylon, captured by Mursilis ca. 1750 B.C., 51 173; excavations at, 22 27; landmarks of, 22 28; first dynasty of, began 2225 B.C., 44 289; Indian trade with, 33 352; introduction of into Sumerian creation story, 36 279-280, 284 ff.
Babylonia, Babylonian, barley, dates and garlic chief products in later times, 58 547; began with painted pottery peoples, neither Sumerians nor Semites, 45 14; boats and rafts used at earliest periods; ships not equipped with sails until 7th cent. B.C., under Phoenician influence, 44 173; climate, dessication of, 45 27; cock appears there under Achaemenid influence, 33 393-394, 396; influence in Old Persian inscriptions, 48 71 f.; land controlled by state, temples and wealthy landowners, 58 547, feudal tenure of 547; libraries not proved to have existed in temples, 27 147-182; Semites, Eastern, entered Babylonia from Arabia, 45 14; transportation by water in early times, references to, 43 173; writing, influence on Phoenician alphabet, 22 177-198; writing, invented by Sumerians 45 14; see also Akkadian Language and Sumerian Language, Art and Architecture, Astrology (Greek, Islamic, Zoroastrian), Astronomy, Calendar, Divination and Hepatoscopy, Etana Myth, Festivals, Guilds, Law, Magic, Marriage, Mathematics, Mesopotamia, Metrology, Near East, Oneiromancy, Seals, Slaves, Sorcery, Sumer, Sumerians, Sumerian, Textiles
Cosmology: conceptions of, 22 138-144; 23 opp. p. 388; Babylonian and Indo-Aryan cosmology, 26 84-88
History: antediluvian king-lists and chronology compared with Berossos, 43 323-329; fall of Neo-Babylonian empire predicted by Ezekiel, 42 372; Isin era, fell at close of reign of Rim-Sin, 38 329; king-lists, discovery and interpretation of, 41 242ff.; Mes-šár-kalama period and First Dynasty of Ur, no violent break between, 51 67-68; method of classifying soldiers in reign of Cyrus, 41 466-467; Nabopolassar Chronicle account of campaign against Harrān in 610 B.C. confirmed by letter of Nebuchadrezzar, 46 362; Nabopolassar, critique and analysis of his Chronicle, 44 122-129; Neolithic not represented, 41 253; prices of staples under Achaemenid rule were double what they had been in the Neo-Babylonian period, 52 305; sea-trade with Egypt, early, 45 239, 245; settled 8000-6000 B. C., 41 261; Western Semites arrived during dynasty of Isin, 28 138-144
Literature: catalogue of love songs found at Aššur, 52 52; epic, religious expression in, 37 35-42; epistolary formulae, 43 26-40; medical texts, titles of, 37 250; Neo-Babylonian practice of redacting short inscriptions into longer versions, 26 98; posthumous journey, theme of, 47 298-301
Religion: deification of rulers, 41 252; deities of justice were: Anu, Bêl, Šamaš and Adad, 52 177, 178; Ekimmu, "departed spirits," three classes of, 39 311-312; elements borrowed by Iranians, 36 300-320; emperor-worship attested by personal names, 37 162-163; emperor-worship not practised, 36 360-380; 37 331; expressions of religious feeling (prayers, king-deification, hymns, future life, literature, creation), 37 23-42; Ištar an androgynous deity, 21 185-187; monotheism tended towards but not realized, 56 402; Nippur psalms and liturgies published by Barton in vol. I of his Miscellaneous Babylonian Inscriptions, interpretation of, 41 131-149; rise of waters in spring believed to be caused by cohabitation of the gods, 56 155-156; sacrificial ritual, (the horse-sacrifice), a parallel between Indic, and, 54 107-128; Scapegoat in, 21 1-22; Sin, moon-god, travelled by boat, as do Egyptian deities, 46 362; Šitlamtaea and Lugalgira, demoniacal manifestations of Nergal, 38 162; source of Zoroastrian and Islamic Persian lunar omens, 35 294-295; West-Semitic

deities found since dynasty of Isin, 28 138-144
Mythology: male temple prostitutes, Sumerian and Semitic myths explaining origin of, 39 83-85; see also Moon; and under names of characters and themes
Bacarē of Greek writers, identified as Porakād, 33 211
Backgammon, see Games
Bactria, Bactrians, Bactrian, history of the cock in, 33 377-379, 395; silk route ran through, 35 225; on trade route overland fr. China to the West, 35 31, 33, 37-39; trade with China and the West, 35 31-33, 37-39; see also Ta-hsia, Yavanas
Bādāmī, basreliefs in caves of, 49 191-193, bull and elephant design at, 49 192
Bad-tibira (Namgarum), situated at Tell Ṣifr near Larsa, 52 183; third antediluvial dynasty, 43 324, 327
al-Baġdādi, see al-Farq bayn al-Firaq
Baghdad, modern Arabic dialect of (phonetics, morphology, lexicon, loan-words), 22 97-114
Bagobo, see Philippine languages
Bahinā Bāī, story of the Marātha poet-saint, 50 76 f.
Bahinabai, a story of Pundalik as told by, 48 341
Bahing, data on verb changes in, 60 311-312
Bahūdaka, as class of Yogins, 22 348
Bakkal-oğlu Sari Mehmet Paşa, life and works, 51 356
Baku, description of fire-temple at Surakhani nearby, 25 176-178; Indian inscriptions on the Fire Temple at 29 299-304
Bakufu, source materials for study of, 59 38, 39, 40, 41, 43, 44, 46, 47
Balaam, identical with Bela', king of Edom, 35 386, home in *Peter in Bēt 'Eden, 389
Ba'l Šamîn, referred to in Daniel as šiqqûṣ šōmem; earliest mention of is in Zakir inscription, 43 143
Baladeva, modern images of, as imitations of ancient Nāga figures, 49 188 f.
Bälau language, see Palau language
Balinese funeral ceremonies, 51 7 f.
Bamboo, Chinese, for fences, in 18th cent., 49 237, price lists for, 240, 241; fr. Ssŭ-ch'uan, seen by Chang Ch'ien in Bactria, 37 98; purple, 49 134
Bamboo Annals, claims to have been found in a tomb of 281 A.D., 56 66, gives miraculous element in its notes on the model emperors, 66, refers to Yü's journey south and his death and burial there, 61; see also Chronology of ancient China
Bamboo slips, chuan, for writing; significance of length of, 44 280-282
Bāṇa's Harṣacarita, on a passage in, 50 129-131
Bangkok, Siam, note on archeological objects in Wang Nah Museum, 29 283
Banyan-tree in Sāvitrī story and rite, 21 57 f., 63
Baptism, of Christ celebrated every thirty years, 32 274, 323; misuse of by Armenians, 32 271, 317, 318, 330; as symbol of regeneration in Semitic and Egyptian religion, 56 155-165; Syriac term for baptism derived from Rabbinic usage? 46 15-18, baptism by aspersion practised by John the Baptist, 18-20, earliest N.T. tradition on, 21, elements of and agent in, 20-22
Barabudur, lutes and harps, 51 49 f.
Barai-Munda sept of the Hos, origin of the, 50 231
Barakāt, abu-al-, Grand Šarīf of Mecca, sends keys of Ka'bah to Selim I, 37 156
Barbarians, see also Jan, K'un-ming, Mang, Ti, Tsö (Tsê ?), P'o
Barbarik, see Berbera
Bārhaspatya, as title of Indian materialism, 50 138
Barley, used as food in prehistoric Egypt, 39 174
Barons, see Shō-gun
Baroody [Bārūdi] collection of Arabic MSS in Princeton University Library, 46 343
Barqūq, modern copy of door from his madrasah in Cairo, 30 58-60
Bar-Šûšan, patriarch, letter of to Armenian Katholikos on Armenian customs contrary to the canon of the church, 32 268-342, sketch of his life, 268-269, Christology of, 306-311
Bartholomae's views on the Avestan preterite tenses, 21 113 f.
Baruch, Greek Apocalypse of, Persian influence in, 33 370
Barygaza, Indian port for ancient export of iron, 35 236
Bašgali, see Piśāca
Basilicas and stoas, early Hellenistic Near Eastern, rabbinical references to, 50 338
Baskets, Chinese, Han and later, see Tomb of Painted Basket
al-Baṣri, al-Ḥasan, critique of his essay on qadar, 55 138-162
Batak (Sumatra), Bataks, alphabet of Phoenician origin, 47 25-35; use of camphor in burial customs of, 42 356, camphor-gathering ceremonies among, 358-359, camphor, legends about, 366-370; see also Folklore
Batán, treatment of original l in, 36 191-193; see also Philippine languages
Bau, Babylonian feast of, 31 253ff.
Baudhāyana, approximate date of, 51 81 f.
Bawlah, King, Egyptian legend of in ibn-'Abd-al-Ḥakam is prototype of Ballad of King John and the Abbot of Canterbury, 22 221-226
Bāyazīd Šāh, Sultan of Bengal, his existence proved from coins, 43 254
Bayer, Gottlieb S., author of Museum Sinicum, 1730, see also Asiatic Studies in Europe; Müller, Andreas
Bàyon, date of the, 50 265
Beads, earliest (ca. 3500 B.C.) inscribed Egyptian examples from Memphis, 36 349; Chinese, Han, coral, glass, see Lo-Lang
Bear, the story of Yü, 56 59
Bear Ceremonialism, in Asia and America, 51 99-100
Bears, dreams of, 49 141-142 n.6
Beast, number of in Rev. 13:18, 26 315-317
Beast fable, stories of animals shamming asceticism, 44 210-212, 232-236
Bechtel's views on the Vedic dual endings, 23 318
Bedauye Language, see Hamitic
Bedjan, Paul, works of, 22 88-90
Behistun inscription of Darius, column V, 58 675 f.; metrical arrangement in, 58 677; rock and inscriptions re-examined, 24 77-95
Beirut, songs, proverbs and stories in modern Arabic dialect of, 23 175-288
Bela', Edomite king, identified with Balaam, 35 386
Bêl-bânia, nâgir êkalli under Shalmaneser III, 34 346, 348
Bêl-dân, nâgir êkalli under Šamši-Adad V and Sammuramat, 34 348-349
Belshazzar, not ruler of Babylonia while Nabonidus was in Têmâ, 42 312-313; prominent in affairs of Uruk, 39 147
Ben-Ammi and the Fairies of John Godfrey Saxe, originally a Jewish tale, 45 363
Benedictus, Petrus, Maronite author, works of, 22 94
Bengal, Tantras and Vedas in, 23 65; see also Bāyazīd Šāh, 'Alā' al-Dīn Fīrūz Šāh and Numismatics, Indian
Bengal, Bay of, important trade of under Andhra rulers, 37 245
Bengali system of accounts, ancient, 52 306
ben Gorion, Joseph, editions and versions of his History of the Jews, 59 260-261
Benjamin of Tudela, fragment of his travels translated by George Borrow, 52 310
Ben Naftali, Masoretic authority, methods of isolating MSS of his school, 51 371
Ben-Sira Hebrew text composed ca. 190 B.C.; Aramaisms and Arabisms in, 23 39-42, not possible to fix original as a whole, 42, two independent lines of tradition, one in the Hebrew, the other in the versions, 42-43; historical substance of, 56 245-247
Benni, Behnām, Syrian patriarch of Mosul, works of, 22 93
Berbera, Africa, described in early Chinese accounts of 7th cent. and later, 30 46-57

van Berchem, Max, death of, 41 160
Berlin Genesis, dates from 3rd cent.; characteristics of, 44 173-174
Berossos, futility of attempting to restore the chronology in his Babyloniaka without cuneiform sources, 46 86; his list of antediluvian kings compared with cuneiform sources, 43 323-329
Bes, cult of, of Indian origin, 43 169
Besbalik, Uigur capital, identified with Po-cheng-tsu, 56 453
Bestiality, associated with deities of animal fertility in Near East and Rome, 40 323-324, 325-328, 330, 332
Bethel, West-Semitic deity, sources where mentioned, 59 81-87, worshipped in Canaan, Babylonia, Syria and Elephantine, 82-87, Akkadian and Aramaic names compounded with, 82-84, found at Ugarit, 87, Phoenician origin of, 89-90, type-parallels to, 91-93
Bethlehem, folk story of Iḥdayd and the She-Ghoul in local dialect, text and translation, 52 168-173; name Fu-lin derived fr., 30 3-4, 17; 33 199
Beth-Ṣûr (Palestine), Greek coins from; height of prosperity in reign of Antiochus Epiphanes; abandoned after Judaizing of Idumaea, 52 301
Bezeklik, see Central Asia, Painting
Bhaga, association with Indra as god of fertility, 36 244, 263
Bhagavad Gītā, comparison of Kashmirian Recension with vulgate, 52 68-75; date of the, 52 391 f.; the "four causes" in the, 57 415 f.; influence on American intellectuals, 56 415; meaning of guṇa, 52 249 f.; meaning of sāṃkhya, 52 250; meaning of yoga, 52 250 f.; and the principal Upaniṣads, recurrent and parallel passages in, 42 1-43; Sānkhya and Yoga in the, 43 167
Bhairava, Śiva as, worshipped by Kānphaṭa yogīs, 45 356
Bhājā reliefs, interpretation, 54 220
Bhāmaha, date of, 50 173
Bhānudās, the Maratha poet-saint, life of, 39 150
Bharadvāja, association with Dhanvantari and Divodāsa, 42 333 f.; associated Indra with Maruts, 36 249
Bharata, on the use of dialects in drama, 44 110-114; treatise on dramaturgy (Nāṭya-śāstra), 40 359 f.
Bharata war, ages of combatants, 24 47-54; date of, 24 7 f.; 52-55
Bharaṭakadvātiṃśika, as Jaina satire, 46 73
Bhartṛhari, Abraham Roger's life of, 25 226 f., translated, 228-230; cave at old Ujjain described, 23 313 f., version of story of his wife Piṅgalā, 314
Bhartṛharinirveda of Harihara, translated, 25 200-225, position in Hindu dramaturgy, 198, Yoga philosophy in, 198 f., duration of the play, 199
Bhāsa, Māgadhī in the plays of, 44 101 f.; the relationship between the Mṛcchakaṭika and the Cārudatta of, 42 59-79, theories, 60 f., significant textual differences, 61-70, technique, 61 f., Prākrit, 62-64, versification, 64-66, dramatic incident, 66-70, time-scheme, 70, summary and conclusion, 70-74; studies in, 40 248-259, fields of inquiry, 248-250, archaisms in Prākrit, 250 f., alphabetical list of selected archaisms, 251-259, summary, 259; treatment of the Udayana legend, 43 169; versification of metrical portions, 41 107-130, analysis of metres, 106-118, list of phrases and comparisons borrowed from epics, 116 f., grammatical solecisms for sake of metre, 118-130, list of solecisms, 121-130, summary, 130
Bhāṣās and vibhāṣās, 44 93-95
bhava, see nidānas
Bhavabhūti, bibliography of his Mālatīmādhava, 25 189-191, 339; of his Mahāvīracarita, 25 191 f.; of his Uttararāmacarita, 25 192-194; Uttara-Rāmacarita, stage emendations in, 34 428-433
bhavacakra, "Wheel of Life", see Symbols, Symbolism
Bhaviṣyottara, source of Hemādri's account of Sāvitrī story and rite in Caturvargacintāmani, 21 53
Bhikṣugītā, or Mendicant's Song, 46 289-296; Eknath's version of, 45 357
Bible, see also Hexapla, New Testament, Old Testament, Septuagint, and under names of various books
Arabic: Syriacisms in Polyglot version of Zechariah, 59 401-402
Armenian: I and II Kgs. and its affinities, 54 53-59
Coptic: St. Luke, description of 6th-cent. Garrett Sahidic MS of, 55 451-457
English: anachronisms in, 48 361; literary importance due to its freedom from Latinisms; is full of Hebrew idioms, 52 51
Greek: Berlin Genesis, characteristics of, 44 173-174; Joshua, Washington MS of, relation to Codex Alexandrinus, 31 365-367; method of identifying Greek vocabulary with its Semitic equivalents, 30 301-312; ὁ Σύρος, a Semite writing in Greek, 47 367; serious differences in text of LXX before time of Origen, 58 101, at least two pre-Origenian traditions of LXX existed, 102
Hebrew: Kethîb and Qerê, problems of, 60 30-45; Masoretic text of 7th and 6th cent. documents fairly represents the original, 59 423; Qaraite commentaries on from the Cairo Genizah, 41 179-180
Old Latin: Hexaplaric elements in the first nine chapters of Joshua, 33 254-258; possibly based on Jewish Latin version, 49 83-84
Syriac: Gen. 32:25, text of, 33 263-264; loss of Urumiah concordance to Peshitta in 1919, 43 128-129; problem of relation of Kt. to Qr. in Ezra, 43 432-433
Bibliography, Maurice Bloomfield, supplementary, 1911-1928, 48 199; Clay, Albert T., 45 295-300; Gottheil, Richard J.H., 56 480-489; Guidi, Ignazio, 55 458-463; Jackson, Abraham Valentine Williams, 58 241-257; A. V. Williams Jackson, addenda to, 58 473; Jastrow, Morris Jr., 41 337-344; Laufer, Bertold, 54 352-362; Salisbury, Edward Eldridge, 22 2-6; Ward, William Hayes, 36 238-241
Asia, Eastern: bibliographical notes, two Far Eastern, 57 421; authors and titles of Western, Japanese and Chinese works suggested as additions to the lists in Merrill and Walker, A Bibliography of Eastern Asiatic Botany, 59 139-140; additional titles for A Bibliography of Eastern Asiatic Botany, 60 258-260
Asia, Northeastern: critical notes on various works on, 60 429-432
Australia, Northwestern: and the question of influences from the East Indies, 58 79 f.
Chinese: grammar, list of Western authors and works on, 58 156, 157, 158, 161, two Chinese dictionaires, 166 n. 15; notes on, evaluations, and suggestions, in connection with Gardner's Union List--Western Books on China---, 2nd Ed., 59 283-286; source materials listed for study of treaty negotiations oi 1842-3-4 opening China to western commercial exploitation, 59 469-484, Footnotes; Taoism, 53 217-218; titles of important ts'ung shu, 51 40-46; Buddhist, see Wei Shih: Hsüan Chuang; early western works on, see Müller, Andreas; see also Ts'ê fu yüan kuei; Yen T'ieh Lun
Indian: chāyānāṭaka genre of Indian dramaturgy, 32 58-63; works of Dāsopant, 42 253 f.; Indian folk-tales, 39 43-54; references to Indian language of gesture, 48 280 f.; the Mahāvīracarita by Bhavabhūti, 25 191 f.; the Mālatīmādhava by Bhavabhūti, 25 189-191; Kālidāsa's Mālavikāgnimitra and Vikramorvaśī, 23 93-101; the Prabodhacandrodaya by Kṛṣṇamiśra, 25 194-196; editions and translations of Śakuntalā, 22 237-248; the Uttararāmacarita by Bhavabhūti, 25 192-194; additions to M. Winternitz, Geschichte der indischen Litteratur, 43 333-336
Japanese: History, Kamakura Period, 1192-1333, Source materials (112 works) noted as to contents and their value for study of, 59 38-55, Primary works: historical, 38-42, diaries, 42-45, war narratives, 45, miscellanies, 45-46, works on culture and morality, 46, law and administration, 46-48, documentary records kept by temples, monasteries, etc. and by prominent families, 48-50, on religion and religious life and thought, 50-52, biographies, 50, writings of Buddhist and Shinto priests and thinkers, 50-52, on antiquities, ancient practices and Court etiquette, 52,

cyclopedic works, 52, on genealogy, 52, on origins of things, 52, Secondary works: present day studies of the feudal period and the manorial system, 52-54, on the Mongol invasions, 54, on Buddhist monasteries and temple economy, 54, on the history of thought, 54-55, on the history of the Kamakura period in general histories of Japan, 55; 102 Japanese works, sources for Notes on Village Government in Japan, After 1600, by K. Asakawa, 30 291-298; sources for Notes on Village Government in Japan After 1600, by K. Asakawa, 4 additional works, 31 151
Manchu: survey of works on Manchu language and literature written since 1908, 60 554-559, unpublished Manchu-French dictionary by Stanislas Julien is in Cleveland Public Lib., 559, important materials in an unpublished ms. in Newberry Library Chicago, see Manuscripts, Manchu; see also Book Reviews, Walter Fuchs
Mandaean: 46 49-55
Old Persian: of studies in Achaemenian religion, 21 161; Old Persian studies, 1912-1936, 56 222-225; supplementary to that in "The present status of Old Persian studies", 58 329 f.
Palau: phonology of language, 35 1 f.
Philippine languages: 40 25-70, bibliographical works, 27 f., printed works, 29-62, manuscripts, 62-67, index of subjects, 68-70; U. S. Government publications dealing with Philippine languages, 42 150-158
Siamese: references on the subject of Siamese tone-accents, 31 283
Tibetan: list of materials containing references to Chinese Turkestan, 57 125-126
Tirurai: phonology of the Tirurai language, 33 150
Bicol, people and language, 25 173 f.
Bigelow, William Sturgis, (d. 1926), In Memoriam, 47 344
Bikol, see Philippine languages, comparative grammar
Bilin Language, see Hamitic
Biography, Chinese, attitude toward facts of private life, in writing of, 59 153; comparison of arrangement of in the Han-shu and the Shih-chi, 54 186-193; Empress Têng, of Later Han, 51 138-159, childhood, 139, scholarly tastes and ability, 139, 150-151, 156-157, death of her father, 139, prophecy of her greatness, 139-140, entering the palace, 140-141, struggle with Yin Hou and elevation to be Empress, 142-143, death of Ho Ti, Têng made regent, 144, her communiqué to the ladies chosen as guardians of Ho Ti's tomb, 144-145, the affair of the theft of the chest of pearls, 145-146, of the false charioteer, 146, Têng's economies at the court, 146-149, 150, 153, 154, her justice, 149-150, death of Shang and boy An placed on throne, 148, feast and ceremony for expelling demons and driving away pestilence, 150, admin. of the gov., 151, death of her mother, 151-152, performs the great sacrifice in the ancestral temple of the imperial family, 152, edict against eating fruits and vegetables out of season, 152-153, the memorial of P'ing-wang Hou Liu I, 153-156, a school estab. for children at the court, 156-157, the incident of Têng K'ang, 158, final illness and death of Empress after reign of 20 years, 158-159, burial in the Shen Tombs, 159, 148 n. 55 of the Monk Pu-tai (d. 916 or 917), 53 49-52; Widow of Pa, 巴寡婦清, one woman of wealth listed among the rich merchants of Pre-Han period, tr. of her Biography fr. the Han shu, with attitional comment fr. the Shih chi; conditions of the times; sources of her wealth, 54 186-193; see also Wên Ta-ya
Bird, development of design of on early Chinese Bronzes, 51 16-18; feeds child exposed by King of Wu-sun in wilderness, 37 100; in T'iao-chih, see Ostrich; see also Raven
Bird-like soul, see hamsa
Birth-tabus, Semitic, 37 14
Bisayan, dialects, 26 120-136, comparative syntax, 134-136, comparative morphology, 125-134, comparative phonology, 124 f.; differences between Tagalog and, 25 162-169; infixes la, li, lo in, 27 142-143; an l "cockneyism" in, 36 181 f.; see also Philippine languages, comparative grammar
Bishop, blessing of by Armenian priest criticized by Ignatius of Antioch, 32 274-275, 325-326
Bishop, Carl W., opinion concerning Yü the Great, 56 62-63; see also Far East, Archeology
Bistām ibn-Qays, ca. 590-615, little known of his life, 43 436
Bît-Âdini, Aramaean state in bend of Euphrates, conquered by Ashurnasirpal II, 38 224-225, 245; Shalmaneser III's campaigns against, 41 353-354, 358, 361
Bît-Iâkin, see Sealand of Arabia
Bitis (Bt), the original Egyptian Tammuz, replaced by Osiris, 39 73 n. 15
Bitumen, obtained by Gudea from Mt. Madga in Elam, 43 44
Bkra śis lhun po monastery, residence of the Paṇchen Lamas, 52 344, 348, 349
Black Magic, called ku, 蠱, 55 1-30, antiquity of the character, early definitions and usage, 1-9, use as a divination symbol, 4-9, a disease caused by worms, frogs, centipedes, etc., 2-5, 8-10, 21-24, 29, various forms of, 7,8,11,13, 15-16, 17, 18, 20-23, warded off by sacrifice of dogs, 3, by sitting cross-legged, 19, by burial of food at street intersection, 19, geographical extent of the practice, 9-10, practiced especially among the aborigines, 10, 11, 17-19, 22-23, manufacture as a "love medicine", 11-13, methods of manufacture as a poison, 1, 8-9, 10-11, 13, 17-18, 21, 23-24, "flying ku", 8, 18-20, 22, antidotes and counter charms, 6, 7, 8, 12, 14 n.34, 15, 16, 17, 18, 19, 20-21, 24, used to acquire wealth, 1, 13-15, 20, 21-29, used as means of revenge, 1, 9, 10, 12-13, 17, laws and methods used to suppress practice of ku, 6, n.13, n.14, 10, 14, 17, 18, 19, 20, 24-25, chin-tsan, a variety of ku, 13-15, 19, 23, 25-27, 28, t'iao-sheng, a variety of ku, 15-16, 18, ku witches, or sorcerers, 6, n.13, 13, 15, 16, 17, 18, 19, 20-21, 23, virtous scholars safe from, 25-29
Blancardo, Solomon, Jewish merchant trading between Genoa and the Levant in the 12th cent., 38 181-182
Blau Monuments, notes on, 22 118-125; new collation of, 24 388-389
Blind, person or persons, as a symbol of "ignorance", one of the nidānas, 60 357
Blo bzaṅ chos kyi rgyal mçhan, one of the earliest Paṇchen Lamas and an incarnation of the Paṇchen Lama represented in a Tibetan temple painting belonging to von Staël-Holstein, 52 348-349
Blo bzaṅ dpal ldan ye śes, Paṇchen Lama who visited Emperor Ch'ien Lung, appears on a Tibetan Temple painting, 52 345, accompained by portraits of his spiritual ancestors here listed, 345-346, 349 n.45
Blo bzaṅ hjam dpal rgya mçho, the eighth Dalai Lama, represented on Tibetan temple paintings, 52 345, the 58th of the spiritual line, 339, represented with 26 of his spiritual ancestors, 340
Blo bzaṅ ye śes dpal bzaṅ po, Paṇchen Lama, 1663-1737, appears on a Tibetan temple painting, 52 349
Block-printing, on textiles, 47 72, 75; see also Printing
Blood, Semitic view of its relation to the soul, 36 151-153
Blood-revenge, Israelite, believed necessary because soul of victim would not rest until avenged, 39 303-321; Arab, soul of victim would not rest until avenged, 39 304 ff.; Greek, murder punished with temporary exile or death, 39 306 ff.
'Blood-sweating horses', see han-hsüeh
Blood-test, as proof of kinship in Jewish folklore, 24 129-144
Bloomfield, Maurice, life and works of, 48 193-199, supplementary bibliography, 199; classification of Vedic hymns, 22 309-320; translation of prānas, 22 255 f.; Vedic Concordance, additions to, 29 284 f.
"Blue Piebald", see Horses of T'ang T'ai Tsung
Blumentritt on Bisayan dialects, 26 121
Boats, Babylonian, not provided with sails until 7th cent. B. C., 44 173; open felucca rigged craft carried Indian Ocean trade in Roman times, 37 241, represented on coins, in painting and sculpture, 241, of the Far Eastern trade in Tamil ports described in poems, 245, quote the Periplus

on large vessels for the voyage to Chryse and the Ganges, 246; represented on pottery from Naqādah, Egypt, 41 192; used for distant journeys in An-hse, 37 97; boat as symbol of the 4th nidāna, nāma-rūpa, or the "in-dividual", 60 359

Bod'aštart, inscription of from temple of Ešmun in Sidon, 24 211-226; inscription of from temple of Ešmun at Sidon, notes on, 25 324-331; king of Sidon, inscription of from temple of Ešmun, 23 156-173; Phoenician king reigning between 320 and 280 B.C., 57 240

Bodhāyana, conjectured author of Vṛttikāra, 31 17 f.

Bodish, see Languages, Sino-Tibetan

Bohol dialect of Bisayan, 26 123

Böhtlingk's translation of prānas, 22 255 f.; 22 301-302

Boloki, concepts of right and left among the, 58 203, 213

Bombay, Neo-Babylonian contract from, 40 142-144; origin of the name Pāe Dhonī in Old, 53 391

Bon Religion, see Literature, Tibetan

Bontok, loss of intervocalic l in, 36 184 f.

Book of Changes, consulted by Han Wu Ti, 37 103; see also I-Ching

Book of Filial Piety, place in the Canon, 44 282

Book of Hsing, 行, an ancient book used in schools in the State of Ch'i, 44 278

Book of Mencius, its place in the Canon, 44 282

Book of Mourning, commentary on, see Sang-fu-chuan

Book of Music, said by Pan Ku to have disappeared after Burning of the Books, 44 280; see also "Four Shu"

Book of Odes, describes hairdress, knot unfastener, 41 297; tells of tribute in ivory fr. Huai River region, 41 298

Book of Rites, see Li Chi

Books, see also Bibliography

Chinese: Buddhist see abstract, Swann; The Classics, history of the Canon of, 44 273-284; criticism of Ferguson's sources for study of mythology, 53 54-65, religious books of Taoism all late, 58; earliest form and terms for, 44 273-276; earliest printed work, 56 535; Harvard-Yenching cards for, and Catalogue of; classifications of titles, see abstract, A.K. Chiu; import into Japan prohibited by the Edict of Kanei, bet. 1630 and 1720, of all western and Chinese books dealing with Christianity, 57 290-303, list of books first prohibited, 292-294, 35 more burnt or destroyed bet. 1685 and 1720 by fanatical officials, 295, 296, 301, Yoshimune's interest in astronomy and the calendar resulted in the Edict of Kyôhô and lifting the ban on 19 scientific books in 1720, 297, 298, method of censorship, 299-301, duties and responsibilities of book inspectors, 299-300, secret possession of prohibited books by scholars, 301-303; private imperial library of Han, contained interpretations of the Classics fixed by the Council on the Classics, held by Han Hsüan Ti, 58 444; Sutras in Tangut (Hsi Hsia) in the National Library of Peiping, 52 190; works quoted from in the Yen T'ieh Lun (1st cent. B.C.), 51 267-275, large number of works listed in the Han Shu, 268, destruction of books at the beginning of Han, 268-269; see also Wei Shu: Four Books

Japanese: tr. of Complete Manual of the Old Sword, 26 334-410;

Mahayana: Sanskrit-Chinese-English Glossary useful for reading Mahayana texts, 52 92-93

Siamese: palm-leaf manuscript books described, 29 282

Boomerang, 55 163-181, Australian missilesticks, 164-166, returning boomerangs, 166 f., origin of boomerangs, 167-169, so-called boomerangs of other areas, 169-179, bibliography, 180 f.

Boran (Baurana), Queen of Persia, leans on Yeshu' yabh in her difficulties after the death of Ardeshir III, 33 201

Borneo, elephant still occurs in, 41 294; harvest gods of the Land Dyaks of, 26 165-175; Borneo, influence of war and of agriculture on the Kayans and Sea Dyaks of, 25 231-247; Islam in, 33 313-344

Borrow, George, translated a part of Benjamin of Tudela's travels, 52 310

Borsippa, Ē-ur-imin-an-ki, ziggurat of temple of Nabû, is Tower of Babel, 40 276-281; ziggurat of is the biblical Tower of Babel, 41 157-159

Botany, importance of in study of ancient Near East, 39 175; question of date of introduction of sorghum vulgare into China, and other bibliographical notes, 60 258-260; Chinese, see also Sunflower; East Asiatic, see also Bibliography

Botel Tabago, loss of l in, 36 185

Bow, composite, appears in Egypt ca. 1600 B.C. and passed from there to Eastern Asia and America, 39 172-173; see also Weapons

Bowls, incantation, Aramaic, from Nippur, notes to, 33 279-280; Christian, from Babylonia, 37 9; Hebrew, in the U.S. National Museum, 23 45, 36 154; Islamic magic and medicinal bowls, with translation and interpretation of inscriptions and symbols, 55 237-256; astrological bowl, 58 366-383; Syriac, in U.S. National Museum, 23 45; 36 154; Syro-Mandaean, from Nippur, 32 434-438

Bows and Arrows, see Military, Archers

Boyer, Père Augustin M., died Jan. 2, 1938, in Paris, 60 439

Boym, Father Michel, see Kircher, Father Athanasius

Brahmā, identification of the Buddha with, 57 342 f.; in Mokṣadharma story of world creation and dissolution, 45 51-61

Brahma Sūtra, date of, as determined from refutations of Buddhist doctrines, 31 1-29

Bráhman, and Ātmán, and animism, 52 82; Bráhman-Ātmán equation, 36 197-202; in the Upaniṣads, 49 116 f.

Brahman, Brāhmans, as a class, origin of the, 48 295; influence on the Purānas, 43 132-141; part in Srāddha ceremony, 22 228-236; physical types, 53 184 f.; position in the Veda, Brāhmanas, and Sūtras, 53 181-183; priests originally Dravidian, 43 136; restriction of constraint by suicide to, 21 156-158; wedding, described, 22 323-328

Brāhmaṇas, caste system in the, 53 182 f.; literature, contributions of the Jaiminīya Brāhmaṇa to the history of, 26 176-196; prāna and apāna in the, 39 111; verbal correspondences of Jaiminīya with other, 23 323-349

Brahmāṇḍa Purāṇa, relation of the Vāyu to, 43 130 f.

Brahmanism, and Hinduism, the main current of, 46 199-201; religious paraphernalia of in U.S. National Nuseum, 23 46-47

Brāhmī, (?) script in a Babylonian contract tablet, a line of, 56 86-88; Brāhmi script, supposed, on Babylonian tablet, is series of European Arabic numerals, 56 490-491; the connection of the Harappa with, 59 Sup. 38

Brāhui, etymologies, 56 351-360; relation to other Dravidian languages, 56 350

Brass, see Bronze

Braut von Korinth, Die, of Goethe, resemblance of the plot to that of the Περὶ Θαυμασίων of Phlegon of Tralles, 39 295

Brazilian Gypsey dialect, 50 139-143

Bread, unleavened, Armenian use of in offerings condemned, 32 337-342

Breasted, James Henry, life and works, 56 113-120

Breath, Hindu conceptions of the functions of, 22 249-308

Bṛhaspati, apāna as, 22 295; approximate date of the writer on law, 51 81 fn.

Bṛhatī, the 12-syllable verse of, in Vedas, 22 316 f.

Bṛhatkathā, source of Harṣa's dramas, 21 88; abridged by Kṣemendra and Somadeva in their works, 53 125 f.

Bṛhatkathāmañjarī compared with the Kathāsaritsāgara, 53 124-143

Bridgman, Rev. E.C., co-founder of the Chinese Repository, contributions of to Chinese studies, 38 100

British General Staff maps of the Near East, criticism of, 39 58-59

British power in India, a political theory of the rise of, 48 348

Bronze, frequency of in lands N. of Assyria, 38 239, 246, 221, 234-235; used by Aztecs and Incas, 39 163; Chinese reference to foundry rules for casting sacrificial vessels for temples, 49 240, 242, regulations for casting the bronze pavilion at Wan Shou Shan, 240, reference to a recipe for "antiquing" bronze, 241; use of in Shang period, 52 242; see also Metals: Wu Jen-chieh

Bronze Age, in China, thought to have begun with the advent of the Shang, 52 244, may have begun with the Hsia about 1800 B.C., 244-246, no trace of a gradual evolution in China, 247

Bronzes, Chinese, Famous ones, the Hsiao Ch'ên Chih, the the Ta Yü Ting, the Mao Kung Ting, dates and inscriptions, 56 343-344; of Hsia, no inscribed ones known, 56 346; sacrificial vessels, pien and tou, 49 130; sacrificial vessels, a Tsun, early Chou or earlier, in the Univ. Museum, Phila., 51 16-22; shape and design compared eith other known examples, 16-18, evolution of t'ao-t'ieh and phoenix bird designs, 16-18, lost wax process of casting, 18, Shang type inscription, shan tso fu keng pao tsun i, kung, 18, sign of bow a family "coat of arms"? 18, the probable origin and development of the character i 彝, 19-20, patination, analysis of the bronze and microphotography, 20-22; of Shang, many extant, 56 346 n.33; three examples inlaid with secular scenes, see abstract, A.R. Hall; of Western Chou, great numbers, inscribed, are extant, 56 337, length and historical value of their inscriptions, 337-339, 342, 346 n.33, occasions for which cast, 339; dating by the inscriptions, 344-345, tr. of a typical inscription on, 346-349; see also Animal Style in Tibet; Karen, of Burma; Mirrors

Brooke, Sir James, god among the Land Dyaks, 26 169 f.; 33 335

Brugmann's law (IE o = Skt. ā in open syllables), and agent nouns -kāra, etc., 21 52

Brunei, Malay kingdom of, founded in middle of 13th cent., 33 316, Islamized ca. 1530, 316, deification of officials in, 325, feuds with Spaniards, 335

Brünnow, Classified List of Cuneiform Ideographs, additions, to, 22 201-220

Bsod nams phyogs glaṅ, first abbot of the Bkra śis lhun po monastery, one of the incarnations of the Panchen Lama appearing on a Tibetan temple painting, 52 348

Bsod nams rgya mcho, the third Dalai Lama, represented on a Tibetan temple painting, 52 344

Bucranium, with solar disc between horns represents Pn-B'l, 32 433

Buddha, cross-cousin marriages in the genealogy of the, 59 220-226; and Devadatta, the supposed joking-relationship between, 59 221 f., 226; evidence as to the historicity of the, 53 204-209; footprints, cult of, note on origin, 57 340; identification with Brahmā of, 57 342 f.; or images of, called burkhan in Mongol, Tungusian, Uigur and Turkish, origin of the word in pre-Buddhist shamanistic images, 36 390-395; his position in Manichaean text from Turkistan, 43 19; prayer to, 49 132-133; family name Chu Tan, 瞿曇, or Ch'iao Ta Mo, 喬答摩, 133 n.3; teaches Yoga-technique is not conducive to perfection, 22 336, 373

Buddha image, Indian origin of, 46 165-170, date of the Greco-Buddhist school of Gandhāra, 166, date of the Mathurā type, 166 f., independence of the Mathurā type, 167 f., Mathurā the centre of type-distribution in India, 168 f., Gandhāran type did not profoundly affect Indian art, 169 f.; crowned, antiquity and Indian origin of, 50 263 f.; monastic type, 50 264; in sculpture, turban replaced by crown, 51 57; in U.S. National Museum, 23 47

Buddhism, Buddhist, the Anatta doctrine in, 49 351 f.; Arhats, standing epithets, of, 40 339-343; and the Ātman, 57 339; compared with Christianity, see also Book Reviews, Anesaki, Katam Karaniyam; dates of introduction into other countries, 53 206f.; doctrine of gifts and giving in the Divyāvadāna, 49 50-51; doctrines, 58 679-686; dramas edited by Lüders, Māgadhī in the fragments of, 44 104 f.; as Dravidian reaction, 39 125; hybrid Sanskrit, the aorist in, 57 16-34; iconography, Vedic sources of elements of, 57 116 f.; instruments of ritual of, in U.S. National Museum, 23 47; Khotanese version of the Rāma story, 59 460-468; literature, the cetiya in, 52 77; Mahāyāna and Hīnayāna as aspects of, 57 339 f.; miracles in the canonical scriptures of, 44 162; non-injury in, 27 455-464; nuns in Hindu fiction, 44 204, 236-242; oldest Buddha cult, that of the Śākya Buddha, flourished ca. 250 B.C., 53 206; among the Palaung, 45 188-189; passage in Manu, 43 165; passage in Manu, 43 244-246; problems connected with the origin of, 53 204-209; purgatory, 44 166; recent trends in the study of, 48 343; religious paraphernalia of in the U.S. National Museum, 23 47; rule against eating meat, 27 455-464; sacred texts, plea to make them accessible, 38 333; Sanskrit, correspondences with Jaina Sanskrit, 40 343 f.; Sanskrit, a Pālism in, 44 73-75; stupa, nature of, 57 340-342; suicide in, 27 455 f.; terminology, in matter of breath control, 22 307; see also Art; Mysticism; Divyāvadāna; Gautama Buddha; nidānas; Religion, Tibetan

Central Asia: legends illustrated in wall-paintings fr., 49 63

China: beginnings in China, A.D.65, 60 585; Ch'an Buddhism and Vedantism, 59 278-280; correlated with earlier Chinese thought, 46 79, 80; criticism of Dr. Ferguson's chapter on myths, 53 63-64; into China, introduction of, 49 354; identity of Mi-lo Fo, the "Laughing Buddha", with Monk Pu-tai, 53 47-52; method of transliteration of names of Buddhist monks, both Chinese and foreign, 52 159-162; remarks on trs. of the Mahāyānasaṃgraha and the Vijñaptimātratāsiddhi, both fr. Hsüan Tsang's tr., 60 115-116; revival of in Boxer times, items, 45 356; in Sung period, illuminated by the pagodas of Zayton, 56 374; value of the Laṅkāvatāra Sūtra to the study of Zen (Ch'an) and of Yogācāra, 52 91-93; see also Hsüan Chuang: Wei Shih; K'uei Chi

Japan: Bibliography of source materials concerning the affairs of monasteries, religious life and thought of the time, lives and writings of famous priests, 59 48-51; close association with Shinto, 54 282, 285, see also Gozu Tennō; Hōdō; Zen, brief summary of Suzuki's answer to "What is Zen?", 57 445-446, training of a Zen monk, definition of the koan exercise, place of prayer, of meditation, 446-447, the Four Great Vows, the sutras most read, the Yü-lu, 447

Bugis, migrated from Celebes to Borneo ca. 1600, 33 318, 320

Buḫārā, see Calendar, Persian

ibn-Buḫtīšū', life of, 36 384-385; see also Manāfi' al-Ḥayawān

Building Supplies, for Chinese imperial palaces, 1727-1750, 49 234-243

Bukē Myōmoku-shō, 武家名目抄, value of, as source for study of the feudal system in Japan, 59 47

Bull, image of, used in ceremonies of the Reception of Spring, Foochow; symbolism of measurements and coloring of, 42 54-58; worshipped by Israelites under name of Jacob, 34 417

Bündahishn, statements regarding the location of the Farnbāg fire in the recensions of the Pahlavi, 41 84-92

Burial

Arab: dead should be buried in their native land, 39 316

Assyrian: refused to woman who practises abortion, 41 47-48 n. 46

Batak (Sumatra): use of camphor in, 42 356

Chinese: on death of an Emperor Palace ladies go to live in the courtyards of the Imperial Tombs as guardians, 51 144-145, 148 n.50, Emperor Shang buried in section for heirs-apparent, 148; in Han Period, of soldiers killed in battle, 57 173; Wên Ta-ya's father, anecdote about reburial of, 57 370, 371-372

Greek: connected with worship of chthonic gods, 39 309 ff., 320

Hebrew: bodies must be buried, 39 311 ff., burial must be in one's native land, 39 316, 319

Semitic: connected with worship of chthonic gods, 39 309

Burial Mounds, see Tombs

Burj-Nāmah, Dekkan parallels to, 35 293-296; Parsi-Persian book of omens, text and translation, 33 286-289, 291-293; text and translation; predominantly Zoroastrian in tone, 30 336-342, possible Babylonian influence in, 337-338

Burkhan, Mongol designation of the Buddha, means deity, god, or image of a god. An ancient and indigenous word of the Altaic languages originally meaning a shamanistic image, 36 390-395; notes on the word "burkhan", and on the Manchu term Fučihi, 37 167-168
Burma, Burmese, chronology, 43 348; harp, 51 47; 'boog-harp', 51 50; lute, 51 50; original home of domestic fowl, 33 373, 395; see also Aloes; Languages, Sino-Tibetan
Buruçaskī, a language of northern Kashmir, 41 60-72, system of pronominalization, 60-63; vigesimal system, 63 f., linguistic affinities, 64-72; elements in Dardic, 46 177 f.
Bushido, the Azuma Kagami most valuable for study of, 59 39
Būzan, see Art, Islamic
Buzeta and Bravo on the dialects of Bisayan, 26 120 f.
Byblos, an Egyptian colony, 48 78; statue of Osorkon I from with inscription of Elība'al, 46 237-240
Byelovodiye, see Utopia, Russian
Bylina, influence on and parallels to legend of Kostryuk, 46 28-32
Byzantium, its influence on Russia, 37 58-61; no political relations with China in Sui period, 33 193, identified with the Ta Fu-lin (Greater Fu-lin) of Sung accounts, 199, 202-208; ruled by pretender Melissenus, 30 25-30; see also Art and Architecture; Fu-lin
Cabbage, eating of prohibited by certain oriental sects, 29 73
Caesarea (Palestine), temple of Hadrian standing there in A. D. 538, 36 342
Caesarean Section in India, aspects of, 59 17-21
Caesura, an ancient phenomenon, 56 405
Cagayân people, 25 173
Cairo, see Genizah
Cala Ataperistan (in Marco Polo), identified with Kāšān, 26 82
Calamian and Bisayan, 26 120, 122
Calendar, see also Yoshimune
Akkadian: based on year beginning in spring, 37 15
Armenian: month-names, Avestan influence on, 28 331-344
Assyrian: Ḫubur, Cappadocian month paralleling Old Assyrian Ḫibur, 46 181; old and Middle Assyrian month-names correspond to the Old Babylonian; stem from Amorites; refer to recurring annual events; presuppose 365-day year, 58 548-549
Babylonian: beginning of year in astronomical spring may go back to kings of Ur, 39 198; in reigns of Lugalanda and Urukagina, 31 251-271, de Genouillac's view of criticized, 253ff.; Kugler's criterion for determining order of months in earliest calendar not valid, 33 297-305, intercalary months in, 300-301, agricultural seasons, importance of for determining calendar, 302-303, months, Barton's order of, 304-305; seventh month (Tašrītu) may once have marked the beginning of the year, 36 298 n. 63
Canaanite: year divided into seven periods of fifty days each, which is still done in some parts of Palestine, 41 182
Chinese: a book on the calendar, or Time, 時, taught in the schools of the State of Ch'i in ancient China 44 278; the chia tzu, the 10 Stems and 12 Branches combined to make 60 cyclical signs, applied in Han dynasty to years, 42 56, used very early for numbering days, 56, the 12 Branches used to name the hours, 56, division of the year into 8 seasons and 24 solar periods, 53, 56, 57; of the Hsia dynasty, 52 245 and n.39; knowledge of the calendar gave power to royalty, 56 67-70, belief that the seasons were made to function properly by the king's performance of the correct ritual, 67-69;
Egyptian: introduced in 2780 B.C., 39 150; solar calendar adopted in 3251 B.C., 59 403
Ḥarrānian: world-year a modification of the older Babylonian, 43 328
Hebrew: borrowed from Babylonia, 36 297; double calendar system recognized by Ezekiel, 37 220; New Year's day falls on first of Tišri with introduction of Babylonian calendar, 37 220-221; lunar substituted for solar calendar after Exile; disappearance of Jubilee Year; intercalary months, 49 355-356; Sabbath, not a Babylonian institution, 45 150; three distinct calendar systems employed in ancient Israel, 43 167
Indian: Faṣli ("harvest") era established by Akbar for NW India, 59 372
Persian: month-names, Avestan influence on, 28 331-344; omens derived from Babylonia, 35 294-295
Seleucid: Greek month-names shifted with relation to the Babylonian, 56 518
Sumerian: based on year beginning in fall, 37 15; months, order and identification of, 33 1-9, no uniform Sumerian calendar in Babylonia, 2, year began with autumn down to time of Gudea, 5, began with vernal equinox after Gudea, 5, intercalary months, 3-6
Syriac: Karkaphensian MS containing description of the Old Syriac Calendar dates from A.D. 1003/4, 52 303; translation of the Karkaphensian MS, 54 129-142
Tibetan: notes on correlation of Tibetan dates with Chinese, 54 312-313
Caligula, number of in Rev. 13:18, 26 315-317
Caliphate, Ottoman, not recognized by the Arabs, 37 153-154
Callahan, James M., contribution of to Chinese historical studies, 38 102
Calligraphy, Chinese, Ts'ai Yung's eight canons of the character yung, 永, see also abstract, Driscoll
Camara, see Kaviripaddinam
Cambodian, Cambodians, monuments, dates of the, 50 264 f.; monuments, the dating of, 49 330 f.; stone terminal in the Toledo Museum, 51 374; see also Conjurers
Cambyses, religion of, 21 179
Camels, Bactrian, in southern Asia Minor in Assyrian times, 41 349; made possible the use of central Asian trade routes, 35 33; used in Chinese performances at court, Later Han, 51 150; not extensively domesticated in Near East till late in 2nd millennium B.C., 60 283 n. 1; as symbol for "unhappiness", "badness", one of the nidānas, 60 357
"Camel Crane" (ostrich), (Chinese, lo-t'o-hao), a product of Po-pa-li (Berbera), 30 49-50
Campanile, an adaptation of the minaret, 30 151-154
Camphor, introduced to the western world probably by Arabs, 42 358, first mentioned in 4th-cent. works, 359, ceremonial use of became general in Sasanian times, 359, imitated by Chinese, 357-358, obtained fr. the tree laurel of Southern China and Formosa, 355, discovered by the Chinese and called "dragon's brains", lung-nao, 364; trade in ancient world and in medieval Eastern Asia; names for, 42 355-356, Batak (Sumatra) legends concerning, 366-370
Canaan, Canaanites, Canaanite, see also Calendar
History: East Canaanites do not appear E of the Tigris in the 3rd millennium B.C., 49 326; a mixed Syrian people speaking Hebrew, 47 363
Language: -a ending of stative and perfect, 60 415, t- prefix of 3rd masc. pl. imperf. an analogical extension of collective use of fem., 416, -n plurals and duals fairly common, 415, antepenultimate stress in words without long syllables, 420, diphthongs, retention of during period of Eg. New Empire, 416-417, sibilants in South Canaanite, 417, yaqtulu- type preterite does not exist in Canaanite, 418-419
Religion: high-places inherited by Israelites, criteria for recognizing, 38 331; Rašap-Makal and 'Anat-'Aštart, nature of, 50 339; see also Rešep
Cāṇakya, Kanika identified with, 44 77
Candlestick, Jewish seven-branched, modeled after Babylonian sacred tree, 45 362
Candra, influences traceable in the grammar of, 56 364
Candraprabha temple of Tiruparuttikunram, date of, 54 440
Cannibals, 300 Chinese victims of, on Rossel Island, see H.U. Hall's review of W.E. Armstrong's Rossel Island, 49 183
Canon, Chinese, see China, Chinese Literature
Canticles, not an Adonis liturgy, 46 154-164, Akkadian loan-words in, 159-160; date of redaction and material, 52 51; its canonicity assured by its ascription to Solomon,

46 190, Greek and Indian analogies to, 191; its terminology is religious rather than secular; Babylonian influence in, 44 174; not a Tammuz-Adonis litany, 45 357

Canton, capital of Nan-yüeh at, see Lu Chia; ivory shops of, 41 296; see also Elephant; Li-chih-wan

Cappadocia, Semitic dialect of related to Old Akkadian; dates from ca. 2500 B.C., 48 357; Cappadocian tablets, Sign 乒 = 1/4, 46 179-180, causative of the verb in, 180, Eašar = Iašar; Ea = Yah, 180-181, Nin-Šubur, name element, 181, Ḫubur, month, 181; texts, West-Semitic names in, 49 126-127, influence of alphabetic writing in, 122-127; see also Calendar, Persian

Caravans, through Central Asia, developed by Han Wu Ti's demand for horses, 37 103-104, size and frequency of, 103-104, 107, frequency causes Chinese articles to be less appreciated by the West, 104, loss of half their number en route, 109

Carchemish, its mineral wealth indicated by Assyrian tribute lists, 38 246-247

Cardahi, Gabriel, Maronite author, works of, 22 95

Careers, for students of Chinese language and civilization, great promise but few positions, 53 364-365

Caritas of the Jains, as chronicles, 36 55

Carter, Rev. Thomas Francis, death of, Aug. 1925, 46 333

Carthage
  History: colonized from same Phoenician mother-city as Motya, Sicily, 48 359
  Religion: Tanit a Libyan name, 32 429-433, Anna, principal deity of Carthage, 432

Cartography, Assyrian, begins ca. 1100 B.C., 38 258; see also Geographical Knowledge in China; Matteo Ricci

Carts, used for distant journeys in An-hsi, 37 97, carried supplies to Tun-huang for the expedition against Ta-yüan, 102 B.C., 112, 136

Cārudatta and the Mṛcchakaṭika, relationship between the, 42 59-79

Carus, Paul, Chinese studies by in the Open Court, 38 101; death of, Feb. 1919, 40 206

Cārvāka, as title of Indian materialism, 50 132-138, earliest reference to, 137

Caspian region, South, occurrence of elephants in, in ancient times, 41 292, 293-294

Cassia, native to East Africa; name anciently applied to various spices, including leaves of the Indian laurel, 40 263-270

Castes in India, origin and development, 53 181-186

Castration, among Ṣābians as religious rite, 47 333

Cat, domesticated, question of, in early China, 60 581-582

Cataleo, Lazar, see Asiatic Studies in Europe (Mattei Ricci, etc)

Categories, Chinese passion for categories of 5 in the Han period, 44 278; see also Chinese Thought; Aristotle

Catholics, Catholicism, in Japan, see Japan, Japanese, Religion, Christianity

Cattle, long-horned Egyptian, its ancestor found in Egypt, 39 177

Cavalry, in China, see Horse

Celadon, see Yüeh Ware

Centipedes, used in making a variety of ku poison, 55 8, 23, 25

Central Asia, Archaeology, remarks on the Citroën Expedition 1931, 57 329-330; Chinese accounts of the Mohammedan conquest differ fr. Arab accounts, 43 434; history of cock in, 33 373-374, 395; elephants, no evidence of in ancient times except imported tame ones, 41 293-294, elephants sent by petty states of to China, 294; government of States in, early Han: Kings: Ta-yüan, 37 94, 109-115, Yüeh-chih, 94, 96-97, An-hsi, 97, Hsiung-nu, see Shan-yü; Wu-sun, see K'un-mo; petty chiefs (city government): T'iao-chih, 97, Ta-hsia, 97-98; Satraps: see Hun-hsieh, Barbarians: 99; the ming-oi of Kyzil and Bezeklik, and style of paintings in several of the caves, 57 329-330, at Kumtura and Subashi, 330, Chinese influences and dev. of Uigur style, 329-330, Manichaean style, 329

Caturvargacintāmaṇi of Hemādri's account of Sāvitrī rite and story, 21 53, 57, 60, 62 f.

Caucasian languages, classification of the, 50 268 f.; parallels to Persian perfect, 39 118 f.

Cebuan dialect of Bisayan, 25 162-169; infixes la, li, lo, in, 27 142 f.

Celebes throwing-stick, 55 172

Ceramics, Chinese, evaluation of Sir Percival David's "A Commentary on Ju Ware", in TOCS, 1936-37, 59 284; shards of celadons found on east coast of Africa, associated with Chinese coins of 11th and 12th cent., 30 55, 57; see also Lo-Lang; Mu-yang-ch'eng

Ceremonies, see also Bear Ceremonialism; Conjurers
  Chinese: commemorated by the casting of bronzes, 56 339, 342; at the Han Court, origin of, see Shu-sun T'ung; see also Ming-t'ang; Pupils, of an image; Festivals, Reception of Spring
  Japanese: Kamakura period, original sources for study of, 59 42-44, 46, 50, 52

Cetaka, refuses to accept Śreṇika as son-in-law, 45 304; war with Kūṇika, 45 308 f.

Ceylon, elephant existed in, 41 294; one of termini of Roman trade with the East, 36 442; see also Aloes; Tobacco

Chaitya-symbol as a mountain, 54 297

Chalcedon, Council of, opposed by Bar-Ṣûṣan, 32 271, 309

Chaldea, see T'iao-chih

Chaldaeans, kept Dec. 25 as feast of winter solstice, 32 322; see also Nestorians

Chalfant, Rev. Frank H., work of on Chinese writing and weights and measures, 38 101; see also Oracle Bones

Chamberlain, Basil H., death of, Feb. 1935, 55 347

Cham, Champa, excavations near Binhdinh and at Chaban, note on, 57 335; see also Aloes

Ch'an sect, see Buddhism

Ch'an-fêng, 蟬封, Mu-kua's brother, King of Ta-yüan, 37 115, 136, 138, his son sent to Court of Han Wu Ti as a hostage, 115

Ch'an-fông, see Ch'an-fêng

Chang, The Three, identity of, 53 229 n.64

ch'ang, 倀, spirit of a person who has been eaten by a tiger, 55 24 n.56, spirit of victim of ku magic similar to, 18, 24

Ch'ang-an, 長安, capital of China in time of Han Wu Ti, the Salt Lake 5000 li fr., 37 96

Chang Ch'ao, Ming antiquarian, visit to the Chao Ling in 1611, 55 424, 426

Chang Chieh-pin, on tobacco, 58 648, 652

Chang Ch'ien, 張騫, his journey to the West, and results, tr. of the account in the Shih-chi, with notes, Chinese text, chronological tables, and index, 37 89-152, his position, 93, sent by Han Wu Ti on mission to the Yüeh-chih, 93-94, captured by the Hsiung-nu and held 10 years, 94, escaped and reached Ta-yüeh-chih via Ta-yüan and K'ang-chü, 94, return, recapture by the Hsiung-nu, and escape to China, 94-95, his report to the Emperor, 95-98, title of 'Marquis of Po-wang' bestowed upon, 99, his failure in the campaign of 122 B.C. against the Hsiung-nu, and consequent loss of rank, 99-100, his proposal to the Emperor concerning the Wu-sun, and his mission as ambassador to, returning with many horses and emissaries, 100-102, rewarded with high rank, 102, death of, 102, influence of his name among western nations, 103, gifts carried by later expeditions imitated those sent in time of, 103, tradition of his tracing the Yellow River to its source, 107, 116, tradition that the grape, pomegranate, garlic, etc. were introduced into China by Chang Ch'ien not substantiated by the Shih-chi, 92, paragraphs 1-79 of Chap. 123 of the Shih-chi considered based on his original reports to the Emperor, 91, chronological data on, 135, 'Chang Ch'ien's Tablet', 138; see also Chang-k'ien-ch'u-kuan-chi; Hai-wai-i-wu-ki-(chi)

Ch'ang-ch'iu Kung, 長秋宮, to establish the, a conventional request made when a new empress is about to be proclaimed, 51 143 and n.23

Ch'ang-chou, a virtuous scholar of, his defiance of frog-ku magic, 55 27

Chang Chün-fang, 張君房, see Yün chi ch'i ch'ien
Chang Hsien, 張仙, God of Birth, a prayer to, 49 153
Chang K'ien, see Chang Ch'ien
Chang-k'ien-ch'u-kuan-chi, (Chang-ch'ien-ch'u-kuan-chih), lost record of Chang Ch'ien's expedition to the West, 37 91-92
Chang-ku, title of certain scholars in the Imperial University, 58 441
Chang Liang, adviser to Han Kao-tsu, 57 177, 179, 180
Chang Ling, 張陵, "Taoist Pope", legend of, 53 221-222 and n.25, 229 and n.64
Ch'ang-lo T'ang, 長樂宮, a hall in the Palace, in Han period the dwelling of the Empress Dowager, 51 156
Ch'ang-t'ing-tzu, 長汀子, name for Pu-tai, 53 47, 49
Chang-yé, see Chang-yeh
Chang-yeh, Western Kansu, residence of P'ei Chü and key position on the western trade route, 33 195-196; Chang Yeh, 張掖, district on western border of China, 37 112
Chang Yeh-yüan, data on dates of his works, 55 476
Chanhu-daro, beads and bead drills excavated at, 57 1-15
Chaṅs dbyaṅs rgya mcho, the sixth Dalai Lama, represented on a Tibetan temple painting, 52 344
Chao Ch'ang, Sung painter, his "sunflower" a species of mallow, 52 94
Chao Ling, Royal cemetery of T'ang T'ai Tsung near Li Ch'üan; visit of Chavannes to, 55 420-421, visit of Chang Ch'ao in 17th cent. to, 424, 426, Horses of T'ang T'ai Tsung at, 421-422, 424, 427-428
Chao ming wen hsüan, 昭明文選, general collection of poems of 6th cent., not a true ts'ung shu, 51 40
Chao P'o-nu, 趙破奴, general sent against the Hsiung-nu, 37 106, captures the King of Lou-lan and defeats Ku-shih in 108 B.C., 106, 135, created Marquis of Cho-yeh, 106, losses against the Hsiung-nu, 111
Chao Shih-ch'êng, 趙始成, general under Li Kuang-li, 104 B.C., 37 110, consulted by Li at siege of Ta-yüan, 113, a vigorous fighter, 114-115, ennobled as kuang-lu-ta-fu, 115
Chao Ti, 趙弟, cavalry officer who beheaded the King of Yü-ch'êng, 37 114, created Marquis of Hsin-chih, 115
Ch'ao T'o, king of Nan-yüeh, see Lu Chia
Ch'ao Ts'o, 鼂錯, and Kia I, 賈誼, (Chia I), statesmen of Western Han; their plan to reduce the power of the feudal kingdoms, 40 184-185; see also Classics, Chinese
Chao-wa, 爪哇, see Names, Geographical, Chinese
Chao Wan, high official at Court of Han Wu Ti, he and Wang Tsang jailed and committed suicide, 58 438-440
Characene, Arab state on Persian Gulf, 35 32, 35, 37
Charads and Charabayads, origin of these septs among the Hos, 50 232
Chariot, Chinese, a gift of a, 51 145; a two horse one in Shang, 52 242 and n.29, with four horses in Chou, 240 and n.25
Charlemagne, regarded as protector of 'Abbāsid interests in Spain, 47 364
Chau Ju-kua, author of the Chu-fan-chih, tr. by Hirth and Rockhill; on Arab and Chinese trade and trade routes in medieval times; passages pertaining to Africa, 30 49-57; on aloe wood, 42 178, 183; on Ta-ts'in and T'ien-chu, 30 10-11, his debt to Chou Ch'ü-fei's Ling-wai-tai-ta, 12-14
Chau Po-Nu, see Chao P'o-nu
Chau Shï-ch'öng, see Chao Shih-ch'êng
Chau Ti, see Chao Ti
Chavannes, Édouard, death of, Jan. 1918, 38 322; belief concerning the model-emperors, 56 57, beliefs in regard to Yü's burial place at K'uai-chi, and a stone there, 62; note on his tr. of the Shih-chi (Les Mémoires historique de Se-ma Ts'ién traduits et annotés), 5 vols. finished, 37 94; on the tr. of san i fen shen, on the Nestorian Tablet, 58 391; visit to the Chao Ling in 1909, where photographed the Horses of T'ang T'ai Tsung in situ, 55 420-421, 427
Chāyānāṭaka genre in Indian dramaturgy, 32 58-63
Chê-chiang t'ung chih, 浙江通志, History of Chekiang province, 53 47; tr. of History of Yüeh-lin Temple, 52
Cheikho F. Louis, works of, 22 90
Ch'ê Ling, 車令, a turfman (?) sent by Han Wu Ti with the expedition to buy horses in Ta-yüan, 37 109
Chemistry, see Science
Ch'êng-hsiang, title of the highest minister, Former Han period, 58 436
Ch'eng-kung Hsing, 成公興, servant and teacher of K'ou Ch'ien-chih, 53 226-228
Ch'êng-wei-shih-lun, 成唯識論, Chinese tr. by Hsüan Chuang of the Wei Shih treatise, the Triṁśikā, with its 10 combined commentaries, 51 292, 293, 302-303, 304; tr. in 659, before the Wei-shih-er-shih-lun, 53 147
Ch'ên Ssŭ, sources for biographical data on, 55 476
Chēra, one of the three kingdoms of southern India, important in the trade bet. East and West, 37 246; Tamil state of first two centuries A. D., 33 209-212, see also Seres
Cherubim, Hebrew origin of, 25 279-286
Chhoṭū Rām Trivēdī, his edition of Mālatīmādhava of Bhavabhūti, 25 339
Chia I, 賈誼, see Ch'ao Ts'o; Chia Yi
Ch'iang, 羌, (Tangutans), southern neighbors of the western Hsiung-nu, 37 94, 96, the Little Yüeh-chih take refuge among them, 97, bar the middle way to Bactria, 98
Chiang Lüeh, 絳略, practiced Taoist callisthenics, 53 239, 54 293
Chiang-nan, = "South of the Yangtse" in the Shuo-wen; Anhwei and Kiangsi in Ming times, 41 304; South of the River, old name for a political division, 49 139 n.4
Chiang-tu, 江都, princess of, given in marriage to old King of Wu-sun, who marries her to his grandson, 37 106
Chiao-chih, see Kattigara
Chia tzu, the 60 cyclical signs, see Calendar, Chinese
Chia Yi, official of Han Wen Ti, 58 437; conversant with several philosophies, 437
Chi Chang, 擊壤, name of an ancient game, 49 154 n.2
Chï-chï, see Chih-chih
Chiefs, see Central Asia, Government of States in
Chien, 簡, single bamboo slips for writing on, 44 273-274
Ch'ien, 潛, a small country west of Ta-yüan which sent envoys to China in early Han dynasty, 37 107
Ch'ien-chih, see K'ou Ch'ien-chih
Ch'ien Han-shu, (chapter 62) authenticity of letter written by Ssu-ma Ch'ien to Jen-an in 91 B.C. is suspect, 55 332-333; Biogr. of Chang Ch'ien, chap. 61, p.2, parallel passage to the Shih-chi in chap. 123, Wylie's tr., 37 90; gives account of way in which Confucianism won victory in the Former Han period, see Confucius, Confucianism; mistake of Pan Ku in placing conjuction of the 5 planets in 207 B.C., correction: May 205 B.C., 55 310-313; song of the Pai Canal, 55 304-305, the proposal to run the Yellow River through the Hu country, 305, changes in the course of the Yellow River in Han period, 304, 305-306; chronology of Ancient China; Han-shu; Tables, Chinese
Ch'ien-lung, Emperor, estimate of his reign, with special ref. to his literary inquisition, 55 477
Chien-mi, 煎靡, a notable of Ta-yüan, captured by the Chinese at the siege of Erh-shih, 37 112
Chien-wei, 犍為, Hsü-chou-fu, starting point of exploring expeditions to find way to India, in time of Han Wu Ti, 37 99
Chiera, Edward, life and works, 53 308
Chi fu ts'ung shu, 畿輔叢書, a geographical ts'ung shu, 51 43, 44-45
Chih-chih, the Shan-yü of the Hsiung-nu, founder of Hunnic power on the confines of Europe, 30 40
ch'ih piao, 尺表, measurement of the Heavens by, mentioned, 54 96-97
ch'ih shou, 赤綬, see Court Manners, Dress
Ch'i Hsien, 郗纖, physiognomist, 53 239, appointed a shang-ta-fu, 239
Chih pu tsu chai ts'ung shu, 知不足齋叢書, pub. in 18th cent., 51 41
Chi Hsin, 紀信, of Han, some legends say became City God, 49 139 n.2

Ch'ih Yu, 蚩尤, divinity hero of a flood legend, 56 60-61
Ch'i-jen shih p'ien, 畸人十篇, by Matteo Ricci, included in the list of books barred fr. Japan, 1630, 57 292, postscript added by Sorai, 301-302
Ch'i Kan, 棋杆, objects at the altar of the Earth-Gods, 49 151 n.1
Chi-ku, see Yen Shih-ku
Chi Ku Ko Library, see Mao Chin
Ch'i-lien-shan, 祁連山, a hill southwest of Kan-chou-fu, where Ho Ch'ü-ping defeated the Hsiung-nu, 37 97, 100, references to and location of, 143, see also Ho Ch'ü-ping
Ch'i Lin, 麒麟, unicorns, 49 141-142 n.9; see also Giraffe
Ch'in, 秦, (China); a man of, at Ta-yüan, who knew how to bore wells, 37 113
Chin-cheo, see Names, Geographical, Chinese
Ch'in Dynasty, government of, 40 175-177; see also Ts'in
China, Chinese, civilization, beginnings of, 39 166; date of introduction of stirrups, 52 85, history of cock in, 33 373-374, 395; influence of in Borneo, 33 329, 344; remarriage of patricians, ancient period, 56 340 n.12; Slaves, freed by Han Kao-tsu, 57 173; stele of Yu Shih-hsiung, with the engraved Picture of the Six Horses of T'ang T'ai Tsung, 55 423-427, the Chao Ling Map Stele, 426; see also Aloes, Archeology; Art; Astronomy; Biography; Ceremonies; Encylopedias; Chronology; Festivals; Games; Languages; Mathematics; Medicine; Military; Music; Nestorians; Newspapers; Printing; Sculpture; Secret Societies; Songs; Tattooing; Taxes; Tone-accent; Trade; Wall-paper; Women
Anthropology: Chinese not all from one original stock, 56 70-71
Archaeology: data on the temple to Yü at Lung Mên, 56 60, on the grave and temple of Yu at Mt. K'uai-chi, 62-63; Palaeolithic and Neolithic sites in China, Manchuria, and Inner Mongolia and the Ordos, see Licent, Father Emile; resumé of archeological work done in 1916 in the Far East, 36 353-354; Szech'uan, tomb caves in, 36 354; see also Lo-Lang
Art: evolution of the t'ao-t'ieh and the phoenix bird on ancient bronzes, 51 16-18; Han pottery tomb tiles fr. West Honan, possibly Ch'in, 57 249; influence upon cave paintings of 8th and 9th cents. in Central Asia, 57 329-330; small jade carving of sage with peach, riding a deer (?), found in Darwin, Australia, during road excavation, 58 75-76; reproductions of the famous Ten Oxherding Pictures, see Book Reviews, Suzuki, Manual of Buddhism; Yüeh ware, see abstract, Plumer
Astronomy: 2nd cent. B.C. concept of Heaven as comprised of nine parts, 59 201; Hsi and Ho, astronomers ? 56 64, 67, the calendar of supreme importance to holder of royal power, 67-69; the Ptolemaic theory promulgated by Ricci in his Map of the World, 1584, 59 342-343
Economic and Social:
Interest rates: attempt to limit, fr. Han on, 58 534-535, rise of expression i pen i li, 一本一利, in Yüan period, 535, not over 3% Ming to 1911, 535; discussion of material in the Han-shu and Shih-chi in connection with biographies of wealthy persons, 54 186-193; Han Wu Ti reign, struggle of the nobles to remain in residence in the imperial capital, 58 439; Shryock's criticism of Granet's reconstruction of the organization and development of Chinese society in the earliest periods, 51 186-188; under Empress Têng of Later Han, 51 143-159; annual expenses of certain court officials, 147, economies practiced by Empress Têng, 143-150, 153, luxuries of the court, 146-148, 150, 152, 153, 157, general conditions, 148-150, Empress Têng's mother given income fr. taxes, 149; waterways in Han Wu Ti's time, transport and irrigation, 55 303-306
Education: civil service examination system, origin of, 57 175; civil service examination system in T'ang dynasty, officials appointed according to their moral and mental "categories", 59 205-206; controlled by government, 53 93-94; educational system, in Han, 51 266-267; see also Huan K'uan; examinations, competitive, abolished 1905, reasons given in Memorial to Throne, 27 79-87, plans for establishment of schools and courses of study, 82-83, appointments from these schools, 83, preferment to old school scholars, 83-84, new system likened to that in China before the Three Dynasty period, 84, 85-86, text-books for the new system, 86, primary schools to be established in every town and hamlet, 86; 4th cent. B.C. period characterized by rise of a scholar class among the lowly, 56 73; initiation of civil service exam. system under Han Kao-tsu, 58 436, exam. system extended by Emp. Wen, 437, education of Emp. Wu, 437, founding, by Wu Ti, of a government university, staffed by Confucian scholars, for training of gov. officials, 435, 441-442, Council on the Confucian Classics in reign of Han Hsüan Ti; interpretations taught in the univ., 443-444, education of Emp. Hsüan, 445, second examination for gov. service, 445-446, advantages of a Confucian education in China, up to present day, 447-449; primary schools of the li, 31 194; school text-books in ancient times, 44 276-278, education in Chou dynasty not so uniform as has been supposed, 278; students in foreign countries encouraged by abolition of competitive examinations in China, 27 81; see also Schools
Geography: China in time of Yu as described in the Yü Kung, 56 53, as described by Mencius, 55, the opening of Lung-men, according to the Shan Hai Ching, 59, according to Huai-nan-tzu, 59, Yü's name and Kun's associated with all celebrated sites near Lung-men, 60, Yü's journey south and site of his tomb and temple near Shao-hsing, Chekiang, at foot of Mt. K'uai-chi, 55, 61-62, ancient China of the Oracle Bones and the Odes, 71, new geographic concepts of the 4th cent. B.C., 74-75; climate at Anyang in late Shang like that of today, see abstract, K.A. Wittfogel; climate in North and South China in the prehistoric period, 41 294-296; Tsou Yen's (3rd cent. B.C.) concept of the world as nine continents, 59 202; see also Gazetteers; Geographical Knowledge in China
Government: administration of canals and rivers in early Han, personal advantage to officials, 55 303, 304, 306; administration of the villages by the li, lin and pao system of house groups; began in Chou period, adopted by Japan after 645 A.D., 31 192-194, variations in the organization under different dynasties, 192-193, monthly assemblage of the li members, 193, the li temple to Earth, where sacrifices were offered spring and autumn, 193; in the Chou period, 40 170-175; feudalism, of Chou and of Western Han, 40 170-193; in Han period, 40 170-193; Han ruler makes important appointments only at suggestion of his high officials, 57 173-175; Han Dynasty, see also Confucius, Confucianism; model-emperor lore the official guide for government since Han, 56 52, character of the ideal government of Yao, Shun and Yü, 51, 67, basis of concept of divinity of kings, 69-70, ancient custom of minister replacing the king, 58, China at time of Golden Age not under one rule, the Golden Age a myth, 71; Sung compared with T'ang, in foreign policy, 57 442; in the Ts'in dynasty, 40 175-177; see also Han Kao-tsu; Legalism; Memorials to the Throne: Edicts
History: abundant source materials for end of Ming and early Ch'ing exist only in Manchu, 60 556; archives of closing years of Ming dynasty not extant, 58 650 n.9; Chang Ch'ien's mission to the West, see Chang Ch'ien; China known in Ta-yüan, 37 94, plan to extend sphere of Chinese influence throughout Central Asia and its success, 98-99, 107-108, waning desire for Chinese products, 98, 104, attempts to open a trade route to Bactria through India unsuccessful, 99, expedition against the K'un-ming tribes in 109 B.C. to open route through their country, 104, embassies to, and conquest of small Central Asian countries, 98-116, embassies fr. Parthia and small countries near, 107, 114, campaigns against the Hsiung-nu, 123-119 B.C. clear them out of the Kan-su corridor, 99-100, proposal to the Wu-sun to occupy the corridor, 100-102, marriage alliance with the Wu-sun and the trade in horses, 102-103, 106-107, missions to Ta-yüan to obtain the 'superior horses', 103, 104, Ta-yüan's refusal to sell the horses, 109, first campaign against Ta-yüan, to get the horses by force, suffers

disaster, 110, remnants of army forbidden to return home, 111, Li Kuang-li's second campaign against Ta-yüan suffers huge losses but succeeds in over-coming Erh-shih and Yü-ch'êng and obtaining the horses, 111-116; China had no relations with Rome, Byzantium or Ta-ts'in at time the new name Fu-lin was first used, 33 193, Yang Ti's attempt to open intercourse with Fu-lin not successful, 193-196, contacts with the Nestorians of Persia, 197-198, the Nestorian church in China known at first as the Persian church, 198-199, account by Hui-ch'ao of the country of Ta Fu-lin, 202-208; contact with western countries in Sui and T'ang dynasties; attempts to open intercourse with Fu-lin, 30 5-8, Sung records of Fu-lin, 30 24-31; contributions of American scholarship to a knowledge of, 38 97-106; diplomatic Service, under Han Wu Ti, demoralized, 37 104-106, for Missions to the West see Envoys: Chang Ch'ien: Po-Wang; earliest written correspondence with Tibet, 38 34-35, marriage of the Chinese princess Wen-ch'êng to King Sroṅ-btsan sgampo, 34, reconquest of the Four Garrisons of Central Asia in 692, 45, Wang Hüan-ts'e's campaign against Magadha, 34, 36; Former Han, fall in 8 A.D. was result of the Confucian theory of government, 57 246-247; influence of the Golden Age Ideal on the writing of Chinese history, 56 52, conditions in the 4th cent. B.C. when the "model-emperor lore" was evolved, 70-75, origin of custom of circumambulation, 68, traditions of Yao, Shun and Yü, 53-67; International Relations, see also Trade Routes: Tong-King; Mongol invasion of Japan, 1281, Japanese source materials for study of, 59 44; of Northern Liang in the 5th cent. 30 33-34, 43; the policy of Ch'i-ying, who negotiated the treaties of 1842-3-4 opening China to western commerical exploitation, one of appeasement, 59 469-484, his policy of personal friendship with Sir Henry Pottinger an effort to apply Confucian principles, 469-471, 477-484, parts played by Ch'i-ying's colleague I-li-pu and his subordinates Hsien-ling and Huang En-t'ung, 471-477, 477-478, letters of Ch'i-ying to Pottinger, 480-482, failure of Ch'i-ying's method, 469, 483-484; prehistoric North and South China compared, 41 294-296, legendary evidence of elephants in North China, 297-298, tribute in ivory fr. Huai River basin, 298, elephants in Ch'u, 298-299, the State of Ch'u 300-301, connection bet. people of Ch'u and the Shan race, 300-301, Ch'u invaded by Wu, 302, 304, conquest of Ch'u by the Chinese, 303-304, the "Kwang" provinces and their absorption in the 7th cent., 304, the elephant in early Yünnan and historical notes, 305-306; regarded as a mirror, 55 183; rule over Tong-King and use of its port as southern seaport for China in sea trade with the West 37 242, 244, 246-249, conquest of Yünnan, 242, see also Yün-nan; story that Shi Huang-ti was son of Lü Pu-wei probably erroneous, see abstract, Derk Bodde; textual criticism, question of Han Kao-tzu's reported sacrifice to Confucius on passing through Lu, 55 331-333; the Tientsin Massacre, se abstract, Clyde; Wei expeditions to Korea, Manchuria, and Siberia; first knowledge of the Philippines, and Borneo; the P'i-she-ya the Visayas of the Philippines, 56 378; see also Cannibals; Confucius, Confucianism; Edicts: Memorials to the Throne; Formosa; Han Kao-tsu; International Relations; Wang Mang; Wên Ta-ya

Language: grammar, early studies of followed method used in Latin, 58 156-157, Chinese syntax one of order, not of form, 158, 159-166, classification of words into "real" 實字 and "empty" 虛字, 159-160, 165, various uses of an 安 to demonstrate, 160-166; lexicons by early Western scholars, 43 6, 8, 9, grammars by early Western scholars, 6, 8, 9; Semitic roots for Chinese and Japanese words nonsense, 55 130-133; multindex system of indexing Chinese characters, 41 185; study of the particle yen, 焉, A. its meaning, 60 1-22, B. its form, 193-207, dictionary meanings, 1-5, characteristics of the Chinese verb, 5-10, yen as equivalent to yü 於, plus a 3rd person pronoun, i. e. yü chih, 7-22, evidence that pronunciation of yen was originally the same for both interrogative and final particle, 193-196, fusion words in Chinese, 196-204, yen probably a fusion word morphologically related to a pair of prepositions, 204-207; Summer Courses, 58 218-219; see also Writing

Law: see also Confucius, Confucianism; Han Kao-tsu

Literature: canon of Chinese Classics, hist. of, 44 273-284, names of the classics during the Chou dynasty, 273-279, the canon after the Chou dynasty, 279-284; Classics; late origin of records of early periods testified to by the analysis of the "Table of Ancient and Modern Men", 59 214; considerable even in Shang times, 56 335 and n.3, nature of, in Western Chou, 336, parts of the Shu-ching which are genuine documents of Western Chou, 336-337, the "P'an Keng" a forgery, 343-344, literary style of inscriptions on oracle bones and bronzes throws light on other early documents, 341-345; no epic poetry, due to Confucian influence, 59 408; T'ang poetess, see Yü Hsüan-chi; use of quotations in Chinese literary composition, 51 266-275; writers of the time of Matteo Ricci and later, see Geographical Knowledge in China

Philosophy: Confucianism, in becoming the official philosophy of the Han gov., developed into the dominating feature of Chinese culture, 58 435, 446-449; of the Stems and the Branches, correlated with the Five Elements and with colors, as applied to the ceremony of Welcoming the Spring, 42 55-58, see also Yang and Yin; writings of the great philosophical period developed the ideals of the model-emperor lore, 56 52, model-emperor lore the official guide for philosophical thought since Han, 52, the ideal of kingship, 67-70, the philosophers' solution for the chaos of the Chou dynasty, 73, 75, sanction for a moral rule based on a Golden Age in antiquity, 75-76, earliest philosophical system of China attributed to Yü, 67; see Chinese Thought; Hsüan Chuang; Jen Wu Chih

Psychology: classification of scholars based on mental and moral qualities used in government in T'ang period 59 205-206;

Records and knowledge of other Nations: Hui-ch'ao's travels to central and western Asia, with tr. of part of his record, 33 202-208; Shih-chi, chap. 123, is oldest source, 30 38, see also Hsiung-nu; see also Africa, early Chinese notices; Fu-lin; Borneo; Philippines

Religion: ancient ceremonies in honor of ancestors with songs and dances, 56 57, 63; note on Buddhist objects in U.S. National Museum, 23 47; prayer, and offer of a play, to drive away pestilence, 49 146; see also Confucianism

Science: attitude towards geographical science in Ricci's time and later, 59 348, 349, 355, 356-359; development of scientific method retarded by traditional system of categorical thinking, see also Chinese Thought

Thought: belief that a drought in 108 A.D. was caused by wrongful imprisonment of an innocent person, and could be broken by righting the wrong, 51 149-150; belief that wealth and prosperity of the people depend upon the "virtue" of the king, 56 68-70; Chinese method of explaining all phenomena has been based on orderly classifications in categories, not on the "logical method" of reasoning, 59 200, search for order and balance shown in every aspect of life, 200-201, numerical categories, 201-202, Tsou Yen's conception of the world, 202, the Five Element system, 202, classification of human beings under various categories, mental and moral, 203-219, Liu Hsiang's examples of 20 types of men, 203, Liu Shao's categories for fitting men to office and occupations, 204, classification based on moral qualities, carried into practice in government through the examination system, in T'ang dynasty, 205-206, the "Table of Ancient and Modern Men", compiled in Hou Han dyn., classified 1, 955 famous personages under nine diff. categories, 207-219, Pan Ku and Pan Chao's "moral ratings", 207-219, table reveals belief of the time in a Golden Age of "Model Emperors", 213-215, relative standing of the various philosophic schools, 215-218, Pan Chao's attitude towards leaders of the Ch'in dyn., 218-219

Trade: aloes, storax, etc, imported from Arabs, 42 176; with Roman Empire, 35 31-41, 224-239, 37 242-249;

Writing: astrological elements underlying Chinese script, see abstract, Moran; directional value of signs was highly developed in early Chinese, see abstract, Britton; pictograph bears evidence to former existence of the elephant in North China, 41 298; script on early tomb tiles, 57 249

China Illustrata (1667), work of Athanase Kircher in, 43 6

Chin-ch'êng, 金城, = Lan-chou-fu's name in Han period; no Hsiung-nu to west of, after Ho Ch'ü-ping's campaign, 37 100

Chinese name An-ts'ai, identified with Antae, 59 60 f.

Chinese Dragon and the Tao concept, 55 327 f.

Chinese jade statue found in North Australia, 58 75-78

Chinese Repository, see Williams, Dr. S. Wells, and Bridgman, Rev. E.C.

Chinese river of life, 26 28 f.

Chinese sculptured stela, early, illustrating scenes from 'Lotus of the Good Law' and Vimalakīrti Sūtra, 51 366

Chinese Studies in U.S.A., contributions of American scholars to historical studies, (prior to 1918), 38 97-106, cannot hold place with work of French, English or German scholars, 97-99, scant attention paid to in U.S. schools and colleges, 99, works by missionaires, 99-101, by diplomats and consuls, 101-102, by historians, 102-103, by foreign born and trained scholars in America, 104-105, by Chinese youth trained in American schools in the U.S. or in China, 105; see also Asiatic Studies in U.S.A.

Chinese Studies in Europe, eminent Scholars in France, England and Germany, 38 97-98; of Andreas Muller (1630?-1694), 60 564-575, the mystery of his Key to Chinese, 565-569, 573-575

Chinese Thought, note on the position of Hsuntzu 49 88-91

Ching, 經, newer name for the Classics than shu, 44 276-279

Ching-chiai, written long after Confucius; added I-Ching and Ch'un Ch'iu to the Canon, 44 278

Ching tai mi shu, 津逮栽[=秘]書, a ts'ung shu issued by Mao Chin, 51 41

Ching-tê chuan têng lu, 景德傳燈錄, biographies of Buddhist monks, 53 47, biography of Monk Pu-tai, 49-52

Ching T'u, 淨土, monastery at Loyang where Hsüan Chuang studied, 51 295

Ch'in Shih Huang-ti, burning of the books and burying of the scholars, 51 186-187; rating of, in "Table of Ancient and Modern Men", see also China, Thought

Chin-shih-t'u-shu-pu, contains picture of a coin of Melissenus, 30 28

chin-tsan, a variety of ku magic, 55 13-15, 25-27, 28

Chin wen text, of the Shu-ching, date and difficulty of, 56 336 n.4, 341

Chiu-ch'üan, 酒泉, district in the Tun-huang region, near the Great Wall, established in early Han to facilitate Chinese trade with the Far West, 37 103, military stations near, 106, 116, army to protect boundary in, 112, resident military governor for 116

Ch'iu Hsing-kung, T'ang General, represented on the sculpture of the horse "Autumn Dew", 55 421-423

Chiu Hua Shan, 九苹[=華]山, S. Anhuei, sacred mt. of the Buddhists, assoc. with Ti Tsang, 49 136 n.2-10, 142 n.2

Chiung Chou, 邛州, a district in Ssŭ-ch'uan; bamboo from, seen by Chang Ch'ien in Bactria, 37 98, Han Wu Ti's attempt to open route through, to India, 99

Ch'iung Hua Lou (Hortensia Tower), see Yüan Ming Yüan

Chiu-t'ang-shu, records vain wish of Emp. Yang Ti to open intercourse with Fu-lin, 30 5, Arabs' siege of capital of Fu-lin, note 16; tr. of Biography of Wên Ta-ya from the, 57 370-372; see also T'ang-shu

Chi Yen, Taoist advisor to Han Wu Ti, 58 440

Ch'i-ying, 耆英, see China, Chinese, History, Ch'ing Dynasty; abstract, J.K. Fairbank

Chiyo, see Tchiyo

Ch'ŏkiang, see Chekiang

Chola, one of the three kingdoms of S. India in 1st cent. A.D., capital, Uragapura Argaru, 37 246, description of Kaviripaddinam, chief port of, 245, 246, mariners to Chryse and the S. China Sea from, 241; Tamil state of first two centuries A. D., 33 210-213

Ch'ö Ling, see Ch'ê Ling

Chota Nagpur Plateau, origin of totem clans among tribes of, 50 227-232

Chou Dynasty, chronolgy of the, 52 234-241; feudal organization of, 40 170-175; summary of conditions from 771-221 B.C., a period of disintegration and unrest, 56 71-75, two waves of foreign influence, 74, unification propaganda, 74-75

Chou Ch'ü-fei, 周去非, 54 145; author of the Ling-wai-tai-ta, main source of Chau Ju-kua's accounts of Ta-ts'in and T'ien-chu, 30 12-14

Chou K'ü-feï, see Chou Ch'ü-fei

Chou Li, 15th cent., story of his poisoning with ku, and cure, 55 12

Chou-li, describes the government of villages, administration by house groups of 5s and multiples of 5s, the pao, lin and li, 31 192-193; ivory in the, 41 296; its place in the Canon, 44 282; tells of tribute in ivory fr. the districts of Yang and Ching, 41 298-299

Chou pi suan ching, 周髀算經, compiled probably by Chao Chün-Ch'ing, 趙君卿, end of second Han, considered oldest group of texts on astronomy and math. in China, see Book Reviews, Noda, Churyo

Chou P'o, a General under Han Kao-tsu, 57 175

Chou Tan, 周澹, Grand Physician (Wei dyn.), attempt to abolish Taoist concoctions of medicines, 53 225

Chou Ya-fu, Imperial Chancellor 150 B.C., 57 174-175

Cho-yeh, 泥野, Marquis of, see Chao P'o-nu

Christ, apocryphal teaching of in Ethiopic Ardeʾet, 25 27-31; born Dec. 25 (solar), Jan. 6 (lunar) in 309 of Alexandrian Era, or 41st year of Augustus, 32 322, 333, baptized in his 30th year, 333-334, descended to dead on Saturday evening, 338; no messianic references to in Old Testament, 32 120-121; saga of in Gospels compared with the Šāh-Nāmah, 55 Supp. 1, 10-11; a special creation, between God and man, 32 271; see also Jesus

Christianity, in China, tradition unreliable which dates it earlier than the entry of the Nestorians, 60 585; descent of Christ into Hell had its ultimate basis in theodicy, 53 291-292; doctrine and cult not originated by Jesus, who is not proved to have been a historical personage, 53 212; eucharist not connected with Passover, but with Qiddûš, 47 83-84; eunuchism and hygeine among, criticized by al-Jāḥiẓ, 47 332-333; God, early Christian and late Jewish ideas of, 45 370; history of, in Asia Minor and Persia, 33 197-202; Christian and Indian miracle of walking on the water, 47 359; persecution of Catholics in Japan in 1612 and after; prohibition of all books mentioning Christianity, see Edicts, Japanese, of Kanei; problems connected with the origin of, 53 212 f.; Christian Purāṇa of Thomas Stevens, discovery of a manuscript of, 43 164; rabbinic influence on ritual, 49 354; see also Arabs (Religion); Armenians; Art and Architecture; Dimmis; Festivals; Nestorians; Syria (Church)

Christmas, celebrated by Armenians on Jan. 6, 32 272, 276, 320-323, 330-332, why celebrated by others on Dec. 25, 320-323

Chronology of Ancient China, the San Tai, 三代, 52 232-247, sources for, 232-234, 237, 242-245, "orthodox" dates of the Ch'ien Han Shu compared with those of the Shih chi and the Bamboo Books, 232-233, 236, 240-243, 244, average length of reigns, 234-235, 236-237, 241-242, evidence fr. Mencius, 235, 237, 239, genealogies of princely houses, 233-234, 235-237, 238-240, Shang King lists, 241-242, fabricated "history" of Hsia, 243-244, evidence for Hsia Dynasty, 244-246, earliest historical date 841 B.C., 235, founding of Chou about 1051 B.C., 236, 237, 241, rise of Shang about 1558 B.C., 242, Shang family records go back to about 1800 B.C., 243, Hsia dynasty founder Ta Yü about 1800 B.C., 246, bronze age civilization, 244-247

Chryse, the coast of Burma, "an island opposite the Ganges", 37 246; where commercial Chinese and Arabs met, 42 364

Ch'u, Kingdom of, elephants in, and historical notes on, 41 299-304; see also Elephants, in Asia
The Chu 洙, and the Szu 泗, rivers in China, 49 129 n.4
Chu Tan, 瞿曇, see Buddha
Chuan, 傳, commentaries, origin of the term, significance of the length of the bamboo slips, 44 280-282
Ch'üan-chou, see Zayton
Chuang-tzŭ, mentions the "Twelve Classics" and the books Confucius revised, 44 278-279; the mind of a Sage like a mirror, Legge S.B.E., vol. 39, pp. 331, 55 184; rating of, in "Table of Ancient and Modern Men", see China, Thought
Chü chen pan ts'ung shu, 聚珍版叢書, pub. in 18th cent., 51 41, rare works fr. Palace Library, copied in 1773, 45
Chu-fan-chï, see Chu-fan-chih
Chu-fan-chih, by Chau Ju-kua, describes the country of Pi-pa-lo, identified as Berbera, Africa, 30 49-50, describes Chung-li (Socotra), 51-52, describes Ts'êng-pa, probably Zanzibar, 56, tr. by Hirth and Rockhill, 49-57
Chu Hsi, declared Hsüntze unorthodox 50 233, 235, but followed his teaching, 237, accepted as continuing the orthodox Confucian tradition, 237; Hocking's studies of his philosophy premature, 56 382; Mencius preferred to Hsün-tzu before time of, 51 30
Chün-cheng, 軍正, a title, adjutant general (?), held by Chao Shih-ch'êng, 37 110, 114-115
Ch'un Ch'iu, 春秋, and its commentaries, 18 quotations fr. in the Yen T'ieh Lun, 51 267, 274-275; named by Confucius as one of the Six Classics and added, by the Ching-chiai, to the Canon, 44 276-278; see also Tso-chuan
Ch'ung-hsü-ssu, Taoist monastery near Ta T'ung Fu, founding of, 53 242
Chün T'ai-shou, a Han title, see Imperial University
Chü-she-lun, 俱舍論, Chinese tr., by Paramārtha, of the Abhidharmakośaśāstra, see Vasubandhu: Wei Shih
Chu shu chi nien, "Annals of the Bamboo Books", see Chronology of Ancient China
Ch'u T'zu, Book of Poetry of South China, full of tales of Yü, 56 61
Chü-yen, 居延, district on western border of China, established by Han Wu Ti, 37 112
Chu Yi-jen, the calligrapher, story of the ku frog in his head, 55 22
Ch'ü Yuan, his Li sao a great repository of Chinese myths, 53 61
Cilicia, archeological reconnaissance, 28 155-163; Aramaic boundary inscription from, 28 164-167; inscription, Aramaic, from Kesecek Köyü near Tarsus, 35 370-374; population in 7th cent. B.C. same as at beginning of Christian era, 59 11; see also Art and Architecture; Sandon monument; Tarsus
Cinnamon, Arab monopoly of the trade in, bet. India and the Roman Empire, 35 230-231, from India, did not grow in Africa, 230; not found in Somaliland or tropical Africa; uses and name of in ancient world, 40 262-270; supposed to have been an export of the Berbera coast of Africa in early times, 30 50
Ciphers, Greek, used in Coptic medical papyrus, of type using key, 45 78
Circe, her prototype is the Ištar of the Gilgameš Epic, 38 332
Circumambulation, of the kingdom, by early emperors of China, 56 68
Circumcision, practised in prehistoric Egypt, 39 174
Citroën Expedition, through Central Asia, see Bachhofer, review of Hackin
Citrus fruits, no species of native to Arabian peninsula, 57 381-382; see also Lemon
City Dwellers, in Central Asian countries in early Han period, see Population
City God, 城隍神, tutelary divinity of the town, prayer to, 49 138, 139, n.1-9
City-planning, topographical and social planning of modern cities was established in ancient Egypt and Mesopotamia, 52 302
Clans, totemism and the origin of, 50 221-232
Clark, Herbert, collection, weights from, 27 400-401
Classics, Chinese (Confucian), became, in Han period, the foundation of education for official position, 58 436-449, studied by emperors, 437, 443, 444, 446, 447, Ch'ao Ts'o took down fr. Master Fu tradition re the Book of History, 437, Shen P'ei, authority on the Book of Odes, 437, Council on interpretation of the Classics held in presence of Emp. Hsüan, 443-444, study of the Classics monopolized by the Confucians, a scholarly education resulting in Confucian indoctrination, 447, 449; see also China, Chinese, Literature
Classic of History, see Shu-ching
Clay, Albert T., life and works, 45 289-294, bibliography of, 295-300
Clementinism, influence of its "true prophet" doctrine on al-Muġīrah, 29 85-86
Clements, Dr. Paul H., contribution to Chinese historical studies, 38 103
Cleveland Public Library, John G. White collection of oriental literature in, 36 421-422; 57 239; Persian legal documents from Mughal India in, 60 99-100
Cloth, Chinese, Han, gift of 7200 feet of "fine white cloth", 51 145, 30,000 rolls of, provided for a funeral, 152, gift of, 151, 158
Clothing, the American Indian moccasin of Asiatic origin, 51 100
Clouds, Arab proverbs about, 52 155-156
Cochin China, Siam used elephants in war with, 41 302
Cock, borrowed by Hebrews in 3rd cent., 33 370, from Aramaeans, 396; date of its introduction into Western Asia, 54 108 f.; origin, history and symbolism of, 33 363-396; original home in Burma-Malaya, 33 372, came from India in 11th-8th cents. B.C., 379-380, Sacred to Ares and Hermes, 381, sacred to chief deity of Gauls, 384, no common word for in Indo-European, except Teutonic languages, 385, sacrificial bird, 371, 380-383, 386-387, 393, symbol of Nergal? 393, 395
Cockfighting, in Greece, 33 374, n. 1, 381
Coffins, see also Lo-Lang; Mu-yang-ch'eng
Coins, see Numismatics
Coins, Chinese, Han, see also Lo-Lang; Mu-yang-ch'eng
Colic, of horse, treated by Assyrians, 37 331-332
Collado, Diego, his Arte della lingua Japonese, 1631, and the Vocabolario, 1632, see Asiatic Studies in Europe
Colorado-Telingana Mss. of portions of the Mahābhārata, 51 357
Columbia University Library, Arabic, Persian and Turkish manuscripts in, 49 219-233
Columbus, Asiatic influences on, 51 87-96; missionary purpose behind his voyages, 38 72
Communion, Christian who has not partaken of it for forty days is not worthy of an oblation after death, 32 339
Compass, and log, use of in navigation not known 1st to 3rd cent. A.D., 37 241, 244
Complete Manual of the Old Sword, 1793, Japanese book on sword judgment, translation, 26 334-410
Confession, Armenian practices concerning criticized by Bar-Šûšan, 32 328-329; Bar-Šûšan's views on, 32 318-319
Conflagrations, automatic, 24 390-391
Confucian, Confucians, Confucianism, first four emperors of Han not Confucians, 53 92; interpreted and edited the ancient writings in light of his own ideas, 56 56; a man of original thought, not merely a "transmitter", 60 117; position of Tablets in the Confucian temple, 57 441-442; a prayer to, 49 129-130, the 5 ancestors of, their post. titles, 129 n.2, sacrifices to, 129 n.3; probable originator of classifications of men according to mental and moral qualities, 59 203, 208, 210, 215, position of the Confucian school in Pan Chao's "Table of Ancient and Modern Men", 216-217; State Cult of, authenticity of the text in the Shih-chi, Biog. of Confucius, stating Han Kao-tsu sacrificed to Confucius, 55 331-333, contradictory accounts of pulling down of Confucius' house, 334, word shu in the Biog. is

suspect, 334-335, Ssu-ma Ch'ien did not see books at Tomb of Confucius, 333-335, ceremonies conducted by scholars in Ssu-ma Ch'ien's time at Confucius' house (冢, "tomb", in the Biography is a mistake for 家, "house"), 335-336, Sung Confucianism probably not closer to the spirit of Confucius than Han, 336, images in the Confucian temple, 336-337; subjects on which the Master did not talk, problem of ming, 命 and of jen, 仁 solved, 53 247-351; teachings regarding Human Nature, 50 233-237, Hsüntze must be regarded as orthodox as Mencius, 235, tr. of passages in Analects VI 17, and XVII 2, shows Confucius made no statement regarding the nature of human nature, 233, Confucius stressed education as all-important; Mencius taught human nature naturally good, no need to train it, 236, Hsüntze's doctrine of evil nature of man not regarded as unorthodox until Chu Hsi declared it so in 12th cent., 235, Hsüntze had greater influence than Mencius upon later Confucian development, 237; teaching regarding human nature, 51 23-32, Mencius orthodox; Hsün-tzu unorthodox in teaching that human nature was evil, 23-32, interpretation of passages fr. the Analects (VI 17 and XVII 2) shows that Confucius considered man's nature naturally good, 24-29, Mencius taught same, 29, Mencius preferred above Hsün-tzu when both were canonized in 1084 A.D., 30, 9 early commentaries on Mencius, only 1 on Hsün-tzu, 31, Yang Liang in 819 attrib. neglect of Hsün-tzu to incoherence and corruption of texts, 31, Hsün-tzu's influence on later Confucianism not so great as Dr. Dubs estimates, 32; "Twelve Classics" he interpreted and the books he revised, according to Chuang-tzŭ, 44 278-279; victory of Confucianism in Former Han a gradual process, 58 435-449, began with Kao-tsu when Confucians helped him overthrow the Legalist Ch'in dynasty, 435-436, set-back under Emp. Hui and Empress Dowager née Lü, 436, impartiality of Emp. Wen; his extension of the Confucian controlled examination, 436-437, Emp. Ching less favorable, 437, gain of Confucians in reign of Emp. Wu; Legalist and Taoist officials replaced by Confucian; a Gov. Univ. founded and staffed by Confucianists for training of Gov. officials,437-442, Wu personally much influenced by Taoist and Legalist doctrines, 442-443, Confucianism strengthened under Emp. Hsüan; Council held on the Confucian Classics which fixed official interpretation; Imperial Univ. filled Gov. offices with Confucian scholars; Hsüan himself held Confucian ideals often impractical and practiced many Legalistic principles, 443-445, final victory of Confucianism under Emp. Yüan; Confucian doctrine became sole guide for rulers, 445-446, continued so under Wang Mang and Later Han rulers, 446-447, four reasons for the victory of Confucianism, 447-448, with ups and downs Confucianists have operated throughout Chinese history until modern period when literature and learning ceased to be synonymous with Confucian teaching, 448-449; Yao, Shun and Yü made to fit into the Confucian ideal, 56 55-56; see also Han Kao-tsu; Ogyû Sorai; Quotations; Utopia

Conjurers, in Cambodia, ceremony for cure of sick, 42 178

Connoisseurship, of Japanese swords, 26 334-410; see Honnami

Consort, left, being superior in rank to right, among the Wu-sun and the Hsiung-nu, 37 106, 139

Constantinople, history of according to Evliya Efendi, 37 232-234; historical significance of site of, 37 57-71; not Fu-lin of T'ang period, 30 2, 3-4, 16-17, 30-31, might have been ref. to as Fu-līn in Sung records, 30 24-31

Contamination as illustrated by lapses, 57 135-150

Convict Regiments, see Military

Cook, Miss Catherine, died Dec. 1938, in New York, 60 439

Copper, found in Babylonia in early strata at Nippur and Šuruppak, 41 254-255; imported by Lagaš from Kagalad and Kimaš in Elam, 43 44; plentiful in lands N of Assyria, 38 220; see also Bronze; Metal

Copts, Coptic, see also Inscriptions and Ostraka; Magic

Muslim polemic against, 41 384, 424-425, 426, 434, 439, 455-456

Language: Perfect with initial h- derived from Ptolemaic and Roman Demotic, 55 258-261; first perfect without h- derived from Late Egyptian-Demotic ỉ-ỉr-, "to do", 55 259; infixed -r-, -re-, denoting 2nd fem. sing. as subj. derived from 2nd present, 55 266-267; h <Eg. ḥ is weak and tends to disappear, 55 258; modern pronunciation in the mass, 23 289-306; phonetics equations with Egyptian and Semitic, 47 236; pronunciation in various dialects, 50 144-149; school language and Coptic-Arabic jargon have traditional contact with living Coptic, 57 242; second present and circumstantial tenses, probable origins of, 55 261-266; very difficult to trace dialectical strains in pre-Coptic texts, 55 263

Texts: letters from monastery of Epiphanius at Thebes, phonetic peculiarities of language in, 47 86-87; Merton ostrakon 1, 58 151-152; Ostraka in New York Historical Society, with translation, 48 147-158; Sahidic ostrakon, with translation, 34 313-314

Coral, Han bead, see Lo-Lang

Corinth, Mycenaean sites in, 36 352-353

Cormorant Fishing, appears to have originated in Japan, 52 268, earliest record of, in China, in the Sui Shu, 268, term wu kuei, "black devil", does not apply to the cormorant, 268

Corpus Inscriptionum Chaldaicarum, notes to the Urartian texts in, 55 294-302

Cosmetics, see Toilet Articles

Cosmology, Babylonian conceptions of, 22 138-144; 23 opp. p. 388

Cottiaris River by Kattigara, probably the Red River of Tong-King, 37 247

Cotton, ki-pei, cloth, trade in on the African east coast in medieval times, 30 51, 56

Cotton-weaving, pre-Columbian, spread from center in Central America, 39 162

Couling, Mr. S., call for subscribers to a new monthly periodical, a sinological Review in China, 38 318

Couling-Chalfant Collection, see Oracle Bones

Council on the Confucian Classics, 53 B.C., 58 444

Court Manners and Customs, Chinese (Han) Dress, ladies at banquet, Later Han, 51 141, a princess's ch'ih shou, 145, 151, a pu-yao for the head, and a huan-p'ei (chatelaine with jade ornaments), 145 n. 36, food, under the Empress Têng of Later Han, 147, stored up grain and dried food, 148, fruit & vegetables to be in season, 153, clothing and ornaments, palace clothing, imperial jewelry, fine articles of beautiful workmanship, engraved vessels fr. Shu and Han, 39 kinds of interior decoration, engraved playthings, 148

Cowell's translation of prāṇas, 22 255 f., 261f.

Cox, Eckley Brinton, death of, 36 350-351

Creation

Akkadian: beliefs concerning, how differing from those of Sumerians, 36 274-99

Babylonian: hymns on, 41 146; story of Amorite origin, 45 140ff.; texts on, 37 35-42; version from before 2000 B.C., in which Enki saves Eridu from the waters, 41 459-460

Gnostic: Marcus, influence of his ideas on al-Muġīrah, 29 81-82

Hebrew: creation made from previously existing materials, 47 357; J version in Genesis is indigenous; P version is borrowed from Babylonia, 36 295-298; not of Babylonian, but Amorite, origin, 45 140 ff.; took place in two cycles, 58 545

Mandaean: from egg, 53 161-164

Sumerian: beliefs concerning, how differing from those of the Akkadians, 36 274-276, 279-299; view of, 36 122-135

Creator gods in primitive religion, development and worship of, 23 29-37

Crete, Cretans, influence on the formation of the alphabet, 22 181-182; references to in ancient Near Eastern sources, 42 319; religion derived from Anatolia or N Syria, 60 551

Cross, see Festivals (Christian)

Cross-bows, used by Chinese in time of Han Wu Ti, 37 110,111

Crow, in the sun, denied by Wang Ch'ung, 55 186
Crown, turreted, does not appear in Near East until Hellenistic period; earlier crowns worn by deities are of feathers, 51 176
Crucifixion, Middle Persian MS of an early Christian tradition on, 39 55; took place on 14th of Nisan, date of sacrifice of Paschal Lamb, 32 334
Crusades, see Amalric and England
Cryptograms, see Ciphers
Ctesiphon, building of a new Antioch at, for the Syrian captives of Khosru I, and called al-Madā'in, 30 7-8, became the see of the Nestorian patriarch of Antioch, who was called "King of Fu-lin" by the Chinese, 9-15; twin city of Seleucia, the two together called al-Madā'in, 33 197-198, site of court of the Nestorian Patriarchs, 198, 200-202, one residence of the Persian kings, 200, called for a time by the Chinese Fu-lin by mistake, 199-202, Ardeshir III's refuge there, 200-202
Cuneiform script, additions to Brünnow's Classified List, 22 201-220; adopted from Sumerians long before time of earliest Akkadian inscriptions, 41 257-258; not of Sumerian origin, 39 269-270
Cuneiform texts, method of copying by inking and bleaching photographs, 55 429-430, preferable to autograph copies, 438
Curiosities, collected by Chinese ambassadors in the Far West in the time of Han Wu Ti, 37 115-116
"Curly", see Horses of T'ang T'ai Tsung
Curse, in cuneiform texts, 34 282-309, begins with time of Entemena of Lagaš, earlier than the oath, 286, deities invoked in, 290, 291-295, 300
Curtiss, Samuel Ives, influence on study of Arab folklore, 60 285
Cushing, Caleb, advocated, in 1844, the adoption of Manchu as the diplomatic language bet. China and the western powers, 60 559
Customs, of the countries of Central Asia, from Ta-yüan to An-hsi, 37 108-109, of Wu-sun, K'ang-chü, An-ts'ai, 96, of the Ta-yüeh-chih, 96-97, An-hsi, Li-kan, T'iao-chih, 97, of Ta-hsia, 97-98
Cyavana, rejuvenation of, 26 45-67
Cyprus, Marburg collection of antiquities, 22 18-19; history of the cock in, 33 383-387, 395; sailors and shipwrights imported by Sennacherib, 50 7-8
Cyril (†444), christology of, 32 309
Cyrus, heroic tradition of, in eastern and western branches, 55 Supp. 1, 9-11; portrayed by Deutero-Isaiah as leader of anti-Babylonian forces, 57 160, expected by Deutero-Isaiah to acknowledge Yahweh, 160-161, 169-170, rôle in Zamyād Yašt like that in Deutero-Isaiah, 162-163; religion of, 21 178 f.
Dagon, Semitic name for the Syrian weather-god Hadad, 45 38 n. 85; worship of spread from Mari on the Euphrates, 44 196
Daic, see Thai, or Tai
Dai-Kwan, 代官, Intendents of the Shō-gun, duties of, 31 155-158
Dakhma (Tower of Silence) at Sanjan, 22 330 f.
Daksina Fire, location in heart, 22 290
Dakšhin Rai, the cult of, 50 224
Dalai Lamas, history of the first eight Dalai Lamas, 52 338, 343-345, the eighth as represented in Tibetan paintings, 338-345, relation to Panchen Lamas, 344-347
Damascus, Jewish songs from, 24 227-264
Damm al-Hawā' of ibn-al-Jawzi, critical edition of under preparation by A.R. Nykl, 57 254
Dānādhikāramahāyānasūtra of the Divyāvadāna, translation of the Sanskrit, Tibetan, and Chinese versions of the, 49 40-51
Dân-Aššur, Assyrian turtânu and eponym, 41 362 ff.; turtânu under Shalmaneser III, 34 346-348
Dānastuti, obscene stanzas in, 21 44 f.
Dances, Dancing
China: legends arising from songs and dances in ceremonies to ancestors, 56 57, 63, dancing matches between sovereign and minister, 58, Yü's dancing as magic, 68; nude, by the T'ung, 獞, women of Kiangsi, in ceremony of making ku poison, 55 11
Hebrews: as religious ceremony, 36 321-32; to celebrate New Year, 37 223
Japanese: Kagura dancers of the Gion Jin-sha borne on floats through the streets at end of the Gion matsuri, 54 289; see also Festivals, Japanese
Daṇḍaka, abbreviated, 41 108-112
Daṇḍin, date of, 50 173
Daniel, Book of, Babylonian tablet from reign of Antiochus Epiphanes, bearing on, 56 247; idea of five world-empires in appears in Roman historians Aemilius Sura, Trogus and Justin, 59 422; not originally written entirely in Aramaic, 51 324-325; Massoretic text is not unreliable, 51 325-326; Old Greek version has an older form of the story than the present Aramaic text, 41 182-183, story of Daniel in the lion's den compared with that of Androcles and the lion, 183; Old Greek version rests on ancient Aramaic text, 46 1, 6, 7, Darius's name possibly an addition, 3, written ca. 250 B.C., 3, possible basis of in fact, 4-5; Persian epic tradition in, 55 Supp. 1, 10-11
Dante, did not draw on an Arabic source for eschatological material in his Divina Commedia, 51 370
Darauni, Joannis Notayn, Maronite author, works of, 22 95
Dardanelles, British campaign against in World War I, criticism of, 40 137-138
Dardic, Dravidian and Burushaski elements in, 46 177 f.
Darius, Kerman inscription of, 27 193 f., photograph of, (opposite) 190; religion of, 21 162-177, 180-184
Daśakumāracarita, authenticity of the introduction, 46 72 f.
Dasara festival at Satara, India, 30 72-76
Dāsopant Digambar, life and works of the Maratha poet-saint, 42 398; the Maratha poet-saint, 42 251-279, sources of information, 251 f., early references, 252, published and unpublished works of, 253 f., historical notes, 254-256, traditions of, 256-279
Dāsopantcaritra, translation (1-313) and summary (314-778) of, 42 257-276
Date-palm, Arabic names of scale-insects attacking, 42 205-206; artificial pollination of in Arab countries, 42 343-354; lexicography of its propagation among the Arabs, 35 207-212; original habitat the eastern shore of the Persian Gulf, but not now found wild anywhere; cult began in Tigris-Euphrates delta and was carried by Phoenicians to Mediterranean, 44 171; as sacred tree, 60 423; symbol of Mother Goddess on Palestinian pottery, 58 548; world distribution of, 45 364
Dates, of Dilmun, were grown in Babylonia, 52 305
David, Mons. Clemens Joseph, Jacobite archbishop of Damascus, works of, 22 92-93
Davis, Sir John, successor of Sir Henry Pottinger, see China, Chinese, History
Dayak, figures of deceased chiefs, 51 6 f.
Dben sa pa blo bzaṅ don grub, a saint, one of the incarnations of the Panchen Lama represented on Tibetan temple paintings, 52 348
Dead, Armenian offerings to condemned, 32 337, 339-340
Death, a semiconscious sleep, according to early Syriac writers, 40 103 ff.
Deborah, song of, date and translation, 34 416
Deborath, ancient capital of Issachar, 34 418
Debs, Joseph, Maronite archbishop of Beirut, works of, 22 95
De Filippi, Lady Caroline, see Filippi
de Guignes, sinologist, disciple of Fourmont, see Asiatic Studies in Europe
Deirmenjik inscription, its light on Achaemenian religion, 21 182 f.
Dekkan, lunar omens from, Parsi-Persian parallels to, 35 293-296
Delbrück's conclusions regarding the preterite tenses in Sanskrit, 21 112 f.

Deluge Story
Babylonian: Akkadian version, translation of beginning, 25 68-75, notes to difficult passages in, 32 1-16; of Amorite origin, 45 140ff.; Hilprecht's fragment, notes on and criticism of his claims for, 31 30-48, not earlier the Kassite period, 45; influence of on Iranian story of Yima's winter, 36 319-320; name of the ferryman in, 23 48-50; not of Amorite origin, 45 28-30; Šuruppak hero of first version, Atraḫasis hero of second, 47 289 ff.; Ut-napištim identical with Sumerian Ziusuddu, 47 290, Egyptian parallels to primitive story of, 292-301; Ziusuddu, was originally hero of a solar myth later incorporated into the Deluge Story, 47 290 ff.; see also Nisir, Mt.
Chinese: myth of connected with name of Yü, 56 53, 54, 54-55, 58-59, connected with flood at origin of world, 59, connection with other early culture heroes, 60-61, Lung Mên and Shaohsing in legend of, 60-63, no connection with Mediterranean deluge lore, 63
Hebrew: of Amorite, not Babylonian, origin, 45 140 ff.
de Mailla, Father, tr. of the T'ung-chien-kang-mu by, into the Histoire Générale de la Chine, one of the early works of French scholarship, 38 97
Demiéville, P., see Ecke, G.
Demons, Chinese, ceremony for expelling, 51 150; use of holly to drive them away, 55 445-450; driven away by toasted beans in the Setsubun festival, 446
Demons of pestilence, see Pestilence
Demotic Chronicle, background of Jewish apocalyptic in, 56 245
Denby, first Japanese to go to Russia, 42 290, opened a school for study of Japanese language in St. Petersburg about 1701, 290
Dennis, J.T., collection of Egyptian antiquities in Johns Hopkins University, 41 186
Denver Public Library, Lansing collection of Arabic MSS and inscription of Baybars in, 60 370-382
Deogam sept of the Hos, origin of the, 50 230
De Plantis (or De Vegetabilibus), translated from Arabic from a Greek paraphrase of an Aristotelian work on plants, 45 331
de Rosny, Leon, author of a Japanese grammar, see Asiatic Studies in Europe
Descent of Christ into Hell had its ultimate basis in theodicy, 53 291-292
Deshauterayes, sinologist, disciple of Fourmont, see Asiatic Studies in Europe
Design, Chinese, and Northwest Coast Indian, similarities, 51 100; see also China, Chinese Art
Deussen, translation of prāṇas, 22 256, 264 f.; 22 276, 287-302; views on prāṇa and apāna, 39 107-110; views on the author and date of Śvetāśvatara Upaniṣad, 22 380-387; on its relation to Sāmkhya system, 22 381-387; views on Upaniṣad philosophy, 36 197-199
Deutero-Isaiah, his belief of divine pardon for Israel a departure from his and other prophets' previous stands, 57 241; under influence of Medo-Persian thought, 57 164-165; adopts idea of Iranian hvareno, 166-169; servant poems in written by follower of Deutero-Isaiah, 46 342
Deuteronomy, Law code and covenant modeled on Ex. 33:12-34:28 and Num. 10:29-32, 38 127-128; origin of individual laws not a safe criterion as to the origin of the code in which they are found, 46 361
Devas, conflict between Asuras and, 39 101 f.
Devadāsa's Vyankatesha Stotra, 46 345
"devadasis", recent legislation against dedication of girls as, in India, 52 285
Devamūrti's Rauhiṇeyacaritra, 44 1
Devi, festival of, celebrated in the Maratha country, 30 72-76
Devil-worshippers, Yezīdīs, around Tiflis, 25 178-181
Dew, ancient Chinese custom of gathering, 55 185-186, possible use of mirrors for collecting, 185, 186, Emperor Ming Ti gathered dew of good augury from trees around his mother's tomb, 189; Arab proverbs about, 52 153-154; see also Words, Kan lu tsiang
Dew, Captain Roderick, in the T'ai-p'ing rebellion, note on, 57 246
Dge ba hbum, appears on a Tibetan painting of the eighth Dalai Lama, 52 343
Dge hdun grub pa, the first Dalai Lama, choice of his successors, 52 338-339, representations in Lamaist paintings, 338, 343-344
Dge hdun rgya mcho, the second Dalai Lama, represented in Tibetan paintings, 52 338, 344
Dharmalakṣaṇa, see Fa-hsiang Tsung
Dharmapāla, Indian priest, teacher of Śīlabhadra, and author of the best commentary on the Vijñaptimātratāsiddhi, 51 302, 304
Diamond Body, a Buddhist term, 49 135 n.6
Diaries, Japanese, Kamakura Period, of Court nobles and Emperors, value of, as source material, 59 42-45
Diatonic scale, indications of its use in ancient Egypt, 44 175
Diaz, Emmanuel, books by, prohibited in Japan, 57 292-294; see also Asiatic Studies in Europe (Matteo Ricci, etc.)
Dice, not at first associated with playing cards in China, nor with ancient divination, said to be first mentioned in China by Ma Jung, second cent. A.D., called po-lo-sai (anciently pa-la-sak), and shu-p'u, 47 75-76
Dietary restrictions and totemism, 50 225-227
Dilbat, lay S of Borsippa, 46 236
Dilmun, dates of, were a Babylonian-grown variety, 52 305; does not appear in the so-called Sumerian Paradise-Epic, 36 291; identified with al-Baḥrayn; seat of early Babylonian culture, 45 237-238; not an island in the Persian Gulf, 36 124; regarded as original home of man in the so-called Paradise Epic of Langdon, 39 66
Dimmis, al-Mutawakkil's measures against, 47 318-322; polemic against in Ġazi al-Wāsiṭi's Kitāb Radd 'ala Ahl al-Dimmah wa-man Tabi'ahum, written at end of 13th or beginning of 14th cent., 41 383-457
Dingle, Edward J., contribution to Chinese historical studies, 38 103
Diṅnāgas and the rain-bringing qualities of elephants, 52 89
Disease, see Black Magic ku
Divālī, the date of, 59 506-508
Divina Commedia, see Dante
Divination, fr. the caws of a crow, among the Palaung, as in ancient India, Tibet, and China, 45 189; Scapulimancy, in Central Asia and America, 51 99; Scrying, American Indian, 51 99; see also Dice; Hepatoscopy; Ophiomancy
Babylonian by gazing on a shiny surface, 42 373
Chinese: ancient diviners used own explanations of the hexagrams, 56 336 and n.5; a book on 卜 taught in the schools of the State of Ch'i in ancient China, 44 278; crowing of ringed pheasant for Kao Tsung Yin Wu-ting, 高宗殷武丁, the furious storm for Ch'eng Wang, 成王, 51 155; dreams of the Empress Têng, 51 139-140; Han divination boards, see Lo-Lang; ku character as a divination symbol, 55 4-9, 29, with wooden figures before poisoning with ku, 24-25; Taoist divinatory text, 54 294; to choose burial place, see also Burial, Wên Ta-ya's father
Islamic: ink, oil and mirror-gazing in modern Egypt, 36 37-53; Indian origin of mandal ceremony, 36 39
Roman: Auspicium and haruspicium of Babylonian origin, 52 296-297
Divodāsa the Bharata, as incarnation of Dhanvantari, 42 324 f., 332-334
Divorce, in Hammurabi Code, 36 6-7, 24-25
Divyāvadāna, notes on, 40 336-352, giving animals intoxicating drink, 336-339, epithets of Buddhist Arhats, 339-343, correspondences between Buddhist and Jaina Sanskrit, 343 f., meaning of āsvāpana, 345, more than one author, 345 f., running comments, 346-352; translation of the Sanskrit text of the Sūkarikāvadāna, compared with the Tibetan and Chinese versions, 48 159-165; translation of the Sanskrit, Tibetan, and Chinese versions of the Dānādhikāramahāyāna-sūtra of the, 49 40-51
Diwan, instituted among Arabs in days of 'Umar, following Persian precedent, 41 419, was run differently in Aleppo and Mesopotamia and in Egypt, 456

Djalatunda-reliefs, the harp of the, 51 50
Dhanvantari, the Indian god, 42 323-337, healing god, 323, sacrifice, 323 f., identified with other deities, 324, incarnations, 324-327, as Divodāsa, 324 f., 332-334, receives the Āyur-Veda, 325, modern traditions, 326 f., shrines, 327 f., meaning of name, 328, as cloud-god, 328 f., cloud-gods outside India, 329-332
Dhanya (śāli), name of Śālibhadra in some texts, 43 261 f.
Dharma Sūri, life and works of, 45 328 f.
Dharmakumāra, original author of Śālibhadra Carita, 43 257
Dharmaśāstras, comparative age of the, 48 294
Dharṇa, practice of, to force payment of debt, 21 146 f., 157 f.
Dhauli recension of the Fourteen-Edicts of Asoka, 30 77 f., 91-93
Dnyāneshwar, Mahārāshtra saint and poet, date of, and reason for composing in Marathi, 37 15
Docetism, influence in Islam, 29 29 f.
Dogs, Chinese (Han) sold fr. the Imperial Park to reduce expenses, 51 147; killed in China to dispel plague 55 3, killed to stop the wind, 3, dog-ku a variety of Black Magic, 7, blood of black dogs an antidote to magic, 3; of Northern Iran, 25 182 f.
Dohada, craving of pregnant women: a motif of Hindu fiction, 40 1-24, scientific and literary treatment, 2, poetic, 2 f., trees have, 2 f., pragmatic, 4, as start motif, 5, injures or endangers husband, 6-14, prompts husband to heroism, 14-16, takes form of pious acts, 16-18, as ornamental incident, 18 f., feigned, 19-23, obviated by trick, 23 f.
Doliche (mod. Duluk), description of site of, 23 85
Dome, earliest representation of on a pre-dynastic Egyptian schist palette, 39 122; goes back to early prehistoric times in Mesopotamia, 56 110; predynastic Egyptian, derived from Babylonia, 41 234; see also Vault
Dome of the Rock, no dome over it before the time of 'Abd-al-Malik, 56 5, 12; not to be excessively venerated by Muslims, 5, 11-12
Dougherty, Raymond P., life and works, 53 308-309
Dove, sacrificed by Hebrews as early as 900 B.C., 33 364; used in early Sumerian sacrifice, 42 98
Dragon, Chinese, connected with the Tao concept, 55 327-328; of the Hsun 荀 Family, 49 141-142 n.11
Dragon Gate, see Lung Mên
"Dragon's Blood", a commercial product of the Berbera coast, isle of Socotra, 30 52, 54
"Dragon's Spittle", see Ambergris
Drama, Chinese, notes on the, 57 205-206
Dravidian, animism in Indian philosophy, 39 125; folk-tales, echo-word motif in, 59 503 f.; mariners, ports, 37 241
Language: elements in Dardic, 46 177 f.; echo-words, 58 553-555, as motif in stories, 555-570; etymologies, 46 309 f.; the comparison of Finnish with, 57 305-307; final i, treatment in Kanara and Tamil, 59 103 f.; *geli and Aryan *gili, 49 60 f.; initial cerebrals, 57 305; the possibility of a connection between the Mitanni and 50 273-305, phonology, 277-283, grammar, 283-301, lexical comparisons, 301-304, conclusions, 305; and Nubian, 52 133-144, phonology, 133-135, grammar compared, 135-139, list of compared words, 140-144; phonology and morphology, 57 112-115; prefixed v in southern, 46 309; possibility of contact with Sumerian, 45 366; words for "bone," 58 472; *wrīghia 'rice,' 47 263-266
Drama, Indian, of Harṣa, time analysis of, 21 88-108; time analysis of Sanskrit plays, 21 88-108; the Viddhaśālabhañjikā of Rājaśekhara, translated, 27 1-71
Dreams, interpretation of, see Oneiromancy
Drehem, Sumerian accounts from, 33 167-179
Drought, in 108 A.D., see also Chinese Thought; ten years of floods or droughts, 51 153
Drugs, knowledge of in 9th-10th cent. Coptic medical papyrus, 45 78-82
Drums, Bronze, used by Karen tribes of Burma, like those of Yünnan, 40 135
Druze, Religion, origin of; Zoroastrian, Christian, Indian and Neo-Platonic sources, 47 366; Revolt (1925), its suppression by the French, 47 108-109; see also Manuscripts
Duke of Chou, legend of driving away the tigers, leopards, rhinoceros, and elephants, 41 298
Du 'l-Šarā' = Semitic Tammuz, 35 222
Dumuzi, king of Bad-tibira, 43 324
Dungi, see also Šulgi
Dungi, Babylonian feast of, 31 253-254
Dura Europos, at Ṣāliḥīyah on the Euphrates, 44 193; architecture, oriental character of, 48 357; cult scenes in frescoes, strong Semitic and Parthian elements in, 51 121 ff.; defenses probably constructed by Parthians sometime after 140 B.C., 48 357; enceinte and plan date from 3rd cent. B.C., 55 211-212; Palmyrene triad (Yarḥibōl, Aglibōl and Ba'al Samîn) in, 51 125-130, of Parthian origin, 128-131, 135-137, Zeus of the triad is associated with Ahura Mazda, 128, possible graffito representation of Zeus, 132-133, cult essentially Parthian, 134; temple at NW corner containing frescoes, description of, 51 119-120, 130, oldest structure built ca. 100 B.C. by Parthians, 130-131, description of frescoes, 120-128, 132, 134, 137, citadel built by Parthians ca. 100 B.C., 135
Duret, Claude, author of Trésor de l'histoire des langues, 1613, see Asiatic Studies in Europe
Durgā, associated with the "seven Indras", 37 86
Dusares, see Du al-Šarā'
Dūtāṅgada of Subhaṭa, translated, 32 58-77
Dutch, people called hung mao, "red hair" by the Chinese, 59 350, 352
Dutch, Middle, works in Cleveland Public Library, 36 421
Dvīpas in Hindu cosmography, 39 209-242; in Indo-Aryan cosmology, 26 85, 88-90
Dyaks of Borneo, contacts of with Islam, 33 317 ff.
Land: agricultural methods among, 29 239 f.; dialects, r for original l in, 36 189; factors in agricultural life of, 29 237-240; harvest festivals, 29 236-280; harvest gods, 26 165-175; origin of order of "barich", 29 266 f.; religious organization, 29 264-274
Sea: deities, 25 240-244; influence of war and agriculture on religion of, 25 231-247; mourning taboo, 25 234, 237
Ea, god of sea, chief authority on ships and shipping, 46 362; see also Enki
E-ana, temple of Uruk, in use down to Seleucid period, 36 336
Eagle, brass, in Zosimos, 26 411 f.
Eagle's fountain in mythology, 26 38-42
Eanna = Babylon, 49 311
Eannatum, calls himself patesi [ensi] rather than lugal, 38 266
Ear, pierced as punishment in Babylonia, 42 87, 89-90
Earth, Babylonian conceptions of, 22 138-144; 23 opp. p. 388; measurement of by the eight ch'ih piao, see Chou pi suan ching
Earth-Gods, 土 神, T'u Shen, prayer to on completion of a building, 49 151, sacrifice to, 151 n.1, also called T'u Ti; compared with God of Land and Grain, 152 n1
Easter, not celebrated by Church Fathers every year, 32 274, 323, meant to coincide with Passover, 334
East India Company, see International Relations, Anglo-Chinese
East Indies, Australia and the question of influences from the, 58 61-80
Easton, Morton Williams, death of, 37 168
Ebedjesus Georgius V Ḥayyāṭ, Nestorian patriarch, works of, 22 84-85
Ecchallensis, Abraham, Maronite author, works of, 22 94
Eclipse, Lunar, primitive ideas of, 39 87-88; Arab ceremonies during, 27 104
École des langues orientales vivantes (Paris), founded 1795 for teaching modern oriental languages, 39 191-192
Economics, as force in development of religions, 24 394-426; effect on Bornean religion, 25 246 f.; (Chinese), prices of building materials, cart hire, man-hours for carpentry, stone cutting, etc., 49 284-243

Eden, Garden of, its site vague, 48 342; located in Babylonian alluvium, not in Amurru, 45 30-34; not in Babylonia, 45 149-150
Edessa, modern Urfa, seat of a famous theological school; see Nestorians
Edicts, see also Memorials
Chinese: against tobacco, 58 649-652, 655, tr. of a Manchu edict of 1639 against tobacco, 652, 657; of Han Wu Ti dismissing all followers of Legalist teachers, 58 438; of 196 B.C., see Hsiao Ho; of Sept. 2, 1905, abolishing the old style competitive examinations, tr. of text of, 27 79, 84-87; see also T'ang-hui-yao
Japanese: of Kanei, 1630, prohibiting import of 32 Chinese works by Matteo Ricci and other Europeans and all books on Christianity, 57 290-303, development of interpretation of the edict, 294-299, 68 titles on early list, 292-294, later every book mentioning Christianity barred, 294-296, ban on scientific books lifted in 1720 by Edict of Kyôhô, 297-298, attitude of the Edo government, 296, 299, method of censorship, 299-303; of Kyôhô, 1720, permitting import of books which do not aim to teach Christianity, see Edict of Kanei
Edom, Edomites, Edomite, origin in North-Arabian Sinai, 35 386-387; did not include territory west of the Wādi al-'Arabah until late Exilic or post-Exilic times, 56 464-467; Wisdom Literature incorporated into the bible; adopted in part from Egypt, 45 353; see also Transjordan
Edrehi, character in Longfellow's Tales from a Wayside Inn, is a real one, 45 360
Egg, Mandaean creation from, 53 161-164
Eggeling's translation of prānas, 22 256 f., 283-286, 300
Eggs, divination by means of, 36 40, 42
Egongot, see Ilongot
Egypt, Egyptians, Egyptian, see also Art and Architecture; Calendar; Fāṭimids; Hyksos; Music; Near East; Science
Archeology: antiquities in J.T. Dennis collection in Johns Hopkins University, 41 186; antiquities in University of Illinois collection, 46 345; antiquities in the U.S. National Museum, 23 45; books on in Cleveland Public Library, 36 421; city-planning, organization of, 52 302; dome, earliest, representation of on pre-dynastic schist palette, 39 122; dome, predynastic, derived from Babylonia, 41 234; excavations in 1915-1916, 36 348-351, 37 86-87; faience "ex libris" plate fragment in Yale University, 53 393; nilometer of Amenemhet III from Nag' al-Der in University of California, 43 49
Culture: Arabs, demonology of, 38 160-166;
History: Chalcolithic culture begins ca. 5000 B.C., 47 355; Menes, accession of ca. 2950 B.C.; is the Mani of Akkadian sources who was defeated by Naram Sin, 39 150; Psammetichus I in 616 and Necho II in 609 B.C. support Assyria against Babylonian rebels, 44 124, 127, 128; Sasanian rule in A.D. 618-629 accepted by landed nobles only; no strong Roman garrison to oppose Sasanians, 48 339; Sennacherib's projected campaign against Egypt in 701-700, 24 265-274; short chronology for period from 12th to 18th Dynasty is the correct one, 53 286-287; 6th and 12th dynasties separated by 160 years, 42 322; ibn-Zūlāq's works on, 28 254-270; cock unknown there before the Roman period, 33 388-389, 396; hunting missile-sticks of, 55 176-178; Phoenician influences on, 48 77, 78; modern, ink, oil and mirror-gazing ceremonies in, 36 37-53; ivory as tribute and booty in the 18th Dynasty fr. Syria, 41 291; Jews in, did not abondon the Aramaic language, 60 131-134; Prehistoric period, 39 164 ff.; source of Solomon's horses, 26 104
Language: chiasm in, 58 545; group-writing not a method of syllabically rendering foreign names, 59 403; parallels with Semitic, 47 198 ff.; meter in, 43 175; blend-forms in, 47 234; numerals, Semitic parallels to, 47 199 ff.; metathesis commoner in Egyptian than in Semitic; examples, 41 177; Old Eg. n corresponds to Semitic l; "snake" has value of palatalized g and corresponds to Sem. ṣ and g, 39 142; š s before labials, 46 351; Sanskrit, alleged relation with, 43 170; scribes among the Assyrians, 48 129; Semitic, parallels to, 35 214 ff.; Semitic, relation to and equations with, 47 198 ff., 237; "snake" represents palatalized g, which should be transliterated ǧ; corresponds to Sem. g, ṣ, ḏ and ẓ, 41 177; what is usually transliterated ṯ represents a palatalized k and should be represented by č, 41 177; y = Sem. l, 44 167
Literature: Legend of King Bawlah is protoype of the Ballad of King John and the Abbot of Canterbury, 22 221-226; Demotic source of Lucian's Φιλοψευδὴς ἢ Ἀπιστῶν, used by Goethe as basis for his Der Zauberlehrling, 39 295-298
Mythology: Nile regarded as semen of Osiris, 39 70; see also Moon
Religion: gods travelled in boats, as did the Babylonian moon-god Sin, 46 362; Hawk was originally totem of a number of tribes worshipping different spirits, 53 170; Isis and Osiris of Semitic origin, 53 170; Isis and Horus compared with Ištar and Tammuz, 35 223; Osiris, resemblances to Tammuz, 35 213 ff.; resurrection, immortality and henotheism found in oldest texts, 39 148; Serapis cult introduced before 311 B.C. from Alexandria; spread to Rhodes and Delos, 52 308; see also under names of deities
Texts: Madīnat Habu texts, corrections in, 52 295; Nilometer with inscription of Amenemhet III from Nāg' al-Dēr, in University of California, 43 49; Summary of contents of Ḏmy text from period between Old and Middle Kingdom, 41 192
Trade: Babylonia, early sea trade with, 45 239, 245; India, ancient commerce with, 35 32, 34; missionary-traders from in Indian Archipelago, 33 315; Roman shipping from went no further east than Ceylon and Dravidian India, 36 442
Writing: alphabet, influence on formation of, 22 177 ff.; Babylonian origin not possible, 39 169-170
Eisagoge, see Porphyrius
Eiselin, Charles Frederick, life and works, 58 550-551
Eknath's version of the Bhikṣugītā, 45 357; translated 46 289-296
Ekoi, concepts of right and left among the, 58 203, 210
El, foremost deity in earliest Babylonian version of Deluge Story, 45 144
Elam, its civilization as old as that of Babylonia, 41 253-255; pottery similar to ware found at Eridu and in prehistoric Egypt, Cappadocia, Turkistan and Syria, 41 253-254; Elamite-Babylonian sign-list (?), 32 103-114; references to in Gudea texts, 43 44; Elamitic king in India (?), 42 194-197; contacts with the Sealand of Arabia, 50 18; Kings of Sumer: texts from Kudur-Mabug to Rim-Sin mention no Elamite, but only Sumerian, deities, chiefly Nannar and Enlil, 51 164-169; see also Susa
Elephant, in Asia; earliest notices of, Egyptian 18th dynasty, concern large numbers in Syria, 41 290-291, Assyrian notices of, 1100 to 9th cent., along the mid. Euphrates and in the south Caspian region, 291-292, mention of in the Shâhnâma, 292, 294, early trade in ivory of western Asia, 292, disappearance of fr. western Asia before time of Alexander, 293, the "Seres" who were "elephant users" undoubtedly Indians, 293, no wild elephants in Central Asia in historic times, 293-294, in the Asiatic islands, 294, occurred in China fr. earliest times through Han, 294-304, Chinese work in ivory fr. prehistoric times to modern, 296-297, fossil ivory, 294, legendary evidence of elephant in North China up to about 1000 B.C., 297-298, early pictograph of, 298, difference bet. Asiatic and African types of, 291, written evidence points to source of ivory as South China, Huai River region and the Yangtse valley where the Shan race was then located, 298-301, the Shan always associated with elephants, 300-301, white elephant sacred, 301, use of for riding and in pageantry, 303, 305, use of in war, 293, 294, 302-303, 305-306, used in construction of a tomb, 302, tamed in Ch'u, 299, 300, the Ch'u State and the trade in ivory, 298-301, inspired few art motives, 298,

304, tamed and kept at court, 294, 299, 300, 301, 303, 304, 306, the hunting of, in Syria, 291; along the Euphrates, 291, in the south Caspian region, 292, in Sulu, 294; in China proper, 297-298, in the Yangtse basin, 302-303, 304, extinction of, in western Asia, 293, in Sulu, 294, in China proper, 297-299, in the lower Yangtse valley, 303, in Ssu-ch'uan, 304, in Kwang-tung, 304, in Yünnan, 305-306, used to put criminals to death in Canton, 304; found in N Assyria, 37 177-178; used in Chinese performances at court, Later Han, 51 150; still found in NE Syria in 9th cent. B. C., 38 246, 250; as rain-bringers, 52 89; role in choosing a king by divine will, 33 158-161; used in Shen-tu (India) in war, 37 98, used in Tien-yüeh, the "elephant-riding country" southwest of China, 99; elephant-science of the Hindus, 50 324
Elîba'al, king of Byblos, inscription of, 46 237-240
Elisha, Islands of, = the Azores, 43 126 n. 10
"Elixir of Life", Taoist, substances used for, or ingredients, 53 216-217, 223, 227, 233, 239, preparation of "medicines", 223, 224-225, 226, 233, 239, 247
Elliot, a rare work by Sir Henry Miers, 41 73 f.
Elliot's Lanao Moro vocbulary, 42 158
Embassies, to China from the Roman Empire, and the West; first fr. Ta-ts'in, in 166 A.D., 30 4-5, fr. Persia, bet. 605 and 616 A.D., 6, first Nestorian mission, 635 A.D., 4, fr. Fu-lin in 643, 667, 701, 719 A.D., 14, 30, mission of priests in 742, Nestorian priest from Ta-ts'in in 744, 15, embassy in Yüan-fêng period (1078-1086), 24-26, 29-30; to China, fr. Ta-ts'in in 166 A.D., 37 243; from the King of the Shan country, in 120 A.D., brought jugglers and musicians of Ta-ts'in, 242-243; to China fr. the West; from Persia bet. 605 and 617 A.D., 33 196, first Nestorian mission established the Persian church 635 A.D., 198-199; from Tibet to China, 634 A.D., 38 34, to ask for workmen to manufacture ink, paper (and writing brushes?), 34-35; see also Hsiung-nu; Hu-ni; International Relations, Anglo-Chinese
Ember, Aaron, life and works, 46 182-184
Emmer, see Wheat
Emperor Hui of Han, see Empress Dowager née Lü
Emperor-worship, apotheosis of Achaemenid kings existed from time of Cyrus, 52 305; not practised in Babylonia, 36 360-380, 37 331; practised in Babylonia, 37 31, 162-163; among the Hebrews, killed by historical events and the development of monotheism, 42 398
Empress Dowager née Lü, of Han, Confucianism suffered set-back under, 58 436; intrigues for succession to throne, 57 173-174, 176, 179, nephew Lü Lu head of army, 174
Empress Dowager (Grand) née Tou, ardent Taoist at Court of Han Wu Ti, conflict with rising power of Confucianists, 58 438, 439-440
Emu Tanggô orin sakda-i gisun sarkiyan, see Manuscripts, Manchu
Emuṣa, the boar, as hoard-keeper, 55 389 f.
Enamel, polychrome, use of in Babylonia, 22 29-34
Encyclopaedias, Chinese, no more reliable than western ones, 47 71
Engineers, hydraulic, attached to the army against Ta-yüan to cut off water supply, 37 111, Chinese, able to bore wells, 113
England, English, expansion in Near East motivated by Crusading ideals, 38 72; change of [a] to [ɔ] after [w] 44 44; change of [ju] to [u] after dentals, 44 44 f.; Middle, works in Cleveland Public Library, 36 421; see also Folklore
English-Rommany jargon of the American roads, 28 271-308; note on, 29 232-235
Eninnû, temple in Lagaš, construction aided by workmen from Susa, 43 44; temple in Lagaš, functions of its fifteen officers appointed by Gudea, 41 192-193; temple of Ningirsu at Lagaš, cult ceremonies in, 42 92-104
Enki, god of Eridu, identical with Enzu and Enlil, 41 138; hero of Eridu version of Sumerian creation story, 36 282-284, 287, 291 ff.; his emblem a fabulous animal compounded of the bearded carp and the wild goat or ibex, 39 71 n. 12; association with metals incicates his mountain origin, 36 294-295; rôle of in the so-called Sumerian Paradise Epic, 39 67 ff.
Enkidu, his identity and relationship to Gilgameš, 40 319-322; identical with fertility-god Gira-Šakan, 37 16; story of civilizing of, paralleled in Gen. 3, 39 287; entirely Sumerian in origin; was originally identical with Gilgameš, 38 332-333
Enki-Ea and Gira-Sumuqan, originally related figures, 40 321-322
Ekimmu, "departed spirits" of Babylonian religion, three classes of, 39 311-312
Enlil, doubles for Enki in the so-called Sumerian Paradise Epic, 39 77 ff.; see also Enki
Enlil-bâni, texts from his reign, 36 34
Enmeduranki, antediluvial king of Sippar, 43 325, 326, 329
Enoch, Book of, versions and translations, 42 44-45, Ethiopic, knowledge of in Europe from 15th to 18th cent., 44-52; Slavonic, two recensions are from two different Greek MSS, 37 16; Slavonic, recensions A and B are independent Greek recensions, B being earlier; A is an expanded text made by an Alexandrian Jew. B was probably translated from Aramaic or Hebrew before A.D. 70, 41 307-312
En-ut, Sumerian deity, form of Enki-Ea, 42 199-200
Environment on religious beliefs, effect of geographical, 41 191
Envoys; from China, to the Wu-sun, as assistants to Chang Ch'ien, 37 101, sent by Chang Ch'ien to several countries of the West, 102, some return with natives of the West, 102-103, regular missions to An-hsi, An-ts'ai, Li-kan, T'iao-chih, and Shen-tu, 103-104, sent by way of Yünnan, robbed and killed by K'un-ming tribes, 104, ill-treated in foreign countries, incite own government to take action, 105-106, sent more & more frequently, 106, 107, loss of prestige in the West, 104, 106, Chinese less honored than Hsiung-nu envoys, 107-108, make false reports, 109, intercepted and killed at Yü-ch'êng, 109-110, deserving army officers appointed to feudal states, 115, sent to Ta-yüan in recognition of Ch'an-fêng as King, 115; collect curiosities, 115-116, To China, fr. the Wu-sun, 101, 103, fr. An-hsi, 107, fr. countries around Ta-yüan, 107, entertainment of the foreign envoys, by Han Wu Ti, 107, 108, prestige of the Hsiung-nu envoys in the West, 108, sons and brothers of kings sent to China as hostages, 114; see also Chang Ch'ien
Enzu, see Enki
E-PA, 7-staged ziggurat at Lagaš, 43 92-95
Ephraim Syrus, his teaching on the soul, 40 104 ff.
Ephthalites, 57 255
Epigraphy, see Inscriptions
Epiphanius, see Panarion
Epiphany and Christmas celebrated by Armenians on Jan. 6, 32 272, 276, 320-323, 330-331, fixing of date of, 334
Eponym-lists, Assyrian, begin with Adad-nirâri III in 911 B.C., 38 211-212
Eponyn system, Assyrian, imitated by Menahem and Pekahiah, 43 165
Equinox, "Obelisk Ridge" at Petra may have been station for observation of equinoxes, 55 464-465; Semitic festival of survives in the Christian feast of the Finding of the Cross, 39 149; vernal, marks time of return of Yahweh's glory, 57 256; vernal, Maṣṣôt festival in celebration of, 46 346; vernal, Palm Sunday connected with it, 38 333; vernal, year beginning with introduced in Babylonia after time of Gudea, 33 5
Equinoxes, precession of, discovered by Babylonian astronomer Kidinas, 46 87
Erh-shih, 貳師, capital city of Ta-yüan (Ferghana) in time of Han Wu Ti, where the 'superior' horses were kept; Chinese campaigns against, to procure the horses, 37 109-113, 135; General, title bestowed on Li Kuang-li, 37 110; campaign of, against Ta-yüan, 110-113; see also Names, Geographical
Erh-ya, its place in the Canon, 44 282; records elephants in the Liang range in Ssu-ch'uan, 41 299; relationship terms

in, not the earliest; represents usage among the nobles, 51 187
Eridu, first settled as a fishing-place by an Asiatic-Elamite people, 54 78; saved from waters by Enki in early Babylonian creation story, 41 459-460; version of the Sumerian creation story, 36 283 ff.
Erkes, Edouard, compares myths on both sides of the Pacific, 56 65-66, earliest traces of sun myth found in stone inscriptions of about 500 B.C., 66
Erytheia, = Cadiz and adjacent islands, 43 126 n. 10
Erythraean Sea, name due to color of rising sun and purple dye obtained from it, 33 358-361; is the ocean surrounding the earth to the E and S in Herodotus, Strabo and Arrian, 33 353-354; see also Prasodes
Erythras, legend of, may reflect struggle between highland and plain peoples, 33 358
Ešmun, = Sem. Tammuz, 35 222; equated with Tammuz-Adonis, 21 188-190; an aspect of Thoth, 48 79; identified with Ugaritic 'Ašmny, 55 98; temple of in Sidon, inscription of Bod'aštart from, 24 211-226; see also Adonis and Tammuz
Ešmunazar, Phoenician king, acceded before 320 B.C., died before 280 B.C., 57 240
Ešmun'azarids of Sidon, genealogical tree of, 23 168-169
Etana, deified king of Kiš, 41 252
Etana Myth, influence on ascensions of Kay Kāvūs and Ganymede, 30 128-129; Pittsfield fragment, text and translation; belongs to Harper's first group, 30 101-131
Ethiopia, Ethiopians, Ethiopic, Arde'et, magical work, ed. and tr., 25 1-48; distributive expressions, formation of, 44 170; Enoch, Book of, knowledge of in Europe from 15th to 18th cent., 42 44-52; gerund developed from stative verb form, 48 283-284; may be a separate African Semitic dialect at bottom; effect of substratum in is questionable, 52 381; name given to tribes on the Gulf of Aden, 35 237-238; specimens of modern popular literature, 23 51-55; statues of kings of from Jabal Barkal, 36 349; see also Abyssinia; Magic; Manuscripts; Semitic Languages
Etruscan, jewelry in Marburg collection, 22 18-19; sign +, ×, 56 406
Eucharist, not derived from Passover; connection with the Qiddûš, 47 83-84; symbolism of ingredients among Syrians, 32 271, 272, 277, 310-316
Euhemerism, model-emperor lore of China an example of, 56 57, 61
E-ul, Sumerian god identified with Nannar (Sin), 43 353
Eunuchism, among Christians criticized by Arab author al-Jāḥiz, 47 332-333
Europe, Europeans, European, knowledge of in China, see Geographical Knowledge in China; Western, history of the cock in, 33 383-386, 395; loan-words in Baghdad Arabic, 22 110-111; "returning boomerang" in, 55 179; see also Folklore
Eusebius, his quotations from Alexander Polyhistor of value for criticism of LXX, 56 251-252; taught Gregory of Nazianza in Caesarea, 32 341
Eutyches, opposed by Bar-Šûšan, 32 309
Evil spirits, see Black Magic ku; Demons
Evliya Efendi, life and critique of his travels, 37 224-239
Examination system in China, see China, Chinese, Education
Exhibition, East Asiatic Art, in Amsterdam, 1919, 43 337
Exodus, Biblical account is of the expulsion of the Hyksos in 1580 B.C., 44 160; Egyptian tales of magic ascribed to Moses and gradually joined to historical narrative of Exodus, 47 363-364; route of, 34 425
Exogamy, origin of not explained, 25 158-159; and totemism, 38 150; relation of totemism to, 50 221 f.
Exorcism, in Japan, for demons of pestilence, 54 283; in Japan, use of holly to drive away demons, 55 445-450; see also Demons; Pestilence
Expeditions, exploring, by Chinese to Western Asia, in direction of India, 37 99, to the Wu-sun, 101; see also Chang Ch'ien; Envoys; Wu-sun; Caravans; China, Chinese, History
Expiation ceremonies among the Hindus, origin of, 34 233-235, care taken to avoid errors necessitating, 235-238, psychological aspects of, 238-241, principal concept in, 241-243, impurities and imperfections of sacrifice necessitating, 243-246, peculiar character of, 247 f., magic formulas in, 250-253, substitutes for materials and participants in, 254-260, simplifications of, 261-263, relation of deity to, 263-266
Exploration, 15th-century, religious element prime mover in, 38 71-72; in China, Manchuria, Inner Mongolia and the Ordos, see Licent, Father Émile
Ezekiel, Book of, no Greek cultural influences in, 52 370, written in 6th cent. B.C., 368-370, 371, 372, pseudepigrahic character doubtful, 370-371, definite Babylonian coloring in, 372, pro-Samaritan features of, 372-373; Scheide Papyrus frequently follows the Hebrew as against the LXX, 58 92-102; Scheide papyri of date ca. A.D. 200; affinities of, 58 533
Ezida, temple of Nabû at Borsippa, is the city referred to in Gen. 11, 40 276-281, pun on its name in Gen. 11:9, 281
ibn-Ezra, Abraham, his philosophical-mystical criticism of the O.T., 55 Supp. 1, 29-32
Fa-hien, see Fa-hsien
Fa-hsiang Tsung, 法相宗, the Dharmalakṣaṇa school of thought in China, of the Wei Shih philosophy, see Wei Shih
Fa-hsien, his attitude contrasted with that of travelers fr. the West to India, 40 227-228, praise of Fa-hsien by an unknown Indian, his host, 228; see also Passages, Chinese
Falconry, in Japan, in Tokugawa period, 31 183-184, 203, 208, 214
Family Records, Japan, see Bibliography
Famine, in Japan, in Tokugawa period, end of 18th, early 19th cent., 30 287
Fang Hu Sheng Ching, see Yüan Ming Yüan
Fang I-chih, on tobacco, 58 649, 651, 653
Fang Yü Sheng Liao, 方輿勝略, geographical work of early 17th cent. errors in, 59 346-347
Fāra, see also Šuruppak, history of excavations at, 52 114-115, antiquities from, 120, peak of its culture after Jemdet Naṣr period, 123-124, history of, 52 125
al-Fārābi, three MSS of his work on the classification of sciences in existence, 45 330-331
Far East, archeology, Mr Bishop's archeological trip to Japan, Korea, and China, in 1916, resumé, 36 354; work in, 1915-1916, 36 353-354; see also India and China
Far Eastern Studies, Committee of American Council of Learned Societies, report of work in 1934-1935, 55 368; in the U.S.A., note on work of Sadajiro Sugiura at Univ. of Penna. in 1900, 57 421
Farhad va-Šīrīn of Vaḥši, modeled after Nizāmi's Ḫusro va-Šīrīn; MS of in Metropolitan Museum copied by 'Ali Riḍā' 'Abbāsi, 44 270-271
Farīdūn, as healer, 38 296-299
Farnbāg fire, location of, 41 81-106, Pahlavi Būndahishn regarding, 84-92, Arab-Persian allusions to, 93-105, summary and conclusion, 105 f.
al-Farq bayn al-Firaq of al-Baġdādi, Damascus MS of dated A.D. 1249, 46 353
al-Farq bayn al-Ṣāliḥ wa-ġayr al-Ṣāliḥ, supposed work of al-Ġazzāli, is another name for his al-Tibr al-Masbūk fi Naṣīḥat al-Mulūk, 43 85-91
Fatḥ 'Ali Ḫān, MS of his Čaġatay-Persian dictionary in Leningrad, 49 186
Fāṭmids, al-Nu'mān family of judges under, account of from ibn-Ḥajar, 27 217-296
Feasts, Babylonian, 31 253 ff.; see also Festivals
Fei-lien Lodge, erected by Han Wu Ti, 58 442
Feng shen yen yi, 封神演義, remarks on date and legends in the, 57 198-200, similarity bet. the Shahnameh of Firdausi and the, 199-200
Fêng-shih-chün, title given to Kan Fu, 37 95
Feng Ying-ching, friend of Ricci, student of western geography, 59 344, 358
Fenollosa, E.F., work of on history of Chinese and Japanese art, 38 103

Ferghana, see Ta-yüan

Ferguson, Dr. John C., answered by Miss Fernald, on the stone horses of T'ang T'ai Tsung, 55 420-428; contributions of to Chinese studies, work on Wang An-shih, 38 101

Fernald, Helen E., answer to Dr. John C. Ferguson on the stone horses of T'ang T'ai Tsung, 55 420-428

Ferreira, Gaspar, see Asiatic Studies in Europe (Matteo Ricci, etc)

Fertile crescent, not situated on the edge of desert country, 44 186-201

Festal Letters, Christian examples of, 60 119-120, Aramaic, from Elephantine, 120-122

Festivals

Arab: circumcision and wedding feasts, 36 325-326

Babylonian: Ištar-Tammuz festival once celebrated in month of Ulûlu, 36 331-332; Zagmuk festival a time for dedicating new temples and kindling new fires, 39 99

Chinese: to the Kitchen God, 24th of the 12th mo., 49 148 n. 3; Mid-Autumn festival, 15th of the 8th mo., when moon is worshipped, 49 149 n. 9; of the Yellow Flowers, alluded to, see Yüan Ming Yüan; Ch'ing Dynasty, reception of Spring, as held in 1911 in Foochow, 42 53-58, date established by position of sun, 53, antiquity of the ceremony, 53-54, held in the eastern suburb at the pavilion of the Spring Bull, 53, 54-55, the procession and ceremony, 54-55, measurements and coloring of the clay bull and the image of the tutelary god of the year, T'ai Sui, symbolic in every detail, 55-58, position of the god in relation to the bull indicates time of New Year and time to plant, 57-58, household ceremonies, 55; Yu Lan Huei,盂蘭會, or Festival of Feeding the Hungry Ghosts, on the 15th of the 7th month, held on Chiu Hua Shan on Ti Tsang's birthday, 49 136 n. 8, 10

Christian: Cross, Eastern Church festival of the finding of, survival of Semitic equinox festival, 39 149; Palm Sunday originally opening of Canaanite maṣṣoth festival; connection with vernal equinox, 38 333

Hebrew: Ab 15th, end of Adonis mourning, 36 324-328; agricultural, 37 209-219; Maṣṣoth, dance at end of, 36 328; vernal equinox festival, 46 346; New Year festival, Babylonian influence on, 37 221; Passover a new moon feast, 46 346; Passover, originally celebrated at new moon of the spring month, 37 214-215; Sukkoth, in honor of Adonis, 36 327; pilgrim feast and water festival, 37 217-219; festival of descent and dedication of fire, 39 98-99; New Year's festival at autumnal equinox, 42 398; weeks, feast of, celebrated on day after Pentecost, 37 215-216; Yom Kippur, 36 324, 327

Japanese: Gion matsuri, held annually in Kyoto, July 17th and 24th, 54 282-289; in Mikawa Prov., named; half-gods Hino and Mizouno represented, 57 127-128, underlying beliefs, 128-129; Setsubun, a New Year's festival, in which toasted beans are scattered to drive out evil spirits, 55 446-450, of Chinese origin, 446, n. 25, use of holly prominent, 447-449

Persian: 'Ašūrā' festival, two popular Azarbayjani poems recited in connection with, 39 113-116

Semitic: agricultural, 36 327-328

Sumerian: at Lagaš, 42 103

Feudalism

China: 40 170-185

Japan: dress and personal adornment of the samurai, 45 89, population statistics of samurai in 1871, 90-91; Tokugawa Period, Rural; 30 259-290; 31 151-216; policy of Ieyasu, dependence of power on peace, 30 259-260; dependence of power on peace, 31 151-152; influence of political wisdom of China and early Japan and adaptation to 17th cent. Japan, 30 260; influence of the political and social ideas of China, 31 152-153; adaptation to 17th cent. Japan, 31 153; social classes, ruler and ruled, warriors and peasants, 30 260-261; population statistics, 30 260, 287-289; Mencius on the rulers and the ruled, 31 153-154; warriors, bu-shi and sumurai, 31 154; distinction bet. warriors and peasants, 31 154-155; landed warriors, 31 155; organization of ruling class, Suzerain, Intendents, and their fiefs, Barons and Barons' Bailiffs, 30 261; organization of ruling class, Suzerain, Intendents, and their fiefs, Barons and Barons' Bailiffs, 31 155-161; organization of the Village and its peasants, 30 261; organization of the village and its peasants, 31 161-162, 163-165; peasants classed according to tenure, 30 261; all under the Village Head, assisted by Chiefs and Elders, 30 261; village officials, head, chiefs and elders, 31 165-168; the Iya-yama villages in the province of Iyo, 31 162-163; District-heads and groups of vilages, 30 261; district-heads and groups of villages, 31 168-170; inviolability of officials; punishment of nobles, 30 261; inviolability of officials, 31 170; joint responsibility of corporate bodies, city wards and merchant and artizan gilds, 30 261-262; joint responsibility of corporate bodies, 31 170; sacredness of the law; peasants' knowledge of it and its bearing upon taxation, 30 261-262, 266-267, 268-269; sacredness of the law, 31 170; law and justice, 30 261-262, 265-266, 267, 268, 275; law and justice, 31 170-172; the peasant as the foundation of the state; the rise of the serfs in the 17th cent., 30 263-266; the peasant as the foundation of the state, 31 172; peasants and warriors as against the rising burgher class, 30 264; peasants and warriors as against the rising burgher class, 31 172-173; ownership of land by the peasant virtual and theoretical, 30 264-265; ownership of the land by the peasant virtual and theoretical, 31 174-175; cultivated and uncultivated land, 30 264, 284, 287-288; cultivated and uncultivated land, 31 175-176; the lord's right of seizure and of mortmain, 30 265; the lord's right of seizure and of mortmain, 31 176-177; succession testate and intestate, 30 265; sucession testate and intestate, 31 177-178; land, capitation, and house taxes, 30 265; land, capitation, and house taxes, 31 178; alienation and division of land, 30 265; alienation and division of land, 31 178-179; fiscal issues affected by tenant farming and change of residence, 30 265, 270-271, 275, 285, 286-287; tenant farming and change of residence, 31 179-181; marriage, 30 265, 275-276; marriage, 31 181; run-away peasants and the right of pursuit, 30 265, 286-287; run-away peasants and the right of pursuit, 31 181-183; what constituted a good lord, 30 265-266; a good lord, 31 183; study of rural conditions, 30 266; study of rural conditions by the good lord a tradition in the political lore of both China and Japan, 31 183-184; paternalism of the village administration, 30 266-269; paternalism of the village administration, 31 184-185; size of peasants' estates, 30 266; size of peasants' estates, 31 185-186; limited publicity of law and finances, 30 267, 268-269; publicity of financial data and of the penal law very limited, 31 187, 189; right of appeal, 30 267; right of appeal, 31 189-192; village organization built upon the Chinese village institution known as pao or lin, the 5 man group, 30 267; the Chinese house groups, 31 192-194; copied in Japan after the 7th cent., 30 267; the group idea copied in Japan, 31 194-196; the system resuscitated after 1600, 30 267; the group system resuscitated after 1600, 31 196-198; villagers told the laws through edicts, sign-boards, and oral command, 30 268; edicts, sign-boards, and oral commands, 31 198-201; village group-records, 30 268; village group-records, 31 201-202; taxation, 30 265, 269-285; inefficiency of feudal system to maintain satisfactory economic conditions, 30 270, 274-275; separation of arms from the land, 30 270-273; seals, 31 202; laws for the peasants of the Domain lands, 31 202-216; evils of peace and luxury, 30 273-277; abbreviations, 30 299-300; more abbreviations, 31 151; bibliography, 30 291-298; additional bibliography, 31 151; Kamakura Period, source materials on, see Bibliography; see also abstract, Asakawa; Shōen

Fiction motif, Coorg, echo word, 58 564-567

Fiction motifs, Hindu, recurring psychic, 36 54-89, books containing stories, 54-56, in modern times and outside India, 56 f., grey hair motif, 57 f., cave call motif, 58 f., tortoise on stick, 60, Brahman cheated out of his goat, 61 f.,

count not your chickens, 62 f.; hasty ingratitude, or, strike but hear, 63-65; how to evade seemingly impossible (trick) conditions, 65-68; laugh and cry motif, 68-89; laughter and crying together, 69-79; laughter by itself, 79-87; crying by itself, 87-89; false ascetics and nuns, 44 202-242; bluff 38 331; disguise as a woman, in the Rig-Veda and Brāhmaṇas, 26 176 f., in Daṇḍin's Daśakumāracarita, 177, in the story of Leukippos and Daphne, 178 f., in the story of Hymenaeus and the virgin, 179-182, in the story of King Ragnar Loðbrók, 182 f., in the Thiðrek saga, 183, in the Roman comedy, 183 f., in the Chanson de Geste 'Auberi of Burgundy', 184, replaced by actual transformation, 185 f., in Daṇḍin's Daśakumāracarita, analogues of the story, 306-309, in the prologue of Guilelmus Blesensis' Alda, with parallels, 309 f., in French pastoral romances, 310 f., replaced by actual transformation, 312 f.; dohada, or the craving of pregnant women, 40 1-24; Evil-wit, No-wit, and Honest-wit, 40 271-275; the goat and the knife, 59 366-368; betrayal of husband's secret by wife, 28 96-98; choosing a king by divine will, 33 158-166; life-index, 39 142; life-index tree, 55 68; change of sex, 47 3-24

Field, Frederick, see Origenis Hexaplorum

Field, oriental metaphor for wife, 36 418-420

Fig, mentioned in Babylonian Deluge story, evidence of the story's West-Sem. origin, 45 146-148; in Babylonian ritual, a Semitic innovation, 45 28-30; Chinese name a-i, see Words

Fihrist of al-Nadīm, account of Manichaeism in, 44 64-68, 70-71

Filippi, Lady Caroline De, née Fitzgerald, death of, Dec. 1911, 32 iii

Fingernails, divination by means of, 36 40-42

Finno-Ugrian languages, separated before morphology became fixed, 56 449

Firdōsi, was probably a Shī'ite, 55 Supp. 1, 7; see also Šāh-Nāmah

Fire, kindling of at feast of the Finding of the Cross, survival of Semitic New Year's rites, 39 149

Fire-crackers, at Reception to Spring Festival, Foochow, 42 55

Fire-making, among primitive and ancient peoples, 39 92-99

Fire-temple, at Surakhani near Baku, description of, 25 176-178; at Baku, Indian inscriptions on the, 29 299-304

Fish-oil, a product of Chung-li in medieval times, 30 52

"Five Classics", canon in Han period, to conform to categories of 5, 44 278-280

Five Elements, the theory of the, 49 140-141; equated with other categories in five; when developed, 59 202; see also Jen Wu Chih

Flood Control, in China, pre-Han canals, 55 303; under Han Wu Ti, 303-306; earliest traditional attempts those of Yü, 56 53-63

Flying Gallop, Reinach's assumption that it was an artistic convention and that its appearance in Chinese and Japanese art was proof of imigration of the motive fr. Mycenaean art, 56 178-179, the posture a real one, therefore no transmission of culture indicated, 180-182, 188

Folklore, collection of works on in Cleveland Public Library, 36 421-422; migration of, Asia and America's common fund of beliefs and traditions, 51 100; see also Magic

Arab: Babylonian influence on demonology; belief in noonday demon, 38 160-166; eclipse, lunar, ceremonies to counteract, 27 104; Wali cult part of general Mediterranean saint-worship; is of Hellenistic-Roman origin, 60 285-286, influence of Ṣūfism on, 286, pagan relics in, 299-300, Popular astrology, magic, divination, etc. derived from literary sources, 294, Stories and songs are of comparatively recent date, 294-295, Hellenistic background of folklore, 283-295, pagan elements in folklore, 295-301; Wāqwāq tree, possible factual foundation of, 42 356

Asiatic: coincidence with tales in America, 51 101-103

Batak (Sumatra): legends concerning camphor, 42 366-370

Chinese: coincidence with tales in America, 51 101-103; criticism of Dr. Ferguson's work on mythology, 53 62; Near Eastern origin of stories of Pigmies and Cranes, of the Kynokephaloi and Amazons, of the Long-Ears, of the Island that was a Turtle, of the Capture of the Rhinoceros, 45 366; a folktale the foundation of the Shun myth, 56 55-56, 66; see also Poetry, Chinese

English: Ballad of King John and the Abbot of Canterbury, Egyptian prototype of, 22 221-226

European Medieval: hairy anchorite, oriental affinities to the legend of, 48 355

Jewish: blood-test as proof of kinship, 24 129-144

Palestinian: Bethlehem folk story of Ihdayd and the She-Ghoul, text and translation, 52 168-173; hair, sacrifice of, 46 341-342; from al-Qubaybah, 50 199-213; see also Palestine; Proverbs

Syria: modern Arabic songs, stories and proverbs, 23 175-288

Föng-shï-kün, see Fêng-shih-chün

Foochow, Ceremony of Reception of Spring, see Festivals, Chinese

Football, see Games

Foreign Countries, Chinese knowledge of, see Hsiung-nu

Foreigners in China; merchants fr. the West taken captive with the inhabitants of Ku-tsang, 30 33-34; see also Mar Sergius

Foreign Relations, China and the British, see China, Chinese, History

Forgeries, Books of the Shu-ching, 56 335 n.1, 336-337, 343-344, the "P'an Kêng", 343-344, forged bronze inscriptions, 345; coin of John Hyracanus imitated in clay, 24 209-210; door from madrasah of Barqūq in Cairo, 30 58-60; gold amulet reputed to have come from Irbid, 33 307-308; Kitāb Dīwān Miṣr, work of Giuseppe Vella, 33 308-312

Forke, Prof. A., contribution of to Chinese historical studies in America, 38 104

Formosa, British nationals shipwrecked on, and beheaded by the Chinese (in 1842), 59 474-475; dialects, r for original l in, 36 188; mountaineers, position of women among, 27 211

Forty, used by Semites in sense of "some, many," 51 371

Foster, Hon. John W., former minister to China, death Nov. 1917, in Washington, 37 336; contribution of to Chinese historical studies, 38 102-103

Fou-ch'iu Po, disciple of Hsün-tzu and teacher of Liu Chiao, 57 176

Fountain of the eagle in mythology, 26 38-42

Fountain of youth, a Chinese parallel, 26 28 f., in European legends, 4-25, 43 f., 415, in Hindu legends, 3-6, 36 f., 44-67, Japanese tale of, 411, origin of stories of, 1-67, in Polynesian stories, 26-28, 414, Semitic parallels, 35-37, sun-set explanation of the, 413 f.

Four Books, use of tao 道 in its philosophical sense, 52 32-34, use of i 義 in any sense, 34

"Four Ching", 四經, in early times meant only the Four Shu, or two, or three of them; whatever documents were used for study in the schools were called ching, i.e. the Classics in general, 44 277-278

"Four Garrisons", the, Kucha, Khotan, Tokmak, and Kashgar, 38 45

Four Great Vows, see Buddhism, Zen

Fourmont, Étienne, author of Grammatica Sinica, 1742, early sinologist, see Asiatic Studies in Europe

"Four Shu", 四術, named in the Li-chi as the Book of Odes, Canon of History, Book of Rites, and Book of Music, 44 276, before Confucius only these four considered school text books, 278

Fourteen-Edicts of Asoka, dialect of the Girnār redaction of, 31 223-250

Fowl, domestic, in early China, 60 582; in the Old Testament, 33 363-396

Foy's conjecture of Arshtāt in Bh. 4.64, 21 169

Francke's theory of Khotan origin of Tibetan writing, 38 38-46; see also Writing, Tibetan

Frankincense, use of for religious purposes among ancient

Arabs, 40 260-261; a product of the Berbera coast of Africa in early times, 30 50, 51, 54; made popular in China by the Arabs, 42 366
Frazer's theories of the origin of totemism, 38 153
French, Old, works in Cleveland Public Library, 36 421
Friday, observed by Syrians as night when Christ was seized by the Jews, 32 319-320, 338, 342
Frogs, frog-ku, a variety of Black Magic, 55 23, the story of Chu Yi-jen and the frog-ku, 22, the story of the scholar of Ch'angchou and the ku frogs, 27
Fuchs, Walter, scholar of Manchu literature, work of, 60 555-556
Fu Chün, 富俊 , see Manuscripts, Manchu
Fu-hsing Textbook of History, see Hsü Ying-ch'uan
Fujiwara Sadaie, 藤原定家 , diary of, as source material for study of the Kamakura period, 59 43
Fujiwara, Tankai, 735 A.D., legend of the magic power of holly, 55 449
Fu-lang-chi, 佛狼机 , see Portuguese
Fu-lin, mystery of identity of, 30 1-31, 33 193-208; identified with Ta-ts'in (Syria), 30 1, 5, 6, 8, 9-10, 16, 30-31, 33 193-194, 199, 202, 207-208; identified with the Court of the Nestorian Patriarchs and captive Christian colony at al-Madā'in, Persia, 30 1, 6-19, 24, 30-31, 33 197-202; arguments for identification of a "Greater Fu-lin" with Byzantium, 30 1, 2-3, 16, 24-31, 33 199, 202-208; relations with China in Sui and T'ang were ecclesiastical, 30 1, 15; derivation of name fr. Bethlehem, 30 3-4, 17; first occurrence of the name Fu-lin in China, 30 2, 4-6, 33 194, 198-199; Yang Ti's desire to open communications with, 30 5-6, 33 194-196; name possibly first known to China through Li Yü, envoy to Persia, 30 4-8, 33 196; embassies to China fr. Ta-ts'in, 30 4-6, 14-15, 24-26, 29-30, 33 196; Nestorian Christians fr. Antioch settled at al-Madā'in, 30 6-15, 33 197-198; the "King of Fu-lin", Po-to-li, identified with Nestorian Patriarch Jesujab II, or orthodox Patriarch Mar Joannes, 30 9-16; language of, as indicated by transcriptians of plant names into Chinese, 30 17-24; Fu-lin of Sung accounts probably a general name for the Byzantine Empire, the Christian world then ruled by Melissenus, 30 24-31; China's lack of communication with Ta-ts'in from Han until Sui, 33 193-194; failure of Yang Ti's emissaries, 33 196; confounded by the Chinese at first with Persia, 33 189-199; as the Nestorians' name for their country may have meant three different places, 33 199
Fuller, Leslie Elmer, life and works, 57 214
Furentai (Ch. Fu Lun-t'ai, 富倫泰), see Manuscripts, Manchu
Furness, William H. 3rd, death of, in Wallingford, Aug. 1920, 41 79, 164
Furniture, Chinese, regulations for making, for imperial palaces, 1727-1750, 49 235, 237, 239, 240, 242, inlaid furniture, materials, finish, use of hot wax, 239
al-Fusṭāṭ, printed and painted Fāṭimid textiles from, 53 394
Futūḥ Miṣr of ibn-'Abd-al-Ḥakam, MS tradition of faulty, 43 146, review of Torrey's edition of, 144-148
Future life, Babylonian belief concerning, 37 34-35; taught in Psalms, 57 255
Fu Yuan Gate, see Yüan Ming Yüan
Galbanum, Chinese name pi-ch'i, see Words
Games, backgammon, football and other ball games, migration fr. Asia to America, 51 100; children's, 48 228-230, 241-242; Chinese, Chi Chang, ancient game of, mentioned, 49 154 n.2; remarks on playing cards, dice, backgammon and polo, 47 75-76
Ganapati in iconography, 57 428 f.
Gaṇḍā method of counting, 24 391 f.
Gandhamādana, incarnation of Nala-Kūbara, 33 66 f.
Gandhāra, Greco-Buddhist school of; date, 46 165 f.; effect on Indian art, 46 169 f.; art, chronology, 46 255; figure, a dated, 24 1-6; heads, implications of Hellenistic resemblance, 52 76 f.; influence in types of Mathurā Buddha, 51 59; sculpture, interpretation, 54 220; stūpa, prototype of the Javanese caṇḍi, 51 2-4; what it symbolized, 51 3 f.
Gandharva and Kandarpa, possible dialectic variations, 51 288
Gandharva-Gandareva myth, possible Semitic influence on, 36 311-312
Gandharvan, Uśanas Kāvya, and Indra, the story of, 28 81-88
Gandharvasena taking the form of an ass, legend of, 23 314 f.
Gaṇeśa in iconography, 57 428 f.
Gaṅgā-stream in Indo-Aryan cosmology, 26 85, 88
Ganymede, ascension to heaven, possible Babylonian influence on, 30 129
Gaokerena, compared with Semitic Tree of Life, 36 303-304, 311, 314
Gārhapatya Fire, apāna correlated with, 22 273, location in belly, 290
Garlic, stated by some works to have been introduced into China by Chang Ch'ien, 37 92
Garrett Collection of oriental MSS in Princeton University Library, 45 350
Garšasp, see Keresāspa
Gārwī, see Piśāca
Gasúr, 200 Sumerian and Akkadian tablets of Agade dynasty from, 52 296; see also Nuzi
Gāthās, the Amshaspands in the, 49 287; meanings of Aṣa in, 21 75 f., 81-87; reference to haoma in the, 49 287 f.; traces of struggle between early Iranians and Hittite and Sumero-Akkadians in, 35 295-296; meanings of Vohumanah in, 21 67-87
Gaubil, Antonio, see Asiatic Studies in Europe
Gauḍapāda's commentary to the Sāṅkhya Sūtras, prāṇa-series in, 22 306
Gaugamela, Battle of, in 331 B.C., elephants used in, 41 293
Gauls, cock an important bird among them at an early period, 33 384, 395
Gautama Buddha, evidence for as an historic figure, 53 204-209; as "first of legal authorities," 51 81 f.
Gavagrīva, Indian Buddhist deity, called Gozu Tennō by Japanese, see Gion Jinsha
Gawar-bati, see Piśāca
Gayo language of Sumatra, r for original l in, 36 188
ġazal, Persian verse form in Rückert, 21 40
Ġāzān Ḫān, patron of abu-Sa'īd ibn-Buḫtīšū', author of the Manāfi'al-Ḥayawān, 36 385-386
Gazelle, associated with deities of animal fertility (Sumuqan-Enkidu, Rešep, Min, Isis, etc.), 40 323-331; as scapegoat in Sumerian texts, 21 1-22
Gazetteers, Chinese, each fu and hsien has its official one; largest collection abroad is in Library of Congress, 41 185; many barred from import into Japan in 17th cent. because they mention Christian monuments, missions, or missionaries, 57 295, 296, 297, 300 and n.10; oldest extant one, 347 A.D., as a source for data on botany of S. Shensi and N. Szechuan, 59 140; complete tr. of one on Mt. Omei, into English, see Book Reviews, Phelps
al-Ġazzāli, see al-Farq bayn al-Ṣāliḥ wa-ġayr al-Ṣāliḥ
'Geben' und 'Nehmen' im Indischen, 43 358-390
Gecko (Ascalabotes fascicularis) in Babylonian medical texts, 39 284-285
Geldner's Translation of the Rig-Veda, etc., 49 349
Geiger, on cattle-tending and agriculture in the Avesta, 39 329
Gempei Seisuiki, 源平盛衰記 , value of, as source for study of Kamakura period 59 45
Genealogies, of ancient China's Princely Houses, 52 234-235, 238-240, 241-242; Japanese, source material for study of, see Bibliography; see also Ancestor Worship
Genesis, Babylonian influence in the list of patriarchs in, 43 327
Genii, Taoist, flying, 53 216 n.4, 219; books of the, 220; mounting to Heaven, 220 n.18, 221, 223; see also Immortals, Taoist: Ch'eng-kung Hsing
Genizah, Cairo, astrological fragment from: text and translation, 47 302-310, 49 291-302; Hebrew Qaraite biblical commentaries from, 41 179-180; Judaeo-Arabic commonplace book from, 52 309-310; Judaeo-Sufi poem from, 49

168-173; medical fragments from, text and translation, 50 112-124

Genkō Shakusho, 元亨釋書, value of, as source for study of Buddhist thought in Kamakura period, 59 50

Genoa, expansion of its trade with the Levant in the 12th cent., 38 176-187

Geographical Knowledge in China, Matteo Ricci's contribution to, and influence on, 59 325-359, I. Ricci's Map of the World, 1584, description of, 325-337, the eight different editions and known extant copies of, 326-327, translation of Ricci's Introduction written (in Chinese) on the side of the map, containing his exposition of fundamentals of geography and cartography, 327-329, translations of the notes on the map, written after the name of each country, 329-337, on the countries of Europe, 329-330, of Africa, 330-331, of America, 331-332, of Asia, 332-336, translation of a description of the equator, 336-337, many other countries named on the map, 337, II. Ricci's contributions, 337-341, the use of the meridians; Ricci's determination of lat. and long. for various places in China, compared with present, 337-338, translation of geographic terms and names, 339, the most recent discoveries in western geography; results of 15th and 16th cent. discovery and exploration, 339-340, a unified conception of the entire world, 340, 341, knowledge of the sphericity of the world, 341, the division of the world into zones, 341, III. Ricci's errors; the popularity of his Map, 341-347, error in estimating length of one degree, 341-342, error in following Ptolemaic system, due (?) to attitude of the Church, 342-343, popularity of the Map led to many orders, other copies, engravings and prints, 343-346, Ricci's pupils and colleagues, Feng Ying-ching and Li Chih-tsao, advanced the study of western geography, 344-345, errors in the compilations of native scholars, i.e. in the Fang Yü Sheng Liao and the Yü T'u Pei K'ao, 346-347, IV. Opposition to Ricci's Map, 347-359, antagonistic writings of Ming scholars, Wei Chün, Shen Ch'üeh, Su Chi-yü and others, tr. of passages fr., 347-349, later misinterpretations, errors and antagonism, ignorance of Ricci's Map, and misinformation by Chinese travelers, 349-354, erroneous ideas concerning western countries, and Ricci and his works, held by Ch'ing imperial scholars, 354-357, the Ming Shih and the Huang Ch'ao Wen Hsien T'ung K'ao of little geographical value, due to refusal to utilize Ricci's information, 354-357, rapid decline of Ricci's influence caused by the self-complacency of the Chinese in the 18th cent., and the connection of the Map with the Catholics, the undeveloped state of science in China, and the carelessness of the Chinese who reproduced the Map, 357-259

Geography, ancient conceptions & misconceptions: Confusion because of assumption that the early sea and land routes to the Far East had same destination, 37 240, 243, 246-249, Ptolemy's calculations, from hearsay, about voyage to Kattigara, fixed coast trending west to join Africa below Zanzibar, 240, 244, 246-249, Marcian of Heraclea's description of the coast beyond the Gulf of Sinae, 247, Marinus of Tyre on sailing from the Golden Chersonese to Kattigara, 246, notions of a southern continent as expressed in the Periplus, 248, Tsin-Lun, an earlier Marco Polo, who came to Kattigara and the Chinese court and observed the coastline of Hainan, 247-249, Gulf of the Sinae = Gulf of Tong-King, 247 ; Asia, four geographical subdivisions of, and the interrelations of their civilizations and religions, 41 190-191; Central Asia, distances: from the Hsiung-nu to Ta-yüan, 37 94, Ch'ang-an to the Salt Lake, 96, bet. Wu-sun and Ta-yüan, K'ang-chü and Ta-yüan, An-ts'ai and K'ang-chü, Yüeh-chih and Ta-yüan, 96, An-hsi west of Yüeh-chih, Li-kan and T'iao-chih west of An-hsi, 97, Ta-hsia fr. Ta-yüan, 97, Shen-tu fr. Ta-hsia, Ta-hsia fr. China, 98, rivers, flowing east, and west, 95, source of the Ho, 96, 107, 116, see also Lopnor; see also Maps

Geology, importance of in Near Eastern archeology, 39 177

Gerasa, visited by Hadrian in A.D. 129-130, 59 362; Semitic influence there slight; chief deities were Pakeidas and Hera, 54 184-185

German, Goethe, Greek and oriental influence on, 39 295-298; Old and Middle High, works in Cleveland Public Library, 36 421; spread of uvular r, 44 45 f.

Geschichte der Araber in Sicilien, of P.W.G. Hausleutner, translation of fictitious Kitāb Dīwān Miṣr, 33 310

Gezer, Amorites in ca. 2500 B.C., 45 25; 2nd-cent. B.C. boundary stone from in Istanbul, 50 341

Ghalchah languages, change of d to l in, 25 339 f.

Ghaselen of Platen, imitated from Ḥāfiẓ, 21 40-41

Ghosaka, medieval French parallel to Buddhist tale of, 42 400

Ghosts, belief in and worship of, 25 333-335

Ghoul, origin and nature of, 38 163, 165-166

Gibeon, not identifiable with Gibeah, 45 182

Gīḥôn, River, = the Nile, 45 32; probably the Kārūn, 48 342

Gilead, see Transjordan

Gilgameš, character of, 40 307-312, 316-320, 328-329; god of sprouting vegetation and fertilizing sun, 37 16; King of Uruk, a historical figure, 41 251-252; motif at Mohenjo-daro, 59 Sup. 41; not connected with Nimrod, 40 202; partly Sumerian and partly Akkadian, Enkidu entirely Sumerian in origin; the two were originally identical, 38 332-333

Gilgameš Epic, address of Ut-napištim to Gilgameš originally belonged to Siduri, 38 61-62; beginning of, 22 7-12; Enkidu, story of civilizing of, paralleled in Gen. 3, 39 287; Gilgameš and Enkidu, their relationship to each other, 40 307-335; journey of Gilgameš to the East because of situation of mountain-paradise there, 48 342; Sumerian originals of among texts from Nippur, 44 160; volcanic eruption in dream of Enkidu before the slaying of Ḫumbaba, 38 336; see also Deluge Story

Ginza, use of Peshitta of Ps. 29:5-9 in, 49 198

Gion Jinsha, Kyoto, Shinto Shrine, 祇園神社, one of the major shrines of Japan. Other name Ya-saka Jinsha, dedicated to divinity Susanoo no Mikoto, 54 282, originally Buddhist, site Banshu, name Gion and divinity Gozu Tennō, founded in middle 7th cent. by Hōdō, a native of India, 283, buildings erected on present site in 9th cent., 283, 285, up to 1868 known as Gion Kanshin In, 282

Gion matsuri, Japanese festival of the Gion Jinsha, Kyoto, held annually July 17th and 24th, 54 282, originated in A.D. 970, in a ceremony to exorcise the demons of pestilence, and was called Goryōe, 283, ceased to be celebrated in late Ashikaga, revived in late 16th cent., since then held annually, 284-285, the procession of, 286-289, phallic significance of the floats in the procession and their names, 285-289; see also Festivals, Japanese

Gira, Sumerian lion-god, identified with Enkidu, 40 320-323, 328-329; Gira and Nergal closely related, 40 328

Giraffe, a product of Po-pa-li (Berbera), in Cantonese tso-lap, 30 49-50; in China, identified by the Chinese as the ch'i-lin, see abstract, J.J.L. Duyvendak

Gira-Šakan, fertility deity, native Babylonian gazelle-type and foreign ass-type; is identical with Enkidu, 37 16

Girnār version of the Fourteen-Edicts of Asoka, 30 77-93; dialect of, 31 223-250

Gírsu, name of a quarter of Lagaš, 57 309-312

Glass, Han ear ornaments, see also Lo-Lang; Mu-yang-ch'eng

Glazing of pottery, known in Egypt ca. 3500 B.C. and introduced into China ca. 2nd cent. B.C.; spread of, 39 166, 173; with metallic oxide referred to in Prov. 26:23, 60 268-269

Glossary, Rommany, 28 275-298; English-Romany, 299-308

Gnosticism, Gnostics, influence on al-Muġīrah, 29 80-88; on al-Mustanīr, 91-92; see also Amulets

Gobryas, governor of Babylon in reign of Cyrus, 41 466-467

God, late Jewish and early Christian ideas of, 45 370; of Birth, see Chang Hsien; of Cattle, 牛王, Niu Wang, a prayer to the, 49 150; Chinese, see Prayers, Chinese; of Fire, 火神, Huo Shen, a prayer to, 49 146-147; of the Green Sprouts of Rice, An Ch'ing Miao, a prayer to the, 49 149-150; of the Land and Grain, 社稷, She Chi, prayer to, 49 152; origin, function, and comparison with the Earth Gods, 152 n.1; sacrifices to, 152; of Locusts, prayer to 49

142-143 n.1; of Vaccination, 迎痘神, Ying Tou Shen, a prayer to, 49 155
Goethe, Greek and oriental influence on, 39 295-298; see also Der Zauberlehrling, Die Braut von Korinth, Der Gott und die Bajadere
Gold, Chinese, Han, gift of 30 chin of, to ladies acting as guardians at the Imperial Tomb, 51 145; from unidentified Mt. Ḫa-Ḫum mentioned by Gudea, 43 45; in ancient Korea, reported by the Arabs, 58 659, 660, 661; pieces of money and a golden horse offered to Ta-yüan for the 'superior' horses, 37 109, rewards of, to Li Kuang-li's soldiers, 115; a product of Zanzibar in medieval times, 30 56; ratio of value to silver rather low in 9th cent. B.C., 38 238; sent to Wu-sun as a gift, 37 101, -pieces and a golden horse sent to Ta-yüan for purchase of horses, 109; see also Metals
Gold dust, use of in Malay magic, 33 335
Gold and Silver Articles, Chinese, Han, engraved vessels fr. Shu and Han to be manufactured no longer, 51 147, 148; see also Lo-Lang
Golden Age of Yao, Shun and Yü, see Model-Emperor Lore
"Golden and Silver Shores", see "Golden Route"
Golden Chersonese, the; the Martaban coast; sailing to Kattigara from, 37 246-247, 248
Golden Gate (Jerusalem), was walled-up before the Islamic conquest to prevent pagan worship of the sun there, 42 398
"Golden Route", called also "Golden and Silver Islands, (or Shores)", see Trade Routes, to Far East
Goldziher, Ignaz, life and works, 42 189-193
Good Friday, celebration of by Syrians, 32 325
Goodnow, Dr. Frank J., died Nov. 14, 1939, in Baltimore, 60 440
Gopatha Brāhmaṇa, prāṇa-series in, 22 259, 302f.
Gorakshanātha, followed by Kānphaṭa yogīs, 45 356
Gordon, Gen. C.G., letter to him from the Mahdi Muḥammad Aḥmad, 31 368-388
Goryōe, 御靈會, old name of Japanese ceremony which was origin of the Gion matsuri, also name of rites connected with worship of the phallic road gods, 54 283-285
Gott und die Bajadere, Der, of Goethe, based on a legend concerning Indra, 39 295
Gottheil, Richard James Horatio, life and works, 56 472-489, 57 251-252
Government, Chinese, Han Dyn., administration of justice by the Empress Têng, 51 145-146, 149-150, 158, cutting down expenses, 146-150, restoration of property, 149, prisoners freed, 146, 149-150, memorial to the throne on the blessings of her government, 153-156, her performance of sacrificial duties and rites, 152
Goyo, see Hashiguchi Goyo
Gñah Khri bcan po, an early King of Tibet, represented on a Tibetan painting as an ancestor of a Dalai Lama, 52 341
Gozu Tennō, 牛頭天王, Japanese name for Gavagrīva, the Bull-headed Heavenly King, original Buddhist divinity of the Gion Jinsha, see Gion Jinsha
Graeco-Romans, see Trade Routes
Grammar, the apparent conflict between practical and scientific, 47 367
Grand Master of Cermonies (T'ai-ch'ang) selected students for the Imperial University, 58 440-441
"Grand Union", see Utopia
Granet, Marcel, position concerning the status of the lore on Yao, Shun and Yü, 56 57-58, 63
Grapes, wine of, in Ta-yüan, 37 95, 108, in An-hsi, 97, seeds of, imported by Chinese envoys, 108; see also Vine
Great Britain, policy in Arab countries during and after World War I, 47 99-112, 115-116, 124-128
Great Plan, ascribed to Chou Period, 56 53: reference to Yü as founder of earliest system of Chinese philosophy, 53-54, 67
Great Planet, the, 太歲, Jupiter, prayer to, 49 139-140 n.1
Great Wall, in Lung-hsi (Kansu), 37 96; at Ling-chü, built to protect trade to the West, 103
Greater Fu-lin (Eastern Roman Empire), tr. of account of, in the Hui-ch'ao-wang-wu-t'ien-chu-kuo-chuan, 33 206, Chinese text, 207; see Fu-lin
Grebnitz, Elias, see Müller, Andreas, imprisonment for heresy
Greece, Greeks, Greek, parallel to a Hindu popular belief, 26 188-190; history of the cock in, 33 380, 395; see also Art and Architecture; Astrology; Blood-Revenge; Burial customs; Inscriptions; Manuscripts; Numismatics; Philosophy; Yavanas
Archeology: "Megarian" type bowl, of Phoenician origin, 58 528; Mycenaean sites in Corinth, 36 352-353
Geography: knowledge of Erythraean Sea, 33 350-362; Greece called Anakù in Akkadian, 45 236-237
Language: transliteration of Old Persian xš, θ, 40 200; sigillata signatures, 58 38-47; proper names, origin of, 46 249-252; names "Ἀσιοι, Ἀσαῖοι, identified with Antae, 59 61-63
Literature: Περὶ Θαυμασίων of Phlegon of Tralles, resembles Goethe's Die Braut von Korinth, 39 295; Φιλοψευδὴς ἢ Ἀπιστῶν of Lucian, is of Egyptian origin and served as basis of Goethe's Der Zauberlehrling, 39 295-298; texts, Persian religion according to, 52 186-189
Mythology: Circe, her prototype is the Ištar of the Gilgameš Epic, 38 332; Marsyas myth, paralleled in Sumerian myth of Lugalbanda and Zû, 40 315; Persius, birth of paralleled in Aelian's account of the birth of Gilgameš, 40 311-312; Priapus, three-legged parallels to in Iran and India, 40 333; myths of rejuvenation, 26 4, 7
Religion: oracle-caves patterned after Semitic models, 38 139
Green Sea, Chinese name of Erythraean Sea, derived from Arabs, 33 355; see also Prasodes
Gregorius Thaumaturgus (210-270), his christology, 32 271, 310, 338; Syriac version of his Λόγος κεφαλαιώδης περὶ ψυχῆς πρὸς Τατιανόν, 35 297-317
Gregory of Nazianza, his christology followed by Bar-Šûšan, 32 270, 307-309; life and teachings of, 341-342
Gṛhaśānti (Grih Shunti) ceremony, performed during Śrāddha ceremony, 22 229
Grierson on the Hindu (gaṇḍā) method of counting, 24 391 f.; on the modern Indian conception of the period of pregnancy, 24 392
Griffith's translation of prānas, 22 255 f.
Gruppe's view of the origin of religion, 25 333
Gud, Sumerian deity, = planet Mercury, 41 45 n. 16
Gudea of Lagaš, rule of, 50 155; texts of dealing with the building of the ziggurat E-PA at Lagaš, 43 92; topography of his texts, 43 41-48
Guhyakas, Kubera as the lord of the, 33 57 f., 68, functions and characteristics of, 61, 65 f.
Guidi, Ignazio, life and bibliography of, 55 458-463
Guilds, organized in Babylonia and Assyria; officially recognized by the government; duties of president; guilds had separate town quarters in Assyria, 60 68-72
Gujarat, ornamentation and paintings in texts, 57 249; Sanskrit of Jains, 46 75 f.
Gujarātī, Old, text of the Kālaka story, with translation, grammatical and lexical notes, 58 5-29
Gukanshō, 愚管抄, value of, as source for study of the Kamakura period, 59 41
Gul ū-Nōrūz of Ḫanīkī, MS of in the Columbia University Library, 23 102-108; possibly modeled on the Nōrūz ū-Gul of Ḫwāju Kirmānī, 102; résumé of plot, 104-108
Gun-powder, introduced into Japan about 1543, 30 271
Gunsho Ruijū, 群書類從, source materials for a study of the Kamakura period contained in, 59 40, 41, 43, 45, 47, 50, 52
Gupta art, chronology, 46 255; dependence on canon, 49 69 f.; sculpture, interpretation, 54 220 f.
Guriel, Joseph, works of, 22 90-91
Guru, symbolic representation of the, 53 307
Guti, Gutians, Empire in Mesopotamia in middle of 3rd millennium B.C., 48 91; not a fair, Indo-European people, 50 338

al-Ġuzūli, see Maṭāli' al-Budūr
Gyokuyō, 玉葉, value of, as source for study of the Kamakura period, 59 42
Gypsey dialect in Brazil, 50 139-143, a modification of Rumanian Gypsey, 139, specimens and commentary, 140-143; of Denmark, 45 97-105; Sigjner and Tatere, 97; etymologies, 98-104; l-element of 3 p. pres. of verbs, 104; probable home of, 104 f.; in New Jersey, 28 271-308
Gypsies, probable origin of, 45 104 f.; of Persia and Lower Iraq, originally came from India, 44 130-133
G'yu brag pa, appears on a Tibetan temple painting as one of the spiritual ancestors of the Dalai Lama, 52 343
al-Ḥabbārīyah, ibn-, good edition of his version of Kalīlah wa-Dimnah by Ni'mat Allāh al-Asmar, 42 394
ibn-Ḥabīb, life and works of, 58 541-542
Ḫabîru, mercenary soldiers of mixed origin, 45 6; a mercenary people (= SA-GAZ); Kassite and Hurrian names among; are the Hebrews, 48 183-184
Hadad, worship of carried to South Arabia by the Amorites, 45 135
al-Ḥaḍra, local saint at Ascalon, reflection of Derketo, 60 300
Hadramawt, missionary-traders from in Indian Archipelago, 33 315
Hadrian, visited Gerasa in A.D. 129-130, 59 362, route of his visit to Palestine and Syria in A.D. 129-130, 364-365, decides to rebuild Jerusalem as Aelia Capitolina in 130, 363; temple of standing in Caesarea (Palestine) in A.D. 538, 36 342
Ḥāfiẓ, influence on German poet Platen, 21 40-1
Hager, Joseph, exposer of Kitāb Dīwān Miṣr, 33 310
Haggai, Book of, poems in, 36 441
Hai-hsi, 海西, Marquis of, see Li Kuang-li
Hail, Rev. Alexander D., death of, in Japan, June 1923, 44 146
Hai-nan, direction of coast of, opposite Tong-King, led to report that coast swung south and west until it joined Africa, 37 247-249
Hair, sacrifice of in modern Palestine, 46 341-342
Hairy Anchorite, oriental affinities with the medieval legend of, 48 355
Hai-wai-i-wu-chi, formerly ascribed to Chang Ch'ien, 37 92
ibn-Ḥajar, account of al-Nu'mān family of Fāṭimid qāḍis from, text and trans., 27 238-296
Hajj, accepted by Muslims of Indonesia, 33 324 ff.
al-Ḥākim, Fatimid Caliph, deification of based on idea of infallible Imām, 47 366
Hākmā, see Ḥikmᵉtā
Ḣalayan dialect of Bisayan, 26 121-123
Halberds, in Ta-yüan, in early Han, 37 95
Ḫaldia, campaigns of Shalmaneser III against, 41 347-350, 358-360, 368, 371, 378-379; not name of country or people, but of a deity only, 55 297-302
ibn-Ḫaldūn, MSS of his works, 46 171-176
Hamburgisches Kolanialinstitut, founded 1908 for study of modern oriental and African languages, 39 193-194
Ḫamir Language, see Hamitic
Ḣamitic Languages, parallels to Semitic, 35 214 ff.; relationship to Semitic, 45 4-5; noun: t-, -t as fem. affix paralleled in Sem., 56 44-45, -t- as accus. exponent found also in Sem., 42-43; verb: sibilant prefixed to caus. stem paralleled in Sem., 56 26
Hammīramadamardana of Jayasiṁhasūri, Māgadhī in the, 44 102 f.
Hammurabi Code, curse in, 34 291; promulgated in Hammurabi's second year, 27 128, existing copy set up in Babylon, not Sippar 128, 134; see also Law, Babylonian
haṃsa, bird-like soul, inhabits the house representing the "seat of the six senses", see House
Haṃsa, as class of Yogins, 22 348
Haṃsa Upaniṣad, literary stratum, 23 67
Ḫana, kingdom flourishing ca. 2000 B.C. near the mouth of the Ḫābūr, 44 191, 193
Ḥanafites, chiefly found in Turkey, India, Russia and Central Asia; numbered about 93,000,000 in 1924, 44 32
Ḥanbalites, chiefly found in central and eastern Arabia; numbered about 2,000,000 in 1924, 44 32; hold excessive regard for Mu'āwiyah and the Umayyads, 54 6-7, successors of Ahl (Aṣḥāb) al-Ḥadīṯ, 11-12, 23, their credo, 18-19
Han Ch'êng Ti, strong Confucian influence in the reign of, 58 446
Han Ching Ti, not so favorable to Confucianism as Wen Ti, 58 437
Hanchow, Ssu-ch'uan, review of Graham's report on excavation at, 56 98-99
Han-chung, 漢中, birth place of Chang Ch'ien, 37 93
Han Dynasty, Canals and Rivers under Han Wu Ti, transportation and irrigation, 55 303-306; Conjunction of the 5 planets in May 205 B.C., 55 310-311, date when "the Han dynasty triumphed", 312; constitutional development of, 40 170-193, feudal system of Chou combined with centralized government of Ts'in during Han forming basis of all later government organization, 170-189, outline of feudal organization, in Chou period, 170-175, centralization under Ts'in, 175-177, Han Kao Tsu's plan of reconstruction, 177-182, feudal kingdoms in Han and their growth in power, 182-184, Rebellion of the Seven Kingdoms, 184-185; enlargement of the royal domain and organization of the central government 185-189, local administration, 189-193, tax system, 192; custom of collecting heavenly dew, 55 185-186, 189, description of Han toilet-box from Lo-Lang, 188, form and decoration of Han mirrors, 185-189; custom of wearing hair in a queue adopted fr. the Hsiung-nu, 56 377; law against practice of ku magic, 55 6, n.13, 9, see also Shou-wen; elephants fr. Ssu-ch'uan sent as tribute to the Court at Ch'ang-an, 41 303-304; origin of Japanese festivals of Tsuina and Setsubun found in China in Han period, 55 446, n.20, n.25; menagerie at Ch'ang-an, 41 303-304; occupations of the Wealthy, see also abstract, N.L. Swann; see also Art, Chinese; Biography, Empress Têng; China, Chinese, History; Confucius, Confucianism; Divination; Han Kao-tsu; Jadestone; Lo-Lang; Mu-yang-ch'eng; Sacrifices; Silk; Tombs; Wang Hsü
Han-hsi-yü-t'u-k'ao, see Passages
Han Hsüan Ti, Confucian education of, 58 443, choice of Confucians for gov. posts, 443, called Council on the Classics, 444, enlarged Imperial University, 444, attitude towards Confucian principles, 444, 446, instruction of his son, later Emp. Yüan, 445
Han-hsüeh, 汗血, "sweating blood", said of the superior horses of Ta-yüan, 37 95, 103, 140
Han-hué, see Han-hsüeh
Ḥanīki, Mīrzā Dōlat Riḍā' Beg, see Gul ū-Nōrūz
Han Kao-tsu, attitude of, towards Confucianism, 57 172-180; early prejudice against Confucians, 175-177; acted upon Confucian principles in his invasion of Ch'in, 172-173, initiated procedure which developed into the Chinese civil service system, 175, gradual turning towards Confucianism, 176-180, early studies and influence of Confucian scholars upon, 176-179, influence of his brother Liu Chiao, of Chang Liang, of Li Yi-chi, 176-177, capture of P'eng-ch'eng, 178, court ceremonial arranged by Shu-sun T'ung, 178-179; Lu Chia's advice and book, the Hsin-yü, 179, tradition of his sacrifice of a suovetaurilia to Confucius, 179, yielding to Confucian officials in appointing his successor, 179-180; began establishment of Confucianism as the official doctrine of the gov., 58 435-436; organization of his government, 40 177-183; question of his t'ai-lao sacrifice to Confucius, 55 331-333
Han-mi, 扜罙, small country to the east of Ta-yüan, 37 95, assistant envoys sent to, fr. China, 102, sends tribute to Han Wu Ti, 107
Han Shu, 625 authors listed in the, 51 268; follows model of Ssu-ma Ch'ien's Shih-chi; arrangement of biographical material and discussion of social and economic phases of the times, compared with cor. material in the Shih-chi, 54 186-192; tr. of biography of Empress Têng fr. Hou Han Shu, 51 138-159. see also Ch'ien Han-shu; Passages
Han-si-yü-t'u-k'au, see Han-hsi-yü-t'u-k'ao

Han T'an, 韓菼, his love of tobacco, 58 654
Han wei ts'ung shu, 漢魏叢書, a collection of rare writings of Han and Wei periods, 51 45
Han Wên Ti, strongly influenced by Confucianism but tried to be impartial, 58 436-437, extended the examination system and encouraged advice fr. candidates, 437; rewards Han Kao-tsu's followers, 57 174-175, 180; care of widows, widowers, orphans, the poor and old, 40 191
Han Wu Ti, Emperor of China, 140-87 B.C., 37 135-136, sends Chang Ch'ien to Yüeh-chih to win them as allies against the Hsiung-nu, 93-94, attempts to open routes to the Far West, 98-99, Chang Ch'ien in disfavor with, 99-100, plans alliance with the Wu-sun, to further procurement of horses, 100-101, 103, his desire to procure good horses, first fr. Wu-sun, then fr. Ta-yüan, led to development of the caravan route through Central Asia, 103-104, pleased to receive embassies fr. Parthia, 107, liked to entertain foreigners, 107, planted vineyards and lucerne fields, 108, his fondness for the 'superior horses' of Erh-shih leads to campaign against Ta-yuan, 109-110, angry at failure, forbids remants of Chinese army to reenter China, 111, sends second army which suffers great losses but gets the horses, 111, 113, calls upon Wu-sun to aid, 114, hostages fr. small countries presented to, 114, rewards officers and army, 115, date of death, 136; feudal states in his time not powerful, 40 185-186; note on Taoism of, 53 231; promotion of scholars under, 57 180; see also Confucius, Confucianism, victory of Confucianism in Former Han
Han Yü, did not consider Hsüntze unorthodox, 50 235; story of banishing the crocodile, 49 143-144 n.4
Han Yüan Ti, complete victory of Confucianism in the reign of, 58 445-446
Hao, 浩, Marquis of, see Wang K'uei
Hapi, see Amset
Harappa culture, beads and bead making of the, 57 1-15; chronology, 59 Sup. 35 f., script, 59 Sup. 37-39, relations with other cultures, 59 Sup. 40-42; "Harappa cemetery," 59 35; see also Indus Valley Culture
Harayan dialect of Bisayan, 26 121-136
Hare, in the moon, denied by Wang Ch'ung, 55 186
Harihara, his Bhartṛharinirveda translated, 25 200-225
Ḥarrān, campaign against in 610 B.C. described in Nabopolassar Chronicle confirmed by letter of Nebuchadrezzar, 46 362; last capital of Assyria, captured by Nabopolassar and the Medes in 610 B.C., 44 127; votive text of Ashurbanipal from temple of Ningal in, 38 167-175; Ḥarrānians use unmixed wine in offering, 32 316-317; see also Calendar
Harṣa's dramas, time analysis of 21 88-108; Priyadarśikā, metres of, 43 171
Harsha, Sonpat copper seal of, possible connection with passage of Bāṇa's Harṣacarita, 50 131
Harṣacarita of Bāṇa, on a passage in the, 50 129-131
Harunori, Uesugi (Yozan), 1751-1822, example of an exemplary lord, sketch of his life, 31 183
Harvard, see Textbooks: Hu Shih
Harvard Journal of Asiatic Studies, see Book Reviews, Elisséeff
Harvest gods of the Land Dyaks of Borneo, 26 165-175
Harvest taboo among the Kayans, 25 244 f.
Hasada sept of the Hos, origin of the, 50 230
Hashiguchi Goyo, titles of his 13 wood-block prints, 57 246
Ḥašwīyah (Muslim sect), identical with the Nābitah, 54 4 n. 5, Firaq al-Šī'ah of al-Nawbaḫti is the most valuable source for them, 5, their views on the Imāmate orthodox, 7-8, share Ḥanbalite attitude toward the Battle of Ṣiffīn and the Battle of the Camel, 11, theology agrees with that of the Ḥanbalites, including literal interpretation of the Koran, 15, 19-20, name applied also to Aṣḥāb al-Ḥadīt, 24, name used as term of insult, 26
Hatalla, see Mahatara
Hatra, see Ninmarada
Ḫatti, dominated by Mari, 41 256; Shalmaneser III's campaigns against, 41 351-353
Haug's translation of prāṇas, 22 255 f.; 283
Haupt, Paul, life and works, 47 1-2
Hausleutner, P.W.G., see Geschichte der Araber in Sicilien
Havret, Father Henri, on the tr. of san i fen shen in the Nestorian inscription, 58 389
Hawk, originally totem of a number of Egyptian tribes worshipping various spirits, 53 170
Hawking, see Falconry
Ḥawqal, ibn-, see Kitāb al-Masālik wa-'l-Mamālik
Ḥawrôn, Canaanite god, 57 402
Ḥaydarābād, noted steel industry of, 35 233
ibn-Ḥazm, Asín's Spanish translation of his Character and Conduct is based on a more complete Cairo edition than the edition of Adham; thesis is that the ultimate goal of all human action is the avoidance of pain, 43 173; see also Kitāb al-Milal wa-'l-Niḥal
Hbrom ston, pupil of Atīśa, appears on a Tibetan temple painting as one of the spiritual ancestors of the Dalai Lama, 52 342
Head-hunting among the Kayans and Sea Dyaks, 25 234, religious aspects of, 25 234-240
Heaven, Taoist, 53 219 n.8, palaces below, 233, 42nd Heaven, 234 and n.97; see also Paradise
Heavens, Babylonian conceptions of, 22 138-144; 23 opp. p. 388; measurement of by the eight ch'ih piao, see Chou pi suan ching
Heaven's Mandate, Confucian doctrine of leading a military force to chastise a wicked ruler, employed by Han Kao-tsu, 57 177-178; employed by Han Kao-tsu, 58 436
Hebrew, Hebrews, Literature in Library of Congress, Washington, 36 355-359; printing in U.S.A., 41 225-229; see also Amulets; Bowls (incantation); Calendar; Festivals; Inscriptions; Israelites; Manuscripts; Marriage; Medicine; Music; Seals; Semites, Home of; Weights
History: accession of Solomon established hereditary kingship; brought centralization of government and concentration of wealth, 57 238-239; Exodus took place in 1580 B.C.; Hebrews were a part of, but not identical with, the Hyksos, 44 160; identified with the Ḫabîru, 48 183-185; Levites must have been in Egypt, 54 301-302; personal names related to Arabic and Amorite, 45 5; people, composition of, 45 6; Temple, Second, first serious work on foundations of begun at end of reign of Cambyses, 46 358-359
Language: a' > e' in northern dialects, 57 156; accent and vocalism: early Hebrew main stress followed by two open syllables gives in Masoretic Hebrew a stressed final vowel with the original stress appearing as a secondary stress, 59 440, short vowels, behavior of with regard to stress, 442, 445, no pre-tone lengthening, 443-444, shewa existing before spirantization began, 446-447, chronology of changes of short vowels under accent shift, 446-453, phonetic position at time of Tell al-'Amārnah letters, 450-451, final short vowels lost ca. 1350-1200, 451, spirantization of stops occurred after orthographic pattern had been well established, 451-453, syncope under influence of accent, 456-457, suffixes of 2nd pl. masc. and fem. stressed in primitive Semitic, 441, early Heb. accent rested on syllable subject to so-called pre-tone lengthening, 443-444, early Heb. accent shift took place before rearrangement of vocalic quantities, 448, 454, chronology of accent shifts, 454-458, early Heb. accent moves in middle Heb. one unit toward the end of the word, 455; accentuation: Metheg, a nota bene sign, 32 78-102, relation to daghesh, 96-97, relation to musical accent, 97-98, Silluq, derived from metheg, 98, Paseq, derived from metheg, 98-100, Raphe, derived from metheg, 100; accusative, uses of, 59 400-401; accusative not used to express point of time, but duration only, 60 224-225, not used with locative significance, 224-228, locative hê is actually terminative, 228-229, terminative hê in Hebrew and Ugaritic, 229-233; adverbial accusative, expressed by subordinate clause without connecting waw, 46 343; analogy in, 26 117-119; characteristic features developed before 2nd millennium B.C., 47 363; co-ordinate adverbial clause, use of, 49 156-159; Daghesh, relation to

metheg, 32 96-97, Ḥaṭef, use of after metheg, 95-96; Fem. suff. *-atu restored under influence of -âtu, 59 457-458; grammars written by Mexican Marrano and Mexican Jew in 1676 and 1873, 52 310; î in the hif'il perf. is derived from the inf. haqṭîl, 44 167; indefinite pronominal ideas, how expressed, 34 115-228; intransitive verb forms in, 24 145-204; lâken, notes on uses of, 30 343-346; letter yôd, its uses with al-Fāsi, 58 167-172; lexicography and syntax influenced by Judah ibn-Tibbon working on Arab models, 46 353-354; m-, nominal prefix, > n- in some proper names, 43 50-51; multiplicative numerals, 35 381-382; mixed constructions, 35 382-385; oration in delivered at Yale by President Stiles in 1781, 51 359; orthography, relation to phonetic development, 59 451-453; passive construction in, 22 45-54; Pi'lel formed from Pi'el of geminated roots, 27 303-316; qᵊ ṭolɛt-type nouns, plural of, 54 425-428; šɛ, relative pronoun, history of its use, 46 163-164; Shewa medium nearly always comes from a full vowel which had quiesced before the introduction of the Tiberian vocalization, 53 355-356; spirantization of stops, 22 13-14; -û, old plural noun ending, 37 165-167; verbs derived from original šaf'el forms, 47 356-357; vocalic similarities to modern Palestinian dialect, 48 361; vowel names, 22 13-17; yaqátalu- type present-future tense, traces of, 60 419; see also Semitic Languages
Poetry: Ps. 120-134, metrical form of, 27 108-122; Strophic structure in Amos, 59 421; too little known about it to be of use in textual criticism, 45 177
Religion: Atonement, Day of, background of Pharisee-Sadducee dispute over manner of high priest's entering the Holy of Holies goes back to time of Zechariah, 47 359; bones of sacrificed animal not broken because of belief in possibility of resurrection, 36 146-153, blood, relation of to soul, 151-153; Cherubim not of Babylonian origin, 25 279-286, Ark of the Covenant had no cherubim, 286; Chosen People idea, why respected by others, 49 366; conservatism in, 21 23-39; Emperor-worship killed by historical events and the development of monotheism, 42 398; "fear" and "love" of Yahweh are technical expressions for "worship", 48 360; has its roots in Arabia, 48 83; high-places inherited from Canaanites, criteria for recognizing, 38 331; Jacob and Israel originally Israelite deities, 46 354; kᵊbôd Yahwɛh paralleled by the Iranian hvareno, 57 166-167; Mɛlɛk (Molech, Moloch) cult introduced by Manasseh and did not revive after its extirpation by Josiah, 49 354-355; monotheism of Moses not dependent on that of Ikhnaton, 44 160; monotheism of Moses not inspired from Egypt, 52 198-199; Moses not mentioned in historical records, 53 194-196, 197-199, possibly originally a deity, 198; mourning, tearing of garments in, 21 23-39; Pharisee-Sadducee controversy over manner of presenting incense in Holy of Holies on Day of Atonement, 47 358-359; problems connected with the origin of, 53 194-199; prophecy, pre-Exilic, scheme of weal following woe found in, 46 352; prophetic movement influenced by Kenites, 38 135-136; sacrificial animals in, 33 363 ff.; Sabbath and festivals in pre-Exilic and Exilic times, 37 209-223; scapegoat sent out to Azazel; Babylonian analogies to, 37 222; slaughtering, method of, produces better meat, 51 366-367, 52 310; solar cult at Jerusalem, 57 256; sun worshipped at Golden Gate in Jerusalem, 42 398; syncretism inaugurated under rule of David, 38 137; Tammuz, 'Aštart and Šɛmɛš, worship of, 46 156-157, 160-164; Tent of Meeting, place where Yahweh met Moses and Israel to reveal his will; patterned after sacred cave on mountain top; originally had no connection with Ark of the Covenant, 38 131-139; wine, place of in ritual, 33 180-192; Yahweh, anthropomorphism of in Little Covenant, 38 129-132; Yahweh not of Kenite origin, 54 301-302, not found in cuneiform literature earlier than 8th cent. B.C., 301; Yahweh represented by image in ark and by bull images of Bethel, 47 358; see also Sabbath; Sacrifice
Texts: amulets, early, from Irbid, 31 272-281; amulet, with translation, 36 160-167
Hebron, ancient solar cult at, 45 356
Hecataeus of Abdera, many historically genuine quotations from him in Josephus and Pseudo-Aristeas, 56 243-244
Hedgehogs, used to combat the Black Magic ku, 55 14, 19, 20, 27
Hell, shown to Disciples by Christ in apocryphal Ethiopic Ar-de'et, 25 44-47; belief in eternity of an Islamic article of faith, 29 73-75
Hellenistic background of Arab folklore, 60 283-295
Hellenistic Greek sigillata signatures, 58 38-47
Helmet of Eannatum, furnished with visor, 38 68-69
Hemādri's account of Sāvitrī story and rite in Caturvargacintāmaṇi, 21 53, 57, 60, 62 f.
Hemacandra's Ayogavyavachedikā and Anyayogavyavachedikā, 49 68; Mahāvīracaritra, historical references in, 45 301-310; Rauhiṇeya story in the Mahāvīracaritra of, 44 1-10; rules for Māgadhī and other Prākrit dialects, 44 82-105; Śrīmahāvīrasvāmistotram, 49 67 f., Vītarāgastotra, 49 68
Heng Shan, 衡山, Hunan, one of the 5 sacred mountains of Taoism, 49 145, 146 n.2
Henke, Dr. F.G., Translation of Wang Yang Ming by, 38 101
Henotheism, found in oldest Egyptian texts, 39 148
Henry the Navigator, Prince, religious element paramount in his explorations, 38 71-72
Hepatoscopy, in Borneo, 26 137-138; Kassite text with translation, from reign of Burnaburiaš II, 38 77-96; originally consisted of gazing at the smooth and shiny surface of the liver, 42 373
Babylonian: importance of its rôle first recognized by Morris Jastrow Jr., 41 330, 335; text, translation and commentary on, 27 91-103
Hepburn System, of Romanization of Japanese, see Japanese, Romanization
Herakles, worship of in Tyre and Thasos, 22 115-117
Hermes, cock sacred to, 33 381
Herod, of Josephus, Jewish War, I, 203-673, a reproduction of the Herod in Nicholas's Universal History, 58 540-541
Herodotus on Persian religion, 52 186 f.
Herringbone pattern in bricklaying, see Mesopotamian Archeology
Hershey, Amos S., contribution to Chinese studies, 38 103
Hertel's edition of Tantrākhyāyika, book ii, 38 274-293.
Hesychius, Persian words in the glosses of, 41 236 f.
Hewitt, J.F., his views on Mahābhārata chronology, 24 8 f.
Hexapla of Origen, second column is work of a Jew, not a Greek, 59 71-80
Hexaplaric elements in the first nine chapters of the Old Latin text of Joshua, 33 254-258
Ḥibbûr Yāpē mē-ha-Yᵊšû'ā, of Nissim b. Jacob, important for study of Judaeo-Muslim cultural history, 45 353
al-Ḫiḍr, legend of, parallel to Koranic version found in ibn-Šāhīn's Kitāb al-Faraj, 51 356; impersonated by jinn in the Lebanons, according to ibn-Taymīyah, 56 6, 15-16; popular Arab saint, his personality a mixture of important pagan Semitic and Graeco-Roman deities, 60 288-290
Hieroglyphic and Sanskrit languages, relationship of, 43 170
Ḥijāz, the, postage stamps of, 37 87-88
Ḥikmᵊtā, Aramaean personification of wisdom, Babylonian Siduri is partial prototype of, 38 64
Hiligayna dialect of Bisayan, 25 162-169
Hiliguayna (Hiligueyna, Hiliguoyna) dialect of Bisayan, 26 121-136
Hillebrandt's views on Indra's sphere of activity, 36 248 f., 267
Hilprecht-Peters Controversy, 26 145-164; Hilprecht's fragment of the Deluge Story, criticism of his claims for, 31 30-48; libraries not proved to have existed in Babylonian temples, 27 147-182; Luštamar letter not written in or sent to Nippur, 29 220-223
Himalayan languages, see Languages, Sino-Tibetan
Himavat, conception of, in the Mahābhārata, 30 364 f.
Himyarites, overthrow Sabaeans and tax trade of Ptolemies, 35 34

Hinckley, Frank E., contribution to Chinese historical studies, 38 103

Hindiisms in Sanskrit, 38 206 f.; 40 84-89, Sanskrit ādeśa 'salutation', 84-87, Sanskrit lāti, 87-89

Hindu, asceticism, economic aspects of, 59 411; astronomy, the Āryabhaṭīya of Āryabhaṭa, 51 51 f.; conceptions of the functions of breath, 22 249-308; calendar, amāvāsyā in the, 59 506-508; date of Divālī, 59 506-508; chronology, the conversion of Vikrama Saṃvat dates, 58 668-669; custom of dying to redress a grievance, 21 146-159: dharṇa, traga, and takāzā, 21 157 f.; dietary restrictions, as sacrifice, 50 225; eponymous observances, 50 224; grammarians, a procedure in studying the, 59 404 f.; proverb 'earth hath ears', parallels to, 28 88-95; popular belief, a Greek parallel to a, 26 188-190; political theories, 43 350; physiology, in the Śāradā-tilaka Tantra, 23 71; people, Vatsa, Vaccha, Vaṃsa, on the names of an ancient, 43 170; numerals, source of, 50 174; mysticism, 48 87 f.; method of counting, 24 391 f.; metres, the epic triṣṭubh and its hypermetric varieties, 59 159-174; medicine, the Caesarean Section in ancient, 59 18-20; tree-marriage, 22 228, 328; woman's achievements, 36 440

Art: the Nāgas in, 49 186-190; trace of 'endlessness' in, 55 417 f.

Cosmography: Śākadvīpa and Śvetadvīpa, 39 209-242; location of Śākadvīpa, 40 356-358; world creation and dissolution, Mahābhārata, Sāṃkhya, and Yoga stories compared, 45 51-67

Drama: portrait painting as a device, 39 144, 299-302; time-scheme of Cārudatta and Mṛcchakaṭikā compared, 42 70

Elephant-science: 50 324; elephant-lore, 52 89 f.; elephants as rain-bringers, 52 89

Epic literature: the oath in, 52 316-337, curse and oath, 316 f., statement of truth in the oath, 317-328, converted into ordeal, 320 f., attestation of the oath, 323-328, by Fire, 323 f., by Water, 324-326, by Earth, 326 f., by gods, 327 f., things sworn by, 328-336, truth and merit, 328-331, touching weapon, head, or feet, or laying hands on one's life, 332-335

Fiction: false ascetics and nuns in 44 202-242, Kāpālikas and their practices, 202-205, Buddhist and Jainist nuns, 204 f., classes of false ascetics, 205, mock descriptions of ascetic get-up, 206-212, ascetics practising atrocities ex professo, 212-218, wicked ascetics smitten by love, 218-221, greedy, gluttonous, or otherwise vicious ascetics, 222-228, rogues shamming asceticism, 228-232, animals shamming asceticism, 232-236, wicked female ascetics, 236-242; bluff in, 38 331; dohada motif, or the craving of pregnant women, 40 1-24; Evil-wit, No-wit, and Honest-wit, 40 271-275; choosing a king by divine will, 33 158-166; life-index motif in, 39 142; the Life-index tree, 55 68; paradox of escaping one's fate, 39 143 f.; recurring psychic motifs in, and the laugh and cry motif, 36 54-89; change of sex as a, 47 3-24, means, 4 f., enchanted water, 6-12, curse or blessing, 12-14, exchange with a Yakṣa, 14-16, magic objects and charms, 16-19, power of righteousness or wickedness, 19-21, origin of notion of sex change, 22-24

Iconography: the Buddha image, 57 336-343; Gaṇeśa in, 57 428 f.; Piṅgala in, 57 328; Sūrya in, 57 327-329

Law: attitude toward suicide, 21 147 f.; meat-eating and non-injury in, 27 455-464; exacting payment by suicide, 21 146 f.; priestly penance and legal penalty, 44 243-257, demarcation between the two systems, 243-247, criminal law a combination of the two, 247 f., how amalgamated, 248-251, assembly of priests, 249 f., relative age of rules of kings and priests, 251 f., the king's chaplain, 253 f., sin and crime, 255-257

Legends: Caesarean section and preternatural birth, 59 20; fountain of youth, 26 36 f., 44-67; the Nāgas in, 49 186-190

Mathematics: algebra, 51 52; the Āryabhaṭīya of Āryabhaṭa, 51 51 f.; numbers and numerical categories of the Mahābhārata, 23 109-155; $\pi = 3.1416$, 51 52; place system, 51 51 f.

Ritual: Caesarean Section in, 59 17 f.; the rite of dantadhāvana in Smṛti literature, 52 163-167, list of texts and passages consulted, 52 167; expiation of errors, 34 233-266; the preta-concept in, 59 412; sun-kiss, breath, smell, and touch in, 60 46-67

Sculpture: identification of Gayā reliefs, 57 191 f.; representations of birth through the side, 59 20 f.

Hindu-Javanese caṇḍi, the meaning of the, 51 1-15

Hinduism, twentieth century tendencies in, 51 369 f.; and Brahmanism, the main current of, 46 199-201

Hippiatry, see Medicine

Hiraṇyagarbha, Kapila as, 22 386 f.

Hirth, Friedrich, (1845-1927), In Memoriam, 47 343; contribution of to Chinese studies in America, 38 104, 102; first to use term "model-emperor lore", 56 51; "Festschrift" published in honor of his 75th Birthday, 40 360

Historiae adversum paganos, see Orosius

Historians, Chinese, of the left and right, 51 155, the Court Historian, 156

Histories, Local, of China, see Gazetteers

History, Chinese, see Chronology of Ancient China; Books: Wei Shu

History of the Former Han Dynasty, see Ch'ien Han-shu

History of Vernacular Literature, see Hu Shih

Hīt, first reference to petroleum springs at found in annals of Tukulti-Ninurta II, 38 214

Hittites, Hittite, as Turanians struggle with early Iranians, 35 295; Indo-European name of, 49 360; civilization, impact on the Occident of, 50 324; wars with Shalmaneser III, 41 352 ff.; see also Art and Architecture; Ḫatti; Seals; Weights

Language: where spoken, 43 68; ḫ, phonetic value of, 48 351; ḫ had secondary value of Sem. ǵ, 57 76; IE *-eγ- > Hitt. -eḫ-, 57 77; ḫ and Saussure's doctrine of the long vowels, 59 175-199; indirect questions in, 59 405 f.; Indo-European element in, 39 257-258; Indo-Europeanicity, historical and cultural background of, 49 360; primitive Indo-European traits in, 49 361; as sister language of Indo-European, 54 207; language, 41 195-209, Hrozný's theory of Indo-European origin, a critical review of the evidence; morphology, 201-209; lexicography, 57 109-111; native name for, 43 68; p corresponds to Indo-European bh, 50 125-128; neuter singular pronouns referring to plural antecedents, 49 351; possible non-Indo-European elements, 41 210-224, application of term, 210 f., pronouns, 212-222, case-endings, 217-220, gender, 221 f., verbal endings, 223 f., conclusions, 224; present stem formations, 47 365; pronouns and morphology, notes on, 47 174-184, ta = IE *to-, 174-177; ašta = Sanskrit tatas, 177-181, ablative, 181-184; -smas 'vos, vobis, eos, eis' and -smes 'vester, eorum,' 53 392; development of stops in, 52 1-12, writing of doubled consonants for original voiceless, single for voiced; phonetic interpretation, 12; suffixal doublets with initial alternation -u̯-/-m-, 47 365; vowel quantity, 48 360

Laws: an obscure passage in (KBo VI., obv. I, line 11 f.), 53 358 f.

Religion: ceremonies before war, 43 69 f.; omina, 43 71 f.

Script: borrowed from the Akkadian via the Amorites, 45 37; cuneiform, source of, 54 208; diagonal wedge not a "Glossenkeil", 58 533; double writing of certain stops, 54 208

Texts: land deed from Tarsus, 59 1-5; on the duties of priests and temple servants, with translation and commentary, 54 363-406; Hittite and Luwian ritual of Zarpiya of Kezzuwatna, text, translation and commentary, 58 334-353

Hiu-chu, see Hsiu-t'u

Hiung-nu, see Hsiung-nu

Hiung-nu River, see Hsiung-nu River

Hjam dpal grags, or Hjam dbyaṅs grags pa, a king whose portrait appears on a Tibetan temple painting of a Pañchen Lama, 52 347

Ḫnsw, the moon, represented as royal placenta, 40 333-335

Ho, Japanese village administrative unit of 5 families, copied from the Chinese 7th cent. system, 30 267, resuscitated in Tokugawa period, functions of, 267-268, 275; 保, (Chinese, pao), group of 5 families, forming the basic unit of Japanese

village administration in the 7th cent. and revived in the Tokugawa period; details of the working of, 31 194-197, more consanguinous in its nature than its Chinese model, 195-197; see also Pao

Ho River, "The Ho", see Yellow River

Hoang Ho, Pai Ho Museum, Tientsin, see Licent, Father Émile

Hocart, his theory of divine kingship compared to that of the Chinese, 56 67-70

Ho Ch'ü-ping, 霍去病, his campaign, and defeat of the Hsiung-nu in 121 B.C., 37 100, 135, death and tomb of, 141

Hōdō, 法道, Indian founder of Gion Jinsha, Kyoto, middle 7th cent., 54 283

Hoen-sié, see Hun-hsieh

Hoffman collection, archaic Sumerian text in, 23 19-20, text and translation of archaic Sumerian text in, 21-28

Ho-hsi, 河西, in modern Kansu, Hsiung-nu driven out from, 37 100

Hōjōki, 方丈記, value of, as source for study of Kamakura period, 59 45

Hoko matsuri, 鉾祭, main celebration of the Gion matsuri, on the 17th, see Gion matsuri

Ho K'ü-ping, see Ho Ch'ü-ping

Holly Grove, Kyoto, legend of, 55 449-450, the metamorphosis of its trees, 450

Holly Magic, in Japan; magic powers of holly mentioned in the Kojiki, 55 444, story of the holly-wood spear of Prince Yamatotake, 444-445, holly wood used for arrow points, 445, magic of the holly spear eight fathoms long, 445, ancient ceremony of driving out evil spirits with staves of holly, 445-446, the setsubun festival, 446-448, holly a favorite motive in art, 448-449, holly used as a family crest or badge, 449, legend of the Holly Grove, 449-450, efficacy of Holly against small-pox, 449-450

Hollow Mulberry, mythological term, 53 243 and n.152

Holt (Wales), Neo-Punic inscription from, 60 578-579

Holy Fire Ceremony, at Church of the Holy Sepulchre, connected with ancient Semitic New Year's ceremony, 39 98; Muslim polemic against, 41 453-454

Honke, Legal Guardian of Manors in the Japanese shōen system, 57 82-83

Honnami, family in Tokyo famous for its connoisseurship of swords, 26 335, 336-337

Hopkins, Edward Washburn, life and works, 52 311-315, bibliography of books and important articles, 314 f.

Hor region of Tibet, population, artifacts and animal style, 53 90 f.

Hornbeck, Prof. Stanley K., contributions to Chinese studies, 38 102

Horses, collected by Assyrians as tribute from N Mesopotamia and Syria, 38 219, 220, 238, 239; brought by Indo-Europeans in their invasion of Asia Minor in first half of second millennium B.C., 39 257-258; obtained by Solomon from Egypt, 26 104; see also Stirrup

China: first mention of riding 60 582; date of introduction of cavalry, and equipment, 52 240 and n.25; gifts of chariots and horses four abreast, 51 145, Empress reduced the number of horses as an economy, 154; time of Han Wu Ti; in Ta-yüan, 37 97, sent as gift to China fr. the Wu-sun, 102, 103, importation of, from the west, led to regular caravan trade, 103, a thousand sent as a marriage gift by the Wu-sun, 106, rich men in Wu-sun own four or five thousand, 107, superior horses kept at city of Erh-shih, 109, horse-breakers accompanied army against Ta-yüan, 112, thirty thousand, in army against Ta-yüan, 111, two breeds of, 'superior' and 'inferior', taken fr. capital of Ta-yüan, 113, 'heavenly horses' and 'blood-sweating' horses, 103; of T'ang T'ai Tsung, sculptures of "Autumn Dew" and "Curly" in the University Museum, Philadelphia, are originals, 55 420-421, Pls. I, II, Figs. 2, 4, all six photographed by Chavannes in situ in 1909, 420-421, Pls. I, II, Figs. 1, 3, position at the tomb at that time, 427; see also Sculpture, Chinese

Horus, see Isis

Hos, origin of totem clans among the, 50 228-232

Hoschander, Jacob, life and works, 54 87-88

Hosea, began to reign in 729 B.C., 44 159

Ho-si, see Ho-hsi

Hostages, to the Chinese Court; small countries of Central Asia send princes as, with Chinese army returning fr. conquest of Ta-yüan, 37 114, son of the King of Ta-yüan one of the, 115

Hotei, see Pu-tai

Hou Chi, 后稷, ancestor of the Chou clans, 56 59, connection with Yü, 61

House, with six openings, as a symbol of the 5th nidāna, ṣaḍāyatana, "seat of the six senses" (the body with its "doors"), 60 359-360

Hsi, 徙, old name for Ya-chou-fu, place on route of Han Wu Ti's abortive attempt to reach India via Ssŭ-ch'uan, 37 99, 148

Hsia Dynasty, chronology of the, 52 243-247; Mencius' description of the period when Yao, Shun and Yü reigned, 56 55, most accurate picture of the period given by the Odes, 70-73; see also Bronzes, Chinese

Hsiang Fei, see Yuan Ming Yuan

Hsiang Shan, regulations for building supplies and furnishings of, 49 234, gravel pits at, 239, the park, 240

Hsiang Yü, gave Han Kao-tsu a kingdom, 57 173, Kao-tsu's crusade against, 177-178; Kao-tsu's crusade against, 58 436

Hsiao Ch'ên Chih, a famous bronze, see Bronzes, Chinese

Hsiao fang hu chai yu ti ts'ung ch'ao, 小方壺齋輿地叢鈔, a ts'ung shu, 51 44, and supplement, 45-46

Hsiao Ho, induced Han Kao-tsu to issue the edict of 196 B.C., re training men for gov. positions, 57 175; through Han Kao-tsu, initiated the Chinese civil service examination system, 58 436

Hsiao Wang-chih, scholar of the five Classics, president of the Council on the Classics held by Han Hsüan Ti, 58 444, put to death by Han Yüan Ti, 445

Hsiao-yüeh-chih, group of refugee Yüeh-chih among the Ch'iang of the Nan-shan, 37 97

Hsi-chang, 西羌, non-Chinese tribes of Kansu and Ssu-ch'uan; traditions concerning Yü origin, 56 62

Hsieh Shou-hao, 謝守灝, see Hun yüan sheng chi

Hsien-ling, 咸齡, see also China, Chinese, History,

Hsi-fan-chi, see Wei Chieh

Hsi-Ho, Mother of the ten suns, myth of connected with Yao, 56 63-66; ancient Chinese sun god, myth of, 53 60-61; see also Tung Chün

Hsi Hsia, kingdom on N.W. frontier of China, people and language, 52 190

Hsin-chih, 新時, Marquis of, see Chao Ti

Hsin-yü, nature of, and influence upon Han Kao-tsu, 57 179

Hsiung-nu, 匈奴, defeat the Yüeh-chih in 176 and 165 B.C., and drive them west, 37 133, furnish Han Wu Ti with information about the Yüeh-chih, 93, Chang Ch'ien held captive among the, 94, 135, their Luk-li prince occupies the throne, 95, Chang Ch'ien's escape fr. them, 95, western division of, bet. Great Wall and Salt Lake, 96, influence of, on K'ang-chü, 96, block northern route to India, 98, Chang Ch'ien's familiarity with their country an advantage in Chinese campaigns against, 99-100, a prince of the western Hsiung-nu tenders allegiance to China in 121 B.C., 100, Ho Ch'ü-ping drives them out of the Kansu corridor, 100, retreat of to the north in 119 B.C., 101, the Wu-sun driven west by, 100, the Chinese invite the Wu-sun to occupy territory formerly held by the, 101, prestige of, among peoples of Central Asia, greater than that of the Chinese, 101, 108, interception of Chinese envoys by, 106, driven away by Chao P'o-nu, 106, give a princess in marriage to the King of the Wu-sun, 106, harass the Yüeh-chih as far as An-hsi, 108, would threaten a Chinese army marching to the west, 109, Chao P'o-nu beaten by the, 111; question of identity with the Huns of Europe, 30 32-45, criticism of Kingsmill's research method, 32-35, Kingsmill's mistake in identifying An-ts'ai, 44-45, Ssu-ma Ch'ien's An-ts'ai, or Yen-ts'ai, later Alan, country of the Aorsi, is not Samarkand, 35-37, Chinese sources of knowledge of the West, 38-39, Ho-su and Suk-tak other

names for An-ts'ai, 40-43, tr. of Chinese text on the conquest of Suk-tak by the Hsiung-nu three generations before the embassy of 457, 43-44, according to European sources the Alans were conquered by the Huns three generations before the embassy of 457, 45, therefore the Hsiung-nu are the Huns, 45; their kingdoms in N. China in 4th cent. A.D., Early and Later Chao, see abstract, McGovern; originators of the custom of wearing queues, 56 377-378; proposal in Han Wu Ti's time to change course in Yellow River to run through their country, 55 303, 305; see also Chang Ch'ien; Huns; Shan-yü; Yüeh-chih

Hsiung-nu River, (Hsiung Ho-shui), 匈河水, Chinese troops march towards, to engage the Hsiung-nu, 37 106

hsiu-tsai, Chinese literary degree (= Bachelor of Arts), annual competitions for abolished in 1905, 27 85

Hsiu-ts'ai yi-teng, title of a highly talented student, see Imperial University

Hsiu-t'u, 休屠, district on frontier of China in time of Han Wu Ti, 37 112

Hsi Wang Mu, development of the myth of, 53 54-55; not seen in Chaldea, according to Chang Ch'ien, 37 97

Hsi Yü, 西域, account of western countries in the Wei Shu said to have been taken from the Pei Shih, 52 45; confused with Europe by Chinese, even in Ricci's time, 59 348; see also China, Chinese

Hsi-yü-t'u-chi, 西域圖記, by P'ei chü, 30 5; mostly lost but subject matter probably absorbed in the Sui-chi, 33 195, its part in firing Yang Ti's desire to communicate with all the western nations, 194-196; see also P'ei Chü

Hsüan Chuang, 玄奘, great teacher and translator of the Wei Shih system of Buddhist philosophy, 51 291-308, founder (?) of the sect in China 291, 299, his translations are basic for western studies, 292, stages in development of his interest in the Wei Shih school of thought, 293-304, the influence of his mind upon the material which he translated, 304-307, problems of translation and Hsüan's fidelity to the original Sanskrit texts, 294-301, 304-307; different forms of his name due to taboos and dialect differences, 52 160-161 n.5; confusion of his Hsi-yu-chi with other works of same title, 53 63-64; reasons for making new tr. of the Viṁśatikā, 53 145, circumstances under which he worked with K'uei Chi, 145-147, his tr. of the Prajñā Pāramitā, the Ta-pan-j'o-po-lo-mi-to-ching, 146-147, his tr. of the Triṁśikā, the Ch'eng-wei-shih-lun, in 659 A.D., 147; see also Buddhism

Hsüan-t'ung Cheng-chi, see Tung-hua Lu

Hsü-chou-fu, Ssŭ-ch'uan, the Sui and K'un-ming tribes to the southwest of, 37 99

Hsüeh t'ang ts'ung k'an, 雪堂叢刻, a modern ts'ung shu of newly discovered ancient writings, 51 42

Hsü Kuang-chi, collaborator of Matteo Ricci, works of, prohibited in Japan, 57 292-294

Hsün Tzu, rating of, in "Table of Ancient and Modern Men", see Chinese Thought; a heretic, not a "moulder of Confucianism", 49 88-91; see also Confucius; Fou-ch'iu Po

Hsü Shih-chi, on tobacco, 58 653

Hsü Ying-ch'uan, author of the Fu-hsing Textbook of History, used by Harvard, 57 196

Hu, 胡, see Tartars

Hua i hwa mu niao shou chen wan k'ao, 華夷花木鳥獸珍玩考, by Shen Mou-kwan, 慎懋官, contains passage on the lemon, 54 149-150, n.14

Huai-nan Tzu, contribution to Hsi Wang Mu myth, 53 54, development of sun myth, 60-61; date of death of, 53 92; conception of Heaven contained in the, 59 201; tells the myth of Kun, Yü, and the Dragon Gate, "Lung-men", 56 59, connects the myth of ten suns with Yao, 64

Huai River, see Elephant

Huan, 驩, small country west of Ta-yüan, in time of Han Wu Ti, 37 107

Huang Ch'ao Wen Hsien T'ung Kao, 皇朝文獻通考, full of gross errors due to refusal to accept Ricci's data on foreign countries; by Hanlin scholars, severe indictment of Matteo Ricci, 59 355-356

Huang ch'ing ching chieh, 皇清經解, a ts'ung shu of the Classics, 51 44

Huang En-t'ung, 黃恩彤, see China, Chinese, History

Huang Ho, 黃河, see Yellow River

Huang Ku and wife, ku sorcerers, story of, 55 24-25

Huan K'uan, 桓寬, early Han author of the Yen T'ieh Lun, use of quotations, 51 266-275, place of, in evolution of Chinese scholasticism, 266, 273

huan-p'ei, 環珮, chatelaine with jade ornaments, see Court Manners, Dress

Hua-yang-kuo-chih, 華陽國志, oldest extant gazetteer, see Gazetteers, Chinese

Hu Ch'ung-kuo, 壺充國, leader in Chinese expedition against Yü-ch'êng in time of Han Wu Ti, 37 114

Hūd, Arab prophet, not from genuine Arab tradition, 60 288

Hui-ch'ao, 慧(or 惠)超, traveller of early 8th cent. in Western and Central Asia; frag. of his record, the Hui-ch'ao-wang-wu-t'ien-chu-kuo-chuan, found at Tun-huang, 33 202-204

Hui-ch'ao-wang-wu-t'ien-chu-kuo-chuan, 慧超往五天竺國傳, frag. of discovered by Pelliot at Tun-huang, 1908, 33 202-204, tr. of parts on Persia, the Ta-shih (Arabs), and Greater Fu-lin, 204-207

Hui Li, 慧立, disciple of Hsüan Chuang and author of the Life of Hsüan Chuang, the Ta-t'zu-en-ssu-san-tsang-fa-shih-ch'üan, note on, 51 295, 296-297, 301

Hūlāgu, decrees toleration for all faiths in Syria, 41 446 ff.

Human Nature, see Confucius, Teachings

Humboldt, author of work on Japanese grammar, see Asiatic Studies in Europe

Hummāma, Manichaean female spirit of darkness, leads last combat of evil against light, 50 198

Hungary, Hungarians, Hungarian, proto-Turkish origins of, 56 448; language, Turkic material in, 56 446-452

Hunger-strike by Hindus to redress grievance, or obtain a request, 21 150-159

Hu-ni, Hsiung-nu prince, King of Suk-tak in 457 A.D., 30 43

Hung Fan, see Great Plan

Hun-hsieh, prince, 渾邪, chief of western Hsiung-nu, tenders allegiance to China, 37 100, his territory deserted, 101, Chavannes' 'Hoen-siĕ', 141

Huns, identified with the Hsiung-nu, 37 141; see also Hsiung-nu

Hun-shŏ prince, see Hun-hsieh prince

Huntington, Dr. Ellsworth, studies by, on the geography and climate of Central Asia, 38 103

Hun yüan shêng chi, 渾元聖紀, on Taoism, by Hsieh Shou-hao, 53 218

Huo Shen, 火神, see God of Fire

Hu pei hsien cheng i shu, 胡北先正遺書, pub. in 1923, a ts'ung shu, 51 42

Hurgronje, Christian Snouck, life and works, 57 215-216

Ḫurrian, Ḫurrians, in Babylonia and Assyria in 3rd millennium B.C., 48 91; cuneiform, as source of the Hittite cuneiform, 54 208; elements among the Ḫabîru, 48 184; appear in second Hyksos period, 57 254; Tušratta Letter (III 110-124), translation of, 59 313-315; entered territory around Upper Zāb from eastern mountains after fall of dynasty of Akkad, 57 108; see also Mitanni; Nuzi; Subartu; θ and z̄ established, 58 173-178, z known, š probably so, 178, θ has sibilant quality, 179, r and l interchange, 182, š and s confused in Akkadian words, 184, two sibilants, expressed by š and s/z respectively; possible affricate, 184, Akk. z and ṣ always written z; Akk. s may appear as z; all three sounds pronounced z by Ḫurrians, 185, voiced sibilant, 185, Akk. š < Sem. ṯ always reproduced by š, 187, similar distinction made by Old Akk., with which the Nuzi syllabary is related, 188-189, š, when corresponding to Ugaritic θ, was intermediate between sibilant and dental spirant; when it replaced s, z or t/d it was probably an affricate, Ugaritic z̄, 192, b fundamentally a spirant, 194-195, p used in alphabetic texts to render f, 197, ġ- like voiced velar spirant represented graphically as ḫ and r, 199-200, ḫ = also Sem. ḫ, 200, k aspirated,

200-201; š not found, 52 351, č found, 351 n.3, stops, voiced and voiceless, not distinguished, 351, voiceless stops are the rule, 358; first person sing. pronominal forms in all cases, 60 267; gutturals appear in western (Mitanni) dialect, but not in the eastern (Arrapḫa), 49 272 n.3; -n (sing.) and -la (pl.) suffixes indicate object of action; are loose elements directly added to their respective nouns only under special syntactic circumstances, 60 219, 223; Nominative ending in (a)š and (a)še, 49 272 n. 3, -wa = "town of," 272 n. 3; verb: passive concept of, 59 291-308, 319, distinction between trans. and intrans. vbs., 294-324, -n, deictic element, 307-308, -š introduces agent of intrans. vbs., 308, suffixes, list of, 308; West-Semitic influence on, 58 188 n. 66
Ḥusayn ibn-'Ali, Grand Šarīf of Mecca, proclaims independence from Turkey on June 27, 1916, 37 161
Hu Shih, author of History of Vernacular Literature, used by Harvard, 57 196
Huvishka, Kushāna ruler, coins of, 56 429-439
Hvarenah, Iranian Kingly Glory, compared with Babylonian Tablets of Fate, 36 308-309
Ḫwārizm, see Calendar, Persian
Hyakurenshō, 百錬抄, value of, as source for study of Kamakura period, 59 40-41
Hyde, Thomas, 1636-1703, early sinologist, 43 8
Hydrography, importance of in Near Eastern archeology, 39 179-180
Hyksos, Semites displaced by Indo-European invasion of Asia Minor, 39 258; period divided into two main phases; Ḫurrians appear in the second, 57 254; their expulsion from Egypt portrayed in the biblical Exodus story; Hebrews were a part of them, 44 160
Hyperboreans, the agelessness of, 26 43
Hypnotism, by Yoga-power, 22 358-360, 377.
Iaḫalu, turtānu under Šamši-Adad V, 34 347-348
Iarimuta, was in Palestine, 42 320-321
Iarmuti, equated with Philistia, 39 150
Ibanag, people and language, 25 172 f.; the article i, 49 362; see also Philippine Islands, Languages
Ibla, unidentified western mountain mentioned in Gudea texts, 43 44
Iblīs, promises to turn woodland spirits into angels if they help him against Muhammad, according to Malay myth, 33 334
I Ching, added to the Canon long after Confucius, 44 278, dropped out in Han but added again, 279-280; absence of the term tao 道 used in its philosophic sense, 52 32; occurrence of i 易 to express the tao idea, 29, 30, 32-33; transmutation system, 53 62, Confucian myth of invention of writing, 55
I-Chou, 益州, district created by Han Wu Ti, modern Yünnan-fu, 37 104, Marco Polo's Yachi, 141
Iconography, of Lama paintings, 52 338-349
Id, see Hīt
Ideographic writing versus phonetic, 55 338 f.
Idolatry, Old Testament, alluded to in terms of unchastity, 48 276-277
Iemitsu, 家光, Shogun, see Japan, Japanese, Religion
Ieyasu, see Tokugawa Ieyasu; Japan, Japanese, Religion, Christianity
Ignatius of Antioch, supplement to letter of Bar-Šûšan to Armenian Katholikos, 32 274, 276, 334
Igorot, see Philippine languages
Iḫdayd wa-'l-Ġūlah, folk story in Arabic dialect of Bethlehem, text and translation, 52 168-173
iḥrām, compared with Hebrew sackcloth, 21 26, 31
Ikhnaton, his solar monotheism had no effect on that of Moses, 44 160
I-King, see I-ching
I Li, its place in the Canon, 44 282; mentions ivory goblets, 41 297; has reference to writing on silk, 56 335 n.2
I-lī-pu, 伊里布, see China, Chinese, History
Illinois, University of, oriental collection in, 46 345
Ilocano, people and language, 25 170-173
Ilokan, see Philippine languages
Iloko, names for anatomical parts, 49 1-21, of man, 1-11, of animals, 11-14, of plants, 14-21; animal names, list of, 48 1-33, mammalia, 1-3, birds, 3-10, reptilia, 10 f., amphibia, 12, fish, 12-22, mollusca, 22-26, worms and larvae, 26 f., insecta, 27-30, arachnida and myriapoda, 30 f., crustacea, 31-33, others 33; plant names, 47 133-173, plants extensively cultivated, 163-173, rice or palay, 163-171, bananas, 171 f., maize, 172, sugar cane, sweet potatoes, 173; names of pathological conditions, 49 244-262
Ilongot, treatment of original l in, 36 194
Imām, Imāmate, beliefs concerning among Shī'ite extremists, 29 22ff., Twelve Imāms, genealogical tree of, 160, Shī'ite doctrine of the return (raj') of, 23-30
Imitation and phonetic law, 44 38-53
Immortality, belief in found in oldest Egyptian texts, 39 148
Immortals, Taoist, Geniehood: 3 kinds of, 53 216, 219, sword in graves of genie, 216 n.4, methods of attaining to, 216, 219 n.11, 221, 222, 223 n.30, 224 n.40a, 244, diet of aspirants to, 216-217, 225-227, 231, 233, 240, 241, 246, 247, 248; see also corrections, 54 290-294; Han, on lacquer ware, see Lo-Lang
Imperial University (T'ai-hsüeh), founded by Han Wu Ti, 58 441-442, 446, enlarged by Emp. Hsüan and continued to fill the bureaucracy with Confucian scholars, 444
Inadahime, The "Japanese Andromeda", wife of Susanoo no Mikoto, 54 282, 284
'Ināyatu'llāh Khān, the life of, 58 357 f.
Incantation bowls, see Bowls, incantation
Incantation, for rain in Ps. 68, 51 366; Babylonian: scapegoat in, 21 1-22
Incarnation (ḥulūl), among Shī'ite sects, 29 13, 45
Incas, used bronze and copper implements, 39 163
Incense, used in offerings to Confucius, 49 130, to Ti Tsang, 135; see also Aloes; Offerings
Incest, figures in Indo-Iranian and Babylonian creation stories, 36 315-316
Incunabula, Hebrew, in the Library of Congress, 36 356
Index, to the Atharvaprāyaścittāni, 33 217-253; of Avestan (Gāthās and Younger Avestan) passages containing preterite tenses, 21 145; to Avestan passages containing subordinate clauses, 22 175 f.; to Hirth's tr. of Chap. 123 of the Shih-chi, on Chang Ch'ien's expedition to the West, 37 137-152; to vols. 21-40 of the JAOS, 44 313-384; to Philo's Quaestiones and De Vita Contemplativa, Armenian-Greek, 53 251-282; of references to the Rāma-story in the Mahābhārata, 50 102 f.
Indexes, new system of indexing Chinese characters, 41 185
India, Indian, Indians, boomerang-shaped instruments of, 55 174-176; castes, origin and development, 53 181-186; the beginnings of civilization in, 59 Sup. 32-44; history of the cock in, 33 375-377, 395; coins, collecting of, 47 186 f.; culture, relations between Mesopotamian and, 54 107 f.; elephants obtained fr. in ancient times, 41 292, 293, 294, the "elephant riding Seres" were Indians, 293; the growing of grapes in, 55 317; the lemon in, 56 47-50; the lemon in, correction, 56 384; some misunderstandings about, 46 193-201, over-emphasis on the spiritual side, 193 f., secular literature, 195, Indians as navigators, colonizers, and traders, 195 f., the main current, 199-201; monetary system of Moghul times, 52 306; musical instruments, parts of a vīṇā, 50 244-252, a lute or mandolin, 50 252 f.; musical instruments, the old vīṇā, 51 47-50, the lute on the Amaravati reliefs, 51 49; musical instruments, upavīṇa = plectrum, 51 284 f., additional references to parts of a vīṇā, 51 285; musical instruments, parts of a vīṇā, 57 101-103; Persian wheel in, 51 283 f.; rhinoceros, as a sacred animal, 51 276-282, kinds of, habitat, the "horn", 279, on seals, 279 f., old references to, 280, present-day customs and traditions centering around, 281 f.; sniff-kiss in ancient, 28 120-134; staff- and pole-dances, 48 281-283; earliest use of stirrups in, 52 85; and the West, 40 225-247, first contacts, 225-228, early Sanskritists, 228 f., printing, 230 f., scholarly collaboration between, 232-241,

need for elementary Sanskrit books, 241-246, of small adequate dictionaries, 246 f.; see also Calendar; Dekkan; Hindu; Iron; Ling-wai-tai-ta; Mathematics; Shen-tu; T'ien-chu; Tobacco; Writing, Tibetan

Archaeology: the problems, 59 Sup. 32-44; solidus of Justinian found at Kalikinayakanpalaiyam, 36 353; works on in Cleveland Public Library, 36 421

Art: the aesthetics of, 54 217 f.; architecture, early, of cities and city-gates, 49 349 f.; architectural terms, 48 251-274; architecture, the kūṭāgāra-sāla, 50 240, the maṇdala-māla, 240 f.; architecture, Pāli kaṇṇikā = circular roofplate, 50 238-243, the meaning of kūṭa, 242 f.; and art of other lands, 46 253 f., supposed foreign elements, 254, chronology, 255; the development from Bhārhut to Sāñcī, 52 83; images, replacing of, 54 222; metal images, South, 53 188; miniature painting, medieval Western, 50 326; miniature painting, elongation of the eye, 53 306 f.; origin of the Buddha image, 46 165-170; painting terms, 52 210 f.; sculpture, interpretation, 54 219-221; sculptures, dating of, 52 84-86; Viṣṇudharmottara chapter XLI, translation and commentary, 52 13-21, lyrical, sacred, and secular painting, 15 f., technical terms in painting, 16-21

Folklore and Mythology: stories of fountains of youth in, 26 44-67; reasons for locating origin of fountain of youth stories in, 26 2-44; Kuvera, three-legged parallels to in Iran and Greece, 40 333; Narāśaṅsa-Nairyosaṅha (Neryosang), associated with royal placenta or umbilical cord, an idea paralleled in Egypt and Mesopotamia, 40 334-335; Pañcatantra in modern, 39 1-54, relation to literature, 1-11, brief survey of published, 1-4, borrowings from literature, 4-11, magic lamp, 5 f., camel's neck, 6 f., son and mother, 8 f., Pañcatantra parallels, 13-43, bibliography, 43-54; legend of Prester John; legend of Oponia based upon, see Utopia, Russian; serpent lore in legend and art, 49 186-190

History: Akbar and Jahāngīr, relations with Shāh 'Abbās the Great, 35 247-268; date of the Aryan invasion, 47 187 f.; a political theory of the rise of British power in, 48 348; and Elam, 42 194-197, the Purāṇic Śiśunāka = Elamitic Susinak, Susunqa, 195, possibility of an Elamitic kingdom in India, 196 f.

Language: dialects, verbs for 'giving' and 'taking' in, 43 358-390, verbs for 'giving', 358-364, forms, 358-362, history, 362-364, verbs for 'taking', 364-383, lē-area, 365 f., origin of the forms, 366 f., area with labh- 'obtain, find', 367 f., area with prāp-, mil-, bheṭ- 'obtain', 368 f., history of isoglosses established by words for 'taking' and 'obtaining', 370-376, grabh- 'take' area, 376-383, forms, 376-378, history, 378-383, analogical spread of preterite -t- from dā-, 383-387, the present stem dē-, 388-390; inscriptions on the Fire Temple at Baku, 29 299-304; names in Aramaic incantation texts from Nippur, 41 159-160; gestures in sign language, 48 279-281

Law: law-books, conception of the king in the, 51 310 f.; legislation, recent, against dedication of "devadasis", 52 285

Literature: reactions to art stated in, 52 213-220; Collection of in Cleveland Public Library, 36 421-422; description of the busy port of Kaviripaddinam in the Tamil poem Paddinappalai, 37 245, scene of jeweller's shops with rich gems in The Little Clay Cart, 245-246; drama, the Dūtāṅgada of Subhaṭa, translated, 32 58-77; drama, the Viddhaśālabhañjikā of Rājaśekhara, 27 1-71; dramas, Māgadhī in, 44 97-105, characters speaking Māgadhī and Ardhmāgadhī, 44 110-114; Persian documents from Mughal, 59 371-374; tales of choosing a king by divine will, 33 158-166; see also Ṛṣyaśṛṅga

Philosophy: atheistic school of, 46 347; materialism, when did it get its distinctive titles?, 50 132-138, Lokāyata, Cārvāka, Bārhaspatya; Rhys Davids' theory, 132 f., nāstikas, 133 f., in the Epic, 134 f., the Arthaśāstra, 135, other works, 135 f., earliest reference to Lokāyata, 136, to Cārvāka, 137, to Bārhaspatya, 138; philosophical ideas, source of, 39 125

Religion: Indic and American Indian religious parallels, 37 72-84, marking a woman's head, 73, ritual use of hair, 73 f., clans, 74, the soul, 74, creation-myths, 76, four divine winds or quarters, 77-79, cosmic ages, 81 f., intoxication part of divine service, 82, proxy gods, 82 f., trinity, 83, Peruvian hymns, 83 f.; Dasara festival at Satara, 30 72-76; divinity of kings in early, 51 309-316; god Aja Ekapād, the one-legged goat, 53 326-334; god Dhanvantari, 42 323-337; iconography, sources of, 51 286; iconography, sources of water cosmology, 51 287; some recent legislation affecting, 52 285; doctrine of man's last end, 57 244; miracle of walking on the water, the Christian and, 47 359; religion of the northern peasant, 47 190 f.; sacrificial ritual, a parallel between Babylonian and, 54 107-128; Yuga-system, Sumerian prototype of, 39 66 n. 3

Trade: with Babylon, 33 352; eastward from India, bet. 1st and 3rd cent A.D., very important, 37 242, 244-245, 249, Graeco-Roman trade with the Malabar Coast, exchange of cargo at Tamil ports and return home, 241; exports, according to classical sources, 35 229-230; missionary-traders from in Indian Archipelago and Borneo, 33 315, 330; as navigators, colonizers, and traders, 46 195-198; with Persia in 16th cent., 35 250-252; Roman and Egyptian trade, ancient, 35 31-33, 35, 39-41; Roman maritime trade with, 37 240-249, references to in Latin literature, 246-249; Roman trade, terminus of, 36 442; India and Roman Empire, commerce between, 51 180-182; exported spices to Roman world, 40 265-270

Indian Ocean, trade winds, see Navigation

Indians, pre-Columbian American, spread of cultural traits of, 39 161

Indo-Aryan cosmology, compared with Babylonian, 26 84-92

Indo-China, archaeology, excavations of Victor Goloubew, and of M. Trouvé, near Angkor Thom, note on, 57 332, restorations at the Bayon of Angkor, 334; language: Grammatical studies, see Asiatic Studies in Europe; see also Aloes

Indo-Europeans, Indo-European

History: appearance of in Asia Minor, 39 254-255, 257; among Amorites of Palestine, 45 38 n. 85; close to Assyrian frontier at accession of Ashurnasirpal II, 38 218; drive Ḫatti out of Asia Minor, 37 173; original home in South Russia, 48 358

Language: abstract suffix -tā- -tāti-, 34 341-343; bh corresponds to Hittite p, 50 125-128; on the chronology of the separation of, 50 325; ē ō became Sanskrit ā before IE e o became Sanskrit a, 33 259-262; grammar, defects in, 36 440, Indo-European did not have schwa or th-spirants; the word for "father"; grammar, suffix -ka, 31 310-312; *ios, originally anaphoric adjective, 22 145 f.; k¹s, Indo-Iranian treatment of, 40 81-84; laryngeal consonants, 58 530; long vowels resulting from earlier loss of h, 51 357; neuter pronouns referring to words of different gender or number, 49 351; origins, the problem of, 51 374; pronominal element -sme/i, 53 392; pronouns and ablative, in the light of Hittite, 47 174-184, IE *to = Hittite ta, 174-177, ablative, 177-184; vocalism, the laryngeal hypothesis and, 60 181-192

Mythology: see Moon

Religion: borrowings from Semites, 36 304 ff.

Indo-Hittite, h, changes of quantity caused by, 51 357; hypothesis, 54 207; laryngeals, phonetic interpretation of the, 60 182 f.; pronoun *sme/i 'thou, you, he, they,' 53 392; vocalism, the laryngeal hypothesis and, 60 181-192

Indo-Iranians, Indo-Iranian

Language: sound-changes, chronology of certain, 33 259-262; treatment of IE. k¹s, 40 82 f., Avestan, 82, Sanskrit, 82 f.; words, notes on, 39 206-207, Sanskrit cāṭaka-, compound adverb prād-u[d]s, sahá, hoḍha- 'stolen property', 206, Avestan puθrā 'with child', vərə-ṭka, 206 f., Indo-Iranian 'root' var 'broad', 207

Mythology: Soma cycle closely associated with Sumerian contest between Lugalbanda and Zû, 40 315-316; water-deities, relationship of names of Greek sea-gods and, 38 303-305

Indonesia, special type of Islam in, 33 322 ff.
Language: sounds in Isinai, reflections of, 35 289-292; l in Philippine languages, 36 181-196, stability of original l, 181, loss, retention, or change of l, 182-194, recapitulation, 194-196; sounds, Palau reflections of, 35 4-12; treatment of original t and s, 38 71; RLD law in, 33 155 f.; sounds, Tirurai reflections of original, 33 151-157
Indoscythians, see Yüeh-chih
Indo-Sumerian seals, 47 284 f.
Indra, rescues Agni and Soma from Vṛtra, 55 385 f.; slays boar with Viṣṇu, 55 389 f.; as god of fertility, 36 242-268; legend concerning used by Goethe in his Der Gott und die Bajadere, 39 295; in the guise of a monkey, disturbs the sacrifice (JB. i.363), 26 192-196; borrowed by Indo-Iranians from Mitanni, 43 428; and Namuci, 55 374 f.; ṛcīṣama as epithet of, 21 51; taking on various shapes, 26 195 f., 314; invoked in Śrāddha ceremony of Kapola Bania caste, 22 229; Uśanas Kāvya, and the three-headed Gandharvan, the story of, 28 81-88; invoked as vṛṣaṇaśvasya mene, 26 176 f.; conquest of Vṛtra, 45 284 f;. and other gods of war and fertility, 37 85 f., American thunder and lightning gods functioning as fertility gods, 85, Durgā associated with "the seven Indras", 86; in the guise of a woman (JB. ii.78), 26 176-188; employs Yoga-power, 22 359 f.
Indus, river of Shen-tu, 37 98, 141
Indus valley civilization, the archaeology of the, 59 Sup. 32-44, extent, 33 f., chronology, 34 f., the various cultures, 35 f., Harappa script, 36-39, relations with other cultures, 37-44; script not related to Sumerian, 49 265-266; style of sculpture, interpretation, 54 220; see also Seals
Inibaloi, treatment of original l in, 36 190 f.
Ink, divination by means of, 36 37, 44-47, 51; as tribute & presents fr. the protectorates to the Chinese Court, began in 102 A.D., 51 144 n.25
In Memoriam
Bigelow, William Sturgis, d. Oct. 6, 1926, in his 77th year, 47 344
Chavannes, Édouard, Life and Works, by B. Laufer, 38 202-205
Hirth, Dr. Friedrich, 1845-1927, 47 343
Laufer, Berthold (1874-1934), 54 349-351; bibliography of works by, 352-362
Inscriptions
Arabic: on modern copy of door from madrasah of Barqūq in Cairo, 30 58-60; reservoir inscription of Baybars, dated A.H. 707, 60 376-377
Aramaic: on Alexander tetradrachms from Egypt, 60 133-134; 5th-4th cent. B.C. inscribed jar handle from Beth Shemesh is earliest sample of Aramaic from Judaea, 55 309-310; Carpentras stele (5th cent. B.C.), syllabic meter in, 46 242-247, Greek parallels to, 244-246; Cilicia, boundary inscription from, 28 164-167; Hadad inscription, notes to, 54 421-423; Hadad (Zencirli), notes to lines 28-29, 37 329-330; al-Jawf inscription from 2nd or 3rd cent. B.C., text and translation, 54 29-33; Panammuwa inscription, notes to, 54 423-424; Sujīn inscription, notes to, 54 424-425; votive inscription of 5th cent. B.C. from Kesecek Köyü, 35 370-374; Zakir inscription, text and translation, 35 353-364, Kilamuwa inscription, translation of, 364-369
Chinese: on Bronzes of Western Chou Dynasty, 56 335-349, hundreds extant, 337, length of inscription compared to texts of the Shu-ching, 337-339, occasions for which the bronzes were cast, and historical value of the inscriptions, 339-342, 29 inscriptions preserve actual documents of Western Chou, 342, similarities to documents of the Shu-ching, 343, study of style for establishing authenticity of other documents, 343, the P'an Kêng a forgery; 343-344, the dating of, 344-345, research on, by Chinese and Western scholars, 345, many inscribed Shang bronzes now known, 346 n.33, Wieger's mistakes in reading a typical inscription of late Chou, and its proper tr., 346-349, important use of in study of history and culture, 349, an "heirloom type" inscription on an early tsun, 51 18; of the Nestorians, at Si-an-fu, 30 3, 10, 14, 15, 17; Nestorian, at Si-an-fu, first pub. in the West in 1630, 43 6; Nestorian Tablet, see also Müller, Andreas; Nestorian Monument, early trs. of, in Latin, French, Italian, see also Words, Chinese, san i fen shen; Ricci's Map of the World engraved on stone and rubbings made, 59 344; on stone stelae, of Yu Shih-hsiung on the Stele of the Picture of the Six Horses, portion of text and tr., 55 423-427; see also Erkes, Édouard; Oracle Bones
Coptic: tombstone from Thebes dated A.H. 280 (A.D. 894), 52 295
Cypriote: on scarab and seal in Marburg collection, 22 19
Greek: from Jewish catacomb in Vigna Randanini (Rome), does not belong to a synagogue of Herodians or Rhodians, 49 318-321; to Zeus Megistos, from second year of Severus Decius, found near 'Azāz in N Mesopotamia, 38 247 n. 67
Hebrew: 'Ayn Dūq, inscribed mosaic floor from dating from 5th cent. A.D., 40 141-142; Beth Shemesh, notes to inscribed jar handles and seal from, 55 307-310; Lachish, reading of Ewer, Bowl, Dagger, Potsherd and Censer Lid inscriptions, 58 Supp. II, 8-41; ossuary inscriptions, 28 355-359; seal and weight, 24 205-208; Siloam inscr., word zdh in means "fissure," 22 55-60; weights, inscribed, 24 384-387; see also Hebrew Language Texts
Indian: at fire-temple of Surakhani, near Baku, 25 177
Moabite: geographical terms Šrn and Š(M)ḥrt in, 22 61-63
Nabataean: Petra, high-place inscription from, notes on, 29 197-202; from high-place of al-'Uzza at Petra, 28 349-351
Neo-Punic: from Holt (Wales), dated in 1st cent. A.D., 60 578-579
Old Persian: Behistun I:65, interpretation of according to the Aramaic version, 33 281-283; textual criticism of, 40 289-299, classifications of variations, 290, the Behistan inscription of Darius, 291-299;
Pahlavi: 8th-century inscription on silver bowl, 28 345-348; notice of Sasanian inscription and relief at Biricik, 28 158; on seals in Yale collections, 52 201-207
Palmyrene: Damascus inscriptions, notes on, 29 194-196; Rep. 721, 743, 746 and Ephem. II 316, notes on, 29 196-197; from Damascus collection, 29 203; Funerary, 21 109-111; Funerary, 25 314-319; Funerary, 25 320-323; Funerary, 26 105-112; Tesserae, 26 113-116; Tesserae, 27 397-399
Phoenician: Aḥîrâm inscription, translation of, 45 269-279; Aḥîrâm inscription dated in early 11th cent. B.C., 48 80; Aḥîrâm inscription dated ca. 1100 B.C., 60 416; Bod'aštart of Sidon, text and translation, 23 156-173, discovery of, 156-158; Bod'aštart inscription from Sidon, notes to, 24 211-226; Bod'aštart inscription from temple of Esmun at Sidon, notes on, 25 324-331; Bod'aštart inscription from Sidon, notes on geographical terms in, 29 192-193; Ešmunazarid inscriptions date in Ptolemaic period, 57 239-240; fragment of votive text from Rhodes, 60 260-264; on seal from Sidon, 28 359; on votive statuette from Sidon, 28 351-354; on late seal, 28 354; statue of Osorkon I with inscription of Elîba'al, from Byblos, 46 237-240, script of a cursive type, 239
Samaritan: on 16th-century Pentateuch case, 27 105-107; synagogue inscription from before A.D. 600 in Jerusalem, 50 340-341
Semitic: list prepared by Yale for "A Library of Ancient Semitic Inscriptions," 39 283-284; word-dividers, use of, 49 123-124
Siamese: earliest example of writing, on stone, at Sukhāthai, 44 13-14
Sinaitic: those containing word nṣb belong to the Hebrew nᵊṣîbîm ruling Edom, 52 296
South Arabic: in Yale University, notice of, 58 528
Interior Decoration, Chinese, a ms. of regulations governing the painting of palace and temple interiors, 49 237, 241, 242, carving, inlaid furniture, etc., 237, 239, prices for materials, 237, 239, 241-242, cost of oil painting per sq. ft., 242, papering, 237-238, 240, mats and awnings, 239-240

International Relations
Between East and West: 44 177-185, anecdote of Japanese Ambassador in Paris, 179, position of Turkey, 179-180, 182-183, the Indian question, 180-181, the Shantung question, 181, Japanese feeling after the earthquake, 181, records of Commodore M.C. Perry of the Expedition to the China Seas and Japan, 1852, 1853, 1854, 182, the AOS and its position in bringing the East and West together, 183-185
Anglo-Chinese: 17th-18th cents. materials on, 57 354, effect of Commutation Act of 1784, 354-355, East India Company's commerce, 353, 354, 355, embassies to Peking, Macartney's embassy in a new light, 355, Mr. Pigou's proposals for an embassy to Peking, 355; Macartney probably performed a compromise ceremony, not the kotow (k'ou-t'ou), see abstract, E.H. Pritchard; see also abstract, J.K. Fairbank
China with the United States: 120 Chinese boys sent in 1871 to Hartford, Conn. for training in the professions, see abstract, T.L. La Fargue
Sino-Korean: see abstract, Goodrich, New Haven, 1936
Interpreters, bet. Chinese and Central Asian countries, 37 98, furnished by Wu-sun to accompany Chang Ch'ien, 102
Ionians, see Yavanas
Ipy, Egyptian wazir in reign of Mentuhotep III (21st cent. B.C.), 44 164-165
Iqbāl-nāmah'i Jahāngīrī, late Mughul illustrations to the, with plates, 58 354-365
Iram (ḏāt al-'Imād), originally a Nabataean sanctuary in N Midian, 60 287
Iran, Iranians, Iranian, Iranians and Slavs in South Russia, 45 68-71, Scythians and Sarmatians, early Russians with Iranian names, 69, Simarg is the Persian Simourg, 69 f., Scythian and Russian legends, 69 f., Iranian influence on Russian culture, 71; dogs of northern, 25 182 f.; see also Medes; Persia
Mythology: Nairyosaṅha (Neryosang), moon-deity called "royal umbilical cord," as in Egypt and Mesopotamia, 40 334-335
Religion: healing and storm gods, Farīdūn, Irman, the tree gōkard, 37 14; gods of healing, 38 294-307, Airyaman, 294 f., Thrita, Thraētaona, Farīdūn, Indian Trita, 296-299, Teutonic and Greek analogues, 299-303, relationship between names of Greek sea-gods and Indo-Iranian water-deities, 303-305, connection of water and healing, 305-307
Iraq, British policy in during and after World War I, 47 111-112; see also Baghdad and Mesopotamia
Irawadi River, see Trade Routes
Irbid (Ḫawrā), early Hebrew amulets from, 31 272-281
Irenaeus, teaching on relationship between body and soul, 40 111 ff.
Iron, common in lands N of Assyria, 38 238-239, 245-246, 247; exported by Kabul in 16th cent., 42 181; people bet. Ta-yüan and An-hsi did not know casting of, in early Han, 37 108, huang-t'ieh='yellow iron', 109 n.6; trade in, from the East to the Roman Empire, 35 224-239, did not come fr. China, 224-230, the Chinese iron industry, 226-227, prohibitive cost of overland trade in iron, 228, Central India the producer of the finest grade of steel then known, used in Damascus blades and by the Persians, 230-235, methods of making steel in early India, 233-235, the fine iron of the Roman trade was Indian steel, shipped by boat, 232-237, iron mines, 226, 231-233, 235, Arab monopoly of the iron trade, 230-231; see also Metals
Irrigation, introduced into Babylonia by the Semites, 41 261-262; earliest in China, growth of the Yü tradition, 56 54, 55-63; Han period, building of canals and river improvements for, 55 303-306
Ĭr-shĭ, General, see Erh-shih, General
Isaac of Antioch, his addition to the letter of Bar-Šûšan to the Armenian Katholikos, 32 272
Isaiah, legends about him connected with those of Adonis, 55 201-202; ch. 40-48 written before the entry of Cyrus into Babylon, 57 158, 160; his attitude in 701 B.C. determined by Ch. 28-31; narrative historically untrustworthy, 45 368; constant opponent of the anti-Assyrian party in Judah, 57 257; does not teach the inviolability of Jerusalem, 37 9; see also Deutero-Isaiah
Isaurians, raid Ṣîṣ and are repulsed by Simeon Stylites, 35 105, 114-115
Isḥāq the Jew, story of from the Kitāb 'Ajā'ib al-Hind, English summary of, 51 365
Išḫara, mistress of Gilgameš, a form of Ištar with chthonic features, 40 311, 316, 320
Isidore of Charax, about time of Christ, traveller over the ancient trade route, with variations, fr. Antioch to Arachosia (Kandahar), 35 36-38
Isin, era of, fell at close of reign of Rim-Sin, 38 329
Isinai language, grammatical notes on, 35 289-292; post-positive article, 291 f.; treatment of original l in, 36 187
Isis, sacred gazelle transferred to her from Min, 40 328; and Horus, compared with Ištar and Tammuz, 35 223; and Osiris, of Semitic origin, 53 170
Islam, Islamic, kingship, idea of derived from the Šāh-Nāmah, 55 Supp. 1, 19-21; religious poetry, formative period down to A.D. 800; predominance of sectarian poets in; penetration of religious motives into love-song, 59 410-411; stability of Islamic states due to political inactivity of the population, 59 122; see also Art and Architecture; Astrology; Bowls, incantation; Divination; Koran; Magic; Medicine; Muhammad; Muslims; Science
Religion: call to prayer copied from Christians and Jews, 30 133-135; heterodox beliefs introduced by Persians and Jews, 29 16, 17ff., 117, 177; in Borneo, 33 313-344, Indonesian Islam a special type, 322 ff., in Sarawak, 340; influence of Iranian dualism on, 59 123-124; integral part is based on Judaeo-Christian tradition; owes little to ancient orient, 60 301; Judaeo-Arabic apology for (Kitāb Masālik al-Naẓar of Sa'īd ibn-Ḥasan), 24 312-383; Malayan, of animistic type, 44 32; qadar defined by al-Ḥasan al-Baṣri as pre-determination and predestination in God's administration of human affairs; is not compatible with human moral and religious freedom, 55 144-162; Sects, see under Shī'ites
Ismā'īlism, anti-Arab origin of, 60 428-429
Israel, Israelites, Israelite, see also Blood-Revenge; Burial; Calendar; Hebrews and Jews
Economy: communalistic features are development of old tribal system, 42 399
Ethics: Truth, little realization of worth of, 48 344
History: began to invade Palestine ca. 1400 B.C., 34 417; occupation of Transjordan, 54 169-177; see also Ahab
Religion: bull worshipped under name of Jacob, 34 417; Israel originally an Israelite deity, 46 354
Issyk-kul, Lake, see Wu-sun
Istambul, not the Chinese Fu-lin of the T'ang period, 30 2, 3-4, 16, 17; survey of books and manuscripts in libraries of, 59 227-246
Ištar, her cult not derived from Amurru, 45 20-24, of Aleppo, worshipped at Nippur, 20, not a deified queen, 22-23; as prototype of Circe, 38 332; may be a deified historical character, 41 252; of Ḫalab (Aleppo), connected with Uruk, 45 135; of Ḫallab (not Ḫalab-Aleppo), 45 217; descent of into the underworld, texts among those from Nippur, 44 160; descent of into the underworld, Ugaritic parallel to, 52 229, 231; was masculine among the ancient Akkadians, 58 548; equated with Nana; is androgynous, 21 185-187; (= Aširta), worship of carried to South Arabia by the Amorites, 45 135; Ištar-Tammuz cult of Semitic origin, 35 213 ff.; see also Festivals (Babylonian)
Išum, Babylonian deity, character of, 32 32
Īśvaragītā, as imitation of Bhagavad Gītā, 54 306 f.; interpretation of the, 54 308-310; metaphysics of the, 54 307
Italy, history of the cock in, 33 383-386, 395; medieval trade with Levant, see Genoa; poetry, sestet probably derived from Arab zajal, 51 370, Dante did not draw on an Arabic source for eschatological material in his Divina Commedia, 370; treaty with the Yaman, 47 123
Itḫia, ruler of Arrapḫa ca. 1500 B.C., 49 273
Ithoter Rivāyat, an eighteenth century Zoroastrian manuscript in Persian, 43 166

Ititi, son of Iakulaba, Gutian prefect of 25th cent. B.C., 48 91
Iti-vuttaka, metrical analysis of the Pāli, 28 317-330
i-ts'ao-lang, 儀曹郎, title, Wei period, 53 224
Ivory, in Ancient China, see Elephant; inlaid (including chryselephantine) found in Assyrian tribute lists from N Syria, 38 215, 239, 246-247, 250, 257; great quantities produced in Po-pa-li (Berbera), 30 48-50, Zanzibar, mart of ivory, 56; Chinese, Han, articles of, mentioned, 51 148; carvings, Chinese and Eskimo, 51 100
Īwān, originated from long-room house in warm climates, 60 168
I-wen-chih, 藝文志, record of literature in the Book of Han: list of the Classics, 44 279
Iya-yama Villages, in Iyo Province, 31 162-163
Izalla, in N Mesopotamia, its wine famous in ancient times, 38 226
Jackson, Abraham Valentine Williams, life and works, 58 221-224, 504-505; bibliography of, 58 241-257
Jacob, his marriage with Laban's daughters closely conforms to the Babylonian errêbu marriage, 57 261-264, payment of bride-price made according to Akkadian-Ḫurrian practise, 268-276; name of bull worshipped by Israelites, 34 417; originally an Israelite deity, 46 354
Jacobites, modern authors among, 22 92-94
Jade, Ancient Chinese ceremonial objects of Chou(?)period, see Hanchow, Ssu-ch'uan; Chinese, Han, articles of, mentioned, 51 148; Chinese, pieces of, and nephrite beads, see Mu-yan-ch'eng; found on hills near Khotan in Han period, 37 95, 107
Jade Capital, Taoist, note on the, 53 219 n.8, 243
Jade Maid, identification of, 53 219 n.11, as the Princess of the Colored Clouds, 228 and n.57, as a teacher of breath control and callisthenics, 231, 248
Ja'far al-Ṣādiq, his position among Shī'ites and Sunnis, 29 104-108, 112
Jagatī in the Pāli Iti-vuttaka, 28 326-329
Jagatī, Hypermetric, in Mahābhārata, 59 159-174
Jahangir, character of, 43 349 f.; relations with Shāh 'Abbās the Great, 35 247-268
al-Jāḥiẓ, criticism of, 29 56-58; style and writings of, 47 314-318, 321-322; see also al-Radd 'ala 'l-Naṣāra
Jāiminīya Brāhmaṇa, Arabic parallel to the story of a friend in need in, 26 296-305; contributions to history of Brāhmaṇa literature, 26 176-196; additions to the fifth series of contributions from, 26 306-314; its contributions to the history of Brāhmaṇa literature, 28 81-98; compared with the Pañcaviṃśabrāhmaṇa, 52 389 f.; story of the rejuvenations of Cyavana, 26 46-50; text of, with notes, 26 58-63; text and translation JB.'s story of Cyavana and Vidanvat, 26 64-67; story of the rejuvenation of Cyavana; text of, with notes; additional notes, 26 413; verbal correspondences with other Brāhmaṇas, 23 323-349
Jain, Jaina, Jainist, Jainism, Caritas and Prabandhas as chronicles, 36 55; categories, 46 268 f.; as Dravidian reaction, 39 125; Kalpasūtra, date of a paper manuscript of, 57 118 f.; Kathā(naka) writings, 36 55 f.; Māhārāṣṭrī, words found in Vedas but not in classical Sanskrit, 44 160; in North India, 52 393-395; nuns in Hindu fiction, 44 204, 236-242; sacred texts, earliest date of, 56 371; Sanskrit, correspondences with Buddhist Sanskrit, 40 343 f.; words and forms, in Śālibhadra Carita, 43 287-290
Jambhaladatta's version of the Vetālapañcaviṅśati, 55 59-65
Jambudvīpa, in Indo-Aryan cosmology, 26 91
Jamšīd, see Yima
Jamuda sept of the Hos, origin of the, 50 231 f.
Jan, 冉, barbarous hill tribe, on southwestern frontier of China; Han Wu Ti's attempt to open a route through country of, 37 99
Jang, name of a ceremony used to expel the Old Year, 56 58; see also shang-jang
Jang, god among the Land Dyaks, 26 170-174
Jantu, the rebirth of, 26 5 f.
Japan, Japanese, resumé of archeological work done in 1916 in the Far East, 36 353-354; costume, see Nō Plays; economic and social Conditions in the Tokugawa Period, Village government after 1600, 31 151-216, see also Feudalism in Japan; education, Tokugawa Period: study of the Chinese Classics in the Baronial schools and the influence of Chinese Political-ethical teachings, 31 152-153, 172, 183, village schools, 202, laws copied in the schools, 212; humor, examples of, 59 150; metal-workers, the Hiiragi-ya, 17th cent., famous for their sword-guards, 55 449; military organization in the Tokugawa Period, separation of the warrior from the land, 30 270-271, 31 173, financial position of barons and warriors, 30 273-274, bu-shi, 武士, and samurai, 31 154, distinction bet. warriors and peasants, 31 154-155; the kingdom of Oponia located in, see Utopia, Russian; political philosophy, source material for study of, 59 41-42; Prester John and, 42 400; first Japanese to come to Russia, 1701, 42 290; tale of a fountain of youth, 26 411; see also Arms, Armor; Dances, Dancing; Festivals; Feudalism; Music; Mysticism; Quippus; Swords; Tobacco
Agriculture: in the Tokugawa Period, 30 266, 270, 271-272, 281-289, edicts to villages on irrigation, water-courses, cultivation of land, 31 204-205, 206, 212-213; 645-1165 A.D., see Shōen
Art: design, influence of the In-Yo philosophy on, 57 249; see also Nō Plays; Wood-block Prints, see Hashiguchi Goyo
Culture: Chinese influence on, in the Tokugawa period, 31 152-153, 172, 183; Chinese influence on, see also Tsuina ceremony, Setsubun festival; Indian influence on, see Gion matsuri
Geography: cartography, Japan on western maps before 1500, 60 275-276, maps of c. 1520 placed "Zipangu" among the North American "islands" near Florida, 276, Portuguese navigators, first arrived in 1542, begin to map Japan in 1550, 276-277, first scientific mapping by Ignacio Monteiro (orMoreira) in 1590, 277, maps by Abraham Ortelius, Mercator, Domingos Teixeira, 1570-1596, 277, Will Adams' exploration and map, 277; identification of road and region in Japan, the Tokaido, see abstract, Hall
Government, Rural: 645-1165 A.D., organization of the Shōen, or Manor, see Shōen; Tokugawa Period after 1600, see Feudalism in Japan
History: argument for proposal of 1769 to permit foreign trade, see abstract, H. Borton; ceremonies in farewell to feudalism, Oct. 1, 1871, in the castles of Japan, 45 88-89; cultural isolation bet. 1630 and 1720 due to prohibition of certain Chinese books, 57 290-303, Edict of Kanei, 1630, development of, 291-303; note on estimating date for beginning of Japanese history, 59 145; 645-1165 A.D., see Shōen; Kamakura Period, source materials for, see Bibliography; Tokugawa Period, see Feudalism in Japan; see also Edicts
Language: efforts to establish Semitic roots for Chinese and Japanese words nonsense, 55 130-133; lexicons by early Western scholars, 43 6, 8, 9; grammars by early Western scholars, 43 6, 8, 9; romanization: the case for Rōmaji (Old Romanization) instigated by Hepburn, as against Rōmazi (Nipponshiki, and Kokutei, or Official, Rōmazi), 60 82-89, chart of differences bet. the 3 systems, 83, Old Romanization better for foreigners, 83-86, none are satisfactory phonetically, 86; opposition to Kokutei in Japan as well as abroad, 86-89
Law: 645-1165 A.D., legal rights and taxation in the shōen system, 57 79-83; prohibition of import of Chinese books on western science and Christianity, bet. 1630 and 1720, 57 290-303, punishment of offenders, 300-301; Kamakura Period, Bibliography for, see Bibliography; Tokugawa Period, see Feudalism in Japan
Literature: diaries of poets, of historical value, 59 43-44, diaries of Emperors, 44-45, poems by Go-Shirakawa, 46; Kaga-no-Tchiyo, biographical notes on, 57 130; see also Nō Plays; Sei Shōnagon
Music: see Nō Plays
Religion: Christian church founded in, by St. Francis Xavier,

1549, 42 289-290; Catholics tolerated by Ieyasu, 57 290, persecuted fr. 1612 on, 290-303, prohibition of books mentioning, 294-296; Christianity, see also Edicts, Japanese, of Kanei; note on Buddhist and Shinto objects in U.S. National Museum, 23 47; Shinto, is as much a religion as it ever was, 60 588; Temples or Shrines as owners of shōen, 57 82; in the Tokugawa Period: Catholic converts excluded from the villages, 30 275, Orders against Catholicism, 31 197, 205, 208, 214, rewards offered for reporting a Catholic, 31 199-200, festivals, and Buddhist and Shinto rituals to be simple, 31 204, 214, laws against making expensive cult statues or building large temples, 31 212, 214, 216; see also Festivals, Gion matsuri; Susanoo no Mikoto; Inadahime; Gozu Tennō; Hōdō; Pestilence; Nō Plays

Sociology: population in the Tokugawa Period 30 260-261, 287-289; figures for various classes, 31 155; comments on Embree's study of a village, Suye-Mura, Kyushu, 60 432-435, social and political divisions, cooperative groups, social strata, village associations, daily life, 434, changes in the social structure as a result of contact with the West i.e. fr. a rice to a money economy, 435

Japanese Studies in the U.S.A., see Asiatic Studies in U.S.A.

Japji section of the Adi Granth, quoted in Baku Fire Temple inscription, 29 299-302

jarā-maraṇa, see nidānas

Jarash (Transjordan), see Gerasa

Jargons, see Secret dialects

Jasmine, Chinese name Yeh-hsi-mi, see Words

Jastrow, Morris Jr., life and works, 41 322-344, as a biblical critic, 322-327, contributions to history of religion, 327-333, as an Assyriologist, 333-336, bibliography of, 337-344

Jātakas, stories of false ascetics, 44 208-242; instances of flesh-eating, 27 461-463; kissing in the, 28 124; Pāli originals of some stories, 38 267 f.; representations of scenes fr., in wall-paintings fr. Central Asia, 49 64

jāti, see nidānas

Jats, degraded tribe of Indian Rajputs, 44 132

Jaugada recension of the Fourteen-Edicts of Asoka, 30 77 f., 91-93

Java, Javanese, caṇḍi, meaning of the, 51 1-15, use as mausoleum, 1 f., 9-15; early Chinese names for, 57 344-345, Kublai Khan's expedition against, 344-345; funeral ceremonies, 51 8-12; lutes and harps, 51 49 f.; settlements in Borneo, 33 316; shadow play, 51 13, the gunungan 'mountain-piece', 13 f.; see also Tobacco

al-Jawf (north Arabia), Aramaic inscription from (2nd or 3rd cent. B.C.), 54 29-33

Jawzi, ibn-al-, see Damm al-Hawā'

Jayasena, 勝軍論師, an Indian scholar, teacher of Hsüan Chuang, 51 303

Jemdet Nasr Tablets, language of is that of an Asiatic-Elamite people, 54 76-77

Jen Wu Chih, 人物志, classification of human personalities as to character and ability, 59 280-282, Tr. of passage on function of the Yin and Yang, and the Five Elements, 281-282, purpose of, to classify statesmen according to their abilities and types of personality, 204

Jeremiah, Book of, Greek and Hebrew versions, differences between show late editing of Hebrew text, 38 74-75

Jerome, derived his idea of four world-empires from Trogus and Justin, 59 422

Jerusalem, its cult of holy places attacked by ibn-Taymīyah, 56 1-21; Hadrian decides to rebuild it as Aelia Capitolina in A.D. 130, 59 363; siege of by Sennacherib, critique of sources on, 24 265-274; solar cult at, 57 256; celebration of water-festival of Sukkoth in, 37 219; see also Golden Gate; Palestine, Archeology

Jesuits, mission press in Japan destroyed by Iemitsu, and Catholics persecuted, 57 290; in China, see Matteo Ricci; Geographical Knowledge in China

Jesus, the evidence as to his historicity, 53 212 f.; no proof of his historicity; not originator of Christian doctrine and cult, 53 212; his position in Manichaean texts from Turkistan, 43 17-19; presides over Manichaean Last Judgment, 50 182, 183-193; as Primeval Man in Manichaeism, 44 63; see also Christ

Jevons, on the effect of development of agriculture on the scope of a deity, 26 173 f.

Jewelry, Etruscan, in Marburg collection, 22 18-19; gold Parthian, from Seleucia-on-the-Tigris, 52 301

Jewels, Chinese, see Pearls

Jews, Jewish, 'Am hā-'ārεṣ, peasant class, growth of their conflict with the clergy, 52 307; blood-test as proof of kinship, 24 129-144; songs from Damascus, 24 227-264; Genoese, trading with Alexandria in the 12th cent., 38 179-184; see also Amulets, Jewish; Apocalyptic Works; Art and Architecture; Calendar; Dimmis; Folklore; Hebrews; Israel; Judaism; Messianism; Songs

History: not settled in Arabia at an early date and did not have a high cultural level there, 54 211-212; persecution of by Leo the Isaurian caused by their messianic expectations, 47 364; relations with Muslims in Egypt, 41 384; ancestors entered Palestine ca. 1100 B.C., 34 417, 419; under Parthian and Sasanian rule: Magian persecution in Parthian times; no distinction in dress; mostly engaged in agriculture and handicrafts, 52 305; homeland in North-Arabian Sinai, 35 386-387; Roman attitude toward in reign of Tiberius, 45 369-370

Language: spoke Aramaic, not Greek, all through the Diaspora, 53 400; Egyptian, did not abandon the Aramaic language, 60 131-134

Law: Mosaic law, relationship to Talmudic, 40 126, commercial law, composed of three elements, 127 n. 1, Asmaktā principle is of Babylonian origin, 126-133

Religion: biblical passages in liturgy, their meaning altered because of absence of context, 44 166; customs retained by Armenians, 32 273, 276-277; religious paraphernalia in the U.S. National Museum, 23 46; seven-branched candlestick modeled after Babylonian sacred tree, 45 362; soul and spirit, distinction between disappeared in later Judaism, 40 117, resurrection, for righteous only, 118-119; wine, unmixed, used in offerings, 32 316-317

Jhangar culture, chronology, 59 Sup. 35 f.; pottery, 59 Sup. 43

Jhukar culture, chronology and characteristics, 59 Sup. 35-37, 42 f., seals, 42 f.

Jichin, Abbot, (1155-1225), author of Gukanshō, biographical notes on, 59 41-42

Jihād, exalted by wealthy Malay Muslims, 33 325-327, 343

Jingoro, Hidari, sculptor; did the woodwork at point of gable of Tsuki hoko, one of the floats used in the Gion matsuri, 54 289

Jinnō Shōtōki, 神皇正統記, value of, as source for study of Kamakura period 59 42

Jirong, god among the Land Dyaks, 26 171-174

Jitaśatru, as an official epithet, 45 309 f.

Jizo, see Ti Tsang

Job, Book of, Chs. 25-35 contain much added material, 53 405; an example of Edomite wisdom literature, 45 353; second set of Jehovah speeches may represent an Alexandrian recension, 46 359

Jōei Shikimoku, 貞永式目, value of, as source for study of Kamakura period, 59 46

Joel, Book of, late date of, 45 361

John, Gospel of, avoidance of first person singular due to Aramaic influence, 49 353

John the Baptist, baptized by aspersion 46 18-20

Johnston, Christopher, life and works of, 36 339-341

Josephus, fragments, many historically genuine, quoted by him from Hecataeus of Abdera, 56 243-244

Joshua, Hexaplaric elements in the first nine chapters of the Old Latin text of, 33 254-258; Washington MS of, relation to Codex Alexandrinus, 31 365-367

Jo-shui, 弱水, the 'weak water' of Chinese legend, located at western edge of the world, 37 143, not in T'iao-chih, 97

Journal of the American Oriental Society, index to vols. 21-40, 44 313-384

Journals, promoting Asiatic studies in 17th cent., see Asiatic Studies in Europe

Juan Yüan, see Wen hsüan lou ts'ung shu 儒學警悟
Judaeo-Arabic, cultural history, Nissim b. Jacob's Hibbûr Yāpē is important for study of, 45 353
Texts: astrological Genizah text and translation, 47 302-310; astrological fragment from the Genizah, 49 291-302; fragment of a commonplace book from the Cairo Genizah, description of, 52 309-310; Kitāb Masālik al-Naẓar of Sa'īd ibn-Ḥasan, ed. and tr., 24 312-383; ophthalmological fragments from the Cairo Genizah, text and translation, 50 112-124; Sufi poem from the Cairo Genizah, 49 168-173
Judah, see Jews
Judaism, began with Jeremiah, 49 366; God, late Jewish and early Christian ideas of, 45 370; Hellenistic, see Philo
Jugglers, from Li-chien (Syria) to China, 30 36; from Ta-ts'in to China, via India, 37 242-243; in T'iao-chih, 37 97, of Li-kan, brought by Parthians as tribute to China, 107, become popular in China, 107
Ju hsüeh ching wu, 儒學警悟, see Ts'ung Shu
Ju-lai Fo, 如來佛, early statues of Maitreya called, 53 47 n.1
Julien, Stanislas, tribute to, 42 392; see also Manchu, Language
Jupiter Dolichenus, representation of, 23 86-87, originally worshipped at Doliche in Commagene, 85, cult obscure, 87-88, mentioned in European inscriptions only, 88-89, 91-92, spread of worship, 84-85, 89-92
Justi's Avestan transcription and the new standard, 21 191
Justinian (Emperor), solidus of found at Kalikinayakanpalaiyam, India, 36 353
Kabāiras or Kubāiras and Greek Kabeiros, 33 55-70
Kabeiroi of Greek mythology, 33 69 f.
Kābul, site of Farnbāg fire in Indian recension of Būndahishn, 41 84-88
Kaīka sept of the Hos, origin of the, 50 231
Kadphises, dynasty of, 35 33-34
Kagalad, Elamite source of copper and clay for Lagaš, 43 44
Kailāsa mountain in the Mahābhārata, 30 365
Kaiserlich-Königliche Oeffentliche Lehranstalt für orientalische Sprachen (Vienna), founded 1851 for teaching modern oriental languages, 39 193
Kaiserliche und Königliche Konsularakademie (Vienna), established 1754 for teaching modern oriental languages, 39 191
K'ai-yüan-shih-chiao-lu, 開元釋教錄, T'ang dynasty catalogue of all trs. of Buddhist books into Chinese, up to 730 A.D.; gives biographical data on Paramārtha, 51 298-299
Kal, Sumerian guardian spirit of the doors, 42 342
Kālāgnirudra Upaniṣad, literary stratum, 23 67
Kālaka story, an Old Gujarātī text of the, 58 5-29
Kalāša, see Piśāca
Kalḫu, became capital of Assyria under Ashurnasirpal, 38 240, 256-257
Kali, worshipped by Karhādā Brahmans, 30 72, 76; and Vikrama, legend of, 23 316 f.
Kali Yuga, beginning of, 24 6 f., 43
Kālidāsa, the date of, 49 75 f.; bibliography of his Mālavikāgnimitra, 23 93-97; of his Vikramorvaśī, 23 98-101; Śakuntalā of, editions and translations of, 22 237-248; Kṛṣṇanātha's commentary on the Śakuntalā of, 23 79-83; Ujjain legend about, 22 331 f.
Kalīlah wa-Dimnah, comparative translation of Ch. VI, 42 215-250; good edition by Ni'mat Allāh al-Asmar of ibn-al-Ḥabbārīyah's text of, 42 394; world's greatest collection of texts of in the University of Chicago, 45 367
Kalpas, Taoist, names of, 53 222, four periods of, 243-244
Kālsī recension of the Fourteen-Edicts of Asoka, 30 77-93; special points of contact of dialect of Girnār redaction with dialect of, 31 247 f.
Kalundi sept of the Hos, origin of the, 50 230
Kalyāṇa, disciple of Rāmdās, folk-story about, 25 186-188
Kamang, spirits of the Land Dyaks, 26 167
Kāmatantra passage cited in Kañcanadarpaṇa of Śivarāma, 24 62
Kamrun, Mountains of, see Aloes
Kanara, treatment of Dravidian final i, 59 103 f.; early, sounds of, 52 133; morphology, 52 135-139; Kanara-Tamil noun-ending -m, origin of, 57 304 f.
Kanauri, notes on phonetics of, 60 311, 312 n.23, 319
Kāñcanadarpaṇa, commentary on the Vāsavadattā of Subandhu, by Śivarāma, 24 57-63
Kan chu chi, 甘珠集, compiled by Chu Sheng-fei c. 1100 A.D., see Ts'ung Shu
Kandahar, became part of Mogul India in 1593; retaken by Shāh 'Abbās in 1622, 35 248-249, 253-254, 263-267
Kandarpa and Gandharva, possible dialectic variations, 51 288
Kanesian, native name of Hittite language, 43 68
Kan Fu, 甘父, Chang Ch'ien's Tartar companion, 37 93-94, 95, 148, an excellent bowman, 95, also called T'ang-i Fu, see T'ang-i Family
K'ang-chü, 康居 (Sogdiana), postal roads to, fr. Ta-yüan, 37 94, visited by Chang Ch'ien, 95, location and description of according to Chang Ch'ien, 95, 96, Chang Ch'ien's visit to, and report of, 95, 96, strong army of; plan to extend Chinese influence to, 98, assistant ambassador sent to, 102, sends help to Ta-yüan against the Chinese, 113, delivered fugitive King of Yü-ch'êng over to the victorious Chinese, 114, 143
K'ang Hsi Emperor, on tobacco, 58 654
K'ang Ling, 康陵, may be a section of the Shên Tombs, 51 148
Kaṇika, identified with Cāṇakya, 44 77
Kanishka, Kushāna ruler, coins of, 56 429-439; dates of, according to various authorities, 35 33, 40, 41, n.1, dynasty of, 35 33-34, 40-41
Kanjur, division of the Tibetan Tripiṭaka, reviews of two studies in the, 52 398-399
Kankanai, loss of intervocalic 1 in, 36 185
K'ang-kü, see K'ang-chü
K'ang Yu-wei, Manchu and early Revolutionary period scholar, on Confucius and antiquity, 56 56
Kānphaṭa yogīs, 45 356
Kan Ying, ambassador to Ta-ts'in from China, 97 A.D., got only as far as T'iao-chih, 35 35-36
Kāpālikas and their practices, 44 202-205
Kapila, sage of the Sāṃkhyas, 22 382-387, called Prajāpati, 386 f.; as Hiraṇyagarbha, 22 386 f.
"Kapola Bania" caste, death ceremonial of, 22 227-236
Karakhoto, see Paper money
Karen, tribes of Burma, language, race, tradition of migration fr. the north, 40 135, monotheistic legend parallel to Genesis account of creation and fall, 135-136; use of bronze drums, distribution of throughout South China, 45 186, relation of to some Philippine tribes, certain Malays, and South China stock, 186-187; Writing, Tradition
Karhādā Brahmans, devotees of Kali, 30 72, 76
Kāriyān, location of Farnbāg fire, 41 89-106, description of modern, 91 f.
Karlgren, his reconstructions of Old Chinese, notes on, 60 303, 304, 306, 309, 310, 315, 316, 319, 320, 322, 323, 330, 334, 335
Kārlī reliefs, interpretation, 54 220
Karyun, see Kāriyān
Kāšān, identified with Cala Ataperistan of Marco Polo, 26 82
Kashgar, see Su-lo
Kashmirian Atharva-Veda, books 1-12, contents of, 46 8-14, comparison with Śaunakīya; charms, 9-12, prayers and imprecations, 10 f., hymns, 12 f., individual themes, 13 f.; contents of, 45 351; book one, edited with critical notes, 26 197-295; book two, edited with critical notes, 30 187-258; book three, edited with critical notes, 32 343-390; book four, edited, with critical notes 35 42-101; book five, edited with critical notes, 37 257-308; book six, edited, with critical notes, 34 374-411; book seven, edited with critical notes, 40 145-169; book eight, edited with critical notes, 41 264-289; book nine, edited with critical notes, 42 105-146; book ten, edited with critical notes, 43 96-115; book eleven,

edited with critical notes, 44 258-269; book twelve, edited with critical notes, 46 34-48; book thirteen, edited with critical notes, 48 34-65; book fourteen, edited with critical notes, 47 238-249; book fifteen, edited with critical notes, 50 43-73; book eighteen, edited with critical notes, 58 571-614

Kashimirian Recension of the Bhagavad Gītā compared with vulgate, 52 68-75

Kashmirian Pañcatantra, position among other versions, 37 15 f.; one of five streams of tradition

Kāśmīrī, see Piśāca

Kassite, Kassites, as an Aryan people, 51 338; elements among the Ḫabīru, 48 184; Indo-European element in, 39 257; Šuriyaš (Sūrya) and Maruttaš(Marut), 51 338

Kāśyapaśilpa, Ch L, vv. 1-7, translated, 52 208 f.

katana, Japanese long sword, 26 349

Kāṭhaka Upanisad, contains earlier conception of yoga-discipline, 22 333-336

Kathakali variations from classical nāṭya, 51 180

Kathā(naka) writings of the Jains, 36 55 f.

Kathāsaritsāgara, contains themes of Harṣa's plays, 21 89; compared with the Bṛhatkathāmañjarī, 53 124-143

Katholikos, office of hereditary among Armenians, 32 275-276, 327-328

Kattigara (Cattigara), on the Red River of Tong-King, the final port of the long sea route fr. Roman Empire to the Far East bet. 1st and 3rd cent. A.D., 37 243, 244, called by the Chinese Kiao-Tsi (Chiao-chih), 243, 244, Roman author's confusion in sailing courses to, and general geography of, due to fact no Graeco-Roman ships got that far, and rarely a traveller, 246-249

Kātyāyana, writer of the Vārtikas, date of, 45 93; approximate date of the writer on law, 51 81 fn.

Kauśāmbī, the site of ancient, 42 396; war between Avantī and, 45 305, location of, 306, besieged by Campā, 307

Kauṣītaki Brāhmaṇa, date of the, 52 391

Kauṣītaki Upanishad, contains earliest reference to constraining by suicide, 21 159

Kauṭilīya Arthaśāstra, notes to Meyer's translation of the, 48 289-322, relative age of, 294, editions and translations of the, 290-294; some allusions to magic in, 42 75-79

Kautilya, character of, 44 76; date of, 51 82 f.; the name, 52 81

Kaviripaddinam, port of the Chola Kingdom of India in early Christian era, busy trade of described in a Tamil poem, 37 245, called Camara by the author of the Periplus, who describes the ships there, 246

Kayans of Borneo, deities, 25 240-244, mourning taboo, 234, 237, influence of war and of agriculture upon the religion of, 231-247; position of women among, 27 211

Kayānids, home around Lake Urumiah and Lake Van; struggle with Hittite and Sumero-Akkadian Turanians, 35 295-296

Kay Kāvūs, attempted ascension to heaven, influence of Etana Myth on, 30 128-129

Keishu, Korea, roof-tiles found at, 55 218-219

Kenites, influenced Hebrew prophetic movement, 38 135-136

Keresāspa, double of Thraetaona, 36 305

Kerman inscription of Darius, 27 193 f., photograph of, (opposite) 190

Keš, town in Babylonia near Kiš and Opis, 41 150-151

Kesecek Köyü (Cilicia), 5th-cent. B.C. Aramaic votive inscription from, 35 370-374

Key to Chinese (Clavis Sinica), see Müller, Andreas

Keying, see Ch'i-ying

Kha che sgom pa, personage appearing on a Tibetan temple painting as one of the incarnations of the Dalai Lama, 52 342

Khafājah, identified with ancient Niqum, 59 107-108

Khaggavisāṇasutta, correct rendering of, 54 218

Khair Khaneh, excavation of a temple on hill of, 57 326-329

Khan 'Ālam, Jahāngīr's ambassador to Shāh 'Abbās, 35 257 ff.

Kharoṣṭī characters, Prakrit inscription in, 24 4 f.

Khmer, art at the Musée Albert Sarrault, 52 83 f.; see also Aloes

Khosru I, King of Persia, destruction of Antioch by, in 540 A.D., 30 6, building a new Antioch at Ctesiphon for his captives, 6-7, ambassadors to or from, 13, 15

Khosru II, King of Persia, enemy of the Christians, 30 6, ruler to whom Li Yü went as envoy, 6, 8, sack of Antioch, 611 A.D., 30 8; known as K'u-sat-ho to the Chinese, 33 197-198

Khotan, Khotanese, The Four Garrisons conquered by Tibet in 670 A.D. taken again by the Chinese in 692, 38 45; literature contained many works tr. fr. the Sansk., 59 468; native names for the language, also Sansk., Tibetan, etc., 59 460; Khotanese Rāma story, 59 397, 460-468; Khotan origin of Tibetan writing, 38 38-46; see also Tun-huang; Yü-tien

Kho-wār, see Piśāca

Khri ral pa, King of Tibet in the 9th cent. A.D., represented on Tibetan temple paintings, 52 342

Khri sroṅ ldehu bcan, King of Tibet in the 8th cent. A.D., represented in Tibetan paintings, 52 342

ibn-Khurdādhbih, notice on Korea, 58 659

Khvārazm, original site of Farnbāg fire, 41 84-106

Kia I, see Ch'ao Ts'o

K'iang (Tangutans), see Ch'iang

Kiang-nan, see Chiang-nan

Kiang-tu, princess of, see Chiang-tu

Kiao-Tsi, see Chiao-chih

Kidinas (Bab. Kidinnu), Babylonian astronomer, worked out his system in 314 B.C; discovered tropic year and precession of equinoxes, 46 87

Kién-weī, see Chien-wei

Kikia, early Assyrian king with Ḫurrian name, lived just before 2000 B.C., 48 91

Kikki, 吉記, value of, as source for study of the Kamakura period, 59 42-43

Kilamuwa, see Inscriptions, Aramaic

K'i-lién-shan, see Ch'i-lien-shan

Kimaš, Elamite city producing copper for Lagaš, 43 44

Kiṃnareśvara, epithet of Kubera, 33 68

Kimpishō, 禁秘抄, by Emperor Juntoku, value of, as source material for study of the Kamakura period, 59 52

al-Kinānī, 'Abd-al-'Azīz ibn-Yaḥya, see Kitāb al-Ḥaydah wa-'l-I'tidār

Kin-ch'ŏng, see Chin-ch'êng

King-Crane Report, publication of, 47 106 n.13

King John and the Abbot of Canterbury, Ballad of, oriental parallels to, 22 221-226

Kingdom of God, impending idea of in Matthew, 45 371

Kings, Book of, Armenian, I and II Kgs., affinities of, 54 53-59

Kings, First Book of, synchronisms in, 47 357

Kingship, in China, ideals of, as expressed in the Model-Emperor Lore regarding Yao, Shun and Yü, 56 51-52, 67-70, 73-75, the divine right of the king lay in his identification with the sun, and his power, therefore, by means of consecrated ritual, to regulate the seasons and the calendar, 67-70, virtue of the king brought wealth and prosperity to the people, 68-70; Islamic ideas of, derived from the Šāh-Nāmah, 55 Supp. 1, 19-21

Kingsmill, T.W., Hirth's answer to his article on the Huns and the Hsiung-nu, 30 32-45; his tr. as used in his paper, "The Intercourse of China with Eastern Turkestan and Adjacent Countries", JRAS, new ser. 14. 74-104, 37 90; death of, in Shanghai, 1910, 31 ii (2)

Kinipa, Mt., identified by Assyrians with Mt. Niṣir of the Flood Story, 38 231

Kin-shi-t'u-shu-pu, see Chin-shih-t'u-shu-pu

Kinship, blood-test as proof of, in Jewish folklore, 24 129-144

Kircher, Father Athanasius, with Father Boym pub. tr. of Nestorian inscription, 58 387-388; the Si-an-fu inscription pub. in his Prodromus, 1630, and remarks on it in China Illustrata, 1667, see Asiatic Studies in Europe; see also Müller, Andreas

Kirkuk, see Nuzi

Kirkuk Tablets, see Akkadian Texts
Kirurri, land N of Assyria incorporated as an Assyrian province; products of, 38 219
Kiš, First dynasty of, dates back into the 5th millennium B. C., 41 250
Kišar, see Anšar
Kiss, of the sun, 60 46-67; and sniff-kiss in ancient India, 28 120-134
Kisurra, situated at abu-Ḥaṭab, 52 114-115
Kitāb 'Ajā'ib al-Hind, see Isḥāq the Jew
Kitāb Aymān al-'Arab wa-Ṭalāqihā of al-Najīrami, text of, 58 615-637
Kitāb Dīwān Miṣr, forged work of Giuseppe Vella, 33 308-312
Kitāb al-Ḥaydah wa-'l-I'tiḏār, of 'Abd-al-'Azīz ibn-Yaḥya al-Makki al-Kināni, MS of in Yale University Library, 39 142
Kitāb al-'Ibar of ibn-Ḫaldūn, editions and MSS of, 46 171-176
Kitāb al-Masālik wa-'l-Mamālik of ibn-Ḥawqal, written before A.D. 891, 54 84-85
Kitāb Masālik al-Naẓar of Sa'īd ibn-Ḥasan of Alexandria, ed. and tr., 24 312-383
Kitāb al-Milal wa-'l-Niḥal of ibn-Ḥazm, Shī'ite sects according to, 28 1-80
Kitāb al-Mudawwanah al-Kubra, was composed by 'Abd al-Raḥmān ibn-al-Qāsim (†806), 41 457 n. 112
Kitāb al-Muḥabbar of ibn-Ḥabīb, composed in or before A.H. 232; only MS of in British Museum; drew on ibn-al-Kalbi, 58 542
Kitāb Naṯr al-Durar of abu-Sa'īd al-Ābi, pt. II, translation of, 54 240-275
Kitāb Radd 'ala Ahl al-Ḏimmah wa-man Tabi'ahum of Ġāzi ibn-al-Wāsiṭi, text and translation, 41 383-457
Kitabatakė Chikafusa, 北畠親房, works of, as source material for study of Kamakura period, 59 42, 52
Kitchen God, 灶神, Tsao Shen, a prayer to the, 49 147-148, origin of, 148 n.1, festival of, 148 n.3; picture of put up, 149 n.11
K'i-tsuṅ luṅ-tsan, see Sroṅ-btsan sgam-po
Kiung district, see Chiung Chou
Kiu-t'ang-shu, see Chiu-t'ang-shu
Kiying, see Ch'i-ying
koan exercise, see Buddhism, Zen
Königlich-ungarische orientalische Handelsakademie (Budapest), founded 1891 (1883?), teaches modern oriental languages, 39 193
Ko Hung, 葛洪, biographical notes on, 60 195 n.4
Kök Tash, coronation stone of Tamerlane, described and measured by Benjamin B. Moore, 1914, 34 436-437
Kokushi, place in the Japanese Shōen system, 57 80-83
Kokushi Taikei, 國史大系, source materials for a study of the Kamakura period contained in, 59 38, 40, 41, 46, 48, 49, 50, 51, 52
Kokutei, see Japanese, Language, Romanization
Kolarian languages, similarities to Buruçaski, 41 66 f.
Koliya clan, cross-cousin marriage at the origin of, 59 222-224
Kombabos, story of in Lucian, compared with so-called Sumerian Paradise Epic, 39 84
Kondô Morishige, 近藤守重, librarian at the Shogun's court, authority for list of books prohibited entry, 1630-1720, 57 291
Koran, Jewish influence in greater than Christian, 54 209-212; Palmer's translation, corrections to, 56 77-84; polemic of al-Mu'tamin ibn-al-'Assāl against, 41 408-409, 447-448; verses from used in magic, 36 44-53
Korea, Korean, Arab geographers on, 58 658-661, known to Arabs as "al-Shīla", 658, Sulaymān's report, 851 A.D., 658-659, ibn-Khurdādhbih's account, note on, 659, al-Mas'ūdi's account 10th cent., 659, al-Qazwīni's, 13th cent., 660, al-Maqrīzi's, 15th cent., 660, identification of, by name and description, 660-661, mention of Moslems in Korean Histories, 661; cartography, see Japan, Geography; referred to by Arab geographers as al-Šīlah, al-Sīlah, 58 658-661; sorcerer's outfit in U.S. National Musium, 23 47; see also Archeology; China, Chinese, History; Tobacco
Kostryuk, the legend of, 46 23-33, in the historical songs; story and historical basis, 23 f., grouping of songs, 25-28, influence of byliny, 28-32, interpretation, 29-33
Kota story with echo-word motif, 58 559-564, 568-570
Kotow, see Macartney Embassy
K'ou Ch'ien-chih, 寇謙之, Taoist practitioner, life of, fr. the Wei Shu, pursuit of geniehood on Mount Sung, 53 225-238, 248 and corrections, 54 292-293
Kou Mang, tutelary god of Spring and the current year, 42 54, part in ceremonies for dispelling pestilence 55, measurements, coloring and all details of his image significantly symbolic, 57-58
Kramīśvara's rules, for Māgadhī, 44 83-89, for Ardhamāgadhī, 106 f.
Krishna sects, impersonation of women among, 47 23
Kṛṣṇamiśra, bibliography of his Prabodhacandrodaya, 25 194-196
Kṛṣṇanātha's commentary on the Śakuntalā, 23 79-83
Kṣatriyas, position in the Vedas, Brāhmaṇas, and Sūtras, 53 181-183
Kṣemendra, as kavi, his Bṛhatkathāmañjarī compared with the Kathāsaritsāgara, 53 124-143; version of the Vetālapañcaviṅśati, 55 59-61
Kshitigarbha, see Ti Tsang
ku, 蠱, see Black Magic
K'uai-chi, see Mt. K'uai-chi
Kuan Chung, 管仲, biographical note on, 59 209 n.38
Kuang-lu-hsün, Superintendent of the Imperial Household, given power, in Han Yüan Ti's reign, to rank members of the imperial retinue, 58 445-446
Kuang-lu-ta-fu, 光祿大夫, title of nobility, given Chao Shih-ch'êng after the Ta-yüan campaign, 37 115
Kuang ya ts'ung shu, 廣雅叢書, a true ts'ung shu, in 560 vols. 51 45
Kuan Yin, 觀音, prayer to, 49 134
Kuan Yü, 關羽, God of War, 49 131 n.1
Kua-wa, 瓜哇, see Names, Geographical, Chinese
Kubēra in Indian mythology, 33 55-70
Kuča, wall-paintings from, 49 62-64
Ku Chieh-kang, author of "Government and History under the cycle of the Five Elements", 56 52, 75, n.4, interpretation of Yü traditions, 54, 56, 61, discards four assumptions concerning ancient period of Chinese history, 70-71, dates Analects of Confucius as earlier than the first few chapters of the Shu-ching, 54, 58, 70, author of Ku-shih Pien, 56, n. 21, 71, n.69, 74, n. 73, propaganda for idea of unification spread in 4th cent. B.C., 74
Kudedah sept of the Hos, origin of the, 50 231
K'uei Chi, 窺基, disciple of Hsüan Chuang and author of commentaries to his writings, 51 293 n.7; entrusted with Hsüan's explanations while translating the Viṃśatikā, 53 144-146, circumstances under which the Wei-shih-er-shih-lun-shu-chi was compiled, 145-148, characteristics of work of, 147-151, method of translation of, 148, abstract of beliefs of various schools of Buddhist philosophy, 148-149, citation of other scriptures, 149-150, use of technical terms, 150-151; see also Wei Shih
K'uei Hsing, 奎星, star deity, patron of Literature, prayer to, 49 137-138 and n.1-5
Kuei-jên, 貴人, notables, leading men of Ta-yüan, decided the policy of their country, 37 109, 112-113, 115
Kuei-shui, 媯水, = the Oxus. The Ta-yüeh-chih live to the north of, 37 96, 97
Kui-jön, see Kuei-jên
K'ui-shui, see Kuei-shui
kü-jen, Chinese literary degree (=Master of Arts), old style examinations for abolished in 1906, 27 83, 85
Kujō Kanezane (1164-1206), author of Gyokuyō, see Jichin
Ku-Khan, Mongol leader, see also Prester John
Kukish, notes on comparative phonetics of, 60 307, 310, 314, 317, 329, 331, 332, 335, 336
Ku-liang Commentary on the Spring and Autumn, study of, revived by Han Hsüan Ti, 58 443, led to calling of the council on Interpretation of the Classics, 443-444; see also Tso-chuan

Kullab, unidentified town in Babylonia, but near Uruk, 40 308
Kultur-Kreis school, tenets of, see Schmidt, Father
K'u-lun, see Urga
Kumārila's evidence on the authorship of the Vṛttikāra, 31 15-18
Kumtura, see Central Asia, Painting
Kun, father of Yü, legend of and interpretation, 56 58
Kün-chöng, see Chün-chêng
Kuṇḍalī, in the Śārada-tilaka Tantra, 23 68-70; origin of name, 23 69
Kundalini, position of, 48 185
Kung Kung, 共工, deity hero of a flood legend, 56 60-61
Kung-sun Hung, Confucian raised by Han Wu Ti to high rank and office; induced the Emp. to establish a Confucian Imperial University, 58 440-441, 446
Kung-yang Commentary on the Spring and Autumn, the authority in time of Han Wu Ti, 58 443, comparison of, with the Ku-liang, led to calling of the Council on Interpretation of the Classics, 443-444; see also Tso-chuan
Kūṇika in the Mahāvīracaritra, 45 305, 308-310
K'un-lun, 崑崙, name of a hill occurring in old books as that where the Ho, or Yellow River, rises; given to hills near Khotan by Chinese ambassadors in early Han, 37 107, 116, 143
K'un-ming, 昆明, tribes southwest of Hsü-chou-fu, given to robbery, 37 99, prevent opening of route to Bactria via India, in time of Han Wu Ti, 99, 104
K'un-mo, 昆莫, title of the King of the Wu-sun, 37 100, 143; see also Wu-sun
Kuo Ch'ang, 郭昌, general sent against the K'un-ming tribes in 109 B.C., 37 104
Kuo Hsiang, a Han title, see Imperial University
Kuo Yü, gives detailed story of Yao, Shun and Yü, 56 55
Kuria Muria Islands, see Abasa and Sacaea
Kuril, dialect words of, compared with Ainu of Yezo and Saghalin, 37 201, 202, 204, 205, 206, 207, 208
Kuroda Yoshitaka, story of the gambling of his vassal Katsura, 31 171-172
K'u-sat-ho, = Khosru, 33 197
Kushan, see Yüeh-chi
Ku Shih Pien, see Book Reviews, Ku Chieh-kang
Kushans, Kushāna, rulers and coins of late, 56 429-439; art, chronology, 46 255; position in Bactria on trade route from China to the West, 35 32-34, 37-39, 41
Ku-shī, see Ku-shih
Ku-shih, 姑師, a city on the Salt Lake, 37 96, interfered with Chinese missions to the west in early Han, 106, defeat of, in 108 B.C., raises prestige of China further west, 106, sends tribute to China, 107
Kuśikas, associated Indra with Maruts, 36 248
Kutīcaka, as class of Yogins, 22 348
Ku-tsang, 姑臧, capture of in 439 A.D. 30 33-34, 43-44, ruins of, close to Liang-chou-fu, Kansu, 34
Kuvera, see India, Mythology
Ku wen text, of the Shu-ching, a forgery, 56 336-337 and n.7
Kü-Yen, see Chü-yen
Kwang-tung and Kwang-hsi, not absorbed by China until 7th cent.; many elephants there up to 10th cent., 41 304
Kwei hai yü heng chi, 桂海虞衡志, by Fan Ch'eng-ta, 范成大, earliest reference to lemons in China, 54 145
Kyzil, see Central Asia, Painting
Labor, Chinese, man-hours in building and furnishing imperial palaces, 1727-1750, the carpenters, 49 236-237, stone cutters and carvers, 237, cart hire, 238-239, 241, painters, 237, reference to papering walls, windows, etc., 237-238; Old Testament attitude toward, 41 193
Lachish, Letters, show that Masoretic text of 7th and 6th cent. documents fairly represents the original, 59 423; seige of by Sennacherib, critique of sources on, 24 266ff.; see also Alphabet and Inscriptions
Lacouperie's theory of the origin of the Tibetan alphabet, 38 37 f.
Lacquer Ware, Chinese, dates on vessels excavated at Lo-Lang, Korea, 54 98, lacquered shoes, 99; inscription on vessels excavated at Lo-Lang, Korea, note on, 56 103; Han toilet-box from Lo-Lang, 55 188; Han, see also Lo-Lang; see also Varnish
Lagaš (Tello), description of site, 50 150, earliest reference to in text of Enḫegal (ca. 3100 B.C.), 151, history of, from Ur texts, 151-158, destroyed by Lugal-zaggizi of Umma, 154; closely associated with Nippur, 42 91-92, worship of Ningirsu at, 91-104, temples at, 95-96, festivals at, 103; divided into quarters of Gírsu, Urukugga, Ninâ and Uru, 57 309-312; E-PA, 7-staged ziggurat at, 43 92-95; war with Umma occurred well along in the reign of Eannatum, 38 266; see also Eninnu; Gudea
Lakṣman, author of Śāradā-tilaka Tantra, 23 66
Lalitavigraharājanāṭaka, Māgadhī in the, 44 100
Lama, Lamaistic, Lamaism, manuscripts, two pub. by Clark in Two Lamaistic Pantheons, 58 695; pantheons, the Staël-Holstein collection of, 51 363 f.; see also Dalai Lama: Paṇchen Lama; Padmasaṁbhāva; Calendar
Lamb, see Paschal lamb
Lamsacos dish, figures on the, 51 181
Lan-chou-fu, = Chin-ch'êng (its name in Han period), 37 100
Land Dyaks, see Dyaks, Land
Lang, 郎, title of an officer in the Imperial household, held by Chang Ch'ien, 37 93, 144; lang, 郎, "chamberlain, page", Han title, 51 269
Lang-chung, "Gentlemen-of-the-Palace", title of lesser scholars of the Imperial University, 58 441
Lang-chung-ling, title of Chief-of-the-Gentlemen-at-the-Palace, Former Han period, 58 438
Language, irreducible minimum in learning a foreign, 43 81-84; learning by foreigners, 33 148 f.; scientific study of vocabulary and idiom, 45 363 f.
Languages, Chinese, Phonetics, see abstract, Kennedy, New Haven, 1936; and dialects, bet. Ta-yüan and An-hsi in early Han, 37 108; Manchu, articles showing Manchu to be a living language, 60 558-559; Comparative philology, Sino-Tibetan, problem of vocalism of, 60 302-337; attempts by Houghton, Simon, and Bonnerjea to establish phonetic laws for, 303-305, recent progress due to Maspero, Wulff and Karlgren, 303-307, aid fr. study of the Daic (Thai or Tai) languages, 303, 305, 306, 307 n.14, present work on phonetic laws of, 302 n.1, 304-307, value of studies of Chinese, especially Old Chinese, 303, 304-307, 309, Old Bodish, 304, 307, list of names of Tibeto-Burmic linguistic groups, 306 n.14, Lušei has the most highly developed vocalic system in, 307, data on initials, Loloish, Old Bodish, Lušei, Burmese, 308-310, final consonants, 310-312, vowels, 312-315, Tables comparing Old Bodish, Burmese, Lušéi, Chinese and Siamese (with Lao), demonstrating phonetic equations, 316-337; schools for study of living oriental languages; needed in America, 39 144-145, 185-188, schools abroad, 189-195, and see also Asiatic Studies in Europe
Laṅkāvatāra, character and doctrines, 52 91-93
Laṅkāvatāra Sūtra, character of, 53 88; translations of, see Book Reviews, Suzuki
Lan-shī, see Lan-shih
Lan-shih (Lan-shī), 藍市, capital of Ta-hsia (Bactria), in the great markets of which Chang Ch'ien saw bamboo and cloth fr. Ssŭ-ch'uan, 37 98
Lao, see Languages, Sino-Tibetan
Lao Lang, the 老郎, three officials of Ch'in Shih Huang Ti, a prayer to, 49 154
Laos, Laotian, writing is alphabetic, 58 693; note on similarity of their script to Siamese, 29 283
Lao-tsu (Lao-tse), little evidence for as an historic figure, 53 209-211, ref. to him by Ssu-ma Ch'ien, 209-210; evidence as to his historicity, 53 209-211; sources for legend of, 53 218-220, and n.6a, 7, 8, 234, n.96, g-grandson of, 247; rating of, in "Table of Ancient and Modern Men", see Chinese Thought
Lao Shang, 老上, the Great Khan, 165 B.C., of the Hsiung-nu, 37 96, killed the King of the Yüeh-chih and made a drinking vessel out of his skull, 96, 133

Lapses, analogical creation and contamination as illustrated by, 57 135-150
Lara Jonggrang, description of the Javanese caṇḍi, 51 4
Larakku, antediluvian Sumerian city mentioned later only in Achaemenid period texts, 41 260
Larissa, in Xenophon (Anab. 3 4, 7) refers to Kalaḫ, 28 102
Larsa, Dynasty of, date formula, discovery of new, 38 329; second antediluvial dynasty, 43 324, 327
Laryngeal hypothesis and Indo-Hittite, Indo-European vocalism, 60 181-192
Laṭakamelaka, Māgadhī in the, 44 100 f.
Latin sigillata signatures, 58 47-60
Lat. and long. of places in China, Ricci's compared to present, 59 338
Latourette, K.S., contributions of to Chinese historical studies, 38 103
Laufer, Dr. Berthold, contributions of to Chinese studies in America, 38 104-105; answer to Francke and Hoernle's theory of Khotanese origin of Tibetan writing, 38 34-46; appointed Honorary Curator of Chinese Antiquities in the Art Institute of Chicago; elected to Finnish Archaeological Society, 40 360; death of, Sept. 1934, 55 348, 368; Committee appointed to plan for a Laufer Memorial, 55 367, American Council of Learned Societies, Committee on Far Eastern Studies, recommend a Laufer Memorial, 368; note on Bibliography of work of, and Biographical Memoir of, by Latourette, 57 421
"Laughing Buddha", see Pu-tai
Laurel, varieties of not found in Somaliland or tropical Africa, 40 262-263, 268-270
Lau-shang, see Lao Shang
Law
Assyrian: Code of ca. 1500 B.C. from Aššur, translation and commentary, 41 1-59; right of primogeniture recognized, 51 371
Babylonian: defaulter, definition of and penalty against, 48 354; deities of justice were: Anu, Bêl, Šamaš and Adad, 52 177, 178; deposit and trust law, compared with that of the Old Testament, 47 250-255; esip-tabal transaction, a type of pawn mentioned in Hammurabi Code but attested from Elam; perhaps an Elamite concept, 52 256-257; Hammurabi Code; arranged according to logical relation of individual laws to each other, 25 248-265; Hammurabi Code compared with the Assyrian, 41 1-59; Hammurabi Code: old and later elements in, 36 1-33, family laws, 3-11, 16-17, 24-31, divorce, 6-7, 24-25, lex talionis, 17-24, woman's status, 10, 24-31; labor contracts, four types of; "harvest-worker" contracts, 58 476-481; loafing during work, penalty for, 56 494; oath in court; terms for; two types, affirmative and promissory, 49 22-29; oath in Sumerian texts, 33 33-50, importance of right hand in, 35, swearing by net (šušgal) of deities, 48-49, oath not found in earliest contracts, 49, contracts with oath but no invocation, 37-42, name of king invoked, 42-48; right of primogeniture recognized, 51 371
Chinese: efforts to combat practice of ku magic, 55 6, n.13, n.14, 10, 14, n.34, 19, punishment of ku witches, 17, 18, 20, 24-25; note on divorce and concubinage, 56 535; Han Dyn., the Empress Têng as detective and judge, 51 145-146, 149-150, 158, her imperial orders and edicts, 147-150, 152-153, 156-157; Han, repeal of law for suppression of literary works, 51 269; notes on Chinese concept of law; Confucian and Legalist schools compared, 49 77-78
Hebrew: blood-revenge passed into lex talionis, then into individual responsibility for sin, but idea of responsibility of children for fathers' sins was revived after the Exile, 28 309-316; defaulter, definition of and penalty against, 48 354; deposit and trust law, compared with the Babylonian, 47 250-255; deuteronomical law-code and covenant modeled on Ex. 33:12-34: 28 and Num. 10:29-32, 38 127-128; Mosaic code antedates Elijah by a generation, 38 127; oath, terms for; methods of taking, 49 26-29; defaulter, punishment of, 49 27; pe'ā, grain left at edges of field for poor, common origin of idea with Ḫurrians, 52 365-366; pentateuchal codes represent continuous tradition, 33 191; pre-Israelite laws in the Book of the Covenant, 41 193; right of primogeniture not recognized until Deuteronomic times; estates divided according to will of parents, 51 371; sale of daughter into slavery to prospective husband paralleled in Nuzi law, 55 190-195; type of law found in Ex. 21:15-17 is of early post-Exilic priestly-oracular origin, 50 338-339; "war legislation" in Deuteronomy is probably early post-Exilic, 52 293
Nuzi: ditennûtu and kaška texts are security transactions, 52 350-367; inheritance, distinction between older and younger son in, 47 53-54; marriage contracts not uniform; brides purchased, 52 296; notes to JEN 333 (lawsuit), 55 439-440; right of primogeniture recognized, 51 371; sale of daughter into slavery to prospective husband paralleled in Hebrew law, 55 190-195; security transaction (ditennûtu) texts and translations, 53 24-46
South Arabic: terms for "law," witness" and "to establish," 37 164-165
Sumerian: ĝul-gik [ḫul-gig] "obstinate resistance," use of term in family code, 38 66-68; oldest laws credited to Nisaba, goddess of writing, and her husband Ḫani, 52 174-175, 177-178, deities of justice were: Gu-silim, Nanše, Ningirsu, Utu, 175-178; right of primogeniture recognized, 51 371
Talmudic: should be studied from point of view of Babylonian law, 38 73
Lazarev Ecclesiastical-Academic Institute for Oriental Languages (Moscow), founded 1815 for teaching modern oriental languages, 39 192-193
Lead, common in lands N of Assyria, 38 220, 215, 238, 247; see also Metals
Leang K'i-tch'ao, see Liang Ch'i-ch'iao
Leaven, symbol of belief in Holy Trinity and return of Christ, 32 312, 316, 338
Lebanon, Lebanese, converted by Simeon Stylites, 35 163-165; dominated by Mari, 41 256
Lebanons, not to be visited by Muslims as sacred place; inhabited by jinn, 56 5-6, 15
Le Brethon de Caligny, in the T'ai-p'ing rebellion, note on, 57 246
Le Coq, see Painting, Central Asian
Legalism, as practiced by the Ch'in State, 57 172, in time of Han Kao-tsu, 172, persistence of, 180; in Former Han, gradual triumph of Confucianism over, 58 436, 437, 438, 440, Legalist character of acts of Han Wu Ti, 442-443, 448, and Hsüan Ti, 444-445, 446, followers of the Legalists, Shen Pu-hai, Shang Yang, Han Fei, Su Ch'in and Chang Yi, dismissed fr. Court of Han Wu Ti, 438
Legends, Chinese, see Feng shen yen yi; Model Emperor Lore; Tung Chun; Hsi Ho; Yü Huang; Mythology, Chinese
Legge, James, on the tr. of san i fen shen in the Nestorian inscription, 58 389; opinion concerning Yao, Shun and Yü, 56 56-57
Legs ldan hbyed, an Indian philosopher whose portrait appears on a Tibetan temple painting of a Panchen Lama, 52 347
Leibniz, see Müller, Andreas
Lei shuo, 類說, compiled by Tseng Tsao in 1146 A.D., see Ts'ung Shu
Lemon, origin India, 54 143, 147, 156-157, word-type "lemon" of Indic origin, 143, 147, n.6, names for in various tongues of India, etc., 146-147, Malayan words for not deriv. fr. Port., 147, 156, Dravidian names, 147 n.6, Manchu, Tibetan, Mongol names, 153, Chinese names for, 144-146, 148-150, 152-154, not introduced into China by foreigners, 143, 147, 154, earliest mention of the li-mung-tzu, 黎朦子, in Chinese records about A.D. 1175, 145, earliest important description, 145-146, not mention in the Pen ts'ao kang mu, 145, probably introduced into Kuangtung province in Sung, 12th cent. or earlier, 143, 145-147, migration fr. India to Indo-China, thence to S. China, 146, steps in migration not traceable, 155-156, Buddhists, had no part in propagation or naming, 147, lemonade, 144, 148-152,

159, lemonade as tribute to the Imperial court, in Yüan period, when it was called she-li-pie, 舍里別, or she-li-pa, 舍里八, (fr. Arabic sherbet or sharbat), 149-151, Mar Sergius, famed sherbet maker, 151, word sherbet used in Yüan period for lemonade, 151, composition of sherbets, 151, use of water ices learned fr. the Near East persists in China to this day, 152, lemon medicinally employed, 145, 148-149, 157, still cultivated in Kuangtung and Se-ch'wan; in northern China mainly in dwarf form, in pots, as an ornamental shrub, 144, 145, 154, 155, established in the Philippines long before Spanish colonization, 155, does not occur wild in the Archipelago, 156, cultivation of began in India bet. 4th and 9th cent., 157, earliest ref. to lemon of India is by Arabic geographers of 10th cent., 157-158, Odoric of Pordenone, and Jordanus first European travelers to mention lemons in India (Ceylon) 157, migration fr. India to Near East under the caliphate, 158, in Syria in 13th cent., 158, Malaga 13th cent., 158, Morocco 14th cent. 158-159, introduced into S. Europe fr. Palestine by Crusaders ?, 159, Arabs took it to Spain ?, 159, culture well established in Italy by 16th cent., 159, fr. Italy to Germany in 16th cent., lemons cultivated in England beginning 17th cent., 159-160; origin not India but Arabia, 56 47-50, word type "lemon" is Arabic, 47-49, wild lemon not recorded as found in India, 49, lemon often confused with sour lime in India where the latter is native, 47-50, lemon well-known in India only in recent time, 47 n3, Laufer, misled, transferred the Skr. and vernacular names of the sour lime to the lemon, 47; origin not India but Arabia, 56 384; not native to Arabian lands, 57 381; Semitic names for of non-Semitic origin, 381, description of in Arabic sources, 382-385; not known to Arabian lands and India before 9th or 10th cent. A.D., 388; not native to Malaysia, 388-390, but to Upper Burma and South China, 395; more Arabic literature on the, 60 97-99, the lemon in al Basrah, Sindh, Iran, 97-98, in Egypt, 98, in Palestine, fr. India, 99; in Persia, Sindh and Egypt, additional references to, 60 97-99
Lemonade, a name given to limeade in India, 56 47; see also Lemon
Lemon grass, used by ancient Arabs for religious purposes, 40 260-261, 263-264, 267-269
Leo (Pope 440-461), opposed by Bar-Šûšan, 32 271, 309
Leo the Isaurian, his persecution of the Jews caused by their messianic expectations, 47 364
Leprosy, see abstracts, Moon, Lewis C.
Levant, Genoese trade with in the 12th cent., 38 176-187
Levi, Sylvain, death of, Oct. 31, 1935, 56 390
Levi, tribe of, established in Judaea before rise of David; never were in Egypt, 57 240; predominant worship was Canaanite Ba'alism, 57 376, four clan families of; list composed as early as Saul's reign, 377-379, championed Moses against rival cult, 378, established in Hebron before it became the capital, 379, foreign names among, 379-380; must have been in Egypt, 54 301-302
Lewis, John Frederick, collection, three Turkish and Persian MSS from, 57 88-94
Lex talionis, in Hammurabi Code, 36 17-24; in the other world (a parallel to JB. i.43), 26 196
Leyte dialect of Bisayan, 26 123-136
Lhasa, headquarters for official correspondence bet. Tibet and China, 38 35, T'on-mi worked on the alphabet there, 35, 36, 42-43
Lha tho tho ri, an early King of Tibet, represented on a Tibetan painting as an ancestor of a Dalai Lama, 52 341
Li, 里, the Chinese mile, a stadium, as used in the time of Han Wu Ti, 37 95, 96, 97, 98, 115, 144; (Jap, sato), Chinese institution of village government copied by the Japanese in the 7th cent., 30 267; 50 family group in rural organization in ancient China, system highly developed in Ming dynasty, 31 192-194; see also Weights and Measures
Liam-po, see Names, Geographical, Chinese
Liang, country of the "Northern Liang" dynasty, ruled by Mu-chien in 5th cent., 30 33-34, capture of capital city, Ku-tsang, by the Toba emperor T'ai-wu in 439 A.D., 34
Liang Ch'i-ch'iao, biographical notes on, 49 76-78
Liang-chou-fu, see also Ling-chü
Liang Wu Ti, friendship of with T'ao Hung-ching, 53 247
Libit-Ištar, controlled Bad-tibira, 52 182-183
Libraries, National Library of Peiping, notes on the, 52 189-190; Palace Library, see Chü chen pan ts'ung shu; John G. White Collection of Orientalia, Cleveland Public Library, 57 239; see also abstract, Chiu; Chi Ku Ko Library; Müller, Andreas; T'ien I Ko
Library loan, see Literature, Chinese
"Library of Ancient Semitic Inscriptions," proposed by Yale University, 39 283-284
Library of Congress, Hebrew books and MSS in, 36 355-359
Li-byin, traditional name of the teacher of T'on-mi in India, 38 36, the distorted etymology of this name forms a basis for the theory of a Khotanese origin for Tibetan writing, 38-41
Licent, Father Émile, S.J., biographical notes, archaeological and palaeontological work of, 57 449-451
Li Ch'ê, 李哆, general under Li Kuang-li in the campaign against Ta-yüan, 37 110, 113, strategical adviser, 115, appointed prefect of Shang-tang, 115
Li Chi, b. 1527; biographical notes on, 59 276-277; comments on the religious philosophy of, 277-280
Li Chi, 禮記, contains the ritual used by the Emperor in regulating the seasons; shows why calendar was important to royalty, 56 67-68; its place in the Canon, 44 282; notes observance of a Reception of Spring ceremony, 42 53; see also Passages
Li-chien, see Names, Geographical, Li-kan
Li Chih-tsao, books by, prohibited in Japan, 57 292-294
Li Chih-ts'ao, friend of Ricci, convert, and engraver of his Map, 59 326, 344
Li-chih-wan, 荔支灣, an Imperial fruit orchard at Canton, 54 148-150
Li-ching, 禮經, Chinese ritual Canon kept at the Royal Court, 44 275; see also li-fa
Li Ch'ŏ, see Li Ch'ê
Li Ch'üan, Tomb of T'ang T'ai Tsung five miles north of, 55 420-421, T'ang T'ai Tsung's memorial temple at the West Gate of, 422, 424, 426, Yu Shih-hsiung, Governor of in 11th cent., 422, 423
Li Ch'üan Hsien Chih, contains text of inscription on the Stele of the Picture of the Six Horses (the Stele of Yu), 55 423
Li Ê, ode in praise of tobacco, 58 655
Li-fa, 禮法, Chinese ritual Canon kept at court of feudal princes, 44 275; see also li-ching
Li, Dr. Fang-kuei, appointment to Yale, 57 208
Life-index in Hindu fiction, 39 142
Li Fu-jên (Li Fu-jŏn), 李夫人, Madame Li, favorite concubine of Emperor Han Wu Ti, sister of the general Li Kuang-li, 37 110
Li Hung-chang, effort to open direct relations with the Vatican, see abstract, Hail; memorials of, concerning Chinese Education Commission to U.S., see abstract, T.L. La Fargue
Liḥyanite, language, full form of article ha- was han-, 56 415; see also Semitic Languages
Li-kan, 黎軒, (Syria) called Ta-tsin in later records, 37 97, China's regular traffic with, 103, 107, identity of, 144
Li-kiẽn, see Li-chien
Li (Kuang ?), General, 李將軍, Chang Ch'ien's chief in 122 B.C., 37 99
Li Kuang-li, 李廣利, generalissimo in campaign against Ta-yüan, is given title of "General Ïr-shï" (Erh-shih) (Nish ?), 37 110, 144, disaster to his armies, 110, forbidden to return inside China, 111, second campaign, 112-115, created Marquis of Hai-hsi, 115; account of his submission to the Hsiung-nu suspect, 55 333
Li Ma-tou, 利瑪竇, see Ricci
Lime, sour, native of India, called nībū, nēbū, nimbū, libū, 56 49; Laufer (and most Indians) confuse it with the lemon, 47-50; bought today in India under name of "lemon", 47
Lin, 隣, an administrative unit of 5 houses, in ancient China, 31 192-194

Lin, of Ch'in, underofficial of Ch'uan-chou, his defiance of the ku magic, 55 28
Linen textiles in Babylonia in third millennium B.C., 36 415
Ling-chü, 令居, near Liang-chou-fu in Kansu; Great Wall at, 37 103
Ling-kü, see Ling-chü
Ling nan tsa ki, 嶺南雜記, by Wu Chen-fang, 吳震方, 17th cent., refers to the lemon, 54 145, 148
Ling Tai Fu, note on parallel idea of 'whiteness' = leprosy, in Arabic and Chinese, as illustrated in a poem by, 46 355
Linguistic, Linguistics, method, canons of, 55 121; linguistic science and the orientalist, 55 115-137; linguistic terminology, 55 122 f.; Chinese, one of main divisions of oriental field, together with other monosyllabic tonal languages, 55 119, Chinese words cannot be compared with words from unrelated languages, 121, efforts of C.J. Ball to establish Semitic roots for Chinese and Japanese words is nonsense, 130-133; advantages of ideographic writing over phonetic, 55 338-339
Ling-wai-tai-ta, 嶺外代答, by Chou Ch'ü-fei, 周去非, contains notice on fruits cultivated in S. China about 1178 A.D., 54 145; Chau Ju-kua's debt to, 30 12, 13, tr. of passages about the King of Ta-ts'in and his appointing the ruler of India, 10, 12
Lion, first mention of in China, 60 582
Lion-god, predecessor of Gilgameš loved by Ištar, 40 321, 328-329, 331
Li P'u-wen, great grandson of Lao-tzu, 53 231, 248
Lisān al-Ṭayr of Navāyi, twelve of its tales borrowed from 'Attār's Manṭiq al-Ṭayr, 49 185-186
Li Sao, 離騷, refers to Hsi Ho, and the sun myth, 56 64
Li Shih-min, see T'ang T'ai Tsung; Wên Ta-ya
Li Ssu, rating of, in "Table of Ancient and Modern Men", see Chinese Thought
Lists, of Ainu numerals, 37 195, of Ainu words in the Yezo, Saghalin and Kuril dialects, 201-203, 205-207; of duals in Atharva-Veda after dual antecedents, 35 28 f.; of Avesta words with k-suffix, 31 306-310; of the divine and demonic epithets in the Avesta, 46 97-153; Bahing, changes in the verb in, 60 311-312; Old Bodish and Burmese words compared, 60 309; of Bahuvrīhi ka-words, 31 122 f.; of forms, found in Bhāgavata Purāṇa, not quotable except from Epic and Veda, 25 92; of Buddhist Sanskrit words tr. into Chinese, 53 148; of 8 schools of Buddhist thought with notes on doctrines of, 149, of 12 sūtras and śāstras cited by K'uei Chi for Wei Shih doctrines, 149-150, of Chinese technical terms in logic, 150-151; Buddhist Sanskrit words trs. into Chinese, 51 300, 305; Chinese Books, import of, into Japan prohibited in 17th cent., 57 292-294, 295, 296, 298; Chinese, uses of the word An, 安, 58 161-162; Chinese, the twelve Princely Houses of Chou, 52 234; Chinese definitions of the word yen, 焉, 60 1-3; of the 58 incarnations of the Dalai Lama, 52 339-340, of the spiritual ancestors of the Panchen Lama, 346; of forms found in Epic, quotable in earlier, but not classical Sanskrit literature, 25 94 f.; of Iloko names for anatomical parts, 49 1-21, of man, 1-11, of animals, 11-14, of plants, 14-21; of Iloko animal names, 48 1-33; of Iloko names of pathological conditions, 49 244-262; of Iloko plant names, 47 133-173; of Indian architectural terms, 48 251-274; Japanese, chart of differences bet. 3 systems of Romanization, 60 83; Japanese, table of Intendants of the Sho-gun in 1867, 31 158; of Pāli originals of some Jātaka stories, 38 267 f.; of Pañcatantra parallels to modern Indian folk-tales, 39 13-16; of principal elements used in formation of pronouns in Philippine languages, 27 388-396; of Piśāca-Rommany equations, 29 233-235; of archaisms found in Rāmāyaṇa, but not in Mahābhārata, 25 95 f.; of Rāmāyaṇa forms unrecorded by Whitney, 25 96 f.; of peculiarities of Rāmāyaṇa not yet noted in Mahābhārata, 25 96; of duals in Rig-Veda after dual antecedents, 35 16-18; of dual dvandvas in Rig- and Atharva-Vedas, 32 47-53; of elliptic duals of Rig- and Atharva-Vedas, 32 41-44; of proverbs and proverbial expressions in the Śālibhadra Carita, 43 287-290; of characteristic Jaina words and forms in the Śālibhadra Carita, 43 290-297; of words in the Śālibhadra Carita, not in lexicons, 43 297-306, quoted only in lexicons or grammars, or quoted in present meaning only in same class of texts, 43 306-313; of new denominal verbs and participles and elative verbs in tarām in the Śālibhadra Carita, 43 313 f.; of words in the Svapnavāsavadatta of Bhāsa not in either of St. Petersburg lexicons, 35 269-271; of Tagalog polysyllabic roots with initial p, which contain, or may contain an initial prefix, 25 290-301; names of Tibeto-Burmese linguistic groups, 60 306 n.14; Sino-Tibetan; examples of sonancy in Loloish, 60 308; tobacco, terms for, in Chinese, Manchu, Korean, Japanese, 58 657; of Vedic duals, 30 157-164; of Vedic words with unclassifiable ka-suffixes, 31 124 f.; of Vedic words, with suffix -ika, without vriddhi, 31 296, with vriddhi, 297 f., with suffix -aka, 298-300, with suffix -uka 300-302, with suffix -īka, 302 f., with primary suffix -ka, 303 f.; of Vedic k-words, 31 312-341
Lisu, see Loloish
Litanies, Christian, compared with invocation to Tammuz and Nanâ, 33 345
Li Tao-yüan, at Lung Mên in 6th cent., 56 60; tr. of his commentary on the Shui-ching, part dealing with Indo-China reviewed, 56 96
Literature
Chinese: fiction, began in Han era, 60 586; library loan groups in 18th cent., see abstract, Swann
Tibetan origin of the epic poem of Gesar, 52 95, extant copies, 95-96, identification of Gesar with Kuan-ti, 96, notes on texts of the Bon religion, 96-97; see also Bibliography
Lithang Ms. of Padma thang yig, date of, 54 312 f.
Lithuanian, klónas, kluonas 'a place where something is spread out', 40 353-355, list of words containing base of, 354 f.; etymologies: výdraga "virago", 42 186, żógis "meadow-drain, gully", 187 f.
Li Tschi, see Li Chi
Li tse ts'ung shu, 笠澤叢書, first used term ts'ung shu in title, but the writings are all by one author, 51 40
Liu Chên, 劉珍, scholar of Later Han, at court of Empress Têng, 51 151-152 n.83
Liu Chi, see Han Kao-tsu
Liu Chiao, Confucian scholar, influence upon his brother Han Kao-tsu, 57 176-177
Liu Chieh, expert on bronze inscriptions, 56 335
Liu Chung, older brother of Han Kao-tsu, 57 176
Liu, Chungshee H., biographical data on, 57 198
Liu Hsin, see Tso-chuan
Liu-i, the Six Dep'ts of Art, the six arts of propriety, music, archery, chariot driving, language, mathematics, taught in the schools in ancient China, 44 280, term later applied to text-books, 280
Liu Li Ch'ü, town near Peking where glazed tiles were made in 18th cent., 49 241
Liu Po, oldest brother of Han Kao-tsu, 57 176
Li Yen-shou, 李延壽, author of the Pei Shih, see Wei Shu
Li Yi-chi, official of Han Kao-tsu, 58 436; biography of, 57 176, Confucian advisor of Han Kao-tsu, 177
Li Yü, 李昱, envoy of Yang Ti to Persia to persuade Persians to send an embassy to China, which arrived bet. 605 and 616 A.D., 30 6, 8; 33 196
Li Yüan, see T'ang Kao-tsu; Wen Ta-ya
Liver-omens, see Hepatoscopy
Livingston, Robert R., first American Egyptologist and orientalist, 51 364
Līwān, see Īwān
Lo Chen-yü, a publisher of ts'ung shu, 51 42; see also Hsüeh t'ang ts'ung k'an
Lo Ch'ung-chih, 羅崇之, Taoist practitioner accused of being an imposter, 53 240-241, 54 293
Locusts, devastate country when Chinese army starts against Ta-yüan, 37 110; four stages of mentioned in the O.T., 53 405
Lo Fu-ch'ang, principal author of the Volume on Tangut Studies, see Book Reviews

Λόγος κεφαλαιώδης περὶ ψυχῆς πρὸς Τατιανόν of Gregorius Thaumaturgus, Syriac version of, 35 297-317
Lohaśāstra passage cited Kāñcanadarpaṇa of Śivarāma, 24 63
Lokāyata, as title of Indian materialism, 50 132-138, earliest reference to, 136
Lokeśvara, see Avalokiteśvara
Lo-Lang, 樂浪. Korea, review of Harada's report on excavation of, 54 97-99; description of a fitted toilet box of Han, from excavations at, 55 188; see also Tomb, of the Painted Basket
Loloish, words in, compared with Old Bodish, Burmese, Ahi, Nyi, Lisu, Moso, PKS, KSY, 60 308-309, phonetic data, 322
Longfellow, Henry Wadsworth, see Scanderbeg, Edrehi
Lopnor (the Salt Lake), region cleared of Hsiung-nu in 121 B.C., and Wu-sun invited to occupy, 37 100-101, Chinese victories near, 106, dangerous region for travelers, 109, Chinese army against Ta-yüan crosses, 110, military stations in Han times line road as far west as, 106, 116; see also Salt Lake
'Lotus of the Good Law', scenes fr., illustrated on early Chinese Buddhist sculpture, 51 366
Lou-lan, 樓蘭, a city on the Salt Lake, 37 96, interfered with Chinese missions to the West, in early Han times, 106, defeated in 108 B.C. and King of captured, 106, 110, 135
Love magic, "love medicine" made for ku magic, 55 11-13
Lowell, Prof. Percival, death of Nov. 13, 1916, at Flagstaff, Arizona, 37 5
Loyang, site of a Taoist altar, 53 248
Lubbock on religion, 25 332 f.
Lucerne, see Mu-su
Lu Chia, adviser to Han Kao-tsu; envoy to Nan-yüeh, 57 179, author of the Hsin-yü, 179; official of Han Kao-tsu, 58 436, helped enthrone Han Wên Ti, 436
Lucian, see Φιλοψευδὴς ἢ 'Απιστῶν
Lugalbanda, deified king of Uruk, 41 252; character and rôle in mythology; influence on Gilgameš epic, 40 311-316; and the Zû bird, text of found among Sumerian tablets from Nippur, 44 160
Lugaldaudu, king of Adab, 33 295-296
Lugalgira, see Šitlamtaea
Lugalkinišududu, king of Uruk and contemporary of Entemena of Lagaš, 51 262
Lugalsabar-ininni, Babylonian deity, 51 264
Lugum sept of the Hos, origin of the, 50 229
Luke, Gospel of: author modified his sources, 58 82 ff., employed Pauline Epistles, 83-91, Luke-Acts not earlier than end of 1st cent., 84; description of 6th-cent. Garrett Sahidic MS of, 55 451-457
Luk-li, 谷蠡, title of a Hsiung-nu prince, 37 95, usual pronounciation "ku", here "luk", 145
Lullabies, 48 235-238, 247-249
Lü Lu, see Empress Dowager née Lü
Lung-hién, see Lung-hsien
Lung-hsi, 隴西, = modern Kansu, Chang Ch'ien set out fr., 37 94, 96
Lung-hsien, see Ambergris
Lung Mên, ancient legends of, 56 59-60, n.28; establishment of Taoist monastery at, 53 223-224, 242, 54 291
Lung-nao, "dragon's brains", camphor, 42 364
Lung-si, see Lung-hsi
Lun-t'ou, 侖頭, a city on the route west fr. China in the Han period, able to harass Chinese expeditions, 37 111, refused provisions to the Chinese army and was laid in ruins, 112, soldier farmers stationed at, to raise supplies for embassies, 116, bibliographical ref., 145
Luṅ-tsan, see Sroṅ-btsan sgam-po
Lun Yü, quotations fr. in the Yen T'ieh Lun, 51 267, 273; see also Passages
Luqmān, native Arab sage of comparatively recent origin, 60 288
Lurs, Zuṭṭ of Lower Iraq are probably related to them, 44 132-133
Lus̈ei, see Languages, Sino-Tibetan
Lushais, assumption of appearance of opposite sex among, 47 22 f.
Lü Su, printed before the Diamond Sutra, 56 535
Lu Wan, close friend of Han Kao-tsu, 57 176
Luwian and Hittite ritual of Zarpiya of Kezzuwatna, text, translation, and commentary, 58 334-353
Lü-yüeh-jên, 呂越人, unsuccessful leader of caravans to Bactria, in time of Han Wu Ti, 37 104
Lü-yüé-jŏn, see Lü-yüeh-jên
Luzon, some minor languages of, 25 170-174
Lycian sign X, 56 406
Lyman, Benjamin Smith, death of, in Philadelphia, Aug. 1920, 41 164
Macabebes, language of, 25 173 f.
Maccabees II, festal letters prefixed to, textual and historical notes on, 60 122-130, Greek is translation from Aramaic, 127, 134-137, 139, translated by the Epitomist himself, 139-141, originally written in Aramaic, 130-137, reconstructed Aramaic text and translation, 141-150
Mac Donald, Duncan Black, appreciation offered to, 53 94-95
Mac Donald Presentation Volume, announcement of publication of, 52 402
Macao, see Tobacco
Macartney Embassy, see International Relations, Anglo-Chinese
MacKinlay's Tagalog Handbook, 42 156 f.
Madain, see al-Māda'in
Madame Li, 姬字氏, see Li Fu-jên
Madanasundarī, the story of, in the Bṛhatkathāmañjarī and Kathāsaritsāgara, 53 141-143
Madga, Madqa, Mt., Elamite source of bitumen, 43 44
al-Madīnah, ibn-Jubayr's visit there in A.D. 1184, 50 26-42
Madjapahit, Hindu-Javanese kingdom, influence of in Borneo, 33 330
Maes, Macedonian silk merchant, on the silk route, see Ptolemy's Geography
Mafigliastro, Buongiovanni, 12th-cent. Byzantine-Genoese merchant in Levant trade, 38 184-185
'Māgadhan' dialects of the Fourteen-Edicts of Asoka, special points of contact of dialect of Girnār redaction with, 31 248-250
Māgadhī, and Ardhamāgadhī, 44 81-121, according to the grammarians, 82-93, in the manuscripts, 95-97, dramas, 97-105, in the quotations of Hemacandra, 104, characters speaking, 110-114, manuscripts versus the grammarians, 118-121
Māgadhisms, in Girnār redaction of Fourteen-Edicts of Asoka, 31 223-229; in the recensions of the Fourteen-Edicts of Asoka, 30 77-93
Magan, included Egypt, 42 321; probably is not Egypt and the east coast of Africa, 43 45-48; early Babylonian name for Egypt and surrounding countries, 45 238-240
Magi, identification of their native cities according to Marco Polo, 26 79-83, reputed tombs of in Sāvah, Urumiah and Cologne, 83
Magians, regard days as named after planets, 32 319 n.5, kept Dec. 25 as winter solstice feast, 322
Magic, referred to in a prayer, 49 145, 146 n.3; see also Amulets; Black Magic, ku
Babylonian: Marduk patron of magic and exorcism, 34 308
Chinese: later Han mirrors considered to have occult power, 55 187-188; sacrifice of dogs to stop wind, 55 3, blood of black dogs an antidote to magic, 3, incantations and spells as a protection against ku, 6, 8, 16-17, 18, bronze chop-sticks as charm against ku, 12, t'iao-sheng, the bewitching of food, 15-16, cowhide ku, 16-17, burial of food at street intersection to turn the ku on the witch, 19, ceremonial preparation of ku "love medicine", or poison, 10-11, 21, for practice of ku in general see Black Magic; the "magic poison affair" in 102 A.D., 51 143 n.22, 146 n.37; spells for dispelling annoyances, 53 245, 54 293; to prevent swords from cutting and foes from burning, 53 246, 54 293; charm books, 53 241, 244-249; magicians, 53 249, 54 294; theory that performance of ritual by the king gave him power over Nature and Man, 56 67-70, Yü's dancing caused submission of the Miao, 68

Coptic: papyri at University of Michigan, Sethianic origin of, 48 358
Ethiopic: Arde'et, magic book of the Disciples, ed. and tr., 25 1-48
Indian: in Kautilya's Arthaśāstra, some allusions to, 42 75-79; in the Sanskrit drama, 45 110-114
Islamic: magic bowls, meaning of symbols on, 55 237-256
Japanese: holly vested with magic power from earliest times, 55 444-450, magic holly in ancient court ceremony of driving out evil spirits and in the Setsubun festival, 445-449, efficacy of the shrine of Holly against small-pox, 449-450
Malay: 33 331-333, 335
Oriental: works on in Cleveland Public Library, 36 421-422
Magic circle, see Rāma Story, in Khotanese
Magindanao Moro, see Philippine languages, comparative grammar
Magnetic needle, early known to Chinese, 37 244
Mahābhārata, chronology and divisions of time, 24 7-56; Colorado-Telingana Mss. of portions of the, 51 357; the critical edition of the, 48 186-190; date of the pseudo-epic, 22 379; emendation of ii.2193 (Calcutta), ii.66.8 (Bombay), 59 366-368; hypermetric triṣṭubh and jagatī in the, 59 159-174; metre of, 22 389; Mokṣadharma story of world creation and dissolution; compared with Sāṃkhya, Manu, and Yoga forms, 45 51-67; mythological aspects of trees and mountains in, 30 347-374; numbers (form and syntax) and numerical categories in, 23 109-155; the oath in, 52 316-337; omissions in recensions of Ādi, 52 253 f.; passages referring to materialism in the, 50 134; phrases of time and age in, 23 350-357; theory of prose beginnings of metrical verses, 43 54 f.; allusions to the Rāma-story in the, 50 85-103, Śānti, 88-90, 100-102, Rāmopākhyāna, 92, passages anticipating the Rāma-story, 93, Bhīma's references, 94 f., Droṇa later than Bhīṣma and and Karṇa, 96, 99, Droṇa, 90-92, 96-100; Rome and (?) Antioch in the, 58 262-265; Sāvitrī story in Vana-parvan, sections 292-299, 21 53-59; suicide in general, 21 148-150; suicide by starvation, 21 150-155; Sukthankar's edition, 49 282-284; war, ages of combatants in, 24 47-54; war, date of, 24 6 f., 52-55; text with Yoga tendencies, 45 64-66; yoga-technique in, 22 333-379
Māhārāṣṭrī, Jaina, words found in Vedas, but not in classical Sanskrit, 44 160
Mahatara, supreme deity of Dyaks of Kotei, 33 336
Mahāvīracaritra, of Hemacandra, the story of Rauhiṇeya in the, 44 1-10; historical references in the, 45 301-310
Mahāyāna Buddhist Scriptures, relation of adhiṣṭhāna-power to projection of Nirmāṇa-kāyas, 56 415
Mahāyānasaṃgraha, see Buddhism
Mahāyānasaṃparigrahaśāstra, by Asaṅga, Chinese tr., She-ta-sheng-lun, 51 296
Mahdi, Muḥammad Aḥmad, letter of to Gen. Gordon, with translation, 31 368-388
Maheśvara's commentary on the Nirukta, 50 175
Mahīpālacaritra by Vīradevagaṇin, 53 391
Maimonides, his theory of conciliation between the O.T. and philosophy does not question the former, 55 Supp. 1, 26, his attitude toward the O.T., 27-29, first to use comparative religion in the study of the O.T., 28
Maitrāyaṇīya Upaniṣad, date of the, 52 391
Maitreya, legend of his dictating to Asaṅga the Yogācarya-bhūmiśāstra, 51 297, 301; see also Pu-tai
Maitri Upaniṣad, yoga terminology of the, 22 333-336
Maize, spread from original home in Yucatan, 39 162
Ma Jung, see Dice
Makal, see Rašap
Makha, the Titan, the significance of his decapitation and head, 55 377-382
Makha Saumya, his identity with Prajāpati, 55 381 f.
Malabar caste system, position of Nayadis, 59 130
Malabar Coast, Graeco-Roman trade with, 37 241, pirates off the, 241, vessels peculiar to the, 246
Malachi, Book of, title was originally "Utterance of Yahweh through his Messenger," 42 396
Malanao Moro, see Philippine languages, comparative grammar
Mālatīmādhava of Bhavabhūti, bibliography, 25 339
Mālavikāgnimitra of Kālidāsa, bibliography of, 23 93-97
Malaya, Malays, Malay, name of Malay given to all Muslims in Borneo, 33 321-322; see also Islam; Magic
Ethnology: Malay Archipelago, custom and race in, 27 195-216, cultural divisions, 199 f.; in North Australia, 58 71-78; source of Sea Dyaks' sea-faring and piracy, 25 232, 239
Language: Malayan "Bahasa Kapor" speech, 45 93
Religion: paganism, its contact with Islam in Borneo, 33 314 ff.
Malgundi sept of the Hos, origin of the, 50 231
Mālikites, chiefly found in Upper Egypt and North Africa; numbered about 20,000,000 in 1924, 44 32
Mallinātha Carita, chronicle of the woman Mallī, nineteenth Tīrthaṃkara of the Jainas, 44 166
Malliṣeṇa Sūri's Syādvādamañjarī, 49 67 f.
Mālobā, the Marāthā saint, translation of his life in Mahīpati's Bhaktalīlāmṛta, 40 300-306
Malta, not settled from Carthage, 48 359; see also Semitic Languages
Malto sound written "q", 56 350
Ma'lūlah, dialect of, see Syriac Language and Semitic Languages
Māmalla style of sculpture, 49 70
Man, Primal, is Jesus in Manichaeism, 44 63, is Ormazd, 69, 71
Manāfi' al-Ḥayawān of ibn-Buḫtīšū', MS of in the Morgan Library, 36 381-389
Manas, udāna and, 22 272 f.
Mānavadharmaśāstra story of world creation, the Mokṣadharma story compared with, 45 56-59
Manchu, Manchuria, Manchurian, Dictionary in MS. prepared by Stanislas Julien, now in Cleveland Public Lib., 40 140; Language: Grammatical studies, see Asiatic Studies in Europe; prohibitions of Tobacco in, see Tobacco; resisted in Yünnan by war elephants 17th cent., 41 306; see also China, Chinese, History
Mandā dᵊ Ḥayyē, partial prototype of in Babylonian Siduri, 38 64
Mandaeanism, Mandaeans, Mandaean, Mandaic, bibliography on 46 49-55, a Mesopotamian gnostic system, 49, preserves Neo-Babylonian elements, 50, an East Aramaic dialect akin to Syriac and to that of the Babylonian Talmud, 49, original home in the Ḥawrān, 50; originated in north Palestine, 46 347; influence on al-Muġīrah, 29 80-88; see also Bowls (incantation)
Language: see Semitic Languages
Magic Bowls: Mandaean-Syriac magic bowls from Nippur, 32 434-438; Mandaean-Syriac incantation bowls from Nippur, notes to, 33 279-280
Religion: first discovered by the West in the 16th cent., 49 195, Sunday observance taken from Christians, 198, classed as dimmis by Muslims, 199, not identical with Ṣābians, 199 ff., origin in Palestine, 211-218, Compared with other Gnostic sects, 205-210; Ptahil, his character influenced by that of Yima-Jamšīd; is supreme beneficent creator deity, 53 157, 164, Abaṭur, identified with Iranian Rašnu, 163, 165, Creation from egg, 161-164; possible intermediary between Zoroastrianism and Manichaeism, 43 21-22; Christ believed to be false Messiah, 49 197
Script: closely related to Nabataean and Palmyrene, 49 211
Mandalay, see Trade Routes
Maṇḍapa, construction of a, 23 69
Mandaya, treatment of original l in, 36 186 f.
Mang, 駹, a barbarous hill tribe of China's southwestern frontier; Han Wu Ti's attempt to open a trade route through the country of the, 37 99
Mangyan, affinity with Tagbanua, 60 271; bamboo manuscripts, 59 496-502; bamboo writings, 60 271 f.
Mani, his name and portrait presumed to exist on Characenian and Kūšān coins; problematical portrait of him from Khocho, 58 235-236, personal description of him; his

lameness, 235-240; his position in Manichaean texts from Turkistan, 43 16-19; referred to as Messiah, 45 250; referred to himself as the "Apostle of Jesus," 49 34
Manichaeism, Manichaeans, Manichaean, Biblical, especially New Testament, influence on, 56 198-207; βῶλος, doctrine of; sectarian belief that a small portion of Light was irredeemable, 58 225-234; Christian influence on, 53 387; compared with Christians by al-Jāḥiẓ, 47 331-332; confession-prayer xv'stv' nyft, a reading of, 52 79; denies bodily resurrection, 45 247, mankind divided into Elect, Hearers, Sinners; parallels in Indian philosophy and in Gnosticism, 247, metempsychosis as a form of retribution, 246-268, compared with Ṣūfi Ladder of Evolution, 266; passed on Docetic doctrines to Islam, 29 29, influence on al-Muġīrah, 80; Jesus, reappearance of, 50 182, 183-193, borrowing from judgment scene in Matt. 25:31-46, 190, world conflagration lasting 1468 years, 195-198, Hummāma, female spirit of darkness, leads last combat of evil against light, 198; not derived from Mandaeism, 49 207; metempsychosis as a form of retribution, 44 161; Miyazdagtāčīh, a food and drink offering, 49 34-39; "Mother of the Living" in Arabic, Pahlavi and Chinese texts; doctrine of the seven seals, 44 61-72; Painting, see Central Asia, Painting; soul, fate of after death; Zoroastrian, Buddhist and Gnostic-Christian elements in, 50 177-181, balance, weighing in, 179, metempsychosis, 178, 180, last judgment and end of the world, 181-198, messianic and apocalpyptic influence in, 50 181; script, similar to that on Syro-Mandaean incantation bowls from Nippur, 32 437-438; weighing soul in balance, borrowed from Zoroastrianism, 43 20-22, account of life in hereafter borrowed from Zoroastrianism, 22-24, Zoroaster, Jesus and Buddha in, 17-19; see also Art
Maṇimekhalai, character and date, 49 71-72
Maṇiprabhā, commentary to Patañjali's Yoga-sūtras, translated, 34 1-114
Mansehra, inscriptions of Asoka, language of, the proposed connection with modern Piśāca, the writing of r, 36 210 f.; redaction of the Fourteen-Edicts of Asoka, 30 77-93; redaction of Fourteen-Edicts of Asoka, special points of contact of dialect of Girnār redaction with dialect of, 31 245-247
Manṭiq al-Ṭayr of Farīd al-Dīn 'Aṭṭār, translation of allegory of moths and the flame from, 36 345-347; influence on the Lisān al-Ṭayr of Navāyi, 49 185-186
Mantra formation in the Śāradā-tilaka Tantra, 23 70-76
Manu, Buddhistic passage in, 43 165, 43 244-246; divinity of kings in, 51 311; and the Manu-smṛti, 51 83; penalties and penances in the laws of, 44 243-257
Manuscripts
Arabic: at the University of Chicago, 45 366; in Cleveland Public Library, 57 239; in Columbia University Library, 49 219-232; Damascus MS dated A.D. 1249 of al-Baġdādi's al-Farq bayn al-Firaq, 46 353; in Garrett Collection, Princeton University, 45 350; of ibn-Ḫaldūn's works, 46 171-176; version of Historiae adversum paganos of Orosius in Columbia University, 51 171-172; Kitāb al-Ḥaydah wa-'l-I'tidār of al-Kināni, in Yale University Library, 39 142; in Lansing collection, Denver Public Library, 60 371-376; Risālat Qawānīn Ḥikam al-Išrāq of al-Šādili, MS of in Princeton, 57 100-101; in Turkey, notice of, 59 227-243; Widgery and Baroody collections in the Princeton University Library, 46 343; ibn-Zūlāq, descriptions of MSS of his works, 28 255-270
Buddhist: fr. Tun-huang, in the National Library of Peiping, over 8,000, 52 190
Čaġatay-Persian: Dictionary of Fatḥ 'Ali Ḫān in Leningrad, 49 186
Chinese: description of MS (now in Lib. of Congress) giving Regulations for building and furnishing imperial palaces, and certain temples, bet. 1727 and 1750, 49 234-243; edicts and proclamations of Emp. Shun Chih 1644-61, 3 ms. vols. loaned to Univ. of Calif. by Mr. John Gilbert Reid, June 1932, 52 180-181; see also Tun-huang
Coptic: St. Luke, 6th-cent. Garrett Sahidic MS of, description of, 55 451-457
Druze: at the University of Chicago, 45 366
Ethiopic: Bibliothèque Nationale eth. 26 text of Acts (15th cent.) is of mixed or Antiochene type, 49 353
Greek: Codex Venetus, sub-Origenian; photo of in Philadelphia, 46 340; Joshua, Washington MS of, relation to Codex Alexandrinus, 31 365-367
Hebrew: in the Library of Congress, 36 355-359; methods of isolating O.T. MSS of school of Ben Naftali, 51 371
Khotanese: see Rāma Story, Khotanese
Manchu: Manchu studies since 1908, 60 554-559, collections in the U.S.A.; unpublished ms. of Stanislas Julien's dictionary of, in Cleveland Public Library, 559, description of ms. Emu tanggô orin sakda-i gisun sarkiyan ("Record of the Words of One Hundred and Twenty Old Men") compiled by one Sungyun, unpublished, in Newberry Library, Chicago, 559-563, order of vols. follows list of the pa kua in Manchu, 560, two prefaces, one (1789) by the author, other (1791) by Furentai, 560-561, 120 chapters on all sorts of subjects, 561, a tr. (1809) into Chinese by Fu Chün exists in ms., 561; see also Manchu, Language
Persian: bequest of Ṣafavid Sultan Ḥusayn, dated A.H. 1118, 56 413, 57 92-93; poem in praise of 'Ali, once property of Awrangzīb, dated A.H. 1122, 56 413, 57 93-94; at the University of Chicago, 45 366; in Cleveland Public Library, 57 239; in Columbia University Library, 49 220, 222, 232; Farhad and Vaḥši, MS of in the Metropolitan Museum copied by 'Ali Riḍā' 'Abbāsi, 44 270-271; in Garrett Collection, Princeton University, 45 350; Gul ū-Nōrūz of Ḥanīki, MS of in the Columbia University Library, 23 102-108; legal documents of 18th cent. from Oudh and Allāhābād, 59 371-374; legal documents from Mughal India in Cleveland Public Library, 60 99-100; Manāfi' al-Ḥayawān, MS of in the Morgan Library, 36 381-389; in Turkey, notice of, 59 227-243
Siamese: the making of palm-leaf manuscripts in Siam, 29 281-283, made by Buddhist priests and students, 281, method and materials, 281-282, original mss. hard to obtain from the temples, 283, loan of Shan and Laos mss. and Peguan text fragment, 283, plans for a national library in Bangkok for preservation of mss. and copies, 283
Syriac: Brit. Mus. 5442, 16th-17th century physiognomic treatise, text and translation, 39 289-294; Brit. Mus. Add. 14,658 of 7th cent., containing philosophical treatises, mostly by Sergius of Riš'aynā; text of his Syriac version of Gregorius Thaumaturgus's Περὶ ψυχῆς from, 35 297-317; Karkaphesian MS of A.D. 1003/4 contains description of Old Syriac calendar, 52 303
Tibetan: see Turkistan, Discoveries
Turkish: in Columbia University Library, 49 222, 230, 232-233; in Garrett Collection, Princeton University, 45 350; in Turkey, notice of, 59 227-243; will of Ahmet Paşa, dated A.H. 917, 56 413, 57 88-92; works of Za'ifi, 57 239
Manvantara theory in the Mahābhārata 24 46 f.
Mao Chin, owner of the great Chi Ku Ko Library, 51 41; dates should be 1598-1659 A.D., 55 475-476
Mao-tun, 冒頓, Great Khan of the Hsiung-nu, 37 96, defeated the Yüeh-chih in 176 B.C., 133
Maps, British General Staff maps of Near East, criticism of, 39 58-59; Japan, see Book Reviews, Haushofer; Kirḫi, Syria, Mesopotamia, Babylonia and Elam in 1100-745 B.C., with Assyrian place-names, 38 260-263; Mersina and Guzney region, 28 163; topography of Sargon of Agade's empire according to Isin Dynasty treatise, 45 opp. p. 193; see also Cartography; Geographical Knowledge in China
al-Maqdisi, Jalāl (or Šihāb) al-Dīn, preparation of his treatise on the merits of Jerusalem, 59 400
Mar, supposed Sumerian god identified with Amurru, 45 11, 12
Mar Amr, biographies of the Nestorian patriarchs, 30 7, 8, 13, 14; tr. of record on Yeshu' yabh, 33 201

Marātha country, celebration of Devi festival in the, 30 72-76; Marāṭha poet-saints, stories of the, 50 76 f.
Marburg collection of Cypriote antiquities, 22 18-19
March, Benjamin F., death of Dec. 1934, 55 114, 348
Marcian of Heraclea, gave details of the Far Eastern voyage to the land of the Sinae, and described the angle of the coast near the Gulf of the Sinae, 37 247, his sailing course down Martaban coast is correct, 247
Marco Polo, identification of the cities mentioned by him as homes of the Magi who came to worship Christ, 26 79-83; on the enchanters of the island of Socotra, 30 53-54, return of Marco Polo in suite of a Mongol Princess, 56; on iron and steel in Persia, 35 233, the steel trade, 232; states Mongols first encountered war elephants in Burma, in 1277, 41 306; tells of use of aloes wood by conjurers in Cambodia to cure the sick, 42 178; "Zayton" of, identified as Ch'üan-chou, 56 373; see also Marko, Monk of the Topozersky Monastery
Marcus Aurelius Antoninus, embassy of to China, 35 39; probably the "An-tun" of Chinese records, 37 243
Marduk, identified with Sumerian Asar, 39 198-199, his emblem (qaqultu) identical with that of Osiris, 203; made hero of Akkadian translation of Sumerian creation story, 36 285-287; lord of magic and exorcism, 34 308
Marduk-bêl-zêr, Babylonian king of 9th-8th cent. B.C., 41 313
Mār Elia Mellûs, Chaldaean bishop of Mārdīn, works of, 22 85-86
Mār Eremia Maqdasi, Chaldaean bishop of 'Aqra, works of, 22 87
Marinus of Tyre, on the sea route fr. the Golden Chersonese to Kattigara, 37 246, 249
Mārkaṇḍeya, rules for Māgadhī, 44 84 f., 89, rules for Ardhamāgadhī, 105-109
Markets, in An-hsi, reported by Chang Ch'ien, 37 97, in Lan-shih, Ta-hsia, where he saw bamboo and cloth from Ssŭ-ch'uan, 98
Mar Michael Ni'imo, Chaldaean bishop, of Baghdad and Basrah, works of, 22 86
Mār Thoma Audo, Chaldaean bishop of Urmia, works of, 22 86
Margolis, Max Leopold, life and works, 52 105, 106-109
Mâri, capital of Amorites in 4th millennium B.C., 44 186 ff.; capital of Amurru on the Euphrates, 45 129 ff.; dynasties, role in Babylonian history, 41 251, 255-256; not seat of Semitic rule before 24th cent. B.C., 45 8-12; site of at Tall al-Ḫarīrī? 46 223-224; situated near Tall Madkūk, 44 195
Marko, Monk of the Topozersky Monastery, his account of the route to Oponia, 42 287-289, 293, possibly a Romanized form of Marco Polo, 290
Maron, St. John, Maronites, origin obscure, 43 435
Maronites, modern authors among, 22 94-96
Mâroti, worship of, introduced by Rāmdās, 25 186, 188
Marriage
Babylonian: errêbu marriage in the O.T., 57 261-264, in the Assyrian Code, 261-262, in the Hittite Code, 262, relation to Arab mut'ah marriage, 262, relationship between terḫâtu, "bride-price" and rîḫtu, "dowry," 271-276
Hebrew: Jacob's marriage to Laban's daughters closely conforms to Babylonian errêbu marriage, 57 261, concept of "stranger-wife" found in Assyria also, 264-265, father's use of income from bride-price found in Nuzi also, 265-269, a practise condemned by the Aramaeans, 269, part of bride-price delivered to her instead of to father, 268-276
Nuzi: bride-price originally used by father; tended later to become endowment for bride, 57 265-276; contracts not uniform; brides purchased, 52 296
Palestinian: custom of so-called bride-price among Arabs has background in economic necessity of receiving a quid pro quo, 53 77-78, polygyny not resented by Arab wives, 76-77
Marriage Alliances, Chinese, early Han; with the Wu-sun, 37 101, 103, the Princess of Kiang-tu (Chiang-tu) sent to the K'un-mo, 106, Hsiung-nu with the Wu-sun; the Hsiung-nu princess given precedence over the Chinese consort of the K'un-mo, 106
Mar Sergius, founder of the Nestorian church at Chen-kiang in 1281 A.D., famed sherbet maker to the Emperor, 54 151
Marsh Arabs of Lower Iraq, description of their life; possible connection with Indian gypsies, 44 130-133
Marsyas myth, paralleled in Sumerian myth of Lugalbanda and Zû, 40 315
Martaban, Gulf of, see Trade Routes
Martin, Dr. W.A.P., historical works of on China, 38 100
Martini, M., his Atlas Sinensis pub. in 1655, see Asiatic Studies in Europe
Martu, myth of his marriage to Namrat in Ninab found in Sumerian tablet from Nippur, 43 164
Maruts, association with Indra as god of fertility, 36 242-268
Masai, concepts of left and right among the, 58 209, 212-214
Maṣāri' al-'Uššāq of al-Sarrāj, tale of a friend in need from, used by al-Ġuzūli in his Maṭāli' al-Budūr; Indian parallel to, 26 296-305
Masorah, their practise of combining alternative readings, 43 229 ff.; see also Ben Naftali
Maspero, H., interpretations of traditional material on the reigns of Yao, Shun and Yü, 56 55, 60, 61, 63, 64-65, characterization of methods and stages by which earliest accounts evolved, 57, origin of kingly custom of circumambulation, 68, conditions in the 4th cent. B.C. when the model-emperor lore was evolved, 70-75
Maspero, père et fils, death of, 36 350
Maṣṣoth, see Festivals (Hebrew)
Master Fu, Former Han, transmitted the Confucian tradition re the Book of History, 58 437
Masturbation, played part in primitive Near Eastern myths about the origin of life, 40 324-326
Masukagami, 增鏡, value of, as source for study of Kamakura period, 59 39-40
Maṭāli' al-Budūr of al-Ġuzūli, story of a friend in need from, ed. and tr., 26 296-305
Mātañga-Līlā of Nīlakaṇṭha, Edgerton's translation of the, 52 89 f.; only published work in Sanskrit on elephantology, 50 324
Mathematics
Babylonian: decimal system, two ways of representing, 33 30; highly developed by 2000 B.C., 60 106, Pythagorean theorem and algebraic methods known, 106; Plato's nuptial number, Babylonian origin of, 29 210-219
Chinese: see Chou pi suan ching; abstract, Gardner, Pythagorean doctrines
Greek: Plato's nuptial number, Babylonian origin of, 29 210-219
Indian: borrowed from Babylonia during Achaemenid period, 51 69-70
Near Eastern, Ancient: based on concepts with no analogy in modern arithmetic; compound-reckoning and calculation by deficients, 44 158
Mather, Increase and Crescent, John Leusden's Latin, Dutch and English Psalter (Utrecht, 1688) dedicated to them, 52 310
Mathurā, art, chronology, 46 255; type of Buddha image, date of, 46 166f.; independence of, 46 167 f.; distribution in India, 168 f.; Buddha, the dating of the various types, 51 59; Nāga images, 49 188 f.; sculpture, the iconography of, 51 56 f.; style of sculpture, interpretation, 54 220
Matrukas, installed in Śrāddha ceremony, 22 229
Mats, Chinese, reference to straw mats and awnings for imperial palaces, 1727-1750, 49 239-240
Mattei Ricci, see Ricci, Matteo
Matthew, Gospel of, Kingdom of God, impending idea of, 45 371
Mauryan sculpture, interpretation, 54 220
Mau-tun, see Mao-tun
Māyā in the Śvetāśvatara Upaniṣad, 22 385 f.
Mayas, originated cultivation of maize; system of writing, 39 162

Mazdaism, problems connected with the origin of, 53 199-204; the Persian religion described by Strabo, 52 187

mDo-maṅ, abridgement of the Kanjur, editions and existing copies of, 52 398-399

Measurements, Chinese, foot, 尺, of T'ang dynasty, K'ai-yüan period, 713-742 A.D., 9 1/4 English inches; chang, 丈, of T'ang period, 7 3/4 English feet, 30 19n.1; Han foot-measure, 51 140 and n.13, cloth measure, 145n.35; length of one degree on Matteo Ricci's Map incorrect, 59 341-342; terms used in regulations for building materials for palaces, 18th cent., 49 236, of timbers, 236, 238, pillars, 237, of building stone, 239, of glazed tiles, 241, size of Chinese "foot", 236, weight of Chinese "catty", 236; see also Heavens; Earth

Mecca, history of the Grand Šarīfate of, 37 154-156, 160-161; missionary-traders from in Indian Archipelago, 33 315

Medea's cauldron as a fountain of youth, 26 6 f., 13

Medes, first appear in history on the Assyrian borders in the reign of Shalmaneser III, 41 347, 376, 378; begin descent upon Assyria in 615 B.C., 44 124-125; rôle of in fall of Nineveh, 22 20-22

Medicine

Assyrian: horse-colic treated with poultice, 37 331-332

Babylonian: Gecko (Ascalabotes fascicularis) in, 39 284-285; medical texts, titles of, 37 250

Chinese: illness of the Empress Têng, 51 150, 158; coughing and expectoration of blood, 159; made of blood of black dogs, 55 3, made from roots of orange tree, 7, ku 蠱 as "love medicine", 11-13, antidotes for ku, 14 n. 34, 16, 18, 20-21, case of surgery, 22; Taoist concoctions; corrections to translation in, 53 217-249, 54 290-294, medicines inefficacious, 293; Taoist concoctions and genie-elixir, 53 247, see also Alchemy; treatment of sick, 246; use of the lemon, 54 145, 148-149, 157; vaccination serum, note on, 49 155

Hebrew: Biblical idea of menstrual poison substantiated by chemistry, 44 165-166

Judaeo-Arabic: ophthalmological fragments from the Cairo Genizah, text and translation, 50 112-124

Muslim: prescriptions in the Manāfi' al-Ḥayawān of ibn-Buḫtīšū', 36 381

Medieval literature, collection of in Cleveland Public Library, 36 421

Megalithic monuments, in Tibet and Central Asia, see Book Reviews, Roerich

"Megarian" type bowl, Phoenician origin of, 58 528

Megiddo, history and meaning of the name, 34 413, 415 ff.; battles at, 416 ff.

Mehmet Fatih, Ottoman Sultan, pious foundations (vakfs) of, 58 527

Mehri Language, article, question of, 32 149 n. 1; see also Semitic Languages

Meigetsuki, 明月記, value of, as source for study of Kamakura period, 59 43

Meillet, Antoine, life and works of, 57 214 f.

Mei-ts'ai, 昧蔡, King of Ta-yüan, succeeding Mu-kua, 37 113, killed by his people for favoring the Chinese, 115, comments on the name, 145; see also Ch'an-fêng

Melanesian, languages of British New Guinea, loss of original l in, 36 186; treatment of t and s, 38 71

Melchizedek, King, a fictitious personage, 38 332

Melek (Molech, Moloch), his cult among Hebrews introduced by Manasseh and did not revive after its extirpation by Josiah, 49 354-355

Melissenus, pretender in Asia Minor in late 11th cent., with title "Kaisar," 30 25-31, coin of described in the Sung-shu, 28-29, identified with Chinese names Mi-li-i-ling-kai-sa, 24-29

Meluḫ(ḫ)a equated with Egypt, 45 230, 239, with Punt, 238, with Africa and South Arabia, 240; included Egypt, 42 318 ff.; probably is not Egypt and the east coast of Africa, 43 45-48; identified with Sinai, 56 247

Members: Deceased 22 1-6, 36 233-241, 36 339-341, 36 426, 429-430, 37 3-5, 37 168, 45 289-294, 46 182-184, 46 331-333, 45 338, 341-342, 47 1-2, 51 86, 51 104-107, 52 105, 52 106-109, 52 272-274, 52 403, 53 308-309, 310, 54 87-88, 55 458-463, 56 113-120, 56 472-489, 57 211-212, 214-217, 57 251-252, 58 221-224, 58 504-505, 58 550-551

Memorials to the Throne, practice of making started with Han Kao-tsu, 57 173; of Kung-sun Hung to Han Wu Ti re the founding of a gov. university, 58 441, 446, of Tung Chung-shu in 141 B.C. concerning statecraft, 448; of Wei Wan to Han Wu Ti, 58 438, decisions of the Council on the interpretation of the Classics memorialized and ratified by Emp. Hsüan in 53 B.C., 444; of 1905, abolishing the old style competitive examinations,, tr. of text of, 27 79-87

Menagerie, of Ashur-nazir-pal at Kalhu, 41 291, of the Chinese Emperor at Ch'ang-an in Han Dynasty, 303-304

Menahem and Pekahiah, introduced Assyrian eponym system into their administration, 43 165

Menant sign-list, notes on, 33 16-23

Mencius, describes character of the period of the model emperors, 56 55, connects Yü with a deluge at the origin of the world, 59, story of Shun's persecution fits with similar tales elsewhere, 66; rating of, in "Table of Ancient and Modern Men", see Chinese Thought; see also Confucius, Teachings

Menes, accession of ca. 2950 B.C.; is the Mani of Akkadian sources who was defeated by Naram Sin, 39 150

Meng T'ien, Chinese general of third cent. B.C., no foundation for ascribing to him invention of writing brush, 47 74; writing brush not invented by, 56 534

Meng Tzu, 孟子, 10 quotations fr. in the Yen T'ieh Lun, 51 267, 275

Menstrual poison, existence of proved, 44 165-166

Mercator, see Japan, Geography

Mercer Museum, Doylestown, Pa., collection of Chinese tools in, 58 690

Meringer's views on the Vedic dual endings, 23 318-323

Merom, Waters of, Waters of Megiddo, 34 416

Meropes' rivers of pleasure and pain, 26 43 f.

Meru mountain in the Mahābhārata, 30 366-374

Meryteti, son of Mereruka and Watetkhethor, 57 242

Mesene, Arab state on Persian Gulf, 35 32, 35

Mêšitug, king of Adab, 33 296

Meskingašer, king of Uruk, Egyptian elements in tradition about him, 49 305-306

Mesopotamia: complex population of N Mesopotamia in 4th millennium B.C., 57 105-106; Mesopotamian culture, relations between Indic and, 54 107 f.; Mesopotamian motifs in Harappa culture, 59 Sup. 41; writing begins at end of Uruk period, 59 Supp. IV, 20-21, 25, 26; see also Art and Architecture; Assyria; Babylonia; Iraq; Near East; Seals; Sumer

Archeology: Assyro-Babylonian antiquities in the U.S. National Museum, 23 44-45; books on in Cleveland Public Library, 36 421; city-planning, evidence for in Sargonid and Chaldean texts, 52 302; city-planning, organization of, 52 302; herringbone pattern made with plano-convex bricks is a foreign importation, 55 205, Ur "Royal Cemetery'' dates from Early Dynastic to Akkadian period, 206-208; house and temple types: Assyrian "corner-entrance" type house, examples of, 60 151-155, found in Mesopotamia from earliest times, 159, of Eastern Mediterranean origin, perhaps brought to Mesopotamia by Semites, 173, 177, "Broad room" type commoner in late times, 155-156, replaced "corner-entrance" type after end of 3rd millennium B.C., 157, less common in Assyria, 157, arises from fusion of "corner-entrance" and broad types, 176-177, introduced into Mesopotamia by highlanders, 178, "Double broad room" type rare and of relatively late date, 157-158, "Long room" type (entrance on short side) is contemporary with "corner-entrance" type from earliest times, 158-159, is primarily Assyrian, 161, variations of, 162, earliest examples in 5th millennium, 167, spread from European Russia, 167-168, 177, modifications of, 168-169, fusion of center courtyard type house with "long room" and "corner-entrance" types

produces a new plan seen at Uruk, 159-160, "Square room" type rare in Mesopotamia; originated in Anatolian and Persian highlands, 165-167, "Central court" type originated in Mesopotamia from highland antecedents, 169-171, tower connected with house, a Mediterranean feature of obscure origin, 173-174; libraries not proved to have existed in temples, 27 147-182; painted pottery a Ḫurrian product; not found all over N Mesopotamia; does not occur throughout entire history of mounds, 57 106, Tell Ḥalāf ware precedes 'Ubayd stage; stratification of Tell Ḥalāf not worked out, 106; plano-convex bricks introduced by stone-using invaders, 57 84-87, herringbone pattern in brick-laying imported into Mesopotamia and reached Anatolia from there, 85-87; Tell Ḥalāf includes beginning of Chalcolithic period; at latest contemporary with Badari, 58 672-673

Geography, Topography: geographical treatise on Sargon of Agade's empire, composed in Isin Dynasty, 45 193-245; topographical-archeological account of northern part, 44 186-201; climate has dessicated in the past 2000 years, 44 197; identification of Akkadian place-names, 46 220-230

History: Early Dynastic begins ca. 3000 B.C., 59 Supp. IV, 17, dates of Jemdet Naṣr, Uruk, al-'Ubayd, Ḥalāf-Sāmarrā and Sakce-gözü periods, 17-18, these cultures not localized, 19, Gawra, al-'Ubayd and Susa I related, 20, predynastic cultures, overlapping and characteristics of, 21, 24-25, diffusion of cultural elements throughout the Near East, 22-24, foreign trade, 25, social framework of Sumerian origin, 25-26; invasion of highlanders at beginning of Uruk and Early Dynastic periods, 60 178; no struggle between Sumerians and Semites as such, 59 485-495; Sumerians in lower Mesopotamia in latter half of Uruk period; do not appear in N before Jemdet Naṣr times, 59 Supp. IV, 28-31, foundations of historic civilization laid by Sumerians in Uruk times, 31; see also Ḫurrians, Guti, under names of rulers, etc.

Mespila, in Xenophon (Anab. 3 4, 7) refers to Nineveh, 28 102-103

Messiah, term applied to Mani, 45 250

Messianic prophecies, not found in Old Testament, 32 120

Messianism, among Shī'ite sects, 29 37-39, 94-95; in Old Testament prophets, 46 347; Jewish, collapsed after Pacorus's invasion of Palestine in 40 B.C.; did not revive until generation before Christ, 56 256; Jewish hopes of Messiah aroused by Umayyad-Byzantine struggle over Constantinople, 47 364

Metallurgy, Hebrew acquaintance with, 43 126-127; Indian methods of making steel in ancient times, 35 233-235

Metal Work, Chinese, regulations for, in building imperial palaces and temples, 1727-1750, 49 239, 240, 241, reference to pavilion at Wan Shou Shan, and incense burners at the Yung Ho Kung, 240, reference to pewter, 239, 241, see also Bronze

Metals, bronze long preferred to iron for edged tools in early China, 35 226, production of fine steel in India in early Christian era, 230-237; mentioned in Assyrian tribute lists, 38 215, 216, 219, 220, 221, 225, 234-235, 238-239, 246, 247, 250; from N Syria and S Asia Minor in Assyrian tribute lists, 41 355, 357, 373; comparative value of in Babylonia in the 6th cent. B.C., 42 399-400; Hebrew names for, 43 116-127; smelting of, taught by Chinese deserters in Central Asia, 37 108-109, bibliography, 145

Metempsychosis, among Shī'ite sects, 29 12, 26-27, 45, 64; as a form of retribution in Manichaeism, 45 246-268; Druze, of Indian origin, 47 366; and totemism, 38 152 f.; Manichaean doctrine of, 44 161

Metrology, Babylonian, mûbal, môbal, fraction of a zûz, 29 207-209; see also Numismatics

Mexico, cultural center of pre-Columbian America, 39 161-163

Meyer's translation of the Kauṭilīya Arthaśāstra, notes to, 48 289-322

Miao, aborigines of S.W. China, women kept ku, 55 22, 6 n. 13; see also Yü, the Great

Midianites. worshipped Yahweh in North-Arabian Sinai in 13th cent. B.C., 35 386

Midnight, demon of related to noonday demon, 38 160-161

Midrash proverb, 'walls have ears', parallels to, 28 89 f.

Mieh-li-i, see Names, Personal

Mieh-li-sun, see Names, Personal

Mié-li-i, see Mieh-li-i

Migrations, of the Wu-sun to the West, 37 100-101; see also Yüeh-chih

Mi-li-i-ling-kai-sa, identified with Melissenus, ruler of the Byzantine Christian world in 1080 A.D., 30 24-29

Military

Central Asia, early Han: archers, mounted, in Ta-yüan, 37 95, number of, among the Wu-sun, the Yüeh-chih, 96, 100, in K'ang-chü, in An-ts'ai, 96, use of, by Chinese in battle with Ta-yüan, 110-112, see also Kan Fu; army, reported weak in Ta-hsia, in An-hsi, in Ta-yüan, 37 98, 110, strong with the Yueh-chih and K'ang-chü, 98, supposed difficulties a Chinese army marching to the West would have, 109; Cavalry, extensively used in time of Han Wu Ti, 37 102, 106, 107, 110, 114

China, early Han: army, difficulties in marching through Central Asia, 37 109, 110, 114; commissariat, Lucerne fields planted in China for fodder for the 'heavenly horses', 37 108; generals, in campaign against Ta-yüan, relative merits of, 37 114-115, rewards bestowed upon, 115; graft, in army administration, 37 114-115, rewards bestowed in spite of, 115; stations, line of, bet. Chiu-ch'üan and the Yü-mên, 37 106, to protect the road fr. Tun-huang to Lopnor, 116; soldiers as farmers at Lun-t'ou, 37 116, use of archers in battle with Ta-yüan, 110-112, use of cavalry against the Hsiung-nu and Lou-lan, 106, 110, the Wu-sun send cavalry aid to the Chinese, 114, convict regiments, used in dangerous campaigns, as against Ta-yüan, 104, 111, 112, commissariat, provisions for the armies and embassies to the West in the time of Han Wu Ti, 108, 110, 111-116; see also Engineers; Horses; Wagons

Millet, used as food in prehistoric Egypt, 39 174

Mīmāṃsā system, date of, 50 173

Mīmāṃsā Sūtra, date of, as determined from refutations of Buddhist doctrines, 31 1-29

Mīmāṅsā Nyāya Prakāśa of Āpadeva, 48 340

Min, gazelle sacred to him, 40 328, 331

Minaean origin of alphabet, theory of, 22 185 ff.; Semitic Languages

Minamoto Family, sources for study of, 59 45

Minaret, origin and history of, 30 132-154

Μινδαλοέσσα, Babylonian astronomical work cited by Hesychius, < Akk. mindâtu ša šamê, "organization of the heavens," 46 87

Mindoro, bamboo writings from, 60 271 f.

Ming-t'ang, a ceremonial building for sacrifices and court receptions, 58 439, Confucian advisors of Han Wu Ti proposed the establishment of one, 439, Shen P'ei sent for, to direct the, 439

Ming Shih, 明史, section of, on foreign countries, full of errors and omissions, 59 353, 354-355

Miracles in the canonical scriptures of Buddhism, 44 162

Mirrors, Chinese, Ancient, comment on term "Sunlight Mirrors" and method of designation by first two characters of their inscriptions, 57 444, no conclusions fr. chemical analysis, 444-445; Chinese, early significance of, 55 182-189, Chou and Ch'in mentions of, 182-184, forms and decorations of early mirrors, 182, 185, 186-187, as symbol of reflection of character of the ruler in the people of his State, 182, 183, symbol of intelligence of Heaven and the Sages, 184-185, used to obtain fire from the sun and water (dew) from the moon, 185-186, worn as a talisman, 186-187, invested with magical power itself only after the Han Dynasty, 187, authorities' erroneous ideas as to use of, 187-188, original and chief use always as a toilet mirror, as attested to by excavations at Lo-Lang, 182, 186, 187-189, see also Lo-Lang; divination by means of, 36 51, 53; Medieval, made of Indian steel, 35 232

Mirzas, Shī'ite holy men of the marsh Arabs of Lower Iraq, 44 131
Misamis dialect of Bisayan, 26 123
Mission Paléontologique Française (1923-24; 1926-27), see Licent, Father Émile
Missions, see Embassies
Mitanni, Sauššatar first known king, ca. 1500 B.C., 49 273, extent of ca. 1500 B.C., 273-274; Indo-European element in, 39 257; language, the possibility of a connection between Dravidian and the, 50 273-305, history, 273 f., sources, 274 f., phonology, 277-283, grammar, 283-301, lexical comparisons, 301-304, conclusions, 305; origin of Vedic deities, 43 428; see also Ḫurrians
Mithra, in Old Persian inscriptions, 21 169
Mitra, borrowed by Indo-Iranians from Mitanni, 43 428; consubstantial with Varuṇa, 55 410; development from a god of accords to a sun-god, 45 282
Mizpah, probably identifiable with Nabi Ṣamwīl, 45 182
Mkhas grub, one of the incarnations of the Pañchen Lama, appearing on a Tibetan temple painting, 52 348
Mṅah bdag ñañ, a Buddhist saint who is represented on a Tibetan painting of the eighth Dalai Lama, 52 343
Moab, see Transjordan
Moabite Language, see Semitic Languages
Model-Emperor Lore of China; Yao, Shun and Yü set up in 4th cent. B.C. as model emperors of a Golden Age, embodying fundamental Chinese ideals of government and kingship, 56 51-76, doubts as to their having been real persons, 53, traditions and personalities, 53-70, mention of Yao, Shun and Yü in earliest writings, 53-56, traditions of Yü, originally a water divinity, 53-63, the Yao tradition connected with a sun myth, 53-56, 63-66, story of Shun from a folk-tale, 53-56, 66-67, position of modern scholars on the status of the Lore, 55-58, early Chinese belief as to function of kingship; its likeness to Hocart's ideal, 67-70, background and conditions out of which the Lore arose, 52, 70-76, war, unrest and change in Chou period, 771-221 B.C., 71-74, new geographical ideas and world view, 74-75, traditional views of ancient period of Chinese history, 70-71, the Lore a product of 4th cent. B.C., evolved by necessity, 52, 70, traditional materials interpreted to form the Model-Emperor Lore, under influence of the kingship ideal, 56, 67, 70, 73-76; influence upon Japan of the Tokugawa period, 31 152-153; see also Chinese Thought; Shun; Yao; Yü
Modiera, Pliny's name for Madura, see Pāṇḍya
Moffatt's translation of the Old Testament, criticism of, 45 368
Mohammedans, settled in Korea 9th-15th cents., 58 658-661
Mohārājaparājaya of Yaśaḥpāla, Māgadhī in the, 44 103
Mohenjo-daro, beads excavated at, 57 1-15; "meditating yogī" statue, 57 245; see also Indus Valley Culture
Mohists, no adherents of this school mentioned as among Han Wu Ti's officials, 58 440; rating of, in "Table of Ancient and Modern Men", see Chinese Thought
Mokṣadharma, meaning of *yoga*, 52 251; story of world creation and dissolution, 45 51-67
mon, Japanese family crest or badge; crests featuring holly, 55 449
Money, Chinese, value of the tael, 1727-1750, 49 236, exchange rate for gold and silver, 239; see also Paper money; Numismatic
Mongolia, Mongolian, Mongols, note on texts, 54 315; first encountered war elephants in battle of Yung-ch'ang against Burma, 1277, 41 306; invasions of Japan, 1281, Japanese sources for study of, 59 44, 48, 54; Mongols in Manchu service, see Sungyun; Furentai (?); Fu Chün; language: grammatical studies; see Asiatic Studies in Europe
Monkey climbing a Tree, as a symbol for the 3rd *nidāna*, *vijñāna* or "consciousness", 60 358-359
Monkeys, in the Rāma story, see Rāma Story, in Khotanese
Mon-Khmer words, compared with Munda, 52 46-50
Monks, Buddhist, see Names, Personal
Monotheism, of Moses, not influenced by that of Ikhnaton, 44 160; of Moses, not inspired from Egypt, 52 198-199; unfulfilled tendency towards in Sumerian and Babylonian religion, 56 402; and henotheism, 55 480-482
Monumenta Serica, see Book Reviews, Biallas
Monuments, Lhasa, tablets with the Sino-Tibetan text of the treaty of 822, 38 35; Chinese, see Nestorian stone
Monteiro (or Moreira), Ignacio, see Japan, Geography, Cartography
Moon, associated with the ass, 40 332-333, with placenta as source of life in Egypt, Babylonia, Iran and India, 333-335; Chinese belief in mystic connection between mirrors and, 55 184-187, collection of heavenly dew from, 185-186, 189, moon made of water, could not contain hare, 185-186; new, omens from in the Dekkan, 35 293-296; new, festival of Ningirsu at Lagaš, 42 103; Parsi-Persian book of omens from, 30 336-342; Parsi-Persian book of omens from, 33 286-293; new, Passover festival in celebration of, 46 346; represented as male in Parthian religion, 51 129; as measurer of time among the Semites, 37 212, new moon, connected with Hebrew Sabbath, 209-214, 7th new moon especially honored by Jews, 220; connected with rain and fertilizing waters in Semitic and Indo-European mythology, 39 72, 77, regarded as fecundating bull and as eunuch in Egypt and Babylonia, 86 ff.; as Osiris, mutilation of, 39 88-89; see also Eclipse
Moon Palace, 月宮, 49 154 n.4
Moore, Benjamin Burgess, letter fr., describing visit to the Kök Tash, coronation stone of Tamerlane, 34 436-437
Moore, George Foot, life and works, 52 273, 274
Morocco, its progress under French rule since 1907, 54 231-239
Morse, Charles J., death of, Dec. 1911, 32 iii
Morse, Edward S., death of, Dec. 1925, 46 332
Mortuary Figures, Chinese, Han or later, horses excavated from the Tomb of the Painted Basket, Lo-Lang, Korea, notes on, 56 102
Mosaic, technique of originated in the highlands of Anatolia, 59 247-250
Mosaics, from Antioch-on-the-Orontes, show shift from painting style to abstraction, 59 399; Hebrew inscription (5th cent.) on, from 'Ayn Dūq near Jericho, 40 141-142
Moses, does not appear in historical records, 53 194-196, 197-199, possibly originally a deity, 198; his monotheism not affected by that of Ikhnaton, 44 160; his monotheism not inspired from Egypt, 52 198-199; tales of Egyptian magic later ascribed to him, 47 363-364; secondary stratum of J document characterized by exaltation of him, 38 124
Moses bar Kepha, his teaching on the soul, 40 106-107, 115-116
Moses of Khorene, *History*, résumé of theories as to its date, 60 73-81
Moslems, see Mohammedans
Moso, see Loloish
Mosques, earliest, had no minaret; not always used in later times, 30 133-138; Mosque of the Prophet in Medina, History of, with plan of re-buildings, 50 26-29, description of by ibn-Jubayr in A.D. 1184, 31-38, Mosque of Hamzah near Medina, ibn-Jubayr's description of, 38, Mosque of Quba near Medina, ibn-Jubayr's description of, 39-40
Mōt (Ugaritic deity), a close parallel to Tammuz, 59 410
Mother Goddess, represented by date-palm on Palestinian pottery, 58 548; represented by palm-tree on Canaanite-Hyksos Palestine Painted Pottery, 59 251-259
Motya (Sicily), colonized from same Phoenician mother-city as Carthage, 48 359
Moulds, for bronze vessels, many found at Anyang, 56 346 n.33
Moule, Arthur C., on the tr. of *san i fen shen*, on the Nestorian Tablet, 58 391
Mount Chiu-i, 九疑, resort of Taoists, 53 231
Mount Chung-t'iao, 中條, as Taoist retreat, 53 240-241
Mount Hua, 華, K'ou Ch'ien-chih in a cave on, 53 227
Mt. K'uai-chi, 會稽, mountain near Shaohsing, Chekiang, where Yü is said to be buried, 56 55, Yü's connection with the Yueh, 61-62, 62-63, legend of Yü's journey there, 61-63, monuments at the grave of Yü at, 62

Mount Ku-ming, 鵠鳴, where Chang Ling studied the Tao, 53 221 n.26, 229 n.64
Mt. Omei, see book Reviews, Phelps
Mount Sung, 嵩, K'ou Ch'ien-chih's sojourn on, 53 227-235, sacrifice to, 236, as Taoist retreat, 236, Wei Wen-hsiu from, 239
Mount Wang-wu, 王屋, mixing Taoist elixir on, 53 239
Mount Yo, 岳, site of Taoist monastery, 53 242
Mountains, sacred, see Chiu Hua Shan; Heng Shan; Sung Shan
Mourning Customs, Hebrew and Arab, tearing of garments and ceremonial nudity in, 21 23-39
Mouse, jumping, Babylonian representation of, 38 140
Mṛcchakaṭika, Śūdraka's vocabulary and grammar, 27 19 f., notes on the, 418-454, translation of Nīlakaṇṭha's interpolation, 452-454; and Cārudatta, relationship between, 42 59-79
Mu-chien, 牧健, Prince of Ho-hsi, 河西, Northern Liang Dynasty, capture of his city Ku-tsang, 30 33-34
Muchiri, seaport on west coast of India trading with Romans, 37 245
Müller, Andreas, biography and work of, in Chinese studies, 60 564-575, access to Chinese library of Admiral Giesel van Lier and additions in Berlin, 565, invented his Key to Chinese in 1667, never published, 565-569, 573-575, published his Disquisitio geographica et historica de Chataja, 1670, 566, edited a Latin version of Marco Polo's Travels, 1671, 566, edited the Nestorian inscription Monumenti Sinici, 1672, 566-567, his Hebdomas Observationum Sinicarum, 1674, 570; the chronological table of Chinese emperors, Basilicon Sinense, 1679, 570; Imperii Sinensis Nomenclatur Geographicus, 1680, 570-571, tr. into Latin and edited Historia Sinensis fr. the Persian of Banakati, 1678, 571, cataloguing works, Catalogus Librorum Sinicorum Bibliothecae Electoralis Brandenburgicae, 1679, 571-572, a second catalogue in 1683, 572, his De Eclipsie passionali disquitio, 1685, 572, contacts with Father Kircher, 565, 566-567, Bayer's and Abbé Renaudot's comments on Müller's work, 568, Leibniz's interest in the Key, 568-569, 575, imprisonment for heresy, 573, fate of his books and mss., 573, modern estimate of the man and his work, 574-575
Müller's translation of prāṇas, 22 255 f., 288-292
Mughal India, Persian documents from, 59 371-374
Mughal school of miniature painting, the Indian precursor of, 50 326; contributions of, 54 441 f.; miniatures, late, illustrating the Iqbāl-nāmah'i Jahāngīrī, 58 354-365; with plates
al-Muġīrah, Shī'ites extremist and his gnostic-Mandaean doctrine, 29 79-88
Muḥammad, contends with Iblīs in Malay myth, 33 334; factors conditioning his revelations, 48 136-146; his Arab biographers are not completely trustworthy, 59 123; his information about Judaism and Christianity not derived from a Jewish informant, 54 211-212
Muḥammad, in Turkish names, see Mehmet
Muḥammad 'Ali, his war with the Wahhābis, 37 156-159
Mukai, Gensei, inspector of imported books at Nagasaki, 1685, 57 299-301
Mu-kién, see Mu-chien
Muk-suk, see Words, Chinese, mu-su
Mu-kua, 毋寡, King of Ta-yüan; killed by his people and head sent to Chinese general to end the siege of the capital, 37 112-113, his younger brother made king, 115; see also Mei-ts'ai; Ch'an-fêng
Mūladeva's pills for sex-change, 47 16-18
Mulberry wood, yang principle predominate in, 42 56, 57
Mule, striped brown, white and black, a product of Po-pa-li (Berbera), 30 50, identified as the Hippotigris Burchelii, the "Tiger-horse" of the ancients, 50-51
"multilocation", believed in by Buddhists as well as by Ancient Catholic Fathers, 58 389-390
Mummers, at court of Han Wu Ti, 37 107
Munda, abstention from eating new crop before festival, 50 226; languages, similarities to Buruçaskī, 41 66 f.; words, comparison with Mon-Khmer and nearby languages, 52 46-50; possible connection with Sumerian, 45 366
Mung T'ien, see Meng T'ien
Munisundara, conjectured author of the Bharaṭakadvātrimśika, 46 73
al-Muqaddamah of ibn-Ḫaldūn, editions and MSS of, 46 171-176
al-Muqayyar, see Ur
Mura, 村, "village", see Feudalism in Japan
Murad IV, Sultan, personal description of by Evliya Efendi, 37 234-235
Muramasa, Japanese sword maker, legend of, 26 334
Murder, expiatory sacrifice for in modern Palestine, 25 313
Musée Guimet, see Book Reviews, DuPont
Museums, see Mercer
Mušallim-Ninib, Assyrian governor of Tille, 34 349
al-Mūsāwi, abu-Muḥammad Ja'far, first Grand Šarīf of Mecca, 37 155
Music, see also Songs
Chinese: connected with the tonal structure of the Chinese language, 57 202; Han period music not known to show any traces of Greek origin, 56 95; singing and flute playing mentioned in a prayer to the Lao Lan, 49 154; abstract, Gardner, Pythagorean doctrines
Egyptian: diatonic scale, indications of use of, 44 175
Hebrew: in the Library of Congress, 36 359
Near Eastern (Ancient): woodwind instruments, types of, 48 360
Japanese: Gion bayashi, 祇園囃, orchestral pieces for the Gion festival, 54 287
Sumerian: cult, 42 102
Musicians, from Ta-ts'in to China, via India, 37 242-243
Musiris, a port of Chera, see Chera
Musk, from Tibet, 42 177
Muslims, world census of in 1924, 44 29-37, illiteracy among, 33
Musri, Land of, variously located, 41 292
al-Mustawfi, al-Mu'tamin ibn-al-'Assāl, see al-Sayf al-Murhaf fi 'l-Radd 'ala 'l-Maṣḥaf
Mu-su, 苜蓿, identified as lucerne (=medicago-sativa); seeds of, brought fr. Ferghana; large tracts planted in China for feeding the 'heavenly horses', 37 108, derivation of the name, 145
al-Mutawakkil, his restrictions against Jews and Christians, 47 315-322
Mu-yang-ch'eng, Manchuria, notes on excavation of, in review of Harada's report on, 52 191-192
al-Muzayyarah, Egyptian Arab female demon of noonday, 38 164-166
Mycenaean, sites in Corinth, 36 352-353
Myrrh, an ancient product of Po-pa-li (Berbera), 30 49, 50
Myrtle, Chinese name mo, see Words
Mysticism
Chinese: practices of the Taoists, 53 215, 216-217, 223-224, 54 291; note on relation of Taoism to an earlier group of mystics, 53 211
Islamic: close parallels between Illuministic Ṣūfis and Nuṣayris, 58 541; in Persian poetry, 36 345-347; see also Ṣūfism
Japanese: satori, a mystic state attained by practice of the koan exercise; attainment of Enlightenment in Zen Buddhism, 54 224-225
Mythology, Chinese, criticism of Dr. Ferguson's work in book Chinese Mythology, 53 53-65, development of the Hsi Wang Mu myth, 54-55, the eight diagrams of Fu Hsi, 55, development of sun myths, 60-62, Huai-nan Tzu, 60, Chung Kuei, 62, story of the "White Serpent", 62, mixed sources, 63-65, treatment of Chinese myths, 61; sources discussed, 54 85-87; see also Model Emperor Lore
Nabataeans, mentioned in texts of Ashurbanipal, 45 6-7; discovery of probable palace and sanctuary of Aretas III at Petra by Horsfield in 1929, 52 286; trade with Rome and the East, 35 32, 34-35, 38-39; position on the trade route from Petra to China and India, 35 32, 34, 35, Chinese

annals refer to, 35, toll collections, 38, destruction of kingdom of, 39; architecture, square-room type temple related to Persian examples, 60 166; see also Du 'l-Šarā'; Inscriptions; Semites, Home of
Nābitah, Muslim sect identical with the Ḥašwīyah, 54 4 n. 5
Nabonidus, absent from Babylonia in 7th, 9th, 10th and 11th years of his reign, when he was probably in Têma, 41 458-459; had his Arabian headquarters at Taymā', 45 354; in Têmâ in 7th, 9th, 10th and 11th years of his reign, 42 310-314
Nabopolassar, analysis and critique of his Chronicle, 616-609 B.C., 44 122-129; saved from Sin-šar-iškun by the Medes, 22 21; was king of the Sealand before ascending the throne of Babylon, 50 20-21
Nabû, Akkadian deity introduced to Western Semites; originally connected with Lagaš, 45 25-27; a West-Sem. deity, 45 144-146
Nabû-aḫ-iddin, šaqû šarri and bêl piqitti of Eanna at Uruk in time of Cyrus, 41 466-467
Nabû-mukîn-aplu, šatammu of Eanna (at Uruk) in time of Cyrus, 41 466-467
Naburianus (Bab. Nabû-rimmannu), Babylonian astronomer, worked out his system in 427 B.C., 46 87
nadd, a kind of fragrant ointment, recipes for preparation of, 43 226
Nag'al-Dēr, inscribed Nilometer of Amenemhet III from, in University of California, 43 49
Nāgas in Hindu legend and art, 49 186-190
Nāgānanda of Harṣa, time analysis of, 21 89, 101-108
Nagasaki, only open port in Japan in 17th cent.; censorship of foreign books centered there, 57 291, 294-295, 297, 299-301
Nag dbaṅ blo bzaṅ rgya mçho, the fifth Dalai Lama, biographical data, represented on Tibetan temple paintings, 52 344, 349
naginata, see Phallism, Symbols, Japanese
Nairyosaṅha, see Iran, Mythology
al-Najīrami, life of; text of his Kitāb Aymān al-'Arab, 58 615-137
Nakane, Genkei, translated western scientific works for Yoshimune, see Yoshimune
Nala-Kūbara, son of Kubera, 33 66 f.
Nālandā, site of a great Buddhist monastery in India, where Hsüan Chuang studied the Wei Shih philosophy, 51 301-303
nāma-rūpa, see Boat
Names, Personal
Akkadian: Adad-qarnaia, 55 288; Amêl-Ea, name of boatman in Deluge Story, changed from Puzur-Bêl and Amêl-Bêl, 23 48-50; Benenima, ancestor of the tribe of Benjamin? 51 359-360; Bir-idri, not = biblical Ben-Hadad, but Hadad-ezer, 41 365-366, 369, 370; Bît-ili, etc (Bethel), names compounded with, 59 82-84; Ḫammurabi, <West-Sem. 'Ammurawiḫ, 37 250-253; Ḫammurabi, names compounded with, 55 285, 288; Ḫattiš, early Babylonian, 26 95; Iašuia, the historical Joshua? 51 359-360, 53 196; i-ti in Old Akkadian names corresponds to later iddin, "has given," 57 243; Kù-bâba as element in, 57 243; Nuṭuptum, "dewdrop," a woman's name, 57 366; Šamaš-inaia, 55 288; Šanduarri, Sanduarri, <Eg. s'-n-dw'-R', "worshipper of Rē'," 42 201-202; = Cilician Šattuara (pron. Sǹtuara), 48 93; Sin-aḫi-êriba, pronounced, according to 5th-cent. B.C. Aramaic transcriptions, as Sanaḫarib or Sanaḫ'arib, 44 159; Theophorous compounds, 36 362
Arabic: 'Ād, perhaps from Heb. minnî 'ad, "from of old," 60 288; Hūd, perhaps contraction of Yahūd, "Jews," 60 288; Idrīs< Ποιμανδρης, 60 287 n. 14; Lugmān, translation of Heb. Bil'am, 35 386
Aramaic: Bethel (deity), names compounded with, 59 84; Klmw, probably not Semitic, 35 365; Nnšt, read Nanašt, 35 372-373; 'Nwšt, names compounded with, 29 205-207; Š'l, vocalization uncertain, 35 366; Šlmw, connected with the Nabataean Šalamians? 54 33; Zkr, pronunciation uncertain, 35 357
Avestan: Zaraθuštra, possibly a priestly title, 53 203
Canaanite: Brgš (Zakir inscr.) = Br+Gawiš<Games, Akk. Mâr Gûsi, 40 319 n.26
Chinese: An-tun, = Anton(ius), Marcus Aurelius (?), 35 39, 37 243; transliteration of names of Chinese Buddhist monks, 52 159-162, of monks fr. abroad, with Sanskrit names, 161, Chinese taking the name Shih (Chinese for Sakya) as their family name, 161-162; I-ta-chi, identified as Ardeshir III of Persia, 33 200; K'u-sat-ho=Khosru, 33 197; Lao-tse, possibly an epithet of Huang-ti, 53 211; Mieh-li-i, 滅力伊 (Cantonese, Mit-lik-i), i probably a mistake for 遜 sin or sun, therefore Mieh-li-sun, or Mit-lik-sun, a transcription of Melissenus, 30 27-29; O-lo-pên, name of leader of first Nestorian mission to China, probably a transcription for Raban or Rabban, 30 4; Po-to-li, 波多力 (Cantonese, Po-to-lik), <Aramean batrirk, "patriarch", 30 13, 14-15
Cilician: Ipparunate, 59 9; Kurunizurumeri, 59 9; Piridauri, 59 10-11; Sandapî, 59 10
Coptic: Ammak(o)uri < Ar. al-mukāri, "camel-driver," 34 313-314; Bapsistia, cf. Gr. Παψις, 48 153 n. 7; Jōrke, < Gr. Σωκράτης ? 48 153 n. 8
Egyptian: pꜣ-Ḫꜣ-rw, "the Syrian," pronounced Piḫuru, 51 65
English: Humphrey, cf. Fr. Onfroi, Ger. Humfrid (Hunifred), "support of peace," 56 190-191, 197; Lilly, Lilian, Lilias, < Lat. lilium<Copt. hlēli, "flower"? 56 197; Mary, <Eg. Mrt, "the beloved"? 56 194-197; Miriam, see Mary; Moses, <Heb. Môšɛ, <Eg.? 56 192-194, 197; Phineas, < Heb. Pînᵊḥâs<Eg. P'-Nḥsy, "the Nubian," 56 192, 197; Susan, <Heb. Šôšannā<Eg. zšn, "lotus," 56 189-190, 197
Greek: Αββαθα <Palm. Ḫabbātā, 25 316; Αβιδλαας <Aram. 'Ab(i)d-lâhā, "servant of the god," 57 318-319; Αγγαθ <Palm. Ḥaggat, 25 316; Αλωρος < Sum. Làl-úr[-alim] 43 323-324, 327, 329; Αμαθθαβειλη <*Amat-Tâb'el? 57 321; Αμηλων <Sum. -en-lù-an-na, 43 325, 329; Αρδατης [Αρδαγης] <Sum. Aratta, 43 326, 329; Βαιδα = Palm. Byd', 25 321; Βαργιναιχου, scribal error; orthographic conflation with Palm. Μαλιχου, 57 319; Belyses = Akk. Marduk-balaṭsu-iqbi, 41 382 n. 78; Γαδδριος, perhaps for * Γαδραιος, hypocoristicon for Γαδραθη, " 'Atê has decreed," 57 318; Δαως <Sum. Dumuzi, 43 324-325, 329; Ειαθ <Palm. Ḥayyat, 25 316; Ευεδορα(ν)χος <Sum. Enmeduranki, 40 312; Ευεδωκος <Sum. Enmedúga, 40 312; Θημαρσας <Tēm Arṣu, "client of Arṣu," 57 319; Μανεεμος = Μαναημος (Heb. Mᵊnaḥem), 57 319; Μαχ(γ)ωσομας, an Iranian name, 57 318; Μεγαλαρος <Sum. [...]làl-gar, 43 324, 326, 327, 329; Ξισουθρος [Ξισουθος] <Sum. Ziusuddu, 43 326, 329; ὄρχαμος <Akk. âlik pâni? 40 308 n. 3; Πυγμαλίων <Canaan. deities P'm and 'Alēyân, 53 104-105; Ραχιμμαιου, from Raḥîmmai <Raḥîm-Nanai, 57 318; Σαθθαδα[τ], perhaps Pers. *Šatadāta, "joy-given," 57 319; Σαμμαχαιος, perhaps hypocoristicon for *Ṣamm-mal(i)k, "Ṣamm is king," 57 318; Σεμψινος [Αμεμψινος] < Sum. Sibzianna, 43 325, 329; Σευηχορος, error for Ευηχορος <Sum. Enmerkar, 40 312; Σημαθ = Σεμαθη, 57 319; Σιλαας <Aram. *Š 'îl-lâhā, "asked of God," 57 319; Σκυθης [Σισυθης] = Ξισουθος <Sum. Ziusuddu, 43 326; Σολομῶν, an Aramaic diminutive used ad honorem, 58 138-139; Συμβελύλος, compounded with divine name Bethel, 59 86, 87
Hebrew: 'Abrāhâm, composed of 'āb, "father," + *rhâm, "multitude," cf. Ar. ruhām, "multitude;" is of Canaanite or Amorite origin, 49 32-33; 'Abrâm, of Babylonian origin, 49 32-33; 'Ādām, <Sum. addamu, "my father" ? 39 272-273; 'Aryôk, a Ḫurrian name, 43 324 n. 1; 'ᵃšāyāhû, on seal, 24 205-206; B'd'l, cf. Eleph. B'dyh, 55 309; Bildad, <Akk. Bil-Adad<Apil-Adad, 49 360; 'Ester, later from of Akk. Ištar, 28 112, 119; 'Ester, late Babylonian form of Ištar, 31 356; Gômer, wife of Hosea, <*gumr, "burning coal," 48 276-277; Ḥawwā, < Sum. ama, "mother"? 39 272-273; ‖ Ar. ḥawā, "to bring forth," 49 31-32; Ḥsy, abbreviation of Ḥᵃsadyā, 55 308; 'Iyyôb, "the man who came back," ‖ Ar. 'iyyāb, "return," 41 185; Ks', theophoric? 55 307-308; Malkîṣɛdɛq, name based on mis-

interpretation of malkî-ṣεdq, "rightful king," 38 332; Mnḥm, identified with O.T. Menahem, 55 308; Môšε, "the deliverer," 53 199; Mûšî, gentilic from Môšε, 57 377 n. 2; Naptālî, cf. Ar. maftalah, "bobbin," 43 50; Nimrôd <Sum. nin, "hunter" and gud, "hero," and is translated by gibbôr ṣayyâd, 40 203 <Sum. Nin-Marada? 40 314 n. 14, 335 n. 57; Šamgar, a Hittite name, 34 419; Šhpr, < Pahl. Šahpuhre, 31 276; Sîs^{ə}rā', a Hittite name, 34 419; Ya'^{a}qôb, "descendant," 46 354; < √*'qb, "to watch over," cf. Sab. √'qb, 52 196; Y^{ə}šûrûn, possibly a hypocoristic from Yiśrā'el, 44 157-158; Y^{ə}hôšûa', originally Y^{ə}šû'ā? 51 359-360; Yiptāh, hypocoristicon of Yiptāh-'El, "El conquers," 58 137; Zk', abbreviation of Zachariah or Zakkûr? 55 307

Ḫurrian: study of formative elements in, 58 462-471; Arip-Ḫurra, contains name of deity Ḫurru, 55 442; Birazzina, Birazzana = Biraššena, from Shechem, 51 66; Dušmana, not an Indo-European name; var. Dumšimana, 55 442; Idaḫakab (Idaḫ-akab, from Tarsus), 59 4-5; Itḫip-Nuzu, contains name of deity Nuzu, 55 442; Mantiya (from Tarsus), 59 4

Khotanese: Lakṣmaṇa, forms of spelling of, 59 465; Sita, forms of spelling of, 59 465; Daśagrīva, forms of spelling of, 59 465-466;

Latin: Marinus, name denoting a rank in the cult of Jupiter Dolichenus, 23 89-90; Onuphrius, < Copt. Ouenŏbr, Ouenŏfre, "he who is continually good," an epithet of Osiris, 56 190

Neo-Punic: M'qryna < Lat. Macrinus, 60 578-579

Pahlavi, Seal: Afrō, cf. Afrō-rāi, 52 206; Anaf, = 'Ανάφης, abbrevation of Anaphernes, 52 206-207; Āpāndāt, a rare name, 52 203; Ašt-Kavātē, "friend of Kavāt," 52 205; Bagašāt, "joy in God," 52 206; Bākī, an abbreviated form, 52 205; Bārvar, "fruit-producing," 52 205; Bāt, = Βάτις, 52 206; Farnabat, = Φαρναπάτης, 52 206; Farnbag, common on Magian seals, 52 204; Fravar(?), connected with Fravarti, 52 206; Gūšnasp, names compounded with, 52 206; Matakān, cf. Ματάκας, 52 206; Mitn, a form of Mithra, 52 206; Mitrpāī, abbreviation of Mihrpanāh? 52 203; Varaḫzuštān, cf. Varaḫzušte, 52 202-203

Palmyrene: 'Abdā, occurs only once in Palmyrene, but known from Nabataean and Sinaitic, 25 323; 'Aqîbā, 21 111; 'Atēšûr, 21 109; Baydā, 25 321; Blṣdq, 27 399; B'ltk, doubtful whether personal name, 26 113; Bwrp', doubtful whether connected with Akk. Burrapi'u, 25 320; Bzbwl, 27 399; Ḥb', from rt. ḥbb, "to love," 25 322; Hdyr', 25 318; see also Greek Ḥn', both masc. and fem., 25 314; Ḥrt', cf. Ar. ḥurrah, "free," 25 321; Kalbā, 27 397; Mrql', <Lat. Marcellus, 25 318; Mtny, hypocoristic, 26 109; Nbûzbd, 25 314; Rūḥā, occurs only once as personal name, 25 319; Šmš (?) 27 399; Tdmr, is not Ar. Tadmur, 26 105-107; 'Ubayhan, an Arabic name, dim. of *Abhan, 57 319; Ytblt(y), 27 397; Zb', hypocoristic of a name beginning with zbd, 26 110

Phoenician: 'Bb'l, has rare form 'B'l, 57 401; B'lpls, "May Ba'al look upon with favor," etc., 45 271; Bod'aštart, 23 161, 169-170; Ṣdqytn, 24 222-223; Tbnt, cf. Heb. Tabnît, 57 410; Trt', Numidian or Libyan, 60 262-263; Yantin-'Ammu, an Amorite name, 60 417; Yantin-Haddu, an Amorite name, 60 417

South Arabic: 'Mnkr, " 'Amm recognizes," 55 316; Sab'-anaŠrawān, a date-name, 55 316

Sumerian: religious conceptions underlying formation of, 34 315-320; Enmerkar, (grand)father of Lugalbanda, > (Σ)ευηχορος, 40 312; Ennamag, "lord of the building, architect," a proper name? 42 341; Lugal-marda, not a late Sem. interpretation of Lugal-TUR-da, 44 288

Tibetan: Li-byin (Lib-yin), transcription of a Prākrit or vernacular form of Sr. Lipikāra, "scribe", 38 38-39, Francke's efforts to trace it to Khotanese, 39-41

Ugaritic: Bn N'bṭ'l, "son of Bethel rules," 59 88; 'Iwr-šr, = Ḫurrian Ewiri-šarri, 55 94, 98, 437-438; Tgẑn, possibly = Ḫurrian Tag[k]i-šenni, 55 98

Names, Divine

Akkadian: Anšar, variant of Aššur, 36 364; Aqtuppîtum, = Ištar of Àktab, 57 360-362; Arwû, Arwu, Arbum, || Heb. 'arye, "lion," Eth. arwê, "beast," Ar. 'arwā', "ibex," 40 328-329; Aššur, originally patron deity of A-usar; not connected with Anšar; other forms of name, 24 282-311; < √*'šr, "to be benign," 28 117-119; IM ('Amārnah tablets) = Ba'al, 48 79; Ištar, old feminine form of Aššur, 28 112-119; < √*'tr with infixed t, and is connected with Asar ('Tr), 39 204 n. 5, 31 355-358; Ištar, not connected with Heb. '^{a}šērā; is from √*'sr with infixed t, 45 21-22; Marduk, < Sum. lù-dug, 39 199; Mari, deity of city of Mari, 41 257 n. 57; Ninurta, <NIN + *'arḍ, "earth," or NIN + uraš (*ǵurs), "planting," if the reading Nin-uraš is correct, 46 232-235; Šulmânîtu, feminine counterpart of N Mesopotamian and Syrian god Šulmân, 48 95; Tammuz (Dumu-zi-abzu), meaning of formation, 40 318; Ummu-ḫubur, title of Tiamat; second element, ḫubur, is West-Sem., 45 143; Ut-napišti^{m} rûqu, mistranslation of Sum. Ziusuddu, "the submerged light of life," 38 60

Arabic: Bahjah (in Fihrist), "Happiness," is the Manichaean "Mother of the Living," 44 64; Kawtar, = Ugaritic Kōtar, Phoen. Kūšōr, Aram. Kawtar, 60 296-297; Ṣamm, N Arabic form of Ṣalm, 57 318

Aramaic: Angarōs < Skt. Angirās, frequently invoked in Indian magic, 41 159-160; Arši < Skt. ṛṣi, 41 160; Bagdānā, contains Pers. bagh, "god," 32 436; Bethel, as theophorous element in personal names, 59 84-85; 'Drswn, possibilities of interpretation, 35 373-374; 'Nwšt, to be read Enmaštu, 28 137; < Akk. In-ušta, etc., 37 329

Avestan: Aešma, < Sum.-Akk. Išmu, 35 295; Akoman, < Sum.-Akk. Akkimu, 35 295; Mahrkuša, identification with Heb. malqôš is late, 36 320

Buddhist: name called upon by a Buddhist god in distress, 48 160 and n.5

Chinese: Hu-lu-she-te, < Pahl. Ḫrōstag, 43 20; P'o-liu-huo-te, < Pahl. Padvaḫtag, 43 20; Shan-mu, "Excellent Mother," is the Manichaean "Mother of the Living," 44 62; Su-lu-she-lu-i, < Pahl. Srōš, 43 20; Su-lu-shih < Uigur Turk. Zrōšč (Zrūšč), 43 16

Edomite: Qōs, < Qaws, Ar. "bow;" confused by Josephus with Ar. Quzaḥ, 60 295 n. 39

Elamite: Amman-kasipar, last element Sum. kašbar, 39 86 n. 41

Egyptian: Ḏḥwty, Thoth, || Eth. dahây, "sun" and Ar. wadah [wadaḥ], "moon," 40 74; Ḫnm, || Ar. hamal, "lamb, ram," 37 21; Mnt, || Heb. mεlεk, "king," 37 21; Mnw, || Ar. Manāt, 37 21; Wśr, Osiris, masculine counterpart of Sem. Aširat and identical with West-Sem. Ašir, 40 317 n. 20

Ethiopic: Jesus, names of in the Arde'et, 25 4-6, 28-29

Greek: Abobas, name of Adonis, cf. N. Heb. 'abbûb, "flute," 36 331; 'Ασσωρός, form influenced by Aššur, 24 305; Δαγων √dg, "to be cloudy," 40 319 n. 27, 314 n. 14; Δερκετῶ <Ugaritic darkatu, "dominion," 60 300 n. 58; Κάβειροι, cf. Kbrw in the Hadad inscription, 54 421; Μισωρ, cf. Akk. Mêšâru, 53 110; Πακειδᾶς, Gerasene deity, <Aram. P^{ə} qîdā, 54 179-183; Σκυθης, misreading for Σισυθης, 38 60; Χυσωρ = Ugaritic Ktr, 53 110

Hebrew: '^{a}šērā (< √*ṯr), Amorite deity of Palestine; name identical with Aššur and S. Ar. Aṯirat, 45 20-21; '^{a}zā'zel < 'Azaz'el, 37 222; Ba'al Z^{ə}bûb, cf. Sum. Za-bà-bà, 37 329; Dāgôn, < √dg, "to be cloudy, rainy," originally a weather-god, 40 319 n. 27; Dāgôn, Semitic name of Syrian weather-god, 45 38 n. 85; Dôd, not name of Tammuz in Canticles, 46 160-161; M^{ə}lεkεt haš-šāmayim = Istar-Venus, 46 157; Nisrôk, corruption of Nimrôd = Nabû, 53 336-337, 338; YHWH, method of solving phonetics of, 46 361

Ḫurrian: Ḫurru, appears in personal name Arip-Ḫurra, 55 442; Nuzu, appears in personal name Itḫip-Nuzu, 55 442

Japanese: Gion 祇園, a transliteration of Jetavana; name of the Gion Jinsha, 祇園神社, 54 283; Yasaka, 八坂, name of the Gion Jinsha, means "many slopes", 54 282

Malay: Juwata, <Skt. devatā? 33 336

Mandaean: 'Abd Ḫwrn, personification of the Jabal al-Ḥawrān? 49 211; Bagdānā, Pers. "God-knowing," 33 285; Ḥawran, Ḥawraran, personification of deity of the Jabal al-

Ḫawrān? 49 211; Hywat, connected with Phoen. Ḫwt, 49 212; Nbat, personification or eponym of Nabataeans? 49 211; Ptahil, < pth, "to create," + 'ēl, "god," 53 152-165; Šamḫîzā, cf. Targ. Šamḫazzā'i, 33 280
Moabite: Kammôš (Akk. Kammusu) < *Kammêš < *Games (in Gil-games), 40 319
Mongol, Tungusian, Uigur, Turkish: Burkhan, = Buddha, see Words
Pahlavi, Book: Kūndag, Manichaean demon, < Av. Kunda, 43 24-25
Pahlavi, Turfan: Aḥarmēn = Av. Aṅra Mainyu, 44 170; Āz = Av. Āzi, 44 170; Azdaḥāg = Av. Aži Dahāka, 44 170; Dūšyārīy = Av. Dužyāirya, 44 170; Mazan(ān), cf. Av. Māzainya, 44 170; Parīgān, pl. of Av. Pairikā, 44 170; Rāmrāṭūḫ, from rām, "joy," + rātīh, "liberality," etc. the Gnostic "Mother of the Living," 44 61-66
Palmyrene: 'Asad, < Ar. Asad, 57 319; Sa'd, < Ar. Sa'd, 57 319
Phoenician: Adonis, = Sum. Damu, 48 79; Ešmun, connected with Ar. samāna [sumāna] "quail," 21 190; Ešmun, < Eg. Ḫmnw, a title of Thoth, 48 79; = Ugaritic 'Ažmny, 55 98
Punic: Pn-B'l, explanation of, 32 433; Tanit, a Libyan name, 32 429-433
Sumerian: Asar-lù-dug || Eg. Wśr, Osiris; connected with Ištar and is source of Sem. Marduk, 39 196-205; Aṣûšunamir, reflex of Tammuz, name connected with Namraṣît and Ṣîsunamrat, names of the crescent moon, 39 86-87; Enkidu, "Lord of the Underworld," derivation and various forms of the name, 40 320-322; Gilgameš, < *Giš-gibilgan-mes, "the torch of Gan-mes," 37 16; Gilgameš < *Gibilganmes; other forms of the name, 40 307-308, 316, 318-319; Gir < Gišbara, 40 311; Gira-Šakan-Sumuqan, identical with Enkidu; various forms of the name, 40 320-335; Gula, a form of Mama, 32 23; Kir-gí-lu, name of Ištar; connected with idea of "plenteousness," 30 325; Lugalbanda, is Lugal-Maráda as god of Marad, 40 313; Mullil, name of Bêl, 30 313; Mummu, from mud-mud, "one who begets many," 58 545; Nana, translated "Ištar," 21 186-187; Ninib, to be read Enmaštu, 28 137-138; NIN-IB, to be read Ninurta, 38 197-201; connected with IB = Uraš, 198, name explained as "lord of iron," 201; to be read Nin-Uraš, 42 210-211; Sâbîtu, wine-goddess, < Mt. Sâbu, 40 315; see also Siduri; Siduri-Sâbîtu, identical with Nin-kasi, 40 315; TAG-TUG, TAK-KU, to be read Taggu, Tagku, 36 91, 92, may be read Šum-tug, Tag-tuš, Tak-Ku, 126, 127, 132, may be read Tag-dûr, 145, to be read Tag-tag or Tug-tug, 271, = Akk. mârat dAnim, "daughter of Anu," 44 54-60; TAG-TUG, to be read Takku, Tikku, 37 163-164; Tišpak, name of Lugalbanda as god of Tupliaš, 40 313 n. 11; Uttu, god of commerce, another form of Utu, 40 73-74; = uttu, "underworld," 42 198, 200; Zamal-mal, to be read Za-bà-bà, cf. Heb. Ba'al Zᵊ bûb, 37 328-329
Ugaritic: 'Al'eyn, 'Alēyân, name underwent transformations; preserved in Greek names Pygmalion and Mygdalion; derived from *'allôn, "oak," 53 104-105; is a distinct name from 'Al'ey, 56 497; 'Ažmny, identified with Ešmun, 55 98; Bt'l, read Bēt'el, 59 88; Gupn, patron deity of Byblos, 53 110; Hd, short spelling of Hadad, 55 56; Hrhb, non-Semitic, 59 409; Ḫss = Akk. Ḫasîs, 53 109-110; Kšr w-Ḫss, cf. Akk. Uznum and Ḫasîs, 55 55; Ktr = Χυσωρ of Sanchuniathon, an artisan deity, 53 110; Mnt, = the Eg. war-god Mont, 55 57; Nkl w-'Ibd (Nkl, 'Ib), identified with Ḫurrian 'Ibnkl, 59 409; Prbht, non-Semitic, 59 409; Rkb 'rpt, "cloud-rider," epithet of 'Alēyân, 55 271; Šḥr, occurs in Phoenician and Punic, 54 82-83; Šlm, occurs in Phoenician and Punic, 54 82-83; Ṯr'l, cf. S.Ar. Tyr B'lm, epithet of 'Lmqh, 53 283; Ym, personification of the sea, 55 57; Zebūl-Ba'al, epithet of 'Alēyân, 55 271
Uigur Turkish: Azrua = Pahl. Zarvān, 44 69; Ög T(ä)ngri, "Mother Goddess," is the Manichaean "Mother of the Living," 44 62; Zrōšč (Zrūšč), Zoroaster, 43 16
West Semitic: Aširat, Aširat, connected with Eg. Wśr, Osiris, 40 317 n. 20

Names, Geographical
Akkadian: identification of names found in Isin Dynasty treatise on Sargon of Agade's empire, 45 193-245; in campaigns of Shalmaneser III, identifications, 41 347-382; Names and sites mentioned in Assyrian annals, identification of, 38 211-252; Alašia, = Cyprus, "the red land," 43 126 n. 10; Amurru, name for Mediterranean, connected with Akk. amirânu and tâmertu, "reservoir" and ammaru, "abundance," cf. Ar. ġamrah, "large body of water," 38 336; = Heb. 'Ûr, 41 257 n. 57; = Ar. ġamrah and Eg. mr, "sea," 43 165; situation and origin of name, 45 203-205; corresponds to Syria, 230; Anâku = Tarshish, "tin land," 43 126 n. 10; Aratta, reading of name; confused with Šuruppak; means "the Euphrates city;" is Assyrian pronunciation of Urat, "Euphrates," 52 117-119; Aššur, < Sum. A-usar, "watersettlement," 45 225; Bikn < Wikn > uknû, > κύανος, "blue," 44 158; Bît Iâkin, later name for the Sealand of Arabia; Iâkin is of West-Sem. origin, 50 14; Buršaḫanda = Hit. Barsuḫanta, 42 320; Gasúr, Old Akkadian name of Nuzi, 55 433; Ḫabirâ'a = Ḫabîru, 48 184; Ḫalab, "Aleppo," name probably originally identical with Ḫallab in Babylonia, 45 241; Ḫanigalbat, geographical name for Mitanni, 49 274; Ḫašur, Mt. = Kašiari-Masius, 40 315; Ḫatti = Mari, 42 318; Ḫubišna = Κύβιστρα, 42 320; Iâmanu = the Yaman? 49 353; is the Yaman, 52 55; Ibla, = Gibla (Gubla), 39 150; = Eg. Ibr on the Syrian coast, 45 197 n. 7; Kannu = Heb. Kanneh, 45 148-149; Kaptara = Eg. Kptr, Heb. Kaptôr, Crete, 42 319; Karduniaš, perhaps originally name of city on frontier of NE Babylonia, 40 319 n. 25; not synonymous with Babylonia, 52 309; Kirḫi, to be read Ḫabḫi 51 65; [K] ismar, cf. Ḫašmar, a land to the E of Assyria, 48 92; Kurṭi, to be read Papḫi, 51 65; Ku-sa-a (pron. Kūšā'a) gentilic from Bît-Gûsi, 42 321; Lab'an, probably Mt. Labnanu near Lake Van, 48 92; Larakku = Gr. Λάραγχα, 41 259-260; Maiteni, uncontracted form of Mitanni; of Indo-European origin, cf. Matai, "Medes," 49 274-275; Marki (in astrological text of Ashurbanipal) is abbreviated from Sum. Mar-tu; earlier Mar is not Amurru, but a place in southern Babylonia, 45 8-10; "Mari," = Mar-tu, Marruki, "Amurru," 45 127 ff.; Mà-rîki = Mari, not Amurru, 45 11-12; Mâri, = MAR-TU and Ḫatti, 42 317-318; = Μερράν, 44 194; name originally identical with Amurru and written MÀ-URU, "ship-city," 45 203-205, 230; Mas'â = Heb. Maśśâ'? 42 306; Mašgun (Armenia) = Mašgungunnu of IIR 51, 12a-d, 48 92; Meluḫa = Eg. Pwnt, 42 320; Mitanni, political name for Ḫanigalbat, 49 274; Namgarum, Semitized version of Sum. Bad-tibira, 52 183; Nusisi = Knossos, in Crete, 42 319 n. 2; Orman [Armanu?] = Armenia, 39 150; Pûṭu, = Punt? 49 353; Qarmatia = Eg. Kꜣ-rꜣ-my-ty, 42 321; Saba'â = Heb. Šᵊbâ', 42 306; Ṣiddirai, early form of Miṣri, 42 319; Subartu, term used 3rd millennium B.C., 49 326; Surmarrâti, = Ar. Sāmarrā, 56 404; mentioned in Sennacherib text in Walters Art Gallery, Baltimore, 57 419-420; Tarsîsu, = Heb. Taršîš, Tartessus in southwestern Spain, 43 163; 48 95; Tegarama, "Tigris-city," mod. Diyarbekir; = Heb. Tōgarmā, 57 435 n. 3; Têmâ = Ar. Taymā', Heb. Tēmâ', Gr. Θαῖμα, 41 458-459; Têmâ = Ar. Taymā', Heb. Tēmâ', Θαῖμα, 42 306, 311; Tibar = Anti-Taurus, 39 150; Tunanat, = Tunip? 56 404; Tawanuwa = Τύανα, 42 320; Udani, hapax legomenon, 41 313
Arabic: Bārawwā < Syr. < Gr. Βέροια, 41 364 n. 39; Dābiq, = Akk. Dabiqu, Δάβεκον, 41 354 n. 23; Halūras = Syr. Holûris (?), Arm. Olorh, Gr. Illyrison, Akk. Uluruš, 41 359 n. 31; Iram, perhaps a corruption of Edom, 35 387; Samālū, Ṣamālū, < Aram. Sam'al, 41 351 n. 13; Sāmarrā, < Akk. Surmarrâti, 56 404; 57 420; Ṣarafand < Ṣarpant < Ṣarpattu < Canaan. √ṣarap, "to smelt, test," 43 116 n. 4; Šaṭṭ al-Qār, may be derived from the old canal du-Qār (Qār = "asphalt"), 46 227; al-Šīlah, al-Sīlah, = Shilla, Korea, 58 658-661; Tail Bāšir = Akk. Til Bašere, O.Fr. Turbessel, 41 354 n. 24; Tall al-Qāḍi, translation of Heb. Dân, 34 415; Taymā' = Akk. Têmâ, Heb. Tēmâ', Θαῖμα, 42 306, 311; Tihāmah, cf. Heb.

təhôm, Akk. tâmtu, "sea," 50 15, 19; Zāb (river), cf. Heb. zûb, "to run," 43 119
Aramaic: Mlz, = Akk. Mêlid, Gr. Melitene, 35 358; Sam'al, > Eg. Samalua, Ar. Samālū, Ṣamālū, 41 351; 'Wr, "Amurru, Akkad," 45 132 ff.
Armenian: Olorh = Ar. Halūras, Gr. Illyrison, Akk. Uluruš, 41 359 n. 31
Canaanite: Amq = Akk. Unqi, Syr. 'Umqā, Ἀμυκή, 41 356 n. 26; 'Arqā = Eg. '-r-q'-tw, Akk. Irqanata, 41 366 n. 45; Ḥazrak = Heb. Ḥadrāk, Akk. Ḫatarika, 41 375; Karkemiš = "Fortress of Chemosh," 40 319 n. 26; La'aš = Akk. Luḫuti, 38 247 n. 67; 41 375
Chinese: An-hsi, Parthia, 35 35; 30 35-36; An-hsi (Cantonese, On-sak), = Arsak, Parthia, 37 137, 150; An-ts'ai, 奄蔡, the country of the Aorsi, or Alans, 30 35, 36, 37-38, changed its name to A-lan, 阿蘭, in later Han, 39, 41, 43-45, identical with Yen-ts'ai, = Alan, = A-lan-na, 35, with Ho-su, 闔蘇, 40-42, with Su-t'ê, or Suk-tak, 33, 43, A-su under the Mongols, 42; An-ts'ai, = Aorsi, called A-lan in later Chinese records; the Alans of history, 37 137, 150; Erh-shih, 貳師, city of Ta-yüan where the 'superior', 'blood-sweating', horses were kept in time of Han Wu Ti, Nīsh (?) (Uratube) Νησαῖα, the home of the Nisean horses of classical lore, 37 141-142, 135, 150; Fu-lin, old pronunciation but-lim > Bethlehem, 33 199; containing the character hsiang, "elephant", occur mostly in west and south China, 41 305; K'ang-chü, 康居, = Sogdiana, 30 34-35, 40; Li-kan, 黎軒, Syria, = Li-chien, 黎軒, 30 36, probably identical in sound, originally, Li-chien= Ta-ts'in (Syria), 36, identical with Rekem, (Petra), 36 n.2; Po-pa-li, (Cantonese, Put-pat-lik) < Barbarik, Berbera, Africa, 30 47-49; Wu-ch'ih-san = Alexandria, 30 46-47; Pu-hien, transcription of Mongol burḫan, a title of Buddha, 36 393-394; Shê-p'o, Chao-wa, and Kua-wa identified with Java, 57 344-345, Danger in identification of place names by resemblance in sound alone, i.e. Liam-po, and Chin-cheo, 345-347; Shen-tu, 身毒, (India), < Sindh, 37 150; Ta-ts'in, = Li-chien = Syria, 30 36; Ta-yüan, 大宛, (Ferghana), real name Yüan, < Yavan ?, 37 148-149, 150; T'iau-chi, = Chaldaea, 30 35-36; Ta-yüan, = Ferghana, 30 35, 40; Yü-lo, al-Ḥīrah, 35 36; see also Geographical Knowledge in China
Coptic: Pemanbij, cf. Ar. Bujah, 34 314
Egyptian: 'Eperu, may be the Ḫabīru, as foreign captive laborers, 53 404; Fnḫw, ∥ Ar. fallāḥ, "peasant," < Aram. pə laḥ, "to cultivate," 46 356; Ḫur(r)u = Syria, 51 66; Ḫ'-r'-bw, may be Aleppo, 41 364 n. 39; Ḫy-r'-b', Ḫy-r'-p', is Aleppo or Ḫerpa, 41 364 n. 39; Ibr = Akk. Ibla, 45 197 n. 7; Kptr = Akk. Kaptara, Heb. Kaptôr, Crete, 42 319; Kꜣ-rꜣ-my-ty = Akk. Qarmatia, 42 321; Mḥw, "Lower Egypt," cf. mḥ, "sea, Mediterranean," 43 165; Pdrw, = Akk. Pitru, 35 388; 'Pr, = Heb. 'Eper of Midian, 48 185; '-r-q'-tw, is Akk. Irqanata, Canaan. 'Arqā, 41 366 n. 45; Samalua, < Aram. Sam'al, 41 351; Tꜣmry, "Egypt," in this, mr = the Mediterranean; properly means "the Sea Land," and originally meant Lower Egypt (Tꜣ mḥ) only, 43 165; 'Tn, = Akk. Bît Adin, 35 388
German: Ungarn, "Hungary," < Ungar < Onugur, 56 447, 448
Graeco-Indian: 37 246-247
Greek: Aisumas = Akk. Sumu, mod. Karaca Dağ, 38 227 n. 42; Ἀμυκή = Akk. Unqi, Syr. 'Umqā, Canaan. 'Amq, 41 356 n. 26; Ἀρζανηνή < Akk. Arsania, 38 220; Ασιχα, error for Σιρχα, = Akk. Sirqu, 45 201; Βαρσαμψη = Akk. Til Barsip? 41 353 n. 21; Γιδδάν = Akk. Ḫindânu, 45 200; Ἑλλάς, as name of Seleucid Empire, 25 302-311; Ἐρυθρὰ θάλασσα, name derived from color of water, 32 115-119; Ἐρυθρὰ θάλασσα, name due to color of rising sun and purple dye obtained from it, 33 358-361; Zama, see Thil Azamana; Θαῖμα = Ar. Taymā', Heb. Tēmâ', Akk. Têmâ, 42 306, 311; Thamana, see Azamana; Thil Azamana, cf. Akk. Zamâni, 38 228 n. 44; Illyrison, Ar. Halūras, Arm. Olorh, Akk. Uluruš, 41 359 n. 31; Καρκαθιόκερτα = Akk. (Karkā) Tušḫan? 38 228 n. 43; Κασπάπυρος < Skt. Kasyapapura, Indus Valley near Peshawar, 33 352 n. 1; Κύβιστρα = Akk. Ḫubišna, 42 320; Λάραγχα = Akk. Larakku, 41 259-260; < Sum. Larak (Larsa), 43 324, 325; Λάρισσα < Akk. Rîsîn, Heb. Resen, 28 102; Μερράν = Akk. Mari, 44 194; Μέσπιλα < Akk. Mušpîlu, "place where shell-limestone is found," 28 102-103; Νίαρα = Akk. Nulia? 41 353 n. 20; Πακτυική, cf. Paḫto; in upper part of Kabul valley, 33 352 n. 1; Παυτιβιβλων, read Παντιβιρων, < Sum. Bad-tibira, 43 324; Συρία, western part of Seleucid Empire; from Ἀσσυρία, 43 237; Canaan. Ṣûr, "mountain," 55 57; Τιγρης < Sum. Idigna(u), 57 56; Τύανα = Akk. Tawanuwa, 42 320
Hebrew: 'amôrā, Gomorrah, derived from same stem as Akk. Amurru, q.v.; 'anāmîm = Akk. Anami? 42 319 n. 2; Bēt-'el, name given to Lûz by Canaanites, 59 95-96; Bēt-Ḥōrôn, with etymological ḥ, not ḫ, 60 421; 'Eber, = Ḫabîru, 48 184; 'Eden, not = Bît Âdini, 45 31 n. 74; 'Ellasar < Akk. Akarsallu? 45 214 n. 56; Gîḥôn < Sum. Gír-nun, 45 34 n. 80; Ḥadrāk = Akk. Ḫatarika, Canaan. Ḥazrak, 41 375; Ḥaṣar-, Ḥeṣrôn, in geographical names, derived from √*ḥḍr and mean "settlement," 59 27-28; Kanneh = Akk. Kannu, 45 148-149; corruption of Kalneh, 149; Kaptôr = Akk. Kaptara, Eg. Kptr, Crete, 42 319 n. 2, 45 236; Kəbûl, var. (Phoen.?) of gəbûl, "border," 58 133; Ləbānôn, probably not Semitic, 45 234; Mā'ôn, = Ar. Ḫirbat Ma'în, 34 424; Maśśâ' = Akk. Mas'â? 42 306; Məgiddô(n), cf. gədûd, "band, troop," 34 415; Mē-Neptôaḥ, < √ptḥ, cf. Ar. miftāḥ, "key," 43 50-51; Merôm, corruption of Məgiddô(n), 34 416, 419; Merôz, corruption of Məgiddô(n), 34 416; Midbar yam = the Sealand of Arabia, 50 22-23; Minnî = Akk. Mannai, "Medes," 41 378 n. 72; Mîšôr, tableland of Moab, 22 62; Nəballāṭ, pi'el participle of blṭ, cf. Akk. balâṭu, "to live," 43 50; Nôp < Môp, "Memphis"? 43 51; Pə tôr, should be vocalized Peter, cf. Akk. Pitru, 35 387; = Akk. Pitru, 41 358; Pîšôn, from Pûšôn, 34 416; < Sum. Pasir? 45 34 n. 80; Qîšôn, from Qûšôn, cf. Ar. qaws, "bow," 34 416; Ṣārə tân, identified with Ar. Ṣarṭabah, 26 331-333; Šārôn, name of district in Transjordan, 22 61-62; Ṣārpat < Canaan. √ṣarap, "to smelt," 43 116; Šəbā' = Akk. Saba'â, 42 306; Śənîr, ∥ Akk. šarâru, "to shine"? 41 186; Šə 'ôl, originally "cleft, ravine," from šā'al, "to cut, split," 41 176; Šin'ār, < Sum. SU-MER < SU-GIR < GIR-SU, 43 252; Sînay, cf. Akk. Šin, "moon," and Ar. al-Badr, 34 415; Śî'ôn, Egyptian form of Śiryôn? 41 186; Śiryôn, was perhaps originally *Śyrôr, 41 186; Taršîš, means "spalling-floor," 43 126; = Akk. Tarsîsu, Tartessus in SW Spain, 43 163, 48 95; Tēmā' = Akk. Têmâ, Ar. Taymā', 42 306, 311; Tōgarmā, < Akk. Tegarama, mod. Diyarbekir, 57 435 n. 3; Tūbal < Phoen. Tūbal = Tabal, Pontus-Cappadocia, 38 200; 'Ūr = Akk. Amurru, 41 257 n. 57; 'Ûṣ, = Ar. al-'Āṣi, the Orontes, 41 184; Yam Sûp, "ultimum mare," 58 131-132; Yāwān, as designation of Seleucid Empire, 25 302-311; Yiśrâ'el, "God flashes," 46 354; Zimrî= Akk. Zumru, 38 235
Hittite: Arzawa, not to be read Arzawi, 55 302; Ḫurru = Mitanni and Ḫanigalbat, 51 66
Hungarian: Magyar, derivation obscure, 56 447-448
Kassite: Karduniaš, perhaps originally name of city on frontier of NE Babylonia, 40 319 n. 25; not synonymous with Babylonia, 52 309
Kurdish: Belqalēn, corruption of Ar. Du-'l-Qarnayn, 41 359 n. 31
Latin: Abarraza = Akk. Apparanzu, 41 370 n. 51
Malay: Pontianak, named after a kind of forest-specter, 33 319 n. 1
Mandaean: Naṣoraya, "the observant," probably as followers of John the Baptist, 49 213-214, 215-216
Moabite: Šrn, plain N. of Moabite tableland, 22 61-2; Š(M)ḥrt, "East," 22 62-63
Old French: Turbessel, < Ar. Tall Bāšir, Akk. Til Bašere, 41 354 n. 24
Palmyrene: Tadmur, occurs in an Akkadian text of 1000 B.C., 53 288
Persian: Lūristān < Akk. Lulli, 45 238; Māh-, as place-name element refers to springs and waters, which were associated with the moon, 39 73

Phoenician: Kmb, Kkb, name of Carthage, origin unknown, 57 404; 'N ydll, second element is a verb, 57 403; 'Rṣ Ršp, district E and N of the cape of Sidon, 23 164-165; district S of Sidon, cf. Ar. Arsūf, 29 192-193; = 'Arsūp <R^{ə} šup<Rεšεp, 57 402; a district of Sidon, 408; Ṣdn Ym, citadel of Sidon, 23 162; cape of Sidon, 29 192-193; Šmm 'Drm, same as Šmm Rmm, 24 214-215; Šmm Rmm, name of hill-district behind Sidon, 23 162-164; district of Sidon, 24 213-215; district N of Sidon, 29 192-193; mountain district of Sidon, cf. Σαμημρουμος 57 401, 409

Sanskrit: Yavana, first designated the Ionian Greek, then the Bactrian Greek, 25 304

Semitic: *Miṣidrīm, "Egyptians," < Eg. *^{e}mḏedrew, 42 319

Sumerian: Adab, < A-TAB, "reservoir, canal," 54 78; Dilmun, various writings of, 36 109; is Baḥrayn Islands or Tālum nearby, 43 45; see also Tilmun; E-^{d}Nin-Mar^{ki}, place near Lagaš, contains element Mar^{ki}, "Mari, Amurru," 45 127 ff.; Eridu, synonym of Apsu in incantations, 38 330; < URU-DUG, "good city," 54 78; etymologies of names, 51 61-64, 66; Ga-súr, pre-Ḫurrian name of Nuzi, forms of, 58 451; GIŠ-ÚḪ^{ki}, to be read Um-ma, 37 255-256; Gubi, = Ġubba in Masqaṭ? 43 45; Ḫašur, Mt. = Kaši-ari-Masius, 38 330; Magan, "Land of the ship-barrier," i.e. Egypt, 35 391; = Ma'an, oldest West-Sem. name of Egypt, 39 150; Mar-tu, meant "the going down of the sun," 45 8; Meluḫa, "Land of Black Servants," i.e. Ethiopia, 35 391; Nippur < Nin-buraššu < Nin-Uraššu, name of a deity, 42 210-211; < *Nibur < *Nibir < *Niĝir, see also Šumer, 59 488 n. 2; NUN^{ki} represents only Eridu, not Babylon, 52 55; ŠES-AB^{ki}-MA, "Ur," read URU-UM^{ki}-MA, 46 310-311; Šit-tab, to be read Àg-tab, Akk. Aq-ṭup, Àk-tab, 57 359-360; Šumer, corruption of Girsu, a quarter of Lagaš, 49 263 n. 1; <*Šimir <*Šiĝir <*Niĝir, see also Nippur, 59 488 n. 2; Šuruppak, various forms of name; confused with Aratta, 52 115-119; Tilmun = Tylos-al-Baḥrayn, 38 330; see also Dilmun; UMMA^{ki}, written for GIŠ-ÚḪ^{ki}, 37 9; Uri, Uru, = Amurru; sign used also for "Akkad" and "palm-tree land, " 42 342

Syriac: Nâṣrat (Nazareth), translation of Heb. Ḥetlôn, 34 415; 'Umqā = Akk. Unqi, Canaan. 'Amq, 'Αμυκή 41 356 n. 26

Ugaritic: Ḫḫ = Akk. Ḫâḫu, N. Syrian people, probably = Ar. Ḫāḫ near Ṭūr 'Abdīn, 53 284; Ṣrrt = Akk. Siraru, 53 283; 'U/egrt, <'U/egr, patron deity of the city, 53 110; Ẓsr, Ẓzr, = Akk. Zinzar, Ar. Šayzar on the Orontes, 53 102-103

West Semitic: Ma'an, oldest name of Egypt, = Sum. Magan, 39 150

Yazīdi: Yazīdi, derived from Pers. ya-zata, īzad, "celestial being," or from Yazd, in Persia? 51 335

Namisādhu, rules for Māgadhī, 44 88 f.

Namrat, see Martu

Nāṇḍillagopa on the dialects of the Prabodhacandrodaya, 44 115 f.

Nanjio, Bunyiu, catalogue numbers for Buddhist works in his edition of the Chinese Tripiṭaka, 51 291-304

Nannar, moon-god, has control of fertilizing waters, 39 72-74, 77

Nan-shan, 南山, range of hills on south side of the Kansu corridor; skirted by Chang Ch'ien, 37 94; home of the Ch'iang barbarians, 97, in 121 B.C. no Hsiung-nu among the, 100

Nan Yang Ta Ti, 南陽大帝, see God of Fire

Nan-yüeh, region now represented by Kwangtung and Kwangsi, 41 304; king and capital of, see Lu Chia

Nan yüe pi ki, 南越筆記, by Li Tiao-yüan, 李調元, 18th cent., reference to the lemon, 54 148-149

Nārada, approximate date of, 51 81 fn.; list of kings in the Mahābhārata, 50 87 f.

Naram-Sin, his accession ca. 2875 B.C., 42 321; ruled ca. 2750 B.C., 41 241; defeated Menes of Egypt, 39 150

Narāśaṅsa, see India, Mythology

Naravāhana, epithet of Kubera, 33 60 f.

Nard, in early Chinese Annals, 43 219; habitat in Himalayas and Hindu Kush; history of its use in ancient world, 43 216-228; Chinese name nai-chih, see also Words

Nāsatyas, borrowed by Indo-Iranians from Mitanni, 43 428

Naṣipīna [Naṣībīn, Nisibis], head of Assyrian provincial cities in time of Ashurnasirpal; site of, 38 216

Nāstikas, as earliest materialists, 50 133 f.

Na't al-Ḥayawān of Aristotle (?), used by ibn-Buḫtīšū' in his Manāfi' al-Ḥayawān, 36 381

Nātaputta, the dental n of, 58 534

Nātya-śāstra, Bharata's treatise on dramaturgy called, 40 359 f.

Navigation, from Egypt to the Far East under the Roman Empire, 37 240-249, discovery of periodicity and use of trade winds in the Indian Ocean, 240-242, sailing craft, 241, winds in the Red Sea, 241, Arab trade fr. ancient times to Graeco-Roman to the Tamil ports of S. India and return, 241, pirates off the Malabar coast, 241, Chola mariners carried on fr. S. India to the Martaban coast, 241-243, importance of the eastern sea trade of India, 242, 244-245, the Far Eastern voyage, fr. the Golden Chersonese to Kattigara, in Tong-King, by Malay and Chinese shipping, 244, 246-249, use of compass and log not known, 241, 244, triple confusion in the sailing courses of the Roman period, 248, Roman ships in the Bay of Bengal and the China Sea (i.e. east of India and Ceylon) were rare, 248-249, Roman ideas of geography beyond India were vague and ports were confused, 243, 244, 245, 246-249, an earlier Marco Polo? 247-249

Nayadis, position in Malabar caste system, 59 130

Nāyin, possibly the Cala Ataperistan of Marco Polo, 26 81; see also Art, Islamic

Naẓm al-'Iqyān fi A'yān al-A'yān of al-Suyūṭi, projected publication of, 45 359

Near East, British expansion in motivated by Crusading ideals, 38 72; British General Staff maps of, criticism of, 39 58-59; difficulty of settling its status at the Paris Peace Conference was due to previously-made secret treaties, 40 138; see also Art and Architecture; Levant; Mathematics; Music; Science

Archeology: excavations, 1915-1916, 36 348-354; painted pottery, distribution of; of Sumerian origin in Mesopotamia, 51 60, 63-64; pottery, Aeneolithic and Early Bronze, 48 78; rise and progress of, 56 121-123, 130-144, progress of decipherment of inscriptions, etc., 123-130

Culture: not static, 60 283-284; beginnings of civilization, 39 164-184; urbanism, early development of, 59 421-422

Prehistory: chronology of, 47 355; common origin of cultural sites from Baluchistan to the Danube and the Dnieper, 41 189-190; paleolithic man in Transjordan, an area then well-watered, 52 286

Nehemiah, itinerary of his night ride, 39 143

Nelnikov, author of Polnoye Sobraniye Sochinenii, containing account of the route to the legendary kingdom of Oponia, 42 287-289, comments on similarities bet. the legends of Prester John and of Oponia, 292-293; see also Utopia, Russian

Neo-Babylonian Empire, interest regularly 20 ^{o}/o annually; barley and dates about equal in value, 52 304-305; of Sealand origin, 50 13-14, 20-21; see also Nabonidus, Arabia

Neolithic remains in Manchuria, see Mu-yang-ch'eng

Nergal, closely related to Gira, 40 328

Nergal-êreš, Assyrian governor of Raṣappa, 34 349

Nergal-ilia, Assyrian governor and turtânu under Adad-nirâri III, 34 348

Nero, number of in Rev. 13:18, 26 315-317

Nēryōsang and other old Parsi Sanskritists, 44 170

Nestorians, Nestorian, brought name Fu-lin to China? 30 2, 4-5, 33 194; embassies to China fr., 30 4, 9, 14-15, 24-26, 30; in Persia, 30 5, 6-15, 33 197-198, 200-202; in China, 30 2, 4, 9, 10, 14, 15, 30, 33 197, 198-199; inscription of Si-an-fu, 30 3, 10, 14, 15, 17; the powerful patriarch Yeshu'yabh, 33 201-202; name Fu-lin as applied to the Patriarchal Court of the, at al-Madā'in, 33 199-202;

name Fu-lin the ecclesiastical designation of the land of the Christians of Syria? 30 31, biographies of Nestorian patriarchs, 7, spoke Aramean wherever they were, 24, patriarchs of Antioch, at Antioch and at al-Madā'in, 6-15, 30, the patriarch at head of the Christians in Asia was the "King of Fu-lin" or "of Ta-ts'in" to the Chinese, 10, early Christians in India were Nestorians, 10-11, church at Balkh, 15; Church at Edessa during rise of Islam, 42 286; nature of teachings of Nestorius, his Book of Heraclides, 58 384-385, centers of Nestorianism in Edessa and Nisibis, 385, Bishop of Seleucia-Ctesiphon leads Persian church the Syriac church into schism fr. Rome, 385, relationship with the Sassanids and the Zoroastrian cult, arrival of the Moslems, flight of Olopên and party to China and Nestorian community established there in 635, Nestorian Monument erected in 781, 385-386, possible trs. of the words san i fen shen on the Monument, 386-393; Nestorius opposed by Bar-Šûšan, 32 271, 309; soul, belief in sleep of founded on Aristotelian psychology, 40 108 ff.; modern study of Syriac among, 22 79-96; see also Inscriptions, Chinese; Mar Sergius

Nestorian Stone, actually discovered at Chang-an, 49 354; at Si-an-fu (Chang-an), 30 3, 10, 14, 15, 17; Nestorian Tablet of T'ang, early Chinese book on, prohibited import into Japan in 17th cent., 57 293

netsuke, see Art, Japanese

New Hebrides "boomerang," 55 171

Newspapers, Chinese, "Peking Gazette" the oldest in the world, 47 74

New Testament, allusion to in Manichaean texts, 56 205 n. 21; Pauline Epistles show knowledge of material underlying the Gospels, 58 549; see also under names of various books

New Year, see also Festivals (Hebrew)
- Babylonian: taken over by Jews, 37 220-221; see also Festivals (Babylonian)
- China: ceremony of Jang used to expel the Old Year and install the New, 56 58
- Israelite: Sukkoth a New Year's festival at autumnal equinox, 42 398
- Jewish: older than Jewish calendar, 36 296-297
- Palestinian, ancient: fell on 10th day of 7th month, 37 220-222, dancing on, 223
- Semitic: festival of survives in Christian feast of the Finding of the Cross, 39 149
- Sumerian: festival of Ningirsu and Bau at Lagaš, 42 103

Ngandjoek statuettes, the harp of the, 51 50

Nichiren, 日蓮 (1222-1282), work of, as source material for study of Buddhism in Kamakura period, 59 51

nidānas, originally prob. 18, as proven fr. Chinese sources, 60 356, Tibetan drawings have 12, 356, symbolic pictures for the, have remained the same fr. early times, 356, connection bet. Buddhist thought and that of the Upanishads indicated, 356-360, parallel found in works attributed to Hermes Trismegistus, 356 n. 4

Nīlakaṇṭha's interpolation in the tenth act of Mṛcchakaṭika, translated, 27 452-454

Nile, River, see Egypt, Mythology

Nīlohaha, name of Varsh Śrāddha ceremony, 22 228

Nimrod, identified with Ninurta, who is of Kushitic origin, 49 312-317; identified with Lugalmarada-Ninurta, 40 335 n. 57; see also Ninmarada

Nimrod Epic, see Gilgameš Epic

Nina, Babylonian feast of, 31 255-256

Ninâ, name of a quarter of Lagaš, 57 309-312

Ninab, locale of Amorite myth of marriage of god Martu to Namrat, found in Sumerian tablet in Nippur collection, 43 164

"Nine Classics", Canon of the T'ang dynasty, 44 282, order of the books fixed in T'ang, 283-284

Nineveh, unsuccessfully attacked by Medes in 614 B.C. 125, fall of, in 612 B.C., 127, 129; fall of, 22 20-22; account of fall of in Xenophon (Anab. 3 4. 7), 28 99-107

Ningirsu, Babylonian feast of, 31 265-266; deity of Lagaš, worship of; names and deities associated with, 42 92 ff., new moon and new year's festival of, 103; may be a deified human being; possibly a priest among the gods, 42 341-342

Ningišzida, a form of Tammuz, 43 92

Ninḫursag, rôle of in the so-called Sumerian Paradise Epic, 39 67 ff.

Ninib, originally a feminine deity, later became masculinized, 28 139-140, an Amorite deity, 138-141, introduced into Babylonia during dynasty of Isin, 141-144

Ninib-ilia, governor of Salmat and turtânu under Shalmaneser V, 34 348, 349

Ninkasi-Sirîs, prototype of Sâbîtu, 40 315

Ninmarada, worshipped under name Nimrod by Aramaeans of Hatra down to 2nd cent. A.D., 40 335 n. 57

Nin-šaḫ, Sumerian deity, changed from female to male, 47 268-269

Nin-Uraš, Sumerian god older than Enlil; = Nin-IB and gave his name to Nippur, 42 210-211

Ninurta, bisexual nature of, 46 233, originally an earth-goddess, 235; associated first with bronze and later with iron, 38 199-201; first mentioned during last dynasty of Ur; a date deity; female consort of Nusku, 46 345-346; later form of Lugalbanda-Horus, 49 315-316; see also Ninmarada

Nipponshiki, see Japanese, Language, Romanization

Nippur, Aramaic business ostrakon from, 29 204-209; Aramaic incantation bowls from, 32 434-438; Aramaic incantation bowls from, notes to, 33 279-280; fragment of Deluge Story from, criticism of Hilprecht's claims concerning, 31 30-48; one of earliest sites in Babylonia, 41 260; Sumerian mythological texts from, 44 159-160; version of the Sumerian creation story, 36 283 ff.; see also Hilprecht-Peters Controversy

Niqum, Babylonian city near Khafājah, 59 107-108

Nirukta = hermeneia, 56 405; authorship and influences, 47 335; relationship of the commentaries of Skandasvāmin and Maheśvara, 50 175

Nisaba, Babylonian deity, unknown to Western Semites, 45 25

Nīšāpūr, (Persia), surface remains at; archeological possibilities of, 48 339; center of Islamic art through period of Səljuq rule, 58 258; see also Art, Islamic

Nish, see Erh-shih

Nisibis, see Nestorians

Nisir, Mt., see Kinipa, Mt.

Niš-pati-bêl, Assyrian governor of Kalḫu and Naṣibîna, 34 348, 350

Niu Wang, 牛王, see God of Cattle

Nō Plays, Japanese lyric drama; aesthetic features, music, costume, spiritual meaning, action, origin, history, present condition, 22 129-137

Noah, similar in character to Utnapištim, 38 61

Noctes Atticae of Aulus Gellius, see Androcles and the Lion

Nöldeke, Theodor, life and works, 51 105-106

Nomad Nations; the Wu-sun, 37 96, K'ang-kü (K'ang-chü), 96, An-ts'ai, 96, Yüeh-chih, 96-97; see also City Dwellers

Non-injury, see Ahiṃsā

Noonday, demon of among primitive peoples, 38 160-166

"Northern Sea", term applied to the Great Marsh, ta tse, (Palus Maeotis), 37 96

Novatians, their confession and teaching compared with those of the Armenians, 32 328-329

Nubian and Dravidian, 52 133-144, phonology, 133-135, grammar compared, 135-139, list of compared words, 140-144

Nudity, ceremonial, among Hebrews and Arabs, 21 24ff.

al-Nu'mān, family of Fāṭimid judges in Egypt, account of from ibn-Ḥajar, 27 217-296

al-Nu'mān (Arab king), forbids Arabs to visit Simeon Stylites, 35 168-169

Numerical Categories, see China, Chinese, Thought

Numismatics
- Byzantine: coins of Melissenus, the Byzantine pretender, described in the Chinese Sung-shu, 30 28-29, one in Bibliothèque Nationale, Paris; pictured in the Kin-shï-t'u—shu—pu ? 28-29
- Chinese: coins of the 11th and 12th cent. found on east coast of Africa, with shards of Chinese celadons, 30 55, 57

Greek: obol, Babylonian origin of, 29 207-209
Indian: dates on Bengal coins frequently misread, 43 253, coins of Danujamarddana Deva ascribed to Ganesh, 254; late Kushāna and Kushāno-Sassanid coins, coinages of Kanishka, Huvishka and Vāsudeva, 56 429-439
Parthian (An-hsi): coins, 37 97, casting of coins not known bet. Ta-yüan and Parthia in time of Han Wu Ti, 108, 139
Nuns, Hindu stories of false, 44 204, 236-242
Nuptial number of Plato, Babylonian origin of, 29 210-219
Nuṣayris, doctrine of, 29 116, 126-127; parallels with Illuministic (išrāqi) Ṣūfīsm, 58 541
Nü Wa, 女媧(女娃，女希)，divinity hero of a flood legend preserving the story of creation of man, 56 60
Nuzi, Semitized at an early date, 58 451-452, Amorites in, 452-453, settled by Ḫurrians at end of 16th cent. B.C., 453; tablets, selected, transliterated and translated, 47 36-60; texts from, résumé of publications and study of, 55 432; see also Akkadian Texts; Gasúr; Law, Nuzi; Marriage
Nyāsa Upaniṣad, literary stratum, 23 67
Nyāya Darśana, date of, as determined from refutations of Buddhist doctrines, 31 1-29
Nyi, see Loloish
Oath, in cuneiform literature, 34 283 ff., tabu-like character of, 283, 302; made by saints in modern Palestine, 25 312-313; pre-Islamic Arab, text of al-Najīrami's Kitāb Aymān al-'Arab, 58 615-637; in Sumerian inscriptions, 33 33-50; see also Law
Oats, wild, found in Egypt, 39 176
Obeid culture, relations of the Amri with, 59 Sup. 39 f.
Obelisk, Black, of Shalmaneser II, mid. 9th cent., gives elephant as an article of tribute, 41 291-292
Obol, Greek, Babylonian origin of, 29 207-209
Obollah (Apologus), port at head of Gulf of Persia, sea trade with India 80 A.D., 35 35, central position on route bet. Kabul and Petra, 37, 38
Odes, see Shih-ching
Odes of Solomon, date in first cent.; proto-gnostic background of, 46 346
Oertel's translation of prāṇas, 22 296, 301
Offerings, mentioned in connection with Chinese sacrifices and prayers to the gods, of: beans, 49 131, beef, 148, calamus, 133, candles, 135, cock, 139 n. 5, ch'i kan, 151, feasting, 131, food, 133, 135, 147, 148, fruits, 129, 145, firecrackers, 151; grain (?), 152, incense, 129, 133, 135, 138, petals of, 141, 145, 147, 150, 151, 154, lights upon the water, 136 n. 10, meat, uncooked, 151, mushrooms, 138, money, paper, 154 and n. 3, a play, 146; porridge, 148, rice (?), 150, 136 n. 10, sacrificial animals, 129, 154, silk, 129, venison, 148, virtue, 135, water, of the P'an (pool in front of a Confucian temple), 130, clean water, 135, 136 n.10, waterplants, 141, willow branches, 135, wine, libations, 131, drinking wine, 138; pure grape wine, 145, pure wine, 155; Han, rice, millet, and all grains for presentation at the temples at the Imperial Tombs to be husked, 51 147, fruits and vegetables for the Imperial Tombs to be in season, 153
Officials, Chinese, Han, Hu Ch'iang chiao wei, 護羌校尉, governor of the protectorate over the Ch'iang people bore this title, 51 138 n. 3; hu-pen chung-lang, 虎賁中郎，144, t'ai-kuan, 太官，146-147, tao-kuan, 導官，146-147, shang-fang, 尚方，147, nei-che, 內者，147, t'ang-kuan, 湯官, 147, ssu-li chiao-wei, 司隸校尉, 148-149, Ho-nan yin, 尹，148-149, Nan-yang t'ai-shou, 太守, 148-149, chung-kuan, 中官，151, chin-ch'ên, 近臣 151, ssû-k'ung, 司空，152, the Court Historian, 156; yüeh-ch'i chiao-wei, 越騎校尉，157, shih-chung, 侍中，158, shang-shu, 尚書，158
Ogyû Sorai, 荻生徂徠，Confucian scholar, attitude of, towards the government ban on books about Christianity, 57 301-302
Oil, divination by means of, 36 40-42, 45-46, 48, 51; symbol of God's mercy, 32 312-314; volatile, distillation of first done by Muslim Arabs and Persians, 42 357
Old Bodish, comparative phonetics of, see Languages, Sino-Tibetan
Old Chinese, reconstruction, data on phonetics of, see Languages, Sino-Tibetan
Oldenberg, Prof. Hermann, death of, at Univ. of Göttingen, Mar. 1920, 41 163
Olive, Chinese name ch'i-t'un, see Words
Old Persian
Grammar and Syntax: anacoluthon, 35 338-340, case usage, with jan-, 349-350, with tarsa-, 340 f., with dāraya-, 347 fn, with parsa-, 351 f., acc. with dauštā bīyā, 348, gen. part. as obj., 346 fn., loc. of specification, 325 fn.; inscriptions, misuse of case forms in, 48 66-73; case usage, with hacā, 35 337-342, pronouns, antecedents, 345-350, enclisis, 347; declension, acc. plur., 35 336 f., locative, 324, pronominal, nom. and acc. sing., 345 fn., fem. sing., 323 f., masc. and neut. sing., 35 338; periphrastic perfect, pre-Aryan origins of, 39 117-121; use of instrumental as accusative or nominative, 23 57-60
Inscriptions: 58 324-330; addendum on a difficult passage (adamšim ajanam, Bh. 4.2), 41 74 f.; as source of knowledge of the Achaemenian religion, 21 160-184; Foy's conjecture of Arshtāt in Bh. 4.64, 21 169; conjectured reference to Avesta in Bh. 4.64, 21 172-175; Behistun rock and inscriptions re-examined, 24 77-95; Behistan inscription, textual criticism of, 40 291-299; Behistun, column V, 58 675 f.; Behistun, metrical arrangement in, 58 677; the restoration of order by Darius, 58 112-121; restoration of order by Darius, 58 324; Darius' Kerman inscription, 27 193 f., photograph of (opposite) 190; the record of Darius's palace at Susa (Dar. Sus. 1), 53 1-23, reconstruction and translation, 1-9, commentary, 8-23; addendum on the Record of Darius's Palace at Susa, 53 166; the record of Darius's palace at Susa (Dar. Sus. 1), 54 34-40, Darius Susa no. 15 Scheil: restoration of order in the empire, 40-50, Accadian version, 47-50, Artaxerxes II Susa no. 28 Scheil, 50-52, Accadian version, 52; Dar. Sus. a, 58 325 f.; Daiva-inscription of Xerxes, 58 324 f.; dubious, 56 215 f.; a dubious tablet in Philadelphia, 56 91-93; dubious, 58 326 f.; the Naksh-i-Rustam inscription of Darius I, 59 406; recently published, 51 189-240, transcription 190-192, restoration, 192 f., bibliography, 193, inscriptions with commentary, 193-232, Dar. Sus. 1, 193-212, Darius 2-16, 212-224, Xerx. Sus. 23, 25, 26, 225-226, Dar. II Sus. 5 A, 24, 226-227, Art. Sus. 28, 228-229, Dar. Ham. b, 229-231, Art. Ham. b, 231-232, grammatical summary, 232-233, concordance and glossary, 234-240; Saqqara glazed title, 58 327-329; textual notes on, 27 190-194; Xerxes' accession to the throne, 58 326
Phonetics and Phonology: epenthesis of i, 44 158; haplology, 35 324 fn., 342 f., rhyming groups, 328 fn., dissimilation, 333; inscriptions, studies in the, 35 321-352, final vowels, 322 fn., 325-329, conventional writing, 322 fn., 328 fn., final vowel of prior element of compounds, 325-329, vowels preceding enclitics, 325-329, h antevocalic, 332-334, haplography, 342, dittography, 342, analogical writing, 348 fn.
Studies: the present status of, 56 208-225
Old Persian provinces, identity of, 56 213-219
Old Testament, canon closed at end of 2nd cent. A.D.; no early canon, 46 189-190; contributions to study of in 1900-1918, 38 114; English, mistakes in translation, 58 122-129; Greek, Alexander Polyhistor's passages on it quoted by Eusebius are of value for criticism of LXX, 56 251-252; Greek, Scheide papyri of Ezekiel dates ca. A.D. 200; affinities of, 58 533, LXX, AQ-type and B-type strata in, 533; J document, secondary stratum of characterized by exaltation of Moses, 38 124; attitude toward labor, 41 193; Maimonides, ibn-Ezra and Spinoza, their attitude toward it, 55 Supp. 1, 22-40, phases in Jewish interpretation of O.T., 23-40; allusions to in Manichaean texts, 56 205 n. 21; manuscripts of school of Ben Naftali, method of isolating, 51 371; messianic predictions in the Prophets, 46 347; no messianic prophecies in, 32 120; Moffatt's translation, criticism of, 45 368
Oldenberg's views on the Vedic dual endings, 23 319 f.

O-lo-pên, leader of the Nestorian mission to China, 635 A.D., 30 4; called a "Persian Priest", 33 198; see also Nestorians

O-lo-pön, see O-lo-pên

Omens, see Astrology; Burj-Nāmah; Divination; Hepatoscopy

Oneiromancy, Babylonian, text in University of Pennsylvania Museum interpreting motions of the body as seen in dream, 38 329

Ophiomancy, Parsi-Persian text on serpent-omens, with translation, 33 289-291, Zoroastrian, derived from Babylonia, 292

Oponia, kingdom of, imaginary, an ideal state pictured by the Old Believers of the Christian church in Russia in the 17th cent., identified with Japan, 42 286-289, details of story based upon legend of Prester John, 289-294

Opis, see Upî

Oracle, see Book of Changes

Oracle Bones, characters on, used with bronze inscriptions, to determine early literary style, 56 343-344; character 之 used sparingly on, 344, discovered in 1899, 345, finds at Anyang dated by inscriptions on the, 346 n. 33, calendric tables on give form of 乙 i, 347, the character 且 tsu on the, 347, name Yin for people or city does not occur on, 335 n.1, brush used for inscribing characters on, 335 n.2, character 天 t'ien probably does not appear on the, 343-344; Bounakoff's criticism of method of deciphering, 56 376, note on bibliographies of, 377; in Couling-Chalfant Collection, spurious specimens, spurious genealogical tables on, 56 529; earliest forms of character i, 彝, 51 19, and Plate III, Fig. 2; early forms of the character i 彝 as found on the, 52 26-29; ancient form of character ku, 蠱, 55 1, 4-6, 9; support data of the Shih chi and the Bamboo Books, 52 233, 241; do not mention Yao, Shun or Yü, 56 53, give names of small localities only, 71; affirmative and negative inquiries, prayer for harvest addressed to a cult figure, place of divination may refer to the Stag Tower, see abstract, R.S. Britton

Orange tree, mentioned by author of 4th cent. A.D., 55 7

Oraons, origin of the kujur sept among the, 50 227

Ordeal, Yao's test of Shun, 56 55, 58, 66

Ordu, Western, of the Hsiung-nu, the Wu-sun King made governor of, 37 100, conquered by the Chinese, 100; see also Ho Ch'ü-ping

Orient, history, works on in Cleveland Public Library, 36 421-422, travel, works on in Cleveland Public Library, 421-422; modern, need for greater understanding of by orientalists, 44 177-185; see also Science; Seals

Oriental Institute of the University of Chicago, foundation of and program, 39 181-183; first expedition to the Near East (1919-1920), report on, 40 282-285

Orientalist, linguistic science and the, 55 115-137; American, task of as seen in 1919, 39 159-184

Oriental languages, modern, need for an American school for the teaching of, 39 185-188, schools for teaching of in Europe, 189-195

Oriental Studies, European, early, 43 1-11; in Syria, 45 356; their place in the world-picture of 1938, 58 403-412; see also Languages

American: outlook for in 1918, 38 107-120; should strive for better interpretation of the modern Near East, 40 138-139; a plea for promoting them to enrich American culture, 48 97-108; see also Asiatic Studies in the U.S.A.

Origen, see Hexapla

Origenis Hexaplorum of Field, additions to Joshua in, 33 254-258

Ormazd, as Primal Man in Manichaeism, 44 69, 71; see also Auramazda

Ormuri, rīdzan 'rice,' 47 265

Ornaments, Chinese, see Gold & Silver; Glass

Orosius, Historiae adversum paganos, MS of Arabic translation of in Columbia University, 51 171-172; derived his idea of four world-empires from Trogus and Justin, 59 422

Ortelius, Abraham, see Japan, Geography

Osiris, his primitive connection with the Nile, 39 73, as moon-god, 88-89; and Isis, of Semitic origin, 53 170; related to Sumerian fertility god Asar, 39 196-205; resemblances to Tammuz, 35 213 ff.; see also Moon

Ostraka

Aramaic: debt-list from Nippur, 5th cent. B.C., 29 204-209; Jewish, from Egypt, description of, 60 132-133

Coptic: Merton 1, text and translation, 58 151-152; in New York Historical Society, text and translation, 48 147-158; text and translation, 34 313-314

Ostrich, in T'iao-chih, 37 97, eggs of, brought to China by Parthians, 107; see also abstract, J.J.L. Duyvendak; "Camel Crane"

Ottomans, Ottoman, see Caliphate

Oxus River, see Kuei-shui

Oyanguni, Melchior, author of a grammar of Japanese, 1738, see Asiatic Studies in Europe

Pa, 巴, part of modern Ssŭ-ch'uan; soldiers from, fought the K'un-mings in early Han, 37 104, 146

Pacific, population problems of the, 48 74-76

Pacorus, his invasion of Palestine in 40 B.C. referred to in Enoch Similitudes, 56 256

Padmasaṁbhāva, putative founder of Lamaism, biography, different texts of, 54 311-312

Padma thang yig, date of Ms. of Lithang of the, 54 312 f.

Padma Vaẓra, appears on the Tibetan painting of the eighth Dalai Lama, 52 343

Pāe Dhonī in Old Bombay, origin of the name, 53 391

"Pagoda-papers", see Wall-paper

Pagodas, Twins, of Zayton (Ch'üan-chou), 56 373-374, stone in imitation of wood, 374

Pahlavi

Texts: Afdīyā va-Sāyakīh-ī Damīg-ī Sagastān (Wonders of Sagastān), transliteration and translation of, 36 115-121; of Yasna ix.49-103, edited with collation, 23 1-18; of Yasna ix.49-103 critically translated, 24 64-76; of Yasna xvii, edited, 26 68-78

Turfan: early Christian account of the Crucifixion in, 39 55-57; etymology, of HPŠYRD, 58 331 f., of 'ŠKRWST', 332, of MNWḤMYD, 333; 'XSVZ = axšōz 'very strong', 53 392; see also Inscriptions

Painted Basket, see Tomb of Painted Basket

Painted pottery, see Mesopotamian Archeology

Painting

Central Asian: mural br. fr. Eastern Turkestan by A. von Le Coq, depicting a Manichaean ceremonial offering, plate and description of, 49 34-39; remarks on the wall-paintings br. fr. Turkestan by von Le Coq, 49 62-64

Chinese: Aesthetic Theory, comments on, 56 530-531, 531-533; painting of sculptures in T'ang dynasty, 55 428; 105 paintings of events and legends concerning Confucius, reproduced in 1923, 52 180-181, paintings of Chinese heroines in a folding book, by Yao Ching-su, 181; Pu-tai as a subject, 53 48, 52; record of painting of Yü Huang by Shih K'o, 53 59; reference to regulations for mounting pictures, 49 238, painting on woodwork of palaces, and pictures painted on the beams, 237, cost of wall paintings in oils per sq. ft., 242; four steps in the painting of mountains and rocks, terms for, 52 298; "sunflower" in Sung painting is a species of mallow, 52 94; wall-paintings at Wan Fo Hsia, 59 155-156; Yuan Ming Yuan wall Painting, in western perspective, 57 127; see also Interior Decoration

Indian: see Ajanta

Tibetan: a painting of the 8th Dalai Lama with 25 of his incarnations, 52 338-345, list of 58 incarnations of the Dalai Lama, 339-340, the Paṇchen Lama with 14 of his incarnations, painting, 345-349, illustrations of the 2 paintings bet. 338 and 339, list of 12 spiritual ancestors of the Paṇchen Lama, 346, relation bet. Dalai and Paṇchen Lamas, 344-347; the nidānas in pictures of the "Wheel of Life", 60 356-360

Paippalāda, fragments, three, 54 70-74; a manuscript at

Poona of the Atharva-Veda, 48 340 f.; manuscripts, description of two, 50 104-111, one at Bombay, 104-109, one at Poona, 109-111; recension of the Atharva-Veda (Kashmirian), 26 197-295; 6.18, reconstruction of, 41 318 f.; and Śaunaka book five, comparison of, 49 350

Pāiśācī Prākrit, on two alleged stanzas in, 44 169; see also Piśāca

Pai Shih-ch'ang, 柏始昌, unsuccessful leader of caravans to Bactria in time of Han Wu Ti, 37 104

Pakeidas, Gerasene deity identical with Σατράπης-Adonis; was chief male deity of Gerasa before dominance of Greek influence; consort was Hera, 54 178-185

Palau language, notes on the phonology of the, 35 1-15

Palaung, a tribe belonging to the Mon-Khmer group of S.E. Asia, notes on the Palaung of Namhsan, 45 187-189, introduction of Buddhism fr. Burma in 1782, and practice of by the, 188, temples and images of Buddha, 188-189, divination among the, 189

Palaeography, Chinese, see Oracle Bones; Bronzes; Inscriptions

Palawan, bamboo writings from, 60 271 f.

Paleolithic man in Transjordan, 52 286

Palestine, see also Folklore; Marriage; Oath; Seals; Songs

Archeology: Beth-Ṣûr, Greek coins from; at height of prosperity in reign of Antiochus Epiphanes; abandoned after Judaizing of Idumaea, 52 301; Chalcolithic settled life spread from the Jordan Valley, 57 240; Jerusalem, third wall, remains and date of, 52 56-58; palm-tree on Canaanite-Hyksos pottery is Mother-goddess symbol, 59 251-259; Rāmallāh, remains at, 46 341; Tell al-'Ajjūl, probably not site of ancient Gaza; comparison of Petrie's and Albright's dates of levels, 53 286, 287; Tell al-Naṣbah, date of tombs at, 52 52-53; Temple of Hadrian standing in Caesarea in A.D. 538, 36 342; toys do not appear until the Iron Age (after 1000 B.C.), 51 176, turreted crown does not appear on deities until Hellenistic period; earlier crowns are of feathers, 176; see also Forgeries

Folklore: songs about enmity between mother-in-law and daughter-in-law, 48 225-228, 238-240

History: Hadrian's visit there in A.D. 129-130, 59 360-365

Religion: bloody sacrifice in modern times, 25 312-313, 27 104; cock and hen emblems of fertility, 33 370; Islamic cult of holy places attacked by ibn-Taymīyah, 56 1-21

Pāli, meaning of ādisati, anvādisati, anudisati, and uddisati in the Peta-Vatthu, 43 410-421; Pālism in Buddhist Sanskrit, diś 'make over merit to', 44 73-75; case-forms for the from-relation, 45 353 f.; commentaries, sources of, 38 267 f.; compounds, on the doubling of consonants in the seam of certain, 41 177; compounds, doubling of consonants in the seam of, 41 462-465; originals of some Jātaka stories, 38 267 f.; kaṇṇikā = circular roof-plate, 50 238-243; kūṭa, the meaning of, 50 242 f.; literature, cleaning the teeth in early, 52 165; muddā, meaning of, 48 279-281; phrase-words and phrase-derivatives, 40 196-198; on a possible pre-Vedic form in, 41 465 f.; relation to Vedic, Sanskrit and Prakrit, 32 414-428; the use of the term, 46 258

Palladas of Alexandria (fl. A.D. 400), his views on birth of man influenced by Jewish ideas, 55 196-199

Pallavas, conquerors of south and west India, 33 210-213; architecture, importance, 49 70

Palm-leaf manuscripts in Siam, note on the making of, 29 280-283; see also Manuscripts, Siamese

Palm Sunday, not celebrated by Church Fathers, 32 274, 323, date fixed, 334; originally opening day of Canaanite mazzoth festival; connected with vernal equinox, 38 333

Palm-tree, on Palestinian Painted Pottery, is symbol of Mother Goddess, 59 251-259; see also Date-palm

Palmer, E.H., corrections to his translation of the Koran, 56 77-84

Palmyra, gods 'Asad and Sa'd of Arab origin, 57 319; fire an important feature of the cult, 51 131, ancestors and rulers deified, 133; mentioned in an Akkadian text of 1000 B.C., 53 288; religious syncretism not influenced by Jews, 43 143-144; see also Alphabet; Dura-Europos; Inscriptions

Palumbe as the site of the fountain of youth, 26 21, 34

Palus Maeortis, Sea of Azov, 37 96

Pampangan, monosyllabic roots in, 31 389-394;see also Philippine languages, comparative grammar

Pampango, people and language, 25 173

Panarion of Epiphanius, Syriac Valentinian hymn in Greek letters in, translation and commentary, 38 1-33

Pân-Aššur-lâmur, Assyrian governor of Aššur and Arbela, 34 349

Panayan dialect of Bisayan, 25 162-169; 26 120-123

Pañcadivyādhivāsa or choosing a king by divine will, 33 158-166

Pañcatantra, Aesop and the, 45 351; in the Bṛhatkathāmañjarī and Kathāsaritsāgara, 53 125 f.; Evil-wit, No-wit, and Honest-wit, 40 271-275; in modern Indian folklore, 39 1-54, lion and bull, 18-20, rams and jackal, 20, unchaste weaver's wife, 20 f., crows and snake, 21 f., heron and crab, 22-24, lion and hare, 24-28, grateful animals, ungrateful man, 28-31, louse and flea, 31, blue jackal, 31-33, strandbird and sea, 33 f., three fish, 34 f., haṃsas and tortoise, 35 f., sparrow and elephant, 36 f., ape and officious bird, 37-39, Duṣṭabuddhi and Abuddhi, 39 f., cranes and mongoose, 40 f., iron-eating mice, 41-43, bibliography of Indian folk-tales, 43-54; Slavonic versions of the, 45 351; text, possibility of reconstructing, 38 273 f.; see also Kalīlah wa-Dimnah

Pāñcarātra texts, close relation to Sāṃkhya, 45 53

Pañcaviṃśabrāhmaṇa, the composition of the, 52 390; compared with the Jaiminīya, 52 389 f.

Pañ Chao, defeated the Yue-chi at Kashgar, 90 A.D., 35 38-40

Pan Chao, part in compiling the "Table of Ancient and Modern Men", 59 207; her moral ratings of the famous men in the "Table", 211-219; foremost woman scholar of China, see also Book Reviews, Swann

Paṇchen Lamas, as represented in Tibetan Paintings, with incarnations, 52 344, 345-349, present Paṇchen Lama, 349 n. 47

Pandu Bing clan of Tamarians, origin of, 50 227 f.

Pāṇḍya, Tamil state of first two centuries A.D., 33 209-213; one of the three kingdoms of southern India, in 1st cent. A.D.; Madura the capital, 37 246

Pangasinán, people and language, 25 173; see also Philippine languages, comparative grammar

Pāṇini, date of the Aṣṭādhyāyī, 59 404 f.; date of, 52 392; tendency toward dichotomy, 59 138 f.; treatment of the indeclinables, 59 136; doctrines on Sanskrit preterite tenses, 21 112; on some rules of, 47 61-70; terminology, 59 136 f.

"P'an Kêng", a book of the Shu-ching, shown by comparison with style of bronze inscriptions to be a forgery of late Chou, 56 343-344

Pan Ku, author of the Ch'ien Han-shu, mistaken in placing conjunction of planets in 207 B.C., 55 310-313; different enumerations of the "Five Classics" by, 44 279-280; part in compiling the "Table of Ancient and Modern Men", 59 207, 210, tr. of his preface to the "Table", 207-209; riming verses in his preface to the Han Shu reveal his part in the organization of the whole work, see abstract, Swann

Pantoja, Diego de, books by, prohibited in Japan, 57 292-294

Pao, 保 (Jap. ho), Chinese village administrative unit of 5 families, system copied by the Japanese in the 7th cent., 30 267; highly developed in the Ming dynasty, 31 192-194; see also Ho

Pao-hsiang Lou, Lama temple in the Forbidden City, Peking, 58 695-696

Paper, as tribute and presents fr. the protectorates to the Chinese Court, began in 102 A.D., 51 144 n.25; Shan and Tibetan processes of manufacture identical, 45 190; see also Interior Decoration

Paper money, Chinese, bill of Yüan dynasty among ms. found at Karakhoto by Sir Aurel Stein, 45 190

Papyri

Arabic: document published by Torrey in JAOS 56 288-292, corrected translation of, 57 312-325; Egyptian, 8th-century, 43 247-248; from Alexandria, dated A.H. 205, text and translation, 56 288-292; tax rolls from reign of al-Muta-wakkil, notice of, 57 248

Aramaic: note to Egyptian Aramaic contract published by Bauer and Meissner, 59 105; notes to Egyptian Aramaic contract published by Bauer and Meissner, 58 394-398

Coptic: magical texts at University of Michigan, Sethianic origin of, 48 358

Greek: Berlin Genesis, dates from 3rd. cent.; characteristics of, 44 173-174; Scheide Papyrus of Ezekiel: dates from 3rd cent.; frequently agrees with Heb. as against LXX, 58 92-102; Scheide papyri of Ezekiel date ca. A.D. 200 and belong to same codex as those of Chester Beatty; affinities of text, 58 533

Papyrus, used as writing material in Assyria and Babylonia, 48 129-135

Paradise, shown to Disciples by Christ in apocryphal Ethiopic Arde'et, 25 47-48; eternity of an Islamic article of faith, 29 73-75; see also Eden, Garden of

Paradise-Epic, so-called by Langdon, really a hymn praising Ea, 36 90-114, is an incantation including Sumerian view of Creation, 122-135, describes Paradise and the Fall of Man, 143-145, is really description of land destroyed by drought, 273, really refers to land devastated by drought, 290-295; describes return of life and fertility to the world at beginning of our age, 39 66, Tilmun regarded as original home of the race, not as Paradise, 66, analysis of text, 67-90, man, position of in, 80 ff., rôles of TAG-TUG, Ninḫursag, Enki, Enlil in, 67 ff., 77 ff., 80-82, curse of disease laid upon off-spring of Nin-ḫursag, 322-328; synopsis of, 41 148-149; does not deal with Paradise and the Deluge, 44 58-59

Paradise Story, Eden located in the Babylonian alluvium, not in Amurru, 45 30-34; not found in Babylonia, 45 148, 150-151

Paramahaṃsa, as class of Yogins, 22 348

Paramārtha, mid. 6th cent. A.D., Indian priest and translator into Chinese of Buddhist Sanskrit works, 51 295, the Viṁśatikā, 295, his tr. compared with Hsüan Chuang's, 299-300, the Mahāyānasaṁparigrahaśāstra, 296, circumstances under which the Yogācāryabhūmiśāstra (Shih-ch'i-ti-lun) was tr., 298-299, 301, 302, author of other Wei Shih texts and largely responsible for diffusion of Wei Shih ideas in China, 299

Parchment, used as writing material in Assyria and Babylonia, 48 109-135; writing material in Parthia, as reported by Chang Ch'ien, 37 97

Paris, see Peace Conference

Parjanya, relation to Indra as god of fertility, 36 244-247, 255 f.

Parlatoria blanchardi, scale-insect attacking the date-palm, 42 205

Parsi, Parsis, Navjot (initiation) ceremony of, 22 322; Parsi-Persian new moon omens, parallels to in Dekkan, 35 293-296; Parsi Sanskritists, 44 170; Tower of Silence at Sanjan, 22 330 f.; see also Persia, Astrology

Pārśvanātha, on the life and stories of the Jaina savior, 38 332

Parthia, Parthians, Parthian, architecture at Dura-Europos, oriental character of, 48 357; control of main overland trade route fr. Antioch, 35 31-32, effort to connect the northern trade route with the Arab sea route, 35-36, control and tolls, 36-38, loss of trade due to internal disorganization, 38, peace with Rome, 38, cut off from being middlemen in the silk trade, 39; intermediaries in trade between East and West, 35 31-33, 35-40; references to wars with Seleucids in Book of Judith, 56 252-253, Pacorus's invasion of Palestine referred to in Enoch Similitudes, 256; Zorastrianism restored in reign of Vologases (A.D. 77-146), 49 369; see also An-hsi; Art and Architecture; Jews; Seleucia-on-the-Tigris; Yavanas

Parvan Śrāddha ceremony, description, 22 228-236

Pašai, see Piśāca

Paschal lamb, bones of not broken as symbol of resurrection, 36 146-153; originally a tabu-sacrifice, 36 150

Passages

Arabic: Arab geographers of 9th-15th cents., writing on Korea, 58 658-660

Chinese: fr. various writers on the use and prohibition of tobacco in China and Manchuria, 58 648-656; Analects IX, 1, Tr. of character yü, 與, according to Shih Sheng-tsu dispels seeming inconsistency, 53 347-351; Analects XVII, 2, on human nature, 51 24-25, VI, 17, states man at birth is upright, 25-28; History of the Former Han Dynasty, (Ch'ien Han-shu Pu-chu), 51, 20b-21a, in "Memoir of Tung Chung-shu" on Emperor Han Wu Ti's promotion of Confucianism, 58 435; Translation of Pan Ku's preface to the "Table of Ancient and Modern Men", Ch'ien Han Shu, 59 207-209; Hsüan-tzu, IX, 4, 57 175; Jen Wu Chih, 人物志, tr. of part of introduction, on the nature of man, 59 281-282; Nestorian Monument, various possible trs. of the passage containing the words san i fen shen, 58 384, 386-393; Li Shuo Huang T'ang Huo Shih P'ien, 利說荒唐惑世篇, by Wei Chün, an indictment of Matteo Ricci and his Map, 59 348, Ts'an Yuan I Su, 參遠夷疏, by Shen Ch'üeh, an attack on Matteo Ricci, 349, Hsieh Tu Shih Chü, 邪毒實據, by Su Chi-yü, an attack on Matteo Ricci and the Jesuits, 349, T'ien Hsia Chün Kuo Li Ping Shu, 天下郡國利病書, by Ku Yen-wu, description of Portugal, 350; Ricci's Map of the World, see Translations; Wei Shu 114, on Taoism, see Translated Works; Sui Shu 35, 12a-13a, on Taoism, see Translated Works; see also Translations

Khotanese: Rāma story ms.: story of conflict of Paraśu Rāma and Daśaratha, 59 464-465, of the birth of Sītā, 465

Passion Week, celebrated every thirty years, 32 323, unleavened bread not to be eaten during, 340-341

Passover, forerunner was spring tabu-offering, 36 327; see also Festivals (Hebrew)

Passy's theory of phonetic change, 44 42

Patañjali, author of Yoga Sūtra, not the same that wrote Mahābhāṣya, 31 25-29; Yoga-sūtras, translated, with the commentary Maṇiprabhā, 34 1-114; Sūtras, Mahābhārata yoga terminology compared with, 22 335-366

Paul, St., knew and used some of the material underlying the Gospels, 58 549; theory of motory sensations, 44 38-43; his trichotomistic view of the soul influenced the early Syriac doctrine of the sleep of the soul, 40 119-120

Pauranic mythology, boar an avatar of Viṣṇu, 55 389

Pa Yi, Shan tribe in S.W. China, practice of ku magic, 55 17; see also Yi

Peace Conference (Paris), Near Eastern representation at; difficulty of settling its problems was due to previously-made secret treaties, 40 138

Pear Garden, 梨園, 49 154 n.5

Pearls, Chinese, Han, affair of the stolen chest of, 51 145, 148

Pedigrees, see Ancestor Worship

P'ei Chü (P'ei Kü), author of the Hsi-yü-t'u-chi, 西域圖記, 30 5, sent to Chang-yeh, western Kansu, 6, could not reach Fu-lin or T'ien-chu, 8; author of the Sui-hsi-yü-t'u, biography of in Sui-shu, 33 194-195, residence in Chang-yeh, Western Kansu, 195, most of his book lost, 195, his part in revival of trade with the West, 196

P'ei Kü, see P'ei Chü

Pei Shih, 北史, by Li Yen-shou, as the source of information about the Wei Shu, see Wei Shu

Pekahiah, see Menahem

"Peking Gazette", see Newspapers

Pelew language, see Palau language

Pelliot, Prof. Paul, manuscripts discovered by at Tun-huang,

1907-1908, 33 202-203; on the tr. of san i fen shen, on the Nestorian Tablet, 58 391

Penal system under Han, 40 191

P'eng-ch'eng, Hsiang Yü's capital, captured 205 B.C., 57 178

P'eng Lai, 蓬萊, one of the 3 isles of the Blessed, 49 141-142 n.8

Pentateuchal codes, represent continuous legal tradition, 33 191

Pen ts'ao kang mu, 本草綱目, does not mention the lemon, 54 145; origin and food of Ku worm, 55 13-14

Pepper, imported by Romans from west coast of India, 37 245

Περὶ κόσμου πρὸς Ἀλέξανδρον, pseudo-Aristotelian work, Syriac version of by Sergius of Rīš'aynā, 35 299

Περὶ Θαυμασίων of Phlegon of Tralles, resemblance of plot to that of Goethe's Die Braut von Korinth, 39 295

Periplus Maris Erythraei, written about 80 A.D., refers to countries and peoples along the Arabian Sea, the Axumites and the land of "Persis", 35 34, 35, the Parthians, 37, n.1, the Nabataeans, 38, the Kushans, 38, 40, information on China, 225, 229-230, on India and the iron and steel trade, 229-230, 232, Kingdom of the Chēra, 236, Ariaca, 236, African coast to Zanzibar, 238; author mentions the three kingdoms of southern India, with their ports, and describes shipping, 37 246, southern extension of India known to the, 248, assumes connection of coast of Hainan, and also of Ceylon, with Africa, 248, draws upon the poets, 249; identification of cities of the Berbera coast, 30 50, products of Berbera coast listed in, 50

Perioco, name on some early maps, stands for Loochoo Islands, 60 276

Père Louis le Comte, on Tobacco in China, 58 649

Perry, Commodore M.C., records of the expedition to the China Seas and Japan, 44 182

Perseus, see Greece, Mythology

Persia, Persians, Persian: lunar and calendar omens borrowed from Babylonia, 35 294; apocryphal acts of Disciples in, according to Ethiopic Arde'et, 25 31-35; history of the cock in, 33 377-380, 394-395; Jackson's notes on his travels there in 1903, 25 176-84; Persian wheel, in India, 51 283 f.; trade with India in 16th cent., 35 250-252; see also Art and Architecture; Calendar; Festivals; Manuscripts; Old Persian; Pahlavi; Parthia; Sasanians; Zoroastrianism

Archeology: Tepe Hissar, correlations of with Mesopotamia, 59 116-117

History: of hostilities bet. the Romans and Persians beginning about 602 A.D., 33 196-197, events following murder of Khosru II, and Ardeshir III's flight to "Fu-lin", 200-202, tr. of Hui-ch'ao's account of Persia, 204-205; members of Arab tribes in Umayyad period, 43 247; sacks of Antioch, Syria, and captivity of Syriac Christians in Persia, 30 6-15, embassy to China, 6; Shāh 'Abbās the Great, relations with Akbar and Jahāngīr, 35 247-268; treaties with Turkey and Afghanistan since 1921, 49 368-369

Language: Pādšāh, an erroneous etymology of, in relation to the pr. n. πατιζείθης (Hdt. 3.61), 40 200 f.; periphrastic perfect, pre-Aryan origins of, 39 117-121; words in the glosses of Hesychius, 41 236-237; ἄρξιφος, βίσταξ, ὀπαστόν, ἀμαζακάραν; yāzdāh, origin of צ z, 42 295-300

Literature: collection of in Cleveland Public Library, 36 421-422; influence of Ḥāfiẓ on the German poet Platen, 21 40-41; poetry, mysticism in, 36 345-347

Religion: Avestan creation compared with Babylonian, 36 300-320; according to Greek texts, 52 186-189; Mithra and Ahura Mazda cults fused after conquest of Media by Cyrus, 57 161-162, Hvareno concept borrowed by Deutero-Isaiah, 166-169; Syrian church in was on way to developing a theology and style free of Western domination, 38 330-331; see also names of deities

Texts: documents from Mughal India, 59 371-374; inscription, at Fire Temple at Baku, 29 302; Parsi-Persian Burj-Nāmah and two ophiomantic texts, with translation, 33 286-293; Parsi-Persian Burj-Nāmah, with translation, 30 336-342

Persian Gulf, character of not understood by Herodotus, 33 352

Persis, place of in trade between China and Rome, 35 32, 35

Perspective, see Painting, Chinese, Yüan Ming Yüan

Peshitta, loss of the Urumiah concordance to in 1919, 43 128-129

Pestilence, in China, salt and rice thrown to drive away noxious vapours (sha ch'i) in the procession of the Reception to Spring, Foochow, 42 55, correspondence to a custom mentioned in the Li-chi ? 55; ceremony for expelling demons and driving away pestilence held at court in Later Han, 51 150; in Japan, efficacy of the Holly Grove against small-pox in the epidemic of 735 A.D., 55 449-450; in Japan, exorcism of the demons of, 54 283; see also China, Chinese, Religion; Plague

Peta-Vatthu, meaning of ādisati, anvādisati, anudisati, and uddisati in, 43 410-421

Petas in Buddhism, 44 166

Peters, John P., see Hilprecht-Peters Controversy

Petra, the ancient Rekem, possible identity with Li-kan, the ancient Chinese name for Syria, 30 36, n.2; capital city of the Nabataeans, at end of southern overland route across Asia, took toll on trade, 35 32-38, conquered by Rome, 104 A.D., 39-40; discovery of probable palace and sanctuary of Aretas III at, 52 286; inscription from the high-place of al-'Uzza, 28 349-351; "Obelisk Ridge" may have been station for observation of the equinoxes, 55 464-465; position as trade center, 35 32, 38-40

Petrie, W.M. Flinders, theory of the origin of the alphabet doubted, 22 182-184

Petroleum springs at Id (Hīt) first mentioned in annals of Tukulti-Ninurta II, 38 214

Phallic symbols, Japanese, the naginata of Susanoo no Mikoto, 54 285, sprouts of a kind of bamboo called Mosodake, 288, sexual significance of order and names of floats in the Gion matsuri procession, 287-289, phallic road gods, 285; emblems and worship at Nippur, Uruk and Tello, 41 132, 141-142

Pharisees, dispute with Sadducees over manner of high priest's entering Holy of Holies on Day of Atonement; background goes back to days of Zechariah, 47 358-359

Philippine, Philippines, known to the Chinese before Ming, 56 378; bamboo manuscripts from Hampangan Mangyan, Mindoro, 59 496-502; linguistic studies, present status of, 41 176; linguistic studies, part played by United States government publications in development of, 42 147-170; linguistic material, a procedure for long-distance collection of, 42 399; see also Tobacco

Language, languages: bibliography of the, 40 25-70; Bisayan dialects, 26 120-136; collection of material on the interrogative sentence in the, 44 169 f.; expression of the ideas "to be" and "to have" in, 30 375-391; comparative grammar of, 27 317-396, subdivision of Malay branch of Malayo-Polynesian, 317 f., number of, 318-320, alphabets of, 320-322, borrowings into, 322 f., materials for study of, 323, general features, 323-329, classification of, 326-329, comparative phonology of, 329-337, pronouns and articles, 337-396, ligatures, 338-340, list of principal elements used in formation of pronouns, 388-396; comparative grammar, the numerals, 28 199-253, cardinals, 200-228, ordinals, 228-234, fractions, 234-237, distributives, 237-244, numeral adverbs, 244-250, restrictive numerals, 250-253; g, three-fold origin of, 31 82-85; i used as pronominal particle, local prefix to nouns and pronouns and as verbal passive prefix and suffix, 49 362-363; Indonesian l in, 36 181-196; the language of education, 46 61-71, suitability of English, 62 f., adaptability of the vernacular, 64 f., political and educational problems, 65 f., advisability of selecting Tagalog, 65-71; minor languages of Luzon, 25 170-174; rgh law (= van der Tuuk's first law) in, 31 70-85, classification of, into r-, g-, l-, y-languages, 72-82; differences between Tagalog and Bisayan, 25 162-169; in the University of the Philippines, department of, 44 169

Philistines, were pre-Hellenic invaders from the Aegean and

Crete, 38 336; language possibly Indo-European, 56 279-281
Philo, did not transform Judaism into a mystery religion, 56 502-503; Quaestiones and De Vita Contemplativa, Armenian-Greek index to, 53 253-282
Φιλοψευδῆς ἢ 'Απιστῶν of Lucian, is of Egyptian origin and was used by Goethe as basis of his Der Zauberlehrling, 39 295-298
Philosophy
Chinese: the tao 道 idea, prevalent in earliest literature but called by other names, 52 22-34, development in meaning of character tao, 25-26, the philosophic concept of tao, 31, tao as a philosophic term not in early use, 32-34, date at which tao crowded out other terms in use 32-34; see also Li Chi, 16th cent.; Wei Shih
Greek: Syriac version of Λόγος κεφαλαιώδης περὶ ψυχῆς πρὸς Τατιανόν of Gregory Thaumaturgus, 35 297-317; see also Mathematics, Greek
Phlegon of Tralles, see Περὶ Θαυμασίων
Phoenicia, Phoenicians, Pheonician, borrowed cock from Cyprus, 33 395; sailors and shipwrights imported by Sennacherib and Ashurbanipal, 50 7-8, 12; trade, goods dealt in revealed by tribute list of Ashurnasirpal, 38 249-250; see also Alphabet; Art and Architecture; Carthage; Seals; Semitic Languages; Weights
History: chronology, Contenau's system compared with the official Palestinian, 48 77; were pre-Hellenic invaders from the Aegean and Crete, 38 336; pays tribute to Ashurnasirpal, 38 248-250; Stone Age; little true Neolithic, 48 77, relations with Egypt, 78; see also under names of various kings
Language: grammar of Aḥîrâm Inscription, 45 271-278, definite article not used, 275, Akkadian influence on lexicon, 269, 273, 275; absolute inf. used as in Hebrew, 57 398, wāw consecutive not used with perf., 398-399, definite article well-established by time of Aḥîrâm inscription, 399-400, accusative of place used, 400; literary style, doubtful evidence for its development, 57 399; not a bilingual people, 57 400; y of the Latin transcriptions may be a sound not capable of representation by the Latin alphabet, 57 398; y for h, appearance of, 60 420, Byblos dialect, archaizing tendency of, 420
Religion: Aštart and Tanit possibly androgynous, 21 187; Ešmun equated with Tammuz-Adonis, 21 188-190; Philo of Byblos and Sanchuniathon too much depreciated, 48 78, pantheon, 78-79; Tyre, pantheon of, 22 115-117
Phoenicoccus marlatti, scale-insect attacking the date-palm, 42 205
Phoenixes, of the Hsieh 薛 Family, 49 141-142 n. 11
Phonemes, choice of symbols for, 53 296; analysis of English compound, 53 297
Phonetic law and imitation, 44 38-53, Paul's theory of motory sensations, 38-43, effect of surrounding sounds, 39 f., impulses toward phonetic change, 41 f., Passy's and Wundt's theory, 42, changes without intermediate steps, 42 f., dissimilation, 43 f., spread of new sound by imitation, 45-48, dialect mixture, 48-50, examples of incomplete spread, 50 f., ways in which phonetic change becomes regular, 51, exceptions to phonetic laws possible, 52 f., necessity of retaining "young grammarians" method, 53
Phonetic writing, compared with ideographic, 55 338 f.
Phrase-words and phrase-derivatives, 40 194-198, in English, 194 f., Greek and Latin, 195 f., Sanskrit, 196, Pāli, 196 f.
Physiognomy, text and translation of 16th-17th century Syriac work on, 39 289-294
Pi in the Mahābhārata, 23 154 f.
P'iao-ch'i, 驃騎, General, see Ho Ch'ü-ping
Piau-ki, see P'iao-ch'i
Pien, 籩, sacrificial vessel, 49 130 n.5
Pig, domesticated, question of origin of, in China, 60 581; pig-ku a variety of Black Magic, 55 7
Pigou, Mr. Frederick, see International Relations, Anglo-Chinese
Pi-hsia-yüan-chün, 碧霞元君, see Princess of the Colored Clouds
P'ing ching kuan ts'ung shu, 平津館叢書, by Sun Hsing-yen, 18th cent., 51 42
Piñgala in iconography, 57 328
Piñgalā, version of the story of Bhartṛhari's wife, 23 314
Pi-pa-lo, see Po-pa-li
Pirates, off Malabar coast of India in 1st cent. A.D., 37 241; see also Navigation
Piśāca languages, comment on the phonology of, 25 340; relationship of language of Shāhbāzgarhi and Mansehra inscriptions to modern, 36 210 f.; equivalents of Rommany words, list, 29 233-235
P'i-she-ya, the Visayas of the Philippines, 56 378
Pīšôn, River, = the Persian Gulf, and the Red Sea, 45 32; probably the Karḫā, 48 342
P'i Ying 辟雍 College, 49 130 n.3
Pi Yün Ssu, builders' regulations for the Hall of the 500 Lohans at, 49 242
Plague, kill dogs to dispel, 55 3
Plano-convex bricks, see Mesopotamian Archeology
Platen, German poet, influenced by Ḥāfiẓ, 21 40-1
Plato, Babylonian origin of his nuptial number, 29 210-219
Playing Cards, of Chinese origin, not important in spread of printing westward, not originally associated with dice, 47 75-76
Pleiades, a favorable mark on sacrificial animals, importance in Vedic and Babylonian horse-sacrifice, 54 123-127, connection with the Babylonian and Vedic constellation, 124, explanation of their position in the Babylonian proto-zodiac and in the list of Vedic nakṣatras, 124-127, calendaric role of the constellation, 126-128
Pliny, on the Aorsi and the Alani, 30 41-42; describes conditions of voyage fr. Egypt to Malabar coast of India and return, 37 241, 246, ignorance in regard to Indian geography, 248; on "silk, furs and iron from the Seres", 35 224-225, 228, 230-232, 236, 239
Plough, history of, in China, noted, 60 583
Plutarch on Persian religion, 52 187
P'o, 僰, = Ya-chou in Ssŭ-ch'uan; Han Wu Ti's attempt to open a route to India through, 37 99
Po ch'üan hsüeh hai, 百川學海, see Ts'ung Shu
Poetry, Chinese, comparison of several of Hart's translations with the literal tr., see Book Reviews, H.H. Hart, The Hundred Names; modern study of folk-lore, popular poetry and childrens' songs, 56 375; Odes, the Yung to be chanted only at the imperial court of Chou, 54 188 n.7; poems by Monk Pu-tai, 53 48, 50-51
Pognon, Paul Pascal Henri, death of, 41 160
Poison, menstrual, scientific proof of its existence confirms biblical ideas of contagion by it, 44 165-166; see also Black Magic, ku
Po Ku T'u, 博古圖, po means "many", 57 444
Polo, see Authors, Laufer, B.; Games
Po-lo-mên, Beluchistan, on route fr. China to Indian Ocean, 33 195
Po-lo-mön, see Po-lo-mên
Polynesian, treatment of t and s, 38 71; cloud-gods, 42 331; stories of a fountain of youth, 26 26-28
Pomegranate, stated by some works to have been introduced into China by Chang Ch'ien, 37 92; in China, first mention of at end of 3rd cent. A.D., 60 582
Pontianak, Malay kingdom in Borneo, founded by Šarīf 'Abd-al-Raḥmān, 33 318-319
Po-nu, see Chao P'o-nu
Pool (p'an 泮) in front of a Confucian temple, 49 130 n.4
Po-pa-li, = Berbera, Africa, see Africa, early Chinese notices
Popular etymology and analogy, 57 145 f.
Population, in Ta-yüan in early Han period, 37 95, in T'iao-chih, 97, in Ta-hsia, 98
Porphyrius, Syriac version of his Eisagoge, 35 298
Porter's Magindanao primer, 42 157

Portugal, Portuguese, exploration in 15th century, importance of religious motive in, 38 71-72; in China, called Fu-lang-chi "Franks", a term at that time designating all Europeans (c. 1515), 59 349, 350, 352-353, 354-355; in Japan, see Japan, Geography

Po-shih, a scholarly degree, given to Shu-sun T'ung, 57 178, at Wen Ti's court, 180;

Po-shih (Erudit), title given in Ch'in dynasty to 70 learned men at Court, 58 436, 70 at court of Han Wên Ti, 437, specialized in each of the 5 Confucian Classics at court of Han Wu Ti, 440, were the Masters at the Imperial University, 441-442, number doubled under Emp. Hsüan, 444

Po-shih Ti-tsu, title of students, see Imperial University

Po-ssī, see Po-ssu

Po-ssu (Persia), account of in the Sui-shu, 30 6; tr. of account of, in the Hui-ch'ao-wang-wu-t'ien-chu-kuo-chuan, 33 204-205, Chinese text, 207

Po Tao, 伯道, a man of the Five Dynasties, 49 141-142 n.5

Potato, American origin of, 59 143

Potato, migration of the, 59 143

Pott, Pres. F.L.H., work of in Chinese history, 38 100-101

Potter's wheel, appeared in Egypt ca. 3000 B.C., 39 172; with or without the potter, as a symbol for the 2nd nidāna, the saṃskāras, 60 358

Pottery, glazing with metallic oxide referred to in Prov. 26: 23, 60 268-269; Chinese glazed tiles, cost of, 49 241; of ancient Ssu-ch'uan, see Hanchow; Chinese and Korean, Han, see Lo-Lang; see also Glazing

Pottinger, Sir Henry, see China, Chinese, History

Po-wang, 博望, Marquis of, title bestowed on Chang Ch'ien in 123 B.C., 37 99, commanded respect in the West, 102-103, successors lower the prestige of, 104-106

Prabandhas of the Jains, as chronicles, 36 55

Prabhūtaratna, with Sakyamuni, appears on early Chinese sculpture, 51 366

Prabodhacandrodaya, Māgadhī in the, 44 97-99, dialects of, according to commetators, 44 114-118

Practical Oriental Academy (Petrograd), founded 1909 for teaching modern oriental languages, 39 194-195

Pradyota, wars of, 45 305-308

Pradyumna, worked over the Śālibhadra Carita, 43 257 f., list of texts re-worked by, 258

Pradyumnasūri, the Śālibhadra Carita by, 43 167

Prajāpati, boar identified with, 55 390; Kapila called, 22 386 f.; identity of Makha-Saumya with, 55 381 f.; prāṇa as, 22 295; sacrifice of, 55 388 f.

Prajāpati-Vāyu, becomes vital breaths, 22 261

Prajñāruci, early 6th cent. A.D. Indian Buddhist translator of the Sanskrit Viṁśatikā into Chinese, 51 295, his style compared with Paramārtha's and Hsüan Chuang's, 300-301, 305

Prākrit, descendants of root aorist, of imperfect and a-aorist in Buddhist hybrid Sanskrit, 57 31-32; in Bhāsa's plays, certain archaisms, 40 250 f., alphabetical list of selected archaisms, 251-259; of the Cārudatta and the Mṛcchakaṭika compared, 42 62-64; grammarians versus the manuscripts, 44 118-121; Prākrit-Indo-European etymologies, fifteen, 60 361-369; inscription in Kharoṣṭī characters, 24 4 f.; Māgadhī and Ardhamāgadhī, 44 81-121, passages preserved in manuscripts, 95, dialects of the Prabodhacandrodaya according to commentators, 114-118; endingless noun case-forms, 59 369-371; origin of, and relations to Vedic and Sanskrit, 32 414-428; on a possible pre-Vedic form in, 41 465 f.; confusion of Sanskrit prepositions prati and pari in, 51 33-39; agreeing with Śiśunāka's limitation of sibilants, 45 73 f.; Prakritisms in the Veda, 32 415-420

Prakṛti, Kuṇḍalī another name for?, 23 69

Pramati in the Disguise of a woman, 26 177, analogues of the story, 26 306-309

Prāṇa, as breath or a form of breath in Hindu literature, 22 249-308; location, 23 71; and apāna, 39 104-112, etymology, 104 f., location of, 105-112, in Vedic and Upaniṣad commentaries, 105-107, Deussen's view of, 107-110, Upaniṣad evidence, 108-111, in the Sūtras and Brāhmaṇas, 111; thoracic and abdominal breaths respectively, 111 f.

Prāṇas, in Yoga-technique of the Mahābhārata, 22 346 f., 362 f.

Prāṇa-series, and points of compass, 22 274 f.; in the Upaniṣads, 22 275-277, 286-302

Prasenajit, father of Śreṇika, 45 302 f.

Prasodes, the unknown land south of the sea, making an angle near the Gulf of the Sinae, 37 247, notion of this southern continent conceived by the Greeks and Romans, 248

Prasthānabheda of Madhusūdana Sarasvatī, the logical and ethical presuppositions of the, 50 323 f.

Pratijñāyaugandharāyaṇa of Bhāsa, legendary material in, 43 169

Praveśikā of Kṛṣṇanātha, 23 79-83

Prayers, Chinese, Translations, with notes; to the five ancestors of Confucius, 崇聖祠文, 49 128-129, to 大成殿文, Confucius, 129-130, to the God of War, 關羽, 130-131, to Ancestors, 拜祖文, 131-132, to Father Buddha, 132-133, to Kuan Yin, 觀音, 134-135, to Ti Tsang, 地藏, 135-136, to Wen Ch'ang, the God of Literature, 文昌, 136-137, to K'uei Hsing, 奎星, 137-138, to the City God, 城隍神, 138-139, for Peace and Health, 祈安文, 139-141, to the Goddess Who Grants Male Offspring, 送子娘娘, 141-142, to the God of Locusts, 142-144, of Thanksgiving for Rain, 謝雨文, 144-145, for Deliverance fr. Plague, 滅瘟疫文, 145-146, to the Fire God, 火神, 146-147, to the Kitchen God, 灶神 147-149, to the God of the Green Sprouts of Rice, 安青苗文, 149-150, to the God of Cattle, 牛王 150, of Thanksgiving to the Earth-God on the Successful Completion of a Building, 架屋謝土神文, 151-152, to the Gods of the Land and Grain, 社公祝文, 152, to Chang Hsien, a God of Birth, 張仙大帝文, 153, to the Lao Lan, 老郎文, 154, to Welcome the Goddess of Vaccination, 迎痘神文, 155

Prefects, post as, given to army officers who had been in the Ta-yüan campaign, 37 115

Pregnancy, duration of, in the Mahābhārata, 24 19, in modern Indian reckoning, 392

Prehistoric Monuments, Central Asia and Tibet: megalithic monuments, see Book Reviews, Roerich

Prémare, Father Joseph Henri de, on tr. of san i fen shen in the Nestorian inscription, 58 388-389

Prester John, legend of, in Russia, 42 290-291, legend of Oponia founded upon that of, 291-294, identity of, 293-294; on the fountain of youth, 26 21 f., 35; and Japan, 42 400

Preta-concept in Hindu thought and ritual, 59 412

Priapus, see Greece, Mythology

Price Lists, Chinese, for building materials and furnishings for imperials palaces and temples, 1727-1750, 49 234-243, value of the tael, 236, terms used, 236; timbers, 236-237, 240-241, kinds of wood, 238; stone, 237, 238-239, brick and glazed tiles, 237, 240, 241, transportation, 238-239, 240, 241, stone carvers' time, 237, painting of interiors, 237, 242

Priests, Armenian, ordination of not complete without offering, 32 338-339; Hebrew, forbidden to drink wine, 33 184-186

Prince Ram Khamhaeng, introduced art of writing into Siam, 44 13-15

Princess of the Colored Clouds, daughter of the deity of T'ai Shan, 53 228 n.57; see also Jade Maid

Printing, invention in China possibly in Sui Dynasty, 47 72, speculation as to dev. from block-printing, 72, invention of revolving wheel for type setting, 73, date of movable type in Korea, 73, Chinese wallpapers intro. into Europe 17th cent. called "pagoda papers", 73-74, wallpapers brought to America in 1735, 74, study of invention of paper, by westerners, 74, tradition of invention of writing brush, 74, sources of information on printing, 74, the oldest newspaper, 74, printing in Ming and Manchu periods, 74, printing on textiles, 72, 75, certificates of membership in secret

societies block-printed on textiles, 75, playing cards not important in spread of printing to Europe; dice and cards two distinct developments, 75-76; Hebrew, in U.S.A., 41 225-229; in Japan, earliest extant printed material, 59 147, Japanese works printed before 1200, 147, intro. of movable type fr. Korea, 148; of Tibetan books, 52 97, metal blocks not used, 97; see also Books, Chinese

Pritchard, Dr. Earl H., biographical notes on, 57 353-354

Priyadarśikā of Harṣa, time analysis of, 21 89, 94-101; metres of, 43 171

Prophets, late Hellenistic-Jewish work on apocryphal lives of, 55 200-203

Prostitutes, temple (male), Sumerian and Semitic myths explaining the origin of, 39 83-85

Prostitution, in early Semitic world, 55 193 n. 11

Proverbs, Arab, dealing with rain, dew, snow and clouds, 52 145-158; Arabic, Syrian, 23 175-288

Proverbs, Book of, antagonistic towards wine, 33 181; parallels to the Wisdom of Amenemopet, 45 372

Pr-wr, Egyptian sanctuary, originally situated close to Pr-nw near Aswān; connected with Osiris, 41 233

Psalms, Book of, oldest psalm is 68:8-9, 16-18, 12-13, 14b, 15, 19, 25-28, 52 294; Ps. 68B, an incantation for rain, is the oldest, 51 365-366; future life and bodily resurrection taught in them, 57 255; no messianic references to Christ in, 32 120-121; 120-134, translation and metrical form of, 27 108-122

Pseudo-Aristotelian literature, see Περὶ κόσμου πρὸς Ἀλέξανδρον

Pseudo-Jeremiah, his Hebrew letter to Babylon reflects true historical conditions, 56 244-245

Ptahil, Mandaean supreme beneficent creator deity; his character influenced by that of the Iranian Yima-Jamšīd, 53 157, 164

Ptolemy's Geography, the stations of the ancient silk route as given in, according to the Macedonian silk merchant Maes, 35 227-228, Casii of, = Sarikol, 229; misconceptions of geography of the Far East based on misinterpretations of reports of travellers, 37 240, his Kattigara = Kiao-Tsi, the port of Tong-King, 244, his criticism of Marinus of Tyre's data, and his drawing of coast beyond, westward to S. Africa, 246-249, ignorance in regard to Indian geography, 248

P'u Hsien, 普賢, see Ti Tsang, prayer to

Punans of Borneo, 25 239

Pundalik, a story told by Bahinabai of, 48 341

Pu Ning Ssu, a temple at Jehol, interior decoration of, 49 242

Puns, Chinese use of in shadow-plays noted, 55 222; in the Śālibhadra Carita, 43 262

Punt, land situated in India, 43 169

Pupils of an image, painting of the, 49 138, 139 n.5

Purāṇas, as history, 43 132-141, Brahman influence, 132-134, genealogies, 135-141, Rig-Veda tradition and the, 138-141; relation of the Vāyu and Brahmāṇḍa, 43 130 f.; research, new methods of, 48 352

Purty sept of the Hos, origin of the, 50 231

Purūravas-Urvaśī saga, reflections of RV. x. 95 in, 29 284 f.

Puruṣa, as blend of elements derived from spheres of Agni, Sūrya, and Viṣṇu, 51 108-114; its dwelling-place, 22 265

Pūrvārcika and Uttarārcika, relative age of, 52 388 f.

Pūṣan, united with Indra as god of fertility, 36 256-258; and Aja Ekapād, 53 327

Pu-tai, 布袋, the "Laughing Buddha", why and how derived fr. the fat monk Pu-tai, 53 47-52, known to Chinese as Mi-lo Fo, 彌勒佛, because of his claim to be an incarnation of Maitreya, 47-48, known to Japanese as Hotei, 48, biography of monk Pu-tai, 49-52, appearance in art in China and Japan, 48, 52, history of Yüeh-lin Temple, 52

P'u-t'au (p'u-t'ao), grapes, see Words, Chinese

Putchuck, a product of Po-pa-li (Berbera), 30 49

pu-yao, 步搖, special cap, see Court Manners, Dress

Pyramid, as symbol of Zeus is of Anatolian origin, 60 549

Pythagorean theorem known in Babylonia, 60 106

Pythagorean doctrine in China, see abstract, Gardner, New Haven, 1936

qadar, critique of al-Ḥasan al-Baṣri's essay on, 55 138-162

al-Qaddāḥ, Maymūn, not identifiable with Muḥammad al-Maktūm, 56 509

Qadesh, battle of between Ramses II and the Hittites, plan of, 46 359

Qāḍis, Fāṭimid, account of al-Nu'mān family from ibn-Ḥajar, 27 217-296

al-Qadri, Šarīf Ḥusayn ibn-Aḥmad, his career in Borneo, 33 318

Qā'idah fi Ziyārat Bayt al-Maqdis of ibn-Taymīyah, text of 18th-cent. Landberg MS of, 56 1-21

Qaraite Bible commentaries from the Cairo Genizah, 41 179-180

Qašīšā Jacob, Chaldaean priest, works of, 22 88

Qatādah line of Grand Šarīfs of Mecca, 37 155, 157

Qāyômā Mār Samuel Giāmil, General Procurator of the Chaldaean Patriarch of Babylon at Rome, works of, 22 87

Quarterly Bulletin of Chinese Bibliography, note on beginning of publication of, 54 319

Qubā (Persia), see Calendar, Persian

al-Qubaybah, Palestine, folklore and songs in local dialect, 50 199-213

Queue, a feature of culture of many peoples in Asia, 56 377-378

Quippus and notched tallies, use of in ancient Tibet, 38 34, in ancient Japan, 34, n.1

Quotations, of Han and Pre-Han works, see Yen T'ieh Lun

Rabbinic belief in sleep and resurrection of the dead, 40 118

al-Radd 'ala 'l-Naṣāra of al-Jāḥiẓ, translation of section of, 47 311-334

Raḥmâni, Ephraem, Syrian patriarch of Antioch, 22 93-94

Rain, Arab proverbs about, 52 147-153, 157-158; controlled by the moon in Semitic and Indo-European mythology, 39 72, 77; falling as a reward for the execution of justice, 51 150; incantation for in Ps. 68, 51 366; prayer for, 49 144-145; invocations for from al-Qubaybah, Palestine, 48 225-249; to terminate plague, 49 145, 146 n.4

Rājaśekhara, life and works of, 27 1 f., his frequent use of proverbs, and diction, 6 f., translation of his Viddhaśālabhañjikā, 8-71; on Śiśunāka, 45 72-75

Rajendra Lala Mitra's translation of prāṇas, 22 255 f.

Rajput, miniature painting, second zenith of, 54 442; painting, 49 72 f.; school of miniature painting, the Indian precursor of the, 50 326

Rāma (commentator on Bombay text) on exceptional forms of the Rāmāyaṇa, 25 90 f.

Rāma Prasād, on the science of breath, 22 307 f.; 23 69

Rāma story, in Khotanese, 59 397, ms. found in Pelliot Coll., 460-461, résumé of, 461-464, style of, 464-465, 468, forms of the names in the, 465-466, spread of the Indian Rāma story; versions and divergences, 466-467, adaption to Buddhist teachings, 467, type of composition Indian, language second stage Khotanese; date of ms. may be 9th cent. A.D., 468; in the Mahābhārata, allusions to the, 50 85-103, five Rāmas, 85 f., Vālmīki, 86 f., the number of kings Nārada told of, 87 f., Rāma's reign, in Śānti, 88-90, in Droṇa, 90-92, the Rāmopākhyāna, 92 f., passages anticipating the, 93, Rāma as Viṣṇu, 94 f., Rāma and Rāvaṇa, 95 f., most allusions of battle-books in Droṇa, 96-99, other battle-books use other sources for similes, 99 f., Śānti, 100-102, death of Śambuka, 101, Viṣṇu's prophecy, 102, index of references, 102 f.; see also abstract, H.W. Bailey

Ramaḍān, observance of among Malays, 33 340

Ramah of Samuel (Ramathaim), identified with Rāmallāh, 45 182

Rāmallāh (Palestine), archeology of, 46 341

Rāmapūrvatāpanīya Upaniṣad, belongs to literary stratum of Tantras, 23 67

Rāmāyaṇa, divinity of kings in the, 51 312-315; linguistic archaisms, 25 89-145, forms unrecorded by Whitney, 96 f., sounds, 97-103, sandhi, 98-103, declension, 103-120, numerals, 115 f.; pronouns, 116-120, conjugation, 120-143, compounds, 143, gender, 144 f.; references to materialism

in the, 50 134 f.; the oath in, 52 316-337; the original, 46 202-219, comparison of the North Western recension with the Bombay and Bengal recensions; hope of restoring an ādi-Rāmāyaṇa vain, 219; suicide in general, 21 148-150; suicide by starvation, 21 151-157; Tibetan version of the, 50 174
Rambhā, wife of Nala-Kūbara, turned to stone, 33 67
Rāmdās, folk-stories about, 25 185-188; influence on Shivaji, 50 159 f.
Rapanui, r for original l in, 36 189
Rank, Chinese, Han, Ladies of the Court: kuei-jen, 貴人, 51 141, hsin-yeh-chün, 新野君, 149, Huang T'ai Hou, 皇太后, 144, chang-kung-chu, 長公主, 151
Rapiqu, western end of Assyro-Babylonian border, 38 214
Rašap-Makal, Canaanite underworld deity closely resembling Nergal, 50 339
Ra's al-Šamrah, see Ugarit
Rašīd, banu-, of Ḥā'il, feuds with the banu-Su'ūd, 37 157-158
Ratnāvalī of Harṣa, time analysis of, 21 89, 90-94; Śivanāthaśarman wrote commentary on, 23 79
Rauhiṇeya, story in the Mahāvīracaritra of Hemacandra, 44 1-10, synopsis and other versions, 1 f., source of translation, 2, translation, 3-10
Rauhiṇeyacaritra of Devamūrti, 44 1
Rāvaṇa and Rāma in the Mahābhārata, references to, 50 95 f., 102
Raven, with 3 feet, in Chinese myth of the 10 suns, 56 63-64
Rawāfiḍ (heretics), history of term, 29 137-159
Rāwandīyah, Shī'ite extremists, 29 121-124
Rdo rje dpal, one of the incarnations of the Paṇchen Lama, appearing on a Tibetan temple painting, 52 348
Rebellion of the Seven Kingdoms, Han period, causes and results, 40 182-187
Records, Chinese, chronicles on bamboo and silk in Han, 51 157; of Parthia, on leather (parchment ?), according to Chang Ch'ien, 37 97
R'edames Language, see Hamitic
Red Sea, name derived from color of water, due to Trichodesmium erythraeum (Cyanophyceae), 32 115-119; navigators used trade winds in, 37 241, S.China Sea too far from, 242; see also Erythraean Sea
Reeds, used as binding material in Babylonian wall-building; texts referring to, 46 297-302
Regio Instituto Orientale (Naples), founded 1727 for teaching modern oriental languages, 39 191
Reid, Mr. John Gilbert, Chinese ms. books and paintings loaned by, to Univ. of Calif. 1932, 52 180-181
Reinach, see Flying Gallop
Reinsch, Paul S., contributions to Chinese studies, 38 102; death of, in Shanghai Jan. 1923, 43 151
Reischauer, Prof. Robert K., killed Aug. 15, 1937, at Shanghai, 57 357
Rejuvenation, myths of, 26 2-67
Rekem, see Petra
Relational words, 52 309
Religion, economic approach to the study of, 24 394-426; effect of geographical environment on, 41 191; historicity of founders of some oriental religions has not been proven, 53 191-214, Moses, 191-199, Zarathuštra, 199-204, Gautama Buddha, 204-209, Lao-tse, 209-211, Jesus of Nazareth, 212-213; universality of, 25 332-335; see also under names of pertinent countries, peoples and sects; also under names of various religious phenomena
 Chinese: many Chinese "gods" are merely patron "saints", 52 98-99, respect is the principle of ancestor worship, 99; pedigrees in connection with ancestor worship, 52 233-234, 236, 238-239, 240; see also Hsüan Chuang; Wei Shih
 Kayans and Sea Dyaks: influence of war and of agriculture on, 25 231-247
 Primitive: creator gods, development and worship of, 23 29-37; influence of geographical environment on, 41 191; Malay paganism, its contact with Islam in Borneo, 33 314 ff., reasons for acceptance of new religions, 342-344; noonday demon among primitive peoples, 38 160-166; sacrifice, animal, as means of communication with deity, 26 137-144; sacrifice, animal, as means of communication with deity, 26 416; totemism, critique of theories of prior to 1904, 25 146-161
 Tibetan: a religious painting of the 8th Dalai Lama and his incarnations, 52 338-345, a painting of the Paṇchen Lama and his incarnations, 345-349; reviews of two studies in the Tibetan Canon, 52 395-399
Religion, etymology of, 32 126-129
Rémusat, Abel, studies on Chinese and Tartar languages, see Asiatic Studies in Europe
Renaudot, Eusebius, student of the Nestorian inscription, 58 388; see also Müller, Andreas
Rešep, Canaanite gazelle-deity, 40 328, 331; corresponds to Nergal; cult partly Mesopotamian in origin, 48 78-79; see also Rašap
Resurrection, belief in found in oldest Egyptian texts, 39 148; of bones of sacrifices, belief in is reason why they were not broken by Hebrews, 36 146-153; bodily, taught in Psalms, 57 255; Jewish, for righteous only, 40 118-119
rGyal rabs gsal-bai me-loṅ, 1328 A.D., edition of E. Schlagintweit, where concerned with the history of the Central-Tibetan kings, is an abridged and corrupted version of, 38 41-43
Rhinoceros, Indian, as a sacred animal, 51 276-282; horn, an ancient product of Po-pa-li (Berbera), 30 49; horn, articles of, in the Han Imperial Palace, mention, 51 148
Rho, Father Jacques, made earliest tr. of Nestorian inscription, 58 386; books by, prohibited in Japan, 57 292-294
Rhodes, fragment of a Phoenician inscription from, 60 260-264
Rhys Davids' views on Lokāyata, 50 132 f., 137
Ribaldo di Saraphia (Ṣaffūrīyah), Syrian merchant trading between the Levant and Genoa in the 12th cent., 38 182-184
Ricci, Matteo, books (in Chinese) by, prohibited in Japan, 1630-1720, 57 291, list of prohibited works by, 292-294, 295, list of scientific works later permitted, 298, ban on the Ti ching ching-wu lüeh, a topographical history of Peking, because of its account of Ricci and of Catholic monuments, 300 and n. 10, postscript to his Ch'i-jen shih p'ien, by Sorai, 301; Chinese name Li Ma-tou, 利瑪竇, 59 350, 355; see also Asiatic Studies in Europe; Geographical knowledge in China
Rice, grown in Ta-yüan, 37 95, in Anhsi, 97, in T'iao-chih, 97, income in, as reward to army officers, 115; found in late stone age sites in China, 60 583; see also Pestilence, China
Riḍā' 'Abbāsi, 'Ali, MS copied by him in the Metropolitan Museum of Art, 44 270-271
Rig-Veda, ā-diś in the, 40 89-92, 97-100; and Atharva-Veda, 22 309-320; caste system in the, 53 181 f.; chāyā in, 55 278-283; death-rites, based on the ritualistic continuity of RV. 10.14-18, 54 276-281, misplacement of RV. 10.18.8-9, 278, 281, liturgical use of verses in post-Ṛg-Vedic ritual, 279 f., interpretation of ṚV. 10.18, 280 f.; diminutive suffixes -ka and -la, 49 279-281, 'late suffix -ika,' 281; enclisis and "mots seconds," 56 363 f.; ethical element in, 40 220; 'Frog-hymn', 7.103, naturalistic background, 37 186-191; 1.115, a hymn to Sūrya, translation and exegesis, 58 419-434; kissing in the, 28 125-127; present márate, the presumed, 59 406; past tenses of, 37 17; pitṛ in later Hinduism, 59 412; prāṇa in the, 22 250-254, 278; the sources and nature of puruṣa in the Puruṣasūkta (RV. 10.91), 51 108-118, lexical and mythological integers drawn from spheres of Agni, Sūrya, and Viṣṇu, 108-114, translation of of the hymn, 114-118; repetition in, 29 287 f.; repetitions, helpfulness in interpreting text, 31 49-69; on the rejuvenation of Cyavana, 26 45; ritual, metaphor of the car as applied to the, 38 330; stylistic criteria and the chronology of parts of the, 49 276-282; tradition and the Purāṇic, 43 138-141; history of the 12-syllable verse, 22 316-318; charge of relative lateness against little Yama-Saṃhitā, 21 43 f.

al-Riḥlah of ibn-Ḥaldūn, texts and MSS of, 46 171-176

Rijksieraden, fetish-insignia of office among Malayan Muslims, 33 328-329

Riley, Athelstan, on the patripassianism of the Nestorians, 58 393

Risālah fi Istiḥsān al-Ḥawḍ fi 'l-Kalām, probably not the work of al-Aš'ari, 56 416

Risālat Qawānīn Ḥikam al-Išrāq of al-Šādili, MS of in Princeton, 57 100-101

Risio, G., Maronite author, work of, 22 96

Riyāḍ, chosen as Wahhābi capital ca. 1824, 37 157

Roads, "postal", from Ta-yüan to K'ang-chu, 37 94

Rockhill, William Woodville, historic works of on China, 38 102, 104; death of, in Honolulu, Dec. 1914, 35 401

Rodriquez, Alvarez, work on Vocabolario da lingua do Japan, 1603, and Arte da lingua do Japan, 1604, see Asiatic Studies in Europe

Röer's translation of prāṇas, 22 255 f.

Roger, Abraham, his life of Bhartṛhari, 25 226 f., translated, 228-230

Rokudai Shōjiki, 六代勝事記 , value of, as source for study of Kamakura period, 59 40

Rōmaji, see Japanese, Language

Romances, medieval, in Cleveland Public Library, 36 421

Romanization of Japanese; Kokutei, a new official system based on a compromise bet. the Nipponsiki and the Hepburn systems, 59 99, important for unification that the West adopt this Japanese official system, 100, table of new spellings, 100-101, tables for conversion, 101, palatalization, 102, advantages of the Kokutei system, 102

Rōmazi, see Romanization; Japanese, Language

Rome, Romans, Roman, attitude toward Jews in reign of Tiberius, 45 369-370; and (?) Antioch in the Mahābhārata, 58 262-265; Roman Greek sigillata signatures, 58 38-47; see also Divination; and also under names of rulers
 Trade: Far Eastern, maritime, 37 240-249; and India, commerce between, 51 180-182; iron trade with the East, 35 224-239; shipping from Egypt went no further east than Ceylon and Dravidian India, 36 442; silk trade with China, 35 31-41; spice importation from Near East and India, 40 265-270

Rommany, English-, jargon of the American roads, 28 271-308; words, list of Piśāca equivalents of, 29 233-235

Roof Tiles, Chinese, for imperial palaces, 18th cent., cost and transportation, 49 241-242; Korean, of Silla, forms and designs, 55 219, reasons for many different patterns being found at one site; tile factories at Keishu, 219, Chinese invention of roof-tiles earlier than in the West, 218

Rossel Island, an Ethnological study of, 49 182-185

Ṛsyaśṛnga, story of a reflection of the Sumuqan-Enkidu cycle, 40 329-331

Ṛta, arta (order), Indo-Iranian idea of compared with Babylonian conception of introduction of order at Creation, 36 307-308, relation to hvarenah, 308

Ṛta nag hgos, one of the incarnations of the Panchen Lama appearing on a Tibetan temple painting, 52 347-348

Ṛtuparṇa, story of, earliest in Indian literature of human being experiencing sex-change, 47 6 f.

"Rubbings" (Ink Squeezes), collection of in National Library of Peiping, 52 189; fake ones of the horses of T'ang T'ai Tsung, 55 421-423, and Pl.III, fig. 5, 424-427 and Pl.III, fig. 6, of designs in flat relief on border and end of sculpture of "Autumn Dew", 427 and Pl. VI, of Stele of the Picture of the Six Horses, 423-424, 426-427, and Pls. IV and V; see also Inscriptions

Rucika on the dialects of the Prabodhacandrodaya, 44 117

Rudra, 43 56-60, destructive beast and benevolent physician, 56, original character, 57, as god of death, 57 f., in Rig-Veda and later Vedic literature, 58, in the ritual, 59, as a storm-god, 59 f.

Rudras, invoked in Śrāddha ceremony of Kapola Bania caste, 22 229

Ruijū Jingi Hongen, 類聚神祇本源 , value of, as source for study of Shinto in Kamakura period, 59 51-52

Russia, Russians, Russian, Byzantine influence on, 37 58-61; early, with Iranian names, 45 69; names Asy, Iasy, identified with Antae, 59 62-64

Rustam, replaces Garšasp in the Šāh-Nāmah, 36 305, story of his birth compared with that of Etana's son, 305

Rye, wild, found in Near East, 39 176

Ryōshu, Lord of Manors in the Japanese Shoen system, 57 81-83

Sabaeans, commercial intermediaries of Ptolemies, overthrown by Himyarites, 35 34; see also Semitic Languages

Sabbath, not a Babylonian institution, 45 150; based on Babylonian full moon celebration; weekly observance of introduced by Deuteronomists, 59 402; connection with the moon, 37 209-214, older than original form of Decalogue, 210, not derived from Babylonia, 209-214

Sabellianism, opposed by Bar-Šūšan, 32 270, 307

Sābians, castration among as religious rite, 47 333

Sâbītu, her character and rôle in the Gilgameš Epic, 40 315, 316

Sabz Pūšān, see Art, Islamic

Sacae, the; at Lake Helmand; their dual subjection to the Yue-chi and to the Parthians, 35 32, 37

Sacaea, see Abasa

Sachau, Eduard, life and works, 51 106-107

Sa chen kun dgah sñiṅ po, son of the founder of a Tibetan Buddhist sect, represented on Tibetan temple paintings as one of the spiritual ancestors of the Dalai Lama, 52 342

Sackcloth, as Hebrew sign of mourning, 21 23-39

Sacrifice, animal, as means of communication with deity, 26 137-144, 416; bloody, in modern Palestine, 25 312-313, 27 104; Christians do not perform, 32 315, 335-336, of lamb condemned, 337-342; purposes of, in primitive tribes, 50 224 f.; see also Offerings
 Assyrian: cock used in, 33 393
 Chinese: to the 5 ancestors of Confucius, 49 129, to Confucius, 129 n.3, 130, to the God of War, 131, to ancestors, 132 n.1, to Buddha, 133, to Ti Tsang, 135, to wandering spirits, or "hungry ghosts", 136 n.10, to Wen Ch'ang, 137, to K'uei Hsing, 138, to the City God, 138, 139 n.5, to the Goddess who Grants Male Offspring, 141-142, to the God of Locusts, 143, to a God of Rain, 144-145, to the God of Fire, 147, to the Kitchen God, 148, 149, to the 5 planets, 149 n.4a, to the God of the Green Sprouts of Rice, 150, to the God of Cattle, 150, to the Earth-God on successful completion of a building, 151, to the God of the Land and Grain, 152, to Chang Hsien, a God of Birth, 153, to the Lao Lan, 154, to the Goddess of Vaccination, 155, other sacrifices, 149 notes; preparation of victims, 147, 149 n.5, music at the, 130, 154; Han Kao-tsu's to Confucius, 57 179; fêng and shan, Han Wu Ti himself decided the rites for, 58 443; reforms of, under Empress Têng of Later Han, 51 146, performance of the great sacrifices at the ancestral temple of the Imperial family, by the Dowager Empress Têng, 152, offering of new and fresh in-season fruits and vegetables, 152-153; t'ai-lao, said to have been performed by Han Kao-tzu to Confucius, doubts on, 55 331, 333; at the Temple of Earth in each li or village unit, held spring and autumn, followed by a feast for the peasants, 31 193
 Greek: cock used in, 33 380-383, 386
 Hebrew: animal bones not broken because of belief in possibility of resurrection, 36 146-153, blood poured on ground to avoid destruction of soul, 151-153; cock as apotropaic and atonement offering, 33 371, animals used in, 363-365, 371; has not one, but many sources; changing ideas of, 47 80-82
 Human: among the Bataks of northern Sumatra, at camphor gathering, 42 358-359, 368-369; in early Lagaš? 42 99; in Yin and Early Chou, 56 341 n.13
 Semitic: tabu-offerings among Semites, 36 327-328

Sa'd, Palmyrene god, of Arab origin, 57 319

sadāyatana, see House

Sadducees, dispute with Pharisees over manner of high priest's entering Holy of Holies on Day of Atonement; causes go back to days of Zechariah, 47 358-359

al-Šādili, abu-'l-Mawāhib, see Risālat Qawānīn Ḥikam al-Išrāq
Ša-Dikanni, Aramaean site on lower Ḫābūr, description of, 38 222-223
Saeki, P. Yoshio, tr. of Nestorian inscription, 58 387
Safaitic Language, see Semitic Languages
Šagastān, Pahlavi treatise on wonders of, text and translation of, 36 115-121; see also Calendar (Persian)
Saghalin, the Ainu of, see Ainu, Language
Šāhīn, ibn-, original title of his Book of Comfort was probably Ḥibbûr me-ha-yᵊšû'ā, 56 507
Šāh-Nāmah of Firdōsi, sources of, 55 Supp. 1, 12-18, became source of Islamic ideas of kingship, 19-21
Šāhpūhragān of Mani, eschatological fragments of, 50 182-197
Saho Language, see Hamitic
Sa'īd ibn-Ḥasan of Alexandria, see Kitāb Masālik al-Naẓar
Sai Hsien, 塞建, a famous priest in China in Hsüan Chuang's time, 51 296
Sails, not used on Babylonian ships until they were borrowed from the Phoenicians in 7th cent. B.C., 44 173
St. Francis Xavier, founded church in Japan in 1549, 42 289-290
St. John's University, Shanghai, founder of, see Schereschewsky
St. Thomas, the Apostle, church of in India, at Trovancór, ruled over by the Nestorian patriarch of Syria, 30 10-11; shrine of, in legend of Prester John, 42 294
Saka, their place in the trade between China and Rome, 35 32, 36-37; see also Khotanese, Language
Śākadvīpa, and Śvetadvīpa, 39 209-242, scholars' locations of, 209-211, cosmography of dvīpas in Hindu texts, 211-242, Śākadvīpa, 218-225, location of, 219-223, castes of, 224 f., Śvetadvīpa, 225-242, description and location of, 225-229, no traces of Christian influence found in conception of, 230-242, inhabitants, 230-232, visits of sages, 231-242; position of, 40 356-358
Šakan, Akkadian ass-god identified with the moon; Egyptian and Indo-European parallels to; identical with Enkidu, 40 320-321, 331-335
Sakaran Sea Dyaks, authority of chief among, 25 237
Sakarra, story of, among the Land Dyaks, 26 167 f.
Sak-chung (Saka tribes ?), driven fr. near Lake Issyk-kul by the Yüeh-chih became the rulers of Kashmir ?, 37 133, originally barbarians of the Yün clan, formerly of Tun-huang ?, 134
Śakti, in mantra formation, 23 70; Śiva as, worshipped by Kānphaṭa yogīs, 45 356
Śakuntalā, editions and translations of, 22 237-248; Kṛṣṇanātha's commentary on, 23 79-83
Śākyas, cross-cousin marriage among the, 59 220-226
Śālibhadra Carita, a story of conversion to Jaina monkhood, 43 166 f., 257-316, composed originally by Dharmakumāra, 257, worked over by Pradyumnasūri, 257 f., résumé, 258-260, a dānadharmakathā, 260 f., other versions, 261, allusions and echoes, 261 f., style, 262, examples of double meaning (śleṣa), 262 f., digest of the story, 263-287, appendices, 287-316, emendations and corrections, 314-316
Ṣāliḥ (Koranic prophet), probably reflection of some biblical character, 60 287-288
Salisbury, Edward Eldridge, life and works of, 22 1-6
Saljuqs, Saljuq, see Art and Architecture, Islamic
Šalmânu-nûnu-šar-ilâni, Aramaean king of Ša-Dikanni in time of Ashurnasirpal II, 38 223-224
Salt, not used when in mourning, 51 139; symbol of God's love for mankind, 32 312-314, blessing of by Armenians condemned, 336-337, 340; see also Pestilence, China
Salt Lake (Lopnor), Yen-tsê, 鹽澤, believed to be at headwaters of the Yellow River, 37 95-96, underground river from, 95; see also History, Chinese; Lopnor
Salween River, see Trade Routes
Samad sept of the Hos, origin of the, 50 232
Samādhi, function of udāna in the state of, 22 277
Samal, loss of intervocalic l in, 36 185
Samāna as a form of breath in Hindu literature, 22 249-308
Samangs of the Malay Peninsula, 27 205 f.
Samarāṅganasūtradhāra by King Bhojadeva, 49 69
Samaritans, Samaritan, see Inscriptions; Semitic Languages
Samaro-Leytean dialect of Bisayan, 26 123-136; the infixes ra, ri, ro in, 27 143
Šamaš, was feminine among the ancient Akkadians, 58 548; worship of carried to South Arabia by the Amorites; became to goddess Šams, 45 135
Šamaš-šum-ukîn, was eldest son of Esarhaddon, 25 79-83
Sāmavedic texts, interrelation and historical development, 52 388 f.
Sambali, treatment of original l in, 36 187 f.
Sambiasi, Francis, books by, prohibited in Japan, 57 292-294
Śambuka, the death of, 50 101
Saṃdhi of stem-finals before -ka suffixes in the Veda, 31 109-113
Śaṃkara's account of Sāvitrī story and rite in the Vratārka, 21 53-66
Sāṃkhya, epic, terms with technical and ordinary meanings in, 22 337 f.; philosophy in Śvetāśvatara Upaniṣad, 22 381-387, Sāṃkhya and Sāṃkhya-Yoga, 383-386; scheme of Tattvas, in epic, 22 366; world creation and dissolution, the Mokṣadharma story compared with, 45 51-67
Sāṃkhya-Yoga, and Sāṃkhya, 22 383-386; terminology, in Śāradā-tilaka Tantra, 23 66, in Śāradā-tilaka Tantra, 72
Samoan story of rejuvenation, 26 414
Šamši-Adad, building operations of, 38 209-210
Šamši-Adad V, extent of Assyrian empire under, 34 353-355
Šamši-ilu, turtânu under Shalmaneser IV, 34 348
saṃskāras, see Potter's Wheel
samūm, baneful wind, types of, 38 161
Sanballaṭ, possibility of existence of a number of persons by this name, 52 199
Sanchōki, 三長記, value of, as source for study of the Kamakura period, 59 43
Sandon, monument of from Tarsus: weapons on it are symbolic of deity's power, 60 551, represents a rock-sculpture, 552-553, dated ca. 150 B.C., 544
Sang-fu-chuan, said to have been written by Tzŭ Hsia, 44 282
Sanjan, first Parsi settlement in India, 22 328-331
Sanjānah, Dārāb Hormazdyār, author of the Parsi-Persian Burj-Nāmah, 30 336-339
Sanjō Nagakané, 三條長兼, diary of, as source for study of Kamakura period, 59 43
Śaṅkara's translation of prāṇas, 22 300-301, 305, commentary to the Vedānta Sūtras, prāṇa-series in, 305
Śaṅkara-ācārya, part in Śrāddha ceremony among the Kapola Bania, 22 229-235
Sāṅkhya, and Yoga in the Bhagavad Gītā, 43 167
Sāṅkhya Sūtra, date of, as determined from refutations of Buddhist doctrines, 31 1-29
Sāṅkhya-tattva Kaumudī, prāṇa-series in, 22 306 f.
San-lao, representatives of the people, under Han Kao-tsu, 57 173, advice of Tung of Loyang, 177
Saṇmukhakalpa, the contents of the, 56 410
Sanskrit, interrelation of Asokan dialects with, 46 257 f.; drama, literary aspects of absence of tragedy in classical, 41 152-156, rule of happy ending, 152 f., tragic possibilities in some plays, 154 f.; drama, magic in the, 45 110-114; reasons for believing that it is related to Egyptian, 43 170; of Jains in Gujarat, 46 75 f.; relation of, to Middle Indic, 33 145-149; proverb, classical parallels to a, 33 214-216; possibility of contact with Sumerian, 45 366; relations of, to Vedic and Prakrit, 32 414-428
Buddhist hybrid: the aorist in, 57 16-34, blends of aorist and optative forms 32-34, descendants of the Sanskrit iṣ-aorist, 19-27, descendants of Sanskrit s-aorists and similar forms, 57 28-31; diśati 'speaks,' 56 406; endingless noun case-forms in, 59 369; the gerund in, 57 244 f.; some correspondences between Jaina and, 40 343 f.; Prakritic descendants of the root aorist, 57 31 f., of imperfect and a-aorist, 32; saṃdhā, saṃdhi (-nirmocana), 57 185-188
Morphology: anomalous formations in Bhāsa, 41 127 f.;

linguistic archaisms of Rāmāyaṇa, 25 89-145, forms unrecorded by Whitney, 96 f., sounds, 97-103, sandhi, 98-103, declension, 103-120, numerals, 115 f., pronouns, 116-120, conjugation, 120-143, compounds, 143, gender, 144 f.; case forms for the from-relation, 45 353 f.; confixes ka- and ku-, 34 334-338; dative singular ending -āya, 52 77 f.; Epic, iyāt, and blends of aorist and optative forms, 57 316 f.; gender-change in words of time in epic, 23 353; gen. plur. type of asmâkam, 34 331-333; infinitive in -tum, in the Vedas, 21 47; neuter plural nasals not appearing in singular, 39 124; passive-stem, 40 199; periphrastic future in Latin, 34 343; phrase-words and phrase-derivatives, 40 196; prepositions prati and pari, confusion in Prākrit of, 51 33-39; pronominal 'stems' in -d, 51 357; solecisms for the sake of metre in Bhāsa, 41 118-130, sandhi, 121 f., middle for active, 122-124, active for middle 124 f., change of conjugation, 125, feminine of participle, 125, absolutive, 125 f., simplex for causative, 126, compounds, 126 f., syntactical combination, 127; tatpuruṣa compounds of the type goghná and gáviṣṭi, 48 166-176, case-dependence, 171-172, structure and accent, 172-176, verbal element first, 175 f.; te for tvām, 51 285

Phonetics: anaḍúd-bhyas, phonetics of, 40 82; treatment of IE. k^ls, 40 82 f.; l = Avestan d, 25 175

Syntax: ablative of time in epic and earlier, 24 56; form and syntax of numbers in the Mahābhārata, 23 109-155

Teaching: books, need for elementary, 40 241-246; books for western students, need and requirements, 43 165 f.; characteristics desirable for a beginner's manual of, 49 351; dictionaries, need for small adequate, 40 246 f.; on presenting, in a small college, 47 366

Words: ā 'near' is cognate with Latin a 'from,' 59 406; ādeśa 'salutation', a Hindiism, 38 206 f.; 40 82-84, 84-87, 95-97; chāyā, implications in early literature, 55 278-283; dhénā = Avestan daēnā = Lithuanian dainà, 32 393-413; garútmant, etymology and meaning, 42 203 f.; lāti, a Hindiism, 40 82 f., 87-89, 93-95; mudrā, meaning of, 48 279-281; ghost-word paḍviṅśat, 51 170 f.; ratha-chidra (Bṛhad Devatā VI.107), a depiction of, at Sāñcī, 51 172; samādhi 'hostage' in the Arthaśāstra, 60 208-216; ṣṭhīv-, 46 60; root varj, etymology and meaning, 35 273-288; yajñopavīta, possible connection with ritual custom of Indus Valley civilization, 57 245; loan-words in Tagalog, 25 287; studies of, 27 402-417; legal language, words of defamation in, 45 39-50

Sanskritists, early, 40 228 f.; Parsi, 44 170

San su ch'üan chi, 三蘇全集, collected writings of the Family of Su Tung-p'o, a ts'ung shu, 51 44

Śāntarakṣita, first employed term Lokāyata for materialist belief, 50 136 f.

Śāntikalpa of the Atharva-Veda, 33 265-278, text, 267-278

San Ts'ai T'u Hui, 三才圖會, geographical work, errors in, 59 347

Saracus, see Sin-šar-iškun

Śāradā, name of Sarasvatī, 23 65 f.

Śāradā-tilaka Tantra, title, author, general character, and contents, 23 65-76

Sarasvatī, called Śāradā, 23 66

Sarawak, influence of war and of agriculture on the religion of Kayans and Sea Dyaks of, 25 231-247; Islam in, 33 340

Sarebas Sea Dyaks, authority of chief among, 25 237

Sargon of Agade, ruled ca. 2847-2791 B.C., 41 241; not an Amorite, 45 13; extent of his conquests, 42 320; Babylonian geographical treatise on his empire, composed in Isin Dynasty, 2300-2100 B.C., 45 193-245

Sargon II, reign and extent of empire, 34 349-350, 357-358; did not reach Lake Urumiah in his 8th campaign, 57 243

Sargonid kings of Assyria, epistolary formulae of, 43 26-40

Šarīfate, Grand, of Mecca, history of, 37 154-156, 160-161

Sarikol, silk-trading center in the Chinese Pamirs, 35 228-229

Sarmatians, influence on Russian Slavs of, 45 68-71

al-Sarrāj, see Maṣāri' al-'Uššāq

Śaryāta and Cyavana, story of, 26 45 f., 48

Śāsanadevīs of a Tīrthaṅkara, 52 394

Sasanians, Sasanian, occupation of Egypt in A.D. 618-629 accepted by landed Egyptian nobles only; no opposition from strong Roman garrisons, 48 339; see also Art and Architecture; Jews; Nestorians; Seals

Sa skya paṇḍita Kun dgaḥ rgyal mḉhan, one of the incarnations of the Paṇchen Lama, appearing on a Tibetan temple painting, 52 348

Śatapatha of the Yajur-Veda, story of Cyavana in, 26 45 f.

Sato, group of 50 families forming a unit in village administrative organization in Japan, 1600; based upon the 5 family group system copied fr. China in the 7th cent., 30 267, functions of the, 268-269, 275; 31 194-196

Σατράπης, see Pakeidas

Śatapatha Brāhmaṇa, accentuation of, 48 89; date of the, 52 391; prāṇa-series in the, 22 258, 280-286

Satara, India, Dasara festival at, 30 72-76

Satobṛhatī, the 12-syllable verse of, in the Vedas, 22 316 f.

Saturn, = Nin-Uraš in Babylonia, 42 211

Satyavant in the Sāvitrī story and rite, 21 54-66, called Citrāśva, 57

Śaunaka and Paippalāda book five, comparison of, 49 350

Śaunakīya, relation of the Kashmirian Atharva-Veda to the, 26 203

Śaunakīya Atharva-Veda, compared with contents of Kashmirian AV., books 1-12, 46 8-14

Śaurasenī Prākrit, inspirer of Śiśunāka's rule of limitation of sibilants, 45 73; locative singular of masculine and neuter i and u stems, 41 461 f.; locative in ē, due to Māhārāṣṭrī influence, 42 212

Saussure's doctrine of the long vowels, and Hittite ḫ, 59 175-199

Sāvitrī story, 21 53-59, Sāvitrī rite, 59-66

Saxe, John Godfrey, see Ben-Ammi and the Fairies

al-Sayf al-Murhaf fi 'l-Radd 'ala 'l-Maṣḥaf, anti-Koran polemic by al-Mu'tamin ibn-al-'Assāl, 41 408-409, 447-448

Scanderbeg, by Longfellow, Jewish source of, 45 360

Scapegoat, gazelle as, in Sumerian texts, 21 1-22, Hebrew, Babylonian prototype of, 4; Hebrew, Babylonian parallel to, 37 222

Scarabs, in Marburg collection, 22 18-19

Scebabi, Augustinus, Maronite author, works of, 22 95

Schall, Johann Adam, see Asiatic Studies in Europe (Matteo Ricci, etc.)

Scheerer's Batan dialect, 42 154 f.; Nabaloi dialect, 42 157 f.

Schereschewsky, Samuel Isaac Joseph, biographical notes on, 58 696-697

Schmidt, Father, exponent of the Kultur-Kreis school of ethnologists, 56 379-380; theory of the origin of Tibetan alphabet, 38 37

School of Names and Circumstances influenced practices of Han Wu Ti, 58 442; see also Legalism

School of Oriental Studies, London Institution, founded 1917 for teaching modern oriental and African languages, 39 195

Schools, Chinese, Later Han, established at court by Empress Têng for children of the court, 51 156-157; see also China, Chinese, Education

Schools, for teaching living oriental languages; ten abroad, 39 189-195, none in America, 144-145, 185-188; see also Asiatic Studies in Europe

Sciadrensis, Isaac, Maronite author, works of, 22 94

Science

Egyptian: unbroken tradition from pagan to Christian times, 45 76

Islamic: Arabs and Persians were the first to distil volatile oils, 42 357

Japan: see Books, Chinese; Matteo Ricci; Yoshimune

Oriental (medieval): its contributions have been discounted in favor of Greek science, 40 137

Scorpion-man in ancient Near Eastern art, 52 288

Sculpture, Chinese, Buddhist, on the pagodas of Zayton (Ch'uan-chou), 56 374; Maitreya, statues of the early type called Ju-lai Fo, 53 47 n.1, the later fat Maitreya called Mi-lo Fo, 47; regulations for stone work and carving at the Yüan Ming Yüan, 49 237, cost of marble; finishing with hot wax, 239, stone cutter's time, 237; statues of Yüan-shih-t'ien-tsun south of Ta T'ung Fu, 53 242, 249; stone horses of T'ang T'ai Tsung; the 2 in U. of P. Museum are the ones photographed by Chavannes, 55 420-421, large fake "rubbings" of the horses, 421-423, Yu Shih-hsiung's copies probably in clay, 423, the Stele of Yu Shih-hsiung or Stele of the Picture of the Six Horses, 423-427, no set of miniature tablets; so-called rubbings of these also fakes, 424-427, the engraved Picture of the Six Horses on the Stele of Yu, 423-424, 425-427, horses not in original position when Chavanes saw them, 427 , T'ang designs in flat relief on border and end of "Autumn Dew", 427, evidence that T'ai Tsung's poems may have been painted on the squares, 428; see also abstract, Hall, Three Bas-reliefs

Scythians, influence on Russian Slavs of, 45 68-71; under Madyes raise seige of Nineveh, 22 21

Scytho-Siberian animal style in northern Tibet, 53 89-91

Sea Dyaks, see Dyaks, Sea

Sealand of Arabia, included N part of Arabian peninsula from Persian Gulf to Red Sea, and as far S as al-Baḥrayn, 50 1 n. 1, 11, 14, 15-17, 19, first dynasty of, founded by Ilumailu, 2, was predominantly Sumerian, 18, second dynasty of, appears at close of 2nd millennium B.C., 3, close affiliation with Neo-Babylonian empire, 13, corridor for Sumerian influence on Egypt, 19-21, relations and struggles with Assyria and Neo-Babylonia, 1-23; was situated on the N and W shores of the Persian Gulf and did not extend into Arabia, 54 94-95; First Dynasty of possibly destroyed by Kassites, 52 55

Seals, cylinder seals of ca. 2000 B.C. from Syria and Palestine, eastern affinities of, 59 398; in Marburg collection, 22 18-19; Oriental, in the U.S. National Museum, 23 45; Sasanian, Aramaic, South Arabic, Hittite, Egyptian, Sumerian and Akkadian seals in the Walters Art Gallery, Baltimore, 58 528

- Aramaean: Mušēzim [b] -Nusku, king of Ša-Dikanni, his seal found at Tarbiṣi in Assyria, 38 223
- Babylonian: impressions on early contract (Harvard Semitic Museum, No. 109), 27 135-141; in University of Illinois collection, 46 345; "Noah in the Ark" seal interpreted as a temple entrance, 48 358-359
- Chinese: wooden, of Han, see Lo-Lang
- Hebrew: double ankh on, 29 193-194; from Beth Shemesh, inscribed, 55 308; inscribed, ca. 9th cent. B.C., 24 205-206
- Hittite: with back carved as human head, 27 400-401
- Indus Valley: inscriptions on not related to Sumerian, 49 264-266
- Japanese, Tokugawa Period: each person had one, 31 202, as used by officials in the villages, 204
- Mesopotamian: cylinder seals introduced in Mesopotamia at end of Uruk period, 59 Supp. IV, 20-21, 25
- Phoenician: inscribed, 28 354; inscribed, from Sidon, 28 359
- Sasanian: in Yale collections, Pahlavi inscriptions on, 52 201-207
- Seleucia-on-the-Tigris: seal impressions range from 300 B.C. to A.D. 220 and show predominance of Greek culture, 52 301-302

Seals, seven, Manichaean doctrine of, 44 68-72

Secret dialects, examples of distortion of words in, 25 55-56

Secret Societies, Chinese, Heaven and Earth League, certificates of membership printed on textile, 47 75; in China, note on, 53 362

Sects, seventy-three, Muslim tradition of, 28 6 ff.

Segalen, Victor, death of, 40 206

Seir, did not include territory west of the Wādi al-'Arabah until late Exilic or post-Exilic times, 56 464-467

Sei Shonagon, 10th cent. Japanese authoress, 57 132, 133-134

Seistan, see Calendar, Persian

Sekino, Dr. T., collection of roof-tiles and bricks of Silla and publication of, 55 218

Seleucia, twin city of Ctesiphon, the two together called al-Madā'in, 33 197-198, Chinese name Su-lin, or Su-li, 197, as capital of Persia, 197(and n.1)- 198; Nestorian patriarchs at, 30 9, n.2, 11, n.2; see also Nestorians

Seleucia on-the-Tigris, destroyed ca. 147 B.C., ca. A.D. 41-43, 112-125, 166, 51 373, autonomous coinage replaced by Parthian in A.D. 41-43, 373, Parthian culture prevails after A.D. 41-43, 373; discovery of Parthian palace and ziggurat dating from Babylonian to Parthian period, 52 287-288, Parthian gold jewelry from, 301, seal impressions from, show predominance of Greek culture, 301-302, no evidence of Parthian administrative organization, 302

Seleucid Empire, Yāwān and Hellas as names for, 25 302-311; see also Calendar

Semedo, Alvaro, see Asiatic Studies in Europe (Matteo Ricci, etc)

Šemeš, worshipped in Jerusalem before the Exile, 46 163

Seminar für orientalische Sprachen (Berlin), founded 1887 for teaching modern oriental languages, 39 193

Semites, Babylonian, Amorite origin of, 41 255-263; carried on no struggle with Sumerians as such in Mesopotamia, 59 485-495; home originally in southern Asia Minor between the Taurus and the Euphrates, 39 243-260; home of, either in Africa or in Arabia, 45 4-5, 7, 14; home of, not in Arabia, 45 123 ff.; prositution in early Semitic world, 55 193 n. 11; western, arrived in Babylonia during dynasty of Isin, 28 138-144; Western, had no civilization earlier than the Babylonian, 45 15

Semitic

- Mythology: prostitutes, male temple, Sumerian and Semitic myths explaining origin of, 39 83-85; legends of the "water of life", 26 19, 35-37
- Religion: birth, puberty, marriage, etc. tabus, 37 14; change of sex in deities, 47 268-269; dancing in honor of mother-goddess, 36 327; Equinox-New Year's festival survives in Christian feast of the Finding of the Cross, 39 149; Ištar-Tammuz cult of Semitic origin, 35 213 ff.; Ištar and Tammuz compared with Isis and Horus, 35 223; moon, new and full, appearance of celebrated, 37 212; Aštarte worshipped as Queen of Heaven, 37 212-213; sacrificial animals, bones of not broken because of belief in possibility of resurrection, 36 146-153; soul of slain believed not to rest until avenged, 39 306; burial customs connected with worship of chthonic gods; bodies must be buried, 39 309-310; tabu-offerings in spring were forerunner of Hebrew Passover, 36 327-8; see also Festivals

Semitic Languages, bibliography of, projected by Frank R. Blake, 56 416; parallels to Hamitic, 35 214 ff.; forms an independent group with Hamitic, 45 4-5; roots originally all triconsonantal, 45 178-179; idioms appear in Sumerian before 3000 B.C.; introduced by East Semites from Arabic, 45 14

- Morphology: blend-forms in, 47 234; causative stem: nuances of meaning, 56 23-24, 29-30, proto-Semitic in origin; original caus. prefixes were š/s, h- and '-, 24, 'a- prefix derived by back-formation from h-, 25, š/s- and h- prefixes not related, 26, originally a compound sentence, 29, derived by prefixing 3rd pers. sing. personal pron., 27-33; genitive ending in, 45 311-315, 355, -t- of passive-reflexive stem is from noun *yât, "to be," 314, 355; imperfect, preformatives of, 41 184-185; internal passive in, 22 45-54, preformatives of imperfect tense, 48 f.; -ka, second person sing. suffix, arose under influence of first sing. suffix -ku, 45 312; nisbah ending is identical with the gen. ending in -i, 45 313; noun: origin of -(a)t as fem. ending is in Sem. -Ham. accus. element -t-, originally used for adverbs, 56 44, t- as abstract preformative not different in meaning from -(a)t; both used in Hamitic, 44-45, numerals originally numerical substantives, 39, -(a)t, fem.

ending, is identical with 3rd fem. sing. perf. vb. suffix, 35-36, a relatively late development, 36-37, extended from abstract nouns; unconnected with idea of fem. gender; used primarily to form derivative and abstract nouns, and later specialized as fem. ending, 39-41; possessed stative verbal form *fa‘il, 58 287; transitive verbs with intransitive forms, 50 340; verb: in perf. and imperf. 3rd person forms are independent; 1st and 2nd pers. are connected with pers. pron; 3rd pers. is later in origin, 56 34-35, -a ending of 3rd masc. sing. perf. is identical with the accusative case, 35, t- stem vbs. formed with old accus. ending -t, 45-46, vb. originally had two aspects, nominal and verbal, 34; West-Semitic, development of aspect-system in, 59 409-410

Phonetics and Phonology: ‘, replaced by ’, etc. at late period, 31 356-357; ḏ an unaspirated alveolar stop, 60 422; h and ’, apparent interchange between, 35 375-377; k was an aspirated stop; Indo-European unaspirated k borrowed in Sem. as q, 57 74-75; l corresponds to Old Eg. n; Sem. ṣ and g correspond to Eg. "snake," or palatalized g, 39 142; l = Eg. y, 44 167; metathesis of dentals and sibilants in hithpa‘el is survival of ifta‘al form, 38 73-74, assimilation of dentals and sibilants in Ethiopic, Akkadian, etc., 74; phonetic equations with Egyptian, 47 236-237; primitive Sem. accent not best preserved in Arabic; law of "enclisis," 59 456; syncope in primitive Semitic, 457; forms quttal, qittal, qattal, etc. not intensive; doubling is caused by r or l in root, 46 56-58; relation to Egyptian, 47 198 ff.; s for š in stems containing a labial, 46 344; vocalic r, l, m, n in, 31 217-222

Syntax: adverbial expressions in, 49 362; nominal: of definite state, 32 141-150, with adjective, 158-169, cases, 150-156, 264, indefinite state, 156-158, 262, with demonstratives, 169-176, 262, 265, with interrogative pronouns, 176-180, 262, quantitative expressions, 180-182, 262, with indefinite pronouns, 182-200, 262, 265, with numerals, 201-217, 262, cases, how expressed, 217-238, 262, qualified by adverbs, 247-252, 263, 267, sentence, qualification by, 252-257, 263, coördination of nouns, 257-261, 263, apposition, 267; of noun and its modifiers, 32 135-267, of numerical constructions, 201-217; 3rd pers. sing. pron. used as copula in proto-Semitic, 56 30; origin of subjectless sentence lies in confusion between parts of grammar and categories of logic, 44 159

Lexicon: idea of "to be" expressed by five types of construction, 47 365; *hû’a and *šī’a, proto-Sem. "he" and "she," 56 28; parallels with Egyptian, 47 198 ff.; numerals, Egyptian parallels to, 47 199 ff.

Senebtisi, tomb of at Lišt, 36 348

Senna, native to Somaliland; history of its use in ancient world, 40 260, 262, 264, 268-269

Sennacherib, projected campaign against Egypt in 701-700, 24 265-274; murdered in temple of Nabu in Nineveh; his murder implied in the Broken Prism of Esarhaddon, 53 338-340, not murdered in Babylon, 340-346

Sentah story of the origin of Land Dyak order of "barich", 29 266

Septs, totemism and the origin of, 50 221-232

Septuagint, Codex Venetus, sub-Origenian, photo of in Philadelphia, 46 340; importance of studying differences between it and the Hebrew original, 38 74-75; see also Bible, Greek

Sera metropolis, = Si-an-fu, 35 227, 230; 37 240

Serapis, cult of introduced into Egypt before 311 B.C. from Alexandria; spread to Rhodes and Delos, 52 308

Serbo-Croatian, surviving Turkish elements in, 51 241-261, specimen of Moslem Bosnian-Croatian, 243-245, phonetic variations, 246-250, grammatical peculiarities, 250 f., vocabulary of most commonly used Turkish words, 251-261

Seres, the silk traders of Chinese Turkestan and the Pamirs, 35 224, 227, 228-229, 236, term mistakenly applied to the Sēri of Chēra, India, 236-237, the "Seres" of Pausanius on the island of Seria, off south coast of Arabia, 237; included the Chēra Tamils and the Arabian tribe of Ausar, 35 236-239; those mentioned by classical writers as "great elephant users" were certainly Indian peoples, 41 293

Sergius of Rīš‘aynā, MS of his work on the Categories of Aristotle, 35 297-299

Seri, region above the Sinae, see Sinae

Seria, Island of, identified as Masira on the south coast of Arabia, confused with the Seres of China, 35 40

Serpent cult, non-Aryan character of, 49 186 f.

Sestet, Italian verse-form, derived probably from Arab zajal, 51 370

Set, appears as Satan in oldest Egyptian texts, 39 148

Sethianic origin of Coptic magical papyri at University of Michigan, 48 358

Setsubun, see Festivals, Japanese

Seven, number, Priestly Code tried to build system of Jewish life on holiness of, 37 220

Sha-chou, 沙州, original home of the Yüeh-chih, 37 96-97

Shadow, Arab belief that man is vulnerable when it is small, 38 160

"Shadow-plays" in Indian dramaturgy, 32 58-63

Shadow-theater in China, review of book by Jacob and Jensen, 55 220-223, collections of figures, 220; types of plot, 221, subjects fr. Chinese folk-lore, 222, use of puns, 222

Shāfi‘ites, chiefly found in Lower Egypt, southern India and Malaysia; numbered about 35,000,000 in 1924, 44 32

Shāh ‘Abbās the Great, relations with Akbar and Jahāngīr, 35 247-268

Shāhbāzgarhi uthanam, 41 460 f.; dental th characteristic of Dardic, 42 211 f.

Shāhbāzgarhi redaction of the Fourteen-Edicts of Asoka, 30 77-93; special points of contact of dialect of Girnār redaction with dialect of, 31 245-247; language of, the proposed connection with modern Piśāca; the writing of r, 36 210 f.

Sháhnáma, elephants mentioned in the, 41 292, 294

Shalmaneser III, reign of, 34 346-348, 353, IV, reign of, 348-349, 352; estimate of, 41 380-382

Shamanism, Siberia, burkhan, the ancient term applied to a spirit worshipped by the shamans, 36 390-395

Shan, origin unknown; located in valley of Yangtse in prehistoric times, 41 300, attachment to the elephant, and beliefs concerning it, 300-301, queer use of elephant in war, 302, Shans in Yünnan, 305; aborigines of S.W. China, women keep ku poison, 55 23; Kingdom of the; as intermediaries in the trade bet. China and the West which passed through Yünnan, 37 242-243, Theinni the capital (or Thinae?) 243, 246-247; note on similarity of their script to Siamese, 29 283; in Burma, a woman's song recorded, 45 191; see also Cochin-China; Pa Yi; Tai, language group

Shang, infant Emperor, son of Empress Têng, 51 144, 148

Shang Dynasty, chronology of the, 52 241-247; a time of small kingdoms, 56 71; writing, use of a brush, 56 335 n.2, character of inscriptions on bronzes of, 346 n.33, sign for an unknown proper name, 346-347; see also Archaeology; Inscriptions; Oracle bones; Sacrifice; Shang-shu; Slavery; Writing; Yin Dynasty

Shang-kuan Chieh, 上官桀, special Commissioner of Government Grain; invests city of Yu-ch‘êng and captures its king in K‘ang-chü, 37 114, broke into enemy's lines, 115, received a court title, 115

Shang-kuan kié, see Shang-kuan Chieh

Shang Kuei, 上邽, prefectural city in present Kansu, birthplace (or garrison ?) of Chao Ti, 37 114

Shang-kui, see Shang Kuei

Shang-lin, 上林, park, 51 147 n.47

Shang-shu, term for earliest parts of the Shu-ching, 56 336-337 and n.6, bronze inscriptions an aide to interpretation of, 340

shang-ta-fu, title, see Ch‘i Hsien

Shang-tang, 上黨, prefecture to which Li Ch‘ê was appointed by Han Wu Ti, 37 115

Shang Ti, 上帝, the Supreme Deity, 49 143-144 n.2; his charge to Yü, 56 59

Shan-hai-ching, the "Hill and Sea" Classic"; Ssŭ-ma Ch‘ien dares say nothing about its tales, 37 116; mentions elephants in Ssu-ch‘uan, 41 299; Hsi Wang Mu myth in, 53 54, sun myth in, 60-61; contains tales of Yao, Shun and Yü with mythical accessories, 56 55, the Bear story of Yü, 59, the

myth of the ten suns and the story of Hai Ho, 64, supposed to have accompanied and explained a book of art, 66, composed 4th-3rd cent. B.C., 55, 74, a product of new geographical ideas, 74-75, contains descriptions of the designs on Yü's tripods, 74
Shantung, the "Shantung question", 44 181
Shan-yü, 單于, title of the Great Khan of the Hsiung-nu, 37 94, 96, 100, 101, explanation of title, 147; see also Hsiung-nu
Shao-fu, 少府, Director in the Imperial Household, a court title given Shang-kuan Chieh, 37 115
Shaohsing, see Mt. K'uai-chi
Shang-jang, 擅讓, an example of, 56 51, 58
Sharp, Gregorius, author of Appendix de Lingua Sinica, 1767, 43 8
Shau Fu, a title, see Shao-fu
Shechem, site of uncertain, 45 182-183; inhabitants were Ḫurrians, 51 65-66
She Chi, the, see Gods of the Land and Grain
Sheep, domesticated, in early China, 60 581
Shen Han-kuang, on tobacco, 58 650
Shen hsien t'ung chien, not a source for origins of mythology, 53 58
Shen-li, 沈黎, a district near modern Ya-chou-fu, Ssŭ-ch'uan, 37 104
Shen P'ei, see Classics, Chinese
Shen-tu, 身毒, (India), southeast of Ta-hsia, 37 98, unrecorded early trade of, with Ssŭ-ch'uan, 98, Chang Ch'ien's plan to discover, 98, abortive attempts to open direct communication with, 99, envoys sent to, by Chang Ch'ien 102, missions to (via Bactria ?), 103
Shen Yi-chi, follower of Han Kao-tsu, 57 176
Shen 慎 Tombs, Empress Têng of Later Han buried in the, 51 159, 148 n.55
Shê-p'o, 闍婆, see Names, Geographical, Chinese
Sherbet, see Lemon
Shield, as apotropaic symbol in Crete and Anatolia, 60 551-552
Shih-chi, availability of to scholars in early Han, 51 271-273, not considered canonical by the Confucianists, 273; comparison of biographical material and discussion of social and economic phases of the times with cor. chapters in the Han-shu, 54 186-193; chapter 123, paragraphs 1-79 probably based on Chang Ch'iens report to the Emperor, 37 91, products brought back by Chang Ch'ien referred to in, 92, Tr. of account of Chang Ch'ien's journey to the west and expeditions of the following years in Chapter 123 of, 93-116; chronology of ancient China according to the, 52 232-233, 234-236, 238-240, 243, 245; date of writing of parts of, 55 331-332, date Ssu-ma Ch'ien stopped writing estimated as bet. 122 and 95 B.C. fr. evidence in his Auto-Biog., 332-333, authenticity of later part of Biog. of Confucius is suspect, 331-333; chap. 123 the oldest source of Chinese knowledge conderning western nations, 30 38; substitutes the name of the Kings of Parthia for that of the country, 30 35; statement on the conjunction of the 5 planets "when the Han dynasty triumphed", 55 312-313; tradition of Yü being connected with the south of China, tomb and temple at Shaohsing, Chekiang, 56 55, 61-62, Emperor Yao like the sun, 63; see also Translations; Passages
Shih-ching, Odes of the Western Chou period; six references to Yü in, 56 53, 55-56, 58, Yao and Shun not mentioned in, 54, refer to many small kingdoms in earliest times, 70-71, gives most accurate picture of earliest period, 72-73; 33 quotations fr. in the Yen T'ieh Lun, 51 267, 274; reconstruction of ancient pronunciation of the, see Karlgren
Shih-ch'i-ti-lun, 十七地論, lost Chinese tr. by Paramārtha, of the Yogācāryabhūmiśāstra, 51 297-299, 301
Shih-ch'ü Pavilion, where were held the discussions on interpretation of the Classics under Han Hsüan Ti, 58 444
"Shih-Destroying Red", see Horses of T'ang T'ai Tsung
Shih Jun-chang, on tobacco, 58 653-654
Shih K'o, painting of Yü Huang's celestial court by, 53 59
Shih lin yen yü pien, 石林燕語辨, first article in the Ju hsüeh ching wu, see Ts'ung Shu
Shih lu, 實錄, record of the Ch'ung-chen period, 1628-1644, not extant, 58 650 n.9; discussed in work by Fuchs, see Fuchs, Walter
Shih Sheng-tsu, 史繩祖, 13th cent. writer, see Passages, Analects
Shih Tsu, 世祖, Wei Emperor, patron of Taoism, 53 225, 235-241, 54 293
Shih wan chüan lou ts'ung shu, 十萬卷樓叢書, pub. by a library in 19th cent., 51 42
Shī'ism, Shī'ites, Egyptian, under the Fāṭimids, 27 217-222; Kling, in Sarawak, 33 340; of Persia and India, numbered about 12,000,000 in 1924, 44 32; sects of, according to ibn-Ḥazm's Kitāb al-Milal wa-'l-Nihal, 28 1-80, 29 1-183; closely related to Ṣūfism, 58 541
Shī-ki, see Shih-chi
Shi-King, see Shih Ching
Shiloh, agricultural festival of Sukkoth at, 37 219
Shintoism, represented by objects in U.S. National Museum, 23 47; Kamakura Period, bibliography of source materials on, and historical documents preserved in Shinto shrines, 59 48-49, 51-52
Shivaji, 300th anniversary of the birth of, 50 159, controversies centering around, 159 f., his killing of Afzul Khan, 159-162; and Rāmdās, folk-stories about, 25 186-188
Shōen, the Japanese Manor, period 645-1165 A.D., description, origin, organization of, administration of, terminology of, 57 78-83; source materials on, 59 48
Shō-gun, the suzerain of Japanese feudal organization in the Tokugawa Period, 30 259, 261, 265-266, 271, 273-274, 281, 282-283, 287, 31 155-158, his Domain lands and Baron's fiefs, 159-160, sale of Domain lands illegal, 178-179, his inviolability, 170, his right of mortmain, 176, his Barons and the Baron's Bailiffs, 160-161
Shōkyū Rebellion of 1221, sources for study of, 59 40, 41, 43, 45
Shŏn-li, see Shen-li
Sho-no, Japanese for camphor, 42 364
Shŏn-tu, see Shen-tu
Shryock, J.K., see Huang K'uei-yuen
Shu, 蜀, (Ssŭ-ch'uan), bamboo and cloth from, seen by Chang Ch'ien in Bactria, 37 98, easiest way to India via, 98, 99, traders of, smuggle goods to Yünnan ?, 99; territories in the southwest of, added to Chinese dominion in time of Han Wu Ti, 104
Shu, 術, name often used in Chou time for the Classics, 44 275-276
Shu, as meaning the Shu-ching, 55 334
Shu-ching, dates and authenticity of parts of, 56 336-337 and n. 4, 6, 7, 335 n.1, the "P'an Keng" a forgery, 343-344; documents in, similar to inscriptions on bronzes of Western Chou, 56 343; occurrence of the character tao 道 as a philosophical term, 52 32, occurrence of the character i 彝 as an equivalent of tao, 29-31, 32-34; traditional view of, 56 52, references to the model emperors Yao, Shun and Yü in, 53-59, 61, 63, 66, hypothesis that the first few chapters, dealing with the model emperors, are forgeries, 70, 71; the "Wei Tzu" of, a Chou forgery, 56 335 n.1; refers to legends regarding source of Yellow River, which seemed confirmed by Chang Ch'ien's discoveries, 37 116; see also Ku Chieh-kang; Ku-wen text; Chin wen text; Words, hsien 獻
Shu fu, 說郛, 14th cent. ts'ung shu of fiction, 51 44
Shui-ching, the "Water Classic", earliest treatise on the waterways of China, 56 96, the commentary by Li Tao-yüan, 96
Shui-ching-chu, review of tr. of the part dealing with Indo-China, 56 96
Shu-king, see Shu-ching
Shun, 舜, one of the three sage heroes of Chinese antiquity, upon traditions of whom was based the Model-Emperor Lore of China, 56 51-76, connection with various folk-tales, 53-56, 66-67; story of Elephants to plow his fields and birds to weed the grain, 41 297; see also Model Emperor Lore of China; Yün Clan

Shuo-wen, definition of ku, 蠱, 55 2, wind generates worms, 5; see also Chiang-nan

Shu-sun T'ung, former Po-shih under 2nd Ch'in Emperor, served Hsiang Yü and was captured by Han Kao-tsu, 57 176, 178, advisor to Kao-tsu and founder of Han court ceremonial, 178-179; surrendered to Hsiang Yü and Kao-tsu in turn, 58 436

Siam, Siamese, note on archeological objects in Wang Nah Museum, Bangkok, 29 283; features of speech and syntax related to Chinese, 44 11-13, source of phonetic writing of Siamese, 13-15, the Siamese alphabet, 15-20, the tones and their notation in writing, 20-26, diacritical marks, 27-28, stone inscription of Prince Rām Khamhaeng the earliest known monument, 13-14; note on the making of palm-leaf manuscripts in, 29 280-283; Siamese edition of the Tripitaka in U.S. National Museum, 23 47; see also Cochin China; see also Languages, Sino-Tibetan; see also Manuscripts; Tone-accent

Si-an (Si-an-fu), the "Sera metropolis" of Ptolemy, also called Thinae, 35 230; ultimate destination of the sea and land trade route fr. Roman Empire to India and up through Yünnan, or to Tong-King and overland, 37 240, 242, 243, 244

Siau-yüé-chī, see Hsiao-yüeh-chih

Siberia, see China, Chinese, History

Sibuyau Sea Dyaks, 25 233 fn., authority of chief among, 237; disappearance of head-hunting among, 25 234

Sibzianna, Babylonian constellation of Orion, = Papsukkal, 43 325

Sidon, ancient extent larger than the present one, 23 156, Temple of Ešmun, Bod'aštart inscription from, 156-173, Ešmun'azarid dynasty, genealogical tree of, 168-169, Bod-'aštart, king of, his inscription from the temple of Ešmun, 156-173; inscription of Bod'aštart from temple of Ešmun in, 24 211-226

Siebold, P.F. Von, author of work on Japanese language, see Asiatic Studies in Europe

Si-fan-ki, see Hsi-fan-chi

Sigillata signature in the Near East, 58 30-60

Sign-lists, cuneiform, 27 297-300; sign No. 572 in Barton's Babylonian Writing is to be read alan, 46 311-312, 353; Elamite-Babylonian (?), 32 103-114; Sumerian, contains many Asiatic-Elamite signs, 54 78-79; uncertain pictographic-cuneiform, notes on, 33 16-23; see also Cuneiform script; Menant

Sijistān, see Sagastān

Śīlabhadra, Indian priest, learned head of great monastery at Nālandā, teacher of Hsüan Chuang in Wei Shih philosophy, 51 301-302, 303

Šilḫ Language, see Hamitic

Silk, culture, in Japan, in Tokugawa period, 30 272, 283-284, 289; eaten by ku worms of Black Magic in China, 55 14, 15, 25, 26; trade in between China and the Roman Empire, 35 31 ff.; growth in silk trade with increase in Roman demand for in time of Pliny, 35 34; increase of Romans' demand for in time of Pliny, 35 228, "Seres" were the traders in silk, not necessarily the Chinese, 228-230, 235-239, transported to Roman Empire in form of raw silk, silk yarn, and as woven stuffs, 225, 230, route of the silk caravans, 227, great cost of the silk transport, 228, silk shipped from India, 229; variegated, gift of; silk of consecration (priest's robe, Buddhist) 49 47

  Chinese, Han: gifts of, to the ladies of the Court acting as guardians at the Imperial Tomb, 51 145; sent by Han Wu Ti as gift to the Wu-sun, 37 101, none in Ta-yüan or countries west of it, 108; trade route fr. China to the West in Han times, 30 46, silk-buying factories of the Phoenician coast, 46; see also Lo-Lang

Śilpaśāstras, origin of, 49 69 f.; purpose of the codifications in the, 54 221

Śilpa texts, the meaning of ābhāsa in, 52 208 f.

Silver, still of comparatively high value in 9th cent. B.C., 38 238; Hittite mines in southern Asia Minor, 41 377; see also Gold & Silver; Metals

Simarg, is the Persian Simourg, 45 69 f.

Simeon Stylites, translation of Bedjan's text of life of, 35 103-198

Siṃhadevagaṇi, rules for Māgadhī, 44 89 f.

Sin, child cursed for parents' sin in Babylonia, 34 301-302; decline and revival of Hebrew idea of children's responsibility for sins of fathers, 28 309-316

Sin, Babylonian moon-god, associated with womb of life, similar ideas elsewhere, 40 333-335; travels by boat, as do the Egyptian deities, 46 362; called "the great carpenter of heaven," 39 81 n. 28; see also Enzu

Šīnā, see Piśāca

Sinae, unknown land east of the, 37 247, the land of the Seri above the Sinae, 247, Thinae the metropolis of the, 247

Sinai, North-Arabian, home of Yahweh-worship in 13th cent. B.C., 35 386-387

Sina Sinorum, see Sera metropolis

Sin-ch'ī, see Hsin-chih

Sind, bead making in ancient, 57 1-15

Sindh, = India, see Shen-tu

Singan-fu, see Si-an (Si-an-fu)

Sin-šar-iškun, last Assyrian king, 22 20-22; his fate not clear from the Nabopolassar Chronicle, 44 126-127, 128

Sippar, fourth antediluvian dynasty, 43 325, 327, 329

Sirach, Book of, original Hebrew text lost at an early date; present Heb. text is translated, 40 219-220

Sirius, Babylonian month of, 31 266-268; in Sumerian month-name, 33 5

Širkūh, al-Malik al-Manṣūr Asad al-Dīn, inscribed bronze magic bowl of, 55 254-256

Ṣīṣ (Syria), birthplace of Simeon Stylites, 35 103, 111, raided by Isaurians, who are repulsed by St. Simeon, 105, 114-115

Sīstān, see Sagastān

Śiśunāga, prohibits use of cerebrals except ṇ, and of ś, ṣ, ḥ, and kṣ, 44 81-121; text and translation of Rājaśekhara's passage on the prohibition of, 45 72, Prākrits agreeing with prohibitions of, 73 f., Susian (Elamite) probable source of prohibition of ha and cerebrals, 74 f.

Sītā, wife of Indra, god of fertility, 36 243 f., 257

Šitlamtaea and Lugalgira, Babylonian demoniacal manifestations of Nergal and equivalent to the Amorite Šarrâpu and Birdu, 38 162

Sittaung River, see Trade Routes

Śiva, as Bhairava and Śakti, worshipped by Kānphaṭa yogīs, 45 356; episode in wanderings of, 53 357 f.; as First Cause, 22 382; as Kapālin requiring human sacrifice, 44 202 f.; the three-peaked mountain as a symbol of, 54 297-299

Śivadāsa's version of the Vetālapañcaviṅśati, 55 59-63

Sivaji, original sources of knowledge of the Maratha king, 44 155 f.

Śivanāthaśarman, brother of Kṛṣṇanātha, wrote commentary on Ratnāvalī, 23 79

Śivarāma's commentary on the Vāsavadattā, 24 57-63, other works of, 58, authorities cited by, 60-63, life of, 59

Si-wang-mu, see Hsi Wang Mu

"Six Classics", named by Confucius; the Four Shu, the I-Ching, and the Ch'un Ch'iu, 44 278-279

Si-yü-t'u-ki, see Hsi-yü-t'u-chi

Skal bzaṅ rgya mcho, the seventh Dalai Lama, represented on Tibetan temple paintings, 52 344-345

Skandapurāṇa, source of Śaṃkara's account of Sāvitrī story and rite in Vratārka, 21 53, source of part of Hemādri's account of Sāvitrī rite in Caturvargacintāmaṇi, 21 62

Skandasvāmin's commentary on the Nirukta, 50 175

Slaughtering, Hebrew method of, produces better meat, 51 366-367, 52 310

Slavery

  China: Yin period, customs revealed by use of character hsien, 獻, 56 340 n.13

  Nuzi: girls sold by parents and married off to purchaser; paralleled in Hebrew law, 55 190-195

  Japan: in Tokugawa period, sales of persons illegal, 30 275, 286, 31 208-214; see also abstract, Sakanishi, New Haven, 1936

Slavonic Enoch, the two recensions of, 37 16

Slavonic versions of the Pañcatantra, 45 351
Slaves, Babylonian, only lowest class marked, 42 80-90
Slavs, domination by Antae of Eastern, 59 64 f.; influence of Iranian peoples on, 45 68-71
Ślesa, examples of double meaning of syllables in the Śālibhadra Carita, 43 262 f.
Śloka, in Bhāsa, frequency and analysis of, 41 113-116; in the Pali Iti-vuttaka, 28 317-326
Small-pox, often fatal to Tibetans in China, 52 349
Smith, Rev. Arthur H., contributions of to Chinese studies, 38 101
Smith, J.M. Powis, life and works, 52 403
Smith College, tablets of the First Dynasty of Babylon at, 37 8
Smṛti literature, the rite of dantadhāvana in, 52 163-167
Snail, analysis of its slimy secretion and its properties, 42 281-284
Snakes, snake-ku a variety of Black Magic, 55 7, 8, 13, 18, 20, 22, 23, story of Lin of Ch'in and the ku snake, 28
Sniff-kiss in ancient India, 28 120-134
Snow, Arab proverbs about, 52 154
Société Asiatique de Varsovie, foundation and publications of, 43 80
Societies, for promoting Asiatic Studies founded in early 19th cent., see Asiatic Studies in Europe
Society of Friends of Asiatic Art of the Netherlands, exhibition held by, in Amsterdam, 1919, 43 337
Society for International Cultural Relations, Kokusai Bunka Shinko Kai, organized in Tokyo, 1934, note on activities, 54 319
Sociology, of Japan in the Tokugawa era, see Feudalism in Japan
Socotra, see Africa, early Chinese notices of; Marco Polo
Sodom and Gomorrah, apocryphal acts of disciples in, according to Ethiopic Arde'et, 25 36-39
Sodomy, apparently common in Assyria; punishment for in the Assyrian Code, 41 10, 20; see also Bestiality
Sogdiana, see Calendar (Persian); K'ang-chü
Solar symbols and the interpretation of Aja Ekapād as sun-god, 53 332 f.
Solomon, his accession established hereditary kingship; brought centralization of government and concentration of wealth, 57 238-239; circumstances surrounding his succession as related in I Kgs. 1-2, 60 383-390; and the Griffon, tale of in Kalīlah and Dimnah, MSS and versions of, 45 367; obtained horses from Egypt, 26 104
Soliman, Sultan of Iconium in late 11th cent. when an embassy was sent to China, 30 24-27
Soliman of Salerno, Jewish merchant trading between Genoa and Alexandria in the 12th cent., 38 179-181
Solstice, summer, ritual of in Ez. 8, 10, 57 256
Solstice, winter, celebrated by Magians and Chaldaeans and some Christians on Dec. 25, 32 322, 333
Soma, breaths identified with draughts of, 22 283-285; relation to Indra as god of fertility, 36 256-262; the production of, by twirling, 55 377; the sacrifice of King, identity with Vṛtra, 55 382 f.; plant, identity of Vedic, 45 351 f.; in Vṛtra's power, 55 385; see also Indo-Iranians, Mythology
Somadeva, Kathāsarit sāgara compared with the Bṛhatkathāmañjarī, 53 124-143; version of the Vetālapañcaviṅśati, 55 59
Somaka, how he increased the number of his sons, 26 6
Somaliland, Somalis, Somali, cinnamon and other varieties of laurel not found there; list of native spices, 40 260-264, 267-269; language, see Hamitic
Sommerville, Maxwell, death of, 26 420
Son of Heaven, see Han Wu Ti
Son of Man, Aramaic phrase meaning originally "son of a man," 37 14
Song of Songs, see Canticles
Songs, children's, 48 233-235, 245-247; see also Shan, in Burma
Arabic: from al-Qubaybah, Palestine, 50 199-213; Palestinian (Arab), from al-Qubaybah and Bayt Jālah, 48 225-249; Syrian Arabic, 23 175-288
China: ancient, in ceremonies to ancestors, 56 57, 63; childrens', see Poetry, Chinese; "Lemon Hot Water Song", by Wu Lai, 吳來, of Yüan, 54 148-149; mention of "The Plum Blossoms are Falling", 54 226; Odes, the Yung to be chanted only at the imperial court of Chou, 54 188 n.7; of the Pai Canal, Han, 55 305
Jewish: from Damascus, 24 227-264
Songs of the Five Sons, genuineness of disputed, 56 53, references to Yü and Yao, 53, 54
Sonpat copper seal of Harsha, possible connection of passage in Bāṇa's Harṣacarita with, 50 131
Sopārā version of the Fourteen-Edicts of Asoka, dialect of eighth edict of, 30 78
Sophar on the brass eagle, 26 412 f.
Soqoṭra, Soqoṭri, language, spirants and velars, behavior of, 60 110-111, ś = Ar. š; s = S. Ar. s_3 (samek), N. Sem. š and s, 111-112; uncertain whether š is original in pronouns, 112; folk-tale motif, betrayal of husband's secret by wife, parallels to, 28 97 f.
Sorai, see Ogyū Sorai
Sorcerers, Sorcery, punished in Assyrian code, 41 44-46; of Chung-li (Socotra), 30 51, 53-54; see also Black Magic
Soul, Chinese ideas of the, 49 132 n.2; nature of and relation to blood among Semites, 36 151-153; nature and sleep of according to the early Syriac church, 40 103-120, distinguished from spirit in O.T. apocrypha and pseudepigrapha, 117; see also haṃsa
South, cardinal direction among Chinese, 37 244
South Arabia, antiquities and inscriptions from in Yale University, 58 528; South Arabic origin of alphabet, theory of, 22 184 ff.; language, sibilants and emphatics, their history and identification with those of other Semitic languages, 60 507-543; religion, criticism of Nielsen's views on, 48 82-83; trade with India and Roman Empire, 35 230-231; worship of Hadad, Ištar, Aširta and Šamaš introduced by the Amorites, 45 135
Soya Bean, wealthy merchant of, 54 191
Spain, Spanish, feuds with Malays of Brunei, 33 335
sparśa, see nidānas
Spectacles, introduction into China, note on bibliography, see abstract, Ch'iu, New Haven, 1936
Spenta-Ārmaiti, character of influenced by that of Babylonian Ea, 36 309
Spiegel's views on the Avestan preterite tenses, 21 113 f.
Spikenard, see Nard
Spinoza, inaugurated critical approach to the Bible, 55 Supp. 1, 33, 35-38, combatted Maimonides's approach to the O.T., 38-40, his contribution to biblical criticism, 40
Spirit and soul distinguished in O.T. apocrypha and pseudepigrapha and by St. Paul, 40 117, 119-120
Spirits of the Stars, prayer to the, 49 139-140
Spirits, Wandering, altars to, 49 151, 152 n.2
Spring, Reception of, see Festivals, Chinese
Spittle, as remedy against evil and disease in oldest Egyptian texts, 41 183
Sports, falcons sold fr. Han Imperial Park to reduce expenses, 51 147; see also Games
Spring and Autumn Annals, see Ch'un Ch'iu
Springs, believed by Palestinian peasants to be inhabited by jinn corresponding to Hellenistic nymphs, 60 261
Śrāddha (Parvan) ceremony, description, 22 228-236; for Javanese Queen Grandmother Gāyatrī, description of, 51 9-12; rhinoceros legends associated with the, 51 281 f.
Śrauta sacrifice, 44 139 f.
Śreṇika, life of, in the Mahāvīracaritra, 45 302-308, son of Prasenajit, 302 f., marriages and progeny, 304 f., retirement and death, 308
Śrīdevī, a goddess of Lama Buddhism, represented in a Tibetan painting, 52 349
Śrī-Lakṣmī, representations of, as "Buddha nativities," 55 323-325

Sroṅ-btsan sgam-po (Chinese, K'i-tsuṅ-luṅ-tsan), first powerful king of Tibet, 617(?) - 650, 38 34-38, 45; represented on a Tibetan painting as an ancestor of a Dalai Lama, 52 341-342

Ssĭ, see Hsi

Ssĭ-ch'uan, see Ssŭ-ch'uan

Ssĭ-ma T'an, see Ssŭ-ma T'an

Ssĭ-ma Ts'ién, see Ssŭ-ma Ch'ien

Ssu-ch'uan, culture of, note on early date of, 56 98; elephant in, in early times, and trade in ivory, 41 299, inhabited by Shans in early times; their connection with modern inhabitants, 300-301, defeated by Wu, 302, elephant extinct in, in After Han, 303-304

Ssu I K'ao, see Huang Ch'ao Wen Hsien T'ung K'ao

Ssu k'u ch'üan shu, a great 18th cent. manuscript library, 51 42; how assembled, 55 478

Ssu-ma Ch'ien, authenticity of last part of his Biog. of Confucius in the Shih-chi, questioned, 55 331-333, date when he stopped writing, 332-333; earliest non-Taoist to ref. to Lao-tzu, 53 209-210; journey to Mt. K'uai-chi to look for Yü's tomb, 56 61-62, on wars in time of Mencius, 73; sojourn in the southwest, 37 135, comment as to year of death, and his father's part in writing of the Shih-chi, 91, 136; Taoist, and Ssu-ma T'an at the Court of Han Wu Ti, 58 440, observation on filling of minor offices, 442; see also Shih-chi

Ssŭ-ma T'an, father of Ssŭ-ma Ch'ien; his part in the writing of the Shih-chi; death in 110 B.C., 37 91, 135; see also Ssu-ma Ch'ien

Ssu pu ts'ung k'an, 四部叢刊, a modern ts'ung shu of rare Sung, Yüan and Ming editions, 51 42

Stadium, see Weights and Measures

Staël-Holstein collection of Lamaistic pantheons, 51 363 f.

Stalactite cupola, earliest dated example of at Sīn, near Isfahān, 59 397-398

Stamps, postage, of the Ḥijāz, 37 87-88

Stcherbatskoi on age of philosophical Sūtras of the Brahmans, 31 4 f.

Steel, trade in between India and Roman Empire, 35 229-237, 239; see also Iron

Stelae, see China, Chinese, Monuments

Stevens, Thomas, 43 163 f., discovery of manuscript of his Christian Purāṇa, 164.

Stiles, Ezra (president of Yale University), delivered commencement oration in Hebrew on Sept. 12, 1781, 51 359

Stirrup, introduction of into China; representation of on Chinese stele of 529 and 554 A.D.; character for, 52 85

Stoas, see Basilicas

"Stone Classics", fragment of the, fr. 175 A.D., in the National Library of Peiping, 52 189

Stone Tower, the station of the silk merchants, on the ancient overland trade route, 35 227-229

Stone Work, Chinese, regulations as to time and cost of carvings for the Yüan Ming Yüan, 49 237, prices for marble, 239, cost of transportation, 239, finishing with hot wax, 239

Storax, Arabian and Javanese, in China, 42 176; a product of Po-pa-li (Berbera), 30 49; see also su-ho-yu

Strabo on Persian religion, 52 187

Stylus, used in Siam for making palm-leaf manuscripts, description of, 29 282

Subandhu's Vāsavadattā, Śivarāma's commentary on, 24 57-63

Šubari first antediluvial Babylonian dynasty of, 43 323-324, 327

Subartu, archaic term for Assyria, 45 233 n. 109; situated in mountains N of Assyria, 57 107-108; bounded by Tigris, Upper Zāb, Zagros and Diyālah, 45 233; see also Ḫurrians

Subāshi, see Central Asia, Painting

Subhaṭa's Dūtāṅgada, translated, 32 58-77

Subhūti, as founder of the line of Panchen Lamas, 52 346

Subrahmaṇya on the dialects of the Prabodhacandrodaya, 44 114 f., 117

von Suchem, Ludolph, question of date of his Description of the Holy Land, 55 102-104

Sū-chou-fu, see Hsū-chou-fu

Sudan "boomerang," 55 173

Śūdras, position in the Vedas, Brāhmaṇas, and Sūtras, 53 181-183

Śūdraka's vocabulary and grammar in the Mṛcchakaṭika, 27 19 f.

Ṣūfism, illuministic (išrāqi), development of, 57 99-100; illuministic (išrāqi), sources and light-doctrine of, 60 90-94; poetry, Judaeo-Arabic 13th-cent. fragment from the Cairo Genizah, 49 168-173; Ladder of Evolution compared with Manichaean metempsychosis, 45 266; in Persian poetry, 36 345-347; closely related to Shī'ism, 58 541

Sugiura, Dr. Sadajiro, note on work of, at Univ. of Penna. in 1900, 57 421

Su-hié, see Su-hsieh

su-ho-yu, (storax?), imported by the Chinese from Arabia, 42 176, 183; see also Aloes

Su-hsieh, 蘇薤, small country east of Ta-yüan, 37 107

al-Suhrawardi, abu-'l-Futūḥ Yaḥya, founder of Illuministic (išrāqi) Ṣūfism; works of, 60 90-94

Suicide, in Buddhism, 27 455 f.; by Hindus in Epic and law, 21 146-159

Sui Dynasty, see Yang Ti; Li Yü

Sui-shu, oldest record in which Fu-lin is mentioned, 30 4, chapter on western countries, 6, Persia described in detail, 5, three trade routes fr. China to the West, 5, Emp. Yang Ti's desire to communicate with all countries of Asia, 6; name Fu-lin occurs in description of Persia in; biography of P'ei Chü in, 33 194, 195, 196, 197, description of al-Madā' in, 198; on Taoism, authors and composition, 53 215 n.2; tr. of remarks on Taoism, with notes, 243-250; see also Wei-shu

Sui-si-yü-t'u, 隋西域圖, see Hsi-yü-t'u-chi

Sujyeṣṭhā and Śreṇika, story of, 45 304 f.

Sukanyā, wife of Cyavana, 26 46, 48-54

Sūkarikāvadāna, translation of Sanskrit text, compared with Tibetan and Chinese versions, 48 159-165; see also Divyāvadāna

Sukkoth, see Festivals (Hebrew)

Suk-tak, (Su-t'e), country of the Alans, 30 33, 43-45

Sü Kuang, scholar, d. 425 A.D., established date of expedition against the K'un-mings, 37 104 n.2

Su Lao Ch'üan, 蘇老泉, Sung author, note on, 49 153 n.1, 2

Sulaymān, account of Korea by, 58 658-659

Šulgi (king of Ur), deified aspect of appears as theophorous element in personal names, 37 162-163

Su-li, see Seleucia

Su-lin, see Seleucia

Su-lo, 疏勒 or 疎勒, Chinese name for Kashgar, 33 204; 30 35

Sultan Beyazid Shah, existence proved from coins, 43 254

Sultan of Brunei, invoked at harvest festival of Land Dyaks as deity, 29 257 f.; god among the Land Dyaks, 26 168 f.

Sulu, elephant exterminated by Moros in, 41 294; loss of intervocalic l in, 36 182 f.; see also Philippine languages, comparative grammar

Sumatra, elephant in, 41 294; see also Aloes

Sumer, Sumerians, Sumerian, see also Arms, Armor; Calendar; Festivals; Law; Music; New Year; Oath

Culture: use of asses and mules as draught animals, 54 117 f.; harp, 51 47; poetry, structure of, 37 25-26; Indo-Sumerian, seals, 47 284 f.; social organization inherited by the Semitic Near East, 59 Supp. IV, 25-26, introduced writing, 26, government and law oriented by strong sense of private property, 26; writing and language pervade Western Asia, 59 Supp. IV, 27-28

History: homeland possibly in 'Umān and eastern Arabia, 49 263-268, 359-360, in Central Asia? 325; possibly in some northern center, 50 81; entered Babylonia before First Dynasty of Kiš, from Central Asia? 41 261; related to the Elamites? 39 249, 256; boundaries of in Isin Dynasty, 54 229; king-lists from University of Pennsylvania Museum, 42 321 n. 3; arrived in Mesopotamia at end of Uruk period, 59 Supp. IV, 28-31; mountain origin of Sumerians, 36 288-290;

authors of painted pottery culture in Mesopotamia; were in Upper Euphrates in early 3rd millennium B.C., 51 63-64; carried on no struggle with Semites as such in Mesopotamia, 59 485-495; as Turanians struggle with early Iranians, 35 295

Language: analogies to other languages, 34 328; Asiatic-Elamite element, 54 78-79, sign-list, includes Asiatic-Elamite signs, 78-79; comparative degree expressed by ablative construction, 43 243-244; compound postpositives in the early language, 43 317-322; consonant doubled after stressed vowel and preceding another vowel, 57 47, 48, vowels in roots are basically short, 47, 48, roots, none with final doubled consonant or orig. long vowel, 47, 48, 49, vowel assimilation is usually progressive, 53, roots ending in labials change following vowel to u, 53-54, 56-57, phonetic complication, esp. of roots, 61-62, a, u pron. as o, 71 n. 95; consonants and vowels, list and quality of; apparent dialectical variations due to inadequacy of cuneiform script, 39 265-279; distorted words in, parallels to in other languages, 25 55-56; Emesal and Emeku dialects, 24 103-106; Emesal-Emeku, phonetic differences between, 25 52-53; Eme-sal, dialect used in litanies and psalms, 39 143; Emesal dialect shows tendency to restore dropped final consonants, 57 49-50; predicative use of genitive case, 58 148-150; homonyms in, 45 372; homophony, problem of, 34 321-327, roots, behavior of final consonant in, 327-328; imperative indicated by root plus suffixes, 49 365; possibility of contact with languages of India, 45 366; k an organic part of the genitive element, 58 148-149; -kam, affix after ordinal numbers < gen. particle -ka + am, 42 304, 393; MAŠ or BAR, developed from a picture of a pair of crossed fire-sticks; meanings of, 39 91-99; structure originally monosyllabic, later developing a bisyllabic tendency, 39 269; orthography does not express doubling of consonant and vowel-length, 57 47; postpositions used as in Turkish and Finnish, 25 54-55, verbal prefixes, Basque and American Indian parallels to use of, 55; source of Harappa script, 59 Sup. 38 f.; stems, related, list of, 39 269-279; -tam, composed of numerical affix ta, "something," + am, 42 301-304, 393; use of third for first person, 37 314-320; tones in, 25 59; tones in, 37 320; tones marked in Emesal dialect, 40 218; not related to Turkish, 44 167; vowel-harmony in, 25 53-54

Mythology: texts concerning in Nippur collection, 44 159-160; waters of Tigris and Euphrates regarded as menstrual flow of earth-mother? 39 70, moon, as fecundating and self-mutilating god, 88-90; cosmology included a system of world-ages, the prototype of the Indian yuga-system, 39 66 n. 3

Religion: conceptions underlying personal names, 34 315-320; creation, beliefs concerning, 36 274-276, 279-299; Lagaš, cult ceremonies at, 42 91-104, temples, description of, 42 93 ff., priests classes of, 96-98, sacrifice at Lagaš, 98 ff., music in, 102; monotheism tended towards but not realized, 56 402; Nisaba and her husband Ḫani credited with oldest laws, 52 174-175, 177-178, deities of justice were: Gu-silim, Nanše, Ningirsu and Utu, 175-178; pantheism, strong movement toward, 39 77

Texts: accounts from Drehem, with translation, 33 167-179; archaic text in Déc. en Chaldée, pl. 1bis, 42 338-342; archaic text in Hoffman collection, 23 19-20, text and translation of, 21-28; Barton, Miscellaneous Babylonian Inscriptions, vol. I, analysis and interpretation of, 41 131-149, text No. 1, note to, 150-151; Bêlit hymn K. 257 (HT 126-131), text and translation, 24 103-128; Blau Monuments, translation of archaic texts on, 22 118-125; Blau Monuments, new collation of, 24 388-389; Brit. Mus. Cun. Texts III pl. I No. 12155, 21 185-187; Chiera's list of duplicates to de Genouillac's Textes religieux sumériens, 54 407-420; Cone of Entemena published by Thureau-Dangin (Déc. en Chaldée, p. xlvii), reading of supported by new net-cylinder, 36 137-139; contract from abu-Jāmūs (near Babylon) from time of Samsu-Iluna, 55 284-293; contract from Nippur of Ur III, 56 494; creation account, translation and interpretation of, 36 279 ff.; creation text from Nippur (first Dynasty of Babylon), 37 37-42; CT, tab. 15821, pl. 18, with translation, 30 94-100; CT XV pl. 7, 8 and 9, tab. 29615, with translation, 30 313-324; CT XV, pl. 11 and 12, tab. 29644, with translation, 29 184-191; CT XV pl. 12 and 13, with translation, 30 61-71; CT XV pl. 23, with translation, 30 325-335; CT XV pl. 24-25, with translation, 31 395-402; Entemena, inscribed cone of, 51 262-265; Fāra (Šuruppak), commercial documents from, 52 110-114, 124, 125-130, list of published texts from, 119-120, date from period before Ur-Nina (2620 B.C. at latest), 120-124; Gen., Dréh. CB, pl. V, No. 22, account, with oath, translated, 33 43-44; incantations, 21 1-22; incantation, 33 345-348; inscribed galet of Eannatum, 38 264-266; inscribed nail head mentioning city of Àktab, 57 359-367; land-conveyance from reign of Enlil-bâni, with translation, 36 34-36; Langdon's Historical and Religious Texts from the Temple Library of Nippur, additions and corrections to, 60 234-257; Libit-Ištar, votive cone of in Yale University; Semitic influence in, 52 182-185; Lugaldaudu, inscription of from Adab, translation of, 33 295-296, 34 facing p. 228; Mêšitug, vase inscription of from Adab, 33 296; Nergal, hymn to, with trans., 28 168-182; "Paradise-Epic," so-called by Langdon, is really a hymn to Ea; text and translation of, 36 90-114, interpretation of, 122-135, notes to text of, 140-145, is a description of Paradise and the Fall of Man, 143-145, refers to land destroyed by drought; textual notes to, 269-273, refers to drought, 290-295; "Paradise Epic," so-called by Langdon, notes to and analysis of text, 39 67-90; pre-Sargonid limestone tablet from Uruk, 38 188-196; provision-lists from Prince collection, with translation, 33 24-32; tablets in University of Illinois collection, 46 345; topography of Gudea texts, 43 41-48; translation of archaic text published by Scheil in Recueil de Travaux XXII, livr. 4, 149 ff., 22 126-128; votive inscription of Libit-Ištar, on eye of statue, 45 154-155

Sumuqan, Akkadian patron of animal husbandry, identical with Enkidu, 40 320-331

Sun, ancient cult of at Hebron, 45 356; associated with the ass in Egypt, 40 332; China, connected with Yao, 56 55, 63-65, comparison with sun myths around the Pacific, 65-66, Yao the sun itself, 63; Chinese belief in mystic connection between mirrors and, 55 184-187, getting fire from the sun by means of a mirror, 185-186, sun made of fire could not contain crow, 186; cock as symbol of, 33 381, 383; worshipped at Golden Gate in Jerusalem, 42 398; worshipped in Jerusalem before the Exile, 46 163; see also Solstice, Equinox

Sunday, honored by pagans because of its dedication to the sun, 32 319-320

Sunflower, intro. into China in late 17th cent., 52 94, earlier so-called "sunflower" a species of mallow, 94

Sung Shan, 嵩山, Honan, one of the 5 sacred mountains of Taoism, 49 148, 149 n.10

Sung-shu, account of Fu-lin differs fr. that of earlier records, 30 24-25, gives composition of an Arab embassy 30

Sung Tzu Niang Niang, 送子娘娘, prayer to, 49 141-142

Sungyun (Ch. Sung Yün 松筠), see Manuscripts, Manchu

Sun-kiss, as life-giving, 60 46-67; among the Hopi Indians, 60 270

Sunnis, in Sarawak, 33 340

Sunqur al-Ašqar, life of, 60 376-382

Sun-tzu, author of On the Art of War, 6th cent. B.C., no mention of use of elephants, 41 302

Śūnyavāda refuted in philosophical Sūtras of the Brahmans, 31 1-29

Surakhani (near Baku), description of fire-temple at, 25 176-178

surimono, see Art, Japanese

Šuruppak, fifth antediluvian dynasty, 43 325; description of ancient site of, 32 1-2; see also Sumerian Texts

Sūrya, in iconography, 57 327-329; characteristics found in Puruṣa, 51 108-114; translation and exegesis of RV. 1.115,

a hymn to, 58 419-434; traits in common with Viśvarūpa, 55 389
Susa, chalcolithic culture begins ca. 5000 B.C., 47 355; workmen from aid in building temple of Eninnu in Lagaš, 43 44
Susanoo no Mikoto, Japanese divinity to whom the Gion Jinsha is dedicated, 54 282, worship possibly brought fr. Izumo, 284, turbulent brother of the Sun-goddess, associate of or successor to Gozu Tennō, 283-284, as god of love and wedlock, 284-285, worshipped at Gion in early 11th cent., 284, symbol and floats in Gion matsuri have sexual significance, 285
Śuṣṇa, foe of Indra, 36 247, 254
Suśruta, prāṇa-series in the, 22 307
Suṣumnā artery, and udāna, 22 266-273, in Mahābhārata 347; in Śāradā-tilaka Tantra, 23 67, 71
Su-t'ê, 粟特, = Suk-tak, country of the Alans, 30 33
Sūtras, of the Brahmans, dates of the philosophical, 31 1-29; caste system in the, 53 183; prāṇa and apāna in the, 39 111; prāṇa-series in, 22 260, 302 f.
Suttee in the Hindu Epic and law, 21 148 f.
Su'ūd, banu-, feuds with the banu-Rašīd of Ḥā'il, 37 157-158
Suvarṇagrāma (Sonargaon), Indian port near one of mouths of the Ganges, 37 244
Ṣuwar-i Aqālīm-i Sab'ah, account of Zoroaster and Zoroastrianism in, translated, 28 183-188
Suye— Mura, see Japan, Japanese
al-Suyūṭi, Arab historian, copied from ibn-'Abd al-Ḥakam, 43 145; see also Naẓm al-'Iqyān fi A'yān al-A'yān
Suzerain, see Shō-gun
Svapnasvāsavadatta of Bhāsa, lexicographical and grammatical notes on, 35 269-272
Svarbhānu, legend of (JB. i.80-81), text and translation, 26 190-192
Svarodaya, Rāma Prasād's translation, 23 69
Śvetadvīpa and Śākadvīpa, 39 209-242; see also Śākadvīpa
Śvetāśvatara Upaniṣad, late character of its yoga terminology, 22 334-336, author and relative date of, 380-387
"Sweating blood", said of the "superior" horses of Ta-yüan, see Han-hüé (Han-hsüeh)
"Sweet dew," 甘露, meaning blessing, term used in Chinese prayers, 49 132, 134 n.4, 140; see also Terms, kan lu tsiang (kan lu chiang)
Swift's Iloko grammar, 42 156
Sword-guards, see Swords, Japanese; tsuba
"Sword judgment", see Connoisseurship, of Japanese swords
Swords
Arab: famous Damascus blades made of Indian steel, 35 232
Indian: made of finest grade of steel known to the Roman world, 35 226, 230, 235, swords of Indian steel made also in Persia and Damascus, 231, 232
Japanese: legends of, 26 334-335, famous swordsmiths, 334-337, 341-342, 352, ancient names of, 349, glossary of terms, 349-352, classification of edge, 355-359, classification of the nakago, 359, classification and description of swords, 362-410; the sword of the samurai, characteristics of, 45 89-90, sword forms, 90, the tsuba, 90, wearing of two swords, 91; sword-guards by the Hiiragi-ya, of 17th cent., famous for fine inlay, 55 449; wearing of two swords a privilege of the warrior nobles, 31 154, exceptions, 154-155, 212, 214
Persian: ancient, made of Indian steel, 35 231, 232, 235
Sykes-Picot Agreement, conditions of, 47 104
Syllabaries, Cuneiform, Chicago Syllabary continued by AO 7661, 52 297
Symbolism, of early Chinese mirrors, 55 182-189; of the Japanese sword, 26 334; of the nidānas in drawings of the Tibetan "Wheel of Life", 60 356-360, pictures representing the "12 links" have remained almost constant fr. early times, 356, the pictures explained, 357-360
Syntactical arrangement, a new method of, 41 176, 467-471
Syria, Syrians, Syrian, Syriac, history of the cock in, 33 386-387, 395; evidence fr. Egyptian monuments of the Asiatic elephant in, 41 290-291; Oriental Studies in, 45 356; Sumerian influence on religion, 51 65; throw-sticks, 55 178; trade with Genoa in 12th cent., 38 181-186; travels in North Syria, topographical and archeological notes, 28 155-163; see also Alphabet; Aramaic; Art and Architecture; Bowls (incantation); Calendar; Folklore; Li-Kan; Manuscripts; Seals; Semitic Languages; Songs
Church: orthodox christology of, 32 307-310; soul, teaching on in early Syriac authors, 40 103-120, trichotomistic view of body and soul due to Jewish influence and to St. Paul, 120; was on point of evolving in Persia a theology and style free of Western domination, 38 330-331; see also Nestorians
History: expedition against by Ashurnasirpal II in 876 B.C., 38 250; campaigns of Shalmaneser III against, 41 350-353, 355, 364-367, 369, 370-376; earthquake, 525 A.D., destruction of Antioch by Persia, 540, and captivity of Antiochian Christians, 30 6-10, the patriarchs of Antioch, 10-15, Antioch and Apameia sacked by the Persians, 611 A.D., 8, known to the Chinese as Fu-lin, 1, 4-6, 8, 9-10, 16, 30-31; power of the Patriarch of the Nestorians fr. Syria, at Ctesiphon, 33 201-202, known to the Chinese as Fu-lin, 193-194, 195-197, 199, in possession of the Arabs, Hui-ch'ao's account of, 205-206, identified as Little Fu-lin, 207-208
Language: a'>ē before medial ', 57 155-156; connecting vowel -â after verbal forms ending in -n extended by analogy from 1st plur. ending, 46 357; anticipatory pronominal suffix, non-Semitic origin of, 47 260-262; loan-words in Baghdad Arabic, 22 109-110; Kurdish and Turkish influence on modern pronunication, 25 76-78; study of among modern Chaldaeans and Nestorians, 22 79-96; vowel-change, history of obscure, 38 9-11
Literature: Aḥīqar Romance, Assyrian influence on, 38 64-65; Simeon Stylites, Bedjan's text of his life is an important example of classical Syriac style, 35 110-111; modern Arabic songs, proverbs and stories, 23 175-288
Texts: Bar-Šûšan, letter of to Armenian Katholikos, with translation, 32 268-342; physiognomic treatise of 16th-17th cent., 39 289-294; Simeon Stylites, translation of Bedjan's text on his life, 35 103-198; Syriac version of the Λόγος κεφαλαιώδης περὶ ψυχῆς πρὸς Τατιανόν of Gregorius Thaumaturgus, 35 297-317; Theodore bar-Khoni's passage on Manichaeism, notes on text, 41 180; Valentinian hymn of ca. A.D. 250 in Greek letters from the Panarion of Epiphanius, with translation and commentary, 38 1-33
Syro-Mandaean, incantation bowl from Nippur, notes to text, 33 279-280; magic bowls from Nippur, 32 434-438
Sze-ch'uan, see Ssu-ch'uan
Szechwan, see Ssu-ch'uan
Taanach, old tradition of two distinct battles of, 38 336
Tabdīl (alteration), Shī'ite doctrine of, 29 61-62, 135
Tables
Chinese: founding of States in early Chou, dates and no. of reigns, 52 238; the "Table of Ancient and Modern Men", fr. the Ch'ien Han Shu, 59 207-219; geographical names, compared fr. three text books, 59 339
Japanese: romanized spellings according to Kokutei Rōmazi, the new Japanese official romanization, 59 100-101
Sino-Tibetan: demonstrating phonetic equations bet. Old Bodish, Burmese, Luśei, Chinese and Siamese (including Lao), 60 316-337
Tablets, Babylonian, at Smith College, 37 8; Neo-Babylonian and Achaemenid period, at Goucher College, 41 179; of ancestors of Confucius, 49 129; in Temple of God of War, 131, of ancestors, in the home, 131, one soul resides in each of the, 132 n.2, jade tablet in Hua Shan, 135, 136 n.2, of the Great Planet and the spirits of the stars, 139, tablet bet. high peaks, 148, of the God of the Rice Sprouts, 149, of the God of Cattle, 150
Tabnit, Phoenician king ruling before 320 B.C., 57 240

Tabu
India: tabu-trees in the Mahābhārata, 30 348
Indonesia: festal, of the Land Dyaks, 29 247-249; mourning, among the Kayans and Sea Dyaks, 25 234, 237; harvest, among the Kayans, 25 244 f.; among Malays, 33 327-328, 330-337
Semitic: at birth, marriage, etc., 37 14; Paschal lamb originally a tabu-sacrifice, 36 150; tabu-offerings among Semites, 36 327-328
Tadkirat al-Kaḥḥālīn of ʿAli ibn-ʿĪsa, Judaeo-Arabic fragments of from the Cairo Genizah, text and translation, 50 112-124
Tagalog, differences between Bisayan and, 25 162-169; expression of case by the verb in, 27 183-189; construction of coordinated words in spoken, 43 170; a new grammar by Pedro Serrano Laktaw, 50 340; formation of infinitive, 25 288, of preterite, 288, of future and present, 288 f., of passive, 289; the infixes la, li, lo in, 27 142-146; loss of intervocalic l in, 36 183 f.; as language of education in the Philippine Islands, advisability of selecting, 46 65-71; ligature and analogies in other languages, 29 227-231; people and language, 25 173 f.; polysyllabic roots with initial p in, 25 287-301, Sanskrit loan-words in, 287; verb, 36 396-414, roots and particles, 396 f., verbs made with verbalizing particles, 397-409, verbal classes, 397-403, secondary and tertiary derivation, 403 f., fully reduplicated roots, 404 f., verbal nouns and adjectives, 405 f., irregularities and peculiarities, 406-409, verbs made with subsidiary particles, 409-411, construction of verbs, 411-413; verbal passive prefix and suffix i, 49 363; see also Philippine Islands, Languages
Tagbanua, affinity with Mangyan, 60 271; bamboo writings, 60 271 f.
TAG-KU [TAG-TUG] is not Sem. Utnapištim, 40 74
TAG-TUG, rôle of in the so-called Sumerian Paradise Epic, 39 80-82
Ta-hia, see Ta-hsia
Ta-hing, title, see Ta-hsing
Tahitian, r for original l in, 36 189
Ta-hsia (Bactria), 大夏, occupied by Yüeh-chih in late second cent. B.C., 37 94, 96-97, visited by Chang Chʿien, 95, his description of, 97-98, bamboo and cloth of Ssŭ-chʿuan seen in markets of, 98, Han Wu Ti consults Chang Chʿien concerning, 100, envoys sent to, 102, abortive attempts to reach, via Ssŭ-chʿuan and India, 104, northern route to, via Chiu-chʿüan, 104
Ta-hsing, 大行, title given Chang Chʿien, 37 102
Ta-i, 大益, small country west of Ta-yüan, in time of Han Wu Ti, 37 107, 148
Tai, a group of allied languages, not a race, 55 340, language group includes Siamese, Lao, Shan, Ahom, Black Tai, Nung, and Dioi, note on their tonal relations to each other, 55 341; see also Siamese
Tʿai Blanc of N. Annam, have a deluge story like the Chinese, 56 60
Tʿai-chʿang, title of the Grand Master of Ceremonies in Han period, 58 440, 441
Tʿai-chung-ta-fu, 太中大夫, title bestowed on Chang Chʿien, 37 95; title given Shen Pʿei by Han Wu Ti, 58 439
Tʿai-fu Têng Yü, 太傅鄧禹, grandfather of the Empress Têng of Later Han, 51 138 n.2, 140
tʿai-lao, sacrifice said to have been performed by Han Kao-tzu to Confucius, doubts of, 55 331, 333
Tʿai-pʿing Rebellion, see abstract, Gaskill
Taira Family, sources for study of, 59 39, 42, 43, 44, 45
Tʿai Shang lao-chün, 太上老君, Lao-tzu, appearance and speech to Kʿou Chʿien-chih, 53 229-231
Tʿai shou chʿêng, 太守丞, deputy governor, Han title, 51 269
Tʿai Sui, 'Great Year', tutelary god of the current year, called Kou Mang; worship of in ceremony of Reception to Spring, 42 54-58
Tʿai Tʿai, 臺駘, deity hero of a flood legend, 56 57, 61
Tʿai-Tsu, 太祖, Wei Emperor, encouragement of Taoism, 53 224-225
Taittirīya Āranyaka, prāna-series in, 22 258 f., 302 f.
Tʿai-wei, 太尉, title, "Minister of War", 53 236; title of next to highest minister, Former Han Period, 58 438
Tʿai-wu, Toba emperor, see Liang
Talismans, Chinese use of Han mirrors as, 55 186
Talmud, legal portions, Babylonian influence in, 38 73; Persian influence in, 33 368 n. 1, 370
Ta-lu, 大祿, a son of the King of Wu-sun, 37 102
Tamarians, origin of the Pandu Bing clan of, 50 227 f., origin of the kamal sept of, 50 228
Tamašeq Language, see Hamitic
Tamil, political divisions in the first two centuries A.D., 33 209-213; ports of S. India, 37 241, 245-246, 248-249, literature and coinage testify to importance of sea trade eastward bet. 1st and 3rd cent. A.D., 245-246; story with echo-word motif, 58 555-558, 568-570; story with echo-word motif, 59 504 f.
Language: treatment of Dravidian final i, 59 103 f.; echo-words, structure of, 59 505; intervocalic li becomes ll, 59 104; lexicon, the forthcoming, 44 134-137; names of God, 45 115-118; phonemic system, 59 505; phonetics, the consonants, 58 665-667; r, the history of, 58 664-668; R, the history of, 57 411-415; sangams, shortened, 52 81; sounds of, 52 133 f., morphology, 135-139; treatment of stops, 47 263 f.; suffix -ia, 59 104; Tamil-Kanara noun-ending -m, origin of, 57 304 f.
Tammuz, not an Arabian deity, but a historical personage, 45 136-138; Babylonian feast and month of, 31 265 ff.; a historical figure; was king of Uruk, 41 252; not a deified ruler, but personification of the apsu, 45 22-23, 35; "Lord of the Net," as divine carpenter, 39 81 n. 28, parallels with Osiris as dying-reviving lunar fertility god, 88-90; successor of Lugalbanda as king of Uruk; closely related to Gilgameš, 40 308, 314, 316-318, 328, related to Akkadian Sumuqan, 323; resemblances to Osiris, 35 213 ff.; name unknown in Palestine and Syria, 21 189; closely parallel to Ugaritic Môt, 59 410; worship of among Israelites, 46 156-157, 160-164, not referred to as Dôd in Canticles, 160-161; see also Adonis and Ešmun
Tan-chu, son of Yao, probable true reason why banished, 56 58
Tancred, varying dates for his death, 52 266-267
Tāṇḍya Brāhmana, story of rejuvenation of Cyavana in, 26 45
Tʿang Dynasty, founding of the, source materials on, 57 368-370, 372-373; see also China, Chinese, Wên Ta-ya
Tʿang-hui-yao, contains text of edict authorizing practice of Nestorian rites, 33 199
Tʿang-i, 堂邑, Chinese family which adopted the Tartar companion of Chang Chʿien, see Kan Fu
Tʿang-i Fu, 堂邑父, see Kan Fu
Tʿang Kao-tsu, see Wên Ta-ya
Tʿang-shu, name Fu-lin in, substituted for Ta-tsʿin just before published ? 33 194, speaks of Pʿei Chŭ, 193-194, passage on history of Persia, 200; passage describing tribes of Po-pa-li (Berbera), Africa, 30 47-48; see also Wên Ta-ya
Tʿang sung pa ta chia wen chʿao, 唐宋八大家文鈔, collected writings of certain Tʿang and Sung poets, a tsʿung shu, 51 44
Tʿang sung tsʿung shu, 唐宋叢書, a collection of rare writings of the Tʿang period, 51 45
Tʿang Tʿai Tsung, reception of embassy from Fu-lin in 643 A.D., 30 14; stone sculptures of his six horses, 55 420-428, his Miao, or memorial temple at Li Chʿüan, 422, 424, 426, poems on the horses, 428; see also Wên Ta-ya
Tʿang Tʿai Tsung Miao, the memorial temple of Tʿang Tʿai Tsung at the West Gate of Li Chʿüan, 55 422, 424, copies made for the miao of the great stone sculptures of the Horses of Tʿang Tʿai Tsung, 420, 423, 424, Stele of the Picture of the Six Horses in the, 424, 426, Stele of the Map of Chao Ling in the, 426
Tangut Studies, see Libraries; National Library of Peiping
Tangutans, see Chʿiang
Tanit, possibly androgynous, 21 187
Tantra, Śāradā-tilaka, title, author, general character, contents, 23 65-76

Tantrākhyāyika, book ii, notes, mainly textual, 38 273-293, possibility of reconstructing original Pañcatantra version, 273 f., Hertel's edition, 274-293; IV, A 286, a note on, 41 76 f.
Tantric lists of Yoga-powers, compared with Mahābhārata, 22 358
Tao, of Heaven, 天道, old phrase meaning the Heavenly Principle, 49 140 n.2, 151; Tao concept and the Chinese Dragon, 55 327 f.
T'ao Hung-ching, 陶弘景, Taoist, a favourite of Liang Wu Ti, 53 247
Taoism, Taoists, Taoist, Han practice of collecting dew, 55 186, decoration of Han mirrors reflect Taoist beliefs, 186; Imperial patronage of, in Ch'in and Han, 53 221, 231, of T'ai Tsu (Wei), 224-225, of Shih Tsu (Wei), 225-226, 235-241, of Hsien Tsu (Wei), 241-242, of Liang Wu Ti, 247, description of origin of universe, 243 n. 151, Han Taoist writers, 246, life of T'ao Hung-ching, 247, life of K'ou Ch'ien-chih, 225-238, 248, Taoist color blue, 237, site of Taoist altar at Loyang, 242, official interest in, 248-249, persecution of, 249, practices of, 221, 222, 223, 230-231, 236, 244-246, charm booklets, 232-233, 237, 238, 241, 244-249, medicine recipes, see also Alchemy; callisthenics, 216, 231, 233, 239, 247, diet of aspirants to geniehood, see also Immortals, Taoist; see also Heaven, Taoist; corrections, 54 290-294; under Emp. Hui and the Empress Dowager née Lü, 58 436, in the time of Han Wu Ti, 438, 440, 442 and n.11, Ssu-ma T'an, Ssu-ma Ch'ien and other Taoists at the Court, 440, influence of, in T'ang dynasty, 449; influence of Buddhism on, 53 222, 227 n.54; Lao-tse an epithet of Huang-ti, 53 211; objections to regarding it as largely a southern influence, 50 168-169; problems connected with the origin of, 53 209-211; Wei-shu and Sui-shu, chapters on; corrections to tr. in 53, 54 290-294, cult pictures on doors, 293, genie-food, 190-192; see also Books, Chinese; see Immortals, Taoist; Lao-tzu; Mountains, sacred; Mythology, Chinese; Tao-tê-ching
Tao-tê-ching, questions of authorship, name, origin of, 53 209-211
t'ao-t'ieh, development of design of on Chinese bronzes, 51 16-18 and plates
Tapa cloth, of Polynesia, method of manufacture of, note on, 45 190
Tar-baby story, place of origin, not original in India, 41 186
Tarshish, see Atlantis
Tarsus, cuneiform texts from, 59 1-16, Ḫurrian names from, 4-5, Cilician names from, 8-11; see also Sandon
Tartar-Manchu, see Manchu
Tartars (hu), usually designating the Hsiung-nu, with their nomadic Turkish, Mongolian, and Tungusic tribes, 37 93-94, 106, 109, 148
Tartessus, see Atlantis
tashi, ancient name of Japanese sword, 26 349
Ta-shih, 大食 or 大寔 (Arabs), tr. of account of in the Hui-ch'ao-wang-wu-t'ien-chu-kuo-chuan, 33 205-206 and notes, Chinese text, 207, discussion on, 204, 207, 208; 30 16; Arabs of the Khalif empire, 30 47
Ta T'ang ch'uang yeh ch'i chü chu, 大唐創業起居注, by Wên Ta-ya, circumstances under which written, 57 368-374, date and other titles of, 372, 373
Tatian, his teaching on the relationship between body and soul, 40 109 ff.; Syriac version of Περὶ ψυχῆς of Gregorius Thaumaturgus directed against him, 35 297-317
Tatpuruṣa compounds of type goghná and gáviṣṭi, 48 166-176
Ta-tsê, 大澤, Palus Maeotis, see An-ts'ai
Ta-ts'in: general term in later Han for Roman Empire, in particular Syria, with capital at Antioch, 30 1, 30, 33 193-194; first mission to China from in 166 A.D., 30 4-5, "King of", referred to by Chinese, was the patriarch of Antioch, or the Nestorian patriarch at al-Madā'in, 6-15, "Greater Ta-ts'in" meant the Roman Empire in its larger sense, 1; reports of, as a store house of jewels, 33 195-196, Nestorian religion from, 199, Fu-lin a later name for, used by the Nestorians, 198-202; Chinese name for Eastern Roman Empire, 37 243; Kan Ying, ambassador to, stopped at T'iao-chih, 35 35-36, Chinese notice, 41; musicians and jugglers in an embassy to China fr. the King of the Shan country, claimed to be men of Ta-ts'in; here seems to mean merely fr. the West, 37 242-243, "An-tun" the King of Ta-ts' in in 166 A.D., 243, the place where the sun sets, 243-244; see also Fu-lin
Ta-tsö, see Ta-tsê
Tattooing, occurs in ancient China and many other places, 57 198, in Hainan Island today, 198
Tattvasaṃgraha of Śāntarakṣita, 49 66 f.
Ta T'ung Fu, Shansi, founding of the Ch'ung-hsü-ssu at, 53 224 and n. 39, 241-242
Ta Tu-tzu, 大肚子, see Pu-tai, 53 47 n.1
Ta-t'zu-en-ssu-san-tsang-fa-shih-ch'üan biography of Hsüan Chuang, see Hui Li
Taxation, under Han Kao-tsu, 57 173; Japan, see Shōen
Taymā', Arabian capital of Nabonidus, 45 354; relations with Babylonia, 41 458-459; relations with Babylonia; description of by modern travellers, 42 305-316, Arabian capital of Nabonidus, 313-316
ibn-Taymīyah al-Ḥarrāni, Aḥmad, see also Qā'idah fi Ziyārat Bayt al-Maqdis was forerunner of Wahhābi movement, 56 3-4
Taymur Paşa, Ahmet, life and works, 51 104-105
Ta Yü, 大禹, mythical founder of Hsia dynasty, probably a water god, 52 244, region connected with his name, 244-245
Taxes, in China, in Han dynasty, no record of exact tax system but taxes on land and mdse. indicated, 40 192
Ta-yüan, (Ferghana), 大宛, first known in China, through visit of Chang Ch'ien, 37 93, 94, 108, connected by postal roads with K'ang-chü, 94, Chang Ch'ien's account of, 95, 98, envoy sent to, 102, its horses stronger than Wu-sun's, 103, prestige of China in and near, 106, 107-108, Han Wu Ti's desire for the 'superior' horses of, 109, the disastrous campaign of the Chinese against, to secure the horses, 109-111, 135-136, the Chinese second campaign, siege of the capital, resulting in supremacy of China, which obtained the horses, 111-113, 136, subsequent relations of, with China, 115-116, comments on the name, 148-149; Kings of, see Mu-kua; Mei-ts'ai; Ch'an-fêng
Ta-yüeh-chih, see Yüeh-chih
Tchiyo (Chiyo), Japanese poetess, see Book Reviews, Hla-Dorge
Tearing of Garments, Hebrew mourning custom, 21 23-39
Tedurai, see Tirurai
Te-hua hsüeh shuo, 德化學說, an example of the Chinese theory of, 56 51
Teixeira, Domingos, see Japan, Geography
Tejas, and the vital breaths, 22 272 f.
Tell al-'Ajjūl, probably not the site of ancient Gaza, 53 286, comparison of Petrie's and Albright's dates of levels, 287
Tell al-'Amārnah, eight new cuneiform tablets found there in 1933-1934, 56 414
Tell Ḥalāf, culture includes beginning of Chalcolithic period; at latest contemporary with Badari, 58 672-673; see also Mesopotamian Archeology
Tell al-Naṣbah, see Palestine, Archeology
Telugu, sounds of, 52 134, morphology, 135-139
Telugus, personality materials for ages preceding 1000 B.C. of the, 48 348, 49 352
Temple, Second (at Jerusalem), first serious work on it begun at end of reign of Cambyses, 46 358-359
Temples
Chinese: to Kuan Yü, God of War, 49 131; Wen Miao, 文廟, 49 129n.1, Wu Miao, 武廟, 131, n.6; see also Prayers, Chinese; Pi Yün Ssu; Pu Ning Ssu; Yung Ho Kung
Sumerian: description of, 42 93 ff.
Temple Records, Japan, see Bibliography
Ten commandments, in Manu, 43 244 f., of the Buddhists, 245 f.
Têng, Empress, of Later Han, biography of, 51 138-159,

Têng kuei-jen, 143, Huang T'ai Hou, 144; see also Biography
Têng Family, at Court, large, 51 140, 149, mother and brothers of Empress Têng allowed to visit her in the palace, 141, Yin Hou's fear of them, 142, raising rank of members of the, 144, brothers of Empress Têng, 144, 151 n.73, 149, Têng Chih, 144, 149, the mother, 149, 151-152, children of the, in school, 156-157, Têng K'ang banished fr. court, 158
Tĕnggĕrese funeral ceremonies, 51 8
Têng Hsün, 鄧訓, father of Empress Têng, of Later Han, 51 138, 139 n.7, 140
Têng Kuang, 鄧光, reproved for advising Han Wu Ti against continuance of war against Ta-yüan, 37 111
Têng Kuei-jen, see Biography, Empress Têng
Têng Yü, 鄧禹, ancestor of the Têng family, 51 157 n. 109; see also T'ai-fu Têng Yü
Tent of Meeting, rendezvous for Yahweh and Israel patterned after mountaintop cave; no original connection with Ark of the Covenant, 38 131-139
Tenubi, god among the Land Dyaks, 26 170-174
Ten Wings, place among the Classics, 44 278-279, 282
Tepe Hissar (Persia), correlations with Mesopotamia, 59 116-117
Terminology, of the Japanese Shōen, or Manor system, terms used in connection with the lands of a Shōen, the people on them, and the owners or officials administering them, 57 78-83
Terms, Chinese, 法門, Fa Men, "The Gate of the Law", 49 134 n. 3, The Purple Han, 紫漢, the Milky Way, 137-138 n.2, ming-mo, 冥漠, the obscure desert, a name for the Desert of Gobi; a syn. for Hades, 147 n.3, ts'ai yün, 採運, lit. "pick transportation", a contractor's or carter's term, 238-239
Tesserae, inscribed Palmyrene, 26 113-116, 27 397-399
Teumman, still alive in 653 B.C., 52 304
Text-books, for Chinese schools in ancient times, 44 276-278; for Chinese schools in 1905, 27 86; the Fu-hsing Textbook of History, see Hsü Ying-ch'uan
Textiles, Babylonian linen weaving ca. 2500-2200 B.C. at Uruk, 36 415; embroidered Han dynasty quilts, 51 152, woven ornamental brocades and embroideries, 147; Chinese satin brocade on MS. book cover of about 1750 A.D., 49 235; printed and painted Fāṭimid, from al-Fusṭāṭ, 53 394; see also Art, Japanese; Silk
Textual criticism of inscriptions, 40 289-299
Thai (Tai), see Languages, Sino-Tibetan
Thamūd, Arab tribe, existed from 8th cent. B.C. to 2nd cent. A.D., 60 287
Thasian Herakles = Ešmun-Adonis, 22 117
Theatre, Chinese, performances in temples, to drive away spirit of pestilence, 49 146 n.5; at the court, for expelling demons and driving away pestilence, 51 150
Theinni, capital of the Shan Kingdom, may = Thinae, 37 243, 246
Thekla, St., and the Lion, possible basis of the story in fact, 46 4-6
Theodore bar-Khoni, account of Zoroaster in, 43 239-242; see also Syriac Texts
Theodore of Mopsuestia, opposed by Bar-Šûšan, 32 271, 309; originator of doctrine of Nestorius, 58 385
Thibet, Thibetan, see Tibet, Tibetan
Thinae, see Theinni
"Thirteen Classics", Canon of the Sung dynasty, 44 283
Thothmes II, received elephants fr. Syria, 41 291
Thothmes III, elephant hunt of, in Northern Syria, 41 291
Thraētaona-Aži-Dahāka combat, compared with Marduk-Tiāmat combat, 36 310-313
"Three Mothers" of the Chou Dynasty, 51 155-156 n. 98
Thrita, as healer, 38 296
Thugs, in Islam, 29 92
Ti, 氐, tribes: prevent expedition to India in time of Han Wu Ti, 37 99
Tiâmat, of West-Sem. origin, 45 143
T'iao-chih, 條枝, (Chaldea), description of, by Chang Ch'ien, 37 97, old Chinese legends known in, 97, regular missions to, fr. China, 103-104; elephant native to ? 41 294; where Kan Ying stopped and turned back, 35 35-36
t'iao-sheng, 排生, a variety of ku magic, 55 15-16
ibn-Tibbon, Judah, created new lexicography and syntax for Hebrew under Arabic influence, 46 353-354
Tibet, Tibetans, Tibetan, origin of Tibetans, organization of first State, 52 341, early kings, 341-342, 347; King Sroṅ-btsan sgam-po responsible for introduction of writing, 38 34-38, aided Wang Hüan-ts'e's campaign against Central India, 34, 36, King Sroṅ's marriage to a Chinese princess, 34, relations with Khotan, 45-46; see also Calendar; Dalai Lamas; Padmasaṁbhāva; Painting, Tibetan; Panchen Lamas; Writing
Art: drawings of the "wheel of life," symbol of the nidānas, 60 356-360; northern, Scytho-Siberian animal style in, 53 89-91; northern, "stone graves" and megalithic monuments, 53 90; see also Book Reviews, Roerich
Literature: version of the Rāmāyaṇa, 50 174; version of the Rāma story, compared with the Khotanese, 59 466 f.
Writing: origin of, 38 34-46, evidence of Chinese annals, 34 f., Tibetan tradition, T'on-mi's mission, 35 f., beliefs of Schmidt and Lacouperie, 37 f., theory of Khotan origin, 38-46, source of name Li-byin, 39 f., the Schlagintweit text, 41-43
Tibeto-Burman group of languages, Himalayan pronominalized branch, resemblances to Buruçaskī, 41 65 f.; see also Languages, Sino-Tibetan
al-Tibr al-Masbūk fi Naṣīḥat al-Mulūk, see al-Farq bayn al-Ṣāliḥ wa-ġayr al-Ṣāliḥ
Ti ching ching-wu lüeh, 帝京景物略, topographical history of Peking, barred fr. Japan, 1695, 57 300 and n.10; see Matteo Ricci
Tidanum, Tidnum, early name of Amurru and land of Ḫumbaba, 41 255
Tien, 典, a large quantity of ts'ê; shuo-wen gives origin as term for the Books of the Five Rulers, 44 274, name of all documents before time of Confucius, 275
T'ien-chu (India), 30 8, 13, lord of was appointed by the "King of Ta-ts'in", 12
T'ien Fen, Lieut. Chancellor under Han Wu Ti, furthered Confucianism in gov., 58 435, 438, 440
T'ien-hsüeh ch'u-han, 天學初函, a ts'ung-shu of reprints published by Catholic missionaries in 17th cent., 20 of its titles prohibited import into Japan bet. 1630 and 1720, 57 292-294
T'ien I Ko Library, Ning-po, smoking prohibited in the, 58 655
T'ien-ma, (t'ién-ma), 天馬, "heavenly horse", the superior horse of Ta-yüan, reference regarding legend of, 37 149, 103; see also Ta-yüan
T'ien Wen, 天問, Book of Poetry of South China, contains tales of the model emperors, 56 55, 61, earliest version of, about 300 B.C.; Hsi Ho and the ten suns myth, 64, 66
Tien-yüeh (Tién-yüé), 滇越, country on the route fr. China to India. Yünnan ?, 37 99
Tiflis, description of Yazīdis in vicinity of, 25 178-181
"Tiger-horse", related to zebra and quagga, see Mule, striped
Tiglath-Pileser, died in January, 726 B.C., 44 159
Tiglath-Pileser I, campaigns of, 37 169-185
Tiglath-Pileser IV, extent of Assyrian empire under, 34 352, 355-357
Tigré, Modern popular literature, translated specimens of, 23 51-55; see also Semitic Languages
Tigriña Language, see Semitic Languages
Tigris and Euphrates, see Sumer, Mythology
Tilak's philosophy, 56 526 f.
Tiles, see abstract, White; Roof Tiles
Tille, Tiluli, Assyrian province, organization of, 38 236
Time analysis of Sanskrit plays, 21 88-108
Timothy (Syriac writer), his teaching on the soul, 40 107-108

Tin, an early export of the Berbera coast, 30 50
T'ing Nien, of Ch'i; proposal to Emp. Han Wu Ti that engineers change course of Yellow River to run through Hu country to remove threat of the Hsiung Nu, 55 303, 305
Tinguianes, people and language, 25 172
Tirqa, capital of Ḫana, at modern 'Išarah on the Euphrates, 44 193
Tiruparuttikunram, dating of the Jain temples, 54 440
Tirurai language, notes on the phonology of, 33 150-157
Titles, Han Dynasty, 51 269; 57 369, 370-373; 58 435-449; see also Officials, Han; shang-ta-fu; t'ai-wei; i-ts'ao-lang
Ti Tsang, 地藏, prayer to, 49 135, 136 n.1, 2, assoc. with Chiu Hua Shan, Anhuei, function to rescue souls fr. purgatory, 136 n.2, 4, 8
Toads, toad-ku a variety of Black Magic, 55 21, 22
Tobacco, in China and Manchuria, early prohibitions of, 58 648-657, dates of importation into the Philippines, Japan, Macao, Java, India, Ceylon, Korea, 648, no refs. to, in Chinese lit., before 1600, 648-655, writers, on the use and prohibition of, Chang Chieh-pin, 648, 652, Yao Lü, 648-649, 654, Fang I-chih, 649, 651, 653, Père Louis le Comte, 649, Shen Han-kuang, 650, article in the Wakan Sansai Zue, 650, Wang P'u (Pu or Fu), 651; Hsü Shih-chi, 653, Shih Jun-chang, 653-654, Wang Shih-chen, 654, the K'ang Hsi Emperor, 654, edicts against, 649-652, 655, Li Ê's ode in praise of, 655, "no smoking" in the T'ien I Ko, Ning-po, 655, prohibitions in other parts of the world, 655-656, East Asian Terms for, 657; in Japan, raising of forbidden in Tokugawa period, 30 272; in Japan, raising of forbidden, 31 204, use of forbidden, 206
Tocharians, possible a Cimmerian people; route of migration, 47 356; prototype of language spoken in western Asia Minor, 56 410
Toda, garments and embroidery, 57 277-289; story with echo-word motif, 58 567-570
Togawa Yasukiyo, 戸川安清, authority for list of books prohibited by the Edict of Kanei, 57 291
Toilet articles, Chinese, description of lacquer toilet-box with mirror, comb, cosmetics, etc. from Han tomb at Lo-Lang, 55 188; see also Lo-Lang
Tokugawa Ieyasu, founder of the feudal system in Japan, 1600 A.D., 30 259, principles of his government based on study of political experience of China and early Japan, 260; anecdote of, concerning dependence of a lord's power on peace, 31 151, his government based on study of political experience of China and early Japan, 152-153, his collection of classical and historical works of China and Japan; encouragement of learning, 152, his saying about taxes, 185
Tokugawa Period, régime based on early Chinese models, 31 153; see also Feudalism in Japan
Tomb, of Yü, near Shaohsing, Chekiang, 56 55, 61-63
Tombs, Chinese, caretakers for, appointed by Han Kao-tsu, 57 173; excavated at Lo-Lang, Korea; of Wang Hsü, 54 97-99; of Painted Basket, excavated at Lo-Lang, Korea, and other tombs, notes on, 56 102-103; pottery tiles from, see abstract, White; tradition of mirrors to light graves a late superstition, not true of early burials, 55 188; use of true vault in Annam, 57 332; see also Aloes; Burial; Lo-Lang; Mu-yang-ch'eng; K'ang Ling; Shun Tombs; Yüan Tombs
Tone (musical, tone-accent), history of use of term; definition of, 37 310-314; representation of, in Oriental Languages, 41 235; in Chinese; analysis of Cantonese, 35 199-204, analysis of Pekingese, 204-206, chart of Cantonese tones, op. 202, chart of Pekingese tones, op. 203; Siamese tone-accents analyzed, 31 282-289, definition of "tones", 282, problems of nomenclature, 283, method of scientific charting of tones, 284-286, analysis, 286-289, chart of the 5 "tones", 286
Tong-King, Chinese rule of, B.C. 214-263 A.D., 37 242, route fr. Chinese capital to its Tong-King seaport Kiao-Tsi (Kattigara of Ptolemy) known, 243-244, the sea route to, according to Roman authors, 246-249; correct description of coast in Marcian of Heraklea, 37 248
Tŏng Kuang, see Têng Kuang
T'on-mi, or T'ou-mi, sent to India by king of Tibet in 632 to gather materials for a Tibetan alphabet, 38 34-37, 42-43
Tools, Chinese, collected for Mercer Museum by Hommel, kinds of, 58 690-691
Topozersky Monastery, in Government of Archangel, see Marko
Tortoise-shell, a product of Po-pa-li, (Berbera), and the island of Socotra in early times, 30 49, 50, 52; Chinese, Han, articles of, mentioned, 51 148; see also Lo-Lang
Totemism, critique of theories of prior to 1904, 25 146-161; background of, 38 145-159; in Australia and elsewhere, 147 f.; exogamy and, 150, totemism of name, 150-152, metempsychosis and totemism, 152 f., Frazer's theories of origin of totemism, 153, principle of food utility, 154 f., prohibition against eating totem, 155 f., Wundt's theory of cult, 157 f., conclusion, 159; and the origin of clans, 50 221-232, relation to exogamy, 221 f., different theories of, 222 f., eponymous observances, 224, purpose of sacrifice, 224 f., dietary restrictions, 225-227, tribes of the Chota Nagpur Plateau, 227-232
Tou, 豆, sacrificial vessel, 49 130 n.5
Tou Ying, Lieut. Chancellor under Han Wu Ti, favored Confucianism, 58 435, 438, 439-440
Trade, Chinese, in camphor, 42 357-358; in early Han period, in An-hsi, 37 97, in Ta-hsia, where Chang Ch'ien saw bamboo and cloth of Ssŭ-ch'uan, 98, goods smuggled fr. Shu to Tien-yüeh, on route to India, 99, bet. China and western countries dates fr. Chang Ch'ien's mission, 102-103, by caravan through Central Asia stimulated by China's demand for good horses, 103; in iron, bet. Roman Empire and the East, 35 224-239, Pliny on silk, furs and iron from the "Seres," 224-225, 228, 230-231, 236, 239, Hirth, Rockhill and others misled, thinking the "Seres" meant China, 224-226, the iron industry in China, 226-227, cost of transport of iron from Shantung, 228, records do not indicate an iron trade with China, 225-230, trade in iron with Africa, 229, all evidence points to India as source of the steel trade with the West, 230-236, Indian ports of export, 230-231, Arab shipping monopoly in iron and cinnamon, 230-231, "Seres" a general term, or result of confusion in names, 236-239; in ivory, Asia, 41 290, 306, fr. Syria to Egypt in 18th dynasty, 290-292, bet. China and the middle East, 296, bet. China proper and the barbarian states of South China in early historic times, 297, 298-299, 304, in hides, Rhinoceros, bet. Ch'u and China proper, 299, in Elephant skins, Assyria, 291-292, 303; in ivory, Asia, fr. Sumatra, 42 180, in iron, Kabul export in 16th cent., 181; Japan (Tokugawa Period), dealings in smuggled foreign wares forbidden, 30 275; bet. the Manchus in Peking and the Ainu of Saghalin in the 18th cent. 37 197; medieval, bet. coast of East Africa and China, 30 46-57, discovery of Chinese coins and shards of celadons and other porcelains on Somali coast, near Mugdishu and Zanzibar, 54-57, products of Po-pa-li (Berbera), 48-50, products of Chung-li (Socotra), 51-52, 54, products of Zanzibar, exchanged for porcelain, 55-57; the overland trade bet. East and West, part played by the Aorsi as middlemen, 30 33, n.1; overland bet. China and the West fr. Han to Sui period, 33 193-197, in Sui dynasty due to extravagance of Emp. Yang Ti, 196, by sea, of Persia with Ceylon, the K'un-lun and Canton, 205; overland between East and West at beginning of Christian Era, 35 31-41; over the sea and land route from Roman Empire to Far East, bet. 1st and 3rd cent., very active, 37 240, silk from the Golden and Silver shores, and Thinae, 240, 246, trade out of China through Yün-nan, 242, products of Yün-nan, 244, description of a trading port in India in Roman times, 245, trade in jewels described in early Sanskrit play, 245-246, trading vessels in the ports of India, 246; see also Arabs, Arabic; International Relations, Anglo-Chinese; Books, Chinese, Import into Japan; Caravans; Expeditions; Trade Routes; Tribute; and see also under names of countries
Trade Routes, overland bet. China and the West; three des-

cribed in the Sui-shu, 30 5; overland bet. East and West at Christian Era: the Antioch, Seleucia, Caspian, Antiochia Margiana route, 35 31, 35, Parthian control of this route, 31, the sea route opened by Rome bet. 50 and 100 A. D., 32, 35, 39, the new overland and sea route fr. Petra to head of Persian Gulf, thru Elam to Lake Helmand, Arachosia and Kabul, 32; growth in Roman demand for silk, 34; Parthian effort to connect the two overland routes, 35-36, the Yüe-chi control of silk routes before and after 100 A.D. 32, 39-40, importance of the Kushan dynasties in the silk trade, 34, 38, route of Isidore of Charax to Alexandropolis, competition on the routes, 38-39, trade bet. Kabul, Obollah and Petra, 38, Chinese remarks on the cause of trade with the West, 41; overland bet. East and West, route of the silk traders according to the Geography of Ptolemy, 35 227; combination Sea and Land route to the Far East under the Roman Empire, 37 240-249, the ancient route of the silk merchants, 240, three stages in the new sea and land route: first, Arab trade by sea fr. Egypt to Tamil ports of S. India, and Ceylon, 240-241, second, Chola mariners plied sea route fr. India and Ceylon to Gulf of Martaban, 241-243, third, overland route up Salwin River valley, across parallel gorges of the Me-kong and Red River to Yün-nan-fu, thence to Cheng-tu and Si-an-fu, 242-243, the so-called "Golden route" (a variation of the 3rd) fr. Yün-nan to the upper Irawadi, down that river to Mandalay, then down the Sittaung, 240, 243-244, an alternate to third stage was a sea route (taken by Chinese and Malay shipping) fr. Gulf of Martaban round the Malay Pen. up to Kiao-Tsi (Kattigara) at head of the Gulf of Tong-King, then up the Red River to Thinae (Theinni, the Shan capital ?) and thence to the Chinese capital, 243,244, 246-249, people often confused as to destination of the various routes, 240, 243, 246-249; new geographical concepts seeped into China in 4th cent. B.C. from the Mediterranean world, 56 74-75; three overland bet. China and the West, described in the Sui-shu, 33 195, by sea, Persia to Ceylon, the K'un-lun and Canton, 205; through Yünnan, a result of effort to reach Ta-hsia (Bactria) through India in early Han, 37 99, 104; to the Utopia called Oponia (Japan ?), from Moscow, see Marko, Monk of the Topozersky Monastery

Trade Winds, of the Indian Ocean, see Navigation

Transcriptions, of foreign sounds into Chinese, 37 150; see also Words; Names

Transjordan, Bronze Age occupation, extent of, 54 171-173, 174, Israelite occupation, 173-177; Paleolithic man in, 52 286; seceded from Palestine over Zionist question, 47 110, al-'Aqabah obtained from the Hijaz in 1925, 110-111; see also Petra

Translation, problems of, 53 298-302; Biography of Yeshu'-yabh, by Mar Amr, 33 201; into Chinese, by Bishop Schereschewsky, note on, 39 149; Japanese, Complete Manual of the Old Sword, 26 334-410; names of Chinese Buddhist monks, by transcription, by meaning, and by a mixture of the two, 52 159-162; The Sūkarikāvadāna of the Divyāvadāna, 48 159-165; see also Edicts; Passages; Prayers, Chinese

Chinese into English: Biography of the Empress Têng fr. the Hou Han Shu, Chüan 10a, 51 138-159; Biography of Wên Ta-ya, fr. the Chiu T'ang-shu, ch. 61, pp. la-lb, 57 370-372; Bronze inscription of late Chou, typical seven character, 56 346, discussion, 347-348, translation, 348; The Four Great Vows of Zen Buddhism, 57 447; Han-shu, Biography of the Widow of Pa, 54 186-193; Hui-ch'ao-wang-t'ien-chu-kuo-chuan, account of the "Greater Fu-lin", 33 206, 207; Letters of Ch'i-ying to Sir Henry Pottinger, 59 480-482; Matteo Ricci's Map of the World, Introduction and Notes on the various Countries, and Names, 59 327-337, 358; Memorial to the Throne, 1905, upon abolishing the old style examinations, 27 79-87, Imperial Edict abolishing the old style examinations, Sept. 2, 1905, 84-87; Shih-chi, Chap. 123, Chang Ch'ien's journey to the West and its results, 37 93-116; Shih-chi, passage on Ch'ing, the wealthy Widow of Pa, 54 193; Wei Shu 114 (completing the tr. in T'oung Pao, 1933) on Taoism, fr. 10b - 13b, with notes, 53 218-243, Sui-Shu, section on Literature: The Taoist Books, 35, 12a - 13a, with notes, 243-250; Wei-shu and Sui-shu, chapters on Taoism, Corrigenda and Addenda to JAOS 53 217-249, 54 290-294

Transliteration, K'uei Chi's method of tr. Sanskrit into Chinese, use of, 53 148; see also Names, Personal

Transmigration, and restrictions on meat-eating in Buddhism and Brahmanism, 27 464

Transportation, by water in early Babylonia, references to, 43 173; Chinese, Han Dyn., gifts of wang-ch'ing-kai carts, 王青蓋車; of chariots and horses four abreast, 51 145; China, Han period, waterways, 55 303-306, pre-Han waterways, 303; Chinese, 18th cent., and costs, of building materials, 49 238-239, of glazed tiles, 241; in Japan in Tokugawa period, restrictions, 30 272, 280; in Japan in Tokugawa Period, evading a barrier, 31 172

Travellers, Chinese, Ch'ing dyn., Yü Yung-ho and T'u Li-chen, 59 349, 350-351; to the Far East, Early, see Tsin-Lun; Marinus of Tyre; Marcian of Heraclea

Treaties, see China, Chinese, History, (Ch'ing Dynasty)

Tree Cult, connected w. worship of Wen Ch'ang, 49 137 n.4

Tribal organization of Land Dyaks, 29 259-274

Tribhowandas Manguldas Nathubai on death ceremonies among the Kapola Bania and others, 22 227-229

Tribute, to China, fr. Parthia and small countries in Central Asia, 37 107; live elephants, 41 290-291, fr. Syria to Pharaoh; fr. Central Asia to Court of China, 294, fr. Ssu-ch'uan to Chinese Court, 303-304, ivory fr. Huai region and Yang and Ching to Chinese Court, 298, 299, see also Obelisk, Black; in furs, from the Ainu to the Manchus, 37 196-197

Trichinopoly, = Uragapura, see Chola

Trichodesmium erythraeum, not responsible for name of Red Sea, 33 349, 355

Trigault, Father Nicolas, probably the first European to see the Nestorian Tablet, 58 386

Trigault, P., see Aesop's Fables

Triṁśikā, see Vasubandhu

Tripiṭaka, Chinese Buddhist Canon, selected works fr., pub. in 1930, 51 292; Siamese, copy of in the U.S. National Museum, 23 47

Tripolis (of Syria), anciently constituted of towns of Maḫalata, Kaiṣa and Maiṣa, 38 248

Trismegistus, Hermes, see nidānas·

Triṣṭubh, epic, and its hypermetric varieties, 59 159-174; in the Pāli Iti-vuttaka, 28 326-329

Trita, as water-god, 38 297 f.

Triu, war-gods of the Land Dyaks, 26 166 f.

tṛṣṇa, see nidānas

Tsai Yuan-pei, see Libraries, National Library of Peiping

Ts'ai Yung, 蔡邕, his eight canons of the character yung, 永, see abstract, Driscoll

Tsang-ko, 牂牁, a region under the Han dynasty comprising parts of modern Ssŭ-ch'uan, Hu-nan, Kuei-chou, and Kuang-si, 37 104

Tsangla, notes on phonetics of, 60 306 n.14, 311, 312 n.23, 335

Tsao Shen, 灶神, see Kitchen God

Ts'ao Ta-ku, 曹大家, tutor of the Empress Têng, Later Han, 51 150

Ts'ao Ts'an, follower of Han Kao-tsu, 57 180; highest official in period following Han Kao-tsu, 58 436

Tsê, 徙, tribes: blocked the route to India in time of Han Wu Ti, 37 99

Ts'ê, 冊, earliest Chinese books, of bamboo slips, 44 273-274

Ts'ê fu yüan kuei, collection of early documents, pub. 1013 A.D., 57 372

Ts'ên-ch'ü, 岑娶, title of the son of the crown prince of Wu-sun, story of, in time of Chang Ch'ien, 37 102, given a Chinese princess in marriage by his grandfather, the K'un-mo, 106

Tseng, old man of Lung-yen, Fukien, story of his struggle against ku magic, 55 28-29

Tseng Kuo-fan, memorials of, concerning Chinese Education Commission to U.S., abstract, T.L. La Fargue
Ts'êng-pa, see Africa
Ts'e yüan, see Encyclopedias, Chinese
Tsién-mi, see Chien-mi
Ts'ién, see Ch'ien
Ts'ien-han-shu, see Ch'ien-han-shu
Ts'in (China), see Ch'in
Ts'in Dynasty, see Ch'in Dynasty
tsing-shih, Chinese literary degree (= Doctor of Philosophy), old style examinations for abolished in 1906, 27 83-85
Tsin-Lun, an earlier Marco Polo who came to Kattigara and was conducted to the Chinese court; told of the lands to the west and observed the trend of the coast at head of Gulf of Tong-King, 37 248-249
Tsiu-ts'üan, see Chiu-ch'üan
Tsö, see Tsê
Tso-chuan, championed by Liu Hsin, 59 218, rated by Pan Chao above the Kung-yang and the Ku-liang commentaries, 218; contains earliest mention of a mirror in Chinese literature, Legge, C.C., vol. V, p. 101, 55 182; on ivory in Ch'u, and the trade with China in ivory and hides, 41 299; not yet studied by important scholars in Han Hsüan Ti's time, 58 443; gives detailed stories of Yao, Shun and Yü, 56 55; on the Yün Clan, ref. to, 37 134
Tso-ch'uen, see Tso Chuan
Tsön-ts'ü, see Ts'ên-ch'ü
Tso-yé, Marquis of, see Cho-yeh
Ts'öng-pa, see Ts'êng-pa
Tsou Lang, virtuous scholar, his defiance of the ku magic, 55 25-27
Tsuba, Japanese sword guard, 45 90
Tsuina, an ancient Japanese Court ceremony for driving out evil spirits, 55 445-446, of Chinese origin, 446
Tsui Shu, 崔述, scholar of the 18th cent., first to point out steps in development of model-emperor lore, 56 56
Tsü-k'ü Mu-kién, see Mu-chien
Ts'ung-p'iao, 從驃, see Chao P'o-nu
Ts'ung Shu, 叢書, collections of reprints and ms. writings, on several subjects by several authors, 51 40-46, earliest use of term in T'ang dynasty, 40, earliest true ts'ung-shu in Sung dynasty, 40, reasons for the rise of, 40-42, still popular, 42, a depository of rare materials, 42, relating to one class of subject, 42-43, recovery of the first one, the Ju hsüeh ching wu, of 1201 A.D., 43, the Kan chu chi, c.1100, and the Lei shuo, 1146, not true ts'ung-shu, 43, the 2nd oldest, the Po ch'üan hsüeh hai, 1273, 43-44, 5 classes of works called ts'ung-shu, 44-45, for library classification how to differentiate bet. true and quasi, 45, the great Hsiao fang hu chai yü ti ts'ung-shu really a class ts'ung-shu (devoted to geography), 45-46
Tsurezuregusa, 徒然草, value of, as source for study of Kamakura period, 59 45-46
Tsurumeso, 弦召, end of the Gion matsuri, on the 24th, a procession and kagura dancers see Gion matsuri
Tu, 牘, writing boards of wood, 44 273-274
Tuan Ch'êng-shih, 段成式, author of the Yu-yang-tsa-tsu, d. 863 A.D. 30 17
Tuan Fang, signer of Memorial to abolish competitive examinations, 1905, 27 79
Tubid sept of the Hos, origin of the, 50 230
Tu Huan, 杜環, author of the Hsing-ching-chi, 行經記, prisoner in Persia for 10 years; describes the captive Christians from Antioch, 30 8
T'u-huo-lo, 吐火羅,= Tokharestan, 30 15; 33 204, 207
Tukaram, dates of, the Mahipati legend of, 51 289 f.
Tukriš, in region N of later Ellipi, called Ḫarḫar by Assyrians, 48 92
T'u-küe, the Turks, 33 206 and n.5
Tukulti-Ninurta II, campaigns against Amme-Ba'li of Bît-Zamâni, against Kirruri, Muški, Urrupna, Išrun, Ladani and Lullu; campaign into Babylonia in 885 B.C., 38 212-216
Tulu, sounds of, 52 134, morphology, 135-139
ibn-Ṭūlūn, minaret of his mosque is of Mesopotamian type, 30 146-148
Tung, old gentleman of Loyang, see San-lao
T'ung, 獞, aborigines of Kuangsi; the women make ku poison, 55 11, 18
Tung-ching, Chinese constellation, usually grouped with the constellation kuei and called shun-shou, 55 310-311
Tung Chung-shu, Confucian advisor to Han Wu Ti, Memoir of, 58 435, his famous replies to examination questions, 435, famous memorials of, concerning statecraft, 448, influence of, upon the Emp., 437, 441, 448
Tung Chün, god of the sun, legend of, 53 61-62; see also Hsi Ho
Tung-hai-kung Wang, 東海恭王, funeral arrangements for Empress Têng's mother like those for, 51 152
Tung-hua Lu (and the Hsüan-t'ung Cheng-chi), derivation of the, see abstract, K. Biggerstaff
Tung-kuan, 東觀, the Palace Library in Later Han times, 51 151
T'ung-t'ien T'ai, erected by Han Wu Ti, 58 442
Tun-huang, Khotanese ms. fragment found at, with text of a Rama story, 59 397; frag. of ms. of the Hui-ch'ao-wang-wu-t'ien-chu-kuo-chuan, found there, 33 202, Chinese photographed some of texts from, 203; old seats of the Yüeh-chih were near, 37 97, locust swarms near, 110, Chinese army returns to, after abortive expedition against Ta-yüan, 110-112, second expedition leaves fr., 111, 112, 113, military governor at, 116; see also Manuscripts; Rāma Story, in Khotanese
Tuppa (Tupa, Tapa), god of Land Dyaks of Borneo, 26 166, 170-175; invoked at Land Dyak harvest festival, 29 257
Ṭur 'Abdīn, dialect of, see Syriac Language and Semitic Languages
Turanians, Iranian name for Hittites and Sumero-Akkadians, 35 295
Turfan Pahlavi, see Pahlavi, Turfan.
Turkey, Turks, Turkish, Oriental studies in, 59 229-231, museums in, 244-246; geographical foundation of her economic and political position, 36 168-180; agreement with Melissenus on division of certain territories; seizure of Anatolia, Phrygia, and Galatia, 30 26; relations with Byzantium and Rome in 568, notes on, 33 193-194, 206 n.1, Yang Ti's relations with the, 194, Persia subject to, 200; background of the Arab revolt of 1916, 37 153-161; treaties with Iran and Afghanistan since 1921, 49 368-369; see also Art and Architecture; Caliphate; Cilicia; Manuscripts; Uigurs
  Language: loan-words in Baghdad Arabic, 22 110; elements in Serbo-Croatian, surviving, 51 241-261, specimen, 243-245, phonetic variations, 246-250, grammatical peculiarities, 250 f., vocabulary of most commonly used, 251-261
  Literature: translated into English, 37 224
  Religion: new religious and moral ideals, eclectic nature of, 48 359
  Texts: Azarbayjani dialect, two poems in recited in connection with the 'āšūrā' festival, 39 113-116
Turki, Amīr, reorganized Wahhābis ca. 1824 and chose Riyāḍ as his capital, 37 157
Turki, Eastern, three periods of literary tongue, 49 185
Turkish-Manichaean script resembles Syro-Mandaean script from Nippur, 32 437
Turkistan, eastern, archeological expeditions to, 56 455-456; discoveries of rich hordes of Tibetan mss. in, 38 38; Buddhist wall-paintings from, 49 62-64
Turtle, kuei, used as a term of abuse, origin of, 53 64
T'u Shen, 土神, see Earth Gods
T'u Shu Pien, 圖書編, geographical work of the early 17th cent., errors in, 59 347
T'u shu tsi ch'eng, see Encyclopedias, Chinese
Tu-yü, 都尉, title of the military governor at Tun-huang in time of Han Wu Ti, 37 116
Tvaṣṭr's sacrifice, 55 387-389
"Twelve Classics", said by Chuang-tzŭ to have been interpreted by Confucius, 44 278

"Two Kwang, the", see Kwang-tung and Kwang-hsi
Tychsen, O.G., deceived by the fictitious Kitāb Dīwān Miṣr, 33 310
Tyre, pantheon of, 22 115-117
tzu, 子, "master" or "teacher", no longer a title of the feudal nobility in the Han era, 51 271
Tzu Ch'an, dates of, 57 441
al-Ubullah, port of Arab states on Persian Gulf, 35 35, 37-38
Ubulu, see al-Ubullah
Udāna as a form of breath in Hindu literature, 22 249-308
Udāyana, war of Pradyota with, 45 307
Udayana legend, Bhāsa's treatment of, 43 169
Ugarit, Ugaritic
Alphabet: developed from Babylonian syllabary in middle of 2nd millennium B.C., 55 101-102, is the original of the Phoenician alphabet, 102; unlikely that various forms of ' represent vowel plus ', 56 496-497, transcription of, 498
Language: a'> e' before medial ', 57 151-157; differs from Late Bronze Age Phoenician only in its more archaic character, 52 309; hwt, hyt, hmt, archaic pronominal forms, 56 440-441; k > g before z, 54 64; locative ending in -h, 58 139; orthography fixed, 55 96; qatala perfect of proto-Semitic origin, 60 418; š- causative used, 58 103-111, h-, '- causative, possible occurences of, 105-111, is historically older than the š- causative, 109-111; ṯ on way to becoming Aram. ṯ, 60 418; terminative hê in Hebrew and Ugaritic, 60 229-233; *yaqatalu used as present-future tense; tense-system difference from the West-Semitic, 57 239; yqtl theme serves as preterite; qtl limited to special circumstances, 58 266-267, qtl indicated continuous state, 268-285, used after imperative, 282-283, passives have force of real perfect, 284, stative form pa'il, 286-288, vocalization of, 285-289, closer to Akk. permansive than to W.-Sem. imperf., 289, yqtl is narrative tense, 289-293, subjunctive (not certain), 293-294, apocopate, 294-296, yaqa(t)tal(u) as present-future stem; vocalization of, 296-309; z̄ a Ḫurrian affricate or sibilant, 55 95-100
Religion: Ba'als crushed by 'Alēyân are deities of the deep and their associates, 55 271; Mōt, close parallel to Tammuz, 59 410; syncretistic character of, 53 101-102, 107, pantheon, 102-110
Texts: Conflict of Ba'al and the Waters, translation and notes to, 55 268-277; Danel text, notes on, 56 440-445; Mōt, conquest of, 52 221-231; notes to mythological texts, 53 97-123; notes to mythological texts, 54 60-66; Poem C, parallelism in, 54 80-82; second liturgical poem, 55 31-58; Virolleaud in Syria (1935), 247-266, myth of a spring, notes to, 56 226-231; Virolleaud Tablets 2 and 3, notes to, 55 89-94
Ugric peoples, divisions of, 56 447
Uigurs, Uigur, tax document from ca. A.D. 1350, 56 458-460, tax assessment, methods of, 460, notes on 11th-14th cent. history, 453-461; see also Central Asia, Painting
Ujjain, modern, a visit to, 23 307-313, remains of observatory at, 311 f., Bhartṛhari's cave in old, 313 f., two legends of old, 314-316
Umanu, unidentified western mountain mentioned in Gudea texts, 43 44
Umayyads, their struggle with the Byzantines over Constantinople gave rise to messianic hopes among the Jews, 47 364
Umm al-Ġayt (Mother of Rain), Muslim surrogate for the Virgin; attached to cult of Atargatis, 60 290-291
Umma, calendar of, 33 2, 7; see also Lagaš
Umman-manda, are not Scythians, but Medes, 44 126, 127
Unicorn, in folklore and religion, 51 276-278, unicorn ram of the Himalayas, 278; see also Ch'i Lin; Giraffe
United States National Museum, Jewish amulets in, 36 154-167; two Jewish amulets from Tunis in, 37 43-56; oriental antiquities in, 23 44-47; note on Far Eastern collections of; Siamese edition of the Tripiṭaka in, 23 47
United States of America, possibility for contribution of oriental studies to, 48 102-108; government publications, role in development of Philippine linguistic studies, 42 147-170; religion, characteristics; factors influencing it, 48 99-102
University Museum, Philadelphia, two great stone reliefs of the Horses of T'ang T'ai Tsung, "Curly" and "Autumn Dew," authenticity defended, 55 420-428
upadāna, see nidānas
Upaniṣads, what they seek and why, 49 97-121, compared with the Atharva-Veda, 98 f., power of esoteric knowledge, 97-121, "releases" and "attainments," 102 f., ātman 112-116, sat, 115 f.; bráhman, 116 f., summary, 118 f., epilog, 119 f.; text and translation of the Avyakta, 60 338-355; and the Bhagavad-Gītā, recurrent and parallel passages in the principal, 42 1-43, conspectus of passages relating to the 'channels of the heart', 6; use of chāyā in, 55 281-283; Deussen's translation of prāṇas, 22 256, 264 f.; Mahābhārata Yoga terminology compared with that of, 22 333-379; significance of the noetical terminology of the, 48 349; philosophy, sources, 36 197-204, Deussen's views, 197-199, spirit of, 199-202, stems from Vedic, 202; prāṇa and apāna in the, 39 107-111; prāṇa-series in the, 22 275-277, 286-302; presentation of a new translation for the principal, 41 182; syntax, dative, 28 388-392, verbs of speaking, 392-406; belonging to same stratum as Tantras, 23 67; the phrase ya evaṃ veda in the, 50 323; see also nidānas
Upī, Babylonian city situated near Iščali, 59 106-107
Ur (al-Muqayyar), description of site, 50 150, history of under rule of Lagaš, 152-153, 154, 155-158; beads from, 57 10 f., 14; herring-bone laid bricks a foreign importation, 55 205, Royal Cemetery dates from Early Dynastic to Akkadian period, 206-208
Uraiyūr, capital of Chōla state, in Greek writers, 33 212
Urarṭu, clashes with Assyria, 34 355; designated same territory as older Armânum (q.v.), 57 418; verb, passive concept of; distinction between trans. and intrans. vbs., 59 294; notes to texts in Corpus Insc. Chald., 55 294-302
Urbanism, early development of in ancient Near East, 59 421-422
Urga, Chinese name K'u-lun, 60 560
Ur-nammu, his accession ca. 2300 or 2475 B.C., 42 321
Ursis, Sabbatinus de, books by, prohibited in Japan, 57 292-294
Uru, name of a quarter of Lagaš, 57 309-312; see also Mar
Uruk, Belshazzar prominent in affairs of, 39 147; earliest kings of according to Hellenistic sources, 50 340; Kushite origin of first dynasty of, 49 312-313, 314-315, kings bore title of Horus, 315, 317; pre-Sargonid limestone tablet from, 38 188-196
Urukagina, calendar of, 33 1-2, 4-5
Urukugga, name of a quarter of Lagaš, 57 309-312
Urumia, lake and city of, 25 182 f.
Urumiah, concordance of the Peshitta, loss of in 1919, 43 128-129; reputed tomb of the Magi in, 26 83
Uśanas Kāvya, the three-headed Gandharvan, and Indra, the story of, 28 81-88; joins the Angels, 55 386 f.
Uṣṇih, the 12-syllable verse of, in the Vedas, 22 316 f.
Ušpia, early Assyrian king with Ḫurrian name, reigned just before 2000 B.C., 48 91
ušu wood, identified with storax (?), the su-ho-yu of the Chinese Annals (?), 42 176
ibn-'Utmān, Muḥammad, Moroccan ambassador to Naples in 1782, his relations with Giuseppe Vella, 33 309
Utnapištim, character of, 38 60-65; primitive account of in Deluge Story; Egyptian parallels to, 47 292-301
Utopia, Confucian, passage in the Li-chi on The Two Utopias, quote Legge tr. 54 68-69, three modern writers on the political theory of China, E.D. Thomas, L.S. Hsü and Liang Chi-chiao, misinterpret passage in Li-chi to refer to a future Utopia, 67-69, time of the Utopia, or "Grand Union", was in past, not future, 69, not Confucius' idea but a later interpolation of the Taoists, 67-69; Russian, of the Old Believers; called Byelovodiye, in the Kingdom of Oponia,

identified with Japan, 42 286-289, story founded upon the legend of Prester John, 289-294
Uttara-Rāmacarita, stage-emendations in the, 34 428-433
Uttarārcika and Pūrvārcika, relative age of, 52 388 f.
Uttu, Sumerian god of contracts, another form of the solar deity Utu, 40 73-74; form of Ištar; patron of commerce and cultural hero, 42 197-200
Vaccination, see Goddess of
Vagina, regarded by ancient oriental peoples as well or fountain, 39 69-70
Vagnoni, Alphonse, books by, prohibited in Japan, 57 292-294
Vaḥši, Persian poet (†1583), see Farhad va-Šīrīn
Vaiśālī, the destruction of, 45 308 f.
Vaiśeṣika Darśana, date of, determined from refutations of Buddhist doctrines, 31 1-29
Vaiśeṣika system, date of, 50 173
Vaiśyas, position in the Vedas, Brāhmaṇas, and Sūtras, 53 181-183
Vallabhadāsa version of the Vetālapañcaviṅśati, 55 59-61
Vallabhī, date of the council of, 52 393 f.
Vālmīki in the Mahābhārata, references to, 50 86 f., 102 f.
Valentinians, Syriac hymn in Greek letters in account of Epiphanius, 38 1-33, dates from middle of third cent., 31, theme is reconstitution of the Pleroma after the destruction of its harmony by the appearance of sin within it, 14, commentary on, 14-33
Van, see Ḫaldia
Vararuci, rules for Māgadhī and other Prākrit dialects, 44 82-96
Vardhamāna temple of Tiruparuttikunram, date of, 54 440
Varnish, (ch'i, 漆, = lacquer); the countries bet. Ferghana and Parthia produced no, 37 108
Varo, Francisco, author of Arte de la lingua Mandarine, 1703, see Asiatic Studies in Europe
Varsh Śrāddha ceremony, named Nīlohaha, 22 228
Varuṇa, assimilation to Ahi-Vṛtra, 55 391; as god of day and night, 55 407 f.; borrowed by Indo-Iranians from Mitanni, 43 428; consubstantial with Mitra, 55 410; as world-king and savior, 45 280-286, etymology of name, 280, relations with the waters, 283 f.
Varvaro family, owners of Arabic MSS forged by Giuseppe Vella, 33 311-312
Vāsavadattā, Sarup's edition of The Vision of, 49 74 f.; Śivarāma's commentary on, 24 57-63
Vasisthas, relation of Indra to other gods among, 36 249, 265 f.
Vasubandhu, Indian Buddhist philosopher 4th cent. A.D., 51 291-292, author of the Vijñaptimātratāsiddhi, Viṁśatikā and Triṁśikā, 291-292, 302, the Viṁśatikā, 295, 299-301, Hsüan Chuang's tr., the Wei-shih-er-shih lun, 291, 295, 299-300, 304-307, the Triṁśikā, 302-304, Hsüan's tr., the Ch'eng-wei-shih-lun, 304, author of the Abhidharmakaśāstra, Chinese tr. Chü-she-lun, 296-297, 302, and of the Pañcaskandhaśāstra, Chinese tr. Wu-yün-lun, 296, 303; note on tr. of his work by Prof. Hamilton, 60 115-116
Vāsudeva, Kushāna ruler, coins of, 56 429-439
Vātadūta, Kṛṣṇanātha as author of commentary on, 23 79
Vatsarāja, in Harṣa's dramas and the Kathāsaritsāgara, 21 89
Vault, primitive method of building described by Theophilus Presbyter (10th cent.), 59 109-110
Vāyu, and breath, 22 251, 288; association with Indra as god of fertility, 36 247, 249; Vāyu Purāṇa, relation of the Brahmāṇḍa to, 43 130 f.; Vāyu Yantra, 23 67; vyāna as, 22 271
Veda, Vedas, Vedic, chant, character, 52 390 f.; chronology, summary of the situation now existing with respect to, 54 112 f.; commentaries, prāṇa and apāna in the, 39 105 f.; concordance of Bloomfield, additions to, 29 284 f.; Concordance, on certain work in continuance of the, 29 286-298; hymns, relative chronology of, 21 42-49; hymns, classification of, 21 45 f., 49; hymns, classification of, 22 309-320; conception of the king in the, 51 309 f.; literature, Rudra in, 43 56-60; metres, development of, 22 313-318; mind as wish-car in, 39 280-282; philosophy, Upaniṣad stems from, 36 202, plan of index of, 202 f.; soma plant, identity of, 45 351 f.; studies in the, 40 89-92; variants, 29 289-298; Vedic and postvedic chronology, 52 391
Language: adhi-brū and adhi-vāc in the, 36 213-225; anyedyúḥ, ubhayedyúḥ (ubhayadyúḥ), 59 425-430; archaisms of Mahābhārata and Rāmāyaṇa, 25 93-96; dhénā 'prayer, song,' 46 303-308; preference for diiambus and syllabic lengthening, 21 50-52; dual ending -āu, -ā, 21 47 f.; forms of the dual, 23 318-324; dual of bodily parts, 30 155-185; dual, elliptic, 32 33-44, dvandva, 34-53, their origin and relationship, 54-57; dual in similes, 35 16-30; instrumental plural endings -ais, -ebhis, 21 48; k-suffixes, kinds, 31 95-108, saṃdhi of stem-finals before, 109-113, diminutives formed by secondary, 125-150; k-suffixes, 31 296-342; perfect, value of, 49 64-66; posterius -pitvam 'cover (night)', 39 261-264; syntactical compounds, 21 51 f.; syntax, dative and genitive after bhū and ásti, 28 260-367, of ūtí and other forms with bhū, 367-371, gerundives hávya and ī́dya with the dative, 371-374, construction of verbs of speaking in RV. and AV. 374-388; Vedic, Sanskrit, and Prakrit, 32 414-428; Vedic, Sanskrit, and Middle Indic, 33 145-149; attraction to the vocative, 31 64 f.
Religion: sources of elements of Buddhist iconography, 57 116 f.; deities, Mitra, Varuṇa, Indra, and the Nāsatyas, borrowed by Indo-Iranians from Mitanni, 43 428; fire-worship, 49 177 f.; hieratic and popular hymns, 21 46-49; horse-sacrifice (aśvamedha), 54 109-114, 123 f., evidence of its performance from inscriptions and coins, 111 f.; its origin, 113 f.; Indra as god of fertility in, 36 242-268; magic in, 55 319-323; mysticism in, 48 87 f.; ontology, an essay in: Angel and Titan; Devas and Asuras consubstantial in essence, 55 373-419; ṛcīṣama, epithet of Indra, 21 50-52; sacrifice, the home of, 48 200-224; hymn to Sūrya, translation and exegesis of RV. 1.115, 58 419-434; vidátha, the place of worship and sacrifice, 48 200-224; vṛjána, spot within the vidátha selected for sacrifice, 48 200 f., 219-224; Yoga practices in, 43 60-65
vedanā, see nidānas
Vedāṅga Jyotiṣa, date of the, 52 391
Vedānta philosophy, in the Bhartṛharinirveda of Harihara, 25 198; in Śvetāśvatara Upaniṣad, 22 386 f.
Vedāntasāra, prāṇa-series in, 22 305 f.
Vedantins, believe veins start from heart, 22 308
Veiling of women practised in Assyria before 1100 B.C., 41 11, 34-38
Vella, Giuseppe, author of the forged Kitāb Dīwān Miṣr, 33 308-312
Vellay on the Adonis myth, 26 413 f.
Veṅgī sculpture, interpretation, 54 220
Venice, Oriental policy at end of 14th and beginning of 15th cent. not consistent, 45 176
Ventriloquism, practised in Babylonian exorcism, 40 218
Verbiest, author of the first Manchu grammar, 60 555
Veron, see also Piśāca
Vetālapañcaviṅśati, in the Bṛhatkathāmañjarī and the Kathāsaritsāgara, 53 125 f.; versions and interpolations, 55 59-62
Veterinary medicine, see Medicine
Vibhāṣās and bhāṣās, 44 93-95
Vidanvat, Tāṇḍya Brāhmaṇa story of, 26 63 f., Vidanvat and Cyavana, Jaiminīya Brāhmaṇa story of, text and translation, 64-67
Viddhaśālabhañjikā of Rājaśekhara, editions of the, 27 2 f.; Prakrit of, 3 f., source of name of, 4, plot of, 4 f., time of, 5, dramaturgy of, 5 f., unusual words in, 7, translation of, 8-71
Vidiśā in the Mahāvīracaritra, 45 308
vijñāna, see Monkey climbing a Tree
Vijñānamātra, see Vijñaptimātra
Vijñānavāda refuted in philosophical Sūtras of Brahmans, 31 1-29

Vijñaptimātra, Vijñānamātra, Indian system of philosophy, Chinese Wei Shih, 51 291-292, 306, distinction bet. the two, 305-307, basic texts the Vijñaptimātratāsiddhi, Viṁśatikā and Triṁśikā, 291; see also Wei Shih
Vijñaptimātratāsiddhi, Viṁsátikā written before the Triṁśikā, 53 147-148; see also Buddhism; Vasubandhu
Vikrama, his birth and accession, a story of, 55 59-88; and Kālī, legend of, 23 316 f.; and Kālidāsa, Ujjain legend of, 22 331 f.; Saṃvat dates, the conversion of, 58 668-669; Vikrama-legend, the motif of "three boys born under the same star," 55 62-88, the version in India Office MS. 2688c (Eggeling 4095), 63-88, new or lexical words, grammatical points, text, commentary, 69-87
Vikramacarita, Persian version, frame-story of the, 55 66-68, Jainistic version, frame story of, 66 f.
Vikramādityacarita story containing reminiscences of Vedic myth of Aja Ekapād, 53 329-331
Vikramorvaśī of Kālidāsa, bibliography of, 23 98-101
Village, Name-terminations, Japanese, 31 161-162; see also Feudalism in Japan: Iya-yama villages
Vimalakīrti Sūtra, as a theme for Chinese Buddhist sculpture, 51 366
Viṁśatikā, see Vasubandhu
Vīṇā, the old Indian, 51 47-50; the parts of a, 50 244-253, representations of the, 244, references in literature, to, 244 f., description and use, 245 f., terms for parts, 246-252, another instrument, 252 f.; the parts of a, 57 101-103; additional references to parts of a, 51 285
Vine, seeds of the grape-, imported fr. Ferghana and planted near the Chinese Imperial Summer Palaces, 37 108; see also Wine
Vinītaprabha, 毘膩多鉢臘婆, Indian monk and author, teacher of Hsüan Chuang, 51 302-303
Vīra, birth and family, 45 301 f.; death, date of, 56 372; nirvāṇa, date of, 52 393
Viracocha-Panchacamac, hymn addressed to Peruvian god, 37 83
Visayan, see Bisayan
Viṣṇu, boar an avatar of, 55 389; slays boar with Indra, 55 389 f.; characteristics found in Puruṣa, 51 108-114; as Rāma in the Mahābhārata, references to, 50 94 f., 102; as savior, 45 288; approximate date of the writer on law, 51 81 fn.
Viṣṇudharmottara, chapter XLI, 52 13-21, translation, 13 f., commentary, 14-21
Viṣṇuite creation story in Mahābhārata, 45 61
Vištāsp, first propagated Zoroastrianism in Sagastān, 36 116, 119
Vištaspa of the Avestan, the identification of the father of Darius with the, 53 201-203
Viśvarūpa, common traits with Agni and Sūrya, 55 389; as a Brahman, 55 387; son of Tvaṣṭṛ, 55 385; and Vṛtra, 55 383-389
Vitae prophetarum, late Hellenistic-Jewish work, Greek, Latin, Armenian, Syriac and Ethiopic versions of, 55 200, earliest Christian interpolations are from 3rd-4th cent., 200
Vohumanah in the Gāthās, 21 67-87
Vonum dialect of Formosa, loss of l in, 36 185
von Zach, Erwin, biographical notes, 56 94
Vratārka of Śaṃkara's account of Sāvitrī story and rite, 21 53-66
Vṛtra, identified with Ahi, 55 390 f.; as a dragon, 45 285 f.; slain by Indra, 55 385-387; as Soma, 55 382; and Viśvarūpa, 55 383-389; as winter cold, 36 267
Vṛttikāra, conjectural authorship of, 31 15-18
Vyāna as a form of breath in Hindu literature, 22 249-308
Vyankatesha stotra of Devadāsa, 46 345
Vyāsabhāṣya, world development as stated in, 45 66
WaChagga, concepts of right and left among the, 58 205, 209
Wagons, and carts with Chinese army against Ta-yüan, 37 112
Wahhābism, Wahhābis, Wahhābi, ibn-Taymīyah its forerunner, 56 3-4; rise of in Arabia, 37 156-159; spread of in Arabia, 47 119 ff.
Wai-alā, see Piśāca
Wakan Sansai Zue, article on tobacco in the, 58 650
wakizashi, Japanese short sword, 26 349
Waley, Arthur, identified figure represented with the horse on the sculpture of "Autumn Dew", 55 423
Walis (shrines), asylums in modern Palestine; bloody sacrifice at, 25 312-313
Wall, see Great Wall
Wall-paintings, Assyrian, 22 31-32; Central Asia, technique of slight relief for jewellry, etc. in use at end of 8th cent., A.D., 57 330
Wall-paper, a Chinese invention, intro. into Europe and America; in colonial houses in Mass., sources of information, 47 73-74
Walters Art Gallery (Baltimore), seals from Western Asia in, 58 528
Wan Fo Hsia, remarks on wall-paintings at, 59 155-156
Wang An Shih, biographical notes on, 56 99-100, Chinese sources for study of, 100-101; placing of his tablet next to that of Mencius in the Confucian temple explained, 57 441-442
Wang Ch'ung, his cynicism in regard to the crow in the sun and the hare in the moon, 55 186; cynicism regarding the Grave of Yü, 56 62
Wang Hsi-ch'i, compiler of the ts'ung shu, Hsiao fang hu chai yü ti ts'ung ch'ao, 51 44, 45-46
Wang Hsü, Chinese official of Han, see Lo-Lang
Wang Hüan-ts'e, punitive expedition of, against Magadha in 648, 38 34, 36
Wang Hu-erh, Taoist, visit to House of Ch'eng-kung Hsing, 53 228
Wang K'uei, 王恢, leader of caravans to the west, 37 106, created Marquis of Hao 浩, 106, attached to the army against Ta-yüan, 110
Wang K'ui, see Wang K'uei
Wang Kuo-wei, modern scholar of the bronze inscriptions, 56 349
Wang Mang, outstanding reforms of, were Confucian ideals translated into governmental practices, 58 446; reforms of ineffective or a burden to the people; list of, see abstract, H.H. Dubs
Wang Nah Museum, Bangkok, archeological objects of ancient Siam, 29 283
Wang P'u (or Pu or Fu), on tobacco, 58 651
Wang Shen-shêng, 王申生, a military governor, a leader of second expedition against Ta-yüan, killed outside Yü-ch'êng, 37 113-114
Wang Shih-chen, on tobacco, 58 654
Wang Shön-shöng, see Wang Shen-shêng
Wan Shou Shan, new summer palace, regulations for building supplies and furnishings of, 49 234, the imperial garden, 235, hauling to north gate; foundry rules for casting the bronze pavilion, 240, references to, 242
Wang Tsang, tutor and advisor to Han Wu Ti, nearly succeeded in making Confucianism the sole philosophy of the gov., 58 437-440
Wang Yang-ming, true follower of Mencius, 50 237
Wan yu wen k'u, 萬有文庫, a ts'ung shu pub. by the Commercial Press, 1928, 51 42
Wāqwāq, see Folklore, Arab
War, influence of, on religion of Kayans and Sea Dyaks of Borneo, 25 231-247; On the Art of War, see Sun-tzu
Warburg, Felix M., life and works, 58 505
Ward, William Hayes, life and works of, 36 233-241
Wāsiṭi, ibn-al-, author of the Kitāb Radd 'ala Ahl al-Dimmah wa-man Tabi'ahum, 41 384
Water, lustration with as symbol of rebirth, 56 157-159; transportation by in early Babylonia, 43 173
Water of life, in Semitic mythology, 26 19
Water-buffalo, domesticated, in early China, question of, 60 581

Waterways, China, pre-Han, 55 303, under Han Wu Ti, 303-306, Hsi-an and the T'ai-hu region centers of canal transportation, 303, boom in waterways for transport and irrigation under Han Wu Ti, 304-305, song of the Pai Canal, tr. from Ch'ien Han-shu, 305, proposal of T'ing Nien to change entire course of Yellow River to remove threat of the Hsiung Nu, 303, 305, the Yellow River changes its course of itself, 305-306, argument of dikes versus new channels, 306, strength of the Yü tradition, 303, 305, 306; see also Flood Control; Irrigation; Shui-ching Yellow River

Weapons, the composite bow as an intrusion fr. Asia to N. America, 51 100; tasselled daggers, fr. Shu and Han, not to be manufactured, 51 147

Weather, Arab proverbs about, 52 145-158

Weaving, see Textiles

Wednesday, Passion revealed to Disciples on, 32 319-320, 338, 342

Weeks, feast of, see Festivals (Hebrew)

Wei Chieh, 韋節, author of a lost work, Hsi-fan-chi, 西蕃記, sent on expedition to Western Turkestan by Yang Ti, 30 6

Weights and Measures

Chinese: foot has 10 inches, 42 56, 57; li, when used in western Asiatic itineraries, is the 30th part of a parasang (or a stadium), 30 54; li, in countries west of Ta-yüan, in time of Han Wu Ti, = a stadium, 37 139

Hebrew: 10-gerā weight, 24 384-386, nsp-weight, 386-387, inscribed half-shekel, 206-208; fifth-shekel weight from Sabastīyah, in Clark collection, 27 400

Hittite: weight in shape of human head, from Clark collection, 27 400-401

Phoenician: prismatic stater weight, 24 208-209

Sabastīyah: stone duck 1/7- shekel from, 27 401

Wei Kuang (Weī Kuang), 衛廣, general sent against the K'un-ming tribes in 109 B.C., 37 104

Wei-lio, An-ts'ai = A-lan according to, 30 39 and n.1, 41; note on, 30 46 n.2, refers to Alexandria, Egypt, as Wu-ch'ih-san, 46-47; see also Passages

Wei Shih, 唯識, Vijñaptimātra system of Buddhist philosophy, Hsüan Chuang as translator of its texts, 51 291-308, doctrine of, 292, translators and teachers in Hsüan Chuang's time and earlier, 295-307, Hsüan's knowledge of the She-ta-sheng-lun, 296, 299, 302, 303, Paramārtha's tr. and influence in spreading the system in China, 298-300, Hsüan promotor rather than founder, 291, 299, the Yogācāryabhūmiśāstra (Shih-ch'i-ti-lun) and Hsüan's tr. of it, the Yü-chia-shih-ti-lun, 297-302, the Wei-shih-er-shih-lun, Hsüan's tr. of the Vijñaptimātratāsiddhi, Viṁśatikā, compared with Paramārtha's and Prajñāruci's, 295, 299-301, the Ch'eng-wei-shih-lun, Hsüan's tr. of the Triṁśikā, with its 10 combined commentaries, 292, 304, Hsüan's trs. of other Wei Shih treatises, 303-304, discovery in 1922 of original Sanskrit texts of the Viṁśatikā and the Triṁśikā, 291-292, publication in 1930, 292, Poussin's French tr. of the Ch'eng-wei-shih-lun, 293, Suzuki's Studies in the Lankavatara Sutra suggest parallel doctrine, 293; K'uei Chi's commentary on Hsüan Chuang's tr. of Vasubandhu's Vijñaptimātratāsiddhi, Viṁśatikā, 53 144-151

Wei-shih-er-shih-lun, 唯識二十論, comments on, by Hsüan Chuang during tr. as compiled by K'uei Chi, 53 145-148, compared with the Ch'eng-wei-shih-lun, 147; see also Vasubandhu; Hsüan Chuang

Wei-shih-er-shih-lun-hui-i, 唯識二十論會譯, collection of the three trs. of the Viṁśatikā, by Prajñāruci, by Paramārtha, and by Hsüan Chuang, 51 295

Wei-shih-er-shih-lun-shu-chi, 唯識二十論述記, commentary on the Wei-shih-er-shih-lun, see K'uei Chi

Wei-shih-san-shih-lun, 唯識三十論, Chinese title for the Triṁśikā by Vasubandhu, 51 291, Hsüan Chuang's study of the Triṁśikā, 302-303; see also Wei Shih

Wei Shou, 魏收, of Northern Ch'i, author of the Wei Shu; see Wei Shu

Wei Shu, 魏書, by Wei Shou, 魏收, history of, 52 35-45, the Pei Shih, 北史, chief source of information about the, 36-41, later history of the work, 41; historical documents available to Wei Shou, 36-38, his helpers, 38-39, completed in four years, 38, 39, dissatisfaction with and revision of, 40-41, other histories of Northern Wei borrowed fr. Wei Shou's, 41-42, Sung editors supplied missing sections fr. unstated sources, 42-43, great mix-up now of parts fr. the various histories, 43-45; on Taoism, tr. of chap. 114, with notes, 53 218-243; see also Corrigenda & Addenda, 54 290-294

Weī Tsié, see Wei Chieh

"Wei Tzu", a book of the Shu-ching, a Chou forgery, 56 335 n.1

Wei Wan, Chancellor in 143 B.C., 57 175; tool of the Confucianists in their fight against Legalists, 58 438

Wei Wen-hsiu, 韋文秀, sent to Mount Sung to mix elixir, 53 239

Well, ancient Semitic metaphor for vagina, 39 69-70; oriental metaphor for wife, 36 418-420

Wen, 文, literature, used by Confucius to indicate the ancient documents, 44 275

Wen Ch'ang, 文昌, God of Literature, prayer to, 49 136-137 and n.1-4

Wên-ch'êng, Chinese princess (kung-chu) married to Tibetan King Sroṅ-btsan, 38 34

Wen Chiao Ch'ang Mīng, 文教昌明, Society, 49 130 n.2

Wen Hsiang (520-548), time of, Taoist temple built, 53 249, 54 294

Wên Hsüan, earliest anthology of Chinese literature, about 530 A.D., important in philology and phonetics, 56 94

Wen hsüan lou ts'ung shu, 文選樓叢書, by Jüan Yüan, 51 41-42

Wên hsüeh, title of certain scholars in the Imperial University, 58 441

Wen-li, Bible and Prayer-Book tr. into, by Bishop Schereschewsky, 39 149

Wen-shan, 汶山, a district created by Han Wu Ti in southwest Ssu-ch'uan, corresponding to modern Mou-chou, 37 104, 151

Wen Shū, 文殊, see Ti Tsang, prayer to

Wên Ta-ya, 温大雅, first Recorder of T'ang history, follower and aide of Li Yüan in his campaigns, author of the Court Journal of the Founding of the Great T'ang which differs fr. other accounts in that it makes out Li Yüan to be the real leader, not Li Shih-min, 57 368-374, tr. of his Biography fr. the Chiu T'ang-shu, 370-372, other sources of information indicate early writing of the Journal, 372-373, probable date of death, 373-374, depicts T'ang Kao-tsu as actual founder, 246

Wen Ta-yu, 温大有, biographical data on, 57 370, 373-374

Wen Yen-po, 温彥博, biographical data on, 57 370, 371, 373-374

The West Chamber, see Book Reviews, Hart, H.H.

West China Border Research Society, organization of, 56 98

Western Chou Dynasty, documents of, in the Shu-ching, the I-ching, the Book of Poetry, possibly of the I Li and the Kuo Yü, 56 336-337 and n. 4, 6, 7, bronze inscriptions of, 337

Western Influence, on Chinese architecture and furnishings, hooks, walls dials, and "western ocean" pagoda top mentioned in lists, 49 242

"Western Sea", 西海, of the Chinese = the Mediterranean, Persian Gulf, or Indian Ocean, according to which trade route was taken, 33 195; Caspian or Aral, 37 95, Persian Gulf, Red Sea, or Mediterranean, 97, terms discussed, 147

Wheat (barley ?), grown in Ta-yüan, 37 95, in An-hsi, 97, 150; wild ancestor (Triticum dicoccum dicoccoides) of, found in Palestine, 39 175, 176; wild (emmer), always found in Near East along with wild barley, 39 176

"Wheel of Life", see Symbols, Symbolism

White, John G., collection of oriental literature in the Cleveland Public Library, 36 421-422, 40 140, 57 239

White, John Williams, death of, 37 168

"White-Footed Crow", see Horses of T'ang T'ai Tsung
Whitney's material on the Atharva-Veda, 44 157
Widgery collection of Arabic MSS in Princeton University Library, 46 343
Widow of Pa, 巴寡婦清, see Biography, Chinese
Wieger, Creel's criticism of his Caractères Chinois and his tr. of a typical bronze inscription, 56 345-349
Wife, referred to in oriental literature under metaphors "well" and "field," 36 418-420
Williams, E.T., contributions of to Chinese studies, 38 101-102
Williams, Prof. Frederich Wells, contributions of to Chinese studies, 38 99-100
Williams, Dr. S. Wells, Founder of the Chinese Repository, contributions of to Chinese historical studies, 38 99
Wind, Chinese belief that it generates worms, 55 3, 5-6; baneful, Arab names of, 38 161
Wine, in ancient China, beer a better term, 60 583; fr. grapes, in Ta-yüan, 37 95, 108, in An-hsi, 97, in China, 107; of Izalla in N Mesopotamia, famous in ancient times, 38 226; unfermented and unmixed, used in communion by Armenians, Jews and Ḥarrānians, 32 273, 316-317, 340, mixed, drunk by Christians, 324, unmixed, not to be used in offering, 337, 340, nor drunk as memorial to dead, 339; favorable and unfavorable views of in Pentateuchal codes, 33 180-192, forbidden to Hebrew priests, 184-186; see also Grapes; Offerings; Vine
Winternitz, Moriz, life and works of, 57 216 f.
Wisdom of Amenemopet, parallels to in the Book of Proverbs, 45 372
Witchcraft, witches, see Black Magic; Magic
Wolf, a She-, legendary wet-nurse of King of the Wu-sun exposed in the wilderness, 37 100, the she-wolf in mythology of many Turkish tribes, 150-151
Woman, Women, created from bicorporal man, 58 545; place of in the Assyrian law code, 41 6-50; of Central Asian countries, reported in China to have great influence with their husbands, 37 108; Chinese, see Biography, Empress Têng; Pan Chao; Widow of Pa; status of in Hammurabi Code, 36 10, 24-31; position in Indian caste system, 53 182 f.; position of, among the Kayans and mountaineers of Formosa, 27 211; position of among Muslims of Borneo, 33 325-327, 332; position and influence among the Sea Dyaks, 25 240-243
Women's Kingdom, confusion of two "Women's Kingdoms", 38 41,n.26
Wonders of Sagastān, see Afdīyā va-Sāyakīh-ī Damīg-ī Sagastān
Wondjina paintings of Australia, 58 66-68
Wŏn-shan, see Wen-shan
Wood, Irving F., death of, Aug. 1934, 55 348
Wood Work, Chinese, regulations for work on large timbers of palaces and temples, 1727-1750, 49 236, pillars, timbers for bridges, gates, etc., 237, wood finishing, 237, painting of woodwork, 237, 242, furniture making, 237, wood carving, 236, 237
Woods, James Haughton, death of, Jan. 1935, 55 348
Word-lists
Akkadian: 24 96-102; 27 297-300; 28 182; 48 179-182
Arabic: 29 182-183; words pertaining to date culture, 35 208-212; date-palm, names for various parts of, 42 344-354; names of scale-insects attacking the date-palm, 42 205-206; root-doublets, 43 422-423; root-doublets with w and r, 43 423-424; medical terms, bibliography of, 50 112-113
Egyptian, Old: Hamitic words in, 37 21
Egypto-Semitic: 37 21; 39 142; 41 177; 43 165; 45 362; parts of body, names of, 46 351-352; 46 356-357; 47 198-237
Greek: philosophical terms with Syriac equivalents, 35 315-317
Hamitic: words in Old Egyptian, 37 21
Hamito-Semito-Egyptian: 46 356-357
Persian, New: names of parts of the date-palm, 42 347-351
Phoenician: 57 398-409
Semito-Egyptian: 37 21; 39 142; 41 177; 43 165; 45 362; parts of the body, names of, 46 351-352; 46 356-357; 47 198-237
Sumerian: 24 116-128; 25 49-67; 28 180-182; 29 187-191; 30 70-71; 30 97-100; 30 319-324; 30 329-335; 31 399-402; 33 25, 27, 28, 30
Syriac: philosophical terms with Greek equivalents, 35 315-317
Ugaritic: 52 229-231
World View, of the Chinese, as contained in Model Emperor lore, 56 52, as grew up in late Chou, 71, 74
Worms, worm-ku a variety of Black Magic, 55 7, 8, generated by the wind, 3, 5-6; see also chin-tsan
Wrestlers, at court of Han Wu Ti, 37 107
Writing, begins in Mesopotamia at end of Uruk period, 59 Supp. IV, 20-21, 25, 26; Chinese, on oracle bones and Yin pottery, with a brush, 56 335 and n.2, a chronological development in the form of characters on oracle bones, 346 n.33, on bronzes, 344-346; changes in the writing of the character kuo 國, "country", due to modern political change, 46 58-60; cuneiform, not of Sumerian origin, 39 269-270; Khotanese, a Central Asian Gupta derived fr. India; similarity to Tibetan due to derivation fr. same source, 38 43-45; Mayan system of, 39 162; Parthian, painted characters on parchment reported by Chang Ch'ien 37 97; pictographic, illustrated by American Indian records, 39 160, Egyptian, not derived from Babylonia, 169-170; Siamese alphabet, 44 11-28; Tibetan, origin of, 38 34-46, no writing before 630 A.D., 34-36, Tradition that King Sroṅ-btsan sgam-po sent T'on-mi in 632 to India to gather materials for a Tibetan alphabet, 35-38, 42-43, system of writing established bet. 630 and 648 based on mid. Indian writing of the 7th cent., 35-38, 43-46, refutation of the theory of Francke and Hoernle that Tibetan writing was based on Khotanese, 38-46; tradition of a former system of writing, which was lost, found among the Kachin, Naga, and Karen, also the Dayak of Borneo and the Ainu of Saghalin, 45 191; see also Records
Writing brush, Chinese, not invented by Meng T'ien, 56 534; see also Oracle Bones; Embassies; Meng T'ien
Wu-ch'ih-san, see Alexandria, Egypt
Wu Jên-chieh, 12th cent. author of the Liang-han-k'an-wu-p'u-i; note on early Chinese terms applying to copper, bronze and other metals, 37 109 n.6
Wu Jŏn-kié, see Wu Jên-chieh
Wu State, Non-Chinese, lower Yangtse, invasion of Ch'u, 6th cent. B.C., 41 302, elephant used in constructing a royal tomb of, 302; rich in the Han period, 40 183
Wu-ku Rebellion under Han Wu Ti, mention of De Groot's misunderstanding of, 55 6 n.13
wu kuei, "black devil", does not apply to the cormorant, 52 268
Wundt's theory of totemism, 38 157 f.
Wu Shao, 吳劭, practiced Taoist callisthenics, 53 239
Wu-sun, 烏孫, a nation near Lake Issyk-kul, probably of Turkish stock, 37 151, location and description as reported by Chang Ch'ien, 37 95, 96, 134, legendary origin of their king, 100, independence won fr. the Hsiung-nu, 100-101, migration west fr. their original territory in the Kansu corridor, 100-101, 134, Chinese embassies to and alliance with, 101-102, marriage alliance with China, 101, 103, 106, horses fr., compared with those fr. Ta-yüan, 103, 107, China's prestige with, 106, 111, half-hearted aid to China against Ta-yüan, 114; attacked by the Hsiung-nu, 30 40
Wu Tso-hai, friend of Ricci, acclaimer of his Map, 59 344, 358
Wu Tsung-tao, artist of 11th cent., engraver of the picture on the Stele of the Picture of the Six Horses, 55 427
Wylie, Alexander, estimate of his tr. of the Story of Chang Ch'ien in the Ch'ien-han-shu, 37 90; on the tr. of san i fen shen, on the Nestorian Tablet, 58 390-391
Xenophon (Anab. 3 4. 7), account of the fall of Nineveh in, 28 99-107

Ya-chou-fu, see also P'o; Hsi
Yahweh, anthropomorphic conception of in Little Covenant, 38 129-132; not found in cuneiform texts before 8th cent. B.C., 54 301; not of Kenite origin, 54 301-302; represented by image in ark and by bull images at Bethel, 47 358
Yājñavalkya, approximate date of, 51 81 fn.
Yajur-Veda, White, prāṇa-series in the, 22 257
Yakṣa, exchanging sex with a, 47 14-16
Yakṣas, functions and connection with waters, 51 286 f.
Yale University Library, Arabic MSS in, 39 142
Yaman, under Turkish control since 1872, 37 159; the, treaty with Italy, 47 123
Yang and Yin, mulberry wood buds early, so possesses much yang, 42 56, mouth of the bull (image used in ceremony of Reception to Spring), if open, indicates the year belongs to the male principle, if shut, to the female principle, 57, if tail of bull on left, the year belongs to yang; if on right, to yin, 57
Yang Chu, rating of, in "Table of Ancient and Modern Men"; see Chinese Thought
Yang Liang, first and only early commentator on Hsün-tzu, 51 31
Yang Ti, Emp. of China, Sui dynasty; his desire to have communication with as many countries as possible, 30 5-6, tried in vain to open intercourse with Fu-lin and T'ién-chu, 5, 8; unsuccessful attempt of to open communication with Fu-lin, 33 193, 194-197, his vanity and extravagance caused revival of trade with the West, 196
Yao, 堯, one of the three sage heroes of Chinese antiquity, upon traditions of whom was based the Model-Emperor Lore of China, 56 51-76, traditions concerning, 53-56, 63-66, connection of myth of 10 suns with, 64
Yao Ching-su, 姚景蘇, painter, in Paris, see Yao Ping-jan; Painting, Chinese
Yao Lü, on tobacco, 58 648-649
Yao Ping-jan, 姚丙然, father of Yao Ching-su; see Painting, Chinese
Yao Ting-han, 姚定漢, former ambassador to Ta-yüan, proposes war, 37 110
Yasaka Jinsha, see Gion Jinsha
Yaughandarāyaṇa, in Harṣa's dramas, 21 89
Yau Ting-han, see Yao Ting-han
Yāvana, merchants of; name included Ionians or Greeks, Graeco-Bactrians and Parthians, Greeks fr. Egypt and Syria; carpenters fr. worked on the Chola palace, 37 245
Yayāti, story of rejuvenation of, 26 3
Yazd, pronunciation of Avestan by Zoroastrian priests of, 25 184
Yazīdis, connect their name with Yazd, in Persia, 51 334, Šayḫān group is situated N of Mosul, 334-335, knowledge of Arabic among, 335, unreliability of their traditions, 335; common origin with 'Ali-Illāhis, 33 ii-iii; of vicinity of Tiflis, description of, 25 178-181
Year, tropic, discovered by Babylonian astronomer Kidinas, 46 87
Year-names, first use of by Han Wu Ti, 59 152, 287
Yeh, 鄴, N. Honan, Taoist altar established at, in E. Wei period, 53 242, 249
Yellow River, 黃河, supposed to pass through Lopnor, 37 95, imaginary source near Khotan, 107, source of, supposed to have been discovered by Chang Ch'ien, 107, 116, 135; changes in its course, in 132 B.C. and later in Han, 55 304, 305-306, canals from, pre-Han, 303, Han canals, 304, proposal of T'ing Nien to change entire course of river to remove threat of Hsiung Nu, 305; legend of Yü connected with opening of Lung Mên and an ancient overflowing of the, 56 59-61, Kun a god of the, 60
Yen Chih-t'ui, 顏之推, biographical notes on, 60 194 n.3
Yen Fa-shih, 嚴法師, a Buddhist teacher of Hsüan Chuang, 51 295
Yen Li-pen, artist of 7th cent., his painting of the Six Horses of T'ang T'ai Tsung referred to in the inscription on the Stele of Yu, 55 427
Yen Shih-ku, great commentator, note on, 55 337
Yen T'ieh Lun, 鹽鐵論, by Huan K'uan, 桓寬, fl. 81-49 B.C., contains 129 quotations and direct citations fr. 20 different books then extant, 51 266-275
Yermak Timofeyevich in Russian folk poetry, 43 206-215, in historical songs, 206-211, in the byliny, 211-215
Yeshu' yabh, powerful Nestorian Patriarch at Ctesiphon, 628-682 A.D., 33 201-202
Yezd, Zoroastrian priests of, their pronunciation of Avestan, 25 184
Yezīdis, so-called devil-worshippers, around Tiflis, 25 178-181, customs of, 180 f.
Yezo, the Ainu of, see Ainu, Language
Yi, East and West, of Yünnan, ku magic among, 55 19; see also Pa Yi
Yima, a solar deity, 36 317-32, story of his winter of Babylonian origin, 319-320
Yin and Yang, 陰陽, pestilence among cattle a result of lack of harmony between, 49 150; when out of balance, cause of trouble in the Empire, 51 150; nature of, in connection with human personalities, see Jen Wu Chih
Yin Dynasty, name Shang preferred, 56 335 n.1; see also Shang Dynasty
Yin Shih, 陰氏, mother of the Empress Têng, of Later Han, 51 138, raised to rank of hsin-yeh-chün, 新野君, 149, rank of chang-kung-chu, 長公主, 151, title ching-chün, 敬君, 152
Ying-ki, Ignatius, on the tr. of san i fen shen, 58 390
Ying Tou Shen, 迎痘神, see Goddess of Vaccination
Yin Hou, 陰后, First consort of Ho Ti, 和帝, Emperor of Later Han, 51 141 n.15, estranged, 142, hatred of Têng family, 142, dethroned 102 A.D., 143, death of, 143, and n.22, post-humously pardoned, 149
Yin ping shih wen chi, 飲冰室文集, collected writings of Liang Ch'i-ch'ao, 51 44
Yi-yen-shou Lodge, erected by Han Wu Ti, 58 442
Yoga, and Sāṅkhya in the Bhagavad Gītā, 43 167; Yoga philosophy in Bhartṛharinirveda of Harihara, 25 198 f.; Yoga-technique in the great epic, 22 333-379; prāya as a form of, 21 150 f.; terminology in the Upaniṣads, 22 333-336; practices in the Vedas, 43 60-65; world creation, compared with that of the Mokṣadharma and of the Sāṃkhya, 45 66 f.; see also Yogācāryabhūmiśāstra
Yoga Sūtra, date of, as determined from refutations of Buddhist doctrines, 31 1-29; Yoga-sūtras of Patañjali, translated, with the commentary Maṇiprabhā, 34 1-114
Yogācāra, see Buddhism
Yogācāryabhūmiśāstra, "Treatise on the Stages of a Yogi", see Hsüan Chuang; Wei shih
Yogī, Yogīs, the Kānphaṭa, 45 356; use of articles derived from rhinoceros, 51 281; nummulite rosaries, legend of origin, 53 357 f.
Yogin, Yogins, state, function of breath in, 22 266; kinds of, 22 348 f.; belief in effect of nostril used in breathing, 22 308; worship of Śiva as First Cause, 22 382; soul-path, in Mahābhārata, 22 346 f.; believe veins start from navel, 22 308
Yoiyama matsuri, 宵山祭, start of the Gion matsuri, see Gion matsuri
"Yoke of the Kingdom of Heaven," not a burden, 52 293-294
Yom Kippur, see Festivals (Hebrew)
Yon tan rgya mc̣ho, the fourth Dalai Lama, represented on a Tibetan temple painting, 52 344
Yoshida Tsunefusa, 吉田經房, works of, as source material for study of Kamakura period, 59 42-43, 44
Yoshida Tsunenaga, 吉田經長, (1239-1309), diary of, as source for study of the Kamakura period, 59 44
Yoshimune, 德川吉宗, interest of, in astronomy and the calendar, resulted in lifting the ban on foreign scientific books, 57 297-298
Yoshimitsu, Japanese sword maker, legend of, 26 334-335
Yü, 禹, the Great, one of the three sage heroes of Chinese antiquity, upon traditions of whom was based the Model-Emperor Lore of China, 56 51-76, various traditions concerning; originally a god of water, 53-63, dissemination of vir-

tue by, brought about submission of the Miao tribes, 68; authority of the Yü tradition in policy concerning waterways in Han period, 55 303, 305, 306
Yüan Chuang, see Hsüan Chuang
Yüan Ming Yüan, old summer palace, regulations for building supplies and furnishings of, 49 234, for work on timbers, 236-237, wood carving, inlaid furniture, stone work of, 237, the An Yu Kung, ancestral hall in, 239, the Ch'iung Hua Lou (Hortensia Tower), 239, the Fang Hu Sheng Ching, 239, 240, the Fu Yuan Gate, 240, the building in shape of a 田, 242; site, apts of Hsiang Fei, Panorama painted on walls, 57 126-127
Yüan Shih-k'ai, viceroy of Chihli Province, signer of Memorial to abolish competitive examinations, 1905, 27 79, 84
Yüan-shih-t'ien-tsun, seems to be a personification of the tao, 53 218 n.7, 221 n.19, starts a kalpa, 243, 244, statues of, 248, writings attributed to, 249
Yüan Tombs, visited by Empress Têng of Later Han, 51 159
Yüan-ts'ê, 圓測, Tibetan Ven-tshig, 57 122, 123-124
Yu-chia-shih-ti-lun, 瑜伽師地論, Chinese tr. by Hsüan Chuang of the Yogācāryabhūmiśāstra, 51 297, 301-302
Yü-ch'êng, 郁成, city on the eastern frontier of Ta-yüan; Chinese envoys of Han Wu Ti intercepted and killed at, 37 109-110, 135, first Chinese army routed at siege of, 110, Li Kuang-li avoids, 112, Chinese army returning fr. siege of Erh-shih fallen upon and killed by people of, 113-114, taken by the Chinese and King fled to K'ang-chü where he was captured and killed, 114
Yü-ch'ŏng, see Yü-ch'êng
Yüé, see Yüeh
Yue-chi, see Kushans, Yüeh-chih
Yüé-chī, see Yüeh-chih
Yüeh, 越, = Nan-yüeh (South China): Kiangsi and Chekiang, 37 94, Tien-yüeh, Yünnan ?, 99, wars against, in 112 B.C., referred to (?), 104, 135
Yüeh Chi, 越姬, concubine of Chao Wang of Ch'u, pledge to suicide, 51 142 n.20
Yüeh-chih, 月氏, Indoscythians, information about, in modern research, 37 152, Han Wu Ti informed of their migration, 93, Chang Ch'ien sent on mission to secure them as allies against the Hsiung-nu, 93-94, 95, 135, they had migrated west, after defeats by the Hsiung-nu, who had made a drinking vessel out of the skull of their King, 96-97, 133; conquer and settle part of Bactria, 97-98, 133-134, political influence over K'ang-chü, 96, strong militarily, 98, ambassadors to, fr. China, 102, 103, identification of the, 133-134; territories on the trade routes fr. 50 B.C. to 50 A.D., 35 32, 33, in India, 33-34, 37-41, defeated by Pan Chao, 38-39, the importance of the Kushan dynasties in the silk trade, 34, 37, 38-41, question of the date of Kanishka, 33; as distributors of animal style, 53 89-91
Yüeh-lin Temple, 岳林寺, history of, tr. fr. the Che-chiang t'ung chih, 53 52
Yuen Ming Yuen, see Yüan Ming Yüan
Yüe-sui, see Yüeh-sui
Yüeh-sui, 越巂, a district on the boundary of Yünnan and Ssŭ-ch'uan, created by Han Wu Ti, 37 104
Yüeh Ware, see abstract, Plumer
Yuga, Indian system of world-ages, Sumerian prototype of, 39 66 n. 3
Yü Han collection, lists 9 pre-Sung commentaries on Mencius, 51 31
Yü han shan fang chi shih shu, 玉函山房輯佚書, a ts'ung shu compiled by Ma Kuo-han, 18th cent., 51 42
Yu-hsiang Chou, = "Country of Docile Elephants", see Yu-kung
Yü Hsuan-chi, T'ang poetess, see Book Reviews, Wimstatt
Yü Huang, the "Pearly Emperor", criticism of Ferguson's sources for study of myth of, 53 58-59, record of painting of by Shih K'o, 59
Yü-kung, Book of Geography, attrib. to Hsia dynasty, now believed composed about 4th cent. B.C., 56 53, 74, interprets Yü as a surveyor of the empire, 53; early 1st millenium B.C., speaks of the "Country of Docile Elephants", in S. Honan, 41 299
Yu Lan Huei, see Festivals, Chinese
Yü-lo, identified as Hira, below Seleucia, 35 36
Yü-lu, see Buddhism, Zen
Yü-mên, 玉門, Gate, in the Great Wall, exit to Turkistan; line of military stations near, established by Han Wu Ti, 37 106, 135, closed against returning soldiers of the disastrous first campaign against Ta-yüan, 111, Chinese second army returns to, greatly depleted, 115
Yü-mŏn, see Yü-mên
Yün chi ch'i ch'ien, 雲笈七籤, on Taoism, by Chang Chün-fang, 53 217
Yün Clan, legend of banishment fr. China, by Emperor Shun; origin of the Sak tribes ?, 37 134
Yung-ch'ang, 永昌, (near Bhamo), a station of the ancient sea and land route from the Roman Empire to the Far East, 37 243; Battle of, 1277; Burmese fought the Mongols with war elephants in the, 41 306
Yung Ho Kung (Lama Temple) Peking, regulations for building supplies and furnishings of, 49 234, rules for the foundry for casting incense burners for, 240, for prayer wheels etc. for, 242; figures of Mi-lo Fo and Ju-lai Fo in the, 53 47 n.1
Yung-lo-ta-tien, 永樂大典, discovery of two "lost" chüan, 52 179-180, these two chüan consist of 45 Funeral Orations (chi wen), 179, part of the set recopied in 1567 and not found on Yuan T'ung-li's list of surviving vols., 180, 33 chüan in 21 vols. which were in process of publication at the Commercial Press have escaped destruction (1932), 180
Yün-nan, importance as a station on the sea and land trade route bet. China and the West, 1st to 3rd cent. A.D., 37 242-244, products of, 244, a description by Marcian of Heraclea may refer to the lakes of Yün-nan and their bamboo bridges, 247; the "elephant-riding country" of Han reports (?), 37 99, trade of with Ssŭ-ch'uan, 99; elephant occurred in up to modern times, 41 305, a center of Shan culture fr. 1st cent. B.C. to Mongol conquest, 305, use of war elephants in Ming and against the Manchus in 17th cent., 306; many ku sorcerers among the women of, 55 12-13; see also Aloes
Yü-pên-chi, 禹本紀, Ssŭ-ma Ch'ien's view of its wonderful tales, 37 116, notes on, 152
Yü-pŏn-ki, see Yü-pên-chi
Yu Shih-hsiung, Governor of Li Ch'üan, 11th cent.; made copies of the Horses of T'ang T'ai Tsung, 55 420, 422, 423, Stele of the Picture of the Six Horses erected by him in 1089 A.D., 420, 423-427, his Chao Ling Map Stele, 426
Yü-shih Ta-fu, 御史大夫, title "Grand Secretary", in Han period, later "Censor General", 51 271; title of third highest minister, Former Han period, 58 438
Yü-tien (Yü-tien), 于寘 (Khotan), location as stated by Chang Ch'ien, 37 95, the watershed of rivers in Central Asia, 95, produces jadestone, 95, 107, envoys sent to, by Chang Ch'ien, 102, Yellow River supposed to rise near, 107
Yü T'u Pei K'ao, 輿圖備攷, geographical work of early 17th cent., errors in, 59 347
Yu-yang-tsa-tsu, 酉陽雜俎, 863 A.D., history of; 18th chap., on trees, gives much information on plants growing in Fu-lin and India, 30 17-19; written before 863 A.D., describes Po-pa-li (Berbera), 30 48
Zach, see von Zach
Zagmuk, see Festivals (Babylonian)
Za'ifi, Pir Mehmet, 16th-cent. Turkish poet, MS of his works discovered, 57 239
Zakir, see Inscriptions, Aramaic
Zamān, Muḥammad Paolo, 17th-cent. Persian painter, life of, 45 106-109
Zamyād Yašt, rôle of Cyrus in similar to his rôle in Deutero-Isaiah, 57 162-163, 167
Zarathuštra, the evidence as to his historicity, 53 199-204
Zarvān, as the Father in Manichaeism, 44 63, 69
Zauberlehrling, Der, of Goethe, based on Lucian's φιλοψευδής ἢ ἀπιστῶν, a story of Egyptian origin, 39 295-298

Zayton, name fr. which word "satin" is derived, identified with Ch'üan-chou, Fukien; twin pagodas of, 56 373-374, harbour greatest in world, 373

Zebra, see abstract, J.J.L. Duyvendak

Zechariah, three persons of this name confused in later tradition, 57 255; his prophetic message delivered in 517 B.C., 47 359

Zechariah, Book of (Arabic), Syriacisms in the Polyglot version of, 59 401-402

Zechariah son of Jehoiada, murder of referred to in Matt. 23:35, 26 320

Zen, see Art, Buddhist; Buddhism; Mysticism, Japanese

Zervanism, the Persian religion described by Plutarch, 52 187

Zeus, identified with Ba'l Šamîn at Palmyra; referred to in Daniel as Šiqqûṣ Šōmem, 43 143; worship of in form of pyramid is of Anatolian origin, 60 549

Ziggurat, as prototype of circular minaret, 30 139-151; symbol of mountain origin of Sumerians, 36 288-289; types of, 43 92-95

Zipangu, see Japan, Geography

Ziusuddu, hero of a solar myth incorporated into the Deluge Story of the Gilgameš Epic, 47 290 ff.; two conflicting Babylonian traditions about, 43 325-326, 327-329

Zodiac, Syriac MS on names of signs of according to school of Bardesanes, 35 299

Zoroaster, the date of, 56 214; infancy, Buddhist tale parallel to apocryphal story of, 38 328; probably active in 8th cent. B.C.; his historicity doubtful, 53 203-204; account of in Theodore bar-Khoni, 43 239-242; made his first convert on southern shore of Lake Urmia, 25 183-184; mentioned in Manichaean texts from Turkistan, 43 16-20

Zoroastrian, Zoroastrians, Zoroastrianism, creation of man, conception of influenced by Babylonia, 36 313-316; calendar omens borrowed from Babylonia, 35 294; fire-temple, the founding of a, 49 174-176; the position of, from Greek texts, 52 187 f.; influence on Manichaeism, 43 15-25; references to in New Persian literature, 28 183-188; restored in Parthia by Vologases (A.D. 77-146), 49 369; first propagated by Vištāsp in Sagastān, 36 116, 119; of Yezd, 25 184; see also Calendar, Persian; Nestorians

Zoku Gunsho Ruijū, source materials for a study of the Kamakura period contained in, 59 41, 43, 47, 49, 50, 51, 52

Zû, and Lugalbanda, myth of contest between sun and storm clouds; closely associated with Indo-Iranian soma-cycle, 40 312-316; myth of, symbolic of Kushite invaders who founded the first dynasty of Uruk, 49 314

ibn-Zūlāq, al-Ḥasan ibn-Ibrāhīm (AH 306-387), works of, 28 254-270

Zuṭṭ, Gypsies of Lower Iraq, of Indian Jat origin; probably related to the Lurs, 44 131-132

III. INDEX OF BOOKS REVIEWED

------. L'Adoption Universelle des Caractères Latins, Dossiers de la Coopération Intellectuelle. Société des Nations, Institut International de Coopération Intellectuelle, Paris, [J. K. Shryock], 55 338-339

------. Annual Bibliography of Indian Archaeology for the Year 1932. Vol. VII, [Ludwig Bachhofer], 57 331-335

------. A Comparative Analytical Catalogue of the Kanjur Division of the Tibetan Tripiṭaka edited in Peking during the K'anghsi Era, and at present kept in the Library of the Ōtani Daigaku, Kyoto. Three parts, [Georges de Roerich], 52 395-399

------. The Cultural Heritage of India. A symposium by some 100 authors, [A. K. Coomaraswamy], 57 426-428

------. Deutsche Gesellschaft für Natur- und Völkerkunde Ostasiens, 60th anniversary vol., see Jubiläumsband

------. Dissertationes in honorem Dr. Eduardi Mahler, [A. Jeffrey], 59 517-519

------. Dīwān Wali al-Dīn Yakan, 45 94

------. Eminent Orientalists, Indian, European, American, 43 76

------. Indian Studies in Honor of Charles Rockwell Lanman, [W. Norman Brown], 50 171-174

------. Iran, vol. I (1926), [N. Martinovitch], 49 91-93

------. Journal of the Indian Society of Oriental Art. Vol. I, Pts. 1 and 2, [A. K. Coomaraswamy], 54 222

------. Jubiläumsband herausgegeben von der Deutschen Gesellschaft für Natur- und Völkerkunde Ostasiens, Teil I, (43 authors), [J. K. Shryock], 53 363-364

------. The Macdonald Presentation Volume, [C. Torrey], 54 89, 90-91

------. al-Muqtaṭaf and its press, [J. Montgomery], 46 92-93

------. Nanking Journal, Vol. I, No. 1, University of Nanking, 1931 [J. K. Shryock], 52 190-191

------. The New Orient: Vol. II, The Far East, symposium, 1933, [J. K. Shryock], 54 316

------. al-Ruwwād, [P. Hitti], 49 327

------. Staatlich Museen zu Berlin, Vorderasiatische Abteilung. Keilschrifturkunden aus Boghazköi. Bde. I-V, [A. Ungnad], 43 67-72

------. Streitberg-Festgabe, [Harold H. Bender], 45 324-328

------. Volume on Tangut (Hsi Hsia) Studies. Bull. of the National Library of Peiping, Vol. 4, No. 3, 1932, [J. K. Shryock], 52 189-190

ABBOTT, Justin E. Bhānudās, [W. Norman Brown], 47 280

------. The Keys of Power, [George W. Briggs], 53 186

------. The Poet-Saints of Maharastra, [Franklin Edgerton], 50 76-77

------. The Poet-Saints of Maharashtra. No. 6, Stotramala: A Garland of Hindu Prayers, [W. Norman Brown], 50 271

------. Tukaram. Translation from Mahipati's Bhaktalilamrita, [W. Norman Brown], 51 289-290

ABRAHAMS, I. The Glory of God, [J. Montgomery], 47 88-89

ACHARYA, P. K. A Dictionary of Hindu Architecture, [Ananda K. Coomaraswamy], 48 250-275

------. Indian Architecture According to the Mānasāraśilpaśāstra. [Ananda K. Coomaraswamy], 48 250-275

ADAM, Maurice. Yuen Ming Yuen, L'Oeuvre Architecturale des Anciens Jésuites au XVIII Siècle, [C. B. Malone], 57 126-127

AEŠCOLY, A. Z. Les noms magiques dans les apocryphes chrétiens des éthiopiens, [F. Hallock], 55 109-110

AIYANGAR, S. Krishnaswami. Manimekhalai in its historical setting, [A. K. Coomaraswamy], 49 71-72

AIYAPPAN, A. Social and Physical Anthropology of the Nayadis of Malabar, [M. B. Emeneau], 59 129-133

AIYAR, R. Sathyanatha. History of the Nayaks of Madura, 46 94

ALBRIGHT, William Foxwell. The Archaeology of Palestine and the Bible, [G. Barton], 52 197-199

------. The Excavation of Tell Beit Mirsim, [O. Sellers], 53 66-68

ALEC-TWEEDIE, Mrs. Mainly East, 43 74

ANDRAE, W. Die ionische Säule, [V. Müller], 54 429-431

ANDRÉ, P. J. L'Islam et les races, [J. Montgomery], 46 89-90

ANESAKI, Masaharu. Katam Karaniyam. Lectures, Essays and Studies, [Shio Sakanishi], 57 448-449

ARAVAMUTHAN, T. G. An Account of the Tamil Academies, [George William Brown], 51 338-339

ARBMAN, Ernst. Rudra, [Harold H. Bender], 43 56-60

ARLINGTON, L. C. and Harold Acton. Famous Chinese Plays, [J. K. Shryock], 57 442-443

ARMBRUSTER, see von Rotter

ARMSTRONG, W. E. Rossel Island: An Ethnological Study, [H. U. Hall], 49 182-185

ARNOLD, Thomas W., and Adolf Grohmann. The Islamic Book, [N. Martinovitch], 50 82-84

------, see also Houtsma, M. T.

ASHTON, Leigh, (ed). Chinese Art, [J. K. Shryock], 56 373

AUTRAN, C. Introduction a l'étude critique du nom propre grec, [Roland G. Kent], 46 249-252

AYSCOUGH, Florence. Chinese Women Yesterday and Today, [J. K. Shryock], 58 691-692

BABINGER, Franz. Die Geschichtsschreiber der Osmanen und ihre Werke, [N. Martinovitch], 48 286-287

BACHHOFER, Ludwig. Early Indian Sculpture, [Ananda K. Coomaraswamy], 51 58-59

BACOT, Jacques. Les Çlokas Grammaticaux de Thonmi Sambhoṭa avec leurs commentaires. [Georges de Roerich], 51 182-185

BADÈ, W. F. Some Tombs of Tell en-Nasbeh, [W. Albright], 52 52-53

BALL, C. J. The Book of Job, a Revised Text and Version, [G. Barton], 45 177-179

BANARSI Das Jain. Jaina Jātakas or Lord Ṛshabha's Pūrvabhavas, 46 94

BANDHYOPADHYAYA, N. C. Development of Hindu Polity, Part I, [E. Washburn Hopkins], 49 52

------. Kātyāyana-Mata-Saṅgraha, [E. Washburn Hopkins], 49 53

------. Kautilya, [E. Washburn Hopkins], 49 52

BANERJI, R. D. Basreliefs of Bādāmī, [Ananda K. Coomaraswamy], 49 191-193

BARAKATULLAH, Mohammad. The Khilafet, [J. Montgomery], 45 336

BARON, Salo Wittmayer. A Social and Religious History of the Jews, [S. Grayzel], 58 482-483

BARTON, George Aaron. Archaeology and the Bible, [J. Maynard], 49 182

------. Semitic and Hamitic Origins, [T. Meek], 54 300-302

BARUA, Benimadhab. Gayā and Buddha-Gayā, [A. K. Coomaraswamy], 57 191-193

BASSET, R., see Houtsma, M. T.

BATES, M. S. (compiler). An Introduction to Oriental Journals in Western Languages, [J. K. Shryock], 53 361-362

BAUER, H., see Houtsma, M. T.

BAUER, Hans. Das Alphabet von Ras Schamra, [J. Montgomery], 53 167-168

------ and P. Leander. Grammatik des Biblisch-Aramäischen, [J. Montgomery], 51 317-320

------ and P. Leander. Kurzgefasste Grammatik des Biblisch-Aramäischen, [J. Montgomery], 51 317-320

BAUER, Theodor. Die Ostkanaanäer, [E. Speiser], 49 325-326
BEAUJARD, André (tr.). Les Notes de Chevet de Sei Shônagon, dame d'Honneur au Palais de Kyôto, [Shio Sakanishi], 57 132
------. Sei Shônagon, son Temps et son Oeuvre (une femme de lettres de l'ancien Japon). Avec une préface de M. Michel Revon, [Lillian E. Knowles], 57 133-134
BIGGERSTAFF, Knight, and Ssu-yü Teng. An Annotated Bibliography of Selected Chinese Reference Works, [J. K. Shryock], 57 350
BEER, G. Mishna Manuscript Codex Kaufmann A. 50, [S. Krauss], 51 78-80
BELLINGER, A. R., see Rostovtzeff, M. I.
BELVALKAR, S. K., and R. D. Ranade. History of Indian Philosophy, [E. Washburn Hopkins], 49 54-55
BENVENISTE, Émile. The Persian Religion according to the Chief Greek Texts, [Maria Wilkins Smith], 52 186-189
BERGSTRÄSSER, G. Einführung in die semitischen Sprachen, [E. Speiser], 50 269-271
BEZOLD, Carl. Babylonisches-assyrisches Glossar, [W. Albright], 48 177-182
------. Ninive und Babylon, [G. Barton], 46 317
BHANDARKAR, D. R. Asoka, [Truman Michelson], 46 256-264
BHATTACHARYYA, B. The Indian Buddhist Iconography, 46 187-189
BHATTASALI, Nalini Kanta. Coins and Chronology of the Early Independent Sultans of Bengal, [H. Wood], 43 253-254
------. Iconography of Buddhist and Brahmanical sculptures in the Dacca Museum, [Ananda Coomaraswamy], 50 82
BIALLAS, F. X. (ed.). Monumenta Serica; Journal of Oriental Studies of the Catholic University of Peking, Vol. I, No. 1, [J. K. Shryock], 56 379-380
BILLIET, Joseph. Cachets et cylindres-sceaux de style sumérien archaïque et de styles dérivés du Musée de Cannes, [T. Meek], 53 70
BINYON, Laurence. Painting in the Far East, 4th ed., [J. K. Shryock], 55 341-342
------. The Poems of Nizami, [A. Coomaraswamy], 49 339
------. The Spirit of Man in Asian Art, [Ananda K. Coomaraswamy], 55 325-329
BIRGE, John Kingsley. The Bektashi Order of Dervishes, [P. Hitti], 59 522-523
BLOCHET, E. Musulman Painting, [N. Martinovitch], 51 71-73
BLONDHEIM, D. S. Les parlers judéo-romans et la Vetus Latina, [M. Margolis], 49 82-84
BLOOMFIELD, Leonard. Language, [Franklin Edgerton], 53 295-297
BLOOMFIELD, M., and F. Edgerton. Vedic Variants, Volume I, The Verb. [LeRoy Carr Barret], 51 73-76
------ and Murray B. Emeneau. Vedic Variants. Volume III: Noun and Pronoun Inflection, [LeRoy C. Barret], 55 110-112
BLUNT, Wilfrid Scawen. Secret History of the English Occupation of Egypt, 43 74
BODDE, Derk, tr. with annotations, of Annual Customs and Festivals in Peking, by Tun Li-ch'en, 57 204
BONNER, Campbell (ed.)., A Papyrus Codex of the Shepherd of Hermas, [H. Comfort], 56 103-104
BOSE, Phanindra Nath. Pratimā-Māna-Lakṣaṇam, [Ananda K. Coomaraswamy], 50 266-267
------. Principles of Indian Śilpaśāstra; with the text of Mayaśāstra, [A. K. Coomaraswamy], 49 69-70
BOUNAKOFF, George. The Oracle Bones from Honan, [J. K. Shryock], 56 376-377
BOUYGES, P. M. Notes sur les philosophes arabes connus des latins au moyen âge, [I. Husik], 45 329-331
BRANDT, J. J. Introduction to Literary Chinese, [J. K. Shryock], 57 351-352
------. Modern Newspaper Chinese, [J. K. Shryock], 57 195
BRÄUNLICH, Erich. Bisṭām Ibn Qais, ein vorislamischer Beduinenfürst und Held, [B. Halper], 43 436-437
BRAY, Denys. The Brāhūī Language. Part II: The Brāhūī Problem. Part III: Etymological Vocabulary, [Edwin H. Tuttle], 56 350-360
BREUER, Isaac. Judenproblem, 43 73
BRITTON, Roswell S. The Chinese Periodical Press: 1800-1912, [J. K. Shryock], 54 316-317
------, (ed). The Couling-Chalfant Collection of Inscribed Oracle Bones, Drawn by Frank H. Chalfant, [H. G. Creel], 56 528-529
BROWN, W. Norman. The Story of Kālaka: Texts, history, legends, and miniature paintings of the Jain hagiographical work the Kālakācāryakathā, [A. K. Coomaraswamy], 53 305-307
BRUNO, Arvid. Gibeon, [W. Albright], 45 181-182
BUCKLER, F. W. Harunu'l-Rashid and Charles the Great, [N. Martinovitch], 52 61-63
BUCKLER, W. H., and D. M. Robinson. Sardis, VII, 1: Greek and Latin Inscriptions, [W. Hyde], 53 178-180
BUDGE, E. A. Wallis. Babylonian Life and History, [G. Barton], 46 318
------. The Bandlet of Righteousness, [H. Gehman], 53 293-295
BŪGA, K. Lietuvių kalbos žodynas. 1 sąsiuvinis, [H. H. Bender], 44 140-141
VAN BUREN, E. Douglas. Clay Figurines of Babylonia and Assyria, [W. Albright], 51 175-177
Al-BUSTĀNI, Fu'ād, see al-Šihābi, Ḥaydar
VON BUTTEL-REEPEN, see von Rotter
CALAND, W. Pañcaviṃśa-Brāhmaṇa, The Brāhmaṇa of the Twenty-five Chapters, [P. E. Dumont], 52 387-390
------. The Śatapatha Brāhmaṇa, Kāṇvīya Recension, [LeRoy C. Barret], 48 89-90
------. Das Śrāuta-sūtra des Āpastamba, aus dem Sanskrit übersetzt, [LeRoy C. Barret], 44 139-140
------. Das Śrautasūtra des Āpastamba, achtes bis fünfzehntes Buch, aus dem Sanskrit übersetzt, [L. C. Barret], 46 272-273
CAMERON, George G. History of Early Iran, [L. Waterman], 56 519-520
CANDLIN, Clara M. The Herald Wind, [J. K. Shryock], 54 316
CLARK, Cyril Drummond Le Gros. The Prose-Poetry of Su Tung-p'o, [J. K. Shryock], 56 95-96
CAPART, Jean. L'art Égyptien, [N. Reich], 43 430-431
CAPPELLER, Carl. Bālamāgha. Māgha's Śiśupālavadha im Auszuge, 43 75-76
CARTER, Thomas F. The Invention of Printing in China and Its Spread Westward, [B. Laufer], 47 71-76
CASSIN, E.-M. L'adoption à Nuzi, [H. Lewy], 59 118-120
CHABOT, J. C. Choix d'inscriptions de Palmyre, [C. Torrey], 43 141-144
CHAKRABERTY, Chandra. A Study in Hindu Social Polity, 43 256
CHALMERS, Lord. Buddha's Teachings, being the Sutta-Nipāta or Discourse-Collection, [W. Norman Brown], 54 218-219
CHALMERS, R. Thomas William Rhys Davids, 1843-1922, 44 79
CHANG TSUNG-CH'IEN, see Creel, H. G.
CHARIGNON, A. J. H. À propos des voyages aventureux de Fernand Mendez Pinto, recueillies et complétées par Mlle. M. Médard, [J. J. L. Duyvendak], 57 343-348
CHARAṆAVIJAYA. Trishashṭiśalākā-purushacharitram-mahākāvyam, by Śrī Hemachandra-āchārya. Parvan First, [Helen M. Johnson], 59 275-276
CHARLES, R. H. A Critical and Exegetical Commentary on the Book of Daniel, [J. Montgomery], 51 317, 323-327
CHARPENTIER, Jarl. The Indian Travels of Apollonius of Tyana, [Helen M. Johnson], 55 316-318
CHASSINAT, Émile. Un Papyrus copte, [W. Schoff], 45 76-82

CH'EN HUNG-SHUN, see Löwenthal
CHIERA, Edward. Joint Expedition with the Irak Museum at Nuzi, [R. Pfeiffer], 49 178-180
------. Joint Expedition with the Iraq Museum at Nuzi, [R. Pfeiffer], 51 76-78
------. Sumerian Epics and Myths, [E. Speiser], 54 432
------. Sumerian Texts of Varied Contents, [E. Speiser], 54 432
CHILDE, V. Gordon. The Most Ancient East, [E. Speiser], 50 79-81
CHRISTENSEN, Arthur. Contributions à la dialectologie iranienne. (Dialecte Guilãke de Recht, dialectes de Fãrizänd, de Yaran et de Natanz) [F. Howland], 52 65-67
CLARK, Walter Eugene. The Āryabhaṭīya of Āryabhaṭa, An Ancient Indian Work on Mathematics and Astronomy, [M. J. Babb], 51 51-52
CLARK, Walter E. (Ed.). Two Lamaistic Pantheons, [J. K. Shryock], 58 695-696
COEDÈS, G. Études cambodgiennes, XIX. La date du Bàyon, [Ananda K. Coomaraswamy], 50 264-265
COHEN, Marcel. Études d'éthiopien méridional, [W. Worrell], 52 380-382
CONTENAU, G. La civilisation phénicienne, [W. Albright], 48 76-80
------. Manuel d'archéologie orientale, I, [E. Speiser], 49 323-325
COOMARASWAMY, Ananda K. Elements of Buddhist Iconography. [W. Norman Brown], 57 115-117
------. Mughal Painting, [N. Martinovitch], 51 71
------. La Sculpture de Bodhgayā, [W. Norman Brown], 57 115-117
------. The Transformation of Nature in Art. [W. Norman Brown], 54 216-218
------. Yakṣas, Parts I and II, [W. Norman Brown], 51 286-288
CORDIER, Henri. Mélanges d'histoire et de géographie orientales, [B. Laufer], 45 185
COTT, Perry Blythe. Siculo-Arabic Ivories, [M. Ross], 60 424-426
COUSENS, H. Chalukyan architecture, [Ananda K. Coomaraswamy], 49 331
------. Somanātha and Other Mediaeval temples in Kāṭhiāwāḍ, [A. K. Coomaraswamy], 53 187
COYAJEE, Sir J. C. Cults and Legends of Ancient Iran and China, [J. K. Shryock], 57 198-200
CREEL, H. G. The Birth of China, [J. K. Shryock], 57 348-349
------, Chang Tsung-ch'ien, and Richard C. Rudolph, Editors: Literary Chinese: Vol. I, the Hsiao Ching, [J. K. Shryock], 59 153-155
------. Literary Chinese by the Inductive Method, [J. K. Shryock], 60 116-117
------. Studies in Early Chinese Culture, [J. K. Shryock], 58 688-690
CROOKE, William. Religion and Folklore of Northern India, [George W. Briggs], 47 189-192
CRUM, W. E., see Winlock, H. E.
CUNY, Albert, see Féghali, Michel
DALAL, C. D. Lekhpaddhati, [Helen M. Johnson], 46 270
DANTHINE, Hélène. Le palmier-dattier et les arbes sacrés, [C. Zirkle], 60 422-424
DANTON, George H. The Culture Contacts of the United States and China, [J. K. Shryock], 52 193-194
DAS, K. N. History of Bengali Literature, [E. Washburn Hopkins], 49 54
DAS, Taraknath. India in World Politics, 43 148
DASGUPTA, S. N. Hindu Mysticism, [Franklin Edgerton], 48 87-88
------. A History of Indian Philosophy, Vols. I and II, [Franklin Edgerton], 52 248-252
DAVID, Martin. Die Adoption im altbabylonischen Recht, [E. Speiser], 49 182
DAVIDS, Mrs. Rhys. What was the Original Gospel in Buddhism? [Ananda K. Coomaraswamy], 58 679-686
DAY, Alfred Ely. Geology of Lebanon and Syria, Palestine and Neighboring Countries, [P. Hitti], 54 438
DESHMUKH, P. S. The Origin and Development of Religion in Vedic Literature, [Franklin Edgerton], 55 319-323
DIKSHITAR, V. R. Ramachandra. Studies in Tamil Literature and History, [George William Brown], 52 80-81
DIMAND, Maurice Sven. A Guide to an Exhibition of Islamic Miniature Painting, [N. Martinovitch], 55 105
------. A Handbook of Mohammedan Decorative Arts, [N. Martinovitch], 51 84-85
DIRINGER, David. Le iscrizioni antico-ebraiche palestinesi, [C. Torrey], 55 469-470
DIRR, Adolf. Einführung in das Studium der kaukasischen Sprachen, [E. A. Speiser], 50 268-269
DODD, Stuart C. A Controlled Experiment on Rural Hygiene in Syria, [P. Hitti], 54 438
DORGE, Mlle. Gilberte, see Hla-Dorge
DOUGHERTY, Raymond Philip. Archives from Erech. Time of Nebuchadrezzar and Nabonidus, [T. Meek], 45 91-92
------. The Sealand of Ancient Arabia, [Z. Harris], 54 93-95
DRISCOLL, Lucy and Toda, Kenji. Chinese Calligraphy, [Nancy Lee Swan], 55 473-476
DRIVER, G. R., and John C. Miles. The Assyrian Laws, [E. Speiser], 56 107-108
DUBS, H. H. Hsuntze; the Moulder of Ancient Confucianism, [J. K. Shryock], 49 88-91
DUCHESNE-GUILLEMIN, Jacques. Études de Morphologie iranienne I. Les Composés de l'Avesta, [Roland G. Kent], 57 429-431
DUMONT, P.-E. L'Īśvaragītā. Le chant de Śiva, [Franklin Edgerton], 54 306-310
DUNNE, J. H. (ed.). Kitāb al-Awrāq of al-Ṣūli, [P. Hitti], 57 322-323
DUPONT, Pierre. Catalogue des Collections Indochinoises, in Musée Guimet, [J. K. Shryock], 56 380
DUTT, Nripendra Kumar. The Aryanization of India, [George William Brown], 51 336-338
------. Origin and Growth of Caste in India, [George W. Briggs], 53 181-186
EBELING, E., Meissner, B. and Weidner, E. Die Inschriften der altassyrischen Könige, [W. Albright], 48 90-93
ECKE, G. and P. Demiéville. The Twin Pagodas of Zayton, [J. K. Shryock], 56 373-374
EDGERTON, Franklin. The Elephant-Lore of the Hindus, [W. Norman Brown], 52 89-90
------. The Mīmāṅsā Nyāya Prakāśa or Āpadevī: A Treatise on the Mīmāṅsā System by Āpadeva, [Walter Eugene Clark], 51 53-54
------ and M. Bloomfield. Vedic Variants, Volume I, The Verb. [LeRoy Carr Barret], 51 73-76
------, Maurice Bloomfield, and Murray B. Emeneau. Vedic Variants. Volume III: Noun and Pronoun Inflection, [LeRoy C. Barret], 55 110-112
------, see also Margolis, Max L.
EDWARDES, S. M. Kharsheji Rustamji Cama, 1831-1909, A Memoir, [G. C. O. H(aas)], 43 256
EDWARDS, E. D. Chinese Prose Literature of the T'ang Period, [J. K. Shryock], 58 687-688
------. Chinese Prose Literature, Vol. II, [J. K. Shryock], 60 586-587
ELISSÉEFF, S., C. S. Gardner and J. R. Ware (eds). Harvard Journal of Asiatic Studies, Vol. I, No. 1, [J. K. Shryock], 56 381-382
EMBREE, John F. Suye Mura - a Japanese Village, [Richard A. Faust], 60 432-435
EMENEAU, M. B. A Union List of Printed Indic Texts and Translations in American Libraries, [Horace I. Poleman], 55 482-483
------, Maurice Bloomfield and Franklin Edgerton. Vedic Variants. Volume III: Noun and Pronoun Inflection. [LeRoy C. Barret], 55 110-112

ENTHOVEN, R. E. The Folklore of Bombay, [W. Norman Brown], 46 265-267
ERDMAN, Paul, see Sa'd, Ḥalīl
ESCARRA, Jean. Le Droit Chinois, [J. K. Shryock], 57 203
EVANS, Ivor H. N. Studies in Religion, Folk-Lore, and Custom in British North Borneo and the Malay Peninsula, [A. Irving Hallowell], 45 92-93
FADDEGON, Barend. The Pravacana-sāra of Kunda-kunda Ācārya, together with commentary, Tattva-dīpikā, by Amṛtacandra Sūri, [Helen M. Johnson], 56 523-525
------. Studies in Pāṇini's Grammar, [Allan Harrison Fry], 59 135-138
FĀRIS, Bāsim A. Post-War Bibliography of the Near Eastern Mandates, [P. Hitti], 54 437-438
FARRUKH, Omar A. Das Bild des Frühislam in der arabischen Dichtung, [P. Hitti], 59 525-526
FAVRE, Lieutenant-Colonel B. Les Sociétés Secrétes en Chine, [J. K. Shryock], 53 362
FÉGHALI, Michel. Contes, légendes coutumes populaires du Liban et de Syrie, [N. Faris], 56 509-510
------, and Cuny, Albert, Du genre grammatical en sémitique, [J. Montgomery], 45 335
------. Syntaxe des parlers arabes actuels du Liban, [P. Hitti], 49 328-329
FEKETE, Ludwig. Türkische Schriften aux dem Archive des Palatins Nikolaus Esterhazy 1606-1645, ed. by Prince Paul Esterhazy, [N. Martinovitch], 53 82-83
FERGUSON, John C. Chinese Mythology; see Feng Han-yi and J. K. Shryock, Chinese Mythology and Dr. Ferguson, 53 53-65
------, see also Hsiang Yüan-pien
FIELD, Henry. Arabs of Central Iraq, [W. Krogman], 57 189-191
de FILIPPI, Filippo. An Account of Tibet; The Travels of Ippolito Desideri, S.J., 1712-1727, with an Introduction by C. Wessels, S.J., The Broadway Travellers series, [J. K. Shryock], 52 400-401
FISH, T. Catalogue of the Sumerian Tablets in the John Rylands Library, [T. Meek], 53 71
FOSSUM, L. O. A Practical Kurdish Grammar, [L. H. Gray], 44 80
FOUCHER, A. On the Iconography of the Buddha's Nativity, [Ananda K. Coomaraswamy], 55 323-325
FRANKE, O. Li Tschi. Ein Beintrag zur Geschichte der chinesischen Geisteskämpfe im 16. Jahrhundert, [L. Scherman], 59 276-280
FRANKFORT, Henri. Archeology and the Sumerian Problem, [E. Speiser], 53 359-360
FREY, J.-B. (ed.). Corpus inscriptionum judaicarum, [R. Marcus], 56 505-506
FUCHS, Walter. Beiträge zur mandjurischen Bibliographie und Literatur, [J. K. Shryock], 58 693
FURLANI, Giuseppe. La Religione degli Hittiti, [Albrecht Goetze], 58 475-476
------. Religione dei Yezidi, [E. Speiser], 51 334-335
FYZEE, Asaf A. A. al-Hiyādatu'-l-Āmirīya, [P. Hitti], 59 527
GADD, C. J. The Fall of Nineveh (reprinted from the Proc. of the Brit. Acad., XI), [G. Barton], 46 316-317
------. The Fall of Nineveh, the Newly Discovered Babylonian Chronicle, [G. Barton], 46 316-317
------. A Sumerian Reading Book, [G. Barton], 46 316
------ and Leon Legrain: Ur Excavations, Texts. I: Royal Inscriptions, [E. Speiser], 49 322-323
GAIRDNER, W. H. T. Egyptian Colloquial Arabic, [W. Worrell], 47 336-337
------. The Phonetics of Arabic, [W. Worrell], 46 318-320
GALE, Esson M. Basics of the Chinese Civilization, [J. K. Shryock], 54 227
GANGOLY, O. C. Masterpieces of Rajput painting, [A. K. Coomaraswamy], 49 72-73
GARDNER, Charles S. Chinese Traditional Historiography, [J. K. Shryock], 59 152-153
------. A Union List of Selected Chinese Books in American Libraries, [J. K. Shryock], 53 92-93
------. A Union List of Selected Western Books on China in American Libraries, [J. K. Shryock], 52 192-193
------. A Union List of Selected Western Books on China in American Libraries, 2nd Ed., [John Pope], 59 283-286
GARDNER, Fletcher, and Ildefonso Maliwanag. Indic Writings of the Mindoro-Palawan Axis, [Horace I. Poleman], 60 275
GARRATT, G. T. The Legacy of India, [A. K. Coomaraswamy] 57 426-428
GAUDEFROY-DEMOMBYNES, Le pèlerinage à la Mekke, [J. Montgomery], 46 88, 91
GEHMAN, Henry Snyder, see Johnson, Allan C.
GELB, Ignace J. Inscriptions from Alishar and Vicinity, [J. Lewy], 57 434-438
GETTY, Alice. Gaṇeśa, [A. K. Coomaraswamy], 57 428-429
GHOSHAL, U. History of Hindu Political Theories, 43 350
GHURYE, G. S. Caste and Race in India, [George W. Briggs], 53 181-186
GIBB, H. A. R. The Arab Conquests in Central Asia, [B. Halper], 43 434-435
------. The Damascus Chronicle of the Crusades, [P. Hitti], 52 265-267
GITANAND, Brahmachari. The Gita Idea of God, [George William Brown], 52 82
GLASENAPP, Helmuth v. Der Jainismus, [Helen M. Johnson], 46 268-269
GOETZ, Hermann. Geschichte der indischen Miniaturmalerei, [A. K. Coomaraswamy], 54 440-442
GOITEIN, S. D. F. (ed.). Ansāb al-Ašrāf of al-Balāḏuri, [P. Hitti], 57 322, 324-325
GOKHALE, Vasudev. Pratītyasamutpādaśāstra des Ullangha, kritisch behandelt und aus dem Chinesischen ins Deutsche übertragen, [J. R. Ware], 54 314-315
GOLOUBEW, V. Ajanta. Les peintures de la première grotte, [Ananda Coomaraswamy], 47 278-279
GOODENOUGH, Edwin R. By Light Light [B. Cohen], 56 500-505
GOODRICH, Luther Carrington. The Literary Inquisition of Ch'ien-lung, [Carroll B. Malone], 55 477-479
GOODSPEED, Edgar J., D. W. Riddle and H. R. Willoughby. The Rockfeller Mc Cormick New Testament, [H. Sanders], 52 376-377
GORDIS, Robert. The Biblical Text in the Making: A study of the Kethib-Qere, [H. Orlinsky], 60 30-45
GOUGH, see von Rotter
GRAHAM, David C. "A Preliminary Report of the Hanchow Excavation," Reprinted from the Journal of the West China Border Research Society, 1934, [J. K. Shryock], 56 98-99
GRAHAM, W. C., see Sprengling, Martin
GRANET, Marcel. Chinese Civilization, Translated from the French by Kathleen E. Innes and Mabel R. Brailsford, [J. K. Shryock], 51 186-188
------. Festivals and Songs of Ancient China, [James R. Ware], 54 100-103
GRANQUIST, Hilman. Marriage Conditions in a Palestinian Village, [H. Spoer], 53 76-78
GRANT, Elihu (ed.). The Haverford Symposium on Archaeology and the Bible, [E. Speiser], 58 670
GRAVELY, F. H., and T. N. Ramachandran. Catalogue of the South Indian Metal Images in the Madras Government Museum, [A. K. Coomaraswamy], 53 187-188
GRAY, George Buchanan. Sacrifice in the Old Testament, [R. Yerkes], 47 79-83
GRIGSON, W. V. The Maria Gonds of Bastar, [M. B. Emeneau], 59 129-133
GRISWOLD, H. D. The Religion of the Rigveda, [George Wm. Brown], 47 187-189
GROHMANN, Adolf, see Arnold, Thomas W.
GROSLIER, Georges. Les collections khmères du Musée Sarrault à Phnom Penh, [Ananda K. Coomaraswamy], 52 83-84

GROUSSET, René. Histoire des croisades et du royaume franc de Jérusalem, [P. Hitti], 56 510, 512
------. Histoire des croisades, II, [P. Hitti], 57 322, 325
GUNSAULUS, Helen C. Japanese Sword-Mounts. [William E. Griffis], 45 88-91
GÜNTERT, Hermann. Der arische Weltkönig und Heiland, [Walter Neisser], 45 280-288
GUNTHER, Hans F. R. Rassenkunde des jüdischen Volkes, [W. Worrell], 50 164-165
GUSTAVS, Arnold. Namenreihen aus den Kerkuk-Tafeln, [P. Purves], 58 462-471
HACKIN, Joseph. Recherches archéologiques au Col de Khair khaneh près de Kābul, [Ludwig Bachhofer], 57 326-329
------. Recherches archéologiques en Asie Centrale (1931), [Ludwig Bachhofer], 57 329-331
HAENISCH, E. Lehrgang der Chinesischen Schriftsprache, [J. K. Shryock], 53 361
------. Monggo Han Sai Da Sekiyen; Die Mandschufassung von Secen Sagang's Mongolischer Geschichte, [J. K. Shryock], 54 315
HAĪDARI, L. A. (tr.). The Prophetship and the Caliphate, 45 94-95
HAIG, Sir Wolseley. Comparative Tables of Muhammadan and Christian Dates, [H. Spoer], 53 175
HALKIN, Abraham S. Moslem Schisms and Sects, [P. Hitti], 56 510, 512-513
HALPER, B. Descriptive Catalogue of the Genizah Fragments in Philadelphia, [I. Davidson], 45 332-334
HAMADA, Kosaku, and Umehara, Sueji, Shiragi Ko-ga no kenkyu, Report upon archaeological research in the Dept. of Literature, Kyoto Imperial University, Vol. XIII, 1934, [Shio Sakanishi], 55 218-219
HAMĪD-ALLĀH, Muḥammad. Documents sur la diplomatie musulmane à l'époque du Prophète et les khalifes orthodoxes, [P. Hitti], 57 326
HAMILTON, Clarence H. Wei-shih-er-shih-lun, [J. K. Shryock], 60 115-116
HARADA, Yoshito, and Tazawa, Kingo. Lo-Lang: a report on the excavation of Wang Hsü's tomb in the ancient Chinese colony in Korea, [Shio Sakanishi], 54 97-99
------ and Kazuchika Komai. Mu-yang-ch'eng; Han and Pre-Han Sites at the Foot of Mount Lao-t'ieh in South Manchuria, Archaeologia Orientalis, Vol. II, [J. K. Skryock], 52 191-192
HARRIS, D. G. Irrigation in India, 44 79
HARRIS, Zellig S. Development of Canaanite Dialects, [W. Albright], 60 414-422
------. A Grammar of the Phoenician Language, [C. Torrey], 57 397-410
------, see also Montgomery, James A.
HART, Henry H. The Hundred Names, [J. K. Shryock], 54 225-226
------. Seven Hundred Chinese Proverbs, [J. K. Shryock], 58 690
------. The West Chamber, [J. K. Shryock], 57 205-206
HASLUCK. F. W. Christianity and Islam under the Sultans, [F. Buckler], 53 73-75
HAUER, J. W. Die Anfänge der Yogapraxis im alten Indien, [Harold H. Bender], 43 60-65
HAUSHOFER, Karl. Japan und die Japaner, [William E. Griffis], 46 81-82
HAWLEY, Charles Arthur. A Criticial Examination of the Peshitta Version of the Book of Ezra, [J. Montgomery], 43 432-433
HAYDON, A. Eustace, (Editor). Modern Trends in World Religions, Chapters by Sprengling, Pratt, Allen, Joshi, Kaplan, Natarajan, Hodous, and Hu Shih, [J. K. Shryock], 55 224
HAYES, William C. The Texts in the Maṣṭabeh of Se'n-wosret-'ankh at Lisht, [H. Ranke], 59 515-517
ḪAYRALLĀH, As'ad, see Sa'd, Ḫalīl
HEFFENING, W. and W. Kirfel (ed.). Paul Kahle, Birthday Volume, Studien zur Geschichte und Kultur des Nahen und Fernen Ostens Paul Kahle zum 60 Geburtstag überreicht von Freuden und Schülern aus dem Kreise des Orientalischen Seminars der Universität Bonn. 23 monographs by Matsumoto, Pippon (of Tokyo), Wang, Roder, Schmitt and others, [James A. Montgomery], 55 472-473
HEMPEL, Johann. Die althebräische Literatur und ihr hellenistisches Nachleben, [J. Montgomery], 55 208-210
HERRMANN, Albert. Historical and Commercial Atlas of China, [J. K. Shryock], 57 200-201
HERTEL, Johannes. Die Arische Feuerlehre, I Teil, [E. Washburn Hopkins], 49 177-178
------. Bharaṭakadvātriṃśikā, [W. Norman Brown], 46 72-75
------, ed. Indische Erzähler. Vols. 1-12, [W. Norman Brown], 46 71-75
------. Die Methode der Arischen Forschung, [E. Washburn Hopkins], 49 177-178
------. On the Literature of the Shvetāmbaras of Gujarat, [Helen M. Johnson], 46 75-76
------. The Panchākhyānavārttika. Part I, [W. Norman Brown], 46 72-75
HERTZ, Amelia. Die Kultur um den persischen Golf und ihre Ausbreitung, [W. Albright], 51 67-70
HERZFELD, Ernst. Altpersische Inscriften, [Roland G. Kent], 59 126-129
HILLEBRANDT, Alfred. Altindische Politik, 44 79
------. Vedische Mythologie, [LeRoy C. Barret], 50 74-75
ḤIMADAH, Sa'īd B. Monetary and Banking System of Syria, [P. Hitti], 56 511-514
------. al-Niẓām al-Iqtiṣādi fi 'l-'Irāq, [P. Hitti], 59 527
HITTI, Philip Khuri. An Arab-Syrian Gentleman, [J. Montgomery], 50 261-262
------. History of the Arabs, [G. Della Vida], 59 121-126
------. Kitāb al-I'ti-bār li-Usāmah ibn-Munqid, [J. Montgomery], 51 327-328, 329-332
------. The Origins of the Druze People and Religion, [J. Montgomery], 50 262-263
HLA-DORGE, Gilberte. Une Poetess Japonaise au XVIII siècle, Kaga No Tchiyo-Jo, [Alfred H. Sweet], 57 130-131
HOBEIKA, Jean. Explication de la liturgie syriaque par saint Jean Maron, [B. Halper], 43 435-436
HODOUS, Lewis (ed.). Careers for Students of Chinese Language and Civilization, [J. K. Shryock], 53 364-365
------. Chinese Buddhism, [Lucius C. Porter], 46 78-81
------. Folkways in China, [J. K. Shryock], 50 169-170
------, see also Haydon, A. E.; Soothill, E. W.
HÖGMAN, C. A. L'Inde et son âme, [W. Norman Brown], 49 95
VAN HOESEN, Henry B. and Frank K. Walker. Bibliography: Enumerative and Historical, [P. Hitti], 49 327
HOLM, Fritz: My Nestorian Adventure, [L. P(orter)], 44 290
HOLTOM, D. C. The National Faith of Japan, [J. K. Shryock], 60 587-588
HOMMEL, Rudolph P. China at Work, [J. K. Shryock], 58 690-691
HOOGT, J. M. van der. The Vedic Chant studied in its Textual and Melodic Form, [P. E. Dumont], 52 390-391
HOPKINS, Clark, see Rostovtzeff, M. I.
HOSPITALIER, J.-J. Grammaire Laotienne, [J. K. Shryock], 58 692-693
HOUO-MING-TSE, Paul. Preuves des Antiquités de Chine, [J. K. Shryock], 52 191
HOUTSMA, M. T., T. W. Arnold, R. Basset and H. Bauer (eds.). The Encyclopaedia of Islām, No. 27, 45 95
------. The Encyclopaedia of Islām, No. 28, [J. Montgomery], 45 336
HOYLAND, J. S. The Commentary of Father Monserrate, S. J., on his Journey to the Court of Akbar, 43 348
HSIANG Yüan-pien. Noted Porcelains of Successive Dynasties, revised, translated and annotated by Kuo Pao-ch'ang and John C. Ferguson, [B. Laufer], 52 93-95

HUDSON-WILLIAMS, T. A Short Grammar of Old Persian, with a Reader, [Roland G. Kent], 57 193-194
HUME, Robert Ernest. The Thirteen Principal Upanishads, [George William Brown], 52 81-82
HÜRLIMAN, Martin. India: the landscape, the monuments, and the people, [Ananda K. Coomaraswamy], 49 190-191
HUMMEL, Arthur W., see Ku Chieh-kang
HURGRONJE, Snouck. The Holy War Made in Germany, [M. Jastrow, Jr.], 36 420
------. Mekka in the Latter Part of the Nineteenth Century, tr. J. H. Monahan, [S. Zwemer], 52 383-387
ḪŪRI AL-MAQDISI, Anīs. (tr.). al-Ḏikra, [P. Hitti], 49 85, 86-87
------. Dīwān ibn-al-Sā'āti, vol. I, [P. Hitti], 59 526
------. Taṭawwur al-Asālib al-Naṭrīyah fi 'l-Adab al-'Arabi, [P. Hitti], 56 511, 514-515
------. Umarā' al-Ši'r al-'Arabi fi 'l-'Aṣr al-'Abbāsi, [P. Hitti], 53 79-81
HUSAIN, H. F. Badshah (tr.). Islam in the Light of Shiaism being a Translation of the Shariatul Islam (Part I), 45 94, 95
HU SHIH. The Chinese Renaissance, [J. K. Shryock], 55 223-224
------, see also Haydon, A. E.
HYDE, Walter Woodburn, see Margolis, Max L.
IPPEL, Albert. Indische Kunst und Triumphalbild, [Ananda K. Coomaraswamy], 52 83
IRELAND, Philip Willard. 'Iraq: A Study in Political Development, [E. Speiser], 59 117-118
IVANOW, W. (ed.). Diwan of Khaki Khorasani, [P. Hitti], 56 510, 513
------ (tr.). True Meaning of Religion, [P. Hitti], 56 510, 513
------ (ed.). Two Early Ismaili Treatises, [P. Hitti], 56 510, 513
'IZZ AL-DĪN, N., see Zurayq, Qusṭi K.
JABBŪR, Jibrā'īl S. 'Aṣr ibn-abi-Rabī'ah, vol. I, [P. Hitti], 56 511, 515
------. Ibn- 'Abd Rabbihi wa-'Iqduhu, [P. Hitti], 54 436-437
JABLONSKI, Witold. Les "Siao-ha (i-eu) l-yu" de Pekin; un essai sur la poésie populaire en Chine, [J. K. Shryock], 56 375-376
JACKSON, A. V. Williams. Zoroastrian Studies: the Iranian Religion and Various Monographs, [Roland G. Kent], 49 286-289
JACOB, Georg and Jensen, Hans. Das chinesische Schattentheater, [T. T. Shui], 55 220-223
JACOBSEN, Thorkild. Philological Notes on Eshnunna and its Inscriptions, [E. Speiser], 54 434
JAMESON, R. D. Three Lectures on Chinese Folklore, [J. K. Shryock], 52 399-400
JANNAWAY, Frank G. The British Museum with Bible in Hand, 43 73
JARRING, Gunnar. Studien zu einer osttürkischen Lautlehre, [N. Martinovitch], 55 105-106
JENSEN, Hans, see Jacob, Georg
JIBRĀN, Jibrān Jalīl. al-Badā'i' wa-'l-Ṭarā'if, [J. Montgomery], 46 92-93
JIRKU, Anton. Die Wanderungen der Hebräer im 3. und 2. Jahrtausend v. Chr., [W. Albright], 48 183-185
JOHNSON, Allan C., H. S. Gehman and E. H. Kase (eds.). The John H. Scheide Biblical Papyri: Ezekiel, [J. Montgomery], 59 262-265
JOHNSON, Helen M. Triṣaṣṭiśalākāpuruṣacaritra. Vol. I. Ādīśvaracaritra, [W. Norman Brown], 52 86-88
JOHNSTON, E. H. The Buddhacarita: or, Acts of the Buddha, [Franklin Edgerton], 57 422-425
JOKL, Norbert. Linguistisch-kulturhistorische Untersuchungen aus dem Bereiche des Albanischen, [Harold H. Bender], 43 427-428
JOUVEAU-DUBREUIL, G. Vedic Antiquities, 43 75
JULIEN, Stanislas. Dictionary of the Manchu Language, unpublished MS. in the John G. White Collection, Cleveland Public Library, [Gordon W. Thayer, from account written by Dr. Berthold Laufer], 40 140
JŪZI, Bandali, and Q. Zurayq. Umarā' Ġassān min Āl Jafnah, [P. Hitti], 54 435-436
KAHLE, Paul. Der Leuchtturm von Alexandria, [H. Spoer], 52 59-61
------. Die verschollene Columbus-Karte von 1498 in einer türkischen Weltkarte von 1513, [N. Martinovitch], 55 106-107
------, M. Mustafa and M. Sobernheim (eds.). Badā'i' al-Zuhūr fi Waqā'i' al-Duhūr, of ibn-Iyās, [P. Hitti], 54 213, 436
KAKINUMA, Katashi. Catalogue of the Library of the South-Manchurian Railway, [J. K. Shryock], 56 381
KAMIL, Murad. Des Josef ben Gorion (Josippon) Geschichte der Juden, [C. Torrey], 59 260-262
KANE, Pandurang Vaman. History of Dharmaśāstra (Ancient and Mediaeval, Religious and Civil Law), [E. Washburn Hopkins], 51 80-84
KARANDIKAR, S. V. Hindu Exogamy, [E. Washburn Hopkins], 49 53
KASE, Edmund H. Jr., see Johnson, Allan C.
KASIR, Daoud S. The Algebra of Omar Khayyam, [P. Hitti], 52 267
KAZUMA KAWASE. Ko katsuji han no kenkyu, [Shio Sakanishi], 59 147-148
KEITH, Arthur Berriedale. Catalogue of the Sanskrit and Prākrit Manuscripts in the Library of the India Office. Volume II. Brahmanical and Jaina Manuscripts. With a Supplement: Buddhist Manuscripts, by F. W. Thomas, [Horace I. Poleman], 55 214-215
------. Classical Sanskrit Literature, [Walter E. Clark], 46 76-77
------. A History of Sanskrit Literature, [Franklin Edgerton], 50 77-79
KERNER, Robert J. Northeastern Asia, a Selected Bibliography, [Wing-Tsit Chan], 60 429-432
KHATAK, S. K., see Spies, Otto
KIMURA, Ryukan. A History of the Terms Hīnayāna and Mahāyāna and the Origin of Mahāyāna Buddhism, [E. Washburn Hopkins], 49 53
KIRFEL, W., see Heffening, W.
KÖNIG, Friedrich Wilhelm. Relief und Inschrift des Koenigs Dareios I am Felsen von Bagistan, [Roland G. Kent], 58 675-679
KOIZUMI, Akio and Shunichi Sawa. Rakuro Saikyu-bo, The Tomb of the Painted Basket and other two tombs of Lo-Lang, a report on the excavations of 1931, [Shio Sakanishi], 56 101-103
KOMAI, Kazuchika, see Harada, Yoshito
KÖSTER, August. Das antike Seewesen, [W. Edgerton], 44 77-79
KOLDEWEY, Robert. Das wieder erstehende Babylon, 4th ed., [G. Barton], 48 95-96
KOSCHAKER, Paul. Über einige griechische Rechtsurkunden aus den östlichen Randgebieten des Hellenismus, [E. Speiser], 52 255-257
KRAMRISCH, Stella. Indian Sculpture. [A. K. Coomaraswamy], 54 219-221
KRAUSE, Max (ed. and tr.). Die Sphärik von Menelaos aus Alexandrien in der Verbesserung von Abū Naṣr Manṣūr B. 'Ali B. 'Irāq, [P. Hitti], 59 524-525
KRAUSS, Samuel. Vier Jahrtausende jüdischen Palästinas, 43 73
KRISHNAMACHARYA, Embar. Tatvasaṁgraha of Śāntarakṣita, with the Commentary of Kamalaśīla, [Franklin Edgerton], 49 66-67
KRISHNASWAMI, P. R. Heber's Indian Journal, 43 349
KROLL, Josef. Gott und Hölle, [C. Kraeling], 53 290-292
KSHETREŚACHANDRA CHAṬṬOPĀDHĀYA. The Date of Kālidāsa, [Virginia Saunders], 49 75-76

KU CHIEH-KANG. The Autobiography of a Chinese Historian, Being the Preface to a Symposium on Ancient Chinese History, (Ku Shih Pien) translated and annotated by Arthur W. Hummel, [J. K. Shryock], 52 100
KU T'ing-ch'ang, see Löwenthal
KUMARAPPA, Bharatan. The Hindu Conception of the Deity As Culminating in Rāmānuja, [Horace I. Poleman], 55 329-330
KUO Pao-ch'ang, see Hsiang Yüan-pien
KURD-'ALI, Muḥammad. Kitāb Ḫiṭaṭ al-Šām, [P. Hitti], 46 321-322, 51 178-179
LACHMANN, Robert, (ed.). Zeitschrift für Vergleichende Musikwissenschaft, Vol. I, [A. K. Coomaraswamy], 54 223
LALOU, Marcelle. Catalogue du Fonds Tibétain de la Bibliothèque Nationale, Quatrième Partie, I. Les mDo-maṅ. Buddhica, IV, [Georges de Roerich], 52 395-399
LAMMENS, Henri. La Syrie. Précis historique, [J. Montgomery], 46 88, 90-91
LAMOTTE, Étienne. Saṃdhinirmocanasūtra, l'explication des mystères, Texte tibétain édité et traduit, [James R. Ware], 57 122-124
------. La Somme du Grand Vehicule, [J. K. Shryock], 60 115-116
LANDSBERGER, B. Die Serie ana ittišu, [A. Götze], 59 265-271
LANGDON, Stephen H. The Babylonian Epic of Creation, [G. Barton], 45 179-181
------. Oxford Editions of Cuneiform Inscriptions, Vol. I, Sumerian and Semitic Religious and Historical Texts; Vol. II, Historical Inscriptions, containing principally the Chronological Prism, W-B. 444, [T. Meek], 44 287-290
------. Oxford Edition of Cuneiform Inscriptions, vols. I and II, [G. Barton], 46 315-316
------, see also Watelin, L. C.
LATOURETTE, Kenneth Scott. The Chinese: Their History and Culture, [Cyrus H. Peake], 56 533-535
------. A History of the Expansion of Christianity, [J. Shryock], 57 438-440
------. (ed.). Progress of Chinese Studies in the United States of America, Bull. No. 1 of the Committee on the Promotion of Chinese Studies, 1931, [J. K. Shryock], 51 340-341
LAUFER, Berthold. The American Plant Migration, Part I: The Potato, prepared for publication by C. Martin Wilbur [L. C. Goodrich], 59 142-143
------. The Domestication of the Cormorant in China and Japan, Field Museum of Natural History publication no. 300: Anthropological series, Vol. XVIII, No. 3, [Esson M. Gale], 52 267-269
LAUTNER, Julius Georg. Altbabylonische Personenmiete und Erntearbeiterverträge, [F. Stephens], 58 476-481
LAW, Bimala Churn. Ancient Indian Tribes, [E. Washburn Hopkins], 49 177-178
------. Women in Buddhist Literature, [E. Washburn Hopkins], 49 52
LAZARUS, L. Zur Charakteristik der talmudischen Ethik, 43 73
LEANDER, Pontus. Laut- und Formenlehre des Ägyptisch-Aramäischen, [J. Montgomery], 51 317, 320-321
------, see also Bauer, Hans
LEANG K'i-Tch'ao (Liang Ch'i-ch'iao). La Conception de la Loi et les Theories des Legistes à la veille de Ts'in, Trs. Intro. et Notes par Jean Escarra et Robert Germain, [G. H. Danton], 49 76-78
LE COQ, A. von and E. Waldschmidt. Die buddhistische Spätantike in Mittelasien, Sechster Teil: Neue Bildwerke II. Mit einem Beitrag über die Darstellung und den Stil der Wandgemälde aus Qyzil bei Kutscha, [F. Edgerton], 49 62-64
------, and ------. Die buddhistische Spätantike in Mittelasien, Siebenter Teil, Neue Bildwerke III, including essays by Friederich Sarre, Otto Kümmel and Heinrich Lüders, [F. Edgerton], 53 360-361
LEGRAIN, Leon, see Gadd, C. J.
LESLAU, Wolf. Lexique Soqoṭri [D. Stehle], 60 110-112
LÉVI, Sylvain. L'Inde et le monde, [E. Washburn Hopkins], 49 177-178
LEVIS, John Hazedel. Foundations of Chinese Musical Art, [J. K. Shryock], 57 201-202
LEVY, Reuben. Deutero-Isaiah, [J. Montgomery], 47 89-90
------. (ed. and tr.). the Ma'ālim al-Qurba fi Aḥkām al-Ḥisba of ibn-al-Uḫuwwah, [P. Hitti], 59 523-524
------. Persian Literature. An Introduction, [A. V. W. Jackson], 44 138-139
LEWIS, Bernard. The Origins of Ismā'īlism, [A. Jeffery], 60 426-429
LIANG, William W. Y., see Löwenthal
LICENT, Emile, S. J. Comtes Rendus de Onze Années (1923-1933) de Séjour et D'Exploration dans le Bassin du Fleuve Jaune, du Pai Ho, et des Autres Tributaires du Golfe du Pei Tcheu ly. (Pub. du Musée Hoang Ho-Pai Ho, No. 38), [Eugene A. Golomshtok], 57 449-451
LIEBENTHAL, Walter. The Sutra of the Lord of Healing, [J. K. Shryock], 57 207
LITTMANN, Enno. Morgenländische Wörter im Deutschen, [R. Kent], 46 248-249
------. Syriac Inscriptions, [C. Torrey], 55 470-471
LIU, Chungshee H. A Study of the Tattooing Custom among the Li of Hainan Island, [J. K. Shryock], 57 198
LÖHR, Max. Untersuchungen zum Hexateuchproblem, I Der Priestkodex in der Genesis, [J. Morgenstern], 46 82-84
LÖWENTHAL, Rudolph, with the assistance of Ch'en Hung-shun, Ku T'ing-ch'ang and William W. Y. Liang. The Religious Periodical Press in China, [Derk Bodde], 60 584-585
LOKOTSCH, Karl. Etymologisches Wörterbuch der europäischen (germanischen, romanischen und slavischen) Wörter orientalischen Ursprungs, [Roland G. Kent], 49 93-94
LOMMEL, Herman. Die Religion Zarathustras, [Maria Wilkins Smith], 53 85-86
LONGHURST, A. H. Pallava Architecture, Parts I and II, [A. K. Coomaraswamy], 49 70-71
------. Pallava Architecture, Part III, [Ananda K. Coomaraswamy], 50 266
LUCE, G. H., and Pe Maung Tin. The Glass Palace Chronicle of the Kings of Burma, 43 348
LUCKENBILL, D. D. Ancient Records of Assyria and Babylonia, I and II, [W. Albright], 48 93-95
LUM, Bertha. Gods, Goblins and Ghosts, 43 75
MACDONELL, A. A. Hymns from the Rigveda, [L. C. Barret], 43 429-430
MC DOWELL, Robert Harbold. Coins from Seleucia on the Tigris, [J. Johnson], 56 517, 518
------. Stamped and Inscribed Objects from Seleucia on the Tigris, [J. Johnson], 56 517-518
MACNICOL, Margaret. Poems by Indian Women, [W. Norman Brown], 46 267
al-Maġribi, Šayḫ 'Abd-al-Qādir. al-Bayyināt fi 'l-Dīn wa-'l-Ijtimā' wa-'l-Abad wa-'l-Ta'rīḫ, [P. Hitti], 47 78-79
MAHMASSANI, Sobhi. Les idées économiques d'Ibn Khaldoun, [P. Hitti], 53 81
MAḤMŪD, 'Abbās. al-Islām wa-'l-Tajdīd fi Miṣr, [P. Hitti], 56 511, 513-514
MAJUMDAR, R. C. The Outline of Ancient Indian History and Civilisation, [E. Washburn Hopkins], 49 55
MALIWANAG, Ildefonso, and Fletcher Gardner. Indic Writings of the Mindoro-Palawan Axis, [Horace I. Poleman], 60 275
MALLIK, G. N. The Philosophy of Vaishnava Religion, vol. I, [E. Washburn Hopkins], 49 54
MALLOWAN, M. E. L. The Excavations at Tall Chagar Bazar, [M. Welker], 58 673-674
------, and J. C. Rose. Excavations at Tall Arpachiyah, [E. Speiser], 56 109-110
MALONE, Carroll Brown. "History of the Peking Summer Palaces under the Ch'ing Dynasty," University of Illinois Bull., XXXI, No. 41, 1934, [J. K. Shryock], 54 443

MAMOUR, P. H. Polemics on the Fatimi Caliphs, [N. Faris], 56 509

MÄNNINEN, I. Die Finnisch-Ugrischen Völker, [N. Martinovitch], 53 84-85

MARCH, Benjamin. Some Technical Terms of Chinese Painting, [J. K. Shryock], 56 382-383

MARCHAL, Sappho. Costumes et parures khmers d'après les Devatā d'Angkor Vat, [A. K. Coomaraswamy], 49 73

------. Dances cambodgiennes, [A. K. Coomaraswamy], 49 73

MARGOLIS, Max L., Montgomery, J., Hyde, W., Edgerton, F., Meek, T. and Schoff, W. The Song of Songs. A Symposium, [N. Schmidt], 46 189-192

MARGOULIES, Georges. Petit Précis de Grammaire Chinoise ecrite, [J. K. Shryock], 56 97

MARSHALL, Harry Ignatius. The Karen People of Burma: a Study in Anthropology and Ethnology, [B. Laufer], 45 185-187

MASSIGNON, Louis. Recueil de textes inédits concernant l'histoire de la mystique en pays d'Islam, [P. Hitti], 51 179

MATSUDAIRA, N. Les Fêtes Saisonnières au Japon, (Province de Mikawa), Étude descriptive et sociologique, [Alfred H. Sweet], 57 127-129

MAYER, Leo A., see Sukenik, E. L.

MÉDARD, M. Le Choei-king Tchou et l'ancienne géographie Indochinoise, [J. K. Shryock], 56 96-97

MEEK, Theophile J. Hebrew Origins, [J. Montgomery], 57 431-434

------, see also Margolis, Max L.

MEHTA, N. C. Studies in Indian Painting, [Ananda Coomaraswamy], 47 275-278

MEILLET, A. Trois Conférences sur les Gāthā de l'Avesta, [Roland G. Kent], 46 273-274

MEISSNER, Bruno. Beiträge zum Assyrischen Wörterbuch, I, [E. Speiser], 54 432-433

------. Die Keilschrift, 43 72

------, see also Ebeling, E.

MENDELSOHN, Isaac. Legal Aspects of Slavery in Babylonia, Assyria and Palestine, [T. Meek], 53 72-73

MENZEL, Theodor (ed.). Festschrift Georg Jacob, [C. Torrey], 54 89-90

MERCER, Samuel A. B. The Ethiopic Text of the Book of Ecclesiastes, [H. Gehman], 52 260-263

------. Études sur les origines de la religion de l'Égypte, [G. Barton], 53 169-170

MERRILL, Elmer D. and Egbert H. Walker. A Bibliography of Eastern Asiatic Botany, [L. C. Goodrich], 59 138-142

MIALL, Bernard, and Franz Kuhn. Chin P'ing Mei (translated), [J. K. Shryock], 60 278-280

MICHALSKI-IWIENSKI, St. F. Atmabodha czyli Poznanie Duszy. Traktat Wedantyczny przez Śankaraczarje, 43 254-255

------. Bhagavadgītā, [Franklin Edgerton], 43 65-67

MILES, John C., see Driver, G. R.

MILNE, Mrs. Leslie. The Home of an Eastern Clan. A Study of the Palaungs of the Shan States, [B. Laufer], 45 187-189

MINGANA, Alphonse. Christian Documents in Syriac, Arabic and Garshūni, [J. Montgomery], 49 284-286, 56 499-500

------. Commentary of Theodore of Mopsuestia on the Lord's Prayer, and on the Sacraments of Baptism and the Eucharist, [A. Vaschalde], 54 91-93

------. Woodbrooke Studies, vols. III and V, [A. Vaschalde], 53 170-173

MITTWOCH, Eugen, see Mordtmann, J. H.

MOELLER, Wächterrufe, 43 73

MONAHAN, F. J., The Early History of Bengal, 46 94-95

MONTET, Edouard. Choix de proverbes, dictons, maximes et pensées de l'Islam, [P. Hitti], 57 326

MONTGOMERY, James A. Arabia and the Bible, [P. Hitti], 54 302-303

------. A Critical and Exegetical Commentary on the Book of Daniel, [M. Margolis], 49 78-82

------ and Zellig S. Harris. The Ras Shamra Mythological Texts, [J. Obermann], 56 495-498

------ see also Margolis, Max L.

MORDTMANN, J. H., and E. Mittwoch. Sabäische Inschriften, [J. Montgomery], 52 194-196

MORGENSTIERNE, Georg. An Etymological Vocabulary of Pashto, [F. Howland], 52 65, 67-68

MULLER, J. A. Apostle of China: Samuel Isaac Joseph Schereschewsky, [J. K. Shryock], 58 696-697

MUNRO, Dana. The Kingdom of the Crusades, [P. Hitti], 56 510, 512

MURGOTTEN, Francis Clark. The Origins of the Islamic State, [P. Hitti], 46 274-284

MUS, Paul. Barabuḍur. [Ananda K. Coomaraswamy], 57 336-343

------. Le Buddha paré: son origine indienne. Çakyamuni dans le Mahāyānisme moyen, [Ananda K. Coomaraswamy], 50 263-264

MUṢṬAFA, M., see Kahle, Paul

NÂG, Kâlidâs. Les théories diplomatiques de l'Inde ancienne et l'Arthaçâstra, [E. Washburn Hopkins], 44 76-77

NARIMAN, G. K. Priyadarśikā, A Sanskrit Drama by Harsha, [Walter E. Clark], 46 77-78

NĀZIM, Muḥammad. The Life and Times of Sultan Maḥmūd of Ghazna, [F. Buckler], 53 75-76

NEISSER, Walter. Zum Wörterbuch des Ṛgveda, [Maurice Bloomfield], 45 157-172

NIELSEN, Ditlef. Handbuch der altarabischen Altertumskunde, [J. Montgomery], 48 80-83

NODA, Churyo. Chou pi suan ching no kenkyu, [Shio Sakanishi], 54 96-97

NOËTTES, Lefebure des. L'Attelage et le cheval de selle à travers les âges: contribution à l'histoire de l'esclavage, [Ananda K. Coomaraswamy], 52 84-86

NYKL, A. R. The Dove's Neck-Ring about Love and Lovers, [P. Hitti], 52 58-59

------ (ed.). al-Niṣf al-Awwal min Kitāb al-Zahrah of Muḥammad ibn-abi Sulaymān al-Iṣfahāni, [P. Hitti], 54 215-216

OBBINK, H. T. De godsdienst in zijn verschijningsvormen, [N. Schmidt], 54 303-306

OBERMANN, Julian. The Arabic Original of Ibn Shāhīn's Book of Comfort, [S. Skoss], 56 506-508

OBERMEYER, Jacob. Die Landschaft Babyloniens im Zeitalter des Talmuds und des Gaonats, [E. Speiser], 50 267-268

OESTERLY, W. O. E. The Jewish Background of the Christian Liturgy, [R. Yerkes], 47 79, 83-84

OGDEN, C. K., and I. A. Richards. The Meaning of Meaning, [A. K. Coomaraswamy], 53 298-303

OLDENBERG, Hermann. Die Lehre der Upanishaden und die Anfänge des Buddhismus, 43 254

OLDENBERG, H. Das Mahābhārata. Seine Entstehung, sein Inhalt, seine Form, [E. Washburn Hopkins], 43 54-56

O'MALLEY, L. S. S. Indian Caste Customs, [George W. Briggs], 53 181-186

VON DER OSTEN, Hans Henning. The Alishar Hüyük. Seasons of 1930-32, [A. Götze], 59 510-515

------ and Eric Schmidt. The Alishar Hüyük, Season of 1927, Part I, [W. Albright], 51 173-175

OSWĀL, Motīlāl Lādhāji. Hemacandrācāryaviracitā Anyayogavyavachedikā, tadvyākhyā ca śrī-Malliṣeṇasūripraṇītā Syādvādamañjarī, [Franklin Edgerton], 49 67-68

PALAK, Naoum Elias. Majmū' al-Alfāẓ al-Suryānīyah min al-'Arabīyah al-'Āmmīyah fi mā bayn al-Nahrayn wa-Ḥuṣūṣān al-'Arabīyah al-Āmidīyah, [P. Hitti], 47 77-78

PARANJPE, Vâsudeva Gopâla. Le Vârtika de Kâtyâyana, 45 93-94

PARET, Rudi. Die legendäre Maghāzī-Literatur, [M. Sprengling], 52 263-265

------ (ed.). Orientalistische Studien Enno Littmann... überreicht, [J. Montgomery], 56 104-106

------. Zur Frauenfrage in der arabisch-islamischen Welt, [P. Hitti], 57 326
PARGITER, F. E. Ancient Historical Tradition, [Walter Eugene Clark], 43 132-141
PAVRY, Cursetji Erachji. Iranian Studies, [Maria Wilkins Smith], 49 174-176
PAVRY, Jal Dastur Cursetji. The Zoroastrian Doctrine of a Future Life from Death to the Individual Judgment, [Roland G. Kent], 48 285-286
PEAKE, Cyrus H. Nationalism and Education in Modern China, [J. K. Shryock], 53 93-94
PEET, T. Eric. A Comparative Study of the Literatures of Egypt, Palestine, and Mesopotamia, [W. Albright], 52 51-52
PE MAUNG TIN and G. H. Luce. The Glass Palace Chronicle of the Kings of Burma, 43 348
PERKINS, P. D. and Ione. Lafcadio Hearn: A Bibliography of His Writings, [J. K. Shryock], 54 444
PETRIE, William Matthew Flinders. Ancient Gaza I. Tell el-Ajjūl, [W. Albright], 53 285-287
PFEIFFER, Robert H. The Archives of Shilwateshup, son of the King, [E. Speiser], 52 257-260
PHELPS, D. L. Omei Illustrated Guide Book, [J. K. Shryock], 57 349-350
PIEPKORN, A. C. Historical Prism Inscriptions of Ashurbanipal, [E. Speiser], 54 434
PODUVAL, Vasudeva. Kathakali (pp. 13), and Diagrams of Hand Poses in Kathakali, [A. K. Coomaraswamy], 51 180
POEBEL, Arno. Das appositionell bestimmte Pronomen der 1. Pers. Sing. in den westsemitischen Inschriften und im Alten Testament, [E. Speiser], 54 433-434
------. The Sumerian Prefix Forms E- and I- in the Time of the Earlier Princes of Lagaš, [E. Speiser], 54 433
POLEMAN, H. I. A Census of Indic Manuscripts in the United States and Canada, [M. B. Emeneau], 59 133-135
POPPER, William. Abū 'l-Maḥāsin ibn Taghrī Birdī's Annals, [J. Montgomery], 51 327, 328-329
------. Extracts from Abu 'l-Maḥāsin ibn Taghrī Birdī's Chronicle entitled ḥawādith ad-duhūr fī madā l'-ayyām wash-shuhūr, [J. Montgomery], 51 327, 328-329
------. Parallelism in Isaiah, [J. Reider], 45 82-88
PRASAD, Beni. History of Jahangir, 43 349-350
------. The State in Ancient India, [E. Washburn Hopkins], 49 52-53
------. Theory of Government in Ancient India, [E. Washburn Hopkins], 49 52-53
PRICE, Ira Maurice. The Great Cylinder Inscriptions A & B of Gudea, [G. Barton], 48 84-87
PRITCHARD, Earl H. The Crucial Years of Early Anglo-Chinese Relations, 1750-1800. Research Studies of the State College of Washington, Vol. IV, Nos. 3-4, [T. K. Fairbank], 57 353-357
QADRI, S. G. Mohiuddin. Hindustani Phonetics, [George William Brown], 52 79-80
QURBĀN, Dāwūd (tr.). al-'Uṣūr al-Qadīmah, [P. Hitti], 49 85, 87-88
RAMACHANDRAN, T. N. Buddhist Sculptures from a Stupa near Goli Village, Guntur District, [W. Norman Brown], 52 90
------. Tiruparuttikunram and its Temples, [W. Norman Brown], 54 438-440
------ and F. H. Gravely. Catalogue of the South Indian Metal Images in the Madras Government Museum, [A. K. Coomaraswamy], 53 187-188
RAMAKRISHNAIAH, K. Studies in Dravidian Philology, [Edwin H. Tuttle], 57 112-115
RANADE, R. D. A Constructive Survey of Upanishadic Philosophy, [E. Washburn Hopkins], 47 274-275
------ and S. K. Belvalkar. History of Indian Philosophy, [E. Washburn Hopkins], 49 54-55
ABU-RAŠĪD, 'Abbūd. al-Riḥlah al-Dāntīyah fi 'l-Mamālik al-Ilāhīyah, [P. Hitti], 54 435
RATHJENS, Carl, and H. von Wissmann. Vorislamische Altertümer, [J. Montgomery], 53 289-290
RAWSON, Joseph Nadin. The Kaṭha Upaniṣad, [Horace I. Poleman], 55 215-216
REICH, N. (ed.). Mizraim, Vol. I, [H. Gehman], 53 292-293
REISCHAUER, Jean, see Reischauer, Robert Karl
REISCHAUER, Robert Karl, and Jean. Early Japanese History (c. 40 B.C. - A.D. 1167), [Hugh Borton], 59 143-146
RELE, Vasant G. The Mysterious Kundalini, [George W. Briggs], 48 185
RENOU, Louis. Études de grammaire sanskrite. Première série, [Franklin Edgerton], 56 362-364
------. La valeur du parfait dans les hymnes védiques, [Franklin Edgerton], 49 64-66
RIBAUD, Michel. Le Vieux Japon: "La Route de la Mer orientale," Voyage du Jeune Stanislas au Japon, ou Essais sur la Civilisation japonaise — Histoire, Religion, Philosophie, Litérature & Beaux-arts. Vol. II, [Shio Sakanishi], 57 131
RICHARDS, I. A. Mencius on the Mind, [A. K. Coomaraswamy], 53 298-303
RICHARDS, I. A., and C. K. Ogden. The Meaning of Meaning, [A. K. Coomaraswamy], 53 298-303
RIDDLE, D. W., see Goodspeed, Edgar J.
RIHANI, Amin. Ta'rīḫ Najd al-Ḥadīt wa-Mulqaḥātihi, [J. Montgomery], 51 328, 332-334
RITSCHER, Walter H. Municipal Government in the Lebanon, [P. Hitti], 54 438
RITTER, Hellmut, (ed.). Kitāb Firaq al-Šī'ah of al-Nawbaḫti, [P. Hitti], 54 214
------ (ed.). Kitāb al-Wāfi bi-'l-Wafāyāt of ibn-Aybak al-Ṣafadi, [P. Hitti], 54 214-215
------. Karagös. Türkische Schattenspiel, [N. Martinovitch], 46 284-285
ROBERTS, Stephen H. Population Problems of the Pacific, [A. J. Saunders], 48 74-76
ROBINSON, D. M., see Buckler, W. H.
ROERICH, G. N. The Animal Style among the Nomads of Northern Tibet, Seminarium Kondakovianum, [E. A. Golomshtok], 53 89-91
------. Trails to Inmost Asia. Five Years of Exploration with the Roerich Central Asian Expedition, [B. Laufer], 52 95-97
RONALDSHAY, Earl of. Lands of the Thunderbolt, 43 349
ROORDA, T. B. (ed.). Choix d'objets d'art d'Extrême-Orient conservés dans les Pays Bas, [B. Laufer], 43 337
ROSE, J. Cruikshank, see Mallowan, M. E. L.
ROSTOVTZEFF, M. Caravan Cities, [J. Montgomery], 53 287-288
------ (ed.). The Excavations at Dura-Europos. Preliminary Report of the Fifth Season of Work, October 1931 - March 1932, [J. Johnson], 55 210-214
------, A. Bellinger, C. Hopkins and C. Welles (eds.). The Excavations of Dura-Europos. Preliminary Report of the Sixth Season ... Oct. 1932 - Mar. 1933, [W. Albright], 57 318-321
ROTHENSTEIN, William. Ancient India, [Ananda Coomaraswamy] 46 253-256
von ROTTER, Gough, von Buttel-Reepen and Armbruster. Die Biene in Aegypten jetzt und vor 5000 Jahren, [N. Reich], 43 431
ROWLAND, Jr., Benjamin. The Wall-Paintings of India, Central Asia, and Ceylon, [W. Norman Brown], 58 484-485
ROWLEY, H. H. The Aramaic of the Old Testament, [J. Montgomery], 51 317, 321-323
RUDOLPH, Richard C., see Creel, H. G.
RUSKA, Julius. Das Buch der Alaune und Salze, [P. Hitti], 57 325-326
RUSTUM, Asad J. The Royal Archives of Egypt and the Disturbances in Palestine, 1834, [P. Hitti], 59 528
------. The Royal Archives of Egypt and the Origins of the Egyptian Expedition to Syria 1831-1841, [P. Hitti], 57 322, 324, 59 528

------, see also Al-Šihābi, Ḥaydar
RYCKMANS, G. Les noms propres sudsémitiques, [J. Montgomery], 55 314-316
SA'D, Ḥalīl, As'ad Ḫayrallāh and Erdman, Paul. al-Mu'jam al-'Aṣri fi 'l-Inki-līzi wa-'l-'Arabi (Centennial English-Arabic Dictionary), [P. Hitti], 49 85-86
SAKANISHI, Shio. Kyogen, [J. K. Shryock], 59 150
SAKISIAN, Armenag Bey. La miniature persane, [A. Coomaraswamy], 50 81
SALEEBY, Najeeb Mitry. The Language of Education of the Philippine Islands, [Frank R. Blake], 46 61-71
SARFARĀZ, 'Abd-al-Qādir. A Descriptive Catalogue of the Arabic, Persian and Urdu Manuscripts in the Library of the University of Bombay, [P. Hitti], 57 322-323
ŚARMĀ, H. Padmapurāṇa and Kālidāsa, 46 95-96
SARUP, Lakshman. Fragments of the Commentaries of Skandasvāmin and Maheśvara on the Nirukta, [Franklin Edgerton], 50 175-176
------. Indices and Appendices to the Nirukta, with an Introduction, [Franklin Edgerton], 50 175-176
------. The Vision of Vāsavadattā. (Svapnavāsavadattam), 46 95
------. The Vision of Vāsavadattā, [Virginia Saunders], 49 74-75
SASTRI, Hirananda. Indian Pictorial Art as developed in Book-Illustrations, [W. Norman Brown], 57 118-119
SASTRI, H. K. Two Statues of Pallava Kings and Five Pallava Inscriptions in a Rock Temple at Mamallapuram, [A. K. Coomaraswamy], 49 70-71
SASTRI, Mahamahopadhyaya T. Gaṇapati. Samarāṅgaṇasūtradhāra by King Bhojadeva, 45 337
ŚĀSTRĪ, S. N. Mojumdar. Ancient India as described by Ptolemy, [E. Washburn Hopkins], 49 55
ŚĀSTRĪ, T. Gaṇapati. Samarāṅgaṇasūtradhāra by King Bhojadeva, Volume II, [A. K. Coomaraswamy], 49 69
ŚĀSTRĪ, Vishva Bandhu Vidyārthī. The Atharva-Prātiśākhyam or the Phonetico-grammatical Aphorisms of the Atharva-Veda, 46 96
SAUNDERS, Kenneth. The Heritage of Asia, [A. Eustace Haydon], 54 103-104
------. Lotuses of the Mahāyāna, 44 290-291
SAWA, Shumichi, see Koizumi, Akio
SAWAKICHI, Kitamura. Grundriss der Ju-Lehre, [J. K. Shryock], 57 196-198
SBATH, Paul. al-Mašra', 44 291
SCHELTEMA, J. F. The Lebanon in Turmoil, [P. Hitti], 43 338-347
SCHERMAN, Lucian and Christine. Im Stromgebiet des Irrawaddy, Birma und seine Frauenwelt, [B. Laufer], 45 189-191
SCHILLER, A. Arthur. Ten Coptic Legal Texts, [W. Worrell and H. Youtie], 52 377-380
SCHJÖTH, Fr. Currency of the Far East. The Schjöth Collection at the Numismatic Cabinet of the University of Oslo, Norway, [Howland Wood], 51 341-342
SCHLOESSINGER, Max (ed.). Ansāb al-Ašrāf of al-Balāḏuri, vol. IV B, [P. Hitti], 59 528
SCHMIDT, Carl. Kephalaia, I, [H. Gehman], 56 520-522
SCHMIDT, Eric. Excavations at Tepe Hissar, Damghan, [E. Speiser], 59 115-117
SCHMIDT, Nathaniel. Ibn Khaldun, Historian, Sociologist and Philosopher, [J. Montgomery], 51 327, 328
SCHNABEL, Paul. Berossus und die babylonisch-hellenistische Literatur, [A. Olmstead], 46 85-87
SCHNEIDER, Anna. Die Anfänge der Kulturwirtschaft: Die Sumerische Tempelstadt, [G. Barton], 43 248-249
SCHOFF, Wilfred H., see Margolis, Max L.
SCHRADER, F. Otto. The Kashmir Recension of the Bhagavad Gītā, [Franklin Edgerton], 52 68-75
SCOTT, Sir J. G. Burma, from the earliest times to the present day, 44 290
SELLIN, Ernst. Das Alte Testament und die evangelische Kirche der Gegenwart, 43 72-73
------. Wie wurde Sichem eine israelitische Stadt? [W. Albright], 45 182-184
SHAH, Chimanlal J. Jainism in North India. 800 B.C. - A.D. 526, [Helen M. Johnson], 52 392-395
SHASTRI, Bhagabat Kumar. The Bhakti Cult of Ancient India, 43 255
SHĀSTRI, Mangal Deva. The Ṛg-Vedaprātiśākhya, with the Commentary of Uvaṭa, 43 350-351
SHIRATORI, Kurakichi (ed.). Memoirs of the Research Department of the Toyo Bunko, No. 4, [J. K. Shryock], 56 377-378
SHRYOCK, John K. Desire and the Universe, a Study of Religions, [George A. Barton], 55 479-482
------. The Origin and Development of the State Cult of Confucius, [J. J. L. Duyvendak], 55 330-338
------. The Study of Human Abilities, The Jen Wu Chih of Liu Shao, [J. J. L. Duyvendak], 59 280-282
------. The Temples of Anking and their Cults, [Esson M. Gale], 52 98-100
SIGURET, J. (Tr.). Territoires et Populations des Confins du Yunnan, [Shryock, J. K.], 57 350-351
al-ŠIHĀBI, Ḥaydar. Lubnān fi 'Ahd al-Umarā' al-Šihābīyīn, ed. A. Rustum and F. al-Bustāni, [P. Hitti], 56 511, 515-516
SILBERSCHMIDT, Max. Das orientalische Problem zur Zeit der Entstehung des Türkischen Reiches, [D. Munro], 45 175-176
SINHA, Jadunath. Indian Realism [J. K. Shryock], 59 151-152
SIRÉN, Osvald. The Chinese on the Art of Painting: Translations and Comments, [Shio Sakanishi], 56 531-533
SKÖLD, Hannes. The Nirukta, [LeRoy C. Barret], 47 335-336
SKOSS, Solomon L. The Hebrew-Arabic Dictionary of the Bible known as Kitab Jami Al-Alfaz [B. Cohen], 60 108-110
SMITH, Margaret. Studies in Early Mysticism in the Near and Middle East, [H. Spoer], 53 173-175
SNEATH, E. Hershey (ed.). Religion and the Future Life, [G. Barton], 43 250-251
SOARES, Anthony Xavier. Portuguese Vocables in Asiatic Languages, [M. B. Emeneau], 60 112-114
SOBERNHEIM, Moritz, see Kahle, Paul
SOOTHILL, W. E. The Lotus of the Wonderful Law, [J. K. Shryock], 51 185
------ and L. Hodous; A Dictionary of Chinese Buddhist Terms, [Shryock, J. K.], 58 694-695
SOWERBY, Arthur de Carle. Nature in Chinese Art, [L. C. Goodrich], 60 580-584
SPEISER, E. A. Excavations at Tepe Gawra, vol. I, [V. Müller], 55 466-469
------. Mesopotamian Origins, [W. Albright], 51 60-66
SPENCER, Arthur Marshman, and Edward J. Thompson. Bengali Religious Lyrics, Śakta, [Walter E. Clark], 46 270-272
SPIES, Otto, and S. K. Khatak (eds. and trs.). Three Treatises on Mysticism by Shihābuddin Suhrawerdī Maqtūl, [E. Jurji], 56 516-517
SPRENGLING, Martin, and W. C. Graham. Barhebraeus' Scholia on the Old Testament, [A. Vaschalde], 52 374-375
STCHOUKINE, Ivan. La peinture iranienne, [E. Schroeder], 57 120-121
STERN, Philippe. Le Bayon d'Angkor et l'evolution de l'art khmer, [Ananda K. Coomaraswamy], 49 330-331
STREET, Julian. Mysterious Japan, 43 75
STURTEVANT, Edgar H. A Comparative Grammar of the Hittite Language, [E. A. Speiser], 54 206-208
------. A Hittite Glossary. Second Edition, [Albrecht Goetze], 57 109-111
SUBHAN, John A. Sufism, its Saints and Shrines, [J. Archer], 59 274-275

SUKENIK, E. L. Ancient Synagogues in Palestine and Greece, [C. Kraeling], 55 107-109
------ and Leo A. Mayer. The Third Wall of Jerusalem, [C. Mc Cown], 52 56-58
SUKTHANKAR, Bhālchandra Sitaram. Translation from the original Marathi of Bal Gangadhar Tilak, Śrīmad Bhagavadgītā Rahasya or Karma-Yoga-Śāstra, [Franklin Edgerton], 56 525-528
SUKTHANKAR, Vishnu S. The Mahābhārata, for the first time critically edited, [Franklin Edgerton], 48 186-190
------. The Mahābhārata, [Franklin Edgerton], 49 282-284
------. The Mahābhārata, [E. Washburn Hopkins], 51 179-180
------. The Mahābhārata, Ādiparvan: Fascicule 5, [Franklin Edgerton], 52 252-254
------. The Mahābhārata. Ādiparvan: Fascicule 7, [Franklin Edgerton], 56 360-362
------. Vāsavadattā, 43 351
SULZBERGER, Mayer. The Status of Labor in Ancient Israel, [J. M. P. Smith], 45 184-185
SUNAVALA, A. J. Vijaya Dharma Sūri, [Helen M. Johnson], 45 328-329
SŪRI, Çrī Vijaya Indra. Reminiscences of Vijaya Dharma Sūri, [Helen M. Johnson], 45 328-329
SUZUKI, D. T. Essays in Zen Buddhism: Second Series, [J. K. Shryock], 54 223-225
------. An Introduction to Zen Buddhism, [Shio Sakanishi], 57 445-446
------ (tr.). The Laṅkāvatāra Sūtra: A Mahayana Text, [Clarence H. Hamilton], 53 87-89
------. Manual of Zen Buddhism, [Shio Sakanishi], 57 447
------. Studies in the Laṅkāvatāra Sūtra, [Clarence H. Hamilton], 52 91-93
------. The Training of the Zen Buddhist Monk, [Shio Sakanishi], 57 446-447
SWALLOW, R. W. Ancient Chinese Bronze Mirrors, [A. G. Wenley], 57 443-445
SWANN, Nancy Lee. Pan Chao: Foremost Woman Scholar of China, [J. K. Shryock], 53 91-92
TARAPOREWALA, Irach Jehangir Sorabji. Selections from Avesta and Old Persian (First Series). Part I, [G. C. O. Haas], 43 255-256
TARRĀZĪ, Fīlīb. Ta'rīḫ al-Ṣaḥāfah al-'Arabīyah, [P. Hitti], 54 437
TAZAWA, Kingo, see Harada, Yoshito
TENG, Ku. Chinesische Malkunsttheorie in der T'ang-und Sungzeit: Versuch einer geschichtlichen Betrachtung, [Shio Sakanishi], 56 530-531
THACKERAY, H. St. John. Josephus the Man and the Historian, [S. Cohon], 53 176-178
THILO, Martin. Die Chronologie des Danielbuches, [J. Montgomery], 47 280-281
THOMAS, Edward J. Vedic Hymns, [L. C. Barret], 43 428-429
THOMAS, F. W. Buddhist Manuscripts. Supplement to Catalogue of the Sanskrit and Prākrit Manuscripts in the Library of the India Office. Volume II. Brahmanical and Jaina Manuscripts. By Arthur Berriedale Keith, [Horace I. Poleman], 55 214-215
------ (tr.). Tibetan Literary Texts and Documents concerning Chinese Turkestan. Part I: Literary Texts, [James R. Ware], 57 125-126
THOMPSON, Edward J., and Arthur Marshman Spencer. Bengali Religious Lyrics, Śakta, [Walter E. Clark], 46 270-272
THOMPSON, Herbert. The Gospel of St. John According to the Earliest Coptic Manuscript, [H. Gehman], 46 286-287
THUREAU-DANGIN, F. Textes mathématiques babyloniens, [H. Lewy], 60 105-107
TILAK, Bal Gangadhar. Śrīmad Bhagavadgītā Rahasya or Karma-Yoga-Śāstra. Translated from the original Marathi by Bhalchandra Sitaram Sukthankar, [Franklin Edgerton], 56 525-528
TODA, Kenji, see Driscoll, Lucy
TORREY, Charles Cutler. The History of the Conquest of Egypt, North Africa and Spain, by Ibn 'Abd Al-Ḥakam, [R. Gottheil], 43 144-148
------. The Jewish Foundation of Islam, [A. Halkin], 54 209-212
------. Pseudo-Ezekiel and the Original Prophecy, [I. Matthews], 52 368-373
TOTAH, Khalil A. Contribution of the Arabs to Education, [P. Hitti], 47 282-284
------ [Ṭōṭaḥ, Ḫalīl]. al-Tarbiyah 'ind al-'Arab, [P. Hitti], 54 436
TOUSSAINT, Gustave-Charles. Le Dict de Padma, Padma thang yig, Ms. de Lithang, traduit du Thibetain, [J. R. Ware], 54 311-313
TUN LI-CH'EN. Annual Customs and Festivals in Peking, tr. and annotated by Derk Bodde, [J. K. Shryock], 57 204
TURNER, Ralph Lilley. A Comparative and Etymological Dictionary of the Nepali Language, [W. Norman Brown], 51 288-289
TYAN, Émile. Histoire de l'organisation judiciaire en pays d'Islam, [G. von Grunebaum], 59 519-522
UMEHARA, Sueji, see Hamada, Kosaku
al-'UNAYSI, Ṭūbīyah. Tafsīr al-Alfāẓ al-Daḫīlah fi 'l-Luġah al-'Arabīyah, 2nd ed. by Tūma al-Bustāni, [P. Hitti], 53 79
UNGER, E. Babylon — Die Heilige Stadt, [R. Dougherty], 52 54-55
UNGNAD, Arthur. Subartu, [A. Götze], 57 104-109
UPADHYE, A. N. Pravacanasāra, Śrī Kundakundācārya's, [Helen M. Johnson], 56 523-525
VAHID BEY, A. A Condensed Dictionary, English-Turkish, [N. Martinovitch], 46 185-186
VAIDYA, C. V. History of Sanskrit Literature. Vol. I. Śruti (Vedic) Period, [P. E. Dumont], 52 391-392
VALLÉE-Poussin, L. de la. Indo-Européens et Indo-Iraniens. L'Inde jusque vers 300 av. J.-C., 46 95
VENKATARAMANAN, S. Select Works of Sri Sankaracharya, 43 76
VOGEL, J. Ph. Indian Serpent Lore, or the Nāgas in Hindu Legend and Art, [Ananda K. Coomaraswamy], 49 186-190
------. La sculpture de Mathurā, [Ananda K. Coomaraswamy], 51 54-58
WADDELL, L. Austine. The Buddhism of Tibet, [J. K. Shryock], 55 225
------. Historical Origin and Economic Purpose of the Tower of Babel and the Name "Shinar," [G. Barton], 43 251-253
------. The Indo-Sumerian Seals Deciphered, [G. Brown], 47 284-285
------. The Phoenician Origin of Britons, Scots and Anglo-Saxons, [R. Kent], 45 172-174
WALDSCHMIDT, Ernst. Die buddhistische Spätantike in Mittelasien. Siebenter (Schluss) Teil, [Franklin Edgerton], 53 360-361
------ and A. von LeCoq. Die buddhistische Spätantike in Mittelasien. Sechster Teil, [Franklin Edgerton], 49 62-64
WALES, H. G. Quaritch. Ancient Siamese Government and Administration, [J. K. Shryock], 55 340
WALEY, Arthur. Zen Buddhism and its Relation to Art, 43 75
WALKER, Egbert H., see also Merrill, Elmer D.
WALKER, Frank K., see van Hoesen, Henry B.
WANG TCH'ANG-TCHE, S. J. La Philosophie Morale de Wang Yang-ming, [J. K. Shryock], 57 352-353
WARDLE, W. Lansdell. Israel and Babylon, [G. Barton], 46 314
WARE, James R. Vocabularies to the Elementary Chinese Texts used at Harvard University, [J. K. Shryock], 57 195-196
------. Vocabularies to the Intermediate Chinese Texts used at Harvard University, [J. K. Shryock], 58 692
WARMINGTON, E. H. The Commerce between the Roman Empire and India, [A. K. Coomaraswamy], 51 180-182

WARNER, Langdon. Buddhist Wall-Paintings, [J. K. Shryock], 59 155-156
------. The Craft of the Japanese Sculptor, [Kojiro Tomita], 56 536
WATELIN, L. C. and S. Langdon. Excavations at Kish, III, [W. Albright], 52 54
WATERMAN, Leroy. Royal Correspondence of the Assyrian Empire, I-III, [T. Meek], 53 68-70
WATTS, Alan W. The Spirit of Zen, [J. K. Shryock], 57 204-205
WEIDNER, E., see Ebeling, E.
WEIL, Gotthold. Tatarische Texte, [N. Martinovitch], 52 63
WEISS, Adolf. Mose ben Maimon. Führer der Unschlüssigen, [H. Davidowitz], 48 190-191
WELLES, C., see Rostovtzeff, M. I.
WENSINCK, A. J. Concordance et indices de la tradition musulmane, [P. Hitti], 56 510-512
WIENER, Harold. Early Hebrew History and Other Studies, [J. Montgomery], 47 90-91
WILBUR, C. Martin, see Laufer, Berthold
WILDES, Harry Emerson. Aliens in the East, [J. K Shryock], 59 149-150
WILHELM, Richard. A History of Chinese Civilization, tr. by Joan Joshua, [J. K. Shryock], 50 168-169
------ (tr.). The Secret of the Golden Flower: A Chinese Book of Life, [A. K. Coomaraswamy], 53 303-305
WILKINSON, J. V. S. The Lights of Canopus: Anvār i Suhailī, [A. Coomaraswamy], 50 170-171
------. The Shāh Nāmah of Firdausī, [A. Coomaraswamy], 52 254-255
WILLIAMS, Charles Allyn. Oriental Affinities of the Legend of the Hairy Anchorite, 45 337
WILLIAMSON, R. H. Wang An Shih, A Chinese Statesman and Educationalist of the Sung Dynasty, Vol. I, [J. K. Shryock], 56 99-101
------. Wang An Shih, Vol. II, [J. K. Shryock], 57 440-442
WILLOUGHBY, H. R., see Goodspeed, Edgar J.
WILSON, C. E. The Haft Paikar (The Seven Beauties) by Nizami of Ganja, [N. Martinovitch], 46 285-286
WIMSTATT, Genevieve. Selling Wilted Peonies, [J. K. Shryock], 57 206
WINLOCK, H. E. and Crum, W. E. The Monastery of Epiphanius at Thebes, [A. Boak and W. Worrell], 47 85-87
WINTERNITZ, M. Geschichte der indischen Litteratur. Dritter Band, [Louis H. Gray], 43 332-336
------. A History of Indian Literature. Vol. II. Buddhist Literature and Jain Literature. Translated from the original German by Mrs. S. Ketkar and Miss H. Kohn, [Helen M. Johnson], 56 371-373
von WISSMANN, Hermann, see Rathjens, Carl
WITTFOGEL, K. A. Wirtschaft und Gesellschaft Chinas; Erster Teil; Produktivkräfte, Produktions- und Zirkulationsprozess, [J. K. Shryock], 53 363
WOLFENDEN, Stuart N. Outlines of Tibeto-Burman Linguistic Morphology, [J. K. Shryock], 51 339-340
WOLFSON, Harry Austryn. Crescas' Critique of Aristotle, [I. Husik], 50 166-168
WOODHEAD, H. G. W. (ed.). The China Year Book, 1921-2, 43 74-75
WOOLLEY, C. Leonard. Ur Excavations, II: The Royal Cemetery, [V. Müller], 55 204-208
WOOLNER, Alfred C. Asoka Text and Glossary, [Truman Michelson], 46 264-265
WORRELL, William H. A Study of Races in the Ancient Near East, [E. Speiser], 49 181
WRIGHT, G. Ernest. The Pottery of Palestine from the Earliest Times to the End of the Early Bronze Age, 58 671-673
WÜST, Walter. Stilgeschichte und Chronologie des Ṛgveda, [Franklin Edgerton], 49 276-282
------. Vergleichendes und etymologisches Wörterbuch des Alt-Indoarischen (Altindischen). Lieferung 1-3, [Franklin Edgerton], 56 364-370
------ and others. Studia Indo-Iranica. Ehrengabe für Wilhelm Geiger zur Vollendung des 75. Lebensjahres 1856-21. Juli - 1931, [Franklin Edgerton], 52 76-79
WULFF, K. Chinesische und Tai, [J. K. Shryock], 55 340-341
YEWDALE, Ralph Bailey. Bohemond I, Prince of Antioch, [A. C. Krey], 45 174-175
YOSHITOMO Okamoto. Jūrokuseiki sekaichizu jō no Nihon (Japan on World Maps of the Sixteenth Century), [Robert Wood Clack], 60 275-278
von ZACH, Erwin. Übersetzungen aus dem Wên Hsüan, [J. K. Shryock], 56 94
ZIYA, Yusuf. Arier und Turanier, [N. Martinovitch], 53 83-84
ZURAYQ, Qusṭanṭīn [or Qusṭi] (ed.). Ta'rīḫ, IX, of ibn-al-Furāt, [P. Hitti], 57 322, 323-324
------ (ed.). The Yazīdis, Past and Present, [P. Hitti], 56 511, 514
------ and N. 'Izz al-Dīn (eds.). Ta'rīḫ ibn-al-Furāt, [P. Hitti], 59 527-528
------ see also Jūzi, Bandali

IV. INDEX OF WORDS

AFGHAN

mas-, 56 357

mrē, 56 358

naγan, 56 355

spīn, 56 359

vrīžē, vrižē, 47 264

xarxēl, 56 356

xuṛīn, 56 357

AINU

kuṅkutu, = numeral 10, became a counting word for sables, 37 195-196, n.13

taṅku, "hundred," adopted from Manchu and common to all Tungusian and Amur tribes, 37 195-196

tunji, "interpreter," a loan word; tsūji in Sinico-Jap., t'uṅ (t'ung)-ši in Chinese, 37 200-201

AKKADIAN

ab(b)uttu, "metal ring attached to a slave," 42 87-88

aklu, "head" of a guild, 60 69, 70

amirânu, "eye-witness," 41 12, 45 n. 15

anâku, means both "lead" and "tin," 45 194 n. 2, 236-237

ânni, "behold," cf. Heb. hinne, 47 49

aplu, "member" of a guild, 60 69

ašâru, "to throw down,"‖Ar. waṯara, "to trample on," 45 362-363

burâdu, purâdu, "bearded carp,"< parâdu, "to be swift,"? 39 71 n. 12

batiqânu, "bâton carried by freeman"? 41 37 n. 42

battu, batti, etc., "all around, all about," reduplication of bantu, "circle," 42 206-207

bêlu, "weapon," < √baḫlu, 46 355

bittu, battu, "girdle, belt," < √*bnṭ, ‖ Eg. bnt, Heb. 'abneṭ, 42 206-207

bukânu, "die or stamp for marking slaves"? 42 83-84

bûlu, "cattle," < √*b'l, 46 355

buṭuttu, "emmer," < Eg. boṭet, 39 176

de'âlu, "scout, spy,"‖Ar. and Syr. dâl, "to go about," 22 23-25

dimtu, "district," 47 38

ditennûtu, "possession," danânu, "to be strong, have power," 52 357-361

dumaqi, "present from husband to bride," 41 24 n. 22, 25 n. 28

dupšikku, "basket carried on the head," a sign of forced labor, 28 146

dûr appi, "cheeks," 22 9

ekêmu, "to take away,"‖Ar. ma'aqa, "to carry off," < 'amuqa, 46 355

erēšu, does not mean "to fashion," 43 354

esirtu, "woman captured in war," 41 35 n. 28

ešmaru, a kind of stone, = Eg. ỉsmr; cf. Heb. šāmîr, "flint," σμύρις, etc., 45 360

gadâmu, II₁, "to crop,"‖Talm. gādam, "to cut off," 44 156, 271-272

galâbu, "to cut off,"‖Heb. gallâb, "barber," 42 82; in reference to marking slaves meaning is uncertain, 80-90

ḫabbatu, "mercenary," 48 183-184

ḫabbûlu, "debtor," 41 12, 33 n. 3

ḫabîru, supplanted ḫabbatu as term for "mercenary," 48 185

ḫalâlu, "to pierce,"‖Heb. ḥālal, Ar. ḫalla; derivatives of, 36 330-332

ḫammû, "usurper," cf. Ar. ḥawa, "to get possession of," 35 392

ḫâmu, "reed, straw," figuratively "small thing, shred," cf. Aram. ḥam in same sense, 54 200-203, 299

ḫarâpu, "to abound," cf. Heb. ḥōrep, "autumn" and Ar. ḫarafa, "to gather fruit;" derivatives of, 29 226

ḫarimtu, "street-walker," 41 36 n. 34

ḫaṣînu, "axe,"‖Eth. ḫaṣīn, "iron," 38 200

ḫittu, ḫîtu, "door-lintel," 43 355

ḫiḫinu, weapon of Ninurta,‖ḫaḫin, "thorn-bush," 39 201

ḫîṭu, "guilt," 41 14 n. 26

ḫubunnu, ḫabattu, "pot,"‖Ar. ḫabana, "to lay away," extension of ḫaba'a, "to hide," 39 85 n. 39

ḫubutâtu, ḫubutûtu, "tax-free property, freedom from tax," < ḫabbatu, "mercenary," 48 183-184

ḫuruptu, a kind of vessel? 41 39 n. 61; "betrothal gift,"‖Talm. ḥ^arûpā, "fiancée," 314-316

ḫuṣâbu, ḫaṣbu, meaning not clear; cf. Jew. Aram. ḥaṣbā, "cabbage with deep roots," 54 201-202

ibaqqan, denom.from buqânu, a kind of implement, 41 n. 79

*igigu, "gecko?" 39 284

ikkibu, "tabu," < Sum. iggib, 39 66 n. 3

ilku, "state tax," 28 154

ilu, often means "king" or "lord," 36 368-369

ina, "in," = Eg. m-, Copt. n-, Heb. ', 45 311

inkaru, "husbandman, farmer," 52 258

irēšu, "resin," (*ġirâšu)‖Ar. 'aġtara, "to exude resin,"Heb. 'ōšer, Akk. mašrû, "wealth," 45 322

imtaḫar, "reached an agreement," 25 275-276

išmeânu, "one who hears a report," 41 12, 45 n. 15

iṭṭittum, weapon of Nabû,‖eṭîdu, "nettle," 39 201

kallatu, "bride, daughter-in-law," 41 28 n. 53

kalmat, "louse," = Ar. qamlah, 36 416

kamir, "eunuch," cf. Ar. kamara, "to be virile," 35 394

kanakku, "door pivot," 43 357

karašku, "mausoleum," 35 396

karpatu, a kind of rectangular vessel, 43 355

kaška, "moiety," 52 362-366

kaspu, "silver,"‖Ar. sakaba, sabaka, "to smelt," 43 117

kîdu, "field," perhaps stands for *kiddu; cf. Ar. kadīd, "trodden ground," and kiddah, "rough ground," 36 230; "loan," 41 12, 15 n. 36

kimmatu, "enclosure,"‖Ar. kamma, "to envelope," 39 71 n. 12

kinâtim šarâqu, "to communicate laws," 25 271-275

kirimmu, "womb," < √kamâru-karâmu, "to cover," cf. Ar. kamara, 39 69

kiuru, "basin," cf. Heb. kiyyôr, 36 232

kulûlu, "door-lintel," 43 355

kunnû, "to fix, appoint,"‖Eg. čnw, "to count," 40 322 n. 32

kurku, kurukku, karakku, "cock?" 33 389-392, 394

kuruštu, "fodder," < Sum., 55 441

lamassu, "divine protecting power," 24 286-290, 300, 302-303

lânu, "aspect"‖Ar. lawn, Eg. 'wn, Copt. eine, "color, image, form," 37 253-255

la'u, meanings of five stems having this form, 32 17-20

lîṭu, "mystery," 46 344

lî'û, "roll," according to which soldiers in Neo-Babylonian army were registered, 41 466-467

mamîtu, "oath, curse," < yama', "that which is pronounced," cf. Ar. wāmi'ah, "misfortune," 34 283-284, 303, n. 1; < √*yamā, cf. Ar. wama'a, "to make a sign with the hand," 49 22

manaḫtu, "outlay for improvements to property," 41 51 n. 75

mangaga, kind of date-palm, dim. of mangu? 39 202 n. 3

marâqu, IV₂, "to be forgiven,"‖Talm. māraq, "to brighten, cleanse," 44 156, 272

mar-nenni, "fastening, adornment," 38 174

mâru, "member" of a guild, 60 69

maškattu (√šakânu), "pledge, deposit," 41 15 n. 35

mummeritu (√amâru), "procuress," 41 22 n. 85

mummu,‖Tiamat, tamtu, < √*hwm, *hmh, 45 36-37

mûnu, "lizard,"‖Syr. āmûnā, 38 88 n. 4

muškênu, "plebs," 36 12-15; "freeborn man," 37 14; "plebeian," in Hammurabi Code, 41 12 n. 18
muttatu, "forehead, hair, headband," 42 80 ff.
naggaru, "carpenter," = Eg. nğr, < Sum. naggar, lamga, 39 81 n. 28
namzîtu, "receiver of a brandystill," || Talm. nāzaytā, 40 219
naqbu, "depth," 22 10
ni'âru, "papyrus (document)"? cf. Heb. nᵊyâyr, 48 131-132
niš, "oath, curse, ban," 34 296, 303; perhaps personified, 284; "lifting up, oath," 49 23
nudunnû, "dowry," > Talm. nᵊdûnyā, 41 25 n. 28
nukušu (Sum. l.-w.), "door pivot," 43 356-357
parîsu, "pole-mast," 32 7-9
pî mâtim, "vernacular," 25 269-271
pêlu, "to exchange," < √*pa'âlu, cf. Heb. pᵊ 'ullā, "compensation," 47 45-46
pû, "vulva," cf. Heb. pôt, 39 69 n. 11
qadištu, "temple-prostitute," 41 35 n. 30
qamâmu, || Ar. qamma, "to sweep off, devour," 39 71 n. 12
qanânu, "to coil, wind, wrap," derivatives of, 29 224-226
qannu, qanqannatu, "boiler of a still," = Talm. qanṣan, 40 219
qannu and rîḫtu money were bride's dowry, 57 272, 274
qanû, "cane," < Sum. gin, 38 67
qaqultu, emblem of Marduk, || qâqûlu, "cardamon," 39 201-202
qâtum, "hand," < *qahtum < √*lqḥ, "to take," 60 95-97
qibû, "to speak, say," 25 268-269
qimmatu, "crown of foliage," || Ar. qimmah, "summit," 39 71 n. 12
qîpu, Babylonian office, higher than šatammu and šaqû šarri, 41 467
qiqqišu (for qišqišu), "cabin, booth," || Heb. qaš, Aram. qaššā, "straw, stubble," 32 6
qû, "thread, cord," || Heb. qaw and Eg. ḳꜣ, 42 210
rabû, "head" of a guild, 60 69, 70
rîḫtu and qannu money was bride's dowry, 57 272, 274
ṣaddu, "sign-post" || Eg. ḏd, "pillar of Osiris," 40 317 n. 20
saḫḫu, "productive, meadow land," = Ar. saḫâḫ, "soft ground," 36 231
šaḫuru, "storehouse," < Sum. saḫur, 39 71
šakultu, a kind of receptacle? 41 39 n. 61
šalû, "to sink, dive," || Ar. salā, 39 75 n. 17
ṣalmu, "statue," 25 266-268
samâḫu, II1, "to carry up," || Ar. šamiḫa, "to be high," 44 156, 272
šanû, "to inundate," || Ar. sanā, "to water," 39 75 n. 17
šâpiru, "agent," not connected with Heb. sôper, "scribe," 48 115-116
šapru, "rump," || Ar. ṯafr, 40 73
ṣarṣar [ṣarṣâru], "water cock," cf. Ar. ṣarṣar, "cock," 35 396-398
šaršên, "eunuch," > Heb. sarîs, 41 18 n. 64, 59
šâšat, connected with Heb. śāśôn, "joy," 38 336
šeriqtu, "father's gift to bride," 41 25 n. 28
sibru, "scribe," in Cappadocian texts, 49 124-126
siparru, "fetters," cf saparru, "net," and supûru, "enclosure," 22 25
sipir, "scribe writing on parchment," (Sum. KUŠ-SAR), Babylonian form was *sipîru or *sipêru, cf. Heb. sôper; wrote in Aramaic and Greek, 48 110-128
šipru, "mission, document," not connected with Heb. sepɛr, "book," 48 115-116
širqûtu, class of branded temple-slaves, 38 335
sisinnu, "swallow," connected but not identical with Heb. sîs, 35 393 n. 3
šuddu, "chest, box," || Talm. šiddā, 32 8
šûdûtu, "proclamation," 52 366-367
šummuṭu, "to tear off (dates)," || Ar. šamaṭa, "to deprive of foliage," 39 71 n. 12
sunnu (sign name), derived from Sum. su(n), 57 65
šûmu, "garlic," < Sum. sum, 57 65
šuru, "next of kin," 55 435-437
šurumma, cf. šurriš, "speedily," 52 256
tadânu, "to be pledged to marry," 41 27 n. 47, 59, 33 n. 7
tadinânu, "person pledged for debt," 41 12
taḫûmu, "boundary," > Talm. tᵊḥûm, 41 54 n. 19
tallalê, "butcher's helpers who throw down the ox before its throat is cut," || Ar. talîl, "prostrated," 38 332
tallu, "ark," 38 174; "door-jamb," 43 356
tamû, "to take an oath," 49 23
târu, a kind of measure, 47 39
tidennûtu, "usufruct, use," 52 256
tîrânu, "zone" into which liver is divided, 38 77-80
tirḫâtu, "bride-price," 41 25 n. 28
tumru, "smoke," from secondary reflexive stem *tamar <*'amar, "to be high," 42 376-377
udru, "Bactrian camel," < Av. uštra, 36 227
ūlâ, "or, or else," < ū, "or" and lā, "not," 22 25-26
ušu, "storax," = Chinese su-ho-yo, 42 176
utte'izzi, pi'el reflexive of na'âdu, "to be exalted," 35 394-396
wardu, "boy, servant," || Ar. walad, 45 321
zakâru, "to say, mention," 25 277-278
zappu, "tuft of hair," 54 115
zittu, "inheritance share," 55 439

ALBANIAN

šemɛrɛ, 43 428

ANNAMESE

tong, 52 50

ARABIC

ājûr, "brick," < Akk. agûru, 32 6
'ālam, "world," < Aram. < Canaan., 60 418
almās, "diamond," < Gr. adamas, 48 180
'arifa, "to know," orig. "to scent," doublet of 'aṯana, 'afana, 'to ascend," 42 376; 43 422
'arūs, lit. "bride," name of jinnîyah inhabiting spring, translation of Syro-Hellenistic νύμφη, 60 291
anā, "I," shortened from anāku, 40 222
asda, asta, "to make a warp," < Eg. śty, "to spin"? 42 209-210
'ašiqa, "to love," || Heb. ḥāšaq, 45 360
'askar, "army, soldiers," possibly af'al from stem of Heb. śākār, "reward, wages," 36 417-418
'aṭar, "scent, perfume," < Aram., 42 376
'awsaj, "brier," < Akk. ašagu, 36 417
badan, "short, sleeveless tunic," < √bdn, "to tie, bind," || Eg. bdn, 42 207
bālah (pl. bāl, bālāt), "iron-shod staff, narrow sword," < Turk. bala, "sword," 50 256-258, 260
dīk, "cock," of Turkish origin? 33 387 n. 1
ḥajar, "stone," || Akk. igaru, "wall," 43 126
ḥalla, "to profane," || Heb. ḥālal; derivatives of, 36 322-323, 330
ḫalla, "to pierce," || Heb. ḥālal, Akk. ḫalâlu; derivatives of, 36 322-324, 330-331
ḫamīs, a military unit; is an old Semitic word and not a loan in Arabic, 56 88-91
ḥanīf, < Nab. ḥanîpā, 58 541
Ḥašwīyah, name derived from ḥašw, "redundant talk," 54 23-24
ḥayy 'ala 'l-ṣalāh, first used in call to prayer by Fāṭimids, 27 220
jinni, "evil spirit," cf. Palm. gᵊnāyā, "gods," and Mand. gina(h), "evil spirit," 57 320; < Aram. genyā, "hidden things, evil spirit," 60 292-293
kāfūr, "camphor," < Malay kāpūr, 42 363-364
kalanbak, "carambola," 57 390
kamaḫa, kamaḥa, kabaḥa, "to hold in, curb," transpositions of makaḥa, 45 319, 355
laysa, "is not," dialectic form of *layṯa, 45 314
līmah, "lime (fruit)," of non-IE Indian origin, 57 387
līmū, "lemon," shortened form of Pers.-Ar. līmūn, 57 387
līmūn, laymūn, "lemon," from Chinese (Canton dial.) li-mung, 57 393-395; Italian, Spanish, French and English words for "lemon," 54 159; > Hindi limū, limbū, nimbū, 56 48

ma'ḏanah, "minaret," various pronunciations of; superseded by manārah in Middle Ages, 30 133
manārah, "minaret," not necessarily from Syr. mᵊnârtā, 30 132
mandal, "magic circle," < Pers. mandal or Skt. mandal [maṇḍalaṁ], 36 38-39
al-marīsi, kind of ghoul so-called in Upper Egypt, < Copt. marēs, 38 163
misk, "musk," < masaka, "to hold," 45 319, 355
nabl, "arrow," orig. "flash," cf. Akk. nablu, "flame," Eg. nby, "to burn," 45 360
nadd, an ambergris compound, 42 177, 181; of Persian origin, 43 226-227
nafl, "gift," || nabl, "arrow," 45 360
nasīb, originally "blood relative," later "relative by marriage," 41 186
qadar, "God's share in man's destiny," 55 143-144
qamlah [quoted as kaemlet], "louse," = Akk. kalmat, 36 416
qašš, "straw, stubble," < Aram. qaššā, 32 6
qirbah, "skin bottle," < Syr. ruqbā, 45 360
qub', "hood," see Heb. qôba', "helmet"
qutār, "smell of roast meat," < Aram., 42 376
Rawāfiḍ, history of the term, 29 137-159
Rāwandīyah, so-called after Rīvand in Ḫurāsān, 29 122-123
ṣabr, "aloes, myrrh," 42 175
ṣād, "copper," < Akk. ṣâdu, "to shine," 43 116 n. 3
samak, "fish," masaka, "to seize," caus. from √*mk, 45 319, 355
ṣanaḫah, "dirt," = Heb. ṣaḥᵃnā, "stench," 43 425
ṣanfi, "Champa aloes," 42 180
šaqā'iq al-Nu'mān, "anemone," orig. meaning "lightning flashes (?) of al-Nu'mān (Adonis)," 60 297-299
saraqa, "to steal," causative from stem preserved in Akk. râqu, "to be empty," 36 418
ṣarṣar, "cock," cf. Heb. zarzîr, 33 396 n. 1
ṣawma'ah, part of a minaret, exact meaning unknown, 30 136-137, 138
sherbet, sharbat (šarbah), "lemonade" < Eng. sherbet, syrup, shrab; Ital. sorbetto; Fr. sorbet; Span. sorbete; Port. sorvete, 54 152; see also Chinese she-li-pie
ṣifr, ṣufr, "copper, brass, gold," < Sum. zabar, Akk. siparru, 43 122
ṣirf, "pure," < Akk. ṣarâpu, 43 116
tahima, "to stink," < taḫima, < √*ḫm > ḫamma, "to stink," 43 424-425
taḫima, "to suffer from indigestion," = ittaḫama < waḫima, 43 425
tūm, "garlic," see Akk. šûmu
'uṣfūr, "small bird," < √ṣfr, 36 417
zindīq, "heretic," etc., is Aramaic equivalent of Heb. ṣaddîq, 28 116-117

ARAMAIC
'ᵃnâ, "I," shortened from anâku, 40 222
bar, "son," doublet of Heb. bin, 44 168
bar-nāšā, "son of a man," cf. Akk. mâr amîli, "full-born man," 37 14
'ᵋlâhîn, used in sense of "god" like Heb. 'ᵋlôhîm, 51 326-327
gō', "inside," an accusative from gawwa, 51 319
ḥam, "reed," figuratively "small thing, shred," cf. Akk. ḫâmu, "reed, straw," in same sense, 54 200-203, 299
ḥᵃrûpā, "fiancée," || Akk. ḫuruptu, "betrothal gift," 41 314-316
ḥᵃwāyā, "difficulty," 46 356
hen, used as emphatic particle, 42 397
ḥērtā, "settlement," see Heb. ḥāṣer
ḥutrā, "enclosure," see Heb. ḥāṣer
'îtay, "is," < *'ît, = Heb. 'et, accusative particle, 35 377-381
kullā, adverbial use of, 43 391-395
lḥyā, "bad," 59 105
mᵊdînā, "province" in Pal. Aram., but "city" in Gentile dialects, 43 230-231
mūbāl, mōbal, fraction of a zûz, > ὀβολός, 29 207-209
nᵊdûnyā, "dowry," < Akk. nudunnû, 41 25 n. 28
nš, "oath," < Akk. niš, 37 329-330
nṣb (Sinaitic), "governor, garrison," 52 296
nwyšā, "cemetery," dim. of ναός, 54 31-32
nyq, "to pour a libation," < Akk. nâqu, 38 65 n. 7
ptkr, "image," < Pers.; in inscription of 5th cent. B.C., 35 372
rᵊgaš, Haf., "to act in concord," 44 168; "to conspire," 46 352
šâ'ā, "hour," originally "moment," a participial form, 51 319
tarnᵊgôl, "cock," 33 369-70, 386-387; not from Sum. tar-lugallu, 389, 390-392, 394
tᵊḫûm(ā), "boundary," < Akk. taḫûmu, 41 54 n. 19
'ûryā, "west," < 'ûr, "Amurru," 45 132
zûz, earliest occurrence of on Babylonian Aramaic ostrakon of 5th cent. B.C., 29 207

ARAMEAN
batrirk, = "patriarch," 30 13

ARAWAK
bimini, 26 414 f.

ARDHAMĀGADHĪ
paḍissuṇe, 36 212

ARMENIAN
hariur, 46 60

ASOKAN
apahaṭā, 36 209
abhītā, 36 205
asvathā, 36 205
asvatha-saṃtaṃ, 36 205 f.
ā Taṃbapaṃnī, 46 258
āsinava, 46 257
-tu, -ti, gerunds, 36 209
nābhake, 36 210
nāsaṃtaṃ, 36 205
nicā, 46 259
paṭivedanā, 36 208 f.
pālanā, 36 207 f.
peṭenika, 46 257
praṣaḍa, 46 257
bhatamaya, 46 259
sukhīyanā, 36 207 f.

ASOKAN DELHI-SIVALIK
anūpaṭīpaṃne, 36 206
abhīhāle, 36 206
isyā, 36 212
lāja, 36 209
siya, 36 209
sukhāyanāyā, 36 209
sukhīyana dukhīyanaṃ, 36 207-209

ASOKAN GIRNĀR
athā, 36 207
-dasaṇā, 36 207 f.
karu, 36 209
kāsati, 36 211
likhāpayisaṃ, 36 211
sruṇāru, 36 212

ASOKAN JAUGAḌA
-saṃtīlanā, 36 209

ASOKAN KĀLSĪ
-dasanā, 36 208
saṃtaṃ, 36 206

ASOKAN MANSEHRA
dhrama-, 36 210 f.
nirathriya, 36 210
śruney[u], 36 212

ASOKAN RADHIA
sukhīyanadukhīyanaṃ, 36 207-209

ASOKAN RĀMPŪRVĀ
sukhīyanadu-, 36 208

ASOKAN SHĀHBĀZGARHI
dhrama-, 36 210 f.
kaṣati, 36 211
niraṭhriyaṃ, 36 210
śruneyu, 36 212
uthanaṃ, 41 178

AVESTAN
aēšasa-, 'petens', 40 121
ašāṯ hača, 31 405
āviš, 40 121-124
daēnā, 32 412; 48 286
dūma, 25 175
hača, 31 403-410
kahrka, "cock," found in Kahrkatāt, cf. Skt, kṛka-vāku, Pahl. kark, Osset, kharkh, Av. kahrkāsa, 33 379 n. 1
puθrā, 'gravida', 39 206
ṯkaēša-, 52 78
vərəṯka, 39 207
vi, 40 122
vīdvaēšām, 47 268
vī-naoiti, 40 125
θwōi, 44 159

BADAGA
-gṛo, -gṛu, 56 356

BAHNAR
kŏtam, 52 49
köpaih, 'cotton', 52 46 f.
ruih, 52 49

BALŪCHI
gandīm, 56 356
guṭh, 56 354
hōḍ, 56 356
kadīma, 56 356
khakhar, 56 357
mēhar, 56 358
pišī, 56 359
tar-, 56 359

BATAK
aloban, "benzoin tree," < Ar. al-lubān, 42 366

BENGĀLĪ
ghāḍ, 56 354
guyā, 52 49
sādā rai, 52 49
sāgum, sēgun, 52 50
tori, 52 49

BISAYAN
naga-buhat, 25 166

BRĀHŪĪ
-a negative, 56 351
-ā suffix, 56 351
all-, 56 351
ant, 56 351
arē, 56 351
asi, 56 351
ass, 56 351
aṭ, 56 351
āvān-, 56 351
bā, 'mouth', 46 309
bā, 56 351,352
balγuṛ, 56 358
balun, 56 352
bāmus, 56 352
ba(r), 56 352
bāṭaγ, 56 352
bē, 56 352
bei, 56 352
bērif, 56 352
bīn, 56 352
bīṛ, 56 352
da-, dē-, 56 352
dā, 56 352
das-, 56 352
dass, 56 352
dāxa, 56 353
dēr, 56 352 f.
dīr, 46 310
dīr, 56 353
ditar, 56 353
dīxa, 56 353
*dōr 'mouth', 46 309
dū, 'hand', 46 178
dū, 56 353
dūī, 56 353
e, 56 353
ē, 56 353
-ē, 56 354
gagall-, 56 354
garau, 56 354
gārr-, 56 354
guṭ, 56 354
hal, 49 60
hal, 56 354
hal-, 56 354
hanēn, 56 354
harf-, 56 354
(h)at-, (h)ata-, (h)ati-, (h)ēs, 56 354
hata-, 56 359
hēf-, 56 354
heṭ, 56 354
hīdž-, 56 354
hilār, 56 354
hīL, 56 355
hin-, 56 355
hōγ-, 56 355
(h)ōr, 56 355
hullī, 56 354
hullī, 56 355
hūlun, 56 355
hur-, 56 355
huš-, 56 355
ī, 56 354
illa, 56 355
īlum, 56 356
īlum, 56 355
īṛ, 56 356
irā, 56 355
iraγ, 56 355
iraṭ, 56 355
istō, 56 356
-k past-suffix, 56 356
-k plural suffix, 56 356
kaḍ, 56 356
kadīm, 56 356
kah-, kask, 56 356
kalūṛ, 56 356
kane, 56 356
karγ, 56 356
kās, 56 356
kōḍ, 56 356
konḍ-, 56 356
kun-, 56 356
littš-, 56 357
littšax, 56 357
lumma, 56 357
maL, 56 358

malxuṛ, 56 358
mār, 56 358
maš, 56 358
maš-, 56 358
masiṛ, 46 310
masiṛ, 56, 358; 57, 308
maun, 56 358
max-, 56 357
mē, 56 358
mir, 56 358
miš, 56 358
mōḶ, 56 358
mōn, 56 358
muh, 56 358
murū, 56 358
musi, 56 358
must, 56 352
ō, 56 359
pin, 56 359
piššī, 56 359
pīun, 56 359
pūskun, 56 359
pūškun, 56 359
raγām, 56 359
-s, 'thou', 56 359
šalāp, 56 359
sī, 56 359
sirōz, 56 359
šūr, 56 359
tar-, 56 359
tēn, 56 359
ti, 56 359
ti-, 56 354
tiss, 56 359
xaf, 56 357
xal, 56 357
xan, 'eye,' 46 178
xan, 56 350,357
xaṛ, 56 357
xarās, 56 357
xaṛīŋk, 56 357
xāxar, 56 357
xazm, 56 357
xīsun, 56 354
xīsun, 56 357
xō, 56 357
xōlum, 56 357
xoš-, xošk-, 56 357
xulkun, 56 357
xutt-, 56 357
urā, 56 359
uṭ, 56 351

BUḪĀRAN
Nawsard, month-name, lit. "new year," cf. Ossetic sārde, etc., "summer," 28 334

BURMESE
chan, 47 266
limmā, "citrus," 57 395

BURUSHASKI
huldžai, 56 355

CANAANITE
b'rrm, "upper" class, 35 367
mškbm, "prostrated" class, 35 367
trp, "to sew," < *trp' < rp', 40 72

CHINESE
------ [illegible], a Shang sign on a bronze for some proper name, 56 347
a-i, 阿驛, (Cantonese, a-yik), the fig, Fu-lin ti-ni 底檷, and Persian anjir, a fig; the Aramean name is te(n)ta, 30 20
An,安, use of, to illustrate problems of Chinese syntax, 58 156-166; Chinese classification of words into "real" and "empty", 159-160, 165; an used 1) as a content-word, 2) with special meanings, 3) as an interrogative particle, lists, 161-162; use as a noun or verb, 163-164; tr. of an min, p'ing an, an an, an jan, 164-165; an as an interrogative particle as in an tsai, an yu, etc., 165-166
An-ts'ai, 59 60 f.
ch'ang, 常, as an equivalent of i 彝, in the Shih Ching and Shu Ching, 52 30-31
ch'ên, 臣, original meaning of is "captive," 56 341 n. 13
chên su, 真塑, tr. "true models," su, "to model in clay," 55 423
ch'i-t'un, 齊暾, (Cantonese, ts'ai-t'ün), olive, < Fu-lin (Aramean) zaita, and Persia ts'ai-t'ün, 30 19
chih,之, use in earliest bronze inscriptions, 56 344
chu,諸, a contraction of 之於, or 之與, 60 197; intermediate state of fusion was 之乎, 60 203
chuan, 傳, "commentaries," > short slips of bamboo called chuan, 44 281
erh,耳, Anc. nźi, as a contraction of 而已, 60 197
fa, 法 used as equivalent for tao 道, and i 彝, 52 31
fu, 弗, a contraction of 不之, 60 197
hê, 盍, a contraction of 何不, 60 201
hsiang, 52 50
hsiang, "elephant"; relation to the Shan word tsang and other tongues, 41 300
hsien, 獻, puzzling use of in the Shu-ching explained by bronze inscriptions, 56 340 n. 13
hsien min, 獻民, or hsien ch'ên, 獻臣, means "captive slaves," 56 340-341 n. 13
hsin, 心, when meaning "general consciousness," 58 694-695
hsing, 行, as an equivalent of tao 道, 52 24
hsing-ch'u, 行廚, meaning "genie-food," 54 290
i, 乙, use of in bronze inscriptions, 56 347
i, 夷, as an equivalent of i 彝, or tao 道, 52 28, 33
I, 彝, origin the picture of a bird held in two hands, 51 19-20; i 彝 character, an early equivalent of tao 道 in its philosophic sense, 52 22-34; absence of tao, in its philosophic sense, fr. oldest texts, 22-23; origin and development of i in form and meaning, 26-29; i used in the Shih Ching and Shu Ching to express the tao idea, 24-25; date of i's replacement by tao, 32-34; i, 彝, use of in bronze inscriptions, 56 348
i-mu, 宜母, or i-mu-tzu, 宜母子, term for the lemon, meaning "beneficial to the mother," 54 148, 149, 154
Jen, 仁, man of, means the man of perfect virtue and goodness, but possibly too naive, 59 210
kan lu tsiang, 甘露漿, "sweet dew beverage," and other meanings, 54 149 n. 11
ku, 蠱, a kind of Black Magic,character indicates insects and reptiles in a dish, 55 1, 2, 4-6, 9
kuan, 觀, see ssŭ
li-mu, 里木, "lemon tree," name in Mongol period < Pers. līmū ليمو, 54 148, 150, 153
li-mung-tzu, 黎濛子, earliest name for the lemon in China, 12th cent., 54 145, 146
List of technical terms used in logic by K'uei Chi, 53 150-151
liu-i, 六藝, the six arts taught in the lower schools in ancient China; term later applied to text books, 44 280
Lo-t'o-hao, "camel crane," < Pers. shutur-murgh, "ostrich," 30 50
lü-hwui, "Soqotra aloes," < Ar. luwīy, 42 183
luk-li, 谷蠡, title of a Hsiung-nu prince, < Uigur, uluk, "great," 37 95, 145, 150
Lung-hsien, "ambergris," lit. "Dragon's Spittle," 30 49, 52
miao, 廟, see ssŭ
mo, 沒, the myrtle (Cantonese, mut), used as transcription for mur, < Pehlevi, mūrd, Fu-lin, a-tz'u < Aramean asa, 30 20-21

mu-su, 苜蓿, (Cantonese: muksuk) "lucerne," probably a transcription of Turk. burchak, 37 145, 150
Nai-chih, 捺祇, the nard, old sound not-ti, < Pers. nard, 30 22
nai-k'i, "narcissus," < Pers. nargis, 43 219
na-lo-t'o, "nard," < Skt. nalada, 43 219
Note on relationship terms in the early Classics, 51 187
o-mo (or a-mo), "ambergris," < Pr. ambar, 30 48; also called ts'eng-p'o, 57
pao, 寶, use of in bronze inscriptions, 56 348
Pi-ch'i, 馝齊, galbanum, (Cantonese pīt-ts'ai), < Pers. bīrzay, 30 21-22
po-lo-sai, dice, < Sanskrit prāsaka, denotes in particular backgammon, 47 75
p'u-t'ao, 蒲陶, "grapes," < Gk. βότρυ-ς, found by Chinese ambassadors in Ferghana, 37 108, 146, 150
san i fen shen, 三一分身, problem of tr. of, in passage on the Nestorian Monument, 58 384-393; translations compatible with Catholic Doctrine rendering fen shen as a noun, 386-387; same, rendering it as a verb, 387-390; trs. not compatible with Catholic Doctrine, rendering shen as a participial adjective, 390-391; aid fr. parallel passage in same inscription, wo san i miao shen, 391-393
she-li-pie, 舍里別, or she-li-pa, 舍里八, "lemonade," > Ar. sharbat (šarbah), 54 149-151, 152
shen, 身, used to tr. saṁtānas, 58 695
shih, 是, use of, as throwing light on the meaning of yen 焉, 60 14-22
Shih, 釋, standing for Śākyamuni, taken for their "Family name" by Chinese Buddhist monks since the 4th cent., 52 161-162
Shih, 識, used by Hsüan Chuang for tr. of both vijñāna and vijñapti, 51 305-307; uses not indicated by Soothill and Hodous, 58 694
shu-p'u, term for dice, 47 75
ssŭ, 寺, as differentiated fr. kuan, 觀, and miao, 廟, 55 337
su-ho-yo, "storax," = Akkadian ušu, 42 176
ta-i, 大藝, a term applied to the Classics, 44 280-281
tao, 道, character, in its philosophic sense, not used in oldest texts, 52 22-34; the tao idea expressed by other characters, chiefly 𢽾, i, 彝, 24-26, 29-34; see also Words, Chinese, i
tau, 'rice,' 47 266
ti, 地, as an equivalent of tao, 道, 52 24, 31
tien, 典, canon; 𠔯, old form, analyzed, 44 274
t'ien, 天, appearance of, on oracle bones, doubtful, 56 343-344 n. 25
t'ien pu, 天步, as an equivalent of tao, 道, 52 25
Tit, planet name, < Pers. Tīr, 28 336
ts'ê, 冊, book; 𠕁, old form, 44 273; length 2 ft. 4 in., 273; frequency of on the oracle bones; early meaning, 56 335 n. 3
ts'e ming, 冊命, meaning of, 56 349 n. 48
tso, 作, use of in bronze inscriptions, 56 347
tsŏng, 52 50
tsu, 祖, use of in bronze inscriptions, 56 347
Tsu-la (Cantonese, tso-lap), < Ar. zarafa, "giraffe," 30 49-50
tsu, 質, meaning in this case "substance" not "essence," 59 282
tsun, 樽, use of in bronze inscriptions, 56 348
Wẹn-hon, planet name, < Sogd. Vunḫān, 28 341
Wun-mut-sī, planet name, < Pers., 28 339
Yeh-hsi-mi, 野悉蜜, jasmine, (Cantonese, ye-sik-mat), < Pers. yasmin and Aramean yasmin, 30 22-23
Yen, 焉, as the equivalent of yü chih, 於之, 60 1-22; as sometimes equal to shih, 是, 14-18; yen[1] and yen[2] originally pronounced alike, 193-196; yen may be a fusion word, 204-207
Yü, 與, as a verb, "to give forth," in passage fr. the Analects, IX, 1, 53 347-351; as a comparative in passage from the Lun Yü, IX, 1, 54 83
Yü, 於, use of, as throwing light on the meaning of yen, 焉, 60 7-14, yü chih never found to occur, 13

COPTIC
boi, kind of drug, of Persian origin, 45 82
karmani, "caraway, cummin," original meaning obscure, 45 80
marabathron, substance difficult to identify with the Gr. malabathron, 45 80-81
nēf, a kind of measure, 48 155 n. 3
pmammiše, "place of fighting," 48 151 n. 2
sitraj, "Indian cinnamon laurel product," 45 79
tam, "barn," abbreviation of ταμεῖον ? 48 155 n. 2
tor(e)p, "to sew," < Eg. *trp < Canaan. *trp, 40 72

CZECH
paloš, "sabre," < Turk.pal(y)uş, 50 259-260

DARDIC
dui, 56 353
natkēl, 'nose,' 46 178
nōzōr, 'nose,' 46 178
thōs, 46 309

DRAVIDIAN
Tamil elumiccai = lemon or lime; Telugu nimma = lemon or lime; Kanara nimbe = lime; Tulu nimbẹ, limbẹ, limbi = lemon, 54 147, and n. 6
*limbūs, "lemon," < Skt. nimbū, 57 388

DYAK
nampok, see Malay bertapar

EGYPTIAN
bdn, "to tie, bind," < bnt, || Sem. *bnṭ, 42 207
bnt, "girdle, belt," || Heb. 'abneṭ, Akk. bittu, 42 206-207
boṭet, "emmer," > Akk. buṭuttu, 39 176
by', "vagina, mine-shaft," cognate with Sem. bi'r, "well," 39 70
byn.t, "harp," = Heb. nebɛl, 44 167
ḏnw, "to count," || Akk. kunnû, Ar. kana, Heb. kinnâ, 40 322 n. 32
ḏd, "pillar of Osiris" || Akk. ṣaddu, "sign-post," 40 317 n. 20
d.t, "hand," < ḏr.t < ḏry.t < ỉḏr, 42 202-203
'ibd, "month," originally meant "moon," || Sem. 'bd, "to wander," 41 186
ỉḏr, "to lock up, bar," || Sem. *ydl, 42 202-203
ỉsmr, a kind of stone, = Akk. ešmaru; cf. Heb. šāmîr, σμύρις, It. smeriglio, etc., 45 360
ḳ³, "thread, cord," || Akk. qû, Heb. qaw, 42 210
ḳśm, "to bend," || Ar. masaka, "to grip," Heb. sāmak, "to hold, support," 45 319, 355
ma-ṯi-pu-(i)ra-ti, "needle," < Canaan. *matpart ca. 1300 B.C., 40 71-72
m'b³, "thirty," = Talm. mᵊ'ubbār, "intercalated," 45 360
mkmrt, < Aram., cf. Talm. mikmôrɛt, "trap, snare," 48 350
nb, "gold," (Copt. nūbe) means "fusible," < nby, "to burn," cf. Akk. nablu, "flame," Ar. nabl, "arrow," orig. "flash," 45 360
nḡr, "carpenter," = Sem. naggaru[m] [naggâru[m]] < Sum. naggar, 39 81 n. 28
rnpt, "year," lit. "name of heaven," 52 295-296
śtk³, "to spin," < śty, "to spin" + ḳ³, "thread, cord," 42 210
śty, "to spin" (> Copt. sote) > Heb. šᵊtî, "warp," and Ar. 'asda, 'asta, "to make a warp," 42 209-210
*trp, "to sew," < Canaan. *trp, 40 72
ṯsm, "greyhound," < ḳśm, q.v., 45 318-320
tyspsy (< √spsy, "to sweeten"), a wood or substance of fragrant or agreeable taste, not cinnamon, 40 263

ELAMITE
is-ma-lu, 56 220

ENGLISH
aloes, < Ar. √lawaya, "to twist," 42 175

benzoin, < Ar. lubān Jāwi, "Javanese incense," 42 176
booze, possible origin from Turk. buza, "millet or barley beer," 49 56-58
cabaret, see cabinet
cabinet, < Sem. *ḫanawa, "to camp," 28 108-111
cedar < Sem. qṭr, "to burn incense," 45 322
chapman, see cabinet
cheap, see cabinet
checkmate, 58 662-664
cipher < Akk. šipru, "message," 42 375
evening, 39 263 f.
gaft, goft, 28 128 fn.
gecko, < Arabic < Akk. *igigu? 39 284
lascar, "East Indian sailor," originally "camp-follower," etc., cf. Ar. 'askar, "army," 36 418
Lemon, word type, of Indic origin, > Ar. limún, > Near Eastern and European names, 54 143, 158, 159; < Ar. limún which, through Per., became Hindi limū, nimbū, 56 48-50
nard, possibly of Iranian origin, 43 217
nectar, see cedar
religion < Lat. relegere, "to heed, have a care for," 32 126-129
saffron, safflower, < Ar. 'aṣfar, "yellow," 43 122
satin < Zayton, a city in China, 56 373-374
Scyth, possibly < sak-ut, "the Sakas," 37 133-134
sesame < Akk. šamaššammu, "sunplant," 40 322 n. 33
zero, see cipher

FRENCH
cabane, see Eng. cabinet
cabaret, see Eng. cabinet
palache, palas, "sabre," < Turk. pal(y)uş, 50 259-260

GADABA
eyam, 52 49

GÂRWI
thair, 'hand', 46 178
thōs, 'head', 46 177

GERMAN
abend, 39 263 f.
kaufen, see Eng. cabinet
Kneipe, see Eng. cabinet
Pallasch, "sabre," < Turk. pal(y)uş, 50 259-260

GŌNDI
allī, 46 310
allī (pl. alk), 49 60
ār, 56 351
arr-, 56 354
āsī, 56 351
aṭ-jār, 56 353
dās-, 56 352
ē-, 56 352
ēr, 56 353
hallē, 56 351
han-, 56 355
hillē, 56 351
huḍ-, hur, 56 355
idd ē, 56 352
karū, 56 356
kōrī-, 56 356
kriār, 56 358
kurrā, 46 310
malā, 56 358
malōl, 46, 310; 56 358
miār, 46 310
miār, 'daughter', 56 358; 57 307
mūnd, 56 358
mussōr, 'nose,' 46 178, 56 351-2
nattur, 56 353
nirū, 56 355
panēkā, 'bone', 58 472
paṛōl, 56 356, 359
pīr, 56 352
ranḍ, 56 355
rō-, 56 359
rōn, 56 360
sī, 56 359
*sōr, 'mouth,' 46 309
ta, 56 354
talā, tallā, 46 310
tirindž, 56 355
ṭuḍḍī, 'mouth,' 46 310
vallē, 56 352
var, 46 309
varēndž, 56 355
vīsī, 56 355

GONDHI
tekām, 52 50

GREEK
ἄγγαρος, 42 334-337
αἰσθάνεται, 40 124
ἀλεκτρυών, ἀλέκτωρ, "cock," of foreign origin, 33 382
ἀμαζάκαρον, 41 237
ἀνεμώνη < Phoen. *Ne'môn (name of Adonis), influenced by ἄνεμος, "wind," 60 297-298
ἄρξιφος, 41 236
βαίτυλοι, βαιτύλια, stones possessing magical properties; nature but not thing is of Phoenician origin, 59 97-98
βίσταξ, 41 236 f.
βύσσος, "byssus," see Heb. bûṣ
γλύφειν, "to carve, write," < Akk. gallupu, [galâbu?], 43 120
γόης, "magician," < Heb. kôhen, "priest"? 42 374
γυναικ-, 34 332
ἔπαιστος, 40 121
ἴθρις, 27 414
ἰσθμός, 27 414
Doric κᾶ, 23 60
καφουρά, καμφορά, "camphor," < Malay kāpūr, 42 363
καπηλεῖον, see Eng. cabinet
κάρταλλος, "basket," < Heb. 'ᵃgarṭāl, 43 235-236
κάρφος, "sticks of dried cinnamon wood," < Ar. qirfah, 40 269
κασσία, applied since Pliny's day to the Indian tree laurel, 40 268
κηρός, "pitch," < Akk. qīr, 28 104
κιννάμωμον < Phoen. equivalent of κάρφεα, 40 265; applied since Pliny's day to Indian tree laurel, 40 268
κοίης, priest of Samothracian mysteries, < Heb. kôhen, "priest," 42 374
κρηπίς, "embankment," < Akk. kipru, 28 103-107
κύανος, "blue," < Akk. uknû, 44 158
μαλάβαθρον < Skt. tamālapattra, "cinnamon;" confused with νάρδος, 40 268
μέγαρον < Sem. *m'rh, "cave," 38 139
νάφθα < Akk. nabâṭu, napâṭu, "to shine," 37 21
νύχα, 27 411
ξύν, 34 333
ὀβολός < Aram. mûbal, môbal, 29 207-209
ὀπαστόν, 41 237
οὐρανός, 39 207
πατιζείθης, 40 200 f.
πείθειν, 27 412 f.
Πιπι, a form of the Hebrew tetragrammaton, 57 241
σμύρις, a kind of stone, cf. Eg. ỉsmr, Akk. ešmaru, Heb. šāmîr, Eng. emery, 45 360
-τος, 38 48
χάλυψ, "steel," < Chalybes, 38 200
χαράσσειν, "to sharpen, whet," a Sem. loan-word, 43 120
χιτών, "tunic," < Heb. kuttônet, 43 123 n. 8
χρυσός, "gold," < Heb. ḫārûṣ, 42 393; a Sem. loan-word, 43 120

HAWAIIAN
wai ora, 26 414

HEBREW
'āb, "father," Talmudic connotations of, 44 168-169
'ābel, "boundary-stone also marking ownership," 27 301-302
'abneṭ, "girdle, belt," || Akk. bittu, Eg. bnt, 42 206-207
'ᵃgarṭāl, "bowl,"< κρατήρ, 43 235
'ᵃhālîm, error for 'ēlîm, "terebinths," 42 173-174
'ālā, "oath, curse," uses of, 49 26
'almuggîm, < Ar. al-muġrah, "myrrh, frankincense," 42 173
'āmmān, "artisan," < Akk. ummânu, 46 159
'ᵃnî, "I," and ānôkî, "I" have conformed to the first person suffix, 40 222
'ap, "person, self," 58 134-135
'argāz, "box, chest," < Philistine *'argaz, argaz, 56 272-281
'āšān, "smoke," see also qîṭôr; primary connotation is "ascending," 42 376
'ᵃṣɛrɛt, "assembly," ||Ar. 'ard, 44 167
'aštê(-'āšār) < *'aštên < Akk. ešt̄ên, "one," < Sum. aštân, "one," 42 301, 393
'āṣûr, "affluent," 44 167; 45 152-153
'āzûb, "destitute," 44 167; "helper," 45 152-153
bāḥel (in Zech. 11:8), a mistake for bāhal, 46 355-356
bānā, "to build," doublet of bārā', "to create," 44 169
bārā', "to create," originally meant "to make a clean job," || bar, "pure, clear," Ar. bāhir, Eth. berūh; and Akk. banû, "to build," 44 168
barbur, "goose," 33 364-365
bɛqa', "half," on weight, 24 207-208
bɛṣɛr, "gold," = zāhāb baḥûn, "tried gold," 42 393; aurum spectatissimum, 43 124-125
bēt-'el, applied to place where deity was worshipped, not to a stone, 59 97
bin, "son," doublet of Aram. bar, 44 168
bûl, "cattle," = Akk. bûlu, 47 368
bûṣ, "byssus," < Skt. picu, "cotton," 57 65
dām, "blood," equivalent of nɛpɛš, "soul," 39 315-316
dârôm, "south, circle of ecliptic," < √dûr, "to turn," 58 130-131
'el, often equivalent to mɛlɛk or ba'al, 36 368
'ɛlôhîm, "god(s)," < Aram. 'ɛlâhîn, 44 161
'ēpā, one of edifices of Yahweh in Palestine after destruction of the Temple, 52 307
'ɛrɛz, "cedar," < Akk. irêšu, "balsamic juice," 45 322-323
'ɛškôl, "bunch of grapes," < 'ɛšɛk, "testicles," 48 277
'ɛtnā, "prostitute's fee," cf. Phoen. ytn, "to give," 58 135
gɛbɛr, "cock," 33 366, 369-370
'ɛpɛs, "end," < √'sp, || Ar. 'sf, "to be sad," Akk. asâpu, "to gather," 45 36
ghd, "to struggle," || Ar. jhd, 58 136
ḥādā, "to rejoice," < Akk. ḫadû < Sum. ḪAD, "joy, pleasure," 45 179
ḥāgag, "to dance," < ḥûg, "to be round," 36 321, 323-324, 328
ḥᵃgôrā, a kind of loin-cloth, 42 208-209
ḥᵃgôrôt, "loincloths," 21 26ff.
ḥālal, "to pierce," related to same verb in meaning "to profane;" derivatives of, 36 321-324, 328-332
ḥallāmîš, "quartz," perhaps a transposed doublet of ḥašmal, "electrum," 43 119
ḥām, "father-in-law," originally "kinsman, blood-relation;" ||Ar. ḥammah, "kinsmen, relatives," and ḥamîm, "kin, relative," < √ḥamma, "to be hot," 41 187
ḥᵃmiššā, ḥᵃmiššîm, formed by analogy with šiššā, šiššîm, 26 117-119
ḥārûṣ, "gold," primary meaning is "dug out," 42 393; stem ||Ar. ḫadira, "to be green," 43 120, 123
ḥāšaq, "to love," ||Ar. 'ašiqa, 45 360
ḥāṣer, "court, enclosure," ||Ar. ḥazîrah, Aram. ḥuṭrā, Ugaritic ḥṭr, Akk. uṣurtu, Phoen. ḥṣr, 59 22-26, can be either masc. or fem., 28-31, LXX equivalents of, 32-35
ḥāṣer, "settlement, village," ||Ar. ḥaḍara, "to be present, settle," S. Ar. ḥḍr, Syr. ḥērtā, Akk. uṣ(â)rum, 59 22-23, 24, 26, 27-28, can be masc. only, 28, LXX equivalents of, 35-37
ḥašmal, "electrum," ||Akk. elmišu, Syr. 'aṣmaḥ, "to glitter," 43 117-118
hen, its use as a conditional particle is not due to Aramaic influence, 42 397
ḥɛsɛd, has meaning of Lat. pietas and N.T. χάρις, 59 401
ḥîrɛq, vowel name, cf. Ar. ḫarq, "narrow opening," 22 15,17
hiššîg, "to reach," < √*wašagu, 36 417
ḥôlɛm, vowel name, descriptive of rounding of mouth, 22 16, 17
hû, "he," h here is a prefixed deictic element, 45 311-312
'im (= Ar. 'am), particle derived from 'a interrogative, 54 295-296, equals Ar. 'imma, 'am and 'innama, 295-297
'îš, "man," perhaps connected with demonstrative 'iš, 'îš, 35 380 n. 1
kāra', "to kneel to drink," 22 73-75
kārar, "to dance," < kûr, "to be round," 36 321-322
kᵊ, "like," shortened form of kî, "as," 45 316-318, 355
kɛsɛp, "silver," not an Akk. loan-word; primary meaning is "fusible," cf. Ar. sabaka, sakaba, "to smelt," 42 393; 43 116
kɛtɛm, "gold," originally meant "subduable," 42 393, 43 123
kî, "as," identical with kî, "burning, branding," 45 317, 355
ki-'im, "but, verily not," 37 10
kiyyôr, "platform, laver," < Sum. ki-úr, kiuru, 40 317 n. 18
kôba', see qôba'
kôhen, "priest," = Ar. kāhin, "diviner;" original meaning was "soothsayer;" stem is a modification of kûn, "to be firm," and is connected with Akk. kêttu, "truth," 42 373-375, 393
kômɛr, "idol-priest," = Akk. ramku, "priest," < √mkr, "to water," < makâru, "a well," < kâru, "to dig," 42 372-373, 393
kōtɛl, "wall," < Akk. kutallu, 46 159
kûk, "subterranean chamber," = Nab. gûḥā, Palm. gumḥā, Akk. kimaḫḫu [qemaḫḫu], < Sum. kimaḫ, 43 121
kullā, adverbial use of, 43 394-395
lâken, notes on uses of, 30 343-346
lîlît, "night-demon," cf. Sum. lilla, 32 25
mal, mil, "tresses," ||Ar. limmah, 37 325-326
māšal, "to rule," originally meant "to shine," 45 317-318
mᵊṣuppɛh, "glazed," 60 268
mᵊ'ubbār, "intercalated," = Eg. m'bᵓ, "thirty," 45 360
miktām, "restricted, conformed" to poetical meter, 32 122-123
ml'k, "grinding," < √*l'k, ||Ar. lāka, "ate, chewed," 37 327
môqeš, "throwing-stick," < √nāqaš, "to strike," 41 185-186
mōrag, "threshing sledge," < Sum. maraḫ, 40 324 n. 38
mz, "wine," ||Ar. muzz, 37 324
nebɛl, "harp," = Eg. byn.t, 44 167
nᵊḥôšɛt, "copper," Nuḫašše? 38 200
nɛpɛš, "monument, tomb," 45 152
neṣaḥ, "juice, glory," || Ar. naḍaḥa, naḍaḫa, "to sprinkle," 45 361
Nōsardi, name of Persian festival, cf. Buḫāran Nawsard, 28 334
nšq, "stacte," 58 137
nûn, "fish," < Aram. nûnā < Sum. NUN, 54 77
'ōpɛn, "wheel," < Akk. epinnu? 40 324 n. 38; cf. Ar. faynah, "moment," and fann, "mode, form," 43 163
'ôt, 'et, accusative sign, derived from *yât, "being," 45 312, 355
paz, "pure gold," cf. Ar. fazza, "to run, flee," Syr. paz, "to leap," Eth. zafana, 42 393, 43 123-124
pɛtɛn, "viper," ||Ar. fitnah, "rebellion," of which basic idea is "fascination," 53 283-284
qādôš, "foreign deity," 32 121
qāmɛṣ, vowel name, denotes slight lip narrowing, 22 16,17
qānɛh, "sweet flag, lemon-grass," other renditions of the name, 40 263-264
qāra', "to tear," 21 24

qāṭar, "to burn incense," = qāṭar, a dialectic doublet of the stem *ġṭr of Akk. irêšu, "resin," 45 322
qaw, "thread, cord," ||Eg. kȝ, 42 210
qᵊṣî'ā, peeled bark of the spice plant, 40 264-265
qibbûṣ, vowel=name, denotes close lip narrowing, 22 16, 17
qiddā (√qdd, "to cut") Bab. kasû, Somali senna; other renditions of the name, 40 263-266
qinnāmôn (√qnn, "to build up, nest"), "spice packed in bundles," 40 264-265
qîṭôr, "smoke," ||Syr. 'ᵊṭar, "to rise like smoke," Akk. qutru, "smoke," Ar. 'aṭan, Heb. 'āšān, 42 375-376; 43 422
qôba', "helmet," < Hitt. kûpaḫi, 57 73-77
rāhîṭ, "panel," < Akk. râṭu? 46 159
rea', "fellow," cf. ra', "evil," Ar. ġayr, "other," 45 361
rεqaḥ, "spice, aromatic," of Arabian origin, 46 159-160
rhṭ, "fillet," ||Ar. rahṭ, "skin garment," 37 326
šāba', Nif. and Hif., "to swear," uses of, 49 26
šablûl, "snail," Rabbinical etymologies of, 42 280
šāḥar, "to look diligently for," Akk. loan-word, 34 421
šaḥat, "pit," < šûaḥ, "to sink," 32 121
šāmîr, a kind of stone, cf. Eg. ìsmr, Akk. ešmaru, σμύρις, Eng. emery, 45 360
sappîr, originally blue Egyptian jasper, then became lapis-lazuli and finally sapphire, or blue Ceylon corundum, 40 269
ṣāra'at, denotes a number of skin diseases, ||Akk. ṣênitu, Ar. naṣā'ah, "whiteness," 43 163; "leprosy," ||Eth. ṣerne'et, "eruption, exanthema," 46 355
ṣārap, "to smelt, test," a doublet of šārap, "to burn" and Ar. šariba, "to drink," 43 116-117
šāraṣ, "to creep," šaf. < rûṣ, "to run," 47 357
sarîs, "eunuch," < Akk. šaršēn, 41 18 n. 64, 59
šāsa', "to split," saf. < nāsa', "to tear out," 47 357
šāsap, "to destroy," šaf. < sûp, "to end," 47 357
šāśôn, "joy," connected with Akk. šâšat, 38 336
šāṭaḥ, "to spread," šaf. < ṭûaḥ, "to daub," 47 357
šāṭap, "to rinse," šaf. < nṭp, "to drip," 47 357
šεbεr, vowel name, cf. Ar. kasr with same meaning, 22 15-16, 17
šᵊbû'ā, "oath," uses of, 49 26
ṣᵊdā, "true," < √yṣd, ||Ar. waṣada, "to be firm," 43 231-232
šegāl, "consort," cf. šegār, "dam" and Akk. šigrêti, "concubines," 22 69 n. 2
śεkwî, "cock," 33 367-370
šεlεg, "snow" < Akk. ašlâku, "washerman, bleacher," < Sum. azalak, 43 163
ṣerē, vowel name, cf. Syr. ṣeryā, "narrow opening," 22 15, 17
ṣᵊrîaḥ, "cellar, vault," transposed doublet of ḥarîṣ, "excavated," 43 121
šᵊtî, "warp," < Eg. śty, "to spin," 42 209-210
šᵊwâ, vowel name, may have been originally šabbā, "chip," 22 17
siqqel, "to clear of stones," caus. from Aram. qᵊlā, "stone," 45 360
šûm, "garlic," see Akk. šûmu
šûrεq, vowel name, denotes close lip narrowing, 22 16, 17
tāmār, "date-palm," < √*'amar, "to be high," 42 376-377
ṭinnep, "to defile," < Akk. ṭanāpu, II1, 46 159
tô'ebā, development of meaning, 52 294
tôrā, "Torah," < √yārâ, "to inform, direct," 47 356
tûšîyā, "support, help," etc. cf. Akk. asū, "to support, help;" Syr. āsyûtā, "help;" Ar. āsiyah, "pillar," etc., 22 35-44
tûšîyā, "wise, skilful," epithet of Adonis-Ešmun, 22 116-117
Waᵓadār, intercalary month, < Akk. Wadar-Adâr, "Extra Adar," 45 320-322, 354
yād, "hand," < √ydl, 42 203
yayin, "fermented wine," foreign origin of indicated, 33 183-184
yôneq, "sucker" of a plant, 48 349
zāhāb, "gold," ||zûb, "to flow, run," Ar. ḏāba, "to melt," 42 393
zānā 'aḥᵃrē, "to run after, desire," 22 64-69
zarzîr, "cock, starling," 33 368-370
zdh, "fissure," < √znd, 22 57-59
zᵊbûl, "dwelling," zābal, "to swell," Ar. balad, "town," 45 362

HINDI
hai, 56 353
har-, 56 354
limū, limbū, see nimbū
nimbū, "lemon" < Ar. limún through Per., usually called pahari nimbū or karna nēbū to distinguish it from the sour lime, 56 48-49
sakwa, 52 50

HITTITE
bu-u-ta^m, 53 358
handa(i)-, "fix, determine," 50 128
har(k)-, "have," 50 128
harnauš, "birth-chair," 50 128
hatk-, "close," 50 128
hurtaiš, "a curse," 50 128
hu-u-us-si-el-li-ya-az, 53 358
huwart-, hurt-, "curse," 50 128
huwiyami, huwai, "run, flee," 50 128
mahhan, 58 533
mekkis, "great," 52 9 f.
nekuz mehur, "evening," 52 10
-smas, -smes, 53 392
suppariya-, "sleep, become weary," 56 282-284
uddar, "word, lawsuit," 52 11 f.
uwatar, 56 284-287

HUNGARIAN
pallos, "sabre," < Turk. pal(y)uş, 50 259-260

ḪURRIAN
ak, "to guide, direct," 59 324
andurâru, "final release," 52 259
aweharu, "1/10 of a homer," 52 256
awenne/a, "anyone," 59 324
aweš-, indef. adverb (?), 59 324
durupi, "need, trouble," 59 313
eman, "ten," 59 324
ewuru, "designated heir," 55 435-436
giraššena . . . šawallaša = Akk. ana dârâti, 59 324
ḫill, "to bring word, inform," 59 311
iri(n), "aid," 59 324
kik-, "three," 56 404-405
kuruštu, "fodder," < Akk. < Sum., 55 441
man(n), "to be," 59 324
-nin, "indeed" (?), 59 324
puḫizzaru, a kind of exchange, adaptation of Akk. pûḫu, 52 259
šatti, "together," 59 324
šawalla, "years," 59 324
šin-, "two," 56 404-405
šû, "to be like, accord with," 59 324
sûdûtu, "proclamation," 52 259
šukk = Akk. ina muḫḫi, el ša elû, 59 324
supîamašten, "shall increase," 59 324
tumn-, "four," 56 404-405
tupp, "to be strong, equal," 59 324
ull-, "to change," 59 324
ulluḫuggu, "hostile"?, 59 324
ur, "to take place," 59 313
ú-ur, "to take place, be present," 59 324
ú-ú-ur, "to desire," 59 324
weš, "to happen," 59 324

HWĀRIZMIAN
Nāwsārči, see Buḫāran Nawsard

INDIAN
agar, "eagle or aloe wood," 42 173, 177, 182-184
nimbū or nēbū, a generic name for citrus fruits; alone it means the lime, see also Hindi, nimbū, and Skr. nimbū.

INDO-EUROPEAN
*bnd [bandh], "to bind," not connected with Sem. *bnṭ, 42 206-207

IRISH
fri, "adversus, in," 31 404

ITALIAN
palascio, "sabre," < Turk. pal(y)uş, 50 259-260

JAPANESE
Bu-shi, 武士, all the military fr. suzerain to lowest foot-soldier, differentiated fr. samurai, 31 154
hiiragi, "holly," connected at first with the name of a deity, 55 444
Shō-gun, 將軍, an abbr. for sei-i-tai shō-gun, 31 155
Tai-kun, 大君, meaning the Shō-gun > Eng. "taicoon," 31 155

JAVANESE
kapas, "cotton," 52 46

KANARA
aḍal, 56 354
akki, 47 264
aḷija, 56 355
añɦ, 56 354
baḍaga, 56 352
bāj, bāji, "mouth," 46 309
bē, bēne, 56 352
beral, beraḷ, 56 355
elabu, "bone," 58 472
elu, elubu, eluvu, "bone," 58 472
eraḍu, 56 355
esaru, 56 353
eṣṭu, 56 351
ili, 46 310
ili, 49 60
itt-, 56 359
kai, 46 309
kāj-, 56 357
kaṇ, 56 350
kāṇ-, kaṇ-, 56 357
ken, kēsu, kisu, 56 357
kesaR, 56 357
magaḷ, 46 310
malar, 56 358
maṇ, 56 358
maRi, 56 358
mej, 56 358
meṭi, 56 352
mī-, 56 358
mola, 56 358
molam, 46 310
mōRe, 56 358
muṛugu, 56 358
nana, 56 356
nāvu, 56 356
nettar, 56 353
oru, 46 309
pesar, 56 359
posa, 56 359
ta-, 56 354
ta-, 56 359
tale, 46 309
tirug-, 56 359
tuṭi, "lip," 46 310
u, 56 359
ul-, 56 355
uri-, 56 355

KANAURI
kar, 56 357

KARIAN
kubda, "weight," < Sem. *kubdu, 56 85

KHASI
ām, 52 48
ūm, 52 48
k'ah, 52 47
kseu, 52 49
kwāi, 52 49
ōm, 52 48
snām, 52 49
snem, 52 48
tham, 52 49

KHERWAN
sail, 52 49

KHMER
amβas, amβāḥ, "cotton," 52 46
ghām, 52 49
jhmōh, 52 48
ktā, 52 49
sruw, 52 50
tārīj, 52 49

KHOTANESE
hvatanai, hvaṃnai, Khotanese name for their own language; Sansk. gaustana; Tibetan ḥu-then, 59 460

KHÔWAR
γetš, "eye," 46 178

KOḌAGU
peda, 56 359

KOLARIAN
lintir, 46 310
manlēi, 46 310
molloi, moloi, 46 310
sēn-, šen-, 56 355
tomod, 46 310

KORWA
yam, 52 48

KUI
ē, 56 353
ena, 56 351
-k, 56 356
kuṛa-mīḍa, 56 358
luhā, 46 310
mrau, 46 310
mrau, 56 358
mūndži, 56 355
mūndži, 56 358
muŋgēli, "nose," 46 178
nīru, 56 353
oḍri, 56 354
paḍa, 56 359
pṛēnu, pl. pṛēka, 58 472
rī, 56 355
rīṇḍe, 56 355
sal-, 56 355
sī, 56 359
siḍe, 56 351
sirō, 46 310
siru, 56 353
sūḍ-, sūṛ, 56 355
sudā, "mouth," 46 309 f.
suḍa, 56 351
ta-, 56 354
tlau, 46 309
ūra, 56 359
ūṛgi, 47 264

vandžu, 56 355
vē-, veg, 56 352
vīa, 56 352
viha, visa, 56 355
vīori, 56 352
vlē, 56 352

KURDISH
jaoz, an initiation ceremony of the 'Ali-Ilāhis, < Av yaozhdāh? 33 iii

KURKU
didom, 52 48
jūmū, 52 48
sunūm, 52 48
urā, 56 360

KURUKH
-ā, suffix, 56 351
ajjā, 56 354
alkh-, 56 357
aula-, 56 351
bai, "mouth," 46 309
bēk, 56 352
eltš-, 56 354
embā, 56 354
ēxā, 56 355
-ia, 56 354
ijjā, 56 359
illē, 56 356
malā, 56 351
mōsgā, 56 358
mōxārō, 56 358
nē, 56 353
olx-, 56 355
osgā, 56 354
pindž-, 56 359
tai, 56 354
tši-, 56 359
xall, 56 357
xebdā, 56 357
xeṛō, 56 358
xos-, xott-, 56 357

KUVI
orli, 49 60; 56 354

LADĀKHI
argon, "half-breed," not connected with a term for the Nestorians, 52 96

LATIN
ā, 59 406
audit, 40 124
cabbana, see Eng. cabinet
cannaba, see Eng. cabinet
caupona, see Eng. cabinet
foedus, 27 413 f.
gallus, "cock," perhaps so-called from Gaulish origin, 33 384
-mōnium, 34 329 f.
nablium, "harp," < Gr. nablion < Heb. nebεl = Eg. byn.t, 44 167
porcus, 27 415
raudus, rodus, rudus, "piece of brass," < Sum. urudu, "copper," 43 122-123
religio, 32 126-129
-tus, 38 48 f.

LEPCHA
nam, 52 48

LITHUANIAN
dainà, 32 412 f.
sù, 34 333
výdraga, 42 186
žógis, 42 187 f.

MĀGADHĪ
ahake, 41 459
kachati, 36 211 f.

MALABARI
tayk, 52 50

MALAY
bertapar, a type of incubation, 33 333
besi, 52 50
bras, beras, 52 50
kapas, "cotton," 52 46 f.
kĕrambil, "carambola," of Indian origin, 57 390
kerbao, 52 49
lima, 46 310
limau, "citrus," 57 389
līmūn, "lemon," < Pers. līmūn, 57 389-390
mulut, 46 310
pontianak, a kind of forest-specter or ghost of unborn child, 33 319 n. 1
semangat, "vital spirit inhabiting people or things," 33 327-328
teliṇa, 46 310
ular, 52 50

MALTO
alx-, 56 357
bēku, 56 352
kei-, ketšk-, 56 356
mala, 56 351
muso, "nose," 46 178; 56 352
nē-, 56 353
olγ-, 56 355
pindž-, 56 359
tāni, 56 359
tei, 56 354
tɔro, "mouth," 46 177, 309; 56 351
tši-, 56 359
ṭuṇḍ-, 56 355

MANCHU
Fučihi = √fut plus -i-hi, 37 167-168

MANDAIC
'abrā, "beam," cf. Talm. 'abrā, 33 280
astānā, "north," cf. Syr. estānā and Akk. ištânu, 33 279-280
gāblā, "south," cf. Heb. nεgεb, 33 280
gina, ginah, "evil spirit," cf. Ar. jinni and Palm. gᵊnē, 57 320
sukrā, "door-bolt," cf. Syr. and Talm. sukrā, 33 279
šûtā, "east," cf. Akk. šûtu, 33 280
tana, "container," form with prefixed t from √'nh, 53 162
uryā, "west," cf. amurru, 33 280
zah, "away with!" 33 279

MARĀTHI
ḍāvā, "left," 57 307

MEDIEVAL
Ondanique, the fine steel used for swords and mirrors, < Ar. Hundwánîy, "Indian," 35 232

MIKIR
chelong, 52 49
kove, 52 49
methan, 52 49
ninkan, 52 48

MINAEAN
būṣ, "byssus," see Heb. bûṣ.

MON
chim, 52 49
coin, 52 50
hnām, 52 48
hum dait, 52 48
kamāo, 52 49
khatām, 52 49

kivet, 52 49
klā, 52 50
me rai, 52 49
neme, 52 48
pasoa, 52 50
preo, 52 49
srō, srō̃, 52 50
yemu, 52 48

MONGOL
burḫan, title of Buddha, a native Ural-Altaic word meaning "deity, image," 36 390-395; not of Turkish origin, 37 167
goša, "bunch of dates," cf. Ar. goš (Persian Gulf pron.) < N. Pers. kušš, ḫušš, "angle," 42 345

MUND
sita, 52 49

MUNDARI
lur-bing, 52 50

NABATAEAN
gûḫā, "subterranean cavern, tomb," < Sum. kimaḫ, 43 121-122

NEPĀLI
debre, "left," 57 307

NICOBAR
arōć, arōś, 52 50

NORTH AFRICAN DIALECTS
hint or al hint, steel, < Hindi metal, or Indian metal, 35 232

OLD IRISH
sech, 31 410

OLD PERSIAN
ἄγγαρος, 42 334-337
aniya-, 35 345 f.
aniyanā, 35 338
āpariyāya, 35 331-336
abaštam, 21 169, 172-175
amānaya, amāniya, 58 678
amuθa, "he fled," 38 121 f.
aruvastam, 38 122 f.
avā (Bh. 4.46), 23 62 f.
avahyarādiy, 35 322-325, 329
asa-, aspa-, 35 343 f.
imam, imām, 35 345 fn.
īy, 35 348 fn.
iyam, 35 345 fn.
[ismar]uv, 56 220
ufrasta-, ufrašta-, 35 351 f.
ufraštādiy, 35 351 f.
ušabārim, 35 343 f.
kā, 23 60
jan-, 35 349 f.
xšapa-, 35 328
taumā, 35 329-331
tarsa-, 35 340 f.
tya-, 35 322 fn., 338 fn.
tyanā, 35 342
θakata^{m}, θakatā, 35 352 fn.
daršam, 35 336 f., 340-342
diš, 35 346 f.
duvitātaranam, 23 63 f.
drauga-, 35 341 f.
nāma, nāmā, 35 324 f., 339
niyaθ^{r}ārayam, 44 171, 285-287
niyasaya, 38 123 f.
māniyam, "estate," 34 329 f.
māniya, "wealth," 33 281-283
māhyā, 35 324 fn., 333
yanaiy, 35 338
rauta, 35 338 f.
viθabiš, τὰ οἰκεῖα, cf. Av. vīsan, "householder," 33 281-283
viθaibiš, 21 181 f.; 23 56-60
[ša]kauθim, 56 220
šakauri[m], 56 220
šām, 35 346
šim, 35 344-350
hača, 31 403-410
hacā, 35 337-342
hadugām, 58 678
ha-miθ^{r}iya-, 31 404
hya, 35 322, 338 fn.
hyāparam, 35 338 fn.

ORMURI
ē, 56 353

PAHLAVI, BOOK
ḫastak, "crippled, lame," epithet applied to Mani, 58 239-240

PAHLAVI, SEAL
apastān 'al Yazdān, "reliance on God," phrase inherited from Assyrian inscriptions, 52 204

PAHLAVI, TURFAN
avīštabēdagīīh, "established lordship," 43 24
axšādīh, "trouble, distress," 53 392
dafēdagīh, derivative abstract from dafēdag < *daftan, "to write," 43 23
miyazdagtāčīh, Manichaean ceremonial offering, compound of miyazdag, "food," + tāčīh, "liquid, drink," 49 34-39; 46 357
MNWḤMYD, 58 333
padišnōḫrēd, derivative passive verb, || Av. ḫšnaoθra, "satisfaction," 43 21-22
nōḫvīr, "Urmensch," 47 193-197
rāsta = rāšta, "true," 39 56
rāstēft, "truth," 39 56-57
'XSVZ, 53 392
'ŠKRWST, 58 332
ḤPŠYRD, 58 331 f.
zādmūrd, "rebirth," 45 267

PALAUNG
hsao, 52 49
krak, kra, 52 49
sāṅ, 52 50
sau, so, 52 49

PALI
akaniṭṭha, "of equal rank," 59 404
anuddayā, 41 462
abhikkanta, 41 462
itthatā, 59 404
kaḍḍh, "draw, plow," 41 465 f.
kaṇṇikā, 50 238-243
kūṭa, 50 242 f.
nāga, "snake," 59 404
paggharati, 41 464
paṭikkulā, 41 462
paribbūlha, 41 462
pādacchida, "stride," 59 404
pādavāra, "stance," 59 404
pāsa, "eye of a needle," 59 404
mokkhacikā, 48 283
muddā, 48 279-281; 52 77
vikkhāyitaka, 41 462
vissussati, 41 464
saṅkha, "species," 59 404
suññatā = annattā, 59 404

PALMYRENE
dk', name of trade or vocation, cf. Ar. dukkān? 26 111
g^{ə}nāyā, "gods," applied to deities 'Asad and Sa'd; name g^{ə}nē originally applied to god of Heliopolis, 57 320

gumḫā, "subterranean cavern, tomb," < Sum. kimaḫ, 43 121-122

PAMPANGA
puk, "to assign," 31 394
tul, "cotton-measure," 31 394

PARJI
pidir, 56 359

PASHAI
antš, "eye," 46 178
dōr, "mouth," 46 177
lē, "die," 46 177

PERSIAN
birindž, 47 264 f.
gurindž, 47 264 f.
γōša, 56 357
kalinbak, "carambola," see Ar. kalanbak
kāz, 56 356
līmū, "lemon," see Ar. līmū
līmūn, "lemon," see Ar. līmūn, laymūn
māt, 58 662-664
pādšāh, 40 200 f.
varindž, 47 264 f.
xalāl, 56 354
yāzdāh, 42 295-300

PHOENICIAN
'gnn, "dove," 33 364 n. 1
ḥsp, "to break," Heb. ḥāśap, "to peel," Ar. ḫašafa, "to crack," 45 273-274
ḫtr, "scepter," fem. as in Akkadian, 45 273
ks', "throne," fem. as in Akk., 45 273
m'š, "statue," of unknown origin; not Semitic, 46 238
šrn, cf. Akk. šurinnu, "column, pillar," 23 171-172
ṣṣ, cf. Samar. Targ. ṣwṣ, "young pigeon," 33 364 n. 1
tammâ', "commander," < Akk. tamû < Amû, "to speak," 45 273
ytn, "to give," < *ntn by backformation, 56 410

POLISH
pałasz, pałasik, "sabre," < Turk. pal(y)uş, 50 259-260

PORTUGUESE
azevre, "aloes," < Ar. ṣabr, ṣibar [ṣabir], 42 175

PRĀKRIT
aṭṭana-, "exercise, gymnastics," 60 361
amhāaṃ (= Skt. asmākam), 40 251 f.
arh-, 40 252 f.
ahake (= Skt. aham), 40 253 f.
āma, 40 254
kaḍḍh, "draw, plow," 41 465 f.
kaḍḍhaī, "draws," 60 361 f.
karia (= Skt. kṛtvā), 40 254 f.
kissa, kiśśa (= Skt. kasya), 40 255 f.
khu (= Skt. khalu), 40 256
caḍaī, "mounts, raises, lays upon" 60 362 f.
cuṭ-, "cut," 60 363
ḍoya-, "wooden object," 60 363 f.
lukkaī, "hide, lurk," 60 368 f.
vaaṃ (= Skt. vayam), 40 258 f.
vaṭṭā, 52 76
haṭṭa-, "market-place," 60 369
hutta-, "facing towards," 60 369
ḍhakkaī, "covers, closes," 60 364
tava (= Skt. tava), 40 257
tuvaṃ (= Skt. tvam), 40 257 f.
dalaī, "gives," 60 365
daṃsaī, "shows," 60 364 f.
disati, 56 406
dissa, diśśa (= Skt. dṛśya-), 40 258
docca-, "second," 60 365 f.
baïlla, "bull," 60 366 f.
rukkha-, "tree," 60 367 f.
laṭṭhi-, "stick, staff," 60 368
lenti, 40 94 f.
lenti, 40 102

ROMANIAN
palos, "sabre," < Turk. pal(y)uş, 50 259-260

RUSSIAN
palaš, "sabre," < Turk. pal(y)uş, 50 259-260
palaška, palašik, "sabre," < Turk. pal(y)uş, 50 259-260

SABAEAN
huwatu, "he," = Granadan Arabic huet and Akk. šu'âtu, 45 313

SAKAI
senam, 52 48

SAMOAN
vai ola, 26 414

SANSKRIT
aṅśa, "quarter," 23 133 f.
āṅgiras, 42 334
aṇḍaja, 48 170-173
adhika, 23 125 f.
adhi-brū, 36 213-225
adhi-vāc, 36 213-225
adhivāsa, 33 162-166
adhivāsana, 33 162-166
adhivāsita, 33 162-166
anaḍúd-bhyas, 40 82
anuyoga, 22 365
antaḥkaraṇa, 45 65-67
anyedyúḥ, 59 425-430
apavarga, 22 343
ápa-varj-, 35 281
ápi-varj-, 35 281
apsarastīrtha, 23 82
abhipitvám, 39 261 f.
abhiprāṇiti, 22 285 f.
abhiśaṅs-, "accuse, accurse," 45 49 f.
abhyadika, 23 125 f.
abhyāsa, 22 356, 360
ámbaram, 27 416 f.
aratni, "cubit," 23 142 f.
arindama, 48 170, 174
ardha, 23 132 f.
arvācīná-, 27 407 f.
arvāñc-, 27 401-407
arvāvát-, 27 407-410
alambuṣā, 23 71
Avantyādhipateḥ, 41 121,129
avara, "almost," 23 126 f.
avyaktam, 45 52-67
aśvattha, 48 170-173
Aṣṭā, 23 113-115
ahaṃkāra, 45 51-66
ahaṃkāra, 22 337, 352
ā, 59 406
ākāśa, 45 52-63
ākṣārita, 45 48
ācarita, 21 146, 147
ātmaja, 48 170, 173
ātmajaya, 48 170, 174
ātmaprabha, 48 170, 173
ātmā, 45 54-63
ā-diś, 40 89-92
ādeśa, 38 206 f.; 40 82-84, 84-87, 95-97
ā-dhā, 60 214
ādhāra, 22 342, 353; 23 68 f.
āpagā, 48 170-173
āpitvam, 39 261 f.
āpṛccha, 41 124, 129
āryajuṣṭa, 48 170, 174
ārṣa, 25 339
ā-varj-, 35 280 f.

ā-vis, "obvious," 40 121-124
āśīrvāda, 48 170, 174
āsana, 22 334, 341-348, 373-379
āsvāpana, 40 345
iḍā, 23 71
indrāviṣṇū, 25 95
indriya, 45 54-67
īḍ-, "revere," 45 158
īśvara, 45 51-52
ukha, 56 357
uttara, 23 125
udāsīna-, 56 363
upakāra, 48 176
upavīṇa, 51 284
upaśuṣyadārdra-, 56 362
upasarga, 22 344
upāsana, 22 334
ubhayedyuḥ (ubhayadyuḥ), 59 425-430
uraga, 48 170, 173
ūrj, 35 287 f.
ṛtvij, 48 170-173
ekarṣi, 22 289 f.
-era-, 33 56
aiśvarya, 22 337, 344, 352, 358, 371-374
kám, 34 333 f.
kampana, "army," 45 326
kara, "cubit," 23 141
karuṇa, 56 50
karpaṭa, 52 47
karpāsa, "cotton," 52 46-48; 56 356
karpūra, "camphor," < Malay kāpūr, etc. < Batak gābū, gāmbū, gāmbūr, 42 362-363, 365
kalayati, 53 391
kalpa, 24 43-45
kalā, "one-sixteenth," 23 135 f.
kāmavāsin, 48 170, 175
kāṣṭhabhūta, 48 170 f., 174
kiṃkara, 48 170, 174
kiṣku, "cubit," 23 142
kulodvaha, 48 170, 174
kuś, 28 128
kuhū, 23 71
kūrma, 23 71
kṛtakṛtya, 48 170, 174
krośa, 23 146 f.
khaga, 48 170-173
khagama, 48 170, 172, 174
khudáti, "futuit," 27 415 f.
gaṇayati, 23 124
gandhārī, 23 71
gábha-sti-s, 31 413
gamiṣye, 41 122, 129
garútmant, 42 203 f.
gala, 56 354
gavyūti, 23 147 f.
giri, "mouse," 49 61
giri, 56 354
guṇa, 22 338, 346, 355; 23 128 f.; 45 51-61; 52 249
guṇita, "multiplied by," 23 128
gurubhakta, 48 170, 174
gṛhīṣyāmi, 25 92
gṛhya, 41 125 f., 129
godhā, "lizard," 51 172
gōdhūma, 56 357
goptā, 25 91
graha, 24 36-39
caturaśratva, 48 282 f.
cātaka-, 39 206
cittam, 45 63-67
codana, 22 342, 345
jagrāsa, 25 92
jambīra, 56 49 f.
jayyāt, 25 95
jaladāgama, 48 171, 174
jīva, 45 60-63
jīvanmṛta-, 56 362
tanūruha, 48 171-174
tanmātra, 45 66
tapas, 22 336, 348, 367-379
tapovṛddha, 48 171, 174
-tas abl., 47 181 f.
-tas, 38 49-59
tasmāt, 47 179 f.
tri, 23 111 f.
Trita, 38 303 f.
daṇḍadhāraṇa, 48 171, 174
daṇḍarāsa, "staff dance," 48 281 f.
dama, 22 334-336, 354
daśa, 23 116 f.
divākara, 48 171
divispṛś, 48 171-173
diśati, 56 406
dīkṣā, 22 362
duryoṇá-, duroṇá-, 34 339-341
duhitām, 25 95
drogdhum, 25 92
dhanaṃjaya, 23 71
dhanu(s), "bow (measure)," 23 144
dharmavṛtti, 48 171 f., 175
dhātu, 23 71
dhāraṇā, 22 335-353, 379
dhārayām āsa, 22 352 f.
dhénā, 32 393-413
dhyāna, 22 334-339, 344 f., 360
dhyānayoga, 48 171, 174
namaskāra, 48 171, 174, 176
namovṛkti-, 35 276 f.
naravāhin, 48 171, 175
nalva (nala), 23 145 f.
nava, 23 115 f.
náhus-, 27 410 f.
nāga, 23 71
nāmadheya, 48 171, 174
niṅs, 28 127
nid, nind, "revile," 45 38 f.
nimbū and nimbūka, names for the lemon, based on vernacular forms of India, 54 147, 156, 157
nimbū and nimbūka, "sour lime," < Ar. limún through Per., 56 48-49, of late date, 50
nimbū, "citrus fruit, lime," 57 395
niśākara, 48 171, 174
nīra, 56 353
nyāsa, 22 334
pañcadivyāny adhivaśitāni, 33 166
paṭa, 52 47
pada, "foot-breadth," 23 143
pada-vī, 40 121
padviṅśat, 51 170 f.
panthā, 21 48
pannaga, 48 171, 174 f.
payodhara, 48 171, 174
paraṃtapa, 48 171, 174
parāvat, 27 409 f.
párā-varj-, 35 280, 281
pariṣvaja(ti), 41 124 f., 129
pariṣvajāmi, 41 124 f., 129
pāraga, 48 171, 174
piṅgala, 23 71
puṇyakṛt, 48 171, 174
puṇyāhavācana, 48 171, 174
putreti, 41 121, 129
punar apāniti, 22 285 f.
pūṣā, 23 71
pṛcchase, 41 122 f., 129
pṛṣṭhataḥ pārśvataś ca, 22 352 f.
prakṛti, 22 337, 352-355; 45 54-56

pratigraha, 60 215
pratibhā, 22 343
pratīcīḥ, 27 417
pratyāyati, 41 128
pratyekabuddha, 43 170
pratyekabodhi, 43 170
pradhānam, 45 66
pradhāraṇa, 22 352 f.
prapitvám, 39 261 f.
prabhāva, 22 337, 378
praveśaka, 25 205 fn., 209 fn.
prasādaja, 48 171, 174
prāṇa, 22 346 f., 353, 362 f.
prāṇayātrā, 48 171
prādus, 39 206
prāya, 21 146-159
prāyaścitta, 34 233
priyavāda, 48 171, 174
prītikara, 48 171, 174
bālabhāva, 48 174
buddhi, 45 51-66
Bṛhácchandas, 23 77 f.
brahma, 45 51-61
brahmacarya, 48 171, 174
brahmacārin, 48 171, 175
brahmavid, 48 171, 174
bhayaṃkara, 48 171, 174
bhayāvaha, 48 171, 174
bhāga, "quarter," 23 133 f.
bhujaṃga, 48 171, 174
bhūtātmā, 45 55-59
bhūtāni, 45 55-66
bhūti, 22 358
maṇīṣā, 22 334, 358
manas, 45 51-66
manuja, 48 171, 174
mánoratha, 39 282
mahat tattvam, 45 66
mahad bhūtam, 45 52-64
mahābrāhmaṇa, 23 79
mahāyoga, 22 365
mahāsiddhi, 22 357-359
mahīdhara, 48 171, 174
mahībhṛt, 48 171, 174
mānada, 48 171, 174
mānasa, 22 334; 45 60-63
mudrā, 48 279-281
mūlādhāra, 23 69
medhā, 22 334
mokṣayoga, 22 365
modiṣyase, 25 92
yajñopavīta, 57 245
yatkṛte, 48 171-174
yaśasvinī, 23 71
yuga, 23 145; 24 43
yudh-, masc., 41 128
yuvākú, 34 333
yoga, 22 333-379; 52 250 f.
yojana, 23 148-154
yoddhum, 25 92
yauvanastha, 48 171-174
rakṣiṣye, 25 92
ratni, "cubit," 23 142 f.
rudantīm, 41 125, 129
rudrapradhāna, 22 340
ruroda, 25 92
lañkha, 48 283
lāti, 40 82 f., 87-89, 93-95
lūma, 25 175
lokapāla, 48 171, 174
vaṃśanartin, "pole-dancer," 48 281 f.
vádhri, 27 414
(vayyà) vayí-a, "attendant," 40 125
váruṇa-, 39 207
vasudhā, 48 171, 174
vasundharā, 48 171, 174
vi, 40 122
vikrama, 22 352, 354
vitasti, "span," 23 142
vidhidṛṣṭa, 48 171-174
vibhūti, 22 337, 358
viṣaya, 22 344, 346, 351
viṣkambhaka, 25 209 fn.
vistara, 22 356
vihaga, 48 171-174
vihaṃga, 48 171
vīṇā, 51 49
vṛṣṭyas, 25 95
vedhás, "worshipper, pious; faithful, true," 27 411-414
vyaktam, 45 52 f.
vyakta, 22 337, 355
vyāma, 23 144
vrīhi, 47 264
śañkhinī, 23 71
śap-, "swear," 45 48 f.
śap-, "entreat," 52 336 f.
śaptvā, 25 91
śamyā, "rod (measure)," 23 144
śiroruha, 48 171-174
śīlavṛddha, 48 171, 174
śṛñgāṭaka, 23 139
ṣṭhīv-, 46 60
saṃyoga, 22 365
sáṃ-varj-, 35 281 f.
saṃskāra, 23 71
saṃskāra, 48 176
sak-thán, 31 412
saṃkṣepa, 22 356 f.
saṃkhya, "times," 23 130
saṃcodana, 22 345
sa'yavāc, 48 171, 174
satyavādin, 48 171, 175
satyasandha, 48 174
saṃtānakara, 48 171, 174
saptan, 23 113
samādhi, 22 335-369; 60 208-216
samāśvāsitum, 41 128
saṃmṛśati, 58 533 f.
sarvarājñaḥ, 41 126, 129
sasmāra, 25 92
sahá, 39 206
sāṃkhya, 52 250
sācís, 31 412
sāmya, 22 334, 346
siddhi, 22 352-359, 367, 371
suvṛkti-, 35 277-280
suśiśvi-s, 32 391 f.
spṛśáti, "touches, grasps, feels, besprinkles," 27 414 f.
syāvas, 25 95
svabhāva, 48 174
svayaṃbhū, 48 171-174
svayāmātṛtṛṇṇāḥ śarkarāḥ, 58 534
svavṛj-, svávṛkti-, 35 282 f.
svastha, 48 171-174
svairavṛtta, 48 171-174
havyavāhana, 48 171, 174
hásta, "cubit," 23 141 f.
hásta-s, 31 413
hastijihvā, 23 71
hitāśraya, 48 171-174
hāhākāra, 48 171, 174, 176
hāhābhūta, 48 171, 174
hoḍha-, 39 206

SANTALI
catom, 52 48
damkom, 52 48

disom, 52 48 f.
guạ, 52 49
hoṛo, huṛu, 52 50
kaḍa (kaṛa), 52 49
kaṭ bel, 52 49
kaskom, 52 46 f.
katkom, 52 49
kŏc bel, 52 49
kul, 52 50
laṛ, 52 50
lodam, 52 48
mayam, 52 49
merom, 52 48 f.
mihū, 52 48
ńum, ńutum, 52 48
odam, 52 48
paha, 52 46 f.
pasra, 52 50
rai turi, 52 49
sadom, 52 48 f.
sągun, sagwan, 52 50
serma, 52 48
seta, 52 49
sunum, 52 48
ṭor, 52 50
ul, 52 50
um ạmin, 52 48
um ḥor, 52 48

SAVARA
ra, 52 49
ti, 56 359

SEMITIC
bi'r, "well," cognate with Eg. by', "vagina, mine-shaft," 39 70
*bnṭ, "to bind," not connected with I-E bnd [bandh], 42 206-207
dam, "blood," < √*dmw, "to be like," 36 152
ḥlp, "to put on," borrowed from Indo-European, 47 356
hu'a, "he," final -a is a remnant of the noun *yât, "being," 45 312, 355
ka, "like," identical with deictic particle k, 37 10
lbš, "to put on," a doublet of ḥlp, 47 356
ydl, "to bolt, shut up," || Eg. ỉdr, 42 202-203

SERBIAN
paloša, "sabre," < Turk. pal(y)uş, 50 259-260

SHAN STATES
tsaṅg, 52 50

SHINA
brīm, 47 264

ŠĪNĀ
mālō, 25 340

SIAMESE
chang, 52 50
khau, 47 266
sak, 52 50

SINDHI
ātā, "pollen of male palm-tree," < Ar. 'aṭa ['aṭā'], "benefit, [gift]"? 42 352

SINGHALESE
div-a, 56 353
ē, 56 353
gala, 56 354
tol, 46 310

SINO-TIBETAN
Comparisons of Old Bodish, Burmese, Lusei, Chinese and Siamese (including Lao), Tables, 60 316-337

SOGDIAN
Nawsarḏ, Nawsarḏīj, see Buḫāran, Nawsard

SOUTH ARABIC
ftḥ, "law," || Eth. feth, 37 164
škn, "to establish," < Akk. šakânu, 37 164
sm'm, "witness," 37 164

SPANISH
acibar, "aloes," < Ar. ṣabr, ṣibar [ṣabir], 42 175
alinde, steel, or steel mirror, < Hindi metal, meaning Indian steel, 35 232
hasta, "until," < Ar. ḥatta influenced by Lat. usque, 56 415-416

STIENG
maham, 52 49
pahi, "cotton," 52 46
rūĕh, 52 49
sou, 52 49
tam, 52 49

SUMERIAN
A-BA, "scribe writing on both clay and parchment," 48 128-131
AN-ZIL-LU, "tabu," < Akk. ^{il}ṣillu, "divine shadow," 39 66 n. 3
apsu, not connected with Heb. 'ϵpϵs, "end," 45 35-36; etymologies of, 142
bir, "gazelle," 21 7-8
DIM, a name including both sesame and dhurah, 31 255
dingir, often means "king" or "lord," 36 368-369
dun ["pig"], meaning uncertain, 33 402-404
DUN, ŠUL, "zebu," 36 140
Eme-sal, "women's speech," 39 279
en-na, sometimes means "when," 39 323-324
E-PA, 7-staged ziggurat, 43 92-95
esir-apin, "dry or kneaded bitumen," 46 301
esir-sun-sun, "liquid bitumen," 46 301
gik [gig], "to resist," and gik [gig], "to bar" are identical 38 67
girman, "reservoir," < kir, "mouth" and man, "two," 39 68-69
ğul-gik [ḫul-gig], "obstinate refusal," 38 66-68
ḫu-rí-in, "horn," < Akk. qarnu, 48 86
id-kana, "source of the rivers," 38 330
kakkul, "receiver of a brandystill," 40 219
kiengi, originally "sacred territory," 49 308-309
KI-NIR, 3- or 4-staged ziggurat, plus temple, 43 94-95
KI-NU-NIR, temple without a ziggurat, 43 95
li, see šim
lu-a-dar-maš, "horned gazelle," 21 7
MIR, "gecko," 39 284
mu-an-na, "year," lit. "name of heaven," 52 295
mummu, "thunder," not related to divine name Mummu, 58 545
nam, particle, meanings of, 47 256-259
nam-erím, "oath," originally associated with idea of curse, 33 37-38; originally "hostile destiny," 34 283; "oath, ban, curse," 49 22
NIM-MEŠ, "fly-whisk," 41 181
par, a type of bitumen used in binding bricks, 46 301-302
sì, "to give," contains roots seg, = mašâlu, and sig, = sapânu, 57 62-63; pronunciation sè possibly Emesal; sì in main dialect; possibility of gradual change in vowel quality, 64; had value sur, zur, 69-70; summary of phonetic values, 72
sì (m), "to give," older form of root than su$_{11}$(m); -u- arises through influence of following m, 57 35-72; was originally sem, cf. Emesal zem, 64; reading sum is post-Sumerian, 65
šim, li, "juniper berries, resin," 42 176
SU = Akk. šiqlu, "shekel," 57 181-184
su11, see sì(m)
suḫur, "foliage, crown of a palm," 39 71 n. 12
Šú.Gé.-tum, = Akk. esirtu, 43 426
zi, "lifting up, oath," 49 23

SYRIAC
'^{ə}mad, "to baptize," possibly derived from Rabbinic ma'^{a}mâd, "presence" of witnesses, 46 15-18

'argāztā, "wallet, chest," < Heb. 'argāz, "chest, box," 56 273
bûṣā, "byssus," see Heb. bûṣ
gurḥā, "monk's cell," < *kurḥā > Ar. kirḥ, 43 121
'ît, "is," < *'ît, = Heb. 'et, accusative particle, 35 377-381
kâpûr, "camphor," < Malay kāpūr, 42 363
kûbā'ā, see qûb 'ā
lam, "to wit," < Aram. lᵊmâ, "with reference to," 43 236
qûbᵊ'ā, "helmet," see Heb. qôba'
ṣāpaḥtā, "snare," causative from Heb. paḥ, "bird-net," 41 186
Tammûz (month), directly < Sum. tamuzi, 57 71 n. 95
taqnâtā, "qualities of mind and character," 39 291-293
tᵊnânā, "smoke," transp. from nᵊtânā, cf. Ar. natānah, "stench," 42 376
tûmā, "garlic," see Akk. šûmu

TAGALOG
halo-, 27 146
pana, 25 298
panag, 25 298
pani, 25 298

TAMIL
alamp-, 56 359
alla, 56 351
añc-, 56 354
ariçi, ari, 47 264
āṭū, 56 354
āvi, 56 351
cejdu, 46 309
cevi, 56 357
eli, 46 310; 49 60; 56 354
elumpu, "bone," 58 472
enakku, 56 356
ennai, 56 356
enpu, "bone," 58 472
ēR-, 56 354
eri-, 56 355
eṛupp-, 56 354
ettanai, 56 351
ī, 56 355
iḷaijaḷ, iḷaijāḷ, 56 356
illai, 56 351
ini, 56 354
irai, 56 355
iraṇṭu, 56 355
iraṭṭu, 56 355
iravu, 56 356
jāvar, jār, 56 352
kai, 46 309
kal, 56 357
-kaḷ, 56 355-6
kaṇ, 56 350
kandru, 46 310
kaṇṇīr, 56 357
karu, 56 358
kātu, 56 357
koḷ, 56 354
koṛunti, 56 358
kōtumai, 56 357
kuti, 56 358
kutirai, 56 355
malai, 56 358
mēj, 56 352
mucal, 56 358
mūnRu, 56 355, 358
nak-, 56 357
nīr, 56 353
nōkk-, 56 355
onRu, 56 351
ōr-, 56 355
oru, 46 309
pejar, 56 356, 359
putu, 56 359
-t (past-suffix), 56 356
ta-, 56 354
talai, 46 309 f.
tēn, 56 354
tin-, 56 356
tuḍi, "lip," 46 310
ukir, 56 355
uṇ-, 56 356
uṇṭu, 56 351
vāj, "mouth," 46 309; 56 351
val, 56 352
veḷ, 56 359
vēṇ, 56 352
viral, 56 355

TANGKHUL
kwāthi, 52 49
silui, 52 49

TANGKHUL NAGA
vat, 52 47
ziñkum, 52 48

TELUGU
alluḍu, 56 355
āvaliñc, 56 351
balu, 56 352
bōke, bomike, "bone," 58 472
chuloo kabri, 52 49
cūc-, 56 355
dīni, 56 353
elike, eluka, 49 60
emuka, emmu, "bone," 58 472
idi, 56 353
īga, 56 355
kannu, 56 350
kundēlu, 56 358
makkelu, "bones," 58 472
nōru, "mouth," 46 309; 56 351
nosalu, 56 358
pati, 52 48
pēru, 56 359
renḍu, 56 355
tala, 46 310
te-, 56 354, 359
teek, 52 50
vēlu, 56 355

TIBETAN
abras, 47 266
nam, 52 48
Saṃdhi, tr. of, 57 123

TULU
āval, 56 351
bāji, "mouth," 46 309
de-, 56 352
duḍi, "lip," 46 310
džānę, 56 352
hū-, 56 355
-kuḷu, kaḷu, 56 356
mei, 56 358
mūdži, 56 358
ondži, 56 351
pudarm, 56 359
sū-, 56 355
tū-, 56 355

TUNGUSIAN, see Words, Mongol

TURKISH, (see also Mongol)
çelebi, "gentleman," < Kurd. ṯeleb, < Syr. ṣᵊlībā, "cross," 54 194-199
cock, names for in various dialects, 33 375
pala, "oar, blade of an oar," < It. pala, 50 255

pala, "saddle-cloth," < N. Pers. pālās, 50 255
pala, "sword," and its European derivatives, 50 254-260

UGARITIC
bṯn, "viper," || Ar. baṯan, but not Heb. pετεn, 53 283-284
dkrn, = zikrôn in Is. 57:8, 55 56
gngn, "bridal chamber," < Akk. gigunu, 53 123
ḥmt, "wall," vocalized ḥômîtu, 60 418
pdr, a Ḫurrian word for "city," 55 52
prʿt, fem. form of "pharaoh," 55 57
ṯpṭ, = Heb. šāpat, "to judge, govern," cf. S. Ar. ṯpṭ, 53 283
ytn, "to give," < √*ntn by back-formation as in Phoenician, 56 410

UIGUR (see also Mongol)
ögütmis, ọgütmis, epithet of the Manichaean "Mother of the Living," 44 68
trazuk, "scales," < Pahl. tarāzūk (NP tarāzū), 43 21

VEDIC
ákava, 45 171
ákāmakarśanaḥ, 48 170, 174 f.
adrí, adrivant, 45 168 f.
ádridugdhās, 48 170 f., 174
adhvaraśríya, 48 169, 173
anūdháḥ, 45 171
antarikṣaprā́m, 48 169, 173
áparājitam, 48 167, 171, 174 f.
aptúraḥ, 48 166, 172
amīvacā́tanam, 48 167, 174
amīvahā́, 48 167, 173
ámbara, 31 52 f.
arí, aryá, "priest," 45 160-168
arídhāyas, 45 162
árvan, 45 170 f.
álakam, 52 78
avadyagohanā, 48 168, 174
aṣṭa, 23 322
asmadhrúk, 48 169, 173
ahám índro váruṇas, 48 201
aharvídaḥ, 48 166, 172
áhigopā, 48 168, 173, 176
índragupta, 48 166
indrapā́nāḥ, 48 170 f., 175
índrāvaruṇa, 23 322
iṣudhínr, 48 168, 173
iṣu-dhyā́, 34 338
iṣmin, 31 49-51
udavāhéna, 48 169, 174
uṣarbúdhaḥ, 48 167, 169, 172 f.
ŕcīṣama, 45 170
ŕcīṣama, 48 201
ṛtájatā, 48 169
ṛtaspṛśā, 48 166, 172
ṛtāvṛdha, 48 166-173
ṛté śrāntásya, 49 361
ṛtvíja, 48 166, 169-173
ṛṣikṛ́t, 48 168, 173
ṛṣidvíṣe, 48 169, 173
auśijáḥ, 48 173
kakṣyaprā́, 48 167, 173
karambhā́d, 40 101 f.
karambhā́d, 40 98-100
karambhā́d, 40 90
kīrí, 31 51 f.
kṣetrajeṣé, 48 168, 174
gáviṣṭi, 48 169, 171, 175
gātuvít, 48 169, 173
girvaṇaḥ, 48 167, 175
gírvāho, 48 168
goghná, 48 166, 171
godā́, 48 166, 173
godúhe, 48 166, 172
gopā́m, 48 166, 172 f., 176
gopīthā́ya, 48 168, 174
gohita, 48 166
ghṛtaprúṣam, 48 169, 173
ghṛtasnúvo, 48 167, 173
camūṣádaḥ, 48 167, 170-173
carṣaṇīdhṛto, 48 166, 172
cākṣmá, 56 368 f.
janā́ṣā́l, 48 170, 173
jyotiṣkṛ́d, 48 169, 173
tanūkṛ́d, 48 168, 173
taraṅgacañcalatara, 48 166
tuvīravān, 21 51
tvā́dātam, 48 167, 171, 174
tvā́vṛdhā, 48 170, 173
dasyuhatyā́ya, 48 174
dasyuhátyeṣu, 48 170, 174
díviṣṭiṣu, 48 169, 172, 175
divispṛ́śā, 48 168, 173
dṛ́bhīka, 56 368 f.
devágopāḥ, 48 170, 173, 176
devavítamaḥ, 48 169, 173
devā́vītaye, 48 167, 175
devā́hūtibhir, 48 167, 175
doṣāvastar, 48 166, 172, 175
draviṇoda, 48 167, 170, 173
dvijottama, 48 166
dhanadā́m, 48 168, 173
dhanaspṛ́tam, 48 169, 173
dharúṇahvaram, 48 170 f.
-dhru, "injury," 45 172
nadīvṛ́tam, 48 170, 172 f.
nṛcakṣasam, 48 168, 175
nṛmā́danam, 48 166, 174
nṛvā́hasā, 48 167, 175
nṛṣā́co, 48 170, 173
nṛṣā́hyāya, 48 168, 174
nemannīṣaḥ, 48 170, 173
nodhā́ḥ, 45 171
paḍbhís, 30 178
patsutaḥśī́r, 48 168, 172 f.
purukṛ́d, 48 170, 173
puruniṣṣídhe, 48 167, 173
púrubhujā, 48 166, 172
puruspṛ́ham, 48 169, 171, 173
puṣṭivárdhanaḥ, 48 168, 174
puṣṭivárdhana, 48 168
bhágabhaktasya, 48 168, 171, 174
bhā́rjīkam, 48 169, 171, 175
madacyútam, 48 169, 171, 173
madrík, madríak, 34 338 f.
madhupébhir, 48 168, 173
madhupéyam, 48 169, 174
mánurhitaḥ, 48 167, 171, 174 f.
máno rúhāṇāḥ, 39 280 f.
manojú, 48 168, 171, 173
manoyúja, 48 167, 170-173
mandayátsakham, 48 166, 175
mayobhú, 48 166 f., 171, 173
mítrāvaruṇa, 23 322 f.
muṣṭihatyáyā, 48 167, 174
yajñanī́r, 48 167, 173
yajñavāhasā, 48 167, 175
yajñaśríyam, 48 166, 173
yudhiṣṭhira, 48 166
ratnadhā́, 48 167, 173
ratnadhātama, 48 166, 168, 172 f.
rathajit, rāthajiteyā, 39 282
ratheśúbham, 48 169, 172 f.
rayiṣā́l, 48 170, 173
ririṣī́ṣtayúr, 48 201
réku padám, "ergiebige Stätte," 52 78
vacoyújā, 48 167 f., 171, 173

vandanaśrúd, 48 170, 173
vamraka, 30 178
vayaskŕt, 48 168, 172 f.
vā́ṣaṭkṛti, 48 167 f., 175
vasudéyāya, 48 170, 174
vasuvít, 48 167, 169, 173
vasuvíttamam, 48 169, 173
vā́syaīṣṭaye, 48 168, 175
vājadā́vnām, 48 167, 175
vājambharā́m, 48 170, 174
vājasā́tamā, 48 168, 173
vā́jasātau, 48 169, 175
vidā́tha, 45 158-160
vidā́dvasum, 48 167, 175
vipaścíta, 48 166, 168, 173
víprajūtaḥ, 48 166, 171, 174
viśvácakṣase, 48 169, 175
viśvatúrā, 48 169, 173
viśvádarśataḥ, 48 169, 171, 174
viśvavedasā, 48 169, 175
viśvasuvído, 48 169, 173, 175
vīrāṣā́ṭ, 48 169, 173
vṛktá-barhis, 35 273 f.
vṛtrahá́ṇam, 48 170
vṛtrahátyeṣu, 48 170, 174
vṛtrahā́, 48 167, 173
vṛṣāyúdho, 48 168, 173
vratapā́m, 48 168, 173
śikṣānaráḥ, 48 170, 175
śuṣṇahátyeṣu, 48 170, 174
śévṛdham, 48 170, 173
śrutkarṇa, 48 169
-śvi-, 32 392
sakā́, 31 410 f.
sā́dmamakhasam, 48 168, 175
sahaskṛta, 48 169, 171, 174
sahasradā́vnām, 48 167
sahasrasā́tamam, 48 167, 173
sahasrasā́m, 48 167, 173
sahojā́, 48 170-173
sahovŕdham, 48 169, 173
sutapā́vne, 48 167, 175
surūpakṛtnúm, 48 166, 175
somaparibā́dho, 48 169, 173
somapā́, 48 166-168, 172 f.
somapā́van, 48 168, 170, 175
sómapītaye, 48 166-169, 175
somapīthā́ya, 48 170
somapéyāya, 48 169, 174
stómavāhasaḥ, 48 167, 175
syonakŕd, 48 168, 173
svadŕśas, 48 169, 173
svarvídam, 48 170, 173
svādhukṣádmā, 48 168, 175
hā́riyogam, 48 170 f., 174
havanaśrútam, 48 167, 173
havanasyádam, 48 170, 173
haviṣkŕtam, 48 167, 173
havíṣkṛtim, 48 168, 175
havyavā́ḍ, 48 167, 169, 173
havyavā́hana, 48 169, 174
hṛdayāvídhas, 48 168, 172-175
hṛdispŕg, 48 167, 172 f.
hotṛvū́rye, 48 168, 174
hvayā́mi, 21 48

WAKHI
mis, "nose," 46 178

WALLACHIAN
pāloš, "sabre," < Turk. pal(y)uş, 50 259-260

WELSH
hep, "sine," 31 410

ZĒBAKI
dust, 56 353

V. INDEX OF PASSAGES

AKKADIAN

'Amārnah Letter 287, line 7, 57 243
Annals of Sennacherib (Taylor), col. ii 34-iii 41, 24 265ff.
Assyrian Laws (Schroeder, KTA), p. 3, col. ii, 80; p. 16, col. iv, 12; p. 18, col. vii, 12, 44 156
Chicago Syllabary, line 220, 37 328-329
Flood-tablet, NE 139, line 127, 46 344; line 164, 41 181
Rassam Cyl. col. iv 70 ff., 53 344-346
Taanach Letter 2, line 19, 57 243
UCP X pt. 1, No. 102, lines 1 f., 59 106-107

APOCRYPHA AND PSEUDEPIGRAPHA

(Old Testament)
Ben Sira 37:16, 58 135-136
Enoch, Slavonic, 16:8, 41 309; 24:2, 41 309; 25, 41 309-310; 30:16, 41 309; 33:1, 2, 41 312; 45:3, 41 312; 49:1, 2, 41 312
Jub. 7:4, 26 333; 23:11-32, 56 255; 34:4, 7, 26 331-333
Judith 16:1-17, 49 361
I Macc. 1:1, 25 307-309
Sirach 4:19, 41 178
(New Testament)
Gospel of Peter, v. 35, 39 55

ARABIC

al-Buḫāri, Ṣaḥīḥ (ed. Krehl), I 105, 21 28-29
Ḥamāsah (ed. Freytag), I 106 v. 4; 107 v. 1, 39 305; 373 v. 3, 39 315; 423 vv. 1-3, 39 319; 457 v. 3, 477 v. 6, 39 317, 318
Koran 2:261, 36 146-148; 7:9, 21 28; 7:71ff., 40 331; 11:67ff., 40 331; 18:60-82, 51 356; 26:155ff., 40 331; 54:27ff., 40 331; 76:5, 42 360; 113, 48 137

AVESTAN

Vidēvdāt 3.7, 31 408; 5.1, 2, 31 409; 5.19, 31 408; 9.53, 31 408; 12.1, 31 409; 18.1, 31 406
Yasna 9.49-103, 23 1-18; 9.49-103, 24 64-76; 10.17, 31 404; 31.14, 31 407; 34.11, 47 267; 37.1, 21 165; 37.2, 31 405; 43.14, 31 405; 44.17, 31 405; 44.17, 31 407; 45.4, 31 405; 49.4, 48 277-279; 51.5, 31 405; 53.1, 31 405; 57, 58 310-323; 61.5, 31 409; 62.7, 31 407
Yt. 8.32, 31 408; 9.10, 31 408; 10.39, 31 408; 19.2, 31 409; 19.34, 31 409

BABYLONIAN

Dar. Pers. g. 1, 21 182

BŪNDAHISHN

Indian recension 17.5-6, 41 84 f.
Iranian recension 17.5-6, 41 88 f.

CHINESE

Analects XVII 2, on human nature, 50 234; VI 17, says nothing about original human nature; meaning twisted by Chu Hsi, 50 234-235
Ch'ien Han-shu, concerning the Pai Canal, 55 305; T'ing Nien's proposal to change course of Yellow River, 305; the Yellow River changed its course, 305-306
Chu-fan-chih, describing the country of Po-pa-li (Berbera), 30 49-50
A collection illustrating the practice of ku magic, covering the entire period of Chinese literature, 55 1-30
Han-hsi-yü-t'u-k'ao, passage fr. the, on an embassy from the Hsiung-nu prince Hu-ni in 457 A.D. to ransom prisoners, 30 43
Han-shu, tr. of passage on how the wealthy acquired and used their wealth, 54 191, tr. of passage on economic and social conditions of pre-Ch'in period, 188-189; tr. of the biography of Ch'ing, the wealthy widow of Pa, 193
Hou-han-shu, An-ts'ai's name changed to A-lan, recorded in, 30 39
Hui-ch'ao-wang-wu-t'ien-chu-kuo-chuan, tr. p. 10-11 on Persia, the Arabs, and Ta Fu-lin, 33 204-206; Chinese text of pp. 10-11, 207
Inscription on the Stele of the Picture of the Six Horses, portion of, tr., 55 426
Li-chi, in Legge, SBE, XXVII, 364-367, the Two Utopias a late interpolation, 54 68-69
Ling-wai-tai-ta, tr. of passage on the lemon, 54 146
Lun Yü, IX 1, note on tr. 54 83; VIII 9, about people following their rulers without being told why, 31 185
Mencius, quotation about the rulers and the ruled, 31 153-154
Shih-chi, Chap. 123, discussion of passage, "skirting the Nan-shan," 37 89-90; tr. of passage fr. naming countries west of Parthia, 30 36; description of An-ts'ai fr., 37; tr. of comments on Ch'ing, the wealthy widow of Pa, 54 193
Shih-ching, Legge, IV, pp. 353, 355; II, pp. 281, 184, 56 72-73
T'ang-shu, passage in chap. 221b, p. 19, on Po-pa-li (Berbera), 30 47-48
Travels of Fa-hsien, his appreciation of the character of the Indians, 40 227; passage by an unknown Indian, his host, in praise of Fa-hsien's attitude, 228
T'ung chien, visit of Emperor Ming in 74 A.D. to his mother's tomb, Chap. 45, pp. 15 a, b, 55 189
Wei-lio, on the trip fr. Alexandria to Ta-ts'in, 30 46-47
Wei-shu, Chinese text and tr. of account of conquest of Suk-tak (An-ts'ai) by the Hsiung-nu, 30 42, 43-44
Yu-yang-tsa-tsu, on the country of Po-pa-li (Berbera), 30 48

EGYPTIAN

Story of the Shipwrecked Sailor, lines 179-186, 45 156

ENGLISH

Gower's Confessio Amantis v. 6670 ff., 26 196

GREEK

Herodotus 1:103-106, 22 21; 1:181, 38 86-87
Homer A. 53-58, 47 175
Josephus, Antiq. 15:158-488, 57 241
Josephus, Jewish War, 1:203-357, 57 241
Iliad 16:234-235, 21 29-30; 22:335-358, 39 315
Odyssey 11:51-73, 39 315
Parthenius (Narr. Amat. XV. 2-3), 26 178
Pausanias VIII. 20.2-4, 26 178 f.
Plato, Republic, Bk. VIII, p. 546 C D, 29 210-219
Strabo, Geog., 779, 32 117-119
Xenophon, Anab., 3:4 7, 28 99-107

HEBREW (see also Old Testament; Apocrypha)

Daniel 3:15, 42 399
Lachish Letter IV, 56 491-493

HITTITE

Keilschrifttexte aus Boghazköi 2.5.2.1-2, 56 286; 3.6.2.8-13 = Götze, Hattušiliš 16.23-29, 47 176; 3.34.2.35, 56 285; 4.4.3.26-28, 56 286; 5.4.2.37-40, 56 283; 5.6.2.26-29, 56 286 f.; Bo. 706.2.24-25, 56 282

JAPANESE

Collection of, on idea of paternalism in government, 31 184-185
An official notice of 1778: on the wisdom of allowing the people free speech, 31 189
Collection of notices fr. signboards, edicts, etc., of the peasant laws of the Tokugawa period, 31 199-200, 202-216
Kinvta, a Japanese Nō Play, tr. of part of, 22 136-137

Tosa Diary (Tosa nikki), passage mentioning holly used at New Year's festival, 55 447
Nihon saiji-ki, on sardines and holly to ward off the devil, 55 447;
A 16th cent. comic interlude; the devil runs into some holly, 55 448
Oni no tsuchi, on a drunken devil scared by holly, 55 448

LATIN
Danish History (Saxo Gram.), 26 182 f.
Lactantii Placidi comment. in Stat. Theb. iii.283, 26 179 f.
Macci Gemini i, p. 103, 25 (Mueller's ed.), 26 183
Macrobius vi. 4.13, 26 183
Mythogr. Vatic. I.75, 26 180 f.; II.219, 26 180 f.; III, tract. xi.3, 26 180 f.
Ovid. A. A. iii.787-788, 26 188
Pliny, on the Alani being formerly called the Aorsi, 30 41-42
Schol. Floriacense ad Verg. Aen. iv.99, 26 179 f.

MARCO POLO
II, 398-399, on the enchanters of Socotra, (Yule, 2nd ed.), 30 53-54

NEW TESTAMENT
Acts 2:29-31, 32 120-121; 9:23-25, 58 88; 13:30 f., 58 87; 18:1-17, 58 89-90;
I Cor. 15, 40 119
II Cor. 2:14-16, 26 329-330
Heb. 2:6, 17, 40 221
John 18:38, 39 56; 19:33-36, 36 146, 43 125
Luke 22:19-20, 58 90; 24:34, 58 86-87
Matt. 23:34 f., 57 255; 23:35 f., 26 317-323; 27:28, 39 56; 28:1, 26 323-329
Rev. 13:18, 26 315-317
I Thes. 4:13-15, 40 119

OLD PERSIAN
Art. Pers. a [b]. 24-26, 21 169
Art. III Pers. 5-6, 48 68; 11-20, 48 68
Art. Sus. a 1-3, 48 67; b, 48 67
Behistun 1.11, 31 404; I. 11-12, 21 162; 1.14, 31 407; 1.20-24, 35 331-336; I. 24-26, 21 162; 1.25-26, 22 150; 1.27-28, 22 150; 1. 33-35, 21 170; 1.47, 24 84; 1.48-53, 35 336 f., 340-342; 1.51, 24 84; 1.54-55, 21 167, 176; 1.55, 27 190; 1.62, 35 345; 1.62-64, 21 176; 1.64-66, 23 60; 1.65-66, 24 84 f.; 1.86, 24 85 f.; 1.86-87, 35 343 f.; 1.87-88, 24 86 f.; 1.92-96, 24 88; 1.94-96, 35 345 f.; 2.2, 31 404; 2.6-7, 22 150; 2.12, 31 408; 2.22-23, 22 150; 2.59-61, 24 88; 2.75, 79, 24 88; 3.87-91, 24 88 f.; 4.2, 41 74 f.; 4.2-8, 35 344-350; 4.5, 31 406; 4.6-7, 58 678; 4.33-35, 21 170; 4.33-36, 35 347; 4.35, 21 162; 4.44, 22 172; 4.44, 23 60-62; 4.44, 58 678; 4.46, 23 62 f.; 4.46, 24 89; 4.49, 24 89; 4.50-51, 24 89 f.; 4.53, 24 90; 4.62-63, 22 157; 4.63-64, 21 170; 4.64, 21 172-175; 4.64-65, 24 90-94; 4.66, 24 94; 4.67-69, 35 347 f., 351 f.; 4.68-69, 24 94; 4.71, 73 (87), 24 94; 4.74-76, 21 167; 4.76, 24 94; 4.77, 24 95; 4.78-80, 21 168; 5.15-16, 35 346 fn.; 5.26-27, 35 346
Dar. Pers. c, 27 190 f.; d, 27 191 f.; d. 1-5, 21 162; d. 2, 31 409; d. 3, 31 406; d. 13-24, 21 167; d. 15-20, 21 171; d. 20-24, 21 176; e. 11-24, 27 192 f.
Elv. 1-8, 21 162
H. 15-20, 21 171
NR a. 1-8, 21 162; a. 32, 21 165; a. 36-37, 35 346; a. 51-55, 21 167; a. 52-53, 21 171; a. 56-59, 21 172; b. 4-5, 38 122
Suez c. 1-4, 21 162; c.8-10, 35 338 f.
Xerx. Pers. a. 14, 19, 27 193; b. 11, 23, 27 193; ca [cb]. 12-15, 21 167; da [db]. 18-20, 21 167

OLD TESTAMENT
Amos 2:7, 50 336; 3:3-4:3, 41 181; 3:5, 41 186; 6:1-2, 50 336; 7:13, 60 422
Cant. 4:14, 42 173; 7:6, 37 324-326
I Chron. 5:25, 22 67
II Chron. 1:16 f., 26 104; 2, 58 135; 9:24, 58 137; 14:1-3, 15, 38 128; 17, 58 135; 21:11, 22 67; 32:1-21, 24 265ff.
Dan. 1-2:4, 58 540; 1-6, 58 540; 1:4, 43 229; 1:12, 47 368; 2:1, 7, 9, 22-24, 43, 48, 43 229-230; 3, 46 6-7; 3:13, 14, 43 231; 3:15, 42 399; 4, 46 6-7; 4:14, 32, 43 232; 5:5, 7, 16, 29, 43 232; 5:6, 51 319; 5:10, 12, 43 232; 5:13, 21, 25-28, 43 233; 6, 41 316-317, 46 6; 6:1-3, 18, 20, 43 233; 6:7, 12, 16, 44 168, 46 352; 7:5, 8, 43 233; 8-12, 58 540; 9:4, 58 136; 10:5, 43 124; 10:20, 25 306-307; 11:2, 25 310-311, 43 233-234; 11:31, 43 143; 12:11, 43 143
Deut. 3:9, 41 186; 9:16, 49 158; 16:1, 37 214; 20, 52 293; 21:23, 52 293; 21:1-9, 39 310-311; 23:5, 35 387; 24:16, 28 309-316; 32, 46 352; 32:24, 44 167; 32:35, 42 390
Eccl. 1:5, 8, 42 390; 1:8, 50 322; 2:1, 42 390; 5:5, 42 390; 9:12, 42 390; 12:1, 36 418; 12:15, 42 390
Est. 9:16, 44 157
Ex. 4:22-26, 37 215; 11:1, 43 394; 12:46, 36 146-153; 14:7, 43 395; 15:11, 32 121; 17:15, 37 330; 19:1, 37 216-217; 21, 49 27; 21:7-11, 55 190-195; 21:15-17, 50 338-339; 22, 49 27; 22:7-9, 47 253-254; 22:10-13, 47 254; 23, 49 27; 32:2, 42 390; 33:7-11, 38 131-132; 33:12 to 34:28, 38 125-139
Ezek. 7:23, 40 221; 8, 57 256; 8:16, 42 398; 10, 57 256; 17:3-4, 42 371-372; 24:1-14, 7-8, 39 314-315; 27:7, 43 126 n. 10; 28, 42 372; 37, 36 148; 40-48, 43 167; 43:1ff., 42 398; 44:1ff., 42 398; 44:6-16, 52 370; 45:18-25, 37 220
Ezra 1:8, 43 234-235; 1:9, 43 235-236; 4:7, 43 236; 4:10, 43 236, 58 397-398; 4:12, 16, 43 236; 5:1, 43 236; 5:2-15, 46 358; 5:7, 43 391-392; 6:8, 15, 43 236; 6:22, 43 237; 7:14, 43 237-238; 7:19, 43 238; 8:17, 43 238
Gen. 1:1-3, 47 357; 1-2:4, 36 295-298; 2:4-25, 36 295-298; 2:8-14, 48 342; 2:10ff., 45 31ff.; 3, 39 287; 3:7, 21 26, 42 208-209; 4:7, 47 366-367; 9:3, 47 368; 9:13, 41 181; 10:8ff., 40 201-203; 10:13-14, 42 319 n. 2; 11, 41 159; 11:1-9, 40 276-277, 279; 14:1, 43 324 n. 1; 14:4, 43 123; 18:21, 43 394; 31:13, 59 94; 31:14-16, 57 259-276; 32:25, 33 263-264; 35:7, 59 94; 36:20-39, 45 353; 37:26, 39 318; 44:12, 49 157
Hab. 3:2, 39 143; 3:17, 50 322
Hag. 46 358-359
Hos. 2-3, 48 276-277; 2:14, 58 135; 4:16, 38 67-68; 5:8, 58 138; 9:1, 58 135; 11:1, 45 353; 11:4, 42 390
Is. 1:2, 45 84-85; 1:3, 39 143; 1:12, 15, 25, 31, 45 85; 1:18, 28, 42 390; 2:6, 16, 45 85; 2:12, 42 390; 3:8, 17, 24, 45 85; 5:1, 45 85; 5:7, 40 221, 42 390, 45 85; 5:13, 44 167; 7:11, 45 88; 7:14, 15, 17, 57 255; 8:6, 45 85; 8:9, 45 85-86; 8:14, 45 86; 9:4, 16, 17, 45 86; 10:4, 33, 45 86; 10:5, 47 366; 10:5-15, 37 9; 10:13, 42 390; 11:3, 58 137-138; 11:4, 6, 8, 45 86; 13, 51 370; 13-14, 42 371; 14:10, 45 86; 14:19, 45 86-87; 14:20, 30, 45 87; 14:21, 28 315-316, 45 87; 16:6, 45 87; 19:17, 45 87; 21:12, 45 87; 22:7, 45 87; 22:17, 33 366; 23:4, 45 87; 23:17, 18, 22 65; 26:14, 30 343; 26:19, 21, 39 313-314; 27:9, 30 344; 28:4, 45 87; 29:18, 45 87; 34:5, 9, 45 87; 35:1-9, 44 174; 36-37, 44 175; 37:27, 45 88; 40-48, 57 158, 160; 40-55, 57 241; 41:2, 50 335-336; 44:19, 47 368; 53:4-5, 44 157; 53:12, 48 357-358; 63:1-6, 46 355
Jer. 4:29, 41 75, 316; 5:2, 30 344; 6:27, 43 124; 11:15, 49 363; 16:18, 58 133-134; 48:13, 59 96; 48:38, 43 394-395; 50-51, 51 370
Job 1:5, 6, 15, 17, 41 184; 2:4, 41 184; 16:18, 39 303ff., 315; 22:23-26, 43 125; 25-35, 53 405; 28:1, 43 119 n. 6; 28:11, 45 319; 31:7, 43 229; 34:25, 30 344; 36:27, 43 119 n. 6; 37:9, 44 167; 37:23, 45 360; 38:36, 33 367-368; 39:13-18, 41 176; 40:20, 47 368; 42:3, 30 344-345
Joel 1:14, 45 361; 4:14, 43 120

Josh. 1:17, 49 158; 11, 34 419; 11:11-12, 49 156-157
Jud. 4, 38 336; 5, 34 416; 5:3-5, 56 409, 462-471; 5:14, 58 138; 7:1-7, 22 70-75; 9:46, 49, 43 121; 16:1-3, 45 356; 21:21, 36 324-326
I Kgs. 1-2, 60 383-390; 1:5, 43 171; 2:1-9, 13-18, 28-31, 59 402; 2:46, 58 137; 4:19, 58 133; 4:20, 54 421, 58 133; 5:3, 33 364; 5:27, 58 135; 5:30, 58 135; 8:4, 38 138; 9:18, 58 133; 9:23, 58 135; 10:11-12, 42 173; 10:20, 60 422; 10:25, 58 137; 10:28f., 26 104; 15:11-15, 38 128; 18:42, 58 136; 19:1-14, 38 129-130
II Kgs. 4:34, 35, 58 136; 8:1, 58 133; 14:6, 28 311-312; 15:13, 43 165, 45 352; 15:17, 23, 45 352; 15:20, 44 159; 17:23, 43 165; 18:13, 17-19:37, 24 265ff.; 18:14-16, 24 265ff.; 18-19, 44 175; 19:26, 32 122; 19:36-37, 53 335-346; 20:4, 59 22
Lam. 4:3, 40 219
Lev. 1-6, 33 363-364; 15:3, 43 119; 16, 21 2-4; 19:4, 49 157; 19:18, 45 361; 19:20, 41 314; 23:15-17, 37 215-216; 23:40, 37 218-219
Mal. 1:1-5, 11, 14, 42 396; 2:12, 44 167; 3:1, 42 396
Nahum 1:12, 58 153-155; 2:14, 37 327
Neh. 8:15, 37 218-219; 2:13, 39 143; 4:7, 43 121
Num. 9:12, 36 146-153; 10:29-32, 38 125-139; 15:35, 49 157; 22:5, 35 387, 389; 22:33, 22 26; 23:7, 35 387; 24:6, 42 173; 24:51, 44 166; 26:58, 57 376-377
Ob. 7, 44 167; 8, 45 353
Prov. 4:25, 50 322; 5:15-20, 36 418-419; 7:17, 42 173; 22:17, 45 353; 22:17-23:10, 45 372; 23:14, 45 353; 25:11, 43 163; 26:23, 60 268-269; 30:1, 45 353; 30:31, 33 368-370, 386; 31:9, 45 353
Ps. 8, 48 349; 16:1-11, 32 120-125; 19, 40 218; 22:1-2, 37 21; 24:7-10, 42 398; 30, 56 249; 33:7, 43 119 n. 6; 45:9, 42 173; 47, 50 322-323; 48, 58 527-528; 49:6, 46 344; 58:9, 42 280-285; 68, 51 365-366; 68:8-9, 12-13, 14, 15, 16-18, 19, 25-28, 52 294; 75:9, 37 324; 79, 56 249; 82, 42 398; 91:6, 38 162; 94:13, 50 322; 104, 45 353; 110:4, 38 332; 144:13, 44 167
I Sam. 1:5, 58 134; 6:8, 11, 15, 56 272-281; 6:13, 56 468-469
II Sam. 1:19-27, 59 402; 21:1-14, 39 313 n. 32; 21:4, 39 308
Zech. 1-8, 47 359; 5:5-11, 52 307; 7:2, 59 96; 9:9f., 57 240; 9:16, 17, 46 355; 10:7, 46 354; 11:8, 46 355-356; 11, 12, 46 343-344; 14:5, 39 143
Zeph. 2:2, 39 143; 2:8, 45 153; 2:14, 45 153; 3:3, 45 153; 3:6, 45 154

PAHLAVI
Dēnkart 6.293, 41 82
Turfan Frag. M. 18, 39 55-57; M. 173, 56 198-207; M. 173, influenced by Rev. 1:8 and Is. 44:6, 53 387
Yasna ix. 49-103 (transl.), 24 64-76

PĀLI
Comm. Khuddaka Pāṭha v, 27 455
Peta-Vatthu I.10.5-6, 43 415; II.1.6, 43 415; II.1.14, 43 416; II.2.6, 43 416; II.2.8, 43 416; II.3.25, 43 416; II.4.7-8, 43 417; II.8.8, 43 417; III.2.8, 43 418; III.6.9, 43 419; IV.1.30, 43 419; IV.1.36, 43 420; IV.1.51-52, 43 420; IV.1.51-52, 44 74 f.

PHOENICIAN
Aḥîrâm inscription, line 1, 57 408; end, 405
Bod'aštart inscription, line 4, 57 404; CIS 14, 406, 407
CIS 4 4, 57 409
Ešmun temple inscription, 57 409
Ešmunazar inscription, line 5, 57 405; line 6, 402; line 9, 21 f., 406; line 16, 406; line 17, 403
Kilamuwa inscription, lines 6 and 10, 57 404
Ma'ṣūb inscription, 57 402
Tabnit inscription, lines 5 and 7, 57 405
Yehawmilk inscription, lines 12 and 13, 57 408

SANSKRIT
Ādīśvaracaritra 2.533, 52 88; 2.618-619, 52 87 f.
Agnipur. 6-7, 34 266; 12-13, 34 266; 16, 34 266
Aitareya Upaniṣad i.1-3, 22 275 f.
Amṛtabindu Upaniṣad 32-35 22 264-266
Atharva-Veda i.16.1, 36 223; ii.27.7, 36 221; iii.1.6c, 30 172; iii.26.1-2, 36 223; iii.29.6, 35 29; iv.8.2, 36 218; iv.13.7a, c, 30 168; iv.14.2b, 30 172; iv.27.1, 36 215; iv.28.7, 36 215; vi.5.3, 36 219; vi.7.2, 36 223; vi.13.2, 36 214; vi.87.3, 36 218; vi.118.1a, 30 168; vi.141.1, 36 220; vii.36.1a, 30 165; vii.38.2, 26 176 f.; vii.116.2, 59 428 f.; viii.2.7, 36 222; viii.2.8, 36 222; viii.6.14b, 30 172; viii.10.21, 59 429 f.; viii.10.28, 33 59; ix.4.8b, 30 165; x.7.39a, 30 168; xi.2.20, 36 222; xi.3.44d, 30 165; xi.3.46d, 30 165; xi.6.22c, 30 181; xi.9.14b, 30 168; xii.1.59, 36 220; xiii.2.26, 30 180; xiii.2.39, 36 201; xiii.3.4, 22 279; xiii,3.4, 39 112; xiv.1.12, 22 280; xviii.3.45, 36 221; xix.32.9, 36 224; xix.51.2b, 30 165; xx.127.7-10, 34 310-312
Bhagavad-Gītā 2.50, 56 528
Bhaktalīlāmṛt 22.48-65, 42 277 f.; 22.79-101, 42 278 f.
Brahma Sūtra ii.2.28-32, 31 13 f.
Bṛhadāraṇyaka Upaniṣad i.5.3, 22 290 f.; iii.1.10, 22 291; iii.2, 22 301 f.; iii.4.1, 22 291 f.; iii.7.6, 36 204; iii.9.26, 22 292; v. 14.3, 22 292
Bṛhatkathāmañjarī 9.2.40-58a, 53 128-131; 9.2.62a, 53 131 f.; 9.2.74b-75a, 53 132; 9.2.186, 53 132 f.; 9.2.392-395, 53 142; 9.2.397-399, 53 142 f.; 9.2.400, 53 133; 9.2.458, 53 133; 9.2.463a, 53 134; 9.2.465, 53 134; 9.2.493-495, 53 134 f.; 9.2.497-500, 53 135 f.; 9.2.559, 53 136; 9.2.575-576, 53 137; 9.2.621, 53 137; 9.2.693-696, 53 138; 9.2.893, 53 139; 9.2.895-898, 53 139 f.; 9.2.1044, 53 140; 9.2.1073, 53 141
Bṛhatsaṃhitā 60.15, 33 164 f.; 78.24, 26 189
Buddhacarita v. 72, 22 387 f.; x.34, 22 388; xii.22, 22 388
Chāndogya Upaniṣad i.3.3, 22 287 f.; i.8-9, 36 204; iii.13, 22 274, 288; v. 19-23, 22 288 f.; vi.2, 35 240-242; vi. 14, 35 242-245; vi. 16, 35 245 f.
Harivaṃśa 382 f., 33 59; 5994, 33 166
Jaiminīya Brāhmaṇa i.42 ff., 26 196; i.125-127, 28 82-88; i.363, 26 192 f.; ii.78, 26 176; ii.79, 26 194; iii.233, 26 194
Jaiminīya-Upaniṣad-Brāhmaṇa i.53.3, 26 188; i.60.5, 22 298 f.; ii.1.15-16, 22 298, 300; ii.1.19, 22 298; ii.5, 22 295; ii.22, 22 295 f.; iv. 22, 22 296 f.
Kāṭhaka Upaniṣad xiii.5, 26 176; v.3-5, 22 293 f.
Kathāsaritsāgara 9.7, 37 328; 75.42-44, 53 131; 75.51a, 53 132; 75.62, 53 132; 77.6, 53 133; 80.9, 53 133; 81.98, 53 134; 81.101b, 53 134; 81.103, 53 134; 84.7-8, 53 135; 84.12-13, 53 136; 85.8, 53 137; 85.26, 53 137; 86.85, 53 138; 88.15-16, 53 138 f.; 90.141, 53 139; 90.147-149, 53 140; 93.47, 53 140 f.; 94.21a, 53 141
Kātyāyana Śrautasūtra 20.1.29-36, 54 110 f.
Kauṣītaki Upaniṣad 2.1, 21 159
Kena Brāhmaṇa xi.3, 26 196
Lalitavistara 119.11, 56 363; 125.16, 56 363; 177.4, 56 363
Lāṭyāyana Śrauta Sūtra 2.2.11, 51 170
Mahābhārata i.1.201, 48 189; i.2.304, 21 154; i.29.30, 23 153 f.; i.71.34, 24 34 f.; i.125.31, 21 148 f.; i.145.34, 24 33; i.147.4, 24 33; ii.5.70, 23 134; ii.66.8, 59 366-368; iii.7.5, 21 152; iii.24.13, 21 57; iii.82.107, 23 152; iii.230.10, 24 35; iii.190.90, 24 32; iii.283.30, 21 155; v.29.15c, 22 389; v.43.21, 23 118; v.48.98, 24 33; v.52.10-11, 24 51; v.55.66, 23 134 f.; v.114.1-4, 53 328 f.; v.151.38, 33 164; vi.11.5-6, 23 150; vi.107.20, 23 118; vii.66.16, 23 152 f.; vii.69.24, 33 59; vii.192.46, 21 151; vii.197.10, 24 54; vii.198.29-31, 21 151; viii.20.30, 23 114; viii.20.49, 23 112; viii.33.19, 23 150; viii.67.6, 23 114; xii.21.7, 23 119; xii.27.23, 21 153; xii.127.7-8, 23 140 f.; xii.148.9-10, 21 149; xii.176.10, 23 127; xii.185.3-5, 45 60; xii.187.15-16, 45 62; xii.187.23-25, 45 60 f.; xii.187.31, 45 63; xii.202.1, 45 63; xii.231.30-32, 45 51 f.; xii.232.1-2,

45 52; xii.232.10-12, 45 57 f.; xii.233.11-15, 45 53 f.; xii.233.13, 45 52; xii.233.17, 45 63; xii.237.3, 22 349; xii.237.14-16, 22 351-353; xii.240.18-20, 45 65; xii.241, 22 343 f.; xii.246.28, 23 141; xii.282.7-8, 23 153; xii.299.18-22, 22 356 f.; xii.299.31-35, 22 356; xii.301. 30-54, 22 350 f.; xii.303.14, 24 44; xii.307.6-10, 22 345; xii.308.14-20, 45 65; xii.317.5, 22 340-343; xii.318.14-16, 45 65; xii.328.40, 45 65; xii.336.9, 23 151; xii.341.29-31, 45 53; xii.349.14-16, 45 53; xii.362.7-8, 53 327; xiii.107.32, 23 128; xiii.110.3, 24 33; xiii.126.48, 24 33; xiii.132.7, 24 33; xiii.134.4, 24 33 f.; xiv.19.48, 45 65; xiv.44.2, 24 15, 34 f.; xiv.58.33-40, 23 153; xiv.69.9, 21 148; xv.11.23, 24 54 f.

Maitri Upaniṣad ii.6, 22 261-295; vi.1, 22 264; vi.5, 22 294; vi.9, 22 290; vi.33, 22 294 f.

Manu i.16, 45 57; i.74-75, 45 59; v.55, 26 196

Nāradasmṛti 15.1-5, 45 41 f.; 15.19, 44 243; 15.20, 44 249; 15.21, 45 39

Nyāya Darśana iv.2.25-32, 31 9-13

Pāṇini 1.1.27-36, 47 61 f.

Pāraskara Gṛhya Sūtra i.16.9-15, 22 274

Pārśvanātha Caritra 6.796-797, 40 3

Prāṇāgnihotra Upaniṣad i, 22 289 f.

Praśna Upaniṣad iii, 22 266-272; iv.3-4, 22 272-274

Rāmāyaṇa 2.21.27-28, 21 156; 2.29.21, 21 148; 2.66.12, 21 149; 2.74.33, 21 148; 2.111.14-17, 21 156; 3.45.36, 21 148; 5.13.38, 21 151 f.; 5.26.7, 21 149; 6.19.41, 21 155; 7.46.21, 54 297-299

Ṛg-Veda i.1.8, 31 69; i.2.3, 32 407; i.2.4ab, 35 274; i.8.5, 31 61; i.10.4, 32 403; i.10.7, 31 57; i.18.7, 32 404; i.22.21, 31 61; i.27.1, 31 69; i.30.21, 31 64; i.32.8b, 39 280 f.; i.32.8b, 39 282; i.32.12, 26 195; i.34.7cd., 35 21; i.35.11, 36 218 f.; i.37.3b, 30 172; i.37.6, 35 23; i.39.6, 31 63; i.45.4, 31 69; i.45.10ab, 27 404; i.46.6, 22 161; i.47.7, 31 52; i.51.13, 26 176; i.55.4, 32 403; i.59.4a, 35 27; i.61.2, 32 402; i.63.7, 35 283; i.64.4c, 30 170; i.64.10c, 30 167; i.65.2cd, 32 391; i.66.1, 22 250; 1.68.2b, 32 391; i.80.10, 31 66; i.80.14, 32 404; i.84.17, 36 220 f.; i.88.6d, 30 167; i.89.8a, 30 171; i.89.8b, 30 171; i.91.20, 48 217; i,92.11-12, 31 59 f.; i.92.16, 27 403; i.95.6, 35 27; i.100.19ab, 36 216; i.101.8, 48 222; i.101.10, 32 405; i.101.11, 48 222; i.103.7, 22 169; i.114.10, 36 222; i.115, 58 419-434; i.116.1ab, 35 274 f.; i.116.10, 26 45; i.120.6c, 30 165; i.124.2, 31 60; i.124.3, 31 58; i.124.5d, 30 182; i.126.5, 45 162; i.132.1, 36 216; i.139.2fg, 30 171; i.140.6d, 30 176; i.141.1, 32 399; i.141.1, 46 306; i.141.11cd, 35 26 f.; i.142.3, 31 67; i.142.5, 35 284; i.143.7, 48 213; i.144.7, 31 68; i.146.2, 30 176; i.152.5, 31 53; i.153.2-3, 48 211; i.159.1, 48 204; i.162.1, 48 212; i.163.11cd, 30 179; i.164.19ab, 27 406 f.; i.164.30, 22 252; i.166.9c, 30 170; i.166.10b, 30 171; i.166.10c, 30 170; i.166.10d, 30 171; i.167.3, 48 217; i.168.3c, 30 170; i.168.3d, 30 172; i.171.2, 32 402; i.173.6, 48 224; i.180.4d, 35 28; i.180.9ab, 35 21; i.181.4b, 30 183; i.181.7, 32 400; i.184.2d, 30 173; i.186.4, 35 20; ii.2.4cd, 30 176; ii.3.6, 35 18 f.; ii.13.4c, 30 177; ii.23.8, 36 216 f.; ii.24.7c, 30 168; ii.27.6, 36 219; ii.27.8, 48 208; ii.27.12, 48 212; ii.30.5, 22 164; ii.37.5ab, 27 405; ii.39.2c, 30 183; iii.1.1, 48 205; iii.1.9, 32 407; iii.3.3, 48 204; iii.4.5, 48 205; iii.4.6b, 30 183; iii.4.8cd, 27 404; iii.8.10a, 30 172; iii.10.9, 31 61; iii.14.1, 48 212; iii.18.1ab, 35 25; iii.19.4, 22 164; iii.20.2, 30 176; iii.22.7, 31 62; iii.26.6, 48 205; iii.28.4, 48 210; iii.29.6a, 30 171; iii.32.4a, 25 336; iii.34.3, 32 408; iii.36.8, 30 180; iii.38.6, 48 215; iii.40.6, 31 57; iii.53.8, 26 195; iii.53.21, 22 251; iii.53.24, 39 262; iii.54.2, 48 207; iii.60.3, 31 62; iv.2.12, 30 177 f.; iv.2.14b, 30 171; iv.3.2d, 27 417; iv.3.10, 31 54; iv.4.8a, 27 406; iv.7.10, 35 285; iv.17.10, 22 150; iv.18.7, 31 67; iv.19.8, 31 67; iv.21.4, 48 211; iv.30.2ab, 35 28; iv.41.8ab, 35 24 f.; iv.52.2, 31 64; iv.56.6a, 30 183; iv.57.6ab, 27 405; iv.58.2abc, 32 401; iv.58.6, 32 399 f.; iv.58.10ab, 32 401; v.1.4b, 30 171; v.2.9d, 30 176; v.30.9, 32 406; v.30.9, 46 308; v.33.9, 45 165; v.34.9, 45 164; v.45.10cd, 27 406; v.54.11a, 30 170; v.54.11c, 30 167; v.54.11d, 30 172; v.54.15, 22 167; v.57.6a, 30 167; v.61.17, 32 405; v.62.2, 32 409; v.64.1c, 30 165; v.64.2a, 30 165; v.64.3, 22 167; v.64.7d, 30 173; v.80.4, 31 58; v.83.6cd, 27 404; v.87.5, 31 49; vi.5.1, 31 65; vi.11.2, 48 205; vi.11.2, 48 208; vi.11.5, 35 274; vi.17.3, 31 66; vi.19.2, 31 62; vi.19.9cd, 27 404; vi.22.2, 31 65; vi.23.3, 31 51; vi.25.3, 27 408; vi.36.1, 31 53; vi.44.15, 31 51; vi.45.33, 45 162; vi.47.18, 26 195; vi.48.14, 40 92; vi.48.14, 40 99 f.; vi.49.10, 31 62; vi.56.1, 40 83; vi.56.1, 40 90; vi.56.1, 40 97-100; vi.59.7b, 30 168; vi.66.1, 31 55; vi.67.1d, 30 173; vi.67.3cd, 35 23; vi.75.12, 36 214; vi.75.13b, 30 171; vii.2.4ab, 35 274; vii.2.5, 35 27 f.; vii.2.6, 35 19 f.; vii.6.5bcd, 27 411; vii.18.3c, 27 406; vii.21.3, 32 404; vii.24.2, 32 410; vii.24.4, 35 284 f.; vii.28.1b, 27 406; vii.32.27, 48 223; vii.39.1b, 27 417; vii.39.2, 35 275; vii.55.2, 31 56; vii.55.6c, 30 171; vii.56.11, 31 49; vii.56.13a, 30 170; vii.61.4, 48 224; vii.62.5a, 30 165; vii.70.5, 32 398; vii.72.1d, 30 183; vii.78.1bc, 27 403; vii.83.2, 36 215; vii.83.3, 27 405; vii.84.3, 48 204; vii.94.4, 32 398; vii.98.4b, 30 171; vii.99.6, 48 206; vii.99.6, 48 220; viii.2.14, 45 163; viii.5.3, 32 398; viii.7.28, 31 64; viii.8.14, 31 52; viii.8.18, 31 69; viii.8.23, 27 407; viii.8.23, 27 410; viii.13.15, 27 409; viii.12.17, 27 409; viii.13.19, 31 67; viii.13.27, 32 403 f.; viii.13.32c, 32 404; viii.14.8, 27 404; viii.16.5, 36 216; viii.19.36, 45 164; viii.20.10b, 30 171; viii. 20.26, 36 221; viii.26.4, 32 398; viii.30.3, 36 220; viii.32.22, 32 398; viii.47.2c, 30 168; viii.47.3b, 30 168; viii.48.14, 36 219; viii.49.6, 32 400; viii.50.4, 32 400; viii.56.1, 31 61; viii.60.13, 30 177; viii.61(50).1, 27 406; viii.67.6, 36 223; viii.72.15, 31 56; viii.73. 17ab, 35 24; viii.73.18ab, 35 24; viii.74.7, 31 68; viii.76.1, 35 286; viii.79.5, 35 285; viii.87.1ab, 35 24; viii.93.11, 40 98; viii.94.3, 45 162; viii.95.1, 32 405; viii.96.20, 36 217; viii.101.4d, 30 165; ix.10.2b, 30 167; ix.13.7c, 30 167; ix.15.4ab, 30 179; ix.20.6b, 30 167; ix.21.5-6, 40 91; ix.24.6, 31 67; ix.24.7, 31 67; ix.34.6, 46 306; ix.36.4b, 30 168; ix.64.5b, 30 168; ix.65.6b, 30 167; ix.70.5cd, 40 89; ix.71.3a, 30 168; ix.79.4d, 30 172; ix.87.2, 48 221; ix.102.8a, 30 171; ix.107.13d, 30 168; ix.108.7, 32 400; ix.110.5c, 30 168; x.7.5c, 30 168; x.4.1, 22 168; x.10.7d, 35 20; x.15.4a, 27 404; x.15.5, 36 221; x.18.14, 25 336-338; x.21.7cd, 30 177; x.27.4ab, 48 224; x.27.5ab, 48 224; x.28.7, 31 66; x.32.8, 22 252; x.41.1, 48 218; x.42.10, 48 223; x.43.6, 32 397; x.55.5, 22 253 f.; x.59.1abc, 35 25 f.; x.59.6, 22 251; x.61.3c, 30 172; x.61.3cd, 40 89; x.63.1, 36 220; x.63.11, 36 224; x.65.2b, 30 183; x.66.13, 31 59; x.71.9a, 27 404; x.79.2c, 30 171; x.81.3, 30 180; x.83.6a-c, 27 405; x.85.12, 39 281; x.85.26-27, 48 202; x.87.3ab, 30 177; x.87.4d, 30 171; x.89.2ab, 35 25; x.89.5d, 27 406; x.89.16d, 27 406; x.90.13, 22 251; x.94.2, 31 63; x.95, 29 284 f.; x.99.12, 30 178; x.100.6, 48 204; x.103.13, 22 165; x.103.13c, 30 171; x.104.3cd, 32 397; x.104.10, 32 394; x.104.10, 46 303; x.105.2b, 30 183; x.106.3c, 35 21 f.; x.106.7ab, 35 22 f.; x.108.7d, 52 78; x.117.5cd, 35 28; x.122.8, 48 207; x.122.8, 48 212; x.121.3, 22 253; x.124, 39 102 f.; x.125.4, 22 252 f.; x.127.1, 30 176; x.128.4, 36 220; x.129.2, 22 252; x.129.6c, 27 406; x.131.1, 22 167; x.131.2cd, 35 276; x.134.2cd, 40 90; x.134.7c, 30 171; x.135.5. 22 173; x.137.7a, 30 168; x.173.3, 36 218; x.188.3c, 32 404; x.189.2, 22 251, 253

Ṣaḍviṃśa Brāhmaṇa i.1.16, 26 176; i.6.9-18, 26 193 f.

Saṃnyāsa Upaniṣad 2(5), 22 275, 288

Śatapatha Brāhmaṇa i.1.1.20, 26 188; i.8.1.5, 47 175; ii.1.2.7, 39 281; ii.2.2.15, 22 285 f.; ii.5.2.17, 26 188;

vi.3.1.30, 26 188; vii.1.2.15, 22 282; vii.5.1.6, 26 188; xi.8.3.6, 22 274 f.; xiii.1.6.1-2, 54 111; xiii.1.9.1-10, 54 109 f.; xiii.4.2.1-4, 54 110
Sāyaṇa on RV.i.51.1, 26 194; x.119, 26 194 f.
Suśruta xi.3, 33 165
Śvetāśvatara Up. 6.13, 22 382
Taittirīya Āraṇyaka 3.9.1, 32 411
Taittirīya Brāhmaṇa 1.5.6.4, 35 286
Taittirīya Saṃhitā iii.1.7.3, 35 286; iv.2.9.6, 32 402
Taittirīya Upaniṣad i.7, 22 293; ii.2, 22 293
Tāṇḍya Brāhmaṇa xiv.6.10, 26 45; xvii.13.9, 27 457
Uttararāmacarita 1.15.5, 49 61
Vājasaneyi Saṃhitā 6.33, 36 221; 15.1, 36 224; 16.5, 36 223; 17.52, 36 219; 22.19, 54 111; 22.22, 54 109 f.
Vikramacarita (SR) 14.0.11, 38 207
Yājñavalkya 3.131, 133, 43 246
Yoga Sūtra iv.15-16, 31 24 f.

SUMERIAN
Gudea Cyl. A col. i, 4-9, 47 259
Gudea Cyl. B. col. vi 11-xii 25, 41 192-193
Myhrman, BE 3, pt. 1, p. 42, 37 330-331

TALMUD
Kethub 85a, 38 73
Berachoth 7a, 36 437
BM 69b, 38 73

VI. INDEX OF ABSTRACTS AND TITLES OF PAPERS READ AT SOCIETY MEETINGS

ABBOTT, J. E. On an Ancient Sword from Tibet, 34 442
------. Bhānudās, the Maratha Poet-saint, 39 150
------. Dnyāneshwar, the Mahārāshtra Saint and Poet, 37 15
------. Eknath's Version of the Bhikshugīta, or 'The Mendicant's Song,' 45 357
------. The Marātha Poet-saint Dāsopant Digambar, 42 397-398
------. The Original Sources of our Knowledge of the Maratha king Sivaji, 44 155-156
------. A Story of Pundalik as told by Bahinabai, 48 341
------. Thomas Stevens and the Discovery of the Devanāgarī Manuscript of his Christian Purāṇa, 43 163-164
------. The Vyankatesha Stotra, or Prayer of Devadāsa, 46 345
ABBOTT, Nabia. Arabic Papyri of the Reign of al-Mutawakkil 'Ala Allah (A.H. 232-47/A.D. 847-61), 57 248
ALBERT, Allen D. Jr. The Debt of Modern Cities to the Ancient Near East, 52 302
------. Some Evidence for Ancient City Planning, 52 302
------. Urbanism in the Ancient Orient, 59 421-422
ALBRIGHT, W. Foxwell. The Canaanite Deities Rashap-Makal and 'Anat-'Ashtart, 50 339
------. Canaanites and Amorites, 47 363
------. The Empire of Sargon of Accad according to the Babylonian Geographers, 51 359
------. Gilgames and Engidu, 37 16
------. Menes and Narāmsin, 39 150
------. The Mouth of the Rivers, 38 330
------. The North Canaanite Epic of 'Al'eyân and Môt, 52 308-309
ALLEN, T. George. The Story of an Egyptian Politician, 41 192
ANESAKI, M. On two Stones with Buddhist Carvings and Inscriptions, 34 442
------. A Comparison of the Relation of the Japanese Kuni-Governorship and of the Frankish Countship to the Rise of Feudalism in the Respective Countries, 45 351
------. Some Problems of the origin of the feudal land-tenure in Japan, 34 441
BAEPLER, Frederick A. (a) Assyr. bûlu, 'cattle,' and bêlu, 'weapon'; (b) The Etymology of Assyr. ekêmu, 46 355
BAILEY, H. W. The Rama Story in Khotanese, 59 397
BAMBERGER, Bernard S. Fear and Love of God in the Old Testament, 48 360
BAR AM, Moshe. The Method of Indicating the Subjunctive in Cappadocian Texts, 56 414
BARRET, LeRoy C. The Contents of the Kashmirian Atharva Veda, 45 351
------. A MS. of the Atharva Veda Pāippalādā at Poona, 48 340-341
------. Myths about Dragon-Fights, 31 vi
------. Pāippalāda and Śāunaka Book Five, 49 350
BARTON, G. A. An Aramaic Loan-Word in the Teachings of Amen-em-ope, 48 350
------. Lexicographical Notes, 44 156
------. Light on the Origin and Early History of Nin-IB (Nin-urta, Nin-urash), 46 345-346
------. (a) On Bindingtwine and Bitumen in Ancient Babylonia; (b) On the Vocalization of the Ideogram ŠES-AB^{ki}-MA; (c) Identification of the Sign No. 572 of Barton's Babylonian Writing, 46 352-353
------. Whence Came the Sumerians? 49 359-360
BATES, Mrs. D. M. Brief mention of Translations into Chinese by the late Bishop S. I. J. Schereschewsky, 39 149
BATES, M. S. Problems of Rivers and Canals under Han Wu-Ti, 54 337
BECKWITH, C. A. Later Jewish and Early Christian Ideas of God, 45 370
BERRY, George Ricker. Messianic Predictions in the Old Testament, 46 347
------. Priests and Levites, 43 167
BIGGERSTAFF, K. Some Notes on the Tung-hua Lu, 59 407
BINGHAM. W. The Rise of Li in a Ballad Prophecy, 60 465
------. Wên Ta-Ya: The First Recorder of T'ang History, 57 246
BLAIR, Dorothy. Influences of In-Yo upon Japanese Design, 57 249
BLAKE, Frank R. The Apparent Conflict between Practical and Scientific Grammar, 47 367
------. Arabic Verbs of Stative Form with Meanings not Clearly Stative, 53 401
------. Connecting Vowel -â after Syriac Verbal Forms in -n, 46 357
------. Construction of Coordinated Words in Modern Spoken Tagalog, 43 170
------. (a) The Department of Philippine Languages at the University of the Philippines; (b) Collection of Material on the Interrogative Sentence in the Philippine Dialects; (c) Distributive Expressions in Ethiopic, 44 169-170
------. (a) The Etymology of the Semitic Particle ka, 'like'; (b) The Compound Particle ki-im in Hebrew, 37 10
------. The Expression man hû elâh dî... in Daniel 3:15, 42 399
------. The Expression of the Idea "to be" in the Semitic Languages, 47 365
------. (a) Long-distance Collection of Philippine Linguistic Material; (b) The Expression man hû elâh dî... in Daniel 3:15, 42 399
------. (a) A New Method of Syntactical Arrangement; (b) The Present Status of Philippine Linguistic Studies, 41 176
------. Relational Words, 52 309
------. (a) The Scientific Study of Vocabulary and Idiom; (b) The Collection of Material Illustrating Indefinite Pronominal Ideas in the Philippine Islands, 45 363-364
------. (a) Spanish hasta. (b) A Bibliography of Semitic Languages, 56 415-416
------. (a) Varieties of the Case of the Direct Object; (b) Semitic Transitive Verbs with Intransitive Form; (c) A New Tagalog Grammar, 50 339-340
------. (a) The Various Methods of Expressing Adverbial Ideas in Semitic; (b) Adverbial Expressions of Time in Syriac; (c) The Particle i in the Philippine Languages, 49 362
BLANK, Sheldon H. The Ben Naftali Bible Manuscripts, 51 371
------. The Death of Zechariah in Rabbinic Tradition, 57 255
------. The Derivation of the word Torah, 47 355-356
------. The War Legislation in Deuteronomy, 52 293
BLOCH, Joshua. Can ὁ Σύρος be Identified with the Peshitta? 47 367
BLOOMFIELD, M. On the Life and Stories of the Jaina Savior Pārśvanātha, 38 332
------. On the Mallinātha Caritra, the Chronicle of the Woman Mallī, the 19th Tīrthaṃkara, or Savior, of the Jainas, 44 166
------. On the Meaning of the Words pratyekabuddha and pratyekabodhi, 43 170
------. On Two Alleged Stanzas in Pāiśācī Prākrit, 44 169
------. The Sālibhadra Carita, A Story of Conversion to Jaina monkhood, 43 166-167
BLOOMHARDT, P. F. The Poems of Haggai, 36 441
BOARDMAN, E. P. Recent New Material for the Study of the T'ai P'ing, 60 465

BOBRINSKOY, George. The Sacred Thread, a Possible Survival of a Ritual Custom of the Indus Valley Civilization, 57 245
BODDE, D. The Early Use of Iron Weapons in China, 60 461
------. Was Lü Pu-wei the Father of Ch'in Shih Huang-ti? 59 413
BONNER, Campbell. A Problem in the History of a Legend, 44 176
BORTON, Hugh. Some Proposals for Opening Japan after 1769, 59 413
BOWMAN, Raymond A. The Scorpion Man in Ancient Art, 52 288
BRADEN, Charles S. Japan and China's Culture, 59 421
------. Konkokyo, a little known Japanese Sect, 55 365
------. Marco Polo on Oriental Religions, 56 421
------. Modern Tendencies in Japanese Religions, 50 326-327
------. Some Modern Tendencies in Chinese Religions, 48 355
------. Some Recent Legislation Affecting Religion in India, 52 285
------. Twentieth Century Tendencies in Hinduism, 51 369-370
BRADY, Thomas A. Ptolemaic Policy and the Cult of Sarapis, 52 308
BRAIDWOOD, Robert J. Gold Jewelry found at Seleucia-on-the-Tigris, 52 301
BRIGGS, George W. Field Work on the Gorakhnathis, 45 356
------. Pāe Dhonī in Old Bombay, 53 391
BRITTON, Roswell S. Clay Block and Wax Block Printing, 53 398
------. Directional Value in Chinese Paleography, 58 531
------. International Law among the early Chinese Kingdoms — Case Studies on Treaties and Treaty-Making, 54 337
------. Studies in Chinese Palaeography, 56 406
------. Three Shang Inscriptions, 59 398
------. Two Series of Anyang Inscriptions, 60 461
------. The Yin Hsü Ossiglyphs, 57 258
BROCKWELL, C. A. Brodie. Calculation by Deficients, 44 158
BROOKS, Beatrice Allard. The Babylonian Practice of Marking Slaves, 42 80-90
BROWN, George William. The Possibility of Contact between Sumerian and the Languages of India, 45 366
------. The Source of Indian Philosophical Ideas, 39 124-125
BROWN, W. N. Bluff in Hindu Fiction, 38 331
------. The Courtier who had Mastered the Seventy-two Polite Accomplishments, 53 391
------. Escaping One's Fate: a Hindu Paradox Illustrated from Fiction, 39 143-144
------. A Hindu Manual of Magic and Ritual for Thieves, 56 410
------. The Indian and Christian Miracle of Walking on the Water, 47 359
------. A Jaina Manuscript from Gujarat Illustrated in the early Western Indian and Persian Styles (illustrated), 57 249
------. The Kālakācāryakathā, 48 343
------. Mediaeval Miniature Painting in Western India, 50 326
------. The Wonderful Tar-Baby Story: its Place of Origin, 41 186
BUCKLER, F. W. The Diplomatic Relations of the Early 'Abbāsid and Carolingian Houses, 47 364
------. The Philological and Historical Setting of the Root ḤLP, 47 356
------. A Political Theory of the Rise of the British Power in India, 48 348
BULL, Ludlow S. A New Egyptian Vizier of the Middle Kingdom, 44 164-165
BURCH, Ernest W. The Kingdom in Matthew, 45 371
BUTTENWIESER, Moses. Deutero-Isaiah's Attitude toward Cyrus, 57 241
------. The Emphatic and Conditional Particles in Hebrew and Aramaic, 42 396-397
------. The Oldest Psalm: Psalm 68B, 51 365-366
------. The Oldest Psalm, 52 294
CAMERON, George G. Media in the Old Testament, 51 370
CAMERON, M. E. The Public Career of Chang Chih-tung (1837-1909), 58 536
CAPART, Jean. An "Ex libris" of King Amenhetep III at Yale University, 53 393
CARNOY, A. J. Healing Gods and Storm Gods in Iran, 37 14
CARTER, Thomas F. The Chinese Background of the European Invention of Printing, 44 164
CASANOWICZ, I. M. A Korean sorcerer's outfit in the National Museum, 36 441
CARUS, Dr. Paul. Traces of Babylonian influence on China, 26 424
CASSADY, M. L. Economic Aspects of Hindu Asceticism, 59 411
CHANG, Y. Z. China's Contribution to Western Civilization, 58 535
------. Why Was There No Epic Poetry in Chinese Literature? 59 408
CHAO, Y. R. Occurrence of the Unstressed Tone in Disyllabic Compounds in Mandarin, 60 459
------. Tone and Intonation in Chinese, 53 398-399
CHAPIN, Helen B. A Document for the study of Yünnanese History, 54 342
------. A Long Roll of Buddhist Images in the Palace Museum, 53 393-394
CHAPMAN, William J. (a) Chronological Table to the Problem of Inconsequent Postdating; (b) Notes on Hosea 11:1, 45 352-353
------. The Earliest Kings of Uruk according to Hellenistic Sources, 50 340
------. The Problem of Inconsequent Post-dating in the Books of Kings, 43 165
------. (a) The Problem of Inconsequent Post-Dating in 2 Kings 15:17, 23, etc.; (b) The Fifth-Century Aramaic Transcriptions of the Name Sennacherib, 44 158-159
------. The Synchronisms of the First Book of Kings, 47 357
CHATTERJI, Jagadish C. The Significance of the Phrase ya evaṃ veda in the Upanishads, 50 323
CHI CH'AO-TING. The Concept of Key Economic Areas and its Relation to the Development of Public Works for Water-control in China, 54 337
CHIERA, Edward. An Amoritic Legend in Sumerian, 43 164
------. Marriage in the Nuzi Tablets, 52 296
------. New Finds in the Sumerian Field, 44 159-160
------. TAK-KU a Female Deity, 44 54-60
CHIU, A. K. Harvard-Yenching Institute Printed Cards for Chinese Books, 59 408
------. Laufer on the Introduction of Spectacles into China, 56 408
------. Library Resources and Book Markets in China: a Preliminary Report, 52 300
CLARK, Walter E. Aryabhaṭa, 47 364
------. Recent Trends in the Study of Buddhism, 48 343
------. The Stael-Holstein Collection of Lamaistic Pantheons, 51 363-364
CLYDE, Paul Hibbert. Frederick F. Low and the Tientsin Massacre, 52 298
COLEGROVE, Kenneth. The Monroe Doctrine of Japan, 40 135
CONANT, C. Everett. Some Changes of Original t and s in Austronesian and Elsewhere, 38 71
COOMARASWAMY, Ananda K. Early Indian Architecture, I. Cities and City-gates, 49 349-350
------. The Indian Doctrine of Man's Last End, 57 244
------. Nirukta = hermeneia, 56 405

------. Some Pali Words, 59 404
------. Svayamātṛṇṇā, 58 534
CREEL, H. G. A New Theory of the Origin of the Chinese Deity T'ien, "Heaven," 56 422
------. On a New Method for the Teaching of Literary Chinese, 57 247
CREIGHTON, J. W. The Communist Period in Canton — October 13, 1924 - December 13, 1927, 52 299
CURRIER, C. W. Gonzales de Mendoza and his work on China, 31 vi
DANTON, George H. Early Sino-American Culture-Contacts, 48 339
------. A Preliminary Announcement of a Study of Chinese Village Names, 41 179
DEAN, James E. The Ancient Syriac Calendar, 52 303
DEBEVOISE, Neilson C. Did the Parthians have an Art? 49 369
------. Some Problems in Parthian Architecture, 48 357
de VRIES, J. D. L. On New Methods of Purāṇic Research, 48 352
DIEZ, Ernst. Naysâbûr in Persia, a Town due for Excavation, 48 339
DIMAND, M. S. Some Fatimid Textiles with Printed and Painted Decoration, 53 394
DOUGHERTY, Raymond P. The Comparative Value of Metals in Babylonia, 42 399-400
------. Cuneiform References to Punt and Yemen, 49 353
------. The Goucher College Babylonian Collection, 41 179
------. The Land of Karduniash, 52 309
------. New Cuneiform References to Belshazzar, 39 147
------. The Shirqûtu of Erech, 38 335
DRISCOLL, Lucy. The Aesthetic of Shen Tsung-ch'ien, 沈宗騫, 53 400
------. The Eight Canons of Ts'ai Yung, 52 297
DUBBERSTEIN, Waldo H. Agriculture and Land Tenure in Later Babylonia, 58 547
------. Interest Rates and Prices in the Chaldaean and Persian Period, 52 304-305
DUBS, H. H. The Economic Reforms of Wang Mang, 59 413
------. The Fall of the Former Han Dynasty, 57 246-247
------. The Victory of Han Confucianism, 58 535
DUMONT, P. E. (a) The Indic God Aja Ekapād, the One-legged Goat; (b) A Note on Bhagavadgītā 10.30, 53 391
------. The Meaning of saṃmṛśati in Āpastamba-Śrauta-Sūtra VI.4.2 and Other Passages, 58 533-534
DUNCAN, George S. The Eden of Genesis and Archaeology, 48 342
------. The Future Life in the Oldest Egyptian Texts, 39 148
------. Spittle in the Oldest Egyptian Texts, 41 183
DUNSMORE, Marion Hiller. The Wisdom of Amenemopet and the Book of Proverbs, 45 371-372
DUYVENDAK, J. J. L. The Auspicious Giraffe, 59 397
------. Hsün-tzu and the School of Law, 49 358
------. New Light on Chêng Ho's expeditions, 53 387
------. The Particle i in Written Chinese, 57 257
DYEN, I. A Procedure in Studying the Hindu Grammarians, 59 404-405
EDGERTON, Franklin. (a) Aesop and the Panchatantra; (b) Slavonic Versions of the Panchatantra, 45 351
------. The Elephant-science of the Hindus, 50 324
------. The Filosofic Materials of the Atharva Veda, 39 148
------. The Gerund in Buddhist Hybrid Sanskrit, 57 244-245
------. (a) Indic diśati, 'speaks'. (b) Indirect Suggestion in Poetry: a Hindu Theory of Literary Aesthetics, 56 406
------. The Kashmirian Pañcatantra, and its Position among Versions of the Pancatantra, 37 15-16
------. A Message from Ancient India to Modern Governments, 53 388
------. The Metafor of the Car as Applied to the Rigvedic Ritual, 38 330
------. The Mīmāṅsā Nyāya Prakāśa of Āpadeva, 48 340
------. Notes on Jaina Māhārāṣṭrī, 44 160
------. On the Doubling of Consonants in the Seam of Certain Pāli Compounds, such as anuddayā, paṭikkūla, 41 177
------. Sāṅkhya and Yoga in the Bhagavad Gītā, 43 167
------. The Sanskrit Pronominal 'stems' in -d, 51 357
EFROS, Israel. Some Glosses to the Hebrew Bible, 42 390
------. (a) Some Glosses on the Hebrew Bible; (b) Some Experiences in Hebrew Lexicography, 50 322
ELISSÉEF, Serge. An Abortive Proposal for Japanese Assistance to the last of the Ming Emperors, 55 365
EMBER, Aaron. (a) The Change of š to s before a Labial in Egyptian; (b) Egypto-Semitic names for the parts of the Body, 46 351-352
------. Echnaton and Moses, 44 160
------. (a) Egyptian T3 mḥ, 'Delta,' and T3 mrį, 'Egypt'; (b) Several Egyptian Etymologies, 43 165
------. (a) The J. T. Dennis Collection of Egyptian Antiquities; (b) The Etymologies of Hebrew ḥām, 'father-in-law,' and of Egyptian 'ibd, 'month,' 41 186
------. (a) New Semito-Egyptian Words; (b) Some African Words in Old Egyptian, 37 21
------. (a) A Note on Job 37:23; (b) Several Semitic Etymologies, 45 360
------. (a) The Phonetic Value of Several of the Egyptian Alphabetic Signs and their Correspondence Etymologically in the Other Semitic Languages; (b) Metathesis in Old Egyptian, 41 177
------. Semito-Egyptian Words, 39 142
------. Some Semitic, Egyptian and Hamitic Etymologies, 46 356-357
EMENEAU, Murray B. The Tibetan and Mongolian Vetālapañcaviṅśati: Introductory story, 54 336
ENGBERG, Robert M. Archaeology and Hyksos Dates, 57 254
ENNIS, T. E. The Influence of Socialism upon Japanese Thought and Action, 60 465
------. Some French Problems in Indochina, 52 299-300
ESTERSON, Sidney I. (a) Restoration of Zech. 9, 16.7, (b) The Alleged Hebrew verb bahál, 46 355-356
EVANS, Kenneth Charles. Geographical Allusions in Josephus' Antiquities, XIV, §§ 158-488 (Jewish War I, §§ 203-357), 57 241
------. The "Hero" as Herod, 58 540-541
FAIRBANK, J. K. Aspects of Ch'ing Finance in the Middle of the Nineteenth Century, 60 465
------. The Policy and Methods of Ch'i-ying in the First Anglo-Chinese Treaty Settlement, 1842-43, 59 413
FAIRBANK, Mrs. J. K. Problems in the Reconstruction of Wu Liang Tz'u, 60 456
FARLEY, M. F. A Brief Record of Archaeological Exploration and Discovery in Fukien, China, 59 399
FAY, Edwin W. Phonetic and Morphological Notes in Sanskrit, 39 124
------. Current Defects in Indo-European Grammar, 36 440
FEIGIN, Samuel I. The Creation of Woman, 58 545
------. "The Humble One Riding on a Donkey" and its Babylonian Parallels, 57 240
FENG, Mr. C. The Social Stratification of the Liao Empire, 60 461
FENG, H. Y., and Shryock, J. K. A Marriage among the Miao, 54 337
FERGUSON, John C. Chinese Bronzes, 35 406
FERNALD, Helen E. The Colossal Chinese Frescoes in the Museum of the University of Pennsylvania, 48 343
------. An Early Chinese Sculptured Stela illustrating Scenes from the "Lotus of the Good Law" and the Vimalakīrti Sūtra, 51 366
------. In Defence of the Horses of T'ang T'ai Tsung: An Answer to Dr. Ferguson's Article in the JNCBRAS, Vol. LXVII, 1936, 59 418
------. A New Chinese Bronze in the University Museum, Philadelphia, 50 326

------. Some Notes on the Horses of T'ang T'ai Tsung, (illustrated), 54 335
FIELD, Henry. The Antiquity of Man in Southwestern Asia, 52 286
FIESEL, Eva. Some New Evidence on the History of the Alphabet, 56 406
FINESINGER, S. B. (a) Heb. ‘açûr u̯ĕ-‘azûb and ‘er u̯ĕ-‘ônê; (b) The Egyptian Prototype of nablium, 44 167
FOX, Gresham G. The Yoke of the Kingdom of Heaven, 52 293-294
FULLER, Leslie E. The Number 40, 51 371
FULLERTON, K. Does Isaiah Teach the Inviolability of Jerusalem at Is. 10:5-15? 37 9
------. Elements in Isaiah's Attitude in 701, 45 368
------. Remarks on Isaiah's Attitude during the Sennacherib Campaign of 701, 57 257
GAECKLER, M. H. A Study of the Aorist, Imperfect, and Perfect Tenses of the Rig-Veda, Early and Late, 37 17
GALE, Esson M. The Public Administration of Salt in China: Origins in the Western Han Dynasty — a preliminary study, 49 359
GARDNER, Charles S. Pythagorean Doctrines in China, 56 407
------. The Romanization of Chinese, 50 337
------. A Series of Illustrations of Imperial Manchu Victories, 60 465
GASKILL, G. E. A Chinese Official's experiences during the first Opium War, 53 399-400
GAVIN, Frank. Aphraates and Jewish Controversy, 38 330-331
------. Rabbinic Parallels in Early Church Orders, 49 354
GEERS, F. W. Prognostics in Ancient Babylonia, 52 296-297
GEHMAN, Henry S. The Buddhist Purgatory, 44 166
------. The John H. Scheide Papyri of Ezekiel, 58 533
GELB, Ignace J. Ishtar and Shamash, 58 548
GIBBLE, Phares B. Mistranslated Passages in Job, 41 184
GINSBERG, H. L. The Aramaic Original of Dan. 1-2:4a; 8-12, 58 540
------. The Dating of the Eshmunazarid Inscriptions, 57 239-240
------. A Hurrian Myth in Semitic Dress, 59 409
GLIDDEN, Harold Walter, and N. A. Faris: The Development of the Meaning of Koranic Ḥanīf, 58 541
GLUECK, Nelson. The Theophany of the God of Sinai, 56 409
------. The Word to‘ebah in the Old Testament, 52 294
GÖTZE, Albrecht. Representation of the Semitic Sibilants in Old Babylonian, 56 409-410
------. The Tense-System of the Ras-Shamra Language, 57 239
GOODRICH, L. C. Early Prohibitions of Tobacco in China and Manchuria, 58 526
------. An Incident in Sino-Korean Relations, 56 407
------. The Ssu-k‘u Ch‘üan Shu and the literary inquisition of Ch‘ien-lung, 53 399
GORDON, Cyrus H. New Tablets from Tell el-Amarnah, 56 414
------. Seals of Western Asia in Walters Art Gallery, 58 528
GORDON, Hirsch L. Rabbinical References to Early Basilicas and Stoas in the Near East, 50 338
GOTTHEIL, Richard J. H. Fragments from an Arabic Commonplace Book, 52 309-310
GRAHAM, Rev. D. C. Religion of the Ch‘uan Miao, 60 464
GRANT, Elihu. (a) Ancient Occupation of Modern Sites: Ramallah and Neighborhood. (b) An Instance of the Modern Sacrifice of Hair in Palestine, 46 341-342
------. Smith College Tablets of the Period of the First Babylonian Dynasty, 37 8
GRICE, Ettalene M. Date Formulae of the Larsa Dynasty, 38 329
von GRÜNEBAUM [or von GRUNEBAUM], Gustave. The Development of Early Islamic Religious Poetry, 59 410-411
GRUENTHANER, Michael J. The Future Life in the Psalms, 57 255
GUNSAULUS, Helen C. Nara-ye-bon, or the Picture Books of Nara, 52 287
HAAS, George C. O. A Medieval French Parallel to the Buddhist Tale of the Luck-Child Ghosaka, 42 400
------. The Meters of King Harsha's Sanskrit Drama Priyadarśikā, 43 171
------. Names of Avestan Demons in the Manichaean Fragments from Turfan, 44 170
HAHN, E. A. Hittite mahhan, 58 533
------. Indirect Questions in Hittite, 59 405-406
HAIL, William J. A Diplomatic Episode: China's Effort to open direct relations with the Vatican, 52 298-299
HALKIN, A. S. Al-Ash'ari's Defense of Kalām, 56 416
HALL, Ardelia R. Chinese Art and Genius (illustrated), 55 365
------. The early Significance of Chinese Mirrors, 54 337
------. Inlaid Chinese Bronzes with Secular Scenes, 59 399
------. Three Bas-reliefs of the late Han Dynasty in the Boston Museum, 56 408
HALL, Prof. R. B. Settlement in the Yamato Basin, 52 286
------. Tokaido: Road and Region, 57 257
HALLOCK, Richard T. The Chicago Syllabary and the Syllabary AO 7661, 52 297
HAMILTON, C. H. An English Translation of Hsüan Tsang's Wei-shih-er-shih-lun, 56 422
------. K‘uei Chi's Commentary to Hsüan Chuang's Wei-shih-er-shih-lun, 52 297
HAMME, Edward R. (a) The î in the Hebrew Hif‘îl; (b) The Original Meaning of Heb. barâ, ‘create,’ 44 167-168
------. The Ostrich in Job 39, 13-18, 41 176
HARDEN, D. B. The Origin of Certain Western Phoenician Settlements in the Mediterranean in the Light of the Earliest Pottery Finds, 48 359
HARDY, Edward R., Jr. New Light on the Persian Occupation of Egypt, 618-29 A.D., 48 339
HARING, D. G. Does the Japanese Emperor Fit Hocart's Theory of Divine Kingship? 59 418
HARRIS, Zellig S. Acrophony and Vowellessness in the Creation of the Alphabet, 53 387
------. Back-formation of itn in Phoenician and Ras Shamra, 56 410
------. Development of the West-Semitic Aspect System, 59 409-410
HARTMANN, G. Symbols of the Twelve Nidānas in the Tibetan "Wheel of Life," 60 458
HAUPT, Paul. (a) Circe and Astarte; (b) Melchizedek, Legitimate King, 38 332
------. (a) Egyptian Boomerangs; (b) The Names of Mount Hermon, 41 185-186
------. (a) The Historical Nucleus of Esther; (b) The Servant of JHVH; (c) Arabic Hypocoristics and Heb. Jeshurun; (d) Epenthesis of i in Old Persian, 44 157-158
------. (a) The Last Words from the Cross; (b) The Babylonian origin of the Term ‘naphtha,’ 37 21
------. (a) Numeratives in Sumerian and Chinese; (b) The Original Meaning of kôhén, ‘priest,’ (c) The Hebrew Names for Silver and Gold; (d) Oriental Philology and Archeology, 42 393-394
------. (a) Ox and ass at the Nativity; (b) Nehemiah's Night-Ride; (c) The Passage Hawk; (d) Accadian and Sumerian, 39 142-143
------. (a) The Rainbow after the Deluge; (b) The Fall of Samaria, 41 181-182
------. (a) The Shepherds in Zech. xi; (b) S for š in Semitic stems containing a labial; (c) Restoration of line 127 of the Flood-tablet; (d) Assyr. lîṭu, ‘mystery,’ 46 343-344
------. The Son of Man, 37 14
------. (a) The Sumerian Origin of the Semitic word for ‘Snow’; (b) Plato's Atlantis; (c) Leprosy and Framboesia; (d) Apples of Gold in Baskets of Silver, 43 163
------. (a) Ventriloquism in Babylonia; (b) The Nuptials of Jahveh and the Sun; (c) Sumerian Stillatories; (d) Suckling Seamonsters, 40 218-219

------. (a) The Volcano in Engidu's Dreams; (b) Assyrian Amurru, Mediterranean, 38 335-336
HITTI, Philip Khuri. The Damascus Ms. of al-Baghdâdi's al-Farḳ bayn al-Firaḳ, 46 353
-------. Naẓm-ul-'Iḳyān fī A'yān-il-A'yān, an Unpublished Manuscript by as-Suyuti, 45 359
------. Oriental Studies in Syria, 45 356
------. The Origins of the Druze Religion, 47 366
HODOUS, Lewis. The Introduction of Buddhism into China, 49 354
HOGG, Willis E. The Foundation of the Second Temple, 46 358-359
HOPKINS, E. Washburn. A Buddhistic Passage in Manu, 43 165
------. The Ethical Element in the Rig Veda, 40 220
------. Ṛté śrāntásya (RV. iv.33.11), 49 361
HORNBECK, Stanley K. The Problem of Republic-Making in China, 36 425
HOUGHTON, Herbert Pierrepont. On Presenting Sanskrit in the Small College, 47 366
HUME, Edward H. A Note on Narcotics in Ancient Greece and in Ancient China, 53 388
------. Some Notes on Medical Education in China Prior to 1600 A.D., 60 464
HUME, Robert E. Miracles in the Canonical Scriptures of Buddhism, 44 162
------. A Presentation of a New Translation of the Principal Upaniṣads, 41 182
HUMMEL, Arthur H. Early Chinese Gazetteers, 49 359
HUNG, William. The Discovery of the Nestorian Tablet, 49 353-354
IRWIN, W. A. The Immanuel Oracle, 57 255
------. Physical Symbols of Yahweh, 47 358
------. Truth in Ancient Israel, 48 343-344
JACKSON, A. V. W. Allusions to Mānī's Fame as a Painter, 49 354
------. The Doctrine of Metempsychosis in Manichaeism, 44 161
------. Notes on Baluchistan and its Folk-poetry, 32 ix
------. A Previously not Noted Parallel between an Apocryphal Story of Zoroaster's Infancy and a Tale in Buddhist Literature, 38 328
------. Traces of Biblical Influence in the Turfan Pahlavi Fragment M. 173, 53 387
------. Turfan Pahlavi miyazdagtāčīh, 46 357
------. See also Yohannan, A.
JACOBS, V. Mot and Tammuz, 59 410
JASTROW, Morris Jr. Gilgamish and Enkidu, 38 332-333
------. The Sumerian and Akkadian Calendar, 37 15
JOHNSON, J. The Date of the Adoption of the Solar Calendar in Egypt, 59 403
JOHNSON, Sherman E. Gospel Material in the Pauline Epistles, 58 549
JORDAN, Conrad W. (a) The Hero of Ephraim; (b) The Name Israel, 46 354
------. (a) 'Thou shalt love thy neighbor as thyself'; (b) Heb. neçh, glory, juice, perpetuity, 45 361
JOSHI, S. L. The Anatta Doctrine in Buddhism, 49 351-352
JURJI, Edward Jabra. Sufi-Shī'ite Affinities, 58 541
KELLOG, Robert J. (a) Historical and Cultural Background of Hittite Indo-Europeanicity; (b) The Indo-European Name of the Hittites, 49 360-361
------. Hittite ḫ, 48 351
------. (a) Hittite Suffixal Doublets with Initial Alternation -u̯-/-m-; (b) Present Stem Formations in Hittite, 47 365
------. Hittite Vowel Quantity, 48 360
------. The Impact of Hittite Civilization on that of the Occident, 50 324
------. Primitive Indo-European Traits in Hittite, 49 361
------. The Problem of Indo-European Origins, 51 374
------. Some Indications of the Eastward Route of the Tocharians, 47 356
KENNEDY, George A. The Phonetics of a rural Chekiang Dialect, 56 408
------. Reflections on the Final Particle yen, 59 407
------. Some Uses of Three Classical Particles in Chinese, 58 531
------. "Why?" and "Why Not?" in Early Chinese, 60 459
KENT, Roland G. Certain Personal Pronouns in Indo-Iranian, 44 159
------. The Naksh-i-Rustam Inscription of Darius I, 59 406
KIANG, Dr. K. H. Chinese Philosophy as a Remedy for the Defects of Western Civilization, 49 355
------. The Cultural Bond between China and Japan, 52 299
KOHUT, George A. 'Ben-Ammi and the Fairies,' a Jewish Apologue by John Godfrey Saxe, 45 363
------. (a) Bibliographical Notes on some Rare Hebraica-Americana; (b) George Borrow's Holograph (unpublished) Translation from the Hebrew of a Chapter from the Travels of Benjamin of Tudela, 52 310
------. A Hebrew Commencement Oration delivered at Yale University by President Ezra Stiles on September 12, 1781, 51 359
------. The Original Jewish Source of Longfellow's Scanderbeg in 'Tales from a Wayside Inn,' 45 360
------. Travels of a hitherto Unknown Jewish Merchant in China in the Tenth Century, 51 365
KRAELING, Carl H. The Odes of Solomon and the Proto-gnostic Hymns of the Manichaean and Mandaean Liturgies, 46 347
------. The Syriac Apocalypse of Paul and the Iranisches Erlösungsmysterium, 51 364-365
KRAELING, Emil G. H. The Ancient Cult of Hebron, 45 356
------. Servant Poems in Deutero-Isaiah, 46 342
KRAFT, C. F. Strophic Structure in the Book of Amos, 59 421
KUKHI, Georges S. Kitab al Haidah wal Itidar, or the Book of Evasion and Apology, 39 142
KURDIAN, Haroutiun. The Date of the Oriental Geography of Ibn Haukal, 54 84-85
------. A Note on the "Description of the Holy Land and of the Way Thither" by Ludolph von Suchem (1350), 55 102-104
LA FARGUE, T. L. Memorials and Decrees on the Establishment and Withdrawal of the Chinese Education Commission to the United States (1871-1881), 59 414
LANMAN, Charles R. (a) The Case-forms used in Sanskrit and Pali to Express the from-relation; (b) The King of Siam's New Volumes of Pali Texts and Commentaries, 45 353-354
------. Geldner's Translation of the Rig-Veda, with Commentary (vols. 33-34-35 of the Harvard Oriental Series) and Historical and Critical Epilogue (36), 49 349
------. Sanskrit Books for Western Students: the Need and the Essential Requirements, 43 165-166
------. Some Characteristics Desirable for a Beginner's Manual of Sanskrit, 49 351
------. Whitney's Material Relating to the Atharva Veda, 44 157
LATOURETTE, K. S. Occidental Studies on Far Eastern History, 1921-1929, 49 358
LAUFER, Berthold. The Buddhist Sculpture of China, 47 355
------. Chinese Pictorial Art, 40 135
------. A Chinese-Hebrew Manuscript, a new Source for the History of the Chinese Jews, 49 355
------. The Game of Polo, 48 357
------. Migrations of Tales from the Near to the Far East, 45 366
------. Recent Archaeological Discovery in China, 36 424, 338
------. Selected Examples of Chinese Pictorial Art from the Imperial Museum at Peking and the Field Museum, 46 360
------. The vigesimal and decimal systems in Ainu numerals and some remarks on Ainu phonology, 37 10-11

LAUTERBACH, Jacob Z. A Significant Controversy between the Sadducees and Pharisees, 47 358-359
LEAVITT, D. A. The Old Testament Attitude Toward Labor, 41 193
LEIDECKER, Kurt F. The Bhagavad-gītā and the St. Louis Movement, 56 415
------. The Logical and Ethical Presuppositions in Madhusūdana Sarasvatī's Prasthānabheda, 50 323-324
------. The Significance of the Noetical Terminology in Upaniṣads and Bhagavad Gītā, 48 349
LEVIS, John Hazedel. A Chinese Musical Renaissance, 53 394
LEVY, Abraham J. Biblical Note — Jeremiah 11:15, 49 363
------. Biblical Notes: (a) Amos 2:7a; (b) Amos 6:1-2, 50 336
------. The Date of Composition of Psalm 47, 50 322-323
------. Notes to Isaiah 10:5 and Gen. 4:7, 47 366-367
------. (a) Some Semito-Egyptian Etymologies; (b) Heb. zĕḇûl and Arab. balad, 45 362
------. Some Vocalic Similarities between Hebrew and the Present Spoken Arabic in Palestine, 48 361
------. (a) Sumerian and Turkish; (b) mizụ̄ád ra'aḇ, 'famine-food,' Deut. 32:24, 44 167
LEWY, Julius. The Assyrian Calendar, 58 548-549
LHEVINNE, Isadore. Gleanings from Old Latin Glossaries, 44 168
LI, F. K. The Hypothesis of a Pre-glottalized Series of Consonants in Primitive Tai, 59 407
------. A Type of Folk-Song in Wu-ming, 58 531
LICHTENSTADTER, I. Ibn Ḥabīb and his Kitâb al-Muḥabbar, 58 541-542
LINFIELD, H. Assyriology and the Study of the Talmud, 38 73
LUDWIG, Dr. Albert P. Chinese Traditional Theories of Foreign Relations, 57 246
LUTZ, Henry F. An Omen-text referring to the Action of a Dreamer, 38 328-329
LYBYER, A. H. The Foundations of Mohammed the Conqueror, 58 527
------. The Four Quadrants of Asia, 41 190-191
------. The Influence of the Crusades upon the Great Discoveries, 38 71-72
------. The Influence of Marco Polo on the Great Discoveries, 52 300-301
------. A Possible Moslem League of Nations, 49 368-369
------. The Religious and Moral Ideals of the New Turkey, 48 359
MC CLELLAND, Hardin T. (a) Critical Historism and Classical Research in Modern Chinese Philosophy; (b) Vitalism and Humanism in Modern Chinese Philosophy, 57 258
MC DOWELL, R. H. Numismatic and other Chronological Evidence from Seleucia, 51 373
------. Sealings and Seal Impressions from Seleucia-on-the Tigris, 52 301-302
MC EWAN, E. W. The Divinity of the Achaemenids, 52 305
MC GOVERN, William M. The Early Inhabitants of Central Asia, 53 403
------. The Ephthalites, 57 255
------. The Historic Relations between Indian, Chinese and Japanese Buddhism, 48 356
------. The Hsiung Kingdoms in Northern China, 58 536
------. Huns, 54 347
------. Some Problems of Asiatic History, in the Light of Buddhist Studies, 49 368
MAC LEAN, J. Arthur. Some Pertinent Facts about the Japanese Wood-Block Designer Hashiguchi Goyo, 57 246
------. The Toledo Museum's Cambodian Stone Terminal, 51 374
MACHT, David I. An Experimental Appreciation of I Kings 1, 5, 43 171
------. Experimental Scientific Appreciation of Psalm VIII, 48 349
------. Experiments concerning šeḥīṭā, or the Hebrew Method of Slaughtering, 51 366-367
------. Further Experiments concerning šeḥīṭā, or Hebrew Method of Slaughter, 52 310
------. A Scientific Appreciation of Biblical References to Menstruation, 44 165-166
------. A Scientific Appreciation of Eccl. 11:7, Gen. 9:3 and Dan.1:12, 47 368
MAGOUN, H. W. The Caesura, an Ancient Phenomenon, 56 405
MALONE, Carroll B. The Old Summer Palace near Peking, 48 356
MANN, Jacob. On some Early Karaite Bible Commentaries, 41 179-180
------. The Struggle between the Omeyyad Caliphate and Byzantium for the Possession of Constantinople, and the Messianic Hopes entertained by the Oriental Jews, 47 364
MANNING, Clarence A. Prester John and Japan, 42 400
MARCH, Benjamin. A New Hypothesis concerning the Use of some Asiatic Bronze Objects, 54 337
------. A Short Note on Chinese Portraiture, 49 358
------. Some Technical Terms of Chinese Painting, 52 298
MARENOF, Shlomo. The Ephah — Zechariah 5:5-11, 52 307
MARGOLIS, Max L. In Psalm 49:6 read 'ēn instead of 'aụōn, 46 344
------. The Text of Sirach 4, 19, 41 178
MARSHALL, Rev. H. I. The Origin of the Karen (of Burma) and their Monotheistic Tradition, 40 135
MARTINOVITCH, Nicholas N. The Garrett Collection of Oriental Manuscripts in the Princeton University Library, 45 350
------. The Widgery and Baroody Collections in the Princeton University Library, 46 343
MATTHEWS, Charles D. The Princeton Muthir on Palestine and Syria, 59 400
MAY, Herbert G. Solar Aspects of the Jerusalem Cult, 57 256
------. Some Scattered Archaeological Notes, 58 548
MAYNARD, John A. The Foundations of Pan-Amurrism, 43 173
MEEK, Theophile J. The Bearing of Deuteronomy 32 on the Form of Hebrew Prophecy, 46 352
------. The Element i-ti in Old Akkadian Personal Names, 57 243
------. Gleanings from the Gasur Texts, 52 296
------. The Grammatical and Poetical Structure of Isaiah 41:2a, 50 335-336
------. Monotheism with the Sumerians and Babylonians, 56 402
------. A New Use of the Adverbial Accusative in Hebrew, 46 343
------. Some Notes on Canticles, 44 174
------. Some Uses of the Accusative in Hebrew, 59 400-401
MEI, K. T. The Influence of Confucius on Chinese Historiography, 49 358
MEILLET, Antoine. Sur la chronologie des langues indo-européennes, 50 325
MENG, Chih. The Education of Chinese Students in America: A Survey and an Appraisal, 60 465
MENZIES, Rev. J. M. Kings and Queens of the Shang Dynasty, as Revealed in the Oracle Bones of Honan, 57 247
------. The Nobles and Officials of the Shang Dynasty, China, 60 459
------. Oracle Bones of the Waste of Yin, 50 337
MICHELSON, Truman. Once more Nātaputta, 58 534
------. Some Middle Indic Notes, 41 177-178
MILLS, Philo Laos. The Journey of Gilgamesh to the Isles of the Blest, 48 342
MONCURE, John. Compensation of Gemination by Insertion of Nasals, 41 177
MONTGOMERY, James A. A Christian Incantation Bowl in the 'Manichaean' Script, 37 9
------. Ethiopic Texts of Acts of the Apostles, 49 353

------. Exhibition of the First Photographic Copy of the Uncial Codex Venetus, 46 340
------. hargîšû, Daniel 6:7, 12, 16, a Word of Kaleidoscopic Interpretations, 44 168
------. Hebrew ḥesed = New Testament charis, 59 401
------. The Meaning of rĕgaš in Dan. 6:7, 12, 12, 46 352
------. The Testimony of the Aramaic Dialects to Oriental Thought and Religion, 44 161
MOON, Lewis Calvin. (a) A Chinese Parallel to Arab. naçâ'ah and baḥâḍ, 'whiteness' = leprosy; (b) A German Parallel to Is. 63, 1-6, 46 355
------. (a) The Seven-branched Lampstand; (b) Assyr. šutêšuru and Arab. ṳâṭara, 45 362-363
MORAN, H. A. The Astrological Elements in Early Chinese Writing, 58 536
------. Possible Sources of the Western Alphabet in the Astrological Signs of the Orient, 43 169-170
MOREY, Charles Rufus. The Mosaics of Antioch, 59 399
MORGENSTERN, Julian. The Gates of Righteousness, 42 398
------. The Historical and Religious Background of Zech. i-viii, 47 359
------. The Historical Beginnings of Judaism, 49 366
------. Holy Cross Day, 39 149
------. Kedesh-Naphtali and Taanach, 38 336
------. The Origin, Date, and Religious and Social Background of the Biblical Laws of the Type of Exodus 21:15-17, 50 338-339
------. Palm Sunday, 38 333
------. The Passover-Mazzoth Festival in the Biblical Period, 46 346
------. Semitic Birth Ceremonies and the Rite of Circumcision, 37 14
------. The Seven Fifties, 41 182
------. The Three Calendars of Ancient Israel, 43 167
NAKARAI, T. W. The Japanese Syllabaries, 55 365
NIES, J. B. Is UMMA^{ki} the Correct Reading for the Ideogram GIŠ-ÚḪ^{ki}? 37 9
NIMS, Charles F. Additions in Job, 53 405
------. Some Notes on the Family of Mereruka, 57 242
NORTON, Ruth. The Life-index in Hindu Fiction, 39 142
NYKL, A. R. Ibn al-Djawzi's Dhamm al-hawā, 57 254
------. Two Editions of Ibn Hazm's 'Character and Conduct,' 43 173
OBERMANN, Julian J. The Impersonalia from a Semitic Standpoint, 44 159
------. An Important Document of Judeo-Muhammedan Religious History, 45 353
------. Notes on the al-Ḫiḍr Legend, 51 356
OGDEN, Charles J. Bhāsa's Treatment of the Udayana Legend, 43 169
------. Note on Kathāsaritsāgara 9.7, 37 328
------. On the Names of an Ancient Hindu People, Vatsa, Vaccha, Vaṃsa, 43 170
------. The Site of Ancient Kauśāmbī, 42 396
------. Two Turfan Pahlavi Etymologies, 53 392
OLMSTEAD, Albert Ten Eyck. The First Chapter of Second Isaiah, 44 174
------. The Historical Joshua, 51 359-360
------. The Last Eighth of Jeremiah, 38 74-75
------. The Oriental Museum of the University of Illinois, 46 345
------. The "Original Home of the Aryans," 48 358
------. Prehistoric Chronology and the Orient, 47 355
PARULEKHAR, N. B. The Atheistic School of Indian Philosophy, 46 347
PATON, Lewis B. The Holy Places of Ancient Canaan, 38 331
PAVRY, Jal Dastur C. Nēryōsang and Other Old Parsi Sanskritists, 44 170
PEAKE, C. H. On the Limitation of Interest Rates in China, 58 534
PELLIOT, Prof. Paul. A New Manichaean ms. in Chinese, 44 161
PETERS, Dr. J. P. The Cock in Oriental Literature, 32 ix
PFEIFFER, Robert H. Edomitic Wisdom, 45 353
PIEPKORN, Arthur Carl. The Annals of Aššurbânapli, 52 304
PLUMER, J. M. The Significance of our Pacific Heritage, 60 467
------. The Site of the Ware of Yüeh, 57 248
------. Tools of the Chinese Potter, 59 397
POEBEL, Arno. The Words for "Year" in Sumerian and Egyptian, 52 295-296
POLEMAN, H. I. The preta-concept in Hindu Thought and Ritual, 59 412
POPE, J. A. The Earliest Dated Chinese Figure, 60 456
POPENOE, Paul. The Distribution of the Date Palm, 45 364
------. 'Your Paternal Aunt the Date-Palm,' 44 171
von PORADA, Edith. Stylistic Development in Syria and Palestine at the Beginning of the 2nd Millennium, 59 398
PRATT, James B. The Buddhist Revival in China, 45 356
PRICE, Ira Maurice. Boats and Ships in Early Babylonia, 44 173
------. The Functions of the Officers of the Temple of Ningirsu, 41 192-193
------. Homonyms in Sumerian, 45 372
------. "Noah in the Ark," or a Temple Entrance, 48 358-359
------. Notes on the Right of the First-born in Early Sumer and the Old Testament, 51 371
------. (a) The Ships of the Gods. (b) Confirmation of Nabopolassar's Campaign against Harran, 46 362
------. Some References to Transportation by Water in Early Babylonia, 43 173
------. Use of the Imperative in Sumerian, 49 365
PRICE, Maurice T. Cooperative Research between Sinologues and other Academic Specialists, 52 300
PRIEST, A. Analysis of the Monster Mask Rebus — Bird or Cicada? 60 456
PRITCHARD, E. H. The Question of the Kotow in the Macartney Embassy to China, 1793, 59 414
------. A Theory of the Historical Development of China, 60 465
REID, R. W. Some Aspects of Piracy and the Mongol Dynasty, 59 418
------. Some Aspects of Piracy in the Mongol Dynasty of China, 60 467
REILLY, John, Jr. Chinese Material in the Museum of the American Numismatic Society, 49 359
REISCHAUER, E. O. Koreans in T'ang China, 60 461
------. Recent Japanese Archaeological Work on the Asiatic Continent, 59 399
REISCHAUER, Robert K. The Japanese Shōen, or Manor, 56 406-407
REISNER, John H. Making available Old Chinese Literature relating to Agriculture, 49 362
REYNOLDS, S. M. Syriacisms in the "Polyglot" Arabic Translation of Zechariah, 59 401-402
RIGG, Horace Abram. The Route of Sargon's "Eighth Campaign," 57 243
ROBINSON, George L. Horsfield's Findings at Petra in 1929, 52 286
------. Moffatt's Translation of the Old Testament, 45 368
------. Needless Anachronisms in our English Bible, 48 361
ROOSEVELT, Q. Moso Pictograph Manuscripts Recently Collected in the Nashi Kingdom, 60 459
ROSENAU, William. Biblical Passages in the Jewish Liturgy, 44 166
------. A Note to Joel 1:14, 45 361
------. Judah ibn Tibbon as a Translator, 46 353-354
------. The Meaning of Talmudic haṳajah, 46 356
------. Some Šafel Forms in Hebrew, 47 356-357

------. The Song of Judith (Judith 16:1-17), 49 361
------. Talmudic Connotations of Abh, 'Father,' 44 168-169
ROSTOVTZEFF, M. The Unity of Ancient Culture in the Copper Age, 41 189-190
ROWE, D. N. The Lower-Division Course on Chinese Culture at Princeton University, 60 465
ROWELL, Teresina. The Relation of the adhiṣṭhāna-power to the Projection of Nirmāṇa-kāyas in the Saddharmapuṇḍarīka and Other Mahayana Buddhist Scriptures, 56 415
ROWLEY, George. A Stylistic Hypothesis concerning Wu Tao-yüan, 53 393
RUDOLPH, A. The Hindu Woman's Achievements: a Note of Appreciation, 36 440
------. Robert R. Livingston as the First American Egyptologist on Record, 51 364
RUDOLPH, R. C. "Emu tanggô orin sakda i gisum sarkiyan," an unedited Manchu Manuscript, 60 459
SACHS, A. Two Cuneiform Place-names, 56 404
------. Unrecognized Uses of Two Cuneiform Ideograms, 57 243
SAKANISHI, Shio. The Holly Myth in Japanese Art and Literature, 54 337
------. Probition of import of certain Chinese and Western books and the policy of the Edo Government, 53 399
------. A Study of the Census Domicile Record of the Slaves owned by the Todaiji Monastery in 772, 56 408
SALMONY, Dr. A. The Possibility of Attributing Chinese Bronzes to Pre-Anyang Times, 60 456
SANTESSON, H. S. The Japanese and the Preservation of China's Antiquities, 58 535
SAPIR, Edward. Loan Words in Western Asia Minor, 56 410
SAUNDERS, V. Portrait Painting as a Dramatic Device in Sanskrit Plays, 39 144
SCHAEFFER, Henry. Hebrew Tribal Economy and the Year of Jubilee, 42 399
SCHANZLIN, G. L. The Indian Monetary System of Moghul Times, 52 306
SCHMIDT, Nathaniel. Daniel in the Lion's Den and Androcles in the Arena, 41 182
------. Is Canticles an Adonis Litany? 45 357
------. The Two Recensions of Slavonic Enoch, 37 16
SCHOFF, Wilfred H. Camphor, and Early Trade in the Indian Ocean, 42 394
------. The eastern Iron Trade of the Roman Empire, 35 405
------. Navigation to the Far East under the Roman Empire, 37 16
------. Roman Sea Trade with the Far East, 36 442
SCHULTHEIS, F. D. The Disaster at T'u-mu in 1449 A.D., 60 465
SCHWARTZ, B. The Diagonal Wedge is not a "Glossenkeil" in Hittite, 58 533
SEIDEL, Moses. Hebrew בול - Ass. bûlu, 'cattle,' 47 368
------. The Root šā'al and the Etymology of Šĕ'ōl, 41 176
SELL, Rev. R. Examples of Religious Polemics in Chinese Literature, 60 465
SELLERS, O. R. Chiasmus in Egyptian, 58 545
------. The Coins of Bethzur and Hellenistic History, 52 301
------. The Lachish Letters and Old Testament Criticism, 59 423
------. Locusts in Palestine, 53 405
------. Meter in Egyptian, 43 175
------. Moses as an Egyptian Magician, 47 363-364
------. Names of Ancient Oriental Woodwinds, 48 360
------. The Scale in Egyptian Music, 44 175
------. Social Implications of Solomon's Accession, 57 238-239
SHIMIZU, Mr. O. An Experimental Method of Cataloguing Japanese Books for Western Libraries, 60 459
SHRYOCK, John K. The Chinese City-God, 47 360
------. A Chinese Machiavelli, 55 363
------. The Cult of Confucius and His Disciples, 49 358
------. Some Medieval Chinese Thinkers of the Six Dynasties and T'ang Periods, 48 350
------ and H. Y. Feng: Chinese Black Magic, 53 388
------. See also Feng, H. Y.
SIEBENS, A. R. Light from the Theory of Law on the Problem of Deuteronomy, 46 361
SIEGEL, Julius L. The Sinaitic Inscriptions: New Interpretation of the Term נצב and its Consequences for Dating, 52 296
SIMSAR, Mehmet A. New Light on Za'īfī, a 16th Century Turkish Poet, 57 239
------. Three Rare Manuscripts from the John Frederick Lewis Collection, 56 413
SMITH, J. M. P. Isaiah and Sennacherib, 44 175
------. The Syntax and Significance of Genesis 1:1-3, 47 357
------. Traces of Emperor Worship in the Old Testament, 42 398
------. The Unique Element in Hebrew Thought, 49 365-366
SMITH, Myron Bement. A Seldjuk Stalactite Cupola at Sīn (Iṣfahān), 59 397-398
SNYDER, J. Edward. Edom's Doom in Malachi, 42 396
------. (a) Habbakuk's Maledictions. (b) The â before the Affixes of the Assyrian Permansive, 40 221-222
SOPER, E. D. Religion and Politics in Present-Day Japan, 40 135
SOOTHILL, W. E. Kingship in China; Early Ideas, 48 350
SPEISER, E. A. Caucasic Influences in the Nuzi Verb, 56 403
------. (a) Letter of Saushshatar, king of the Mitanni; (b) On the Name Bildad, 49 360
------. The Values of three Ḫurrian Numerals, 56 404-405
------. Vocalic n in Assyrian, 45 359
------. Were the Ancient Gutians Really Blond and Indo-European? 50 338
SPRENGLING, Martin. (a) Arabic Manuscripts, etc. at the University of Chicago; (b) The Tale of King Solomon and the Griffon, 45 366-367
------. A Syrian Edition of Ibn al Habbârîya's Kalîla wa Dimna, 42 394
von STAEL-HOLSTEIN, Baron A. On a Lamaistic Pantheon recently discovered in the Forbidden City of Pekin, 49 350
STAPLES, W. E. The Tetragrammaton as Pipi, 57 241
STEARNS, Wallace N. A Possible Reason Why Paul did not Visit Alexandria, 45 369-370
STEFANSKI, Elizabeth. A Ninth-Century Christian Tombstone from Egypt, 52 295
STEINEN, Dr. D. von den. Sigh-poetry in and before the Han Dynasty, 60 465
STEPHENS, Ferris J. Grammatical Evidence for the Date and Origin of the Cappadocian Semitic Dialect, 48 357
------. A "Two-Page" Cuneiform Letter, 59 399-400
STINESPRING, W. F. The Meter of 'David's Lament over Saul and Jonathan,' 59 402
STURTEVANT, E. H. Changes of Quantity Caused by Indo-Hittite h, 51 357
------. The Evidence of Anatolian Languages for Indo-European Laryngeal Consonants, 58 530
------. Neuter Pronouns Referring to Words of Different Gender or Number, 49 351
------. The Pronominal Stem *sme/i- in Hittite and Indo-European, 53 392
------. Sanskrit ā, 'near,' is Cognate with Latin ā, 'from,' 59 406
SWAIN, Joseph Ward. The Theory of the Four Monarchies, 59 422
SWANN, Nancy Lee. An Account of certain favored Eunuchs of the Palace, 54 334
------. Certain Occupational Pursuits of the Wealthy in the Western Han Period of China, 59 408
------. Chao I-ch'ing's Study of the "Water Classic," 57 258

------. The Edition of Sutra No. 1, Collection No. I (Nanjio No. 88, 大方廣佛華嚴經, Buddhâvatamsakamahâvaipulya sutra), of the Gest Chinese Research Library, 52 298
------. The Empress Teng (2nd cent. A.D.): Was She or Was She Not a Tool in the Hands of Powerful Leaders? 50 337
------. Excerpts from and problems in a study of the life and writing of Pan Chao, 49 358-359
------. An inter-library Loan-group in the Greater Hang-Chou, 56 407
------. Pan Ku's Preface to the Han Shu, 58 535-536
------. A War Loan in 154 B.C., 60 461
------. A Woman Among the Rich Merchants: The Widow of Pa, 巴寡婦清, 3rd century B.C., 53 399
SWINGLE, Walter T. An Early Chinese illustrated work on natural history, Cheng lei pen ts'ao, in the Chinese collections of the Library of Congress, 36 442
------. The Multindex System for Finding Chinese Characters and its Uses, 41 185
------. Notes on the Gazetteers and other Geographical Works in the Library of Congress Chinese Collection, 41 185
SZADZUNSKI, Eleazar I. Materials for the Parthian and Sassanid History in the Talmudical Writings, 52 305
TAYLOR, W. R. Recent Epigraphic Discoveries in Palestine, 50 340-341
------. Nestorian Crosses in China, 52 288
TEDESCO, P. The Presumed Rigvedic Present márate, 59 406
THACKER, Nainsinh L. Are the Hieroglyphic and the Sanskrit Languages Related? 43 170
------. Are the Land of PUNT and the God BES African or Indian? 43 169
THAYER, Gordon W. The John G. White Collection of Orientalia, 57 239
TORREY, C. C. The Aramaic Language in the Later Jewish Dispersion, 53 400
------. The End of the 'Molech' Cult in Israel, 49 354-355
------. A Palestinian Aramaic Idiom in the Fourth Gospel, 49 353
------. South-Arabian Antiquities at Yale University, 58 528
TSU, Y. Y. Modern Chinese Scholarship in the Field of Religion, 53 400-401
UHL, Lemon L. Colorado-Telingana Mss. of Portions of the Mahābhārata, 51 357
------. A Contribution towards the Identification of the Soma Plant in Vedic Times, 45 351-352
------. Further Personality Materials of the Telugus for Ages preceding 1000 B.C., 49 352
------. Personality Materials of the Telugus, or Andhras, for the Ages preceding 1000 B. C., 48 348
------. The Shrine Tirupati; its Deity, Lord Venkata; Domestic Images of Venkata, 48 349
VERNADSKY, G. On the Origins of the Antae, 58 527
VOIGT, Edwin E. The Jehovah Speeches in Job, 46 359
WANG, Mr. Y. The Chun Organization of the Ch'in Empire, 60 459
WARE, J. R. A Difficult Phrase in Liu T'ao's Memorial on the Yellow Turbans, 58 531
------. The Final Particle wei, "to do, to be," 60 459
------. Old Persian niyaθ^{r}ārayam, 44 171
------. The Taoist expression hsing-ch'u, 行廚, 54 337
------. Wei Shou on Buddhism, 52 297-298
WATERMAN, Leroy. Method in the Study of the Tetragrammaton, 46 361
------. Pre-Israelite Laws in the Book of the Covenant, 41 193
------. Some Determining Factors in the Northward Progress of Levi, 57 240
------. Some Historical and Literary Consequences of Probable Displacement in I Kings, 1-2, 59 402
------. Some Results of the Season's Work at Sepphoris in Galilee and at Seleucia-on-the-Tigris, 52 287-288
WHITBECK, R. H. The Influence of Geographical Environment on Religious Beliefs, 41 191
WHITE, Bishop W. C. Pictorial Art in Ancient China — Tile Pictures of 3rd Century B.C., 57 249
WILBUR, C. Martin. Economic Aspects of Slavery During the Han, 57 245
WILKINS, Ernest Hatch. [Oriental Influence on Early Italian Literature], 51 370
WILLIAMS, C. A. Oriental Traditions of the Hairy Solitary, 48 355
WILLIAMS, F. W. A Chapter in Early Chinese History, 45 350
WILSON, John A. Ancient Text Corrections in an Egyptian Temple, 52 295
------. The 'Eperu of the Egyptian Inscriptions, 53 404
------. New Texts of the Battle of Kadesh, 46 359
WINNETT, Fred V. Some Recent Researches in Lihyanite and Thamudic, 56 415
WITTFOGEL, K. A. Climatic Conditions during the Later Part of the Shang Dynasty, 59 408
------. The Development of Early Chinese Institutions in the Light of Modern Anthropology, 60 461
WOLFENSON, Louis B. Transposition of ת before Sibilants in the Semitic Languages, 38 73-74
WORRELL, W. H. The Coptic Magical Papyri, 48 358
------. Popular Traditions of the Coptic Language, 57 242
WRIGHT, G. Ernest. Palestine in the Chalcolithic Age, 57 240
------. Some Phoenician Art of the Persian Period and the Origin of the 'Megarian' Bowl, 58 528
WRIGHT, Walter Livingston Jr. Baqqāloghlu Ṣārī Meḥmed Pashā and his Kitāb ül-Güldeste, 51 356
WYNGAARDEN, Martin J. Topic Notes on Is. 53:12, 48 357-358
YAMAGIWA, J. K. Compound Post-positions in Modern Japanese Writing, 59 407
------. Kinahan Cornwallis: Faking and Plagiarism on Japan, 59 423
------. Wants in Japanese Language Teaching, 58 531
YEAWORTH, Eleanor F. F. The Preformatives of the Semitic Imperfect, 41 184-185
YOHANNAN, Abraham. Notes on Theodore bar Khoni's Syriac Account of Manichaeism, 41 180
------. Ithoter Rivāyat, an Eighteenth Century Zoroastrian Manuscript in Persian, 43 166
------, and A. V. Williams Jackson: Notes regarding the Tomb of Tamerlane, 35 405
ZEITLIN, Solomon. The Am Ha-aretz in the Early Tannaitic Literature, 52 307
------. The Jewish Calendar from the Biblical Period up to the Fourth Century C.E., 49 355-356
------. See also Adler, Cyrus